The History of English

The History of English: An Introduction provides a chronological analysis of the linguistic, social, and cultural development of the English language, from before its establishment in Britain around the year 450 to the present. Each chapter represents a new stage in the development of the language from Old English through Middle English to Modern Global English, all illustrated with a rich and diverse selection of primary texts showing changes in language resulting from contact, conquest and domination, and the expansion of English around the world.

The History of English goes beyond the usual focus on English in the UK and the USA to include the wider global course of the language during and following the Early Modern English period. This perspective therefore also includes a historical review of English in its pidgin and creole varieties and as a native and/or second language in the Caribbean, Africa, Asia, and Australasia.

Designed to be user-friendly, *The History of English* contains:

- chapter introductions and conclusions to assist study
- over 80 textual examples demonstrating linguistic change, accompanied by translations and/or glosses where appropriate
- study questions on the social, cultural, and linguistic background of the chapter topics
- further reading from key texts to extend or deepen the focus
- nearly 100 supporting figures, tables, and maps to illuminate the text
- 16 pages of color plates depicting exemplary texts, relevant artifacts, and examples of language usage, including Germanic runes, the opening page of *Beowulf*, the *New England Primer*, and the Treaty of Waitangi.

The companion website at **www.routledge.com/cw/gramley** supports the textbook and features:

- an extended view of major aspects of language development as well as synopses of material dealt with in a range of chapters in the book
- further sample texts, including examples from Chaucer, numerous Early Modern English texts from a wide variety of fields, and twenty-first-century novels
- additional exercises to help users expand their insights and apply background knowledge
- an interactive timeline of important historical events and developments with linked encyclopedic entries
- audio clips providing examples of a wide range of accents.

The History of English is essential reading for any student of the English language.

Stephan Gramley is Studiendirektor at Bielefeld University, Germany, in the Department of Linguistics and Literary Studies.

The History of English

An Introduction

Stephan Gramley

Routledge
Taylor & Francis Group

LONDON AND NEW YORK

First published 2012
by Routledge
2 Park Square, Milton Park, Abingdon, Oxon OX14 4RN

Simultaneously published in the USA and Canada
by Routledge
711 Third Avenue, New York, NY 10017

Routledge is an imprint of the Taylor & Francis Group, an informa business

© 2012 Stephan Gramley

The right of Stephan Gramley to be identified as author of this work has been asserted by him in accordance with sections 77 and 78 of the Copyright, Designs and Patents Act 1988.

British Library Cataloguing in Publication Data
A catalogue record for this book is available from the British Library

Library of Congress Cataloging in Publication Data
Gramley, Stephan, 1943–
 The history of English : an introduction / Stephan Gramley.
   p. cm.
  Includes bibliographical references and index.
 1. English language—History. 2. English language—Variation. I. Title.
 PE1072.G73 2011
 420.9—dc22
                                                                          2011015909

ISBN: 978–0–415–56639–1 (hbk)
ISBN: 978–0–415–56640–7 (pbk)
ISBN: 978–0–203–18224–6 (ebk)

Typeset in Garamond and Parisine
by Keystroke, Station Road, Codsall, Wolverhampton
Printed and bound in Great Britaain by
CPI Group (UK) Ltd, Croydon, CR0 4YY

Contents

Illustrations

Plates

The following plates appear in a color section between pp. 214 and 215.

Figures

Maps

Tables

Texts

Preface

This textbook and its accompanying website are intended to serve as the basic reading and study resources for college and university courses on the history of English. The level of work is aimed at undergraduates and is supported by extensive background material for the less well initiated, but also opens up a number of controversial questions for those who might want to pursue the development of English beyond the bounds of a straightforward narrative. The approach in this book does not treat English as a monolithic entity, but the product of use by diverse speakers through the ages, in differing levels of society, and over a wide geographic spread. Because of its broad focus, this *History of English* can also be employed in classes which deal with language change or with the global varieties of English.

    A History of English has grown out of a general interest in language change and language contact; consequently, it seeks to view the development of the language from these two basic perspectives. For one *HoE* follows the more specifically linguistic course of the language as such, and here it stands in the tradition of books such as Quirk and Wrenn 1957, Strang 1970, Samuels 1972, Millward 1996, Görlach 1997, and many others. The second point of view puts its emphasis on sociocultural and historical factors in change, most especially language contact. Here it resembles books like Leith 1983, Knowles 1997, and Fennell 2001. There are, of course, a number of books in the field which combine both points of view, for example, Blake 1996, Baugh and Cable 2002, and Barber et al. 2009. There is, however, no other one-volume history of English which dedicates anything like as much space to the historical spread of English beyond the British Isles and/or North America. The present book devotes approximately half of its chapters (1–6) to the history of English up to the Early Modern English (EModE) period and the other half (7–13) to the history of English since the beginning of its global spread in the seventeenth century.

    Historical change must be studied as much as is possible in its geographical breadth and its social stratification. Understanding how language varies will deepen and enhance our understanding of society and, we hope, our tolerance of diversity. In addition, the study of the history of the language can give us some of the tools we need to access the literature of earlier periods, and it can give us a better understanding of the social and economic forces that shape language and language attitudes. We can recognize not only the processes of change in language (among other things, typological shift, abductive processes, grammaticalization and lexicalization), but some of the mechanisms of social interaction such as accommodation, bilingualism and bidialectalism, code-switching, creolization, and substrate influence. Furthermore, language change offers an important window on the human mind and how the language faculty works.

The treatment of historical developments requires some initial knowledge of the vocabulary, pronunciation, structures, and practices which are to undergo change. In order to help the user find his or her way, this book introduces the necessary basic material, such as the text-oriented explanation of selected features of Old English (OE) in chapter two and the glosses provided for OE texts given in chapters two and three. With OE, as with Middle English (ME), Early Modern English (EModE), and Modern English (ModE), *HoE* makes frequent use of texts and other authentic material, drawing on manuscripts, corpora, and published sources. All told, a total of over eighty texts appear in the printed book; and additional textual material can be found on the website. As the language dealt with becomes more familiar, it is usually sufficient to add ModE glosses or comparisons to ModE.

HoE has been composed to sketch out the broad currents of change and draws on a selected set of linguistic topics which illustrate these currents. Numerous examples have been taken from the areas of vocabulary, but the idea has been to indicate, characterize, and illustrate rather than to enumerate in long lists. Shift in pronunciation has followed the same principle, taking illustrative and more readily understood examples rather than exhaustive accounts of sound changes. Grimm's and Verner's Laws, the Great Vowel Shift, and examples of feeding and bleeding have been introduced with this in mind. Within the general area of grammar and inflection, a great deal of attention has been devoted to the pronoun system. In addition, both the loss or reduction of old and the introduction of new categories are treated. Among the former we find the case and gender systems of nouns, determiners, and adjectives; among the latter, aspect and mood/modality in the verb. Changes in the use of the language (pragmatics) have been approached in a small selection of examples as well.

Historical language contact has taken place with a wide selection of language neighbors: pre-English substrate languages, Latin, the Celtic languages, French and other later Romance languages, some of its Germanic sister languages, especially "Low Dutch," numerous indigenous languages of North America, Africa, Asia, Australia, and New Zealand, and a wide variety of immigrant languages. Everywhere contact has left now larger, now smaller marks on English. Changes in the language have emerged not only within this overall context, but also within the internal tug and pull between its numerous regional and social varieties. Traditional, regional, and social dialects as well as the many national varieties of Standard English (StE) and what in this book is designated General English (GenE) have exerted mutual influence on each other. How strong the influence in the one or the other direction has been is a matter of the intensity and duration of contact as well as the relative prestige of the varieties involved. Today English is used in local contexts, national ones, and global ones. It has become polycentric, yet does not seem to have lost its basic sense of unity.

As support for those who are linguistically uncertain an extensive glossary of linguistic terms – always with examples – has been added at the end of the book. Furthermore, an extended version of this glossary is available on the book website (**www.routledge.com/cw/gramley**), where historical, social, and cultural entries have also been supplied. In contrast to the alphabetical glossary in the book, the website glossary is structured by topic. Other attributes of *HoE* which are intended to help the user are the large number of tables, maps, figures, and color plates. Each chapter is preceded by a bulleted list of the major points to be examined, and each ends with a short summary, study questions (sample answers and further exercises on the website), and annotated suggestions for further reading.

The general bibliography and the index given at the end document sources and help the reader to find the passages where a particular topic is presented.

Many of the website glossary entries go into more depth than is possible in the book itself. Furthermore, topics which are treated in a number of different chapters are presented on the website in a more synoptic form. There are also links to further exercises and to both new texts and extended ones. All extracts have been carefully selected within the recommendations for fair dealing and are credited in their captions. The publishers would be pleased to hear from any not acknowledged appropriately so that this can be amended at the earliest opportunity.

In closing, there is a long list of people I would like to thank. In a very general sense my colleagues at the Bielefeld University Department of British and American Studies and the excellent Bielefeld University Library, without which this project would have been hopeless. More specifically, thanks go to all the anonymous reviewers for their often very helpful suggestions, not all of which I necessarily adopted. For in the end I carry the responsibility for the material selected, the explanations given, and the positions taken. Everyone at Routledge has been extremely helpful, and the list is long: Nadia Seemungal (commissioning editor, English language and linguistics), Sarah Mabley (deputy production editorial manager, humanities), Marie Mansfield (senior website designer), Kate Reeves (copy editor), and Emma Davis (who searched out high-resolution color plates and their rights). I would especially like to mention Eloise Cook, my desk editor in the early phase of writing, Alex McGregor, who helped me to the deadline, and Moira Taylor, who accompanied me most intensively in all but the final stages of work. Last, but very certainly not least, more thanks than I can express go to

Hedda

for her support and patience. I owe her an enormous debt for lost time together which desperately needs to be made up.

Acknowledgments

The publishers would like to thank the following for permission to reprint their material:

Plate 1.1 Ptolemy. Britain and Ireland
Jacob d'Angelo after Claudius Ptolemaeus, Cosmographia Claudii Ptolomaei – cosmology of Britain and Ireland, Alexandrini (1467), published in the Reichenbach Monastery. Artist: Nicolaus Germanus. Ink and color on parchment. Now held in the National Library, Warsaw
    From http://en.wikipedia.org/wiki/File:Ptolemy_Cosmographia_1467_-_Great_Britain_and_Ireland.jpg
    Website www.bn.org.pl; www.polona.pl
    Accession number Rps BOZ 2/I-II

Plate 1.2 Serpent Stone
(Pictish) English: Aberlemno Serpent Stone. Class I Pictish stone. © Catfish Jim and the soapdish at en.wikipedia
    http://en.wikipedia.org/wiki/File:Serpent_stone.JPG

Plate 2.1 Mercy and Truth (ninth century)
Württembergische Landesbibliothek for kind permission to reprint Carolingian minuscule (ninth century), from the Stuttgarter Psalter, Cod. bibl. fol. 23, 100v. Psalm 85: 10 "Mercy and truth are met together; righteousness and peace have kissed each other" held in the Württembergische Landesbibliothek, Stuttgart, Germany.

Plate 2.2 Medieval Church Music (late thirteenth century)
Government of South Australia and State Library of South Australia for kind permission to reprint Antiphonal page 1 showing an illuminated R. Antiphonarium ad laudes vesperas, et magnificat a nat. Dni N.J.C. usque ad octavam epiphanie. Liber secundus. Image courtesy of the State Library of South Australia. SLSA: Rare Books Room 096 d ++.

Plate 2.3 Runic Pin
© The Trustees of the British Museum for permission to reprint Anglo-Saxon disc-headed pin from Malton, North Yorkshire, engraved with the first seven or eight letters of the *futhorc*, 'f u þ o r c g l a æ e', British Museum, mid-Saxon (650–850).

Plate 2.4 *Beowulf* (c. 1000)
British Library for permission to reprint *Beowulf*, 1st page "Hwæt! Wé Gárdena . . ." The beginning of *Beowulf* (Whole folio). The beginning of the Anglo-Saxon poem about *Beowulf* in the sole surviving manuscript. Originally published/produced in circa 1000. Cotton Vitellius A. XV, f.132. Image no. 010625

Plate 3.1 Anglo-Saxon Chronicle (copied in mid-eleventh century)
British Library for permission to reprint Entries in Anglo-Saxon Chronicle [Whole folio] Entries in the chronicle for the years 991 to 993. Image taken from Anglo-Saxon Chronicle. Originally published/produced in England [Abingdon]; eleventh and twelfth centuries. Cotton Tiberius B. I, f.144v. BL 013094

Plate 3.2 Book of Lindesfarne
© The British Library Board for permission to reprint Book of Lindisfarne, John 1:1 (c. 720) [Whole folio] Incipit page to St. John's Gospel. Text with decorated letters 'INP'. Decorated border. Image taken from Lindisfarne Gospels. Originally published/produced in N.E. England [Lindisfarne]; 710–721. Author: Eadfrith, Bishop of Lindisfarne; scribe, Aldred, Shelfmark/Page: Cotton Nero D. IV, f.211. Language: Latin, with Anglo-Saxon glosses.

Plate 4.1 William the Conqueror (eleventh century).
William the Conqueror, No. 4539 (scene 37). Detail from the Bayeux Tapestry – eleventh century. By special permission of the city of Bayeux.

Plate 4.2 Death of King Harold (eleventh century)
No 4571 (scene 57). Detail from the Bayeux Tapestry – eleventh century. By special permission of the city of Bayeux.

Plate 5.1 The Peasants Revolt (c. 1385–1400)
© The British Library Board for permission to reprint The Peasants' Revolt (Miniature). Two groups of rebels meet outside London. They carry banners of England and St. George. Their leaders John Ball, on horseback, and Wat Tyler, standing left, are labelled 'Jehan Balle' and 'Waultre le Tieulier' respectively. Image taken from Chroniques de France et d'Angleterre, Book II. Originally published/produced in S. Netherlands, circa 1460–1480. Author: Froissart, Jean. Shelfmark/Page: Royal 18 E. I, f.165v. BL 016522. Language: French.

Plate 5.2 Wycliffe
University of Glasgow Library, Department of Special Collections, for permission to reprint John Wycliffe: New Testament – England: late Fourteenth Century. John Wycliffe: New Testament. Manuscript: England: late Fourteenth Century. MS Hunter 191 (T.8.23): Opening of beginning of St. John's Gospel (folio 2v).

Plate 5.3 Chaucer as a pilgrim (early fifteenth century)
Huntington Library for permission to reprint Chaucer the Pilgrim – From the Ellesmere Manuscript, Huntington Library, in San Marino, California, USA (MS EL 26 C 9 153v). This item is reproduced by permission of The Huntington Library, San Marino, California.

Plate 5.4 World map (late fourteenth century)
© British Library for permission to reprint (Double opening) World Map in rounded oval shape. The heads placed round the edge represent the twelve winds. Britain is at the lower left. Image taken from Polychronicon. Originally published/produced in late fourteenth century. Author: Higden, Ranulf. Shelfmark/Page: Royal 14 C. IX, ff.1v–2. BL 002429

Plate 6.1 Shakespeare, The First Folio (1623)
British Library for permission to reprint Shakespeare, The First Folio (1623) Titlepage. Image taken from Mr. William Shakespeares Comedies, Histories, & Tragedies. Published according to the True Originall Copies. [Edited by J. Heminge and H. Condell.] Ed. Pr. Originally published and printed by Isaac Iaggard and Ed. Blount: London, 1623. Shelfmark/Page: C.39.k.15, dedication and frontispiece. BL 072991

Plate 6.2 Bunyan. *The Pilgrim's Progress* (1683 [1677–78])
© The British Library Board for permission to reprint John Bunyan. *The Pilgrim's Progress*, 1683 [1677–78] [The Pilgrim's Progress from this world, to that which is to come: delivered under the similitude of a dream. Wherein is discovered, the manner of his setting out, his dangerous journey; and safe arrival at the desired countrey.] Originally published/produced in London, 1679. Shelfmark/Page: C.70.aa.3, frontispiece and title page. BL 075712

Plate 6.3 Milton. Areopagitica (1644)
© The British Library Board for permission to reprint Milton, John, [Prose Works. Areopagitica] Areopagitica; a speech of Mr. John Milton for the liberty of unlicenc'd printing, to the Parlament of England. (London, 1644.) Ashley1176. C.120.b.12.(1.) C.55.c.22.(9.) G.608

Plate 8.1 Johnson's Dictionary (1755)
Vassar College Libraries for permission to reprint the title page of the 1755 first edition of Johnson's Dictionary

Figure 8.2 Lodwick Universall Alphabet
Lodwick Universall Alphabet. Source: Abercrombie, D. (1965) *Studies in Phonetics and Linguistics.* London: OUP, p. 51.

Plate 8.2 Dickens' Sam Weller (1833)
Characters from Charles Dickens "Sam Weller" Details: Artist: Kyd. Publisher: Raphael Tuck & Sons Size: 3.5" x 5.5" (9 x 14 cm) Other Categories: New Additions Stock #: 303266 Description: Dickens Series 541 III
"Sam Weller" (*The Pickwick Papers*) "We shan't be bankrupts, & we shan't make our fort'ns. We eats our biled mutton without capers, & don't care for horse-radish ven ve can get beef."

Plate 9.1 Middle passage (after 1788)
"Stowage of the British Slave Ship *Brookes*, Under the Regulated Slave Trade Act of 1788, American School, engraving, Library of Congress, Washington DC." Broadside Portfolio 282, #43. Image courtesy of the Rare Book Division of the Library of Congress.

Plate 9.2 Jamaican Creole Alphabet (current)
Source: John Well's phonetic blog archive 1–15 August 2008.

Plate 10.1 New England Primer (1690)
The Pocumtuck Valley Memorial Association Library for permission to reprint the title page from a 1905 facsimile reprint of the 1690 *New England Primer*.

Plate 10.2 Manumission paper (1821)
© Ontario County Department of Records, Archives and Information for permission to reprint letter written by Robert Buchan setting a slave free.

Plate 10.3 Fugitive slave notice (1 August 1810)
© New York Public Library for permission to reprint this slave notice from Geneva Gazette of Geneva, New York.

Plate 10.4 American Spelling Book (1824)
New York Public Library for permission to reprint the facsimile cover of Noah Webster's Blue-Backed Speller.

Plate 10.5 Uncle Remus
Wilson Special Collection Library for permission to reprint title page of *Uncle Remus, His Songs and His Sayings: The Folk-Lore of the Old Plantation*. By Joel Chandler Harris. With Illustrations by Frederick S. Church and James H. Moser. Published in New York, D. Appleton And Company 1881.

Plate 11.1 Convict discipline (1837)
Rare/Special Collections, Morris Miller Library, University of Tasmania for kind permission to reprint Original Essays on Convict Discipline by Captain Alexander Maconochie, 1837, with some letters etc. in further illustration of the same subject by J. Backhouse and G.W. Walker 1937, University of Tasmania Special and Rare Materials Collections

Plate 11.2 Treaty of Waitangi/Te Tiriti o Waitangi
Archives New Zealand for permission to reprint Treaty of Waitangi (1840) showing Maori signatures. Archives New Zeland/*Te Rua o te Kāwanatanga*
Wellington Office. [1A 9/9]

Plate 11.3 South African road sign (current)
Vincent Mounier for permission to reprint "Robot" South African road sign. © Vincent Mounier. www.vincentmounier.com

Plate 11.4 New Zealand road sign (current)
Bob and Joy Hall, Timaru, New Zealand.

Plate 12.1 Bollywood poster
BFI for permission to reprint poster of Bollywood Film, *Shaheed*, by director Ramesh Saigal, 1948 © British Film Institute.

Plate 12.2 Multilingual sign in Singapore
Paul Souders/Worldfoto for permission to reprint photograph "Asia, Singapore, Warning sign outside fence of Cargo Terminal" 2006 ASNG0181.jpg. © Paul Souders/WorldFoto

Disclaimer

The publishers have made every effort to contact authors/copyright holders of works reprinted in *A History of English* and to obtain permission to publish extracts. This has not been possible in every case, however, and we would welcome correspondence from those individuals/companies whom we have been unable to trace. Any omissions brought to our attention will be remedied in future editions.

The origins of English (before 450)

Si civitas, in qua orti sunt, langa pace et otio torpeat, plerique nobilium adulescentium petunt ultro eas nationes, quae tum bellum aliquod gerunt, quia et ingrata genti quies et facilius inter ancipitia clarescunt magnumque comitatium non nisi vi belloque tueare.

(Tacitus, *Germania*, XIV)

If the tribe in which they have grown up is in danger of growing weak in a long period of peace, many of the noble young men by their own decision search for tribes which are currently waging war; for quiet is not congenial to them and it is easier to gain fame among dangers; furthermore, it is only possible to support a large number of followers with acts of violence and war.

Chapter Overview:

This chapter:

- explores some basic points about the origins of human language;
- asks how so many languages came about and looks at how some are related to each other;
- reviews the main principles of language change – internal and external change, including creolization;
- examines the Germanic tribes in Roman times and the influence of Latin, the language of the Romans, on the language spoken by those Germanic tribes who carried what was to be English to Britain.

1.1 The origins of human language

According to some calculations the capacity for language – which is surely one of the most clearly human features we have – emerged approximately 145,000 years ago (± 70,000) (Bickerton 1990: 175). The emergence of human speech depended on both suitable physiological change in what were to become the organs of speech and on changes in the structure of the brain to allow humans to work with the complexity of language neuro-logically (ibid.: chap. 8). Furthermore, the acquisition of language is widely seen as a unique human faculty (e.g. Bickerton 1990: 4). As such it was then passed on to the descendants of the first group of speakers (link: The origins of language).

Just how this mooted first language may have looked is unknown, but the multiplicity and diversity of languages spoken in today's world indicate one of the unchanging principles of human language – change: out of one many have developed. One of these many lan-guages is English, itself a grouping of often very different varieties spoken all over the world by both native and non-native speakers. Just how many speakers is a widely debated question, as is the question of what a native and what a non-native speaker is (see the discussion in 7.4.2 and 13.4). It is the aim of this book to explore how English came into being and developed the enormous amount of diversity which the label English covers.

1.1.1 Divergence, change, and the family model (link: Models of change)

Among those who study language (as such, i.e. not "just" individual languages) there are those who have tried to trace the development from the assumed first or *proto-language* to our own day with its 5000 to 7000 languages. This is done by extrapolating backwards from the known to the unknown in a process designated as reconstruction (link: Example of reconstruction). It notes the similarities between, say, English and *Dutch* and Icelandic or between *French* and *Spanish* and Italian and tries to figure out what earlier shared forms the three languages mentioned in each case might be expected to have had. In the case of French, Spanish, and Italian these languages are known as the Romance (or Romanic) languages, all of them having "descended" from the earlier "parent" language, Latin. (The name Romance is an indication these languages were spoken by the Romans.)

Latin is well documented by the many Latin texts still available today. By tracing changes from Latin to its successor languages it has been possible to discover principles of language change and to classify the resulting languages accordingly. Figure 1.1 is a highly simplified presentation of Latin and its daughter languages (mutual sisters). The division into a western and an eastern branch is only one way of distinguishing the family's *divergence*. And, of course, the nine languages in the bottom line are not a complete list of the present-day *Romance languages*.

For English, Dutch, Icelandic as well as other *Germanic languages* such as German, Yiddish, Frisian, Swedish, Danish, Norwegian, and Faroese there is no documented earlier language. Yet historians of language make the assumption that the same kinds of principles apply here as to Latin and the Romance languages and allow us to reconstruct a language

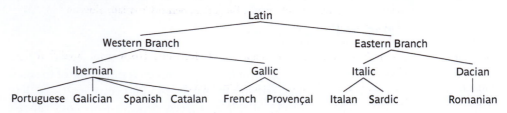

Figure 1.1 The Romance language family

known as **Proto-Germanic**. This proto-language is labeled metaphorically as the mother of a language family and the sublanguages as its daughters or, as it may be, granddaughters. In Figure 1.2, as in Figure 1.1, not every variety has been listed – and the East Germanic sub-family has died out completely.

The Germanic and the Romance language families themselves belong to a larger grouping known as the **Indo-European language family** (link: Indo-European language family). This language family has, in the modern age, spread widely throughout the world at the cost of other languages. In fact, today as much as half the population of the world may well be (native) speakers of an Indo-European language. Table 1.1 lists its nine families (two putative sisters not listed in the table, Tocharian and Hittite, are no longer spoken).

The **family model** has played an important role in the historical study of language and is based on assumptions about geographical distance as a factor which eventually leads to the accumulation of differences between the varieties to the point where we may first speak about dialectal differences (with continued mutual intelligibility). Eventually the differences are so large that the speakers in the separate speech communities can no longer understand each other. It is then usual to speak of different languages.

We should note, however, that the criteria which are applied in deciding whether two varieties which have drifted apart in this fashion are separate languages or not are also political. English is distinct from German, Dutch, and Swedish. But how distinct are English and **Scots** or Dutch and Low German (spoken across the border from The Netherlands in

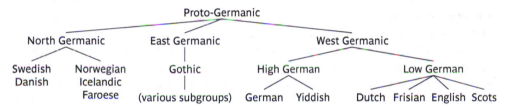

Figure 1.2 The Germanic language family

Table 1.1 The Indo-European language family

Proto-Indo-European

Armenian	Armenian
Albanian	Albanian
Balto-Slavic	Baltic: Latvian, Lithuanian; West Slavic: Czech, Polish, Slovak; East Slavic: Russian, Ukrainian; South Slavic: Bulgarian, Serbo-Croatian, Slovene, Macedonian (etc.)
Celtic	Welsh, Gaelic, Breton (etc.)
Germanic	Dutch, Frisian, English, German; Danish, Icelandic, Norwegian, Swedish (etc.)
Hellenic	Greek
Indian	Bengali, Hindi, Marathi, Punjabi, Urdu (etc.)
Iranian	Baluchi, Farsi (Persian), Kurdish, Pasto
Italic	Latin → Catalan, French, Galician, Italian, Romanian (etc.)

parts of Germany) or Swedish and Danish? Mutual intelligibility as well as questions of power and (language) politics are questions of degree and often cannot be answered definitively.

One of the problems with a simplistic family model is that it assumes divergence and therefore does not take into account *borrowing* and other processes by which languages grow more similar. Yet this is precisely what happens when speech communities come into (renewed) contact with each other. In prehistoric times migrations of peoples often led to the loss of contact and to divergence. But in that world as well as in the historically documented world, renewed contact – in the form of trade, military conquest, cultural and technical diffusion, or whatever – has led to an increase in shared linguistic features (e.g. words, structures, meanings and practices, pronunciations). In the present-day world of intense and frequent long-distance travel and trade as well as of instant communication over long distances, geographical remoteness has become less decisive as a motor for change (see 13.2).

1.1.2 The speech community (link: Speech community)

We may view users of a language according to the attributes they share – be they location, gender, age, ethnicity, social class, or whatever else (including combinations – or *intersectionalities* – of these). In prehistoric times and, indeed, in early historical times location was probably the most significant feature which marked off speakers into separate communities. Speakers in a single community were very likely to speak like other members of the same community and more or less differently from people who, while speaking the "same," mutually intelligible language lived further away.

It is the relatively more intense interaction between speakers which ensures that their language will be more or less homogeneous. While individual speakers will produce speech according to their own internal(ized) rules and may be said to have an independent language system, their system will be relatively more similar to the system of speakers they are in frequent contact with than with speakers located further away. This closeness is based on the principle of *accommodation* (link: Accommodation), a basic principle of communication which dictates that we make our speech more similar to that of our communication partners when we want to:

- improve communication
- gain the listener's social approval
- maintain a positive social identity
- minimize negative outcomes
- reduce social and psychological distance (cf. Giles et al. 1977).

In doing this we converge with our interlocutors, for example, in pronunciation, speech rate, and pauses. Of course, we may also *diverge* from those we are talking to by emphasizing linguistic differences in order to underscore social distinctions or to maintain identities (cf. Winford 2003: 119). In both cases the motives may involve individual likes and dislikes or may be a matter of group identity.

1.2 Language change

Change in language is usually seen as one of two types. The first is termed internal change and covers variation in what might be called the normal "drift of language" ([link: Linguistic drift](#)), as when more and more people within a *speech community* do not pronounce /h/ in words which previously had an aitch. Another example, which will be elaborated below in 1.2.2, 1.2.4, and 1.3.2, is the increasing use of demonstratives before nouns, which in the earliest stages of the language had been preceded by *adjectives*, by an occasional demonstrative, but never by an *article*. At some stage the *demonstratives* became not only normal, but also systematic, and the result was an article system[1] ([link: Articles](#)). It is clear that variant forms will coexist, that is, forms with and without /h/ and nouns preceded or not by a demonstrative or an article. Presumably the spread of such innovations can be credited to accommodation.

1.2.1 Internal change

What is not easily explicable is just why people begin to drop their aitches or to use more and more pre-nominal demonstratives. One speculative, but not completely implausible scenario is that such changes are closely connected with emphatic communication. Aitches have historically been lost first in combination with other consonants. Old English (OE) had words which began with the clusters /hl-/, /hn-/, /hr-/, and /hw-/ (cf. *hláf* (loaf), *hnígan* (lean), *hring* (ring), *hwæt* (what)). This /h/ represents strong *aspiration* and may well have gradually been associated with emphatic expression. Its loss in such combinations would then be expected in non-frenetic speech. This would be a contribution to understanding why the combination /hw-/ has been retained longest: it is most frequent in question words and they are often uttered individually and therefore more emphatically (*What! Why! When!*). While clusters with /h/ have overall declined or disappeared, in some types of English they have actually spread, as when the interjection *Wow!* is pronounced /hwaʊ/ rather than historical /waʊ/ by some speakers in California (Metcalf 1972: 33).[2]

The use of a demonstrative before a noun has a similar motivation: it had the effect of emphasizing (and specifying) the following noun. In emphatic speech *styles* this must have been common usage. From what initially were singular cases speakers would have generalized this usage. In this way the original *deictic* ([link: Deixis](#)) sense, for example, the location of something in time and space, would then have become less prominent and the sense of specification would have been generalized to nouns for which location in space was not prominent, that is, not just deictic *se fisc* (lit. "that fish"), but also *þurh þone hunger* ("by that hunger"), a much more abstract usage.

---

1 This is a highly simplified explanation; it does not, for example, consider indefinite articles.
2 No comment will be made at this point on the loss of initial /h-/ in many urban British *accents* nor on the loss of /x/, the variant of /h/, (spelled <gh> in, for example, *though, right*, etc.). See below 6.3.1.4.

1.2.2 Typological change (link: Typological change)

The kind of change which the development of an article system represents is so fundamental that it is often referred to as typological change. In making a statement of this sort we are employing ideas about classes or types of languages, for example ones with and ones without articles. English has articles; Russian does not. Hence the two are typologically different (in this point). While this example seems clear, it conceals the question about what we are comparing when we make typological conclusions, that is, what is an article? Basically, we can use either a formal or a functional approach (cf. Croft 1990). From the formal point of view we are looking for words which precede a noun. That would be the case for *the* and *a/an* in English and for *la/el/lo* and *un/una* in Spanish, but it would not include the particle added at the end of nouns in Swedish, for example the *-et* in *huset* (literally "house-the"). Consequently, functions, and not form alone, clearly also play an indispensable role. From a functional perspective (definite) articles are *specifiers*: they indicate that the noun which follows is a particular, individual example of the class indicated by the noun. Furthermore, the reason for choosing a particular structure cannot be neglected. That is, the pragmatic motivation for using it needs to be taken into consideration, as our speculation about the reasons for the emergence of the articles in English shows.

In the case of English the sheer quantity of structural changes that took place between the (pre-)Old English period and, say, Early Modern English (EModE) was so great that people (e.g. Strang 1970: 59; Barber et al. 2009: 26–29) speak of a typological change. *Word order* patterns (link: Word order in English) changed, *inflections* (link: Inflection in English) were lost, subject pronouns became mandatory, new noun and verb categories (link: Grammatical categories) emerged while older ones disappeared. *Modes of address* (link: Modes of address), expressions of *politeness*, structures of discourse – all "external" to the narrower linguistic system of the language – also changed. In the course of this book we will look at all of these points and more.

1.2.3 External change

When languages come into contact with one another, they are likely to have an influence on each other, sometimes quite significant, as in the case of *creolization* (see below 3.3, 4.3, and chapter 9), and sometimes relatively superficial, as when words from one language find their way into another language and are assimilated into it. In either case – or in any of the numerous stages that lie between these two extremes – the change within the receiving language may be traced back to its source. Furthermore, this may be a major part of an explanation about why a particular innovation has come about. Very often this lies in the power or prestige of the source speech community or in the convenience of borrowing *vocabulary* for "new" things from the "new" language. In the following the two processes just mentioned, creolization and borrowing, will be explained and exemplified.

1.2.4 Creolization (link: Creolization)

When language communities in which mutually unintelligible languages are spoken come into contact with each other, communication is most often ensured by learning the language of the other group. In some, relatively extreme cases a large subaltern group, itself frequently polyglot, comes to be dominated by a group of powerful speakers of an "outside" language.

The nature of the domination may be political, military, economic, religious, or whatever; it may last for a short time or for centuries; the contact between the dominant and the subordinate groups may be close or distant. All of these factors are likely to have an effect on language use, and one of the results of such *language contact* can be the emergence of a creole.

The conditions for creolization are most likely to come about in a situation in which there is imperfect learning of the superordinate language, the *superstrate*, on the part of those learners who will eventually contribute the basis for a creole. This is due to more distant contact with the superstrate. Such speakers are frequently dependent on devising a means of communication, both between themselves and the dominant group and among themselves. As a result, a great deal of lexical borrowing from the superstrate takes place, but the borrowed vocabulary is used, to a greater or lesser extent, according to the grammar of their *native language*(s), the *substrate*(s).[3] Consequently, what is produced may seem like a word-for-word translation of the speaker's *L1* using vocabulary from the superstrate. This is as if the Latin sentence *ego te amo* were to get English words but retain Latin word order: *I you love*. Such a linguistic state of affairs is referred to as *pidginization* (link: Pidginization), whereby a pidgin is understood as a language which is nobody's native language. There may be as many different grammars as there are native languages of the pidgin speakers. The children of pidgin speakers use the building blocks of the pidgin(s) to produce the language they use when they learn to talk. This is their own first or native language and is what is regarded as a creole.

Creolization has occurred at various times throughout the history of English (see esp. 3.3 and chapter 9). In the case of pre-invasion Germanic we have no direct, documentary evidence of creolization; however, the rather striking changes in the pronunciation of Proto-Germanic in comparison to the other Indo-European languages may well be an indication of contact between Indo-European invaders and a non-Indo-European substrate of speakers (see below 1.3).

Furthermore, the development of article systems in the Romance languages and in the West Germanic languages is an indication of an influence that can hardly have just been "in the air." What is more likely is that some of the substrate languages of the Italian and Iberian peninsulas, of Gaul (more or less present-day France), and of northwestern Europe exclusive of Scandinavia may have had article systems, thus reinforcing an internal, pragmatically motivated typological shift to languages with article systems (cf. Crisma 2009). The definite article developed notably differently in the Scandinavian languages and in Romanian, namely as a suffix added to the noun (see above). And in all the Slavonic languages (except Bulgarian, which patterns like Romanian) there is no definite article at all, suggesting a different set of conditions in different geographical areas.

1.2.5 Borrowing (link: Borrowing)

Cultural and linguistic difference may affect languages without bringing about any significant structural change. When new artifacts, new processes, and new ideas are adopted in a society previously without them, their designations are often the result either of the use

---

3 Other sources including general principles of learning or acquisition are also involved. See 9.5.4.

of native elements in *word formation processes* (link: Word formation processes) or of the borrowing of the words used in the donor language. OE *eorþcræft* (literally "earth-craft") is a combination of two native elements in a familiar process of *compounding* and is used to express the classical concept of geometry. More common in the pre-invasion period, however, was direct borrowing, giving us such present-day words as *cheese*, OE *cēse* (< Latin *caseus*), *street*, OE *strǣt* (< *strata*), and *mint*, OE *mynet* (< *moneta*). Borrowing from Latin in the pre-invasion Germanic period was a very productive way of expanding the Germanic word stock and its effects will be dealt with below (1.4.2).

1.3 Changes in Germanic before the invasions of Britain

Some linguists have advanced the notion that Proto-Germanic differs from the other Indo-European (IE) languages because of the imposition of Proto-Indo-European on a group of speakers with a different substrate language, as mentioned above. This theory of creolization (and variations on it) has not been widely accepted. Yet it would go quite far in explaining the long list of differences between the Germanic branch and the other IE languages: (1) the smaller number of *tense* (link: Tense) and *aspect* (link: Aspect) distinctions of Proto-Germanic; (2) the presence of regular verbs (so-called *weak verbs*) with a {-d} or {-t} ending in the past; (3) the presence of *weak adjective endings* (link: Introduction to OE); (4) the shift of *word stress* (link: Word stress) to the root syllable; (5) the presence of a fairly large number of words which do not seem to be derived from IE sources; and, of course, (6) the effects of Grimm's and Verner's Laws (see next).

1.3.1 Changes in pronunciation (link: Sound change)

Long before the invaders from the northwest of the European continent arrived in Britain, where they would establish the language that was to become English, a subgrouping of the speakers of Proto-Indo-European adopted changes in pronunciation that came to be known as the *First Germanic Sound Shift*.[4] One part of this, *Grimm's Law*,[5] describes the systematic shift in the way people pronounced certain consonants. IE voiced stops, the sounds /b/, /d/ and /g/, lost their *voicing* in Germanic and became /p/, /t/, and /k/. This means that IE /b/ as represented by Latin *lubricus* underwent a change to /p/ as seen in English *slippery*. Likewise /d/ became /t/ as in the pair Latin *ad* and English *at*. Finally, /g/ as in *jugum* became /k/ as in *yoke*. This would have led to a *merger* with words that already had /p/, /t/, and /k/ except that the latter three themselves changed to the corresponding *fricatives* /f/, /θ/, and /h/ (see Table 1.2). As a result IE /p/ as in Latin *piscus* became /f/, as in English

4 There was also a Second Germanic or High German Sound Shift (link: Germanic Sound Shift). It does not concern us since it caused changes seen in present-day German vis-à-vis the Low German languages (Dutch, English, Frisian, etc.).

5 Named after the nineteenth century German linguist Jakob Grimm (1785–1863), also known for the fairy tales he and his brother Wilhelm collected.

Table 1.2 Grimm's Law (simplified)

voiced stops	become	"new" voiceless stops	"old" voiceless stops	become	voiceless fricatives
b (Latin: *lubricus*)	>	p (English: *slippery*)	p (Latin: *piscus*)	>	f (English: *fish*)
d (Latin: *ad*)	>	t (English: *at*)	t (Latin: *tres*)	>	θ (English: *three*)
g (Latin: *jugum*)	>	k (English: *yoke*)	k (Latin: *cordis*)	>	h (English: *heart*)

fish; the **stop** /t/ (*tres*) shifted to the fricative /θ/ as in *three*, and the /k/ of Latin *cordis* was pronounced as /h/ in English *heart*. Needless to say, there are very, very many other instances of this shift. For unfamiliar terminology, see glossary.

Yet these changes do not occur in every case where they might be expected. Some of the exceptions turned out to be easy to describe. Germanic retained /p, t, k/ after /s/ as in Latin *sparus* and English *spear*, also *stella* – *star, scorbus* ("ditch") – *scrape*. Likewise, /p, t, k/ remained unchanged after a voiceless stop, for example as is the case of the /t/ after the voiceless stop /k/ in both Latin *octo* and English *eight*, also *noctis* – *night*.[6] But why, for example, did /t/ in IE as represented by Latin *pater* become not /fɑːθər/ but /fɑːðər/? At this point another nineteenth century linguist, Karl Verner,[7] in the second part of the First Germanic Sound Shift known as **Verner's Law**, explained this by pointing out the effect of word stress. According to Verner both *pater* and *father* originally carried their stress on the second syllable, as did IE **phadēr* (the asterisk "*" meant this word has been reconstructed). Verner discovered that voiceless fricatives (/f, s, θ, ʃ/) became voiced in Germanic if the preceding syllable was unstressed. However, this had been hard to discover because a later shift of stress to the root syllable had removed the original reason for the voicing shift (link: First Germanic Sound Shift).

1.3.2 Changes in grammar

Early Germanic was a language which marked nouns, adjectives, and demonstratives (words like *this* and *that*) for case, number, and gender. These are categories of grammar which have a very much reduced presence in ModE. **Number** is still a marked for count nouns like *apple(s), banana(s),* and *cucumber(s)* though not normally for abstract ones like *beauty,*

Table 1.3 Verner's Law (simplified) (link: Phonetic symbols)

IE voiceless stops	*p*	*t*	*k*
Grimm: became voiceless fricatives	ɸ	θ	x
Verner: became voiced fricatives	β	ð	ɣ

6 Note, however, that voiceless <c> (pronounced /k/) became /h/ in Germanic – originally pronounced like German <-ch> as in *acht* or Spanish <j> as in *hija*.

7 Nineteenth century Danish linguist (1846–1896).

intelligence, and *secrecy* or **mass nouns** like *snow, milk,* and *dirt.* **Gender** is marked grammatically[8] only in the third person singular personal pronouns (*he, she, it*). **Case**, a marking of such sentence functions as subject (nominative), direct (accusative) or indirect (dative) object, and possessor (genitive), is marked today most clearly in the system of **personal pronouns** (link: Personal pronouns) (e.g. possessive *my/mine, your(s), her(s), his, its, our(s), their(s)*), but the {-s} ending is also used to mark the possessive case of nouns (*the book's cover, my* **family's** *summer plans, two* **guys'** *brilliant ideas*).

In Germanic as in other Indo-European languages there was a complex system of inflectional endings. Whoever has learned Latin or modern European languages like Russian or German is familiar with such systems. If we look at (Classical) Latin,[9] we see a language which resembles undocumented, but reconstructed Proto-Germanic in many of its features. By the time Old English came to be written the process was well underway in which inflectional endings were no longer being clearly distinguished. Interestingly enough, the same process was also taking place in the case of (Vulgar) Latin,[10] which was also now losing many of its case **markers**, but – like English – preserving some of them in the personal pronoun system, while maintaining distinctions of gender (e.g. French masculine *le livre*, feminine *la coup* or Spanish masculine *el libro*, feminine *la copa*), and marking number in one or the other fashion.

As both the Germanic and the Romance languages lost more and more endings, there must have been difficulties in making the necessary grammatical distinctions. In both cases the system of **demonstratives** (link: Demonstratives) was used to mark gender (in the Romance languages) and case and gender in Old English. This was done by placing a demonstrative in front of the noun, as for example with the Latin words for *earth* and *fish*, where the definite articles used developed (in varying ways) out of the Latin demonstrative masculine *ille* and feminine *illa*:

Table 1.4 The definite article in some modern Romance languages

Latin	French	Spanish	Italian
terra	la terre	la tierra	la terra
piscus	la pêche (le poisson)	el·pez	il pesce

In the case of English the demonstrative also began to function as the definite article, as we see for the words for *fish* and for *earth*:

Table 1.5 The definite article in some older Germanic languages

Proto-Germanic	Old English	Gothic	Old High German
*erthō	sēo eorðe	so aírþa	diu erda
*fiskōjanan	se fisc	sa fisks	dé fisc

8 Distinctions such as *waitress–waiter* or *he-dog–she-dog* are lexical rather than grammatical in nature.
9 Classical Latin is the variety taught in school; it was decisively formed under the influence of Roman writers such as Cicero and preserved in the work of grammarians.
10 Vulgar (or colloquial) Latin was the language of everyday life. It was the latter which changed, gradually turning into the vernacular languages French, Italian, Spanish, Catalan, Romanian, and so on.

Not only did the two groups of languages develop article systems at about the same time, they also used the same sources, the demonstratives.

1.3.3 Changes in vocabulary

Sound shifts and grammatical restructuring no doubt say a great deal about the *typology* of a language because they are of a systematic nature. Vocabulary, in contrast, is more likely to reveal something about the world the speakers lived in. First we will look at the ancient world of the Germanic peoples and then at the nature of the contact between them and the Romans and at the influence of the Roman Empire and of Latin as seen in a number of the Germanic languages including Old English.

1.4 The world of the Germanic peoples

As early Europe was moving out of the Stone Age into the Bronze and then the Iron Age, larger ethnic units began to form, and contact between them began to grow in significance, both warlike and trade-oriented. During the Bronze Age (roughly the first half of the first millennium BCE)[11] La Tène culture (link: La Tène culture), associated with Celtic peoples and territory, stood in a trade relation with Greek settlements at Marsalis (present-day Marseille) in the south and also exercised influence on the Germanic peoples to the north and east. As the Iron Age set in (second half of the first millennium BCE) major changes in trade and in social organization took place, and Roman influence started on a course of expansion which would go well beyond its Italian basis not only to Africa and the Levant, but also to Gallia, Germania, and Britannia. Our focus will be first on Germania and eventually on Britannia as well.

The designation Germanic (link: Germanic peoples; link: Germanic migrations) is used for a variety of peoples who lived both inside and outside of the Roman Empire and whose unifying feature (from our point of view) is their use of some form of Germanic (as discussed above). The life styles of these peoples differed between their various groupings.   Those within the Roman Empire adopted many features of Roman culture, and gradually even became essential to the survival of the Empire, supplying it, as they did, with slaves, soldiers, generals, and even emperors. The areas just outside the borders such as, for example, the Frisian (North Sea) coast, produced agricultural products for the Romans and were as such well integrated in the imperial economy and familiar with Roman life styles (Todd 1992: 68). The Germanic peoples who lived further away participated in the luxury trade, but were hardly affected by Rome on a more common, everyday basis.

The Germanic peoples lived principally from animal husbandry (esp. cows, pigs, sheep, and horses, in that order of importance). Hunting was of negligible importance, but there was substantial fishing at the coast. Crops included grain (barley, wheat/emmer, rye, and millet), legumes (beans, peas), and various vegetables (e.g. celery, spinach,

---

11 BCE = "Before Common Era"; CE (used below) = "Common Era"

dandelion, radishes, lettuce); furthermore, flax (for linseed oil and linen) was cultivated, but little or no fruit. The grain was also used for fermented beverages such as beer (ibid.: 76–79).

Germanic societies were regarded as relatively egalitarian, yet the power of the leader or king was indisputably great. Young men (warriors) had the possibility to break away from the tribe under the leadership of a strong leader, to engage in raiding and to found a tribe of their own (cf. Todd 1992: 31–32; Price 1994), a feature which was significant for the Germanic invasions of England. Otherwise, it was the family (in which men might have more than one wife and in which slaves were held) which was the basic social unit (Todd 1992: 32–33).

1.4.1 Germanic–Roman contact

Germanic contact with the Roman world ([link: Roman Empire](link)) was often of a military nature, whether facing them as enemies or joining them as members of the Roman army. Some, such as, for instance, Arminius, gained military expertise while serving with the Roman army and then used this experience to install himself as a Germanic leader and organize resistance to Rome. Yet even though the Empire expanded its territorial control by means of military campaigns, its most telling influence among the Germanic peoples was in the area of trade regardless of whether the groups in contact were within the Roman Empire (Germania Superior and Germania Inferior) or outside of it (Germania Magna aka Germania Libera on Map 1.1).

Perhaps most clearly evident was the use of money, which archeologists have found in numerous hoards of coins, in the trade built up along routes established before the rise of

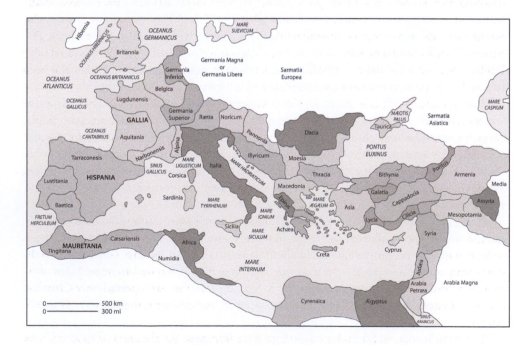

Map 1.1 The Roman Empire

Rome. This trade connected the Mediterranean world with Northern Europe and the British Isles. The major goods that were exchanged were metals. This originally took place without the use of money, though gold coins were introduced as early as 125 BCE. Celtic Britain (link: Celtic Britain), for example, was an important early source of tin, which was alloyed with copper to make bronze (see Cunliffe 1988, esp. chap. 7 and 8). Germania exported slaves, animal hides, meat, and amber in exchange for metallic vessels and pottery, jewelry, textiles, and perhaps some foodstuffs. Once these peoples were integrated in the Roman market world, money exercised considerable power over them and was an instrument of interference and control over areas not directly incorporated in the Roman Empire. Money, trade, gifts, and military aid even allowed Rome to exercise influence on the choice of leaders in Germania Libera (cf. Todd 1992: chap. 5).

1.4.2 The influence of the Roman world and of Latin

As already mentioned, Germanic soldiers served in the Roman army. While most soldiers remained in the Empire, others returned home bringing not only weapons and goods but also raising expectations about life styles and new ways of organizing society. This may be seen in such varied spheres of life as military, trade, religion, and life style.

Roman military structures were hierarchically organized while Germanic ones were largely democratic, allowing groups of young warriors to act independently of the clan. The military success of the Empire was surely a positive model for the Germanic peoples and was one of the factors which led to a more hierarchical organization, but also to an upgrading of Wodon, the Germanic god of war (link: Germanic and Classic pantheons), to the god of social order in general. Latin influence in the military area led to the adoption of words such as *camp*, *mīl* "mile," *pīl* "javelin," *pytt* "pit," *segn* "banner," *strēt* "street, road," and *weall* "wall." Many of these words, like those listed in the following paragraphs, also found their way into other Germanic languages. Latin *strata* (OE *strēt*), for instance, also entered Dutch (*straat*) and German (*Straße*). Others listed here and below disappeared from English, but not necessarily from other Germanic languages, for example *pīl* has not been retained in English, but shows up as German *Pfeil* "arrow."

The significance of trade can be seen in the adoption of words like *cēap* from Latin *caupo* "tradesman," which had a multitude of meanings, for example "purchase, sale, traffic, bargain (cf. present-day *cheap*), payment, goods, market, price." Other words in this area borrowed from Latin include *mangian* "to trade"; *mydd* "a unit of dry measure"; *mynet* "coin," cf. ModE *mint*; *pund* "pound"; and *sēam* "load, harness," but also such southern European goods as *wīn* "wine"; *must* "grape mash undergoing fermentation"; *eced* "vinegar"; *flasce* "bottle"; and *cylle* "leather bottle."

The Roman world did not greatly affect religion in the North, but those who settled in the Empire (or their children) converted to Christianity within a generation or two. It was only in the fourth century that any major change came, when the first Germanic people, the Goths, were Christianized. In the long run, Christianity and its language, Latin, were to have an extraordinarily strong effect on the language. In this early period only Christian *biscop* and pagan *Sæternesdæg* "Saturn's day, Saturday" can be mentioned in the domain of religion.

Roman influence on life styles was sure to have impinged on the areas of food (cf. *wīn*, *must*, *eced* above), clothing, household, and building, as the following table of borrowings

Table 1.6 Latin words borrowed into the early Germanic languages (here: Old English)

food	ModE	household	ModE	building	ModE
butere	butter	cucler	spoon	cealc	chalk
cīese	cheese	cuppe	cup	copor	copper
cires	cherry	cycene	kitchen	pic	pitch
cisten	chestnut	disc	dish	tigel	tile
minte	mint	cytel	kettle	*clothing*	
pipor	pepper	line	rope	gimm	gem
pise	pea	linen	linen	sigel	brooch
plūme	plum	mese	table	pilece	skin robe
senep	mustard	scamol	stool	*other*	
spelt	spelt, a kind of wheat	teped	curtain	mūl	mule
ynne	onion	pyle	pillow	pīpe	pipe, flute

suggests. Note, however, that some of the borrowed items in the list have since been replaced. For example *senep* has given way to *mustard*, a word borrowed from French.

Despite what seems to be an extensive list, there is evidence for few borrowings beyond these items. As we will see when we look more closely at Old English in the following chapters, its word stock contained only a small percentage of borrowings. Of course, it is not possible to come to watertight conclusions since there are no texts available in a Germanic language before the third century, when Ufilas prepared a translation of the Bible into Gothic, fragments of which have survived. The only other early examples of Germanic language use are second century CE *runic* inscriptions (link: Runes) made on weapons and personal ornaments which were found in the western Baltic area (Todd 1992: 120). The use of runes indicates a certain, though probably highly restricted, degree of literacy.

1.5 The Germanic migrations (link: Germanic migrations)

In ancient times the peoples of Europe periodically moved from their homelands to new territories. Just why they migrated is a matter of conjecture and surely differed from case to case (cf. Pohl 2005: 24–26). The major reason mooted is overpopulation, which led smaller groupings (rarely if ever a whole people) to move off to find sufficient land to settle on. On occasion pressure came from outside invaders such as the Huns, who pushed various peoples further to the west and caused them to try to find lands in the Roman Empire. Drought or other natural catastrophes might also have forced groups to pull up stakes and look for (literally) greener pastures. All of these points might be understood collectively as push-factors. The migration of the Angles to Kent was probably such a case since it seems that whole clans moved. Todd writes:

The stimuli to migrate were probably various, including a deterioration of living condi-tions in the coastal areas [not further specified], a rising population and, not least, a growing awareness of the opportunities for material advancement now opening across the North Sea.

(1992: 221)

Pull-factors, as indicated in the preceding quotation ("opportunities for material advancement") are also often seen as motivation for migration. Raids by bands of young warriors, perhaps younger sons without land, seem to have been quite frequent. While many of them were just that, raids, from which the men returned home with booty of all sorts, on other occasions they settled in the areas invaded and, after removing the male competitors they had defeated, took the indigenous women as wives. This may apply to the Saxons, whose pattern of settlement in the English *Midlands* with small and equal allotments suggests a well-regulated system of distributing spoils. Furthermore, since the Saxons practiced primogeniture,[12] smaller allotments would suffice, while the larger ones in Kent suggest more the Angles' system of gavelkind[13] (cf. Price 1994: 77).

Other pull-factors may be found in the changing structure of Germanic society under the influence of Roman expansion and Roman culture. The Roman Empire represented a high standard of living with well-established associations of power and prestige. In the case of England, even after the withdrawal of the Roman legionnaires there would have been no abrupt change.

1.5.1 The northern peoples: the Saxons and Frisians

The Saxons were not mentioned in any of the extant Latin literature until the second century CE, and they first attracted greater notice in the late third century as sea-raiders (along with the better-known Franks). Ptolemy (Plate 1.1) placed them between the Elbe River and the base of the Jutland peninsula. In the later Roman period Saxon was the name given the inhabitants of the lower Weser and Elbe valleys and the adjacent coastlands. Their reputation as sea-raiders was justified inasmuch as they made attacks on northern Gaul and Britain which continued into the fourth century, intensifying toward century end. In the fifth century they began to establish settlements in southeastern Britain (as well as in Gaul). On the Continent the Saxons remained a potent force until they succumbed to Frankish (link: Frankish) control under Charlemagne in the eighth century.

As a "people" they were not centrally organized, but consisted of individual war-bands (third and fourth centuries). For the fifth century it can be said: "Many settlements were abandoned in the first half of the century and not reoccupied. This was partly due to migration to Britain and elsewhere, partly to a major redistribution of settlement in the Saxon region" (Todd 1992: 217). With the movement to Britain in the fifth and sixth centuries the Anglii, probably a subgrouping of the Saxons, disappeared from the scene, "their land in Angeln deserted for a time and then colonized by Danes and Slavs" (ibid.: 218).

The Frisii were seldom mentioned in the later Roman Empire. Although subsumed under the generic designation Saxon, "a Frisian identity was maintained and in the fifth century they again emerge, though into a twilight" (ibid.: 219). Eventually, it seems they

---

12 Primogeniture assigned the inheritance of land to the oldest son.
13 Gavelkind provided for the division of land among all the sons. Daughters had no title to land of their own.

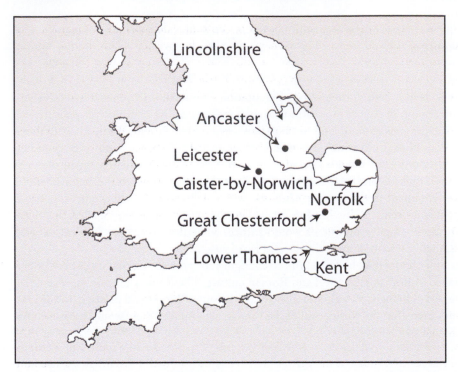

Map 1.2 Pre-Conquest Germanic cemeteries

came under Frankish control. However that may be, there is no doubt about the extent of Frankish cultural influence among them, and the political weakness of the Frisii, as well as their restricted space, may have been a spur to their more adventurous sons to seek their future in trade far from their homeland. For others, migration beckoned, to Britain, according to the Byzantine historian Procopius, and to northern Gaul (ibid.: 220).

1.5.2 The Saxons, Angles, Jutes, and Frisians in Britain

The earliest evidence we have of Germanic settlement in Britain consists of the Anglo-Saxon cemeteries and settlements in the region between the Lower Thames and Norfolk. Others possibly lay in Lincolnshire and Kent. In Caister-by-Norwich there was a large cremation cemetery outside the town dating from about 400. Similar settlements were found near Leicester, Ancaster, and Great Chesterford. One of the most likely explanations for these settlements, virtually always outside the city walls, was that the Germanic invaders were invited there to protect the British settlements, especially after the Romans withdrew. Much as in other western provinces, the Empire relied on barbarian troops and officers from the late third century on.

The formal end of Roman rule by 410 did not mean the end of all efforts to protect Britain from external attacks, the most serious of which came from the Scots and the Picts (link: Scots and Picts) (Plate 1.2) to the north and the sea-borne Saxons among others. It may well have been that the British leaders continued to use Germanic troops after 410 and perhaps even to increase their numbers. For the Germanic newcomers it was probably of no importance who recruited them. They were simply doing what their fathers before them had done. However, without any central power to coordinate defenses the Germanic forces would soon have realized they had a free hand to do as they wished. Soon more would be coming from the Continental coast near the Elbe and Weser estuaries (the Saxons), from Schleswig-Holstein, especially the region of Angeln (the Angels), from northern Holland (the Frisians), and probably from Jutland (the Jutes). Todd's general description is instructive:

> Frontiers maintained for centuries between tribal societies and an advanced centralized state were bound to have impact on both sides in a variety of ways. . . . What is observable on and beyond the northern Roman frontiers, from the third century onward, is the emergence of frontier societies, neither purely Roman provincial nor entirely barbarian. Typically, such societies on long-established frontiers develop a material culture which draws on elements from both sides while remaining part of the dominant political order. When that order weakened or collapsed, a frontier society often remained in being and filled the political vacuum.

> (1992: 147)

This was the probable background against which the writings of Bede ([link: Bede](#)) may be understood. Writing long after the fact, in 731, he described how two Germanic leaders, Horsa and Hengist, were invited by the Celtic king Vortigern to defend his kingdom against the Picts. Horsa and Hengist and their troops were given the Isle of Thanet (in Kent) as their pay. But to the dismay of the Britons, they expanded into all of Kent. In the account of Gildas[14] they went home, but this hardly seems credible in the overall context of the Germanic conquest of England. On the other hand, the figure of Hengist, who is claimed to be the descendant of Wodon (Uoden – Udecta – Uitta – Uictgisl – Hengist) reflects the need for a divine founding myth more than historical fact (cf. Brooks 1989: 58).

Just which Germanic tribes actually settled in Kent is debatable. Bede's claim is that Kent was settled by Jutes, and this is confirmed by archeological evidence: especially jewelry and thin decorative metal floral designs. Despite the closeness of Gaul and the presence of Frankish artifacts (brooches; glass; pottery flasks; weaponry), there is no evidence of Frankish settlements. Conclusions based on the size of land-holdings and settlement patterns point to the Angles (Price 1994: chap. 9). More important than distinguishing which group was involved is their reason for migrating. The motivation for leaving may have been a worsening of living conditions and the pressure of a growing population as push-factors and the wish to profit from the opportunities for material betterment on the other side of the North Sea as a pull-factor.

1.6 Summary

In the history of mankind language has, since its inception, played a decisive role. However the original language may have looked and whatever principles may have been the basis of

---

14 A sixth century historian; cf. *De excidio Britanniae*. Bede drew on Gildas's account in his own work.

its structure and function, it has always been subject to change, which is, therefore, itself a principle. In the course of this change ancient "families" of languages emerged which further diverged to make up the languages we can observe at present. Some of the principles of change explain how, within the group known as Indo-European languages, the Germanic subgroup developed and within it the West Germanic languages, which include English.

The speakers of the various Germanic languages stood, at the beginning of the first century CE in a close relationship to the Roman Empire, which exercised a great deal of influence on the lives of the Germanic peoples, including borrowings into their languages. It was a number of the coastal tribes which first raided and then later settled in Britain, in this way establishing there what was to be known as English.

STUDY QUESTIONS

Social and cultural background

1. What was the way of life of the various Germanic people like? What did they have in common that made them Germanic?
2. Name the areas of activity in which the Germanic peoples and the Romans were in contact. Which of these areas were the most important?
3. The text mentions three types of motivation for the Germanic migrations. Which was the most common, the next most, and which least?
4. What concrete (physical) evidence do we have from the earliest period of Germanic settlement in Britain?

Linguistic background

1. Cognates are words in two different languages which ultimately have the same historical source. For example, both French *père* and Spanish *padre* have their origins in the Latin word *pater*. English *father* and German *Vater* are, together with *père*, *padre*, and *pater* cognates derived from Proto-Indo-European *ph_2'tēr. Now using Grimm's Law find the English cognate of the following Latin words.

Latin cognate	English cognate	Latin	English
rectus		canis	
edere		decem	
tenuis		dentis (genitive)	
per		pecus	

Note that you can use the etymological information in any good desk dictionary about the English word you choose as a cognate to confirm your conclusions – or not.

2. Today /h/ occurs in English chiefly in initial position in a word and always in a prevocalic position, *head* /hed/ or *happen* /hæpən/. In compounds whose second element begins with /h/ it is usually (but not always) retained, *prehensile* always with /h/, but *prehistoric* and *forehead* with or without it. Explain how emphatic vs. non-emphatic speech style may have affected the retention or loss of initial /h/; furthermore, why can /h/ be retained before the consonant /w/?

3. What might have motivated the development of the system of the definite article in the Germanic and Romance languages? What common type of source did the definite article have in German, English, French, Spanish, and Italian?

4. There are numerous similarities between English and German and between English and French. Which of the two pairs are members of the same language family within the Indo-European family? What are the criteria for a language family?

Further reading

Barber et al. gives a reasonable and considerably longer introduction to pre-invasion linguistic developments. Price provides a well-argued background to the differing customs of the invaders of Britain and uses this to make conclusions about who settled where. Todd is a comprehensive treatment of the Germanic tribes.

Barber, C., J.C. Beal, and P.A. Shaw (2009) *The English Language. A Historical Introduction*, 2nd ed. Cambridge: CUP, chapters 3 and 4.

Price, A. H. (1994) *Germanic Warrior Clubs. An Inquiry into the Dynamics of the Era of Migrations and into the Antecedent of Medieval Society*. Tübingen: UVT Lück und Mauch.

Todd, M. (1992) *The Early Germans*. Oxford: Blackwell.

CHAPTER TWO

Old English

Early Germanic Britain (450 – 700)

"Desilite," inquit, "milites, nisi vultis aquilam hostibus prodere; ego certe meum rei publicae atque imperatori officium praestitero." Hoc cum voce magna dixisset, se ex navi proiecit atque in hostes aquilam ferre coepit. Tum nostri cohortati inter se, ne tantum dedecus admitteretur, universi ex navi desiluerunt.

(Caesar, *Gallic Wars*, Book IV, 25)

"Leap," he said, "fellow soldiers, unless you wish to betray your eagle to the enemy. I [the standard-bearer], for my part, will perform my duty to the commonwealth and my general." When he had said this with a loud voice, he leaped from the ship and proceeded to bear the eagle toward the enemy. Then our men, exhorting one another that so great a disgrace should not be incurred, all leaped from the ship.

Chapter Overview:

This chapter:

- reviews pre-Anglo-Saxon England and discusses the cultural and linguistic influence of Celtic and Roman Britain on emerging England and its language, English;
- discusses the formation of the Anglo-Saxon kingdoms and follows with excerpts from the early seventh century laws of King Æðelbirht of Kent; using this language material, a selection of important features of Old English (OE) are introduced;
- reviews the culturally and linguistically important process of Christianization and introduces an early Christian text in OE;
- offers a short look at OE literary texts either written about or during this early period;
- provides two versions of one final text to illustrate some of the regional differences within early OE.

2.1 The First Peoples

The words above record the first Roman invasion of Britain. But before pursuing the Roman invaders or the Germanic ones introduced at the end of the previous chapter, we will outline who was there before them. However, just who the first people were that inhabited the island, how they lived, and what kind of language they spoke – sometime during the last Ice Age in the Early and Late Stone Ages (the Paleolithic and Neolithic periods) – is not known and lies far in the pre-historic past. More relevant for the purposes of this book are the first speakers of an Indo-European language who settled in Britain and who were, very likely, Celts. These people may have arrived as early as 2000 BCE, though probably not until sometime in the first millennium BCE and settled throughout both Britain and Ireland by the time written history records anything about these islands. As pointed out in the preceding chapter, these peoples maintained trade relations with Rome in the final centuries BCE, in which Britain was an important supplier of tin.

2.1.1 Celtic influence

There are no records of the Celtic language(s) these people spoke, but it may be assumed that what they spoke were the Goidelic-Celtic predecessors of Irish and Scottish Gaelic and Brythonic-Celtic ancestors of Welsh (link: Celtic). Yet Celtic left few traces in English. The rural Celtic population would have been enslaved or otherwise subdued; or they would have been driven off the land, which meant moving westward into Cornwall or Wales or leaving Britain for Brittany in present-day France; in cases in which they lived in unattractive or inaccessible places the Celts would have been ignored. In all three cases they would have had little opportunity to add to the word stock of the Germanic newcomers or to exercise influence on grammar or pronunciation. Among the exceptions were a few items such as the now lost words *brat* "cloak" or *bin* "manger" and a small number of survivals in ModE: *bannock* "small Scottish cake" < OE *bannuc* "bit, small piece" < Old British/Cornish *banna* "drop"; *brock* "badger" < OE *brocc* < Old British *broc*; *clock* < OE *clugge*, compare Middle Irish *clocc* "bell"; *curse* < OE *cursian* < Old Irish (OIr) *cūrsagim* "I blame"; *dun* "dull grayish brown" < OE *dunn* < OIr *donn* "dark." Virtually nothing further in the everyday ***vocabulary*** of English testifies to the linguistic presence of the once dominant Celtic-speaking population, and even the words given here are not all accepted as uncontroversially Celtic in origin.

A number of Latin words have also entered OE by way of Celtic: *ancor* "anchorite" < OIr *anchara* < Latin *anachoreta*; *ass* "donkey" < OIr *asan* < Latin *asinus*; and *cross* < OIr *cros* < Latin *cruc-*. Overall, however, there are so few traces of Celtic in English that it is hardly possible to identify a particular domain of Celtic influence, though the presence of these religious words does speak for the influence of the Celtic Church in England (see below). All told, in a generous count, there may be a couple hundred words which are ultimately of Celtic origin, most of them ***place-names***.

2.1.2 Place-names or *toponyms* (link: Toponyms)

The linguistic origins of place-names in England come chiefly from two sources. One is some prominent feature of the topography such as a river, a hill, or a flat plain. The other is the name of the inhabitants of a locality, that is those whose place it is. In both cases linguistic elements of the name provide us with hints about the language once used in a given area. Some toponyms may have sources in one single language; however, hybrid forms are also common. Among the purely Celtic names we find *Bernicia, Devon*, both tribal names, but also *Kent* "border" and the kingdom of *Deira* < Celtic *Deifr* "water" as well as the rivers *Avon* "river," *Esk* and *Exe* < *isca* "water," *Ouse* "stream," *Thames* "dark river" < *tamesis* "darkness," and *Trent*, possibly meaning "strongly flooding" or from a contraction of, *tros* "over" and *hynt* "way."

Examples of hybrid forms include both Celtic–Latin and Celtic–Germanic combinations. *Lincoln* combines *lindon*, a Celtic word for "pool" with Latin *colonia* "colony, settlement," both shortened to *Lin + coln*. *Lancaster* combines the Celtic name for the River Lune, possibly meaning "pure" or "healthy," with *-caster*, which like *-cester* and *-chester* are all ultimately derived from Latin *castrum* "camp, fort" via OE *ceaster*. Germanic–Celtic hybrids give us *Cornwall* < *cornovii*, a Celtic tribe, + Germanic *wealas* "foreigner, servant, slave," from which the name *Wales* also stems. A further example is *Cumberland* < Celtic *Cymry* "Welsh" and Germanic *land*.

Celtic toponyms can be found throughout England, but are understandably more prominent toward the west and north, areas which remained Celtic-speaking longer. In a similar sense we find more West Germanic place-names in the South and Southeast, and a large number of North Germanic, Scandinavian ones in the North and Northeast, where the Vikings settled in large numbers in the period to be treated in chapter 3. West Germanic toponyms include, among others, names ending in {-ham} "homestead" (as in *Birmingham*); {-borough, -bury} "castle," (*Marlborough, Salisbury*); {-ing(s)} "the people/family of" (*Hastings* and *Worthing*); {-ton} "enclosure, village" (*Northampton*); and {-field} (*Sheffield*). Examples of Scandinavian place-names are those ending in {-by} "farm" or "town," (*Barmby*); {-holm} "flat riverside land or island" (*Downholme*); {-thorp(e)} "village" (*Nunthorpe*); {-thwaite} "isolated parcel of land" (*Langthwaite*); or {-toft} "homestead" (*Langtoft*).

In addition to the Germanic, Celtic, and Latin names and elements already mentioned, Romance elements show up in the form of further Latin **borrowings** such as {portus} "harbor" (*Portsmouth*); {strata} "road, street" (*Stratford*); or {vīcus} "farm or village" (*Keswick*).[1] Other **Romance language** place-names were introduced from **French** much later, after the Norman Conquest (see chapter 4), but may be mentioned in this section on toponyms. They include, for example, *Beaulieu* < {beau-} "beautiful" + {-lieu} "place" or *Beaumont* with the element {-mont} "hill," but also {-ville} "farm, village, field" as in *Enville*. These are only a few of the formative elements which can easily be seen in place-names, but they are sufficient to tell us who lived there and was in possession of the land enough to impose their toponyms.

2.1.3 Roman influence

One possible explanation for the limited extent of Celtic influence may lie in the high degree of Romanization of Celtic Britain. Gallia on the Continent, the sister province of Roman

---

1 The elements {-wich} and {-wick} may be traced back, as in *Nantwich*, to Latin *vīcus* via Germanic *wīc/wich/wick/wyke*, sometimes meaning "farm," as in *Keswick*, or to Scandinavian *vic* "bay, port" as in *Greenwich*.

Britannia (see Map 1.1), was also originally Celtic-speaking, but thorough Romanization in Gaul led to the eventual displacement of Celtic by Latin, which itself evolved into French (north) and Provençal (south). In Britain the process of Romanization greatly advanced in the towns and cities, so that there must have been a high degree of Celtic–Latin *bilingualism* in which there was relatively little borrowing from the less prestigious Celtic into the local Latin. Once the Romans had gone and the Germanic invaders had made their incursions (see 2.2), communication with British leaders is more likely to have been in Latin than in Celtic. The rural population would, as already mentioned, have been subjugated, driven off, or ignored. In all three cases the linguistic influence of their language on the Germanic newcomers would have been minimal.

In the case of the Romans, interest in Britain moved beyond the realm of trade when Julius Caesar landed there in 55 and again in 54 BCE. Nothing came of Caesar's attempt to make Britain a Roman province, if indeed that was his intention. He may well have only intended to cow the Britons enough to prevent them from helping their Gallic cousins across the Channel. One further consequence of Caesar's venture was to bind Britain more tightly under the political and economic influence of Rome. Then, less than a hundred years later, in 43 CE, a Roman expeditionary force seriously began with the conquest of what was to be England, which was largely completed by the year 50. Nevertheless, there was Celtic resistance such as the rebellion led by Queen Bodicea in the Southeast, revolts of the more northerly Brigantes, and repeated incursions of the Picts and Scots moving south from Scotland. From the third century on Germanic raids on the southern coast and later Irish raids in the west began to pose further threats to Britain. Yet from 43 CE until the time the Roman armies left sometime around the year 410, Roman cities and towns grew up throughout all but the far West and the North, most densely in the Southeast, where Roman conquest had begun and the influence of Rome was most secure.

Roman culture could be seen in the towns, where trade helped the economy to flourish and the flow of goods from the Continent to increase. Britain continued to be important as a supplier of metals (tin and iron). Both trade and military control were facilitated by Hadrian's Wall and, for a time the Antonine Wall as well as a series of forts and a system of Roman roads, the major ones of which were centered in London (Londinium), which was founded by the Romans (see Map 2.1). As a result of trade the wealthy were able to emulate Roman life styles and to live in large houses with central heating, running water, and tiled mosaic floors. Roman dress, ornaments, utensils, pottery, and glassware were in use, and towns might well have public baths, a theater, and temples. Trade was greatly facilitated by the use of money, which, however, began to drop out of use after the Roman withdrawal. Around the time of Roman departure a certain degree of economic decline could be noted even though many of the economic centers such as Canterbury, Cirencester, Wroxeter, Winchester, and Gloucester remained active into the sixth century, and the farms centering on these towns continued to function. Despite the importance of Roman culture Latin seems to have contributed little to English during this period. This may have been due to the civic and military disorder that characterized the transition from Roman to Celtic to Saxon power. Latin returned, however, with the introduction of Christianity about two centuries later and exerted considerable influence on English, as we will see in 2.4.

Map. 2.1 Roman roads and walls

2.2 The Germanic incursions

Legend has it, as recorded by Bede (673–735) in his *Historia ecclesiastica gentis Anglorum* (*The Ecclesiastical History of the English People*) of 730 (see below 2.5.3–4) and also recorded in the *Anglo-Saxon Chronicle* (initially composed c. 890; Plate 3.1) for the year 449, that the Celtic king Vortigern sought Germanic military help. Vortigern's people and lands were under pressure from the Picts and the Scots, but also from Saxon raiders; consequently, Vortigern followed the example of the Romans in enlisting Germanic reinforcements. Germanic soldiers were well known because some had served in the Roman army in Britain and some seem to have settled in Britain as well. These new allies came in large numbers and settled rather than coming merely as administrators and soldiers of an army of occupation, as had the Romans. Consequently, if the Germanic forces did not enslave the Celts, they drove them off. Thus to the west Wales remained Celtic-speaking, as did Cornwall for a long time. However, in other areas such as Elmet in Yorkshire islands of Celtic settlement remained. Celtic resistance to the Germanic conquest has found its expression in the cluster of stories and legends around King Arthur, a late fifth to early sixth century (Romano-)Celtic leader. Arthur's historical kernel has been greatly embellished by the addition not only of the Roundtable but also the court at Camelot, whose name is an echo of Camulodunum, present-day Colchester, the historical capital of Celtic Britain.

The newcomers, who continued to arrive well into the sixth century, were part of a Germanic farming culture, as pointed out in 1.4. As such they were less interested and involved in urban culture as practiced by Romans and Britons, which contributes to an understanding of why so little was borrowed from Latin or Celtic into the emerging English language. This also helps to explain why they often initially settled in sites outside the towns and cities. Furthermore, Roman culture began to collapse under the neglect it experienced from the invaders.

Germanic settlement patterns followed the rivers and the Roman roads. The Saxons were concentrated on the south coast, in Sussex and Wessex, but also north of the Thames in Middlesex and Essex; the Angles were to be found on the east coast and in the *Midlands* reaching up into Northumbria and southern Scotland by 600; the Jutes settled in Kent, parts of Hampshire, and the Isle of Wight; while the Frisians are not associated with any particular place (see Map 2.2).

It is not clear how distinct the differences among the four tribal groups[2] of Angles, Saxons, Jutes, and Frisians may have been. They probably came as uncoordinated bands, but new arrivals will probably have put down roots near earlier kinsfolk, though it is not impossible that the settler groups may have included some mixing. However this may have been, it is unlikely that there were any major linguistic differences; all of the newcomers were speakers of "***North Sea Germanic***," sometimes also known as Ingvæonic (link: North Sea Germanic). The *speech community* extended not only throughout Anglo-Saxon England, but also, as the designation indicates, to the Continental side of the North Sea as well. Even today English is closely related to Frisian, which is spoken in parts of The Netherlands and Germany. As far as the emerging language of the invaders is concerned, although there were regional dialectal differences, there was such a high degree of similarity that the language spoken by the Anglo-Saxons was uniformly called *Englisc* by all four groups, which is perhaps indicative of a feeling of shared culture and identity (link: Identity) (see 2.5.4 below on variety in OE).

2.2.1 The Germanic kingdoms

Throughout the country a series of small kingdoms under local chiefs began to emerge in groupings in which social organization was by family and clan and there were hereditary nobles (*eorls*) and simple freemen (*ceorls*). Furthermore, decisions were taken in a local assembly (*gemōt*); guilt was established by character reference or combat; and justice was meted out via fines (*wergild*). The chieftains were the heads of (extended) families. Some of them may have effectively replaced pre-existing Celtic kingdoms, something especially likely in the cases of Kent, Deira, Bernicia, and Lindsey, but many will have been newly created by warrior-kings (cf. Bassett 1989: 23ff). Inasmuch as the political boundaries of the kingdoms were often the same as those of the corresponding bishoprics, once Christianization had taken place (see 2.4), the power base was broader than the clan or the dynasty. Yet caution is necessary since Bede, the principal source, with his primarily church-oriented history, was unlikely to mention a kingdom if it did not have a bishopric (ibid.: 4). Further stability is likely to have come from the eventual creation of a hybrid

---

2 Evidence for the presence of the Franks, another Germanic tribe is mixed and controversial (link: Franks).

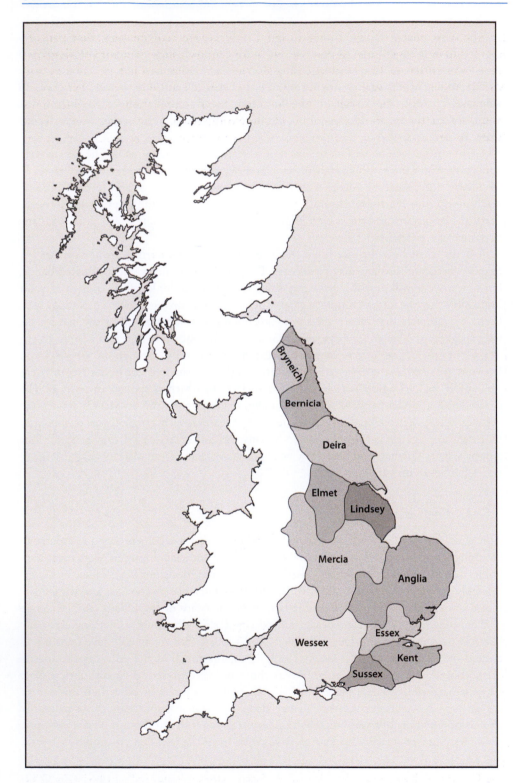

Map 2.2 The ancient kingdoms

British–Saxon people.[3] In the course of time a ruthless process of amalgamation seems to have led to ever larger units so that over the sixth century a loose structure of kingdoms came into existence. They included smaller kingdoms such as Lindsey, Hwicce, and Middle Anglia, which were eventually absorbed by Mercia, and Bernicia and Deira, which combined to form the kernel of Northumbria. Such combinations of smaller units eventually led to a set of seven major kingdoms: Northumbria, Mercia, East Anglia, Kent, Essex, Sussex, and Wessex, traditionally known as the Heptarchy (Map 2.3), which was

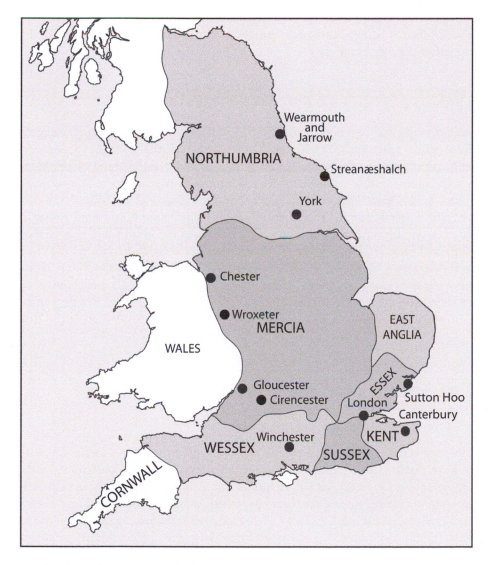

Map 2.3 The Anglo-Saxon Heptarchy (c. 700)

---

3 More recently DNA studies have raised questions about the proportions of the population which were Celtic or Germanic with suggestions that relatively few Saxon males immigrated and mixed with the Celtic population they dominated.

maintained over a longer period in the seventh and eighth centuries. Kent took on early prominence under King Æðelbirht (Aethelbert) (see 2.2.2 and 2.3.3). East Anglia was, like Kent, a late sixth and early seventh century center of power, and the wealth found at the seventh century burial site at Sutton Hoo (link: Sutton Hoo) bears witness to this. In the seventh century, the predominance of power lay in Northumbria. In the eighth it moved south to Mercia, where Offa's Dyke (link: Offa's Dyke) testifies to Mercian power. Later, after the Viking invasions in the ninth and tenth centuries, Anglo-Saxon power was centered in Wessex. Within the context of this book the significance of these kingdoms is that their boundaries more or less coincide with the *dialects* traditionally postulated for Old English, but for which there is little evidence because of the dearth of written documentation of the language before the eighth century.

2.2.2 The laws of the Kent

Æðelbirht was not only an early convert to Christianity, but an important overlord, sometimes termed a *bretwalda*, over Kent and Essex, perhaps with significant influence on East Anglia. His legitimacy was claimed genealogically, as in the case of Horsa and Hengist. One such claim, that of Bede, has him as the son of Irminric (sometimes spelled Eormenric), son of Octa, son of Oeric, surnamed Oisc, son of Hengist. Æðelbirht's law code is the oldest preserved Anglo-Saxon code and stems from the beginning of the seventh century, that is, from 602 or 603. It comprises some 90 laws and governs questions of liability in cases of injury inflicted on the Church or within the feudal hierarchy. It testifies to the close relationship between Church and State. Note that injury may be compensated for in terms of money payments, that is, the *wergild* mentioned above. Text 2.1 in 2.3.3 contains a few excerpts from Æðelbirht's code, laws 1, 2, 3, 57, and 82, which will serve as a first introduction to the Old English language.

2.3 Introduction to Old English (link: Brief introduction to OE)

2.3.1 Alphabet, spelling, and pronunciation

Before looking at the first OE text, a note on the *alphabet* and *spelling* is useful. OE texts did not have the strict convention of spaces between words that we are familiar with. Although most texts use a modified Latin alphabet, not all do (see Text 2.2 for an example). Among the modifications we find the letter <þ>, called "thorn," which is used for present-day <th>, as is <ð>, called "eth." In Text 2.1 <þ> occurs initially only, as in *þis* "this" or *þā* "the/those (nominative plural)"; and <ð> elsewhere, e.g. *frið* "peace, refuge" or *oðerne* "other, second, next." Both of them are pronounced either as voiceless /θ/ or voiced /ð/ depending on their position in a word and the stress pattern of the word. A second, slightly unusual letter is <æ> as in *þær* "there, then." It is called "ash" and is pronounced as a low front vowel, for which the ***International Phonetic Alphabet*** (link: IPA) uses the same symbol /æ/. Other letters which are not in the current alphabet do not occur in Text 2.1. They will be introduced later as necessary (link: Alphabet).

As with <þ> other fricatives are also not distinguished as their voiceless and voiced *allophones* (link: Phonological terms). This means that <f> can be /f/ or /v/; <s>, /s/ or /z/. However, <sc> is always the voiceless *fricative* /ʃ/, as in *biscopes* "bishops." The letter <c> is somewhat difficult to interpret. Before the front vowels <i> and <ea> in this text *palatalization* has taken place, giving us /tʃ/, as in *ciricean* "church"; elsewhere in this text the pronunciation is /k/, as, for example, in *cyning* "king," *diacones* "deacon's," or *drincæð* "drinks." In much the same manner <g> may be /j/ before front vowels, as in *dæge* "days," *gif* "if" or in the verbal prefix {ge-}, but /g/ elsewhere, compare *gylde* "(re-)pay" and *scillinga* "shillings." One final ambiguous letter is <h>. At the beginning of a word it has the value of /h/, as in *him* "him" (third person dative) or *hām* "home," but it is /x/, like German <ch> or *Spanish* <j>, before a consonant, as in *Æðelbirht* or at the end of a word as in *feoh* "property" (ModE *fee*).

The letter-vowels are assumed to have been pronounced much like their "Continental" values, but the use here of letters with macrons – or long marks – over the vowel is a purely modern convention based on the presumed length of the vowel. In this sense we recognize as long <ā, ǣ, ē, ī, ō, ū, ȳ> with a macron and the same letter without a macron as short. Hence the vowels of OE are paired long and short /ɑ(ː), æ(ː), e(ː), i(ː), o(ː), u(ː), y(ː)/. For two vowel-letters together in words like *feoh* or *gebiege* we assume a diphthongal pronunciation /eo/ and /iy/ (cf. Hogg 1992 or Blake 1996 for details on OE pronunciation).

2.3.2 Pronouns

To help with the text, Table 2.1 shows the *system of personal pronouns* in OE. In contrast to ModE there are four grammatical *cases* (link: Grammatical case)[4] – and in the masculine and neuter of the third person singular, an additional case, the instrumental. Furthermore, there are three numbers, singular, dual (for two), and plural although the dual, which only applied to the first and second persons, soon disappeared and was expressed as part of the plural. The second person still regularly distinguished singular (*þū* "thou") and plural (*ge* "ye") (see also (link: System of personal pronouns).

2.3.3 General grammatical information

Word order may be different from ModE; see especially subordinate clauses (all the *gif*-clauses), in which the verb appears at the end, compare *Gif cyning æt manes hām drincæð*, literally "If king at man's home drinketh." See 4.2.3, 4.2.3.1, and 5.3.3; link: Word order).

There are no *articles* in the noun phrase (link: Noun phrase). In *þā dōmas* the word *þā* is the nominative plural masculine demonstrative *determiner* "those". Eventually these demonstratives evolve into the definite article of the emerging article system as well as supplying the morphologically simplified forms of the *demonstrative* system (see discussion in 1.2.2, 1.2.4, and 1.3.2; link: Demonstratives).

---

4 Note that there are two traditions according to which the cases are ordered. Britain and much of the Commonwealth put similar looking cases closer together, thus placing accusative immediately after the nominative. In the US the cases follow the usual order introduced by the ancient Greek and Latin grammarians: nominative–genitive–dative–accusative plus, for Latin, ablative and then vocative.

Table 2.1 **The personal pronouns of Old English**

1ˢᵗ person	singular			dual	plural
nominative	*ic*			*wit*	*wē*
genitive	*mīn*			*uncer*	*ūser, ūre*
dative	*mē*			*unc*	*ūs*
accusative	*mec, mē*			*unc*	*ūsic, ūs*
2ⁿᵈ person					
nominative	*þū*			*git*	*ge*
genitive	*þīn*			*incer*	*eōwer*
dative	*þē*			*inc*	*eōw*
accusative	*þec, þē*			*inc*	*eōwic, eōw*
3ʳᵈ person	masculine sg.	feminine sg.	neuter sg.		plural
nominative	*hē*	*hēo*	*hit*		*hie (hig, hi, heo)*
genitive	*his*	*hire (heora)*	*his*		*heora (hyra, hira, hiora)*
dative	*him (heom)*	*hire (heore)*	*him (heom)*		*him (heom)*
accusative	*hine*	*hī, hēo, hie*	*hit*		*hie (hig, hi, heo)*
instrumental	*hȳ (hēo)*		*hȳ (hēo)*		

Case appears, as with the personal pronouns, in the nominative, genitive, dative, and accusative; *prepositions* require objects with case endings, for example *on dæge* preposition + accusative or *tō him* preposition + dative pronoun. Note that some expressions which appear with a preposition in ModE may appear only with a case ending, but without a preposition, for example *cyninge L scillinga* with dative *cyninge* "to or for the king."

All nouns have **gender**, which does not correlate with biological sex. For examples, see the glossary.

For **personal pronouns**, see Table 2.1 above. The relative pronoun is immutable *þe*; see the Title of Text 2.1: . . . *þā dōmas, þe Æðelbirht cyning āsette* "the(se) laws which/that King Æðelbirht decreed."

There are two *tenses* for verbs: present, for example plural *syndon* "are" or singular *drincæð* "drinks"; and past, for example *āsette* "set" third person singular; and there is both an indicative mood, for example *syndon, āsette,* and a **subjunctive** one, present tense singular *gylde* "must pay, be recompensed." There is nothing comparable to the ModE progressive in the grammar of OE. The verbs themselves fall into numerous classes which cannot be reviewed here (see, for example, Quirk and Wrenn 1957; Smith 2009) (link: The verb classes of OE).

Text 2.1 Æðelbirht's Laws (602 or 603) (excerpts)

Title. *þis syndon þā dōmas, þe Æðelbirht cyning āsette on Augustinus dæge*
These are the laws which King Æðelbirht set up in St. Augustine's days.

1. *Godes feoh and ciricean XII gylde. Biscopes feoh XI gylde. Preōstes feoh IX gylde. Diacones feoh VI gylde. Cleroces feoh VI gylde. Cyrifrið II gylde. M(ynstres) frið II gylde.*
   Property of God and the church is to be recompensed twelvefold, a bishop's property elevenfold. A priest's property ninefold. A deacon's property sixfold. A cleric's property sixfold. The peace of the church twofold. The peace of monasteries twofold.

2. *Gif cyning his leōde tō him gehāteð and heom man þær yfel gedō II bōte and cyninge L scillinga.*
   If the king orders his people (to come) to him and someone then causes them injury, double compensation and fifty shillings to the king.

3. *Gif cyning æt manes hām drincæð and þær man lyswæs hwæt gedō, II bōte gebēte.*
   If the king is drinking at a man's home, and anyone commits any evil deed there, he is to pay twofold compensation.

57. *Gif man ōðerne mid fÿste in naso slæhð, III scill.*
   If someone hits another on the nose with his fist, three shillings.

82. *Gif man mægð-man nēde genimeð, þān āgende L scillingas and æft æt þān āgende sīnne willan æt gebiege.*
   If someone abducts a virgin/maiden by force, 50 shillings for the person she belongs to, and then he may buy her back as desired.

(R. Schmid (1832) *Die Gesetze der Angelsachsen. In der Ursprache mit Übersetzung und Erläuterung.* Leipzig: Brockhaus)

Glossary and grammatical information

nom. = nominative; gen. = genitive; dat. = dative; acc. = accusative; sg. = singular; masc. = masculine; fem. = feminine; pres. = present; p. = person

Title

þis "this" nom. sg. neuter

syndon "are" pres. pl. of *bēon*; agrees with pl. subject

cyning "king" nom. sg. masc.; note reverse word order *Athelbert King*

āsette "established, set up" 3rd p. sg. past of *āsettan*

þā "the" plural; agrees with following pl. noun

on "in, on" prep. here with the acc.

dōmas "laws" nom. pl. masc.

dæga "days" acc. pl. masc.

þe "which" indeclinable relative particle

Law 1: The first sentence has an unnamed but understood third person subject ("someone") of the subjunctive verb *gylde* "is to pay" plus accusative objects as recipients. The translation gives the whole in the ModE passive.

Godes "of God" gen. sg. masc.

gylde "recompense, pay" 3rd p. sg. subjunctive

feoh "property" acc. sg. neuter

Cyrifrið "the peace of the Church" acc. sg. masc. or neuter

ciricean "church" acc. sg. fem.

Mynstresfrið "ditto of the Monastery" as above

Law 2: Note the word order in this and the following sentences: The *if*-clause has the order Subject–Object–Adverbial–Verb; the second half of the *if*-clause has Dative Object–Subject–Adverbial–Direct Object–Verb. The definite noun *cyning* is used without a definite article as is *man* if it is the masc. sg. nom. noun for "man, person"; however, it may be the **indefinite pronoun** meaning "someone."

gif "if" (pronounced /jɪf/)

yfel "evil" acc. sg. neuter

leðde "people" acc. pl.

gedō "make, act, do, cause"

tō "to" with dat.
gehāteð "order" 3rd p. sg. pres. tense

bōte "recompense" fem. pl., cf. ModE (give someone something) to boot

þær "there, then"

gebēte "order" 3rd p. sg. subjunctive

Law 3:

æt "at" takes dat., sometimes acc.

drincæð "drink" 3rd p. sg. indicative

manes "a man's" "man, person" gen. sg. masc.

lyswæs "evil" adjective

hām home masc. sg. dat.

hwæt "something, what"

Law 57:

ōðerne "other" adjective, acc. sg. masc.

naso "nose" fem. sg. acc.

mid "with" takes dat. or instrumental; sometimes acc.

slæhð "hits" 3rd p. sg. indicative of *slēan*

fyste "fists" fem. sg. dat.

scill "shillings" masc. pl. acc. (abbrev.) of *scillingas*

Law 82:

mægð-man "maiden, virgin" masc. sg. acc.

æft "after" adverb

nēde "by force" fem. sg. instrumental case without a preposition, literally "by need"

ætþān "then"

genimeð "take" 3rd p. sg. indicative of (*ge-*)*niman*

sīnne "his (maid)" possessive adjective, masc. sg. acc.

þān "then" adverb

willan "will, want" masc. sg. instrumental "as desired"

āgende "(pay) back" past participle of *āgan*; "again, back"

gebiege "buy" 3rd p. sg. subjunctive of (*ge-*)*bicgan*

2.4 The Christianization of England

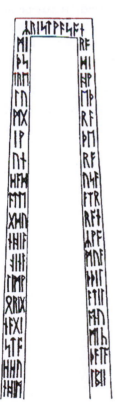

This was the most momentous happening between the arrival of the Anglo-Saxons and the invasion of the Vikings (see chapter 3). Although the Celts had been converted, the practice of Christianity waned and then disappeared under the new Germanic masters. However, at the very end of the sixth century Pope Gregory I (papacy: 590–604), sent a missionary who is known today as St. Augustine of Canterbury from the Roman Church to convert the Anglo-Saxons. In this way he pre-empted the Celtic Church, which had begun missionary work in Scotland. In 597 Augustine together with a band of monks landed at Thanet in Kent, a place reminiscent of the advent of the Germanic invaders almost exactly 150 years earlier. Augustine soon converted the king of Kent, Æðelbirht, whose wife Bertha of the Merovingian Franks was a Christian. This was a crucial event for the Church since Æðelbirht was the most powerful king south of the Humber River. Soon further areas became Christian (East Saxons in 604; King Edwin in 627 in Northumbria; West Saxons in 635; Mercians in 655) so that all England was nominally Christian by the year 700.

Figure 2.1 The runic inscription on the Ruthwell Cross

The Celtic mission had begun earlier with the establishment of a monastery on the Scottish island of Iona in 563. The Celtic Church gradually extended westward and began to establish itself in Northumbria after 635. This led to rivalry between the Celtic and the Roman churches, ostensibly over questions of liturgy and the date of Easter, but this was most likely linked to questions of dynastic power. In any case the dispute was settled amicably at the Synod of Whitby (probably held at Streanæshalch near York) in 664. The laurels went to Rome, thus bringing all England clearly into its sphere. Roman Christianity led to a cultural upswing including church building, the establishment of monasteries with the use of Latin in the services, and a flowering of ecclesiastical learning. The double monastery of Wearmouth and Jarrow was especially prominent (see Map 2.3). Concomitant to this was the new stimulation of vernacular literature and art, stone masonry, and glass production. Manuscripts were produced in the scriptoria of the monasteries, many of them with brilliant illuminations (Plate 2.1). Church music (Plate 2.2) (such as the Gregorian chants) emerged and agriculture, at least at the monasteries, was modernized.

Of the various points just mentioned it is the incipient development of literacy which is surely most significant. This movement began when Augustine, the first archbishop of Canterbury, founded a monastery there which began to produce manuscripts for liturgical and educational use. To a very large extent this meant cultivation and preservation of Latin literature, which was carried out with so much success that it was to be English and Irish monks who would be the propelling force in the Carolingian reforms (**link: Carolingian reforms**) and the revival of classical Latin on the Continent. Next to Latin English itself was widely used in codes of law (see Text 2.1), in religious works, and, of course, in translations from Latin. In general, Latin script adapted for use with English was adopted. Yet the older Nordic-Germanic use of runes can also be found, most impressively on the Ruthwell Cross, a stone cross some five and a half meters (20 feet) high, which was erected in Northumbria in the seventh century. It can be seen today at Ruthwell in Dumfriesshire, Scotland. Figure 2.1 shows part of the runic inscription on one side of the shaft of the cross. The text is part of a well-known religious poem called "The Dream of the Rood." *Rood* (OE *rod*) was the word used for "cross" and *dream* refers to the vision of the cross by the narrator as well as the thoughts of the *rood* on becoming the cross of Christ. The poem contains pagan elements such as the image of a warrior-hero and the animistic quality of the speaking cross. In the following, the text shown in Text 2.2 can be transliterated with the help of the *futhorc*, the Anglo-Saxon **runic alphabet** (**link: Runic alphabet**) (Plate 2.3), which is given in Figure 2.2 (cf. Hogg 1992: 79–83). Each letter has a name and a phonetic value. You might want to try to transliterate the text into the Latin alphabet yourself before looking at the solution as given below.

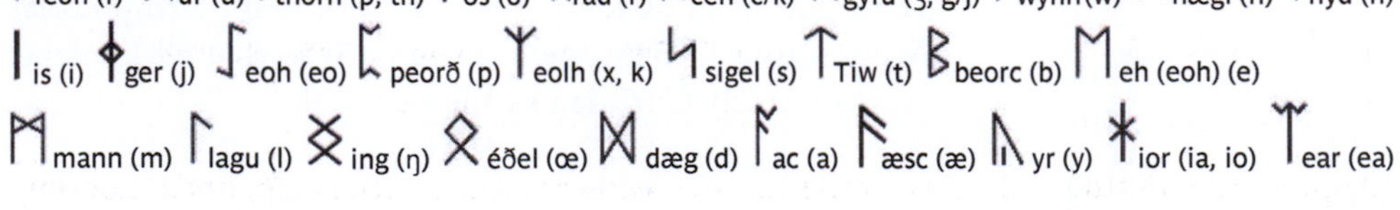

ᚠ feoh (f)　ᚢ ur (u)　ᚦ thorn (þ, th)　ᚩ ós (o)　ᚱ rad (r)　ᚳ cen (c/k)　ᚷ gyfu (ʒ, g/j)　ᚹ wynn (w)　ᚻ hægl (h)　ᛏ nyd (n)

ᛁ is (i)　ᛄ ger (j)　ᛇ eoh (eo)　ᛈ peorð (p)　ᛉ eolh (x, k)　ᛋ sigel (s)　ᛏ Tiw (t)　ᛒ beorc (b)　ᛖ eh (eoh) (e)

ᛗ mann (m)　ᛚ lagu (l)　ᛝ ing (ŋ)　ᛟ éðel (œ)　ᛞ dæg (d)　ᚪ ac (a)　ᚫ æsc (æ)　ᚣ yr (y)　ᛡ ior (ia, io)　ᛠ ear (ea)

Figure 2.2 The Futhorc

Text 2.2 Christic was on the cross

ᚣᚱᛁᛋᛏ·ᚠᚪᛋ·ᚪᛏ·ᚱᛖᛞᛁ·ᚾᚹᛖᚦᚱᚪ·ᚦᛖᚱ·ᚠᚪᛋᚪ·ᚠᛏᚱᚱᚪᚾ
·ᚣᚠᚠᚪᛗᛁ·ᚠᚦᚦᛁᛚᚪ·ᛏᛁᛚ·ᚠᛏᚾᛗ·ᛁᚳ·ᚦᛗᛏ·ᛏᚳ·ᛒᛁᚾ…
ᛗᛁᚦ·ᛋᛏᚱᛖᛚᚪᛗ·ᚷᛁᚹᚾᛏᛞᚪᛞ·ᚪᛚᛖᚷᛞᚪᚾᛏ·ᚾᛁ·ᚾᛁᚾᚪ
ᛚᛗᛗᚢᚱᛁᚷᚾᚪ·ᚷᛁᛋᛏᚪᛞᛞᚪᚾᛏ·ᚾᛁᛗ

On the Ruthwell Cross the text given in Text 2.2 begins at the top left and then moves down the right leg. The continuation (ll. 3 and 4) goes down the left leg. Note below that the rune *cen* is transliterated as <c> and that *eolh* is transliterated as <k>. This has been done in order to maintain the runic distinction. *Eolh* in the word *krist* reflects the Greek letter *chi*. Note, too, that on the left leg line 11 ends with the first half and line 12 starts with the second half of the rune *hægl*. The text, as transliterated and translated, reads as follows, whereby the last four words in the second line reflect a discontinuity in the text in the middle of a word:

krist wæs on rodi.	*hwepræ per fusæ*	*fearran kwomu æppilæ til*
Christ was on (the) cross.	Yet there (the) eager	from far came noble to the
anum. ic þæt eal bih[eold]	*mið strelum ȝiwundad æleȝdun*	*hi hinæ limwœriȝnæ*
One. I that all beh[eld]	With arrows wounded laid	they him weary-limbed down.
ȝistoddun him		
They stood by him		

Glossary

rodi "cross" fem. sg. dat.	*anum* "one" masc. sg. dat.; meant as Christ
hwepræ "yet"	*mið* "with"; takes dat.
fusæ "eager, brave" pl.	*strelum* "arrows" masc. pl. dat.
fearran "from far"	*ȝiwundad* "wounded" past part.
kwomu "come" 3rd p. pl. past	*æleȝdun* "laid away" 3rd p. pl. past
æppilæ "noble" pl.	*limwœriȝnæ* "limb + weary" masc. sg. acc.
til "to, till"; takes dat.	*ȝistoddun* "stood" 3rd p. pl. past

Despite the enormous influence of the Church, earlier pagan practices remained, not only as suggested by "The Dream of the Rood," but also, for example, in the names of the weekdays, Tuesday (*tīwesdæg*), Wednesday (*wōdnesdæg*), Thursday (*þunresdæg*), and Friday (*frīgedæg*), all named for Nordic gods: Tiu, the god of war and the sky; Woden; Thor, the god of thunder; and Frīg, goddess of domestic love and the hearth. Likewise, Easter took its name from *Eastre*, the dawn-goddess. Despite the persistence of Germanic elements in religion, renewed influences on the vocabulary of English came from contact with Latin in the realms of both religion and learning. Besides borrowings which came via Celtic, as mentioned in 2.1.1, for example *ancor*, *cross*, and *clugge*, direct borrowing from Latin in the time before and partially overlapping Christianization includes *mægester* "master," *cugle* "cowl," *mentel* "cloak," *cocer* "quiver," *leahtric* "lettuce," *lafian* "to bathe, wash, lave," *trifulian* "to grind to powder," *dilegian* "to cancel, delete," and *pinsian* "reflect, consider" among others (Kastovsky 1992: 304–305). Obviously, the Latin and Greek words included in Text 2.1, *biscop*, *cirice*, *cleroces*, *cyrifrið*, *diacones*, *mynstres*, and *preōstes*, are early borrowings that were already in use in this period.

2.5 Literature in the early Old English period (link: OE literature)

Relatively little material is available from the period before 700, which we are looking at in this chapter. Texts 2.1 and 2.2, both early texts, represent two very central fields of writing, legal texts and religious ones. Even though the two texts are excerpts from prose and poetry respectively, they do not do full justice to either. The laws of Text 2.1 consist of short, relatively formulaic items with little sense of sustained textual structure. The material in Text 2.2 is two disjoined lines from "The Dream of the Rood" which do not give a fair impression of the "relatively homogeneous poetic language shared by most poems," (Godden 1992: 491) namely lines with four major stresses and a caesura dividing them two-and-two and linked by alliteration and thematic repetition. In the following, three short textual samples are intended to rectify this shortcoming. The choice of the texts reflect three important traditions of OE writing: pagan, Christian, and historical writing. The first is represented in the probably best-known piece of OE poetry, *Beowulf*, the second by a poem of disputed origin and tradition, "The Wanderer," and the third by the *Anglo-Saxon Chronicle*. A fourth additional text, "Cædmon's Hymn," will follow in the final short section on linguistic variety in OE.

2.5.1 *Beowulf*

Text 2.3 has been taken from *Beowulf* (Plate 2.4), which was written at an unidentified time and place and which some feel is a pre-Christian poem. This epic tale is set in Denmark and Sweden in pagan times, but is written in OE as transmitted in a manuscript from the eleventh century. The poem may have been composed considerably earlier and transmitted orally. Some of its formulaic wording would support this, as do its tribal, Germanic setting and its heroic celebration of the warrior-king Beowulf. Yet the idea of a warrior-king who dies for his people is not so far from Christian ideas as to rule out a later time of writing. The passage quoted below from the beginning of the poem tells of the birth of an earlier Beowulf, the son of the Danish king Scyld. This Beowulf is not the heroic protagonist, but he does precede and foreshadow the appearance of the later Beowulf, who kills the marauding monster Grendel and Grendel's mother. Much later, now long a king, Beowulf kills a dragon who threatens his people in a fight in which he is fatally wounded.

Text 2.3 The birth of the first *Beowulf*

ðæm eafera wæs	*æfter cenned,*	To him an heir was afterward born,
geong in geardum,	*þone god sende*	Young in the world, whom God sent
folce to frofre;	*fyrenðearfe ongeat* 15	To the folk as help; he confirmed the terrible plight
þe hie ær drugon	*aldorlease*	That they once endured without an earl
lange hwile.	*Him þæs liffrēa,*	For so long a while. Him then the Lord,
wuldres wealdend,	*woroldare forgeaf;*	the Wielder of Glory, gave worldly renown.
Beowulf wæs breme	*(blæd wide sprang),*	Beowulf was famous: wide spread his glory,
Scyldes eafera	*Scedelandum in.*	Scyld's son, in the Scandian lands.

(www8.georgetown.edu/departments/medieval/labyrinth/library/oe/texts/a4.1.html)

Glossary

eafera "son, heir" masc. sg. nom.

wæs cenned "was conceived"; passive

geong "young"

geardum "dwelling place" masc. sg. dat.

folce "people, folk" neuter sg. dat.

frofre "help, joy"; masc., fem., neuter

fyrenðearfe "terrible plight"

ongeat "confirm" past

ær "once"

drugon "endure" past

aldorlease lit. "earl-less"

liffrea "Lord of Life" masc. sg. nom.

wuldres "glory" neuter sg. gen.

wealdend "wielder" plus gen.

woroldāre "worldly renown"

forgeaf "give" past

breme "renowned"

blæd "glory, success" masc. sg. nom.

The poem has been set to accentuate the division of lines into two parts with a hiatus in between. Line 15 (*folce to frofre; fyrenðearfe ongeat*), for example, has two stresses (in bold) before and two after the break. The two halves are linked by alliteration, here with an <f>. This is realized in ideal fashion in the first three words carrying stress, also the case in lines 14 with <g>, 18 with <w>, and 19 with <b>.

2.5.2 "The Wanderer"

Text 2.4 is an archaic text in the sense that it stands between the pagan and the Christian traditions. It may have been written as early as the time of Augustine's mission, but may also have been considerably later. In any case the one existing manuscript was preserved in the tenth century Exeter Book (see 3.5.2). The poem contains reminiscences of past pagan warriorhood, but is tempered about half way through by thoughts of Christian salvation.

Text 2.4 Excerpt from "The Wanderer" (c. 600) (ll. 8–14)

Oft ic sceolde ana	*uhtna gehwylce*	Often I had, alone	each dawn,
mine ceare cwiþan.	*Nis nu cwicra nan*	To speak of my trouble.	Nor is now anyone living
þe ic him modsefan	*minne durre*	To whom I dare	my innermost thoughts
sweotule asecgan.	*Ic to soþe wat*	Openly to speak.	I in truth know
þæt biþ in eorle	*indryhten þeaw,*	That it is in men	a noble custom
þæt he his ferðlocan	*fæste binde,*	That he [a man] his breast	holds fast,
healde his hordcofan,	*hycge swa he wille.*	Guards his treasure chest,	thinks as he wants.

(www8.georgetown.edu/departments/medieval/labyrinth/library/oe/texts/a3.6.html)

Glossary

sceolde "should, have to"	*nu* "now"	asecgan "say"	*ferðlocan* "breast," metaphor: "mind"
ana "alone"	*cwicra* "quick, alive"	*to soþe* "in truth, forsooth"	*fæste* "fast, tight"
uhtna "dawn"	*þe* relative "who"	*wat* "knew" 3rd p. sg. pres.	*binde* "bind, hold"; 3rd p. sg. pres. subjunctive
gehwylce "each one"	*modsefan* "courage"	*biþ*, lit. *be-eth* "is"	*healde* "hold, protect"; 3rd p. sg. pres. subjunctive
ceare "cares, troubles"	*mine* "my"	*eorle* "nobleman"	*hordcofan* "treasure/ hoard chamber," metaphor: "thoughts"
cwiþan "quoth, say"	*durre* "dare, venture"	indryhten "noble"	*hycge* "think"; 3rd p. sg. pres. subjunctive

Nis . . . nan < *ne*	*sweotule* "openly"	*þeaw* "custom"	*swa* "so, as"
is "isn't" + *ne ane*	adv. fr. adj. + adv.		
"none," a double	ending {-e}		
negative			

2.5.3 The *Anglo-Saxon Chronicle*: Britain

Text 2.5, though a later text, is thematically fitting: it is the introductory passage of Bede's *Historia ecclesiastica gentis Anglorum* (finished in 731), but translated into Old English as the introduction to the *Anglo-Saxon Chronicle* in the ninth century. It may rely on material from lost West Saxon annals which ended in 754. The text used here is from the Peterborough manuscript (aka *Laud Chronicle* or *Peterborough Chronicle*). The text is so relatively clear and easy to follow that a glossary can be dispensed with, but see the linguistic comments following the text.

Text 2.5 The *Anglo-Saxon Chronicle*: Introduction (eleventh century)

Brittene igland is ehta hund mila lang.   *7 twa hund brad.*   *7 her sind on þis iglande fif geþeode.*
The island Britain is 800 miles long,   and 200 miles broad.   And there are on the island five languages;

Englisc. 7 Brittisc. 7 Wilsc. 7 Scyttisc. 7 Pyhtisc. 7 Bocleden.   *Erest weron bugend þises landes Brittes.* 2
English & British & Welsh & Scottish & Pictish & Latin.   The first inhabitants were the Britons,

þa coman of Armenia.   *7 gesætan suðewearde Bryttene ærost.*   *þa gelamp hit þæt Pyhtas coman suþan*
who came from Armenia,   and first peopled Britain southward.   Then happened it, that the Picts came south

of Scithian.   *mid langum scipum na manegum.*   *7 þa coman ærost on norþ Ybernian up.*   4
from Scythia,   with long ships, not many;   and, landing first in the northern part of Ireland,

7 þær bædo Scottas þet hi ðer moston wunian.   *Ac hi noldan heom lyfan.*   *forðan hi cwædon*
and then the Scots said that they must dwell there. But they would not give them leave; for they [the Scots] said

þæt hi ne mihton ealle ætgædere gewunian þær. *7 þa cwædon þa Scottas. we eow magon þeahhwaðere*
                                                           ræd gelæron.   6
that they could not all dwell there together;   And then, said the Scots, we can nevertheless give you advice.

We witan oþer egland her be easton.   *þer ge magon eardian gif ge willað. 7 gif hwa eow wiðstent.*
We know another island here to the east. There you may dwell, if you will;   and if someone withstands you,

we eow fultumiad. þet ge hit magon gegangan. ða ferdon þa Pihtas. 7 geferdon þis land norþanweard.   8
we will assist you, that you may gain it.   Then went the Picts and entered this land northward.

(MS E: Bodleian MS Laud 636, http://asc.jebbo.co.uk/e/e-L.html)

Linguistic features of Text 2.5

Spelling: The use of <7> is conspicuous. This character comes from the Tironian notes ([link: Ideograms](#)) and stands for *ond* "and" in much the way that <&> (ampersand) does today.

Vocabulary: Among the few borrowings from Latin in this text all but *mila* (miles) are proper names.

Grammar: The word order is verb–subject inversion after an introductory adverbial in both the following examples:

adverbial	verb	subject
Erest	*weron bugend þises landes*	*Brittes.*
þa	*gelamp*	*hit þæt Pyhtas coman suþan of Scithian*

Such inversion was common, but not absolute.

There were three types of verb in OE, the weak or consonantal, the strong or vocalic, and the irregular ones. This text offers examples of all three types, though only in a few of their possible forms.

The consonantal verbs are what today are called the regular verbs, that is, the ones that have a regular past tense and past participle, namely {-ed}. In OE the vast majority of verbs were consonantal, though not regular in the sense we are familiar with since they also included cases of vowel and consonant change. The past and past participle endings were, however, often the almost familiar inflections {-ode} and {-od} respectively. In this text *wunian* "dwell, live" is an example:

infinitive	present 3rd p. sg.	past	past participle
(ge-)wunian	*(ge-)wunað*	*(ge-)wunode*	*(ge-)wunod*

The vocalic type of verb depended on a variety of patterns of vowel change and had one further distinct form due to the fact that the past singular and the past plural often had different vowels. From the text we may take as an example *cuman* or *(ge-)limpan*

infinitive	present 3rd p. sg.	past 1st and 3rd sg.	past-plural	past participle
cuman	*cymð*	*cōm*	*cōmon*	*(ge-)cūmen*
(ge-)limpan	*(ge-)limpð*	*(ge-)lamp*	*(ge-)lumpon*	*(ge-)lumpen*

The irregular verbs are a diverse set. The most central of them is the verb *be*, which remains the most irregular in ModE as well. Next to the present indicative *eom, eart, is, sind(on)* "am, art, is, are" there is an alternative paradigm *bēo, bist, bið, bēoð*. The past has 1st and 3rd p. sg. *wæs*, 2nd p. sg. *wǣre* and pl. *wǣron*. In Text 2.5 we find examples of *is, sind*, and *weron* (alternate form of the past plural). The subjunctive has its own paradigms: present singular *sȳ* and plural *sȳn* or *bēo* and *bēon* and past singular *wǣre* and plural *wǣren*. The subjunctive was used, among other things, to express wish or volition, the possible, but not certain truth of a situation, or hypothetical contexts. Only vestiges of the subjunctive are to be found in ModE (link: Mood). An example of volition is the phrase *sī þīn nama gehālgod* from the Lord's Prayer, where *sī* is the present subjunctive of *be*. In the King James Version (KJV) of the Bible it is still rendered in the subjunctive *Hallowed be thy name*, but in a ModE translation we find instead the ***modal auxiliary verb*** (link: Auxiliary verbs) *may*: *May your holy name be honored*. Examples of the subjunctive were also pointed out in Text 2.1.

One final point is the existence of aspectual distinctions in the verbs. What this means is that different facets or aspects of meaning could be expressed by using prefixes. One of the most prominent of these is {ge-}, which emphasized the completed or perfective nature of the action designated by a verb. In Text 2.5 we find *wunian* in l. 5 in the simple meaning of "dwell, live," but *gewunian* in l. 6, where it is the suitable way of emphasizing the idea of togetherness or completeness. In l. 8 we find first *ferdon* "go," but immediately afterwards *geferdon* "enter," compare also *brecan* "break" – *abrecan* "smash"; *slean* "hit" – *ofslean* "kill"; or *bærnan* "burn" – *forbærnan* "burn up" (cf. Samuels 1972: 163ff). These prefixes were, however, generally in decline and were to be replaced by new developments in the language in the ME and EModE periods (link: Aspect).

2.5.4 Variety in Old English

The verb forms just introduced give a hint at the extent of variation in OE. Diversity of forms was normal though it was partly countered in the process of ***standardization*** which eventually took place in OE. Much of the variety was regional, and this was grounded in the four major regional dialects which OE is usually regarded as consisting of: Northumbrian and Mercian, sometimes grouped together as Anglian; Kentish; and West Saxon. The majority of extant texts from the OE period are in the West Saxon scribal tradition (see 3.4), but there are a few good examples of work composed in other dialect areas. Among these regions Northumbria was especially important in the seventh and eighth centuries. Consequently, we will look at Text 2.6, "Cædmon's Hymn," in two versions, a northern one and a West Saxon one. Cædmon (late seventh century) was a contemporary of Bede and associated with the monastery (link: Early Christian England) (link: Viking incursions) at Streonæshalch (present-day Whitby Abbey), as a lay brother; both men were northerners.

We only have Latin writing from Bede (with the possible exception of his five-line *Death Song*) in OE, but "Cædmon's Hymn," composed in the seventh century and available in a manuscript from 737, gives us some idea of Anglian usage. The choice of words in the two versions below is identical with the exception of l. 5, which has Anglian *scop aelda barnum* "created, the High Lord, for men", but West Saxon *sceop eorðan bearnum* "created the earth for men." However, both the Anglian and the West Saxon versions vary in themselves between the two readings. The major differences are to be found in the vowels. It is widely recognized that West Saxon underwent a process of ***diphthongization*** which does not show up in northern texts. Vowel qualities also seem to have varied. Some apparent differences are, however, probably only spelling conventions. Since the two texts come from different regions and from different times, the variation may be due to either factor or both. Table 2.2, drawn from material in the texts, is only a selection of the contrasts to be found in the two versions. Yet despite the differences between the two texts, both share the division of lines into two times two stresses tied together by alliteration.

Table 2.2 Anglian and West Saxon parallel forms

line	Anglian (A)	West Saxon (WS)	contrast A–WS	comment
l. 1	hefænricæs uard	heofonrices weard	e – eo; a – ea	WS diphthongization
l. 2	metudæs maecti end his modgidanc	meotodes meahte and his modgeþanc	æ – e; ae (æ) – ea; e – a; i – e	differing vowel quality
l. 2	maecti	meahte	cC – hC	spelling convention
l. 3	uerc uuldurfadur	weorc wuldorfæder	u – w	spelling convention
l. 4	dryctin	drihten	y – i	WS unrounding of /y/
ll. 2, 5, 7	modgidanc, –, **tha**	modgeþanc, eorðan, **þa**	d, th – ð/þ	spelling conventions
ll. 4, 9	astelidæ, foldu	onstealde, foldan	a – on; u – an	loss of nasal in unstressed syllables

Note that the translation has been given in a fashion which is intended to remain as close to the word order of the original as possible. The result is not highly artistic, but may help you to read the OE version more easily.

Text 2.6 Cædmon's Hymn (in two versions)

Early Anglian (Northumbrian, MS of 737)

Nu scylun hergan   hefænricæs uard,
Now shall we praise the guardian of the heavenly kingdom,

metudæs maecti   end his modgidanc,
The Creator's power and His conception,

uerc uuldurfadur,   sue he uundra gihuaes,
The work of the Father of Glory, as He of every wonder

eci dryctin,   or astelidæ.
Eternal Lord, created the beginning.

He aerist scop   aelda barnum
He first created, the High Lord; for men (A)

heben til hrofe,   haleg scepen;
Heaven as a roof hallowedly shaping it.

tha middungeard   moncynnæs uard,
Then the earth, mankind's guardian,

Early West Saxon (first half of tenth century)

Nu sculon herigean   heofonrices weard,

meotodes meahte   and his modgeþanc,   2

weorc wuldorfæder,   swa he wundra gehwæs,

ece drihten,   or onstealde.   4

He ærest sceop   eorðan bearnum
He first created the earth for men (WS)

heofon to hrofe,   halig scyppend;   6

þa middangeard   moncynnes weard,

eci dryctin,	*æfter tiadæ*	*ece drihten,*	*æfter teode*	8

The Eternal Lord, afterwards brought forth

firum foldu,	*frea allmectig.*	*firum foldan,*	*frea ælmihtig.*

For man the fields, the Almighty Lord.

("Cædmon's Hymn", T. Jebson (ed.) (1994) at: www8.georgetown.edu/departments/medieval/labyrinth/library/oe/minor-poems.html)

Further social, cultural, political, economic, religious, and linguistic developments within the roughly 700 year period of OE will be added in chapter three.

2.6 Summary

This chapter has traced the background and early history of OE and looked especially at linguistic and cultural contacts with the Celts, whose contributions to English and Anglo-Saxon England were relatively restricted. The influence of the Romans was more substantial, but overall the invasions of the Germanic tribes, their settlements, and the kingdoms they set up were largely a new sociocultural and linguistic beginning. A first textual sample of Old English was used to introduce some of the main features of the language as well as to give a hint at the nature and power bias of one of the early kingdoms, Kent. From there we outlined the process of Christianization and supported this with a second OE text, taken from the Ruthwell Cross, this one written in runic script. Of the three further texts, one from *Beowulf*, was largely pagan in character. A second one, from "The Wanderer," was a mixture of pagan ideas and Christian content. And the third was an extract from the *Anglo-Saxon Chronicle*. Each was used to deepen understanding of the language and literary traditions of early Anglo-Saxon England. The chapter closed with an examination of two versions of "Cædmon's Hymn," which served to make the variation in OE – be it in space or in time – clearer.

STUDY QUESTIONS

Social and cultural background

1. What was the social position of the Celtic-speaking population of Britain like in the period after the Anglo-Saxon conquest? What consequences did this have for the Celtic languages? for English?

2. What kind of contact did the Romans and the Germanic peoples have in Britain?
3. Why did conversion to Christianity take place so rapidly? What effect did Christianization have on the society of early Germanic England?
4. What kind of literature is available to us from the OE period?
5. What is the effect of the limitations in the literature which we have from the OE period on our knowledge of the language?

Linguistic background

1. Characterize the influence of Celtic on OE and give some examples.
2. What do place-names tell us about the settlement of England and the ethnic heritage of the various regions? Give examples.
3. How was the Latin alphabet adapted for use in writing OE? What other tradition was drawn on for this?
4. Both OE and ModE have the category of gender in their grammar. In ModE gender is based largely on "natural gender," by which people mean the biological sex of what is referred to. For reference to a man we use *he*; for a woman, *she*; and for a house, *it*. Explain how this differs in OE and give examples.
5. What is the relationship of the Germanic kingdoms to the dialect areas of Anglo-Saxon England?
6. What distinctions are made in the OE personal pronoun system which are not made in ModE?

Further reading

Bassett is a collection of articles with detailed information on the formation of the Anglo-Saxon kingdoms. Ekwall is the classic study of English place-names. Hogg is a comprehensive collection of contributions about all the relevant linguistic aspects of Old English, and Stapleton is a convenient printed, non-internet source of basic information about important authors and texts.

Bassett, S. (ed.) (1989) *The Origins of Anglo-Saxon Kingdoms*. London: Leicester UP.
Ekwall, E. (1970 [1936]) *Concise Oxford Dictionary of English Place-Names*, 4th ed. Oxford: Clarendon.
Hogg, R.M. (1992) *The Cambridge History of the English Language*. vol. I *The Beginnings to 1066*. Cambridge: CUP.
Stapleton, M. (1983) *The Cambridge Guide to English Literature*. Cambridge: CUP.

CHAPTER THREE

Old English

The Viking invasions and their consequences (700 – 1066/1100)

CONTENTS

Chapter Overview:

This chapter:

- follows the development of English from the time of the Viking invasions at the end of the eighth century up to the Norman Conquest of 1066;
- outlines three stages of Viking incursions: raids on the coast; conquest and settlement; dynastic conflict – giving one OE text in connection with each of these phases, always illustrating the Wessex point of view;
- presents the influence on Old English of speakers of Old Norse in Britain in regard to vocabulary, pronunciation, inflection, and syntax;
- explores the nature of linguistic contact by looking at the arguments which speak for and against seeing this as an instance of creolization; in doing this special attention is paid to the features of Danelaw English;
- reviews developments outside of Danelaw, in the areas controlled by Wessex, with an eye to the renewal of learning under King Alfred and the subsequent establishment of a West Saxon standard;
- sketches the further development of this process within the framework of monastic reforms. A final example of OE is offered in the form of the riddles preserved in the Exeter Book.

Text 3.1 The *Anglo-Saxon Chronicle* for 787 – The Invasion of the Vikings

. . . 7 on his [Brihtric cing] dagum comon ærest .iii.   scipu Norðmanna . . . 7   þa   se   gerefa
. . . and in his [King Bertric]   days came first   three ships of Northmen,   and at this the reeve

þærto rad   7 he wolde   drifan to ðes cininges tune,   þy he nyste   hwæt hi wæron,
there rode   and he wanted to drive to the king's town,   for he didn't know what they were,

7 hine man ofsloh þa.   ðæt   wæron þa erestan scypu Deniscra manna þe Angelcynnes land gesohton.
and him they killed there. These were the first ships of the Danes that   England   sought out.

(MS E: Bodleian MS Laud 636, http://asc.jebbo.co.uk/e/e-L.html) *hine man ofsloh þa.*

3.1 The Viking invasions

3.1.1 The first phase of Viking incursions

The passage quoted above from the *Anglo-Saxon Chronicle* for the year 787 (Plate 3.1) is the first record of the new danger of raids on the British coast from abroad. Much like the Anglo-Saxons over 300 years before, the new raiders were also part of a Germanic people, this time from even farther north. They were Vikings from Scandinavia (link: Vikings). The push-factors for them to leave their original homes were probably similar: overpopulation of a homeland with too few natural resources. In addition, they were part of a system in which inheritance was passed on to the oldest son (primogeniture); consequently, younger sons had to search for fame and fortune elsewhere. As a result, once the Franks under Charlemagne (768–814) had destroyed the naval power of the Frisians to the north of the Franks, there was no one to hinder the Vikings, who now had no problem sailing into the North Sea. Like the Anglo-Saxons before them they first raided the coast, pillaging and burning and then returning home with their booty, which consisted of gold, silver, jewels, fine clothing, and slaves. As a result the monasteries of Lindisfarne (793), Jarrow (794), and Iona (795) were sacked and valuable manuscripts were destroyed (Plate 3.2). From the mid-ninth century on they came with large armies and eventually settled, as recounted in the next section.

3.1.2 The second phase: settlement

Eventually Danish Vikings gained control over large parts of northern and eastern England, as did Norwegian Vikings in western Scotland and parts of Ireland (Map 3.1). This was not a matter of raids or temporary incursions, for the Norse settled in the North and East between 865 and 955, at the same time they were also settling Scotland, Ireland, and what

Map 3.1
Danelaw and
Wessex in 878

was to be Normandy. Their language was not maintained anywhere for longer than perhaps two generations, not even in England, where settlement was densest.

In 866 they conquered East Anglia; in 867 they captured York. Large numbers of Scandinavians settled in these areas and began to establish farms. There is no doubt that there was hostility between the original inhabitants and the newcomers, and territorial conflict continued. Yet there seems to have been little of the forced removal that had been typical of the earlier Anglo-Saxon conquest of England, in which a great many Celts fled from the aggressors.

The West Saxons kings consolidated their dynastic claims and undertook defense against the Danes. In the *Anglo-Saxon Chronicle* we learn in the entry for 854 that Æthelwulf, who had been fighting with changing fortune against the Danes, had his right to the throne justified in much the same way as Horsa and Hengist four hundred years before. He is recorded as descending in a long line which led by way of Woden right back to Seth, the son of biblical Adam. This lineage was, of course, convenient to the initiator of the *Anglo-Saxon Chronicle*, Alfred the Great of Wessex, who was Æthelwulf's son (link: Wessex and Danish dynasties). And it was Alfred who was to turn the tide and stop the advance of the Danish Vikings. He managed this in 878 at the battle at Ethandun (Edington), in which he defeated Guthrum, the Danish king of East Anglia. Peace under the Treaty of Wedmore stabilized the kingdom of Wessex by setting a boundary between it and that part of England – namely Northumbria, East Mercia and East Anglia – which was known as *Denalagu* (Danelaw) because Danish jurisdiction was recognized there. As one of the terms of peace, Guthrum agreed to become Christian. Not only did this give the treaty more support, but it was also a major step toward assimilation of the Viking conquerors. Yet despite the peace treaty, conflict persisted as the West Saxons continued reconquering territory in Danelaw until West Saxon control covered virtually all of England. Sixty years after Wedmore, Alfred's grandson Æthelstan was the one who would make a great step toward uniting the kingdom under the West Saxons. This is celebrated in the poem "The Battle of Brunanburh" (link: Battle of Brunanburh), where we read about the victory of the West Saxons in 937 over the Viking raiders and the Scots with whom they were allied. The following lines from the poem show the dynastic claims against those perceived to be the enemy, the Scots and the Vikings (*scip-flotan*).

Text 3.2 "The Battle of Brunanburh" (ll. 7–12)

eaforan Eadweardes,	*swa him ge-aethele waes*	The sons of Edward,	it was only befitting their noble descent
fram cneo-magum	*thaet hie aet campe oft*	from their ancestors	that they should often
with lathra gehwone	*land ealgodon,*	against each hostile people,	defend their land in battle
hord and hamas.	*Hettend crungon,*	horde and home.	The enemy perished,
Scotta leode	*and scip-flotan,*	Scots men	and seamen [Vikings],
faege feollon.	. . .	fated they fell. . . .	

(D. Burnley (ed.) (1992) *The History of the English Language. A Source Book.* London: Longman, 50)

Glossary

eaforan "son"	*lathra* (adj.) "hostile, hateful, hated"	*leode* "people"
swa + waes "it was only"	*gehwone* "each"	*scip-flotan* "seamen"; literally: "ship-floater"
ge-aethele "befitting noble descent"	*ealgodon* (3rd p. pl.) "they might defend"	
cneo-magum "ancestors"	*Hettend* "The Enemy"	*faege* "fated"

campe "battle"   *crungon* (3rd p.pl. past) "fell   *feollon* (3rd p.pl. past) "they
                       in battle, perished"   fell"

3.1.3 The final phase of Danish invasion: dynastic conflict

Despite the sentiments of the lines quoted from "The Battle of Brunanburh," it is likely that settlements of Danes and of Anglo-Saxons existed in relative proximity, and in the towns there was sure to have been mixing between the groups. The ways of life of both were similar, if not identical. Furthermore, with the end of paganism religion offered an additional bond. Hence the attack by Olaf Tryggvason in 991, in which his forces pillaged towns on the southern coast, must be seen as a result of dynastic and not ethnic rivalry. He and his army also fought the Saxons at Maldon. The OE poem, "The Battle of Maldon" (link: Battle of Maldon), commemorates the attack, which took place on the coast northeast of London. The existing version of the poem – an eighteenth century copy – probably stems from the late eleventh century. It tells the story of English forces defeated by the Viking invaders, but the poem celebrates the Saxons' heroic stand, which may have been a telling point at the time the manuscript was composed, namely after the Norman Conquest, when once again invaders had prevailed. The lines given below are the reply of the Saxon leader Byrhtnoð to the demand of the Vikings that the Saxons pay them tribute. The translation is given word-for-word and not in idiomatic English. A glossary has been added in the right-hand column. A more fluent translation follows.

Text 3.3 "The Battle of Maldon"

42 *Byrhtnoð maþelode,*   *bord hafenode,*   *maþelode* (3rd p. sg. past of *maþelian* "herangue";
    Byrhtnoth spoke,   his shield holding,   *bord* "board" (neut. sg. acc.); *hafenode* 3rd p. sg. past)

    wand wacne æsc,   *wordum mælde,*   *wand* "whirled" (> ModE *wind*); *wacne* > ModE *weak*;
    shook the slender   with words spoke,   *wordum* "with words" (neut. pl. dat.); *mēlan* "talk"
    ash (spear),

44 *yrre and anræd*   *ageaf him andsware:*   *yrre* "with ire, angry" (adj.); *an-* "one" + *-ræd* "plan";
    angry and single-minded   gave him answer: *a-* emphatic prefix + *geaf* "gave" (3rd p. sg. past)

    Gehyrst þu, sælida,   *hwæt þis folc segeð?* *Ge-* prefix + *hyrst* "hearest" (2nd p. sg. pres.);
    Hear you, sailor (Viking), what this folk says?   *sælida sæ* "sea" + *lida* < *liðan* "travel, sail"

46 *Hī willað ēow tō gafole* *gāras syllan,*   *ēow* "to you" (2nd p. pl. dat.); *gafol* "tribute"
    They want to you as   spears to give,   (neut. sg. dat.) < *giefan* "give"; *syllan* > ModE
    tribute   "sell"; *gāras* (masc. pl. acc.)

    ættrynne ord   *and ealde swurd,*   *ealde* "old; tried and true"; *swurd* (neut. pl. acc.)
    poisonous point,   and old swords,

48	*þā heregeatu* then armor	*þe ēow æt hilde ne dēah.* that for you in war is useless.	*here* "army" + *geatu* "weapons"; *hilde* "combat, war" (fem. sg. dat. after *æt*); *dēah* "be of value" (3rd sg. pres.)
	Brimmanna boda, Seamen's messenger,	*ābēod eft ongēan,* bear word back again;	*bīmm-* "surf, sea" + *manna* "men" (masc. pl. gen.) *ā-* emph. prefix + *-bēod* "bear" (past participle)
50	*sege þīnum lēodum* tell your people	*miccle lāþre spell,* a very loathsome tale:	*þīnum* "thine" (dat. pl.); *lēodum* "men" > ModE lewd; *miccle* > ModE *much*
	þæt hēr stynt unforcūð that here stands a good	*eorl mid his werode,* earl with his war-band,	*un-* "not" + *-for-* "loss of" + *-cūð* "famous"; *werode*, related to ModE *war*
52	*þe wile gealgean* that will defend	*ēþel þysne,* homeland this,	*þysne* (masc. sg. acc.) note inverted word order
	Æþelrēdes eard, Aethelred's land,	*ealdres mīnes,* land of my prince,	*eard* cf. ModE *earth; ealdres* "elder" (masc. sg. gen.); *mīnes* (masc. sg. gen.) note inverted word order
54	*folc and foldan.* folk and fold.	*Feallan sceolon* fall must	*fold*, "land" cf. ModE *(sheep)fold; sceolon* "shall, must"
	hæþene æt hilde. the heathens at war.	*Tō hēanlic mē þinceð* Too shameful me-thinks	*hēan-* "despised" + *-lic* "like"
56	*þæt gē mid ūrum sceattum* that you, with our wealth,	*tō scype gangon* to (yours) ships went	*gē* "ye"; *sceattum* "treasures" (masc. pl. dat.)
	unbefohtene, unfought against,	*nū gē þus feor hider* now you thus from far hither	*unbefohten* "un+fought-against"
58	*on ūrne eard* to our earth (land)	*in becōmon.* in came (have come).	
	Ne sceole gē swā sōfte Not shall you so softly	*sinc gegangan;* riches gain:	*sōft-* + *-e* (adverbial ending)
60	*ūs sceal ord and ecg* us shall point and edge,	*ǣr gesēman,* first reconcile,	*ǣr* "ere, first"; *ge-* "complete" + *-sēman* "same"
	grim gūðplega, grim battle-play,	*ǣr wē gofol syllon."* before we tribute give."	*gūð-* "combat" -*plega* "quick motion," cf. ModE *play*

(D. Burnley (ed.) (1992) *The History of the English Language. A Source Book.* London: Longman, 58)

Byrhtnoth spoke, lifted his shield and shook his slender spear; angry and determined he answered: "Do you hear, Viking, what this people says? They will give you spears as tribute with deadly points and experienced swords, then armor which is useless to you in battle. Messenger, take back our answer and tell your people a more loathsome story: here stands not so bad a leader with his troops, who will defend their homeland, Æthelred's land, the land of our prince, home and hearth. You heathens must now die in battle. It seems to me it would be shameful if you escaped on your ships with our treasures without any resistance on our part now that you have come here from so far away. You cannot just disappear with our riches: rather things must be settled with our sharp weapons in grim battle, before we will pay tribute.

The renewed attacks by the Danes did, however, lead to the payment of tribute and, eventually, the establishment of a Danish king over all England. First Sweyn Forkbeard (1013–1014), who drove Æthelred into exile, and then his son Cnut (Canute) took the throne (1016–1035). Since Cnut was more or less simultaneously king of Denmark and later of Norway, his reign put an end to the Danish raids, but not to Danish claims to the throne, which followed his death as well as the death of the longest reigning of his pre-conquest successors, Edward the Confessor (1042–1066). Even under the Danish kings it was English and not Danish which was spoken at court.

3.2. Linguistic influence of Old Norse

The enmity indicated by the lines just quoted probably does not do justice to the largely peaceable relations which existed in daily life on a local basis. The two groups lived close together, and there was probably a fair amount of intermarriage. So even if it is not clear whether the languages of the two groups were similar enough to be mutually comprehensible, there was sure to have been a fair amount of *bilingualism* (link: Bilingualism). Indeed, the displacement of Danish is unthinkable without bilingualism. Although Norse language pockets continued to exist into the twelfth century,[1] a renewed set of military incursions by the Danes did not reverse language shift to English. Yet, as Thomason and Kaufman, for example, say, "The Norse influence on English was pervasive, in the sense that its results are found in all parts of the language; but it was not deep except in the lexicon" (1988: 302). It is, therefore, with the lexicon that we will start.

3.2.1 Vocabulary

Many words were virtually identical, though pronunciation and inflection often differed. Yet numerous words did differ, and quite a lot of Scandinavian *vocabulary* was borrowed. Geipel says it was about 400 words, and they were often among the most common. Nordicisms in the rural *dialects* amount to another 2000 (1971: 69–70). Furthermore, the *borrowings* come from all areas of life. This is different from the learned words which had

---

1 In the Shetlands Norn, a Scandinavian language, may have been spoken as late as the nineteenth century.

been borrowed from Latin in the OE period and which came particularly from the area of religion. In 2.1.2 Scandinavian *place-names* ending in {-by}, {-holm}, {-thorpe}, {-thwaite}, and {-toft} were already mentioned, to which family names ending in {-son} can be added here, both ones with a Norse first part, such as *Swainson* or *Orneson* and without, for example, *Johnson*, *Jackson*, or *Paulson* (ibid.: 174ff) vs. OE {-ing} (as in *Browning*). ON influence is visible especially in the area of war and maritime activities, where it provided a fairly large subgrouping of **loan words** such as *barda* "beaked ship"; *cnearr* "small ship or galley"; *liþ* "fleet"; *scegþmann* "pirate"; *dreng* "warrior"; *bātswegen* "boatman, boatswain"; *orrest* "battle"; *rān* "robbery"; and *rannsaka* "ransack." In addition we find a number of words relating to law or the administrative system: *lagu* "law"; *māl* "active at law"; *hold* "landholder (less than a Danish *jarl*)"; *hūsting* "tribunal"; and *riding* (< *thriding* "division of Yorkshire").

What is really remarkable is the huge number of common words which have an ON source. Among the most widely used we find *get*, *give*, and *take*; *dirt*, *dregs*, and *mire*; *nag*, *call*, and *scowl*; *guess*, *want*, and *thrive*, but also farm and animal terms such as *axletree*, *bull*, *down* (feathers), and *egg* as well as words for bodily features: *freckles*, *leg*, and *skin*. Even *birth*, *slaughter*, and *die*; *fellow*, *husband*, and *sister* come from ON. This shows in relatively dramatic fashion the influence of Scandinavian speakers in domestic and working life.

Borrowing ([link: Borrowing and word formation](#)) may be straightforward, especially when there is no exact equivalent in the borrowing language. This was clearly not the case with some words, for example not for *taka* "take," for which the OE word *niman* (cf. present-day German *nehmen*) was available. Just why *take* eventually displaced native *niman* is not clear. However, as with many such pairs of words, the ousted word continued to exist under restricted conditions. Archaic *nim* is still listed in dictionaries in the sense of stealing, as are both *nimble* (< ME *nimel* < OE *numol* < OE *niman*) and *numb* (< the past participle of *niman*). In other cases we have to do with **loan translations**, as in the case of *hāmsōcn* < ON *heimr* "home" + ON *sōkn* "struggle, fight" "attacking an enemy in his house," a kind of ancient breaking and entering. In some cases both Norse and Saxon words remained in use though sometimes with meaning distinctions, as with *anger*, *cast*, *die*, *ill* (< ON *angr*, *kasta*, *deyja*, *illr*) next to OE *wræþþ*, *weorpan*, *steorfan*, *yfel* (> ModE *wrath*, *warp*, *starve*, *evil*). In still other cases the meaning may come from one language but the form from the other: OE *hlāf* meant "bread" (cf. Russian *xleb*) while OE *brēad* meant "fragment"; the latter took on the meaning of ON *brauð* "bread," leaving *hlāf* to become the more restricted ModE *loaf*. Other words continued to be used in the Norse-influenced **traditional dialects** not just of Northumbria and Cumbria, but also of Lindsey, Fourboroughs, Norfolk, Elmet, Lancaster and Chester (see Map 3.2), words like *attlen* "think"; *big* "build"; *bolnen* "swell"; *hoast* "cough"; *laik* "play"; *lait* "search"; *lathe* "barn"; *reike* "path"; *roke* "mist"; *tinen* "lose"; or *gate*, which in the northern dialect means "way, road, street" < ON *gata* as opposed to the StE meaning of *gate*. As a final comment it should be pointed out that most Scandinavian loan words do not appear in writing until the ME period; however, their form shows they were adopted in the late OE period. The fact that written evidence comes so late may be credited to the lack of a literary tradition in Danelaw.

Map 3.2 Ethnolinguistic regions

3.2.2 Pronunciation

In many cases OE and ON words are virtually identical, but often sound changes ([link: Sound change](#)) have led to distinctions. There are five very prominent cases:

(1) ***Proto-Germanic*** /sk/ remained /sk/ in Norse, but became /ʃ/ in OE. Numerous words in ModE which have the ***consonant cluster*** /sk/ come ultimately from ON: *skirt* (vs. native *shirt*), *scrub* (vs. *shrub*), *scatter* (vs. *shatter*), but also *skin, sky,* or *skill* (rather than *hȳd, wolcen,* or *cræft*).

(2) /g/ for /j/ as in *give* (OE *giefan* with in initial /j/) or *egg* (OE *ey*).

(3) /k/ for OE /tʃ/ as in *kid* (OE *cild*) or *kirk* (OE *cirice*).

(4) Proto-Germanic /ai/ became /ei/ in Norse, but /oː/ in OE as in the ModE pairs *nay–no*, *hale–whole*, or *raid–road* (where *raid* originally had the restricted meaning of *highway robbery*).

(5) Proto-Germanic /au/ remained ON /au/, but became OE /eːa/ as in *lauss* (> ModE *loose*) vs. *lēas* (> ModE *-less*, e.g. *hopeless*).

Other pronunciation differences such as Norse loss of initial *w-* (cf. *Ulf* vs. *Wulf*) or *metathesis* (ON *brenna* vs. OE *biernan* "burn") are less frequent.

3.2.3 Inflection

One of the most significant changes between Old and the Middle English was the gradual decay of inflectional endings ([link: Inflection in English](#)). This loss occurred both in the areas where contact with Old Norse was strong as well as within the West Saxon area. Consequently, it would be difficult to claim that contact with ON was its cause. However, the North showed large numbers of Norse borrowings and grammatical influence while the South was a more or less unbroken continuation of OE. Overall, change was more rapid in the North; and where new forms were introduced, ON is the likely source. Inflectional loss shows up in:

(1) loss of grammatical gender;
(2) simplification (not so rapid in the South) of gender, number, and case *agreement* in *adjectives*, qualifiers, quantifiers, and *demonstratives*; and
(3) the general loss of dative and genitive plural cases.

In other words, the *language contact* situation in the Danelaw area, presumably with widespread bilingualism, seems to have led to a grammatically unstable situation in which speakers were uncertain about endings. As one author writes, "The gap between the two is not great but it may well have encouraged speakers to replace inflections with a different system. When all of these differing pronunciations are taken into account, communication may have at times been difficult" (Blake 1996: 80).

The most important innovations were the introduction of the {-es} ending in the third person singular, present tense where the South continued to use {-eð}, which is often spelled <-eth>. The source may be the ON third person singular ending, once an older {-r}, which regularly changed to {-s}. For the inflections in a slightly later stage see Table 4.2 in 4.2.3.1. The North–South opposition so described is an oversimplification which ignores the *Midlands*, where an early ME plural verb form ending in {-n} helped to overcome the possible confusion of the sometimes identical third person singular and plural pronouns *he*: *he comeþ* "he comes" vs. *he comen* "they come" (Samuels 1972: 85).

While number has continued to be an important category in English, grammatical gender and case distinctions were already growing less and less important and would eventually be given up in favor of "natural gender" ([link: Grammatical gender](#)). The OE third person pronoun paradigm began uniformly with <h>. The important differences in case, gender, and number were marked by the inflections. Gradually, however, the distinctions between the vowels, especially in unstressed, rapid pronunciation, were becoming less and less reliable. Furthermore, several forms were identical, for example the dative singular masculine and neuter and the dative plural were the same: *him*. The nominative and accusative singular feminine and the plural of the same cases were also identical: *hie*. This was already leading to what, in ME, would be a significantly modified system (cf. Table 3.1).

Once again innovation came from the North: the replacement of the OE third person plural personal pronouns by forms was influenced by ON ([link: Personal pronoun systems](#)), all the forms of which began with <th> (see 4.2.3.3).

In the case of feminine singular nominative *hēo* the solution lay elsewhere. Although there is dissent about the process, the likelihood is fairly great that *hēo* was replaced by the corresponding demonstrative pronoun *seō*. The latter could have developed into *she* through **palatalization** of /s/ + a high front unstressed vowel which produced /ʃ/ (cf. also Burnley 1992: 416). The vowel /oː/, where *sho* appears instead of *she*, was in common use for a long time (Strang 1970: 236, 420) and is still used in some regional dialects. A more plausibly argued development is given by Samuels, who points out that the convergence of *hē* and *hēo* ("he" and "she") and of *hīe* ("they") to the single homophonous form *hē* led to the use not just of the plural *þei* but also to feminine singular variants along the following lines:

hēo → *heō* → /hjo, hje/ → /ço, çe/ → /ʃo, ʃe/

This change would have begun in Cumbria in the Norse-influenced North and then gradually spread southward. Evidence for this can be found in written forms like <ʒhe(o), ʒho, ghe>, representing /ç/, which was then replaced by <s(c)he, s(c)ho>. This is traceable in a transitional area which gradually moved south and finally ended in Devon, Dorset, and Kent (Samuels 1972: 114ff).

There are a number of further, relatively minor points such as the adoption of the ON prepositions *fro*, *with* (accompaniment), *till*, and *until*.

Table 3.1 The third person pronouns of OE in comparison to ME changes (more advanced in the North)

3rd person	masc. sg.		fem. sg.		neut. sg.		plural	
	OE	ME	OE	ME	OE	ME	OE	ME
nominative	*hē*	*he*	*hēo (hie)*	*she (sho)*	*hit*	*(h)it*	*hīe (hig, hi, heo)*	*they*
genitive	*his*	*his*	*hire (heora)*	*hir(e)*	*his*	*his*	*heora (hyra, hira, hiora)*	*(t)hir(e)*
dative	*him (heom)*	*him*	*hire (heore)*	*hire*	*him (heom)*	*(h)it*	*him (heom)*	*(t)hem*
accusative	*hine*		*hī, hēo, hīe*		*hit*		*hīe (hig, hi, heo)*	
instrumental	*hȳ (hēo)*		like dative		*hȳ (hēo)*		like dative	

3.2.4 Syntax

The major features of English which are very likely to have developed under the influence of ON have, first and foremost, to do with *relative pronouns*/particles.

In OE the relative particle was most usually the word *þe*, which could take an antecedent of any type and which was not further distinguished for case or number, for example with a plural antecendent: . . . *þa ærestan scypu **Deniscra manna** þe Angelcynnes land gesohton* ("then [they] built ships for the Danish men who/that attacked England"); or with a singular antecedent: *þæt her stynt unforcuð **eorl** mid his werode, þe wile gealgean eþel þysne* ("an . . . earl who/that wants to. . ."; from Text 3.3, ll. 51–52).

ON also contributed to the use of the relative particle *as*, which is more common today in northern than in southern English dialects in its non-standard use, for example *the man as came yesterday*. As such it corresponds to Norse *som* "as" (Knowles 1997: 44).

A further innovation in the use of relatives is the zero relative, as in *the man* [zero] *I saw yesterday*. It seems that this structure occurred before the Viking invasions (Quirk and Wrenn 1957: §120b), but it is remarkable that the zero relative is a relatively rare construction in the languages of the world, but one shared by Danish and English. The same applies to what is called "preposition *stranding*," a construction in which the relative is fronted, but the preposition whose object it is remains in its "original" place in the clause. An illustration of this is the preceding sentence in which the words *in which* can be changed to show stranding:

. . . *a construction **which** the relative is fronted **in** . . .* (link: Relative clauses).

In the verb phrase there was little use in OE of the complex forms which are so common in ModE such as the perfect, the progressive, the *will*-future, or the use of *do* as an auxiliary, that is, **do**-periphrasis (link: Auxiliary or periphrastic *do*). These were to become increasingly common in the ME period (see 4.2.3, 5.3, and 6.3.3). Here, too, the question arises as to whether the introduction of these structures was not perhaps facilitated by the linguistic turbulence of OE–ON language contact, or by the submergence of the (West Saxon) written standard during the coming period of Norman dominion. It might be argued that the loss of the standard, whether in Danelaw or under **Norman French** domination, was like taking the lid off the pot and letting **vernacular** forms percolate upward where they would eventually be incorporated into the new standard that would begin to emerge in the Middle English period.

3.3 Creolization

Various historical linguists have mentioned the possibility that the developments in English between the OE and the ME periods were so strongly affected by language contact between ON and OE that this may be a case of *pidginization* and subsequent *creolization*. Leith, for one, writes:

> We cannot say for sure that a process like pidginization caused the abandonment of the Anglo-Saxon system of inflexions. But it would not be surprising if the process was at least hastened in the first instance by contact between the English and their Scandinavian neighbours and subsequently by contact with the Normans.

He adds that pronoun change suggests "a thorough and close mixing of the two speech-communities" (1983: 103–104).

3.3.1 Pidginization and creolization (link: Pidginization; link: Creolization)

These are the result of language contact in which there is significant change in the structure of the resulting languages (see 1.2; chapter 9). In pidginization there is massive simplification including the loss of inflections and the reduction of *grammatical categories* such as gender, case, number, tense, and *aspect* (link: Grammatical categories). For example, in a purely fictitious pidgin made up solely for illustrative purposes, a speaker might say something like *no me buy book*. This is ambiguous due to the missing tense and aspect categories, and could mean the speaker doesn't ever buy books, didn't buy a book on a particular occasion, or doesn't want to buy a book or books. A creole, in contrast, generates grammatical categories such as number, tense, aspect, and *modality* marked by the introduction of individual words or particles rather than the use of inflections. The hypothetical utterance just given might then be expanded as follows: *me no did buy book-them*, where *did* marks the past and *-them* indicates the plural. When a creole comes into existence, the upper or *superstrate* language – in this case English – the *lexifier* language, which is the major source of vocabulary, is used to supply the necessary particles. These, however, are employed in a grammatically non-English way to mark negation and tense. For example, they are frequently put in front of the verb for negation or tense, and they follow the noun to mark the plural. Pronoun case remains unchanged *me*, where GenE uses *I* (and also *my* or *me*). In both pidginization and creolization there is massive borrowing from the lexifier language. Furthermore, the prosody (rhythm, stress, and intonation) of the less prestigious *substrate* language or languages, which are frequently very numerous, is retained. In addition to this, pidgins and creoles come about most often situations in which there is social inequality between the powerful speakers of the upper or superstrate language and the subjugated speakers of the substrate language. The question is: how does this apply to the relationship between ON and OE?

3.3.2 Arguments and evidence

Two strong proponents of the creolization hypothesis are Bailey and Maroldt, who see evidence for creolization, which they define rather vaguely as "a gradient mixture of two or more languages" (1977: 21). They argue that a Norse–English creole arose in the North between 900 and 1066 as a new system and not merely as a new subsystem which internal change could have brought about. It involved substantial change (lexicon, semantics, *syntax*, phonetics, phonology, morphology). This can be seen in such fundamental changes in English as the simplification of inflections and the loss of grammatical gender and most instances of case. For Bailey and Maroldt: "It cannot be doubted that [Middle English] is a mixed language or creole" (1977: 22) (see 4.3). ON and OE stood in close contact in the North, where the Norse population made up over 50% of the total. ON was widely spoken and would have led to a situation of linguistic instability. This in turn would have hastened the reduction of inflections. Consequently, it is understandable that OE inflections, which were being lost everywhere, disappeared more extensively and earlier in the North. The relatively weak status of OE in Danelaw could easily have led to increased borrowing of basic vocabulary from ON, and this, too, is typical of creolization.

This position is rejected by Thomason and Kaufman, who concede that there was important structural change in English and that ON–OE language contact was the source of much of it, but they do not understand this as evidence of creolization. Furthermore, they do not see evidence for assuming such a large Norse element in the population (1988: 302–303). In any case, the type of change observed was happening independently of ON–OE language contact. The loss of final /ə/, which led to the loss of a number of grammatical distinctions in the North, occurred *after* Norse had died out there (1250–1300) even though it came even later in the South (1400). Hence it would be hard to see this as a contact phenomenon. The Norse features of Northern English appeared abruptly and remained until after the development of StE (i.e. from 1250 to 1450 in written documents of **Northern** ME) (ibid.: 279). In the North there was unrounding of /œ/ and /y/, which were kept in the South. In the North /s/ was used for Southern /ʃ/ (cf. *sall* vs. *scal* "shall"). The North lost the infinitive suffix, which was kept in the South as in *give* vs. *giefan* "give." And finally in the North the past of **strong verbs** had only one vowel (ibid.: 278f), for example /a/in *gaf* (all persons, singular and plural), while the South kept the division into two as seen in *geaf* (first and third person singular) with a short **diphthong** and *gēāfon* elsewhere with a long one. "This degree of simplification in the North, versus its rarity in the rest of the Danelaw, correlates with the rather high level of social upheaval prevalent in the North between 920 and 1100. It does not, however, correlate with anything in the structure of Norse" (ibid.: 277). The whole question is complicated by the fact that there are few texts between 900 and 1200 which reflect vernacular English. Vernacular documents after 1200 do indeed show little change in the South, more in the Midlands, and a great deal in the North (ibid.: 312–313).

Danelaw English has numerous features which may be attributed to Norse such as the pronouns mentioned above. This indicates intense borrowing and contact-induced shift (ibid.: 281). The influence of Norse on Danelaw English is clearly present in the lack of **voicing** of initial **fricatives**: /f, θ, s/ as in *fæt* "vat" with Northern /f/, but Southern /v/, or *þow/þoʒ* "though" with Northern /θ/ and Southern /ð/, or *sittan* with Northern /s/ vs. Southern /z/, which was characteristic of the English **Southwest**, but also of **Dutch**. Indeed, this may already have begun on the Continent, but the influence of Norse clearly reinforced the lack of initial voicing in Danelaw. Norsified English did not have the perfect prefix {ge-} used in West Saxon.

3.3.3 Creolization or not?

What does this all mean for the question of creolization? If we look just at what Bailey and Maroldt on the one side of the argument and Thomason and Kaufman on the other say in regard to the features enumerated above we see that there is agreement about many points, but still a differing conclusion.

For Thomason and Kaufman the greater simplicity of Danelaw ME represents internal simplification of English and is not due to Old Norse influence. This would include, for example, the switch to natural gender in Old Northumbrian, the lack of gender and case agreement, elements of Norse grammar and vocabulary (1988: 280). All in all, Norsified English seems to have arisen in the eastern Midlands (Lindsey) and to have contained numerous Midlands elements, but also important Norse grammatical components. It came about while Norse was still spoken, though already in decline as a result of the extension of

Table 3.2 Creolization features applied to OE–ON language contact

creolization feature	Bailey/Maroldt	Thomason/Kaufman
intense language contact	yes	yes
high proportion of Norse speakers	yes	uncertain; rather fewer
social inequality between Norse and English	yes	yes
loss of inflections (gender, case)	yes	yes, but independent of contact
introduction of particles	some	not addressed
major lexical borrowing from Norse	yes	yes

English political dominance (ibid.: 284). Thomason and Kaufman conclude that ME contained 20% Norse features (from a rather long list of 260 features); 75% are English. The remaining 5% are pure innovations. For Thomason and Kaufman this is not enough to justify seeing the Middle English which resulted as a product of creolization (ibid.: 292). The two languages were simply too similar to begin with, and there wasn't any polyglot substrate as is typically the case with pidginization and creolization. This speaks against creolization and suggests that bilingualism with a high degree of lexical and grammatical borrowing is more likely.

Surely the sociolinguistic situation was anything but simple. There would have been pockets of OE speakers in Danelaw, but also ON communities as well as mixed ones. Hence the language spoken would have included both anglicized Norse as well as Norse-influenced English. As Knowles remarks:

> Perhaps the linguistic relations between the two languages can best be described as a continuum, ranging from a relatively unmixed Scandinavian at one end of the scale to a relatively uninfluenced English speech at the other. In between, the languages co-existed, and then merged, with English forms and structures competing at first with the Scandinavian ones, then gradually spreading northwards.
>
> (1997: 24)

The difficulty that prevents us going beyond speculation is the lack of texts which reflect the vernacular in the long period from about 900 to 1250. Lass quotes one of the few pieces of evidence available, an eleventh century runic inscription at Aldburgh (Yorkshire):

Text 3.4 An eleventh century inscription showing OE–ON mixing

Ulf let aræran cyrice for hanum and for Gunware saula

Ulf let build church for him and for Gunware soul

Ulf had (this) church built for him(self) and for Gunwaru's soul.

(R. Lass (1987) *The Shape of English. Structure and History*. London: Dent, 53)

This text is a good example of **code-mixing** ([link: Code-switching and code-mixing](link)). *Ulf* is a Danish name (OE: *Wulf*) and the dative object of the preposition *for* is ON *hanum* rather than OE *him*. However, this text is exceptional, for most of what we have does not reflect the various regional vernaculars, but is written in the West Saxon standard (see next section).

3.4 Alfred's reforms and the West Saxon standard

For all the attention we have given to the Norse invasions it would be a mistake to neglect what was happening in the South. Basically, this means what was happening in Wessex, for, as we have seen, the kingdom of Wessex was the only independent "English" power outside of the areas in England under Norse control after the kingdom of Kent had been absorbed by Wessex in 825. What makes the West Saxon role so significant for us are the reforms which King Alfred ([link: King Alfred](link)) carried out. Countering the decline caused by the invasions of the Vikings – pagans who robbed monasteries, burned books, killed, enslaved, or dispersed monks – Alfred exerted military resistance against the Danes, and he stimulated a revival of learning by commissioning the translation of a number of important Latin works into OE. This was a reversal of the decline following the disastrous Viking raids, which had disrupted monastic life. After all, the only significant form of intellectual life in ninth century Europe was to be found in the monasteries.

The kind of literary work which Alfred initiated is an indication of some of the motives behind his literary revival. Two of the most important were *Cura Pastoralis* ("Pastoral Care") and the *Anglo-Saxon Chronicle*. The former, a set of rules or guidelines, was originally written in Latin in or around the year 590 by Pope Gregory, the pope who sent St. Augustine to Canterbury shortly after composing them. Under Alfred translations of the *Cura Pastoralis* were sent to each of the twelve dioceses which lay under West Saxon control. This had the effect of establishing common religious-intellectual ground within Alfred's territory. With the *Anglo-Saxon Chronicle*, based to a large extent on Bede's *Historia Ecclesiastica*, a common secular historical tradition was invoked. The vernacular language and the literature written in it served as a first move beyond mere military unification toward a consciousness of ethnic identity ([link: Ethnicity](link)). Though Danelaw was not immediately affected by it, the Norse presence was crucial since it triggered the intellectual revival. Furthermore, Alfred's use of English translations was a pedagogically wise move since the level of Latin was probably too low and too restricted to have the kind of influence which was envisioned by the king. We should not forget, however, that Alfred's program of translation into and writing in English reached only the small, albeit important literate elements in the kingdom, which now comprised everything outside of Danelaw, namely Wessex, Kent, and the western part of Mercia. The kinds of texts we have from this effort are, of course, somewhat restricted. By far the most numerous are religious, historical, and legal texts. As a contrast to what we have already seen – excerpts from the *Anglo-Saxon Chronicle*, from "The Battle of Brunanburh," and from "The Battle of Maldon" as well as religious and legal texts – we will have a brief look at a riddle in Text 3.5 (see below 3.5.2).

Following the early, seventh century literary primacy of Northumbria with Bede and Cædmon, as mentioned in 2.4, the literary and political center moved southward to Mercia

in the eighth century. Evidence of the Mercian tradition is to be found in the *Life of St. Chad*, which is preserved in a twelfth century manuscript, but employing ninth century spelling. This text suggests a pre-Alfredian interest in translation and reveals a relatively standardized language (Blake 1996: 76). But clearly Mercian power and the Mercian literary tradition ([link: Cynwulf](#)) were destroyed by the Norse incursions. Consequently, West Saxon was to be the standard language. The new literature instigated in King Alfred's initiative was associated with the power, prosperity, and prestige of Wessex, and by virtue of this the West Saxon dialect of OE soon became the basis of written OE even beyond the borders of Wessex. This meant that writing which had originally been composed in a different dialect was often copied into the West Saxon variety. As a result, most written OE from Alfred's time on is West Saxon or is highly influenced by its scribal traditions. By about the year 1000 West Saxon was essentially the OE written standard. The influence of Wessex was so strong because the efforts of Alfred and his royal successors – his son Edward the Elder, grandsons Athelstan, Edmund I, and Eadred as well as great-grandsons Edwy and especially Edgar – led to the gradual defeat of the Danes as more and more territory came under the control of the West Saxon dynasty. Under Wessex rule the division into counties came into existence, often with the consequence that their new administrative centers also became linguistic focal points.

The kings of Wessex succeeded in unifying England and thus establishing the prerequisites for economic stability and prosperity, but the conflict between the English and the Norse is described somewhat misleadingly with the remark that Alfred and Wessex "saved" the rest of England from the Danes (Barber et al. 2009: 109). Where life styles were basically very similar and there was, eventually, both religious and linguistic assimilation the notion of "saving" is somewhat parochial. In the period of Wessex ascendency England became a unified country, no longer *Angelcynn*, an ethnic designation, but *Englaland*, a political one, whereby the latter "is not a descriptive term but a political claim" (Knowles 1997: 38). Whether the king was West Saxon or Danish reflected dynastic more than demographic forces.

3.5 Monastic reform, linguistic developments, and literary genres

In the tenth century, due to the combined efforts of Dunstan, Archbishop of Canterbury; Æthelwold, bishop of Winchester; and Oswald, bishop of Worcester and Archbishop of York, monastic reforms were introduced along the lines of the changes that had been introduced in Cluny ([link: Early Christian England](#)). These led to further literary and linguistic revival. One of the most prominent effects of this is the rather sizeable set of words borrowed into English from Latin, most of them learned in nature. Among them we find such familiar religious words as *clūstor* "cloister," *crēda* "creed" or *fant* "baptismal font," but also scholarly words such as **accent**, *istoria* "history," or *terminus* "term." There are also words for flora such as *figa* "fig" or *gingifer* "ginger" and fauna including *camel* or *tiger*. All in all some 450 Latin words can be found in OE writings, some before this period. In addition, a large number of Germanic words which had taken on a Christian meaning might be added. Many Latin concepts appeared as **loan translations** or **calques**, as when *prophet*

appears as *wītega* "someone who knows" or *patriarch* as *hēahfæder* "high father." Native words also took on new meanings in the context of the new religion as when *sanctus/-a* "saint" is expressed by *hālga* "the holy one" or *martyr* by *þrōwere* "someone who suffers." Many, but by no means all, of these new Latin words came into relatively wide usage, as can be seen by the fact that they became nativized. This means that they resembled Germanic words in their pronunciation and structure and that they could enter into native ***word formation processes*** such when the noun *culpa(n)* < Latin *culpa* "guilt, fault, sin" became the verb *culpian* "to humble oneself."

3.5.1 Ælfric

As a part of the monastic renewal one of Dunstan's pupils, Ælfric of Eynsham (c. 955–1010), one of the most prolific writers of the Old English period, became a leading figure. He was important because of his strictly religious writing, which consisted of numerous homilies, but also because of his efforts at reviving Latin. This he pursued by means of his *Grammar*, his *Glossary*, and his *Colloquy*. The first of these was a Latin grammar written in English; the second, a word-list arranged by topic; and the third, a manual to help students learn how to speak Latin. Because of his work in this field he is also known as Ælfric the Grammarian. As far as English is concerned he helped to establish the West Saxon standard, which he adopted in his own writing. This meant a more consistent use of the grammatical cases, for example using accusative case objects after prepositions such as *þurh* "through, because of" (otherwise also dative and genitive) and *oð* "to, up to, until," *wið* "against, by, near," and *ymbe* "at, around, near" (all three otherwise also dative). He used the form *bið* rather than *is* in the third person singular present tense; and he helped to establish a more standardized vocabulary, such as *modig* rather than *ofermod* or *oferhygd* for Latin *superbia* "pride."

3.5.2 The Codex Exoniensis

The Codex is one of the most important manuscripts of OE literature (Exeter Cathedral Library MS 3501) and the largest still in existence. It is a collection of tenth century poetry in the West Saxon standard by unidentified authors. It was probably composed in the second half of the tenth century and was given by Leofric, the first bishop of Exeter, to the Exeter Cathedral library in the middle of the eleventh century. As such it is a product of the Benedictine Revival. This Exeter Book contains both religious and everyday texts including such key ones as "The Wanderer" (see Text 2.4), "The Seafarer," and "Widsith" ([link: OE literature](#)), but also some 95 riddles. Many of the latter are familiar from traditions outside of England and the English language, but many are unique to this collection.

Riddles are popular in many cultures. They are chiefly oral in tradition and go back beyond the beginnings of literary expression. They are verbal puzzles that try the wit of the teller against that of the listeners. Like the one given below they are comparisons and usually consist of two parts, a straightforward description and a more precise, but contradictory or misleading block, plus, of course, an answer. In Text 3.5 lines 1–2 are the description; lines 3–7, the block. In addition to this general structure, Riddle 44 (but careful – the numbering varies!), like the others in the Exeter Book consist of lines typical of OE poetry: they are divided into two halves, each with two strong beats and a caesura in between.

Text 3.5 An Old English riddle from the Exeter Book (Riddle 44)

Wrætlic hongað	*bi, weres þeo*	1	*ofer cneo hefeð,*	*wile þæt cuþe hol*	5
Wonderously it hangs	by a man's thigh		over his knee raises	he wants the well-known hole	
frean under sceate.	*Foran is þyrel.*	2	*mid his hangellan*	*heafde gretan*	6
Noble under a cloak	in front a hole.		with its hanging	head to greet	
Bið stiþ ond heard,	*stede hafað godne;*	3	*þæt he efenlang*	*ær oft gefylde.*	7
It is stiff and hard,	has a good stand.		what he even so long	before did often fill.	
þonne se esne	*his agen hrægl*	4			
Then this man	his own coat			Answer: *cæg*[2]	

(www8.georgetown.edu/departments/medieval/labyrinth/library/oe/texts/a3.22.44.html)

Short glossary

weres "man" gen. sg.; cf. Latin *vir*; cf. also ModE *werewolf*

stede "stand"; cf. ModE *stead*

þeo "thigh"

se esne "this man"

frean "master, king, spouse, god"

agen "own"

sceate "cloak", cf. ModE *sheet*

hrægl "coat"; cf. ModE *rail*

foran "in front" cf. ModE *(be)fore*

wile "wish, want" from *willan*; cf. ModE *will*

þyrel "hole"; cf. ModE *drill*

cuþe "well-known"; cf. ModE *uncouth* + meaning change

bið "be-eth, is"

cæg "key"

3.6 Summary

This chapter has traced some of the consequences of the Viking presence in Britain and has demonstrated what kind of changes their language, Old Norse, instigated in Old English. Particular emphasis has been given to an evaluation of the nature of the linguistic contact between OE and ON. Pro-creolization arguments emphasize the very significant borrowing

2 Other answers have also been suggested.

of everyday words from ON, the very conspicuous changes in the pronoun system, and changes in verb inflections. The arguments against creolization point out the basic similarity of the two languages and the great likelihood of ON–OE bilingualism and language shift to OE with significant borrowing from ON. On balance the degree of change and the nature of the social relationship between Danes and Saxons does not speak for creolization, but it does indicate a quality and closeness of contact far different from what we can see anywhere else in the history of the older language. The chapter has also introduced Alfred's reforms, which led to the creation of a written standard in OE. Some final remarks have focused on the types of texts produced in this period and ended with a look at an OE riddle.

STUDY QUESTIONS

Social and cultural background

1. How did the Christianization of the Vikings contribute to the stability of England after King Alfred's victory over the forces under Guthrum at Edington?
2. How do the two poems quoted in the excerpts ("Brunanburh" and "Maldon") reflect "national" self-awareness among the Saxons?
3. The written literature we have from the OE period may not give a balanced view of the language. Explain why this is the case.

Linguistic background

1. What speaks for and what against seeing the weakening of inflections as the result of ON–OE contact?
2. Quite a number of ON–OE lexical doublets exist which may be credited to borrowings from ON which go back to the same roots as the corresponding OE words. Where they continue to exist there is a semantic differentiation between the two. Explain how the following pairs differ:

a. *scoot < skjōta*	vs.	*shoot < scēotan*
b. *skittle < skutill*	vs.	*shuttle < scytel*
c. *kirk < kirkja*	vs.	*church < cirice*
d. *wail < vāla*	vs.	*woe < wā*

3. Assuming a situation of creolization between ON and OE, which language would be the superstrate and which the substrate language? Justify your conclusion.
4. How are the effects of ON on the language evident in ModE? Give examples from the areas of inflection, syntax, and regional dialect vocabulary.

Further reading

Bailey and Maroldt are the major proponents of the creolization hypothesis, and Thomason and Kaufman offer the most explicit rebuttal (cf. 263–331). Both make for interesting reading, but the latter offers rather more detail than beginning students can easily handle. Geipel presents a comprehensive picture of Viking-Old Norse influence in Britain, sometimes a bit overdone. Blake (chap. 4) offers a good introduction to the West Saxon standard. Both Knowles and Leith are very readable and stimulating social-cultural histories. Leith (2007) offers a short, very accessible overview covering the periods treated here in chapters 2–5.

Bailey, C.-J.N. and K. Maroldt (1977) "The French Lineage of English," In: J.M. Meisel (ed.) *Langues en contact – Pidgins – Creoles – Language in Contact.* Tübingen: Gunter Narr, 21–53.

Blake, N. (1996) *A History of the English Language.* Houndsmill: Palgrave.

Geipel, J. (1971) *The Viking Legacy: The Scandinavian Influence on the English and Gaelic Languages.* Newton Abbot: David and Charles.

Knowles, G.O. (1997) *A Cultural History of the English Language.* London: Edward Arnold.

Leith, D. (1983) *A Social History of English.* London: Routledge.

Leith, D. (2007) "The Origins of English," In: D. Graddol, D. Leith, J. Swann, M. Rhys, and J. Gillen (eds.) *Changing English.* London: Routledge, 39–73.

Thomason, S.G. and T. Kaufman. (1988) *Language Contact, Creolization, and Genetic Linguistics.* Berkeley: University of California.

CHAPTER FOUR

Middle English

The non-standard period (1066/1100 – 1350)

7 þa hwile com Willelm eorl upp æt Hestingan on sancte Michaeles mæssedæg. 7 Harold com norðan 7 him wiðfeaht ear þan þe his here come eall. 7 þær he feoll. 7 his twægen gebroðra Gyrð 7 Leofwine. 7 Willelm þis land geeode.
    (*The Anglo-Saxon Chronicle* for 1066, MS E: Bodleian MS Laud 636, http://asc.jebbo.co.uk/e/e-L.html)

And the while, William the earl landed at Hastings, on St. Michael's Day: and Harold came from the north, and fought against him before all his army had come up: and there he fell, and his two brothers, Girth and Leofwin; and William subdued this land.

Chapter Overview:

This chapter:

- looks at how English fared in the aftermath of the dynastic conflict which put a non-English ruling class at the head of both Church and State after the Norman invasion in 1066;
- assesses the linguistic effects of the Norman French presence in the country and the disuse of the West Saxon English standard as well as the introduction of French ways at the top of society;
- reviews attitudes toward English and French in England;
- traces changes – perhaps influenced by the presence of French – in regard to pronunciation and spelling, grammar and morphology, vocabulary and word formation, and regional variation;
- revisits the creolization hypothesis in regard to Norman French;
- using the sparse literature from the period, shows change and continuity in the language and illustrates some of the text types in which English was employed;
- provides examples of the dialectal diversity of Middle English.

4.1 Dynastic conflict and the Norman Conquest

The dynastic conflicts of the early eleventh century (see 3.1.3) continued in 1066 with the death of Edward the Confessor. His successor was King Harold. However, both the Norwegians under King Harald III and the Normans under William, who maintained he had been promised the throne by Edward, also claimed the crown. Harold successfully defeated Norwegian King Harald and his English and Scottish allies in the North at Stamford Bridge. Immediately after the battle he learned that William and his forces had landed in Kent and hurried south to meet him in battle. The two armies fought with each other at Hastings, and in the conflict Harold and his brothers were killed (See Plates 4.1 and 4.2). With this outcome William was able to have himself crowned king of England at Christmas in 1066 and to begin a major reshuffling of feudal lordships. The dynastic events of 1066 are recounted in Text 4.1, excerpted from the *Anglo-Saxon Chronicle*. The language of the account is clearly Old English, which is the starting point for the developments in this chapter. In this excerpt Tostig (aka Tosty), the brother of King Harold of England, had allied himself with the Scots and the Norwegians. In reading the text, do not forget that <7> is the Tironian sign for Latin *et* "and."

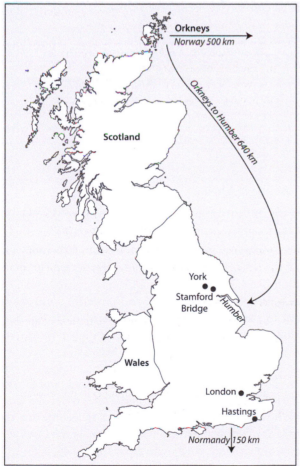

Map 4.1 The military conflicts of 1066

Text 4.1 The Norman Conquest recounted in the *Anglo-Saxon Chronicle* for 1066

7 se cyng Eadward forðferde on twelfta mæsse æfen. . . . .
And King Edward died on the eve of Twelfth-day [of Christmas]; . . . .

7 Harold eorl feng to Englalandes cynerice.   *swa swa se cyng hit him geuðe.*
And Harold the earl succeeded to the kingdom of England,   even as the king had granted it to him,

. . . 7 þy ilcan . . . com Tostig. eorl into Humbran mid .lx. scipum.   *. . . 7 he for to Scotlande mid .xii. snaccum.*

. . . And that same year . . ., came Tosty the earl into Humber with 60 ships. . . . And he went to Scotland with 12 vessels;

7 hine gemette Harold se Norrena cyng mid .ccc. scipum   *7 Tostig him tobeah.*
and Harald, the King of Norway, met him with 300 ships,   and Tosty submitted to him;

7 hi bægen foran into Humbran. oð þet hi coman to Eoferwic.   *. . . 7 man cydde Harolde cyng*
and they both went into Humber, until they came to York.   . . . And it was made known to King Harold

hu hit wæs þær gedon 7 geworden.   *7 he com mid mycclum here Engliscra manna.*
how it there was done, and had happened;   and he came there with a great army of English men,

7 gemette hine æt Stængfordes brycge.   *7 hine ofsloh.*   *7 þone eorl Tostig. 7 eallne þone here ahtlice ofercom.*
and met him at Stamford Bridge,   and slew him   and the earl Tosty, and boldly overcame all the army.

(continuation of the epigraph, *The Anglo-Saxon Chronicle* for 1066 MS E: Bodleian MS Laud 636, http://asc.jebbo.co.uk/e/e-L.html)

4.1.1 The Norman French presence in England

The overall effect of the Norman Conquest on English is controversial. At Peterborough the *Anglo-Saxon Chronicle* was continued in English until 1154 (see Text 4.1). Yet without doubt, the Conquest had a massive effect on **vocabulary**, changed patterns of word formation, and altered the phonological structure of the language. However, there is less agreement about its effects on **word order** and inflection (see 4.2). Literary norms changed as well (4.4). All of this seems to be the result of the presence of well-educated and powerful Normans in influential positions. But in contrast to the Vikings, there was no massive immigration. Consequently, the **Norman French** influence – generally confined to the higher classes – on everyday vocabulary (see 4.2.4) was rather less than that of ON had been (3.2).

Understandably, William replaced with his own followers the English nobles who had been killed both at Hastings and in the mop-up campaigns which followed, and he also replaced many of the others whom he regarded as security risks. The leaders were, of course, the most influential sector of society. It would, however, be exaggerated to assume that the complete leadership of the country was now Norman French. Nevertheless, in the *Domesday Book* (link: *Domesday Book*), the record of landowners which was made in 1086, the overwhelming majority of the feudal overlords were from Normandy, and relatively few were native to England. Most of the high church leaders were French as well: Both the archbishops (Canterbury and York), all but one of the bishops, and eighteen out of twenty-one abbots were French as well. Yet overall no more than 2% of the clergy would have been non-English. The Normans numbered perhaps 20,000 (Traill 1902, qtd. in Thomason and Kaufman 1988: 267–268) in a total population of between 1.25 and 2 million, in other words between 1% and 1.6% of the total population. This number may refer to the actual fief-holders (Thomason and Kaufman 1988: 268), in which case the total would have to be extended to include retainers and soldiers, thus raising the number to perhaps 5%. Thus, the mass of the inhabitants of England were English-speaking peasants who remained linguistically relatively unaffected. Furthermore, the Normans were concentrated in the South and Southeast, especially in the towns. Their numbers included monks and merchants from the Continent, not all of whom were *French* speakers. All the same, this led to an influx of French attitudes[1] and to divided allegiances until Normandy was lost to the English king in 1204 (see 4.1.2). Furthermore, French itself was the language of the upper classes for about 200 years, even though there were sure to have been French–English intermarriages among the lesser nobility. *Bilingualism*, especially in the case of French land-owners in more isolated rural areas, was also certain to have been practiced. In general, the use of French marked class more than ethnic or national identity.

Text 4.2 comes from a history of England which begins with its (legendary) founding by Brutus of Troy to the time of composition. It was written by a monk in Gloucester, as reflected in the language, which is typical of south Gloucester. The passage quoted is of interest because of the comments it contains on the use of French and English.

Text 4.2 Robert of Gloucester's *Chronicle* (c. 1300)

þus com lo engelond. in to normandies hond.	Thus came, lo! England into Normandy's hand
& þe normans ne couþe speke þo. bote hor owe speche.	And the Normans didn't know how to speak then but their own speech
& speke french as hii dude at om. & hor children dude also teche.	And spoke French as they did at home, and their children did also teach;
so þat heiemen of þis lond. þat of hor blod come.	So that high men of this land that of their blood came
holdeþ alle þulk speche, þat hii of hom nome.	Have all the same speech that they took from them.
vor bote a man conne frenss. me telþ of him lute.	For but a man know French men count of him little.
ac lowe men holdeþ to engliss. & to hor owe speche ʒute.	But low men hold to English and to their kind of speech yet.
ich wene þer ne beþ in al þe world. contreyes none,	I think there are in all the world no countries
þat ne holdeþ to hor owe speche. bote engelond one.	That don't hold to their kind of speech but England only.

(5 marked beside line "holdeþ alle þulk speche, þat hii of hom nome." / "Have all the same speech that they took from them.")

---

1 French was used at the pre-Conquest court of Edward the Confessor (1042–1066), who though from the royal house of Wessex had been raised in Normandy.

ac wel me wot uor to conne. boþe wel it is.
vor þe more þat a mon can. þe more wurþe he is.

10   But men well know it is well for to know both,
     For the more that a man knows, the more worth he is.

(D. Freeborn (1998) *From Old English to Standard English. A Course Book in Language Variation.* Ontario: University of Ottawa Press, 81)

Glossary

com(e) (1, 4), *Engelond* (1, 9), *honde* (1), *hor* (2, 3, 4, 7, 9), *lond* (4), *blod* (4), *nome* (5), *mon* (11) <o> for Southern /ɒ/; elsewhere <a> for /a/

couþe (2) past "could"; *conne* (6) 3rd sg. subjunctive, (10) infin. "know"; *can* (11) 3rd sing. pres. "know"

3rd p. plur. pronoun: *hor* (2, 3, 4, 7, 9) gen. "their"; *hii* (5) nom. "they"; *hom* (5) dat.-acc. "them"

owe (2) "own" with loss of final /n/

dude (3) "did"

at om (3) "at home"; this shows the loss of initial /h/

heiemen (4) {high} + {men}

holdeþ (5, 7, 9) 3rd p. plur. pres. tense "hold"

þulk (5) {the} + {ilke} "the same, such"

nome (5) "took" past plural of *niman* + loss of final /n/

vor/uor (6, 10, 11) initial Southern /v/; elsewhere /f/

me (6, 10) plur. of *man* under loss of final /n/

telþ (6) 3rd p. plur. pres. tense of *tell* "to count"

lute (6) "little"; *ac* (7, 10) "but"; *ȝute* (7) "yet"

wene (8) "think, doubt, suppose"

ne . . . none (8) "not . . . none" (double negative)

beþ (8) 3rd p. plur. pres. tense "are"

wot (10) past of *witen* "know"

Without the Norman presence English would probably have changed more slowly. The loss of inflections which had already set in would surely have continued, as it did in other *Germanic languages*. Vocabulary based on native *word formation processes* ([link: Word formation processes](#)) would very likely have been retained to a larger degree. However, the increased presence of French books and laws and other documents in French or Latin made these languages more accessible and led, ultimately, to large-scale *borrowing* from these languages into English. Furthermore, the influence of French was and continued to be visible in the adoption of French writing conventions.

The Norman Conquest is frequently portrayed as monumental for the development of English ("progress" toward "civilization"). Yet some have seen this as a rupture in the continuity of English. This view has propagated the myth of the Norman yoke, which turned out to be opportune for, among others, the monarchy. It has emphasized the idea of English–French competition, which has continued into the twentieth, if not twenty-first, century: the notion of "hostility mixed with admiration." Indeed, French was used at the top and English at the bottom of the social scale, as pointed out above. With the weakening of the French connection there was room for Englishmen at the top, and there was "a general social upheaval that greatly increased the opportunity to move from class to class into social prosperity" (Shaklee 1980: 38).

4.1.2 Separation of France and England

The kings of England, William I and II, then Henry I, Stephen, and later Henry II, ruled over both England and Normandy. Under Henry II the French territories of Anjou and Maine were added through his wife, Eleanor of Aquitaine. The very prominence of the Norman "empire," which encompassed not only England, but large parts of France, led to an inevitable conflict with the king of France, who demanded that he be recognized as the overlord of the Duke of Normandy, who happened to be the king of England as well. This

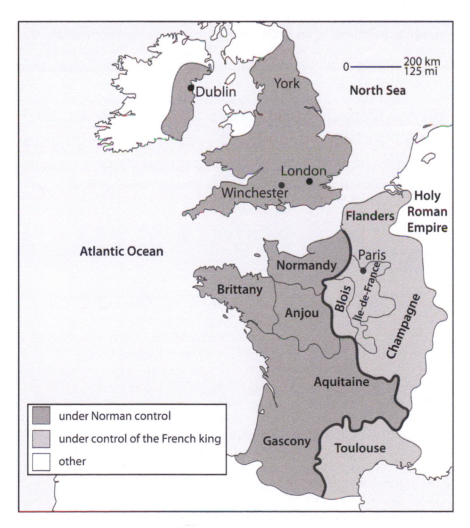

Map 4.2 The Norman empire (c. 1200)

led to armed conflict in 1204 when King John married Isabel of Angoulême against the wishes of King Philip of France. The latter chose to perceive this as disloyalty. The whole affair ended in John's loss of Normandy. As a result, the kings of England were more or less forced to focus their interest on England, and the nobility was supposed to choose between their holdings in France and in England, but not both. By mid-century this did, indeed, become the case despite the further introduction of French office-holders under Henry III (1216–1272). The ultimate end of English ambitions in France came much later in the Hundred Years' War (1337–1453), which settled the matter once and for all (see 5.1.1).

The once natural use of French in the upper classes had become artificial by the thirteenth and fourteenth centuries, and French virtually disappeared in the fifteenth. However, French and English were in general use among the upper classes in the thirteenth century. Whoever could, made a point of learning French: knights, merchants, stewards, and bailiffs on manors. Maybe 1% of the common people did so: *Lewede men cune Ffrensch non, / Among an hondryd vnnepis on* "Common men know no French. / Among a hundred scarcely one" (Brunner, *The Romance of Richard the Lion-hearted.* ll. 23–24). French was still the normal language in polite circles, Parliament, the law courts, and public negotiations at the end of the century. Yet English was beginning to be associated with incipient English nationalism, as the excerpt from *Cursor Mundi* (c. 1300) shows (Text 4.3). This work was very popular to judge by the number of manuscripts which have survived (some 56). Although the original was composed in Northumbrian, there are extant versions which represent the English of different regions; and below in Text 4.9 a short selection is used to show some of the typical regional features of early ME. The text is written in verse and runs to some 30,000 lines. It is a religiously oriented history of the world written in couplets of eight syllables,[2] which helps us to determine whether the final <e> is to be pronounced or not. By the time this text was written, English was the common language in all classes of society though still not widely used in writing.

Text 4.3 *Cursor Mundi* (c. 1300)

þis ilk bok es translate	*ilk* "same"	This same book is translated
Into Inglis tong to rede	*rede* "read" (infin.)	Into the English tongue to be read
For the loue of Inglis lede,	*lede* "people"	For the love of the English people,
Inglish lede of Ingland,		The English people of England,
For the commun at understand. 5	*at* "to" (infin. marker)	For the common people to understand.
Frankis rimes here I redd,	*redd* "read" (1st p. sing.)	French rhymes here I read
Comunlik in ilk[a] sted;	*sted* "place"	Commonly in each place;
Mast es it wroght for frankis man,	*mast* "most"; *es* "is"	Most is written for the French man,
	wroght "did" past of *work*	
Quat is for him na Frankis can?	*quat* "what"; *na* "no"	What is for him who no French can (speak)?

---

2 Within the poem the account of the Christ's Passion adopts a new meter of alternating eight and six syllable lines with an *a-b-a-b* rhyme scheme.

In Ingland the nacion, 10		In the nation of England,
Es Inglis man þar in commun;		English men are there in general;
þe speche þat man wit mast may spede;	*wit* "with"	The speech that one with most may succeed;
Mast þarwit to speke war nede.		Most necessary it is to speak with it.
Selden was for ani chance		Seldom was by any chance,
Praised Inglis tong in France; 15		The English tongue praised in France;
Give we ilkan þare langage,	*give we* condit. inversion	If we give to each their language,
Me think we do þam non outrage.	*me think* dat. subject	I do not think we do them any outrage.
To laud and Inglish man I spell	*laud* "ignorant" (cf. *lewd*)	To the ignorant and English man I write
þat understandes þat I tell.		Who understands what I say.

(Prologue, II, ll. 232–250)

4.1.3 *Magna Carta* (link: Magna Carta)

King John, known for robbing his brother Richard Lionheart of the crown and for playing the antagonist to the legendary figure of Robin Hood, was probably a better leader than his reputation allows. All the same, the loss of Normandy was only one of the setbacks which the royal Plantagenet house suffered under him. The second introduced a major shift in power in the thirteenth century and so was a harbinger of more fundamental changes to come. This was his signing of the Great Charter or *Magna Carta* at Runnymede in 1215. Since King John was forced by the English barons to do this, he later rejected the document. Nevertheless, it has remained one of the centerpieces of Anglo-Saxon democracy, for it smoothed the way to common law and Parliament. Yet reneging led to the first of a series of conflicts with the barons.

4.1.4 The re-emergence of English, reaction to foreigners, and the growth of national feeling

In 1234 the protest of the bishops at Winchester led to the dismissal of foreigners, but they were soon restored to office. Resentment continued, especially on the part of Bishop Grosseteste, who complained among other things about their lack of knowledge of English. This drove the barons and the middle class to make common cause. One of the results of this was the Provisions of Oxford (1258), which was the first proclamation since the Norman Conquest to be issued not only in French and Latin but in English as well, and it was the only proclamation in English under Henry III. The Provisions were intended to promote power-sharing – essentially recognition of a parliament – between the king and the barons, but they were not accepted by the king. This resulted in the Barons' War (1258–1265), which was part of the increasing dissatisfaction with the neglect of English interests. Under Henry III's successor, Edward I (1272–1307), most office-holders were English, and it is interesting to see that the king's appeal for support against the king of France included the latter's alleged attempt to do away with the English language. Some knowledge of English was coming to be seen as the mark of an Englishman (link: Language and nation). Such appeals witness the beginning of larger changes in attitude toward English, which as the language of the lower classes had up to now been regarded as uncultivated. However, with the gradual *merger* of the Norman French with the native population, English became the common language in all parts of the population. This is attested in the lines given in Text 4.4, an anonymous early fourteenth century romance (see *word order* for more on OVS and SOV).

Text 4.4 *Of Arthour and of Merlin* (before 1325), ll. 21–26

Riȝt is, þat Inglische vnderstond,		Right it is that English understand
þat was born in Inglond;		Whoever was born in England,
Freynsche vse þis gentilman,	OVS; *vse* (3rd sg. pres. subjunctive)	The gentleman uses French,
Ac euerich Inglische Inglische can:	SOV	But every Englishman knows English.
Mani noble ich haue yseiȝe,		Many a noble I have seen
þat no Freynsche couþe seye:	SOV	Who could not speak French.

(W. D. Turnbull (ed.) (1838) *Arthour and Merlin, A Metrical Romance*. Edinburgh: Abbotsford Club)

One of the consequences of the re-emergence of English was the decline of French, which various attempts set out to arrest. Novices at Canterbury and Westminster were forbidden to use English; the University of Oxford required students to know both French and English. Consequently, it can be deduced that French was now clearly a foreign language. From 1250 on manuals appeared which were intended to help in the teaching of French. Nevertheless, English as a written language and the use of English in the courts and in Parliament was not to become established until the middle of the fourteenth century, basically within the larger framework of the Hundred Years' War. By the fifteenth century English would be normal in both public and private dealings even though French would still remain the language of the Court and of some elements in the upper class (see 5.1.1 and 5.3).

4.2 Linguistic features of Middle English in the non-standard period

In the 200 years after the Norman Conquest there was no concept of a standard English. This probably opened the language to more rapid change at all levels because it removed the influence of written language, which is generally conservative. In the period after 1250 the concept of Englishness was growing stronger. In this sense the gradual reintroduction of English as a written language of public record may best be regarded as the restoration less of a standard than a national language, that is, the language spoken by the vast majority of the population, albeit in great variety. In the following sections we will look at a selection from among the many changes in pronunciation, in vocabulary and *spelling*, and in inflection and grammar that were transpiring.

4.2.1 Pronunciation of ME and *phonemicization* (link: Phonemicization) (/v, ð, z/)

The high degree of lexical borrowing from French supported the evolution of new phonemes. Contact with and borrowing of words with the ***phonotactic*** features (link: Phonotactic features) of French led to contrasts between initial voiced and voiceless *fricatives*, where OE tended to have voiceless initial /f/ and /s/ and voiced medial /v/ and /z/. This complementary distribution came to an end when ***loan words*** with initial ***voicing*** or medial non-voicing were adopted. Most conspicuous was the presence of initial /v-/ in words borrowed from French, which led the way to meaning distinctions between words with /f-/ and those with /v-/, compare ModE *fan–van*. Function words such as the definite ***article*** were only weakly stressed while lexical words carried stress. As a result the former developed voiced /ð/ and so stood in contrast with the latter which began with voiceless /θ/, compare *þe* "the" /ðe/ vs. *þē* "servant" /θeː/. The loss of /w/ in the combination /sw-/ leads to *so* (< *swā*) and *sword* /sɔː(r)d/ (< *sweord*). The sound /x/ begins to disappear, becoming /f/ or zero as in ModE *dough* /doʊ ~ daʊ/, *cough* /kɔːf ~ kɒf/(link: Loss of /h/).

The changes in the vowels and the ***vowel system*** in the ME period are very complex. In the following the general results for the non-Northern ***accents*** of English are presented and complex processes are collapsed (for more detail see Lass 1992). There are somewhat less obvious changes such as the cases where /l, r, n, m/ + voiced consonant resulted in vowel lengthening or ***diphthongization***, for example in OE *cild* "child" original /i/ becomes /iː/ (and later /aɪ/). This did not occur if a third consonant followed, hence *cildru* "children" has /i/ (and later /ɪ/). In opposite fashion long *ē* shortened before double consonants. For example, *mētan–mētte* developed into "meet"–"met"). A much more far-reaching development was ***Open-Syllable Lengthening*** (link: Open-Syllable Lengthening), the general lengthening of vowels in open syllables in this period, especially in the South. This meant that /a/, /ɛ/, and /ɔ/ as in *faren* "fare," *spere* "spear," and *boren* "borne" became long /aː/, /ɛː/, and /ɔː/ in open syllables. The consequence is that today phonologically short vowels (/ɪ, e, æ, ɒ, ʊ, and ʌ/) do not occur in open syllables.[3] In addition, more and more unstressed vowels were realized as ***schwa*** or lost in final position.

The standard (Wessex) vowel system at the time of the Norman Conquest consisted of paired long and short vowels and diphthongs, and this is reflected in the early ME period. The OE diphthongs eo/ēo ***monophthongize*** to /ø ~ e/ and /øː ~ eː/; and /æɑ/ (*eahta*) and /æɑ/ (*bēam*) to /æ/ and /æː/ (Lass 1992: 42–56; Blake 1996: 122–123; see Table 4.1 for an overview) (link: Vowel change in ME).

---

3 The major exception to this is schwa /ə/, which, of course, does show up in open syllables (e.g. *comma* /-ə/). The minor exception is final /-ɪ/, as in *ready* (esp. northern English and older *RP* pronunciations); however, there seems to be a shift in process as more and more people in England now have final /-i(ː)/.

Table 4.1 The vowels of late OE and early ME

| | late OE (Wessex) | | | | early 14ᵗʰ century (East) | | | |
	front	rounded	back	diphthongs	front	back	diphthongs	
high	i/iː	y/yː	u/uː		i/iː	u/uː	iu	(ui)
high-mid	e/eː		o/oː	eo/eːo	e/eː	o/oː	ɛu	ɔi
low-mid					ɛː	ɔː		ɔu
low	æ/æː		ɑ/ɑː	æɑ/æːɑ	æ/æː		ai	au

4.2.2 Spelling in ME (link: Spelling)

The orthographic system introduced in connection with the **standardization** of West Saxon continued to be practiced after the Conquest. However, the surviving standard was no longer prestigious and gradually grew outdated by change. A number of conventions began to shift, probably largely due to contact with French. Although no standard emerged in the early ME period, it is possible to see some more or less general effects. One of these is that non-Latin letters fell into disuse. <ȝ> begins to cede to <g> and <i>; <þ> and <ð> to be replaced by <th>; and <æ> increasingly to interchange with <e> or <a> (Blake 1996: 118). Wynn <ƿ> is now rare; and <u>, <uu>, and <w> are used in its place. Eventually, <y> would be used as a consonant for /j/, and <ȝ> would be fully retired. Independent of these considerations <k> began to come into use, especially where <c> + <e, i> would lead to misinterpretation as /s/ rather than /k/.

Among the grapheme combinations OE <hw> for /hw/ was somewhat illogically reversed to <wh>, probably under the influence of other combinations which used <h> as a diacritic, especially <th>, <ch>, and <sh/sch>. In the North and East Anglia <qu, u> and in east **Midlands** <w> were also used for /hw/. By this time <c, sc> had been replaced elsewhere by "French-inspired spellings" <ch, sch> (ibid.: 130).

An account of changes in the spelling of the vowels is considerably more challenging since there were significant regional differences in pronunciation. A few examples will have to suffice. OE <y>, originally rounded front /y(ː)/, had become <e> in the Southeast, but rounding was retained in the **Southwest** where <u>, a French spelling, but also <ui> and <uy> occurred. High back rounded /uː/ was frequently spelled <ou> in French fashion. And the raising of OE ā to /ɔː/ led to the use of <o> or <oo>.

One last point concerns the *Ormulum*, a twelfth century East Midlands work, of which some 20,000 short – or 10,000 long – lines remain extant. Its composition, much of which has been lost, may have stretched over several decades, perhaps from mid-century until about 1180. This poetry has not been praised because of its literary quality, for it was dogmatic in the use of consistently long lines of 15 beats in iambic feet, but without rhyme. It also contains a great deal of repetition, as ll. 1–2 and 9–10 in Text 4.5 plainly show. It has relatively few loan words from French, but it provides evidence of the influence of ON in ME since it contains 120 such items (Geipel 1971: 64) and includes English–Danish doublets, for example l. 14 *dredinng 7 aȝʰe* (*dread* < OE *drǣdan*) and *awe* < ON *agi*). What is linguistically most impressive about the *Ormulum* is the use of spelling to indicate the author's pronunciation. Short and long vowels, which had not been orthographically distinguished in OE, were differentiated here: the short ones were followed by double consonant-letters and the long ones by only one, for example l. 5 *follc* ("folk, people") /ɒ/ vs. l. 7 *god* ("good") /oː/. This indicates that the long–short consonant distinction of OE had presumably been lost (Blake 1996: 125). Orm also sometimes used single accents to mark long vowels (l. 2 *tór* "difficult") or double ones (l. 7 *üt* "out"). Orm also distinguished between /g/ using <g> and /j/ or /x/ using <ʒ>, for example *grimme* ("grim, fierce") (l. 2) vs. *ʒiff* ("if") (l. 1). Remember the note on "7" given for Text 4.1. The content of this text is part of Orm's admonitions, occasional passages in which he offers criticism of the social conditions of his times.

Text 4.5 Admonition from the *Ormulum*

Forr ʒiff þe riche mann iss braþ		For if the powerful man is wrathful
7 grimme. 7 tór to cwememm;		And fierce and hard to please,
Hiss lede att iss unnderr himm		His people that are under him
Himm dredeþþ þess te mare		Will fear him all the more.
7 tohh swa þehh ne till þe follc	5	But yet neither for the people
Ne till þe laferrd nowwþerr.		Nor for the lord
Niss þatt nohht þwerrt üt god inoh.		Will it be particularly good
Tell þeʒʒre sawle berrhless.		For the salvation of their souls
þatt he be grimme. 7 aʒʰefull.		That he is fierce and frightening
7 braþ 7 tór to cwemenn.	10	And wrathful and hard to please.
Forr he maʒʒ ben swa gramme mann;		For he may be so fierce a man
þatt he beþ laþ hiss lede.		That he is hateful to his people.
. . .		. . .
7 tohh swa þehh iss ned tatt he.		But nevertheless it is necessary that he
Dreding. 7 aʒʰe sette.		Impose dread and awe
Onn alle þa þatt lufenn toþþ	15	On all those who love [lawlessness]
7 who 7 unnashhtnesse.		And wrongdoing and conflict

(From inserted leaves 11b–c in MS Junius 1: see *The Ormulum Project*, www2.english.su.se/ nlj/ormproj/ormulum.htm)

4.2.3 Grammar

There was a great deal of grammatical change in the ME period. At the center of this was the decay and large-scale loss of inflectional endings. Nouns lost distinctions in case and gender due to altered pronunciation and ***adjectives*** lost their number marking in addition in most cases. ***Adverbs*** which were derived from adjectives in OE with the inflection {a} were marked by a final {-e} (e.g. *faire* < *fair*), by no ending at all (*pleyn*), or by {-ly} (earlier {-liche}) (*trewely*). Grammatical gender was still present in *Ayenbite of Inwyt* (1340), but the tendency toward natural gender was already present in OE, where, for example, Ælfric used masculine *hláf* "bread" but referred to it using the neuter pronoun *hit*. Added to this, phonetic changes and analogy led to a move from final /-m/ to /-n/ thus making the dative singular and plural identical. In a further step the *nasal* disappeared. At same time there was a leveling of inflectional a, o, u, e to schwa. Consequently: <-a, -u, -e, -an, -um> all show up as <-e>. All of this was occurring between the tenth and twelfth centuries, for example OE *muðum → muðun → muðu → muðe*. The most common **declension** (link: Declension) of OE, which followed the pattern for "stone" *stan, stanes, stane, stan* (nom., gen., dat., acc. sg.) and *stanas, stana, stanum, stanas* (plur.), was eventually reduced to two forms, *stan* and *stanes*. The {-es} of *stanes* was to be generalized to most nouns for the possessive singular as well as the complete plural. Initially, however, the South had also favored the {-en} plural on the pattern of the second most frequent OE declension, whose plural was {-an} in the nominative and accusative (e.g. *naman* "name"). The North and northern Midlands went over to {-s} by 1200 as did all the Midlands 50 years later. In the course of the fourteenth century, the {-s} plural was accepted everywhere (cf. Strang 1970: §142).

As the preceding example shows, inflectional attrition started in the North in the late OE period (3.2.3) and spread south, finding its conclusion – with a few exceptions in the extreme South – in the fourteenth century. One of the factors that would have initiated this decay of endings lies in the initial stress of the Germanic languages, including OE. For this process the presence of the Viking settlements and ON **language contact** was probably an important factor (see discussion in 3.3) since it may have destabilized the system in the North to a degree which accelerated the loss of inflections. While language contact, including the presence of dialectal variants of OE, will surely have played an important role in initiating change, once it began, it ran its course independently of the initial impetus. In other words, inflectional loss had wide-reaching consequences beyond morphology: it led to more analytic syntactic forms, especially the spread of periphrastic constructions. As one prominent linguist says, "as far as we know, the major syntactic changes in the Middle English period do not find their origin in dialectal variants, but are a result of the morpho-logical developments discussed above [loss of inflection]" (Fischer 1992: 208; see esp. 4.2.3.1).

Throughout the following, North–South differences will be pointed out again and again. A relatively large number of innovations, but not all of them, came from the North. This may have had to do with changes which took place under Norse influence, but it is also likely that quite a bit of this may be due to the survival in the South of the OE standard in writing. It gradually grew outdated as the spoken *vernacular* changed, and it lost in importance due to the rise of French and Latin, yet it remained a presence and a preserve of older and more conservative features of the language. In the North, less oriented toward the old Wessex standard, changes were quicker to show up.

Scandinavian influences (already mentioned in 3.2) supplied the following non-stigmatized forms: (a) the third person plural personal pronoun, (b) the present tense plural of the verb *be*, and (c) the third person singular present tense verb inflection.

(a) *hey, here, hem* changed to *they, their, them* (Northern forms)
(b) *be* changed to *are* (a Northern form)

Somewhat more slowly (a shift which lasted into the EModE period)

(c) {-th} changed to {-s} (3rd sing) (a prestigious Northern form)
(Shaklee 1980: 58–59).

In each of these cases the advance of the new forms can be traced in documents on their way southward, as they first appear in the North, then in the Midlands, and finally in the South (cf. Samuels 1972: §5.2). In the case of the third person plural pronoun, the switch occurred first in subject function as *they* displaced *hey*. Only later did *their* and *them* push out *here* and *hem*. And indeed even today *'em* < *hem* for *them* continues to be used in the spoken language (*We saw 'em yesterday*).

New grammatical patterns may also have been influenced by the presence of French speakers. Before looking at some of the innovations, note the following list of structures in which French influence has been *suggested*, but often remains very *debatable*:

- *Who*, an interrogative, came to be used more and more for the OE relative *þe* on the model of French *qui* (both a relative and an interrogatory pronoun in French);
- *Weorþan* was replaced by *be* as the passive auxiliary, perhaps under the influence of French *être* "be" + past participle.
- French *faire* "do, make" + infinitive may have indirectly influenced the rise of periphrastic *do* in English (see 5.3.2).
- There was also ***case leveling*** of subject *ye* to object *you* parallel to the model of French *vous* (both subject and object).[4] The loss of the *ye–you* distinction is also credited to a leveling in pronunciation, inasmuch as the unstressed forms of both were more or less indistinguishable.

The most far-reaching changes in grammar were due to the continuing loss of inflections (see 3.2.3 and 3.3). It would be misleading to credit this to French influence, but an indirect effect may be seen in the fact that the West Saxon standard lost its dominant status, thus allowing inflectional loss to proceed unhindered by the written standard. The spread of noun ***plural {-s}***, for instance, where OE had a wide variety of ways of marking the plural, may have been marginally affected by Anglo-Norman plural {-s}, but is basically an independent development.

There was a shift from synthetic to analytic structure, that is, from a syntactic system which was highly dependent on inflectional endings with less strictly fixed word order to a system with few endings and highly prescribed word order. The new word order, whose default setting was SVO (Subject-Verb-Object), led to the gradual abandonment of SOV, which was frequent in dependent clauses in OE (see 2.3.3 and 5.3.3; link: Word order change). Verb-second order, which is the case not only in SVO, but also after initial adverbials (AdvVSO), became increasingly infrequent, yielding to AdvSVO, where V does not come in second position.[5] There was also a move to greater use of periphrastic verb structures, such as the progressive and the perfect, that is, ones which depended more on auxiliaries than on ***mood*** and tense inflections, and on prepositional phrases in place of case endings (see 4.2.3.1; 5.3.3).

Pronoun objects in OE tended to be pre-verbal. Nominal objects were post-verbal in main clauses. Note that only 18% of all noun objects preceded the verb in the early ME *Ormulum*,

---

4 In some varieties of English there was leveling to *ye* for both subject and object.

5 AdvVSO is still a part of ModE in two variants. Variant (1) non-assertive adverb + auxiliary + S+V (*Seldom does she agree with me*; *Never had I seen such a sight*) and – less strongly prescribed – variant (2) adverb of place + V + S (*Down the road came the bus*; *there goes John*).

while 51% of pronoun objects still did (see Fischer 1992: 372). In Text 4.5 (ll. 13–14) we find a pre-verbal noun in the subordinate clause *taat he Dreding 7 aʒᵇe sette*. The noun–pronoun difference is explained as due to lighter weight and ***theme–rheme structure***: noun phrases are "heavier" and heavier elements tend to come later in the sentence. The loss of inflection is frequently given as one of the motivations for fixed word order and the use of prepositions. Certainly, pronouns, with case marking, could follow the older pattern longer, for example *Himm dredeþþ* (Text 4.5, l. 4). Note that OE is in this sense organized by ***discourse structure***, which means that elements can be moved to the front of the sentence in order to come into focus (link: Theme–rheme). In ME, in contrast, word order was much more strictly determined by syntactic factors and no longer allowed the freedom of movement of OE (cf. Fischer 1992: 372ff; cf. the preceding paragraph). Text 4.6 illustrates the continuation of SOV word order in subordinate clauses, where the lexical verb comes in final position as in *that ich you wile telle* "that I want to tell you." Even the two main clauses which follow have the verb in final position: *Wo so it wile here . . .* "Whosoever wants to hear it . . ." and *The tale is of Havelok imaked* "the tale is made/written about Havelok," in which the past participle (*imaked*) of the passive comes at the end. On the other hand, the subclause in the final sentence does not use a final verb position: *Whil he was litel, he yede ful naked* "while he was little, he went fully naked"). What this shows is the variability which word order still had and which could be used to put words at the end of a line for the purposes of rhyme.

Text 4.6 *Havelok the Dane* (1295 – 1310), ll. 1 – 6

Herkneth to me, gode men - *Wo so it wile here and therto dwelle.*
Wives, maydnes, and alle men - *The tale is of Havelok imaked:*
Of a tale that ich you wile telle, *Whil he was litel, he yede ful naked.*

(R.B. Herzman, G. Drake, and E. Salisbury (eds.) (1999) *Four Romances of England.* Kalamazoo: Medieval Institute)

4.2.3.1 The verb

The verb was also affected by inflectional change and loss. Leveling, often by the process of analogy, led to a reduction in the number of strong, that is, irregular, verbs: almost one-third of them had become regular by the ME period, for example OE *helpan–healp–hulpon–holpen* became *help–helped–helped* except in some of the ***traditional dialects*** (link: Traditional dialects), where the strong forms are still to be heard today (e.g. *the medicine holp him a lot*). In other cases there was leveling between the vowel of the past singular and the vowel of the past plural. The unitary vowel chosen was either that of the singular (*write–wrote–written*) or of the past participle (*slide–slid–slid*) (link: Reduction of strong verb classes). Loss or reduction of verb endings meant that person and number distinctions were reduced to a single distinction in the North, but considerably more in the conservative South (see Table 4.2):

Table 4.2 Present tense verb inflections

	South		North	
	indicative	*subjunctive*	*indicative*	*subjunctive*
1st sg.	-e	-e	ø (-is)	ø
2nd	-(e)st	-e	-is	ø
3rd	-eth	-e	-is	ø
pl.	-eth/-e(n)	-e(n)	-is	ø

The Midlands first had, for the indicative, either {-es} or {-eth} for the third person singular and {-es} or {-en} for the plural, but moved quickly to third person singular {-es} and {-en → -e → ø} (Strang 1970: §§119, 131; Thomason and Kaufman 1988: §9.8.6.6).

The progressive

In OE *bēon* + present participle is ambiguous and may be a main verb followed by a participial adjective or may already be a progressive. In ME this sequence can be regarded as a structural unit because *ben* is seldom separated from the main verb by other elements. The loss of such prefixes as {a-, be-, ge-} may have given impetus to the progressive as a way of expressing on-going activity or durative *aspect* (ibid.: §§113, 155; Samuels 1972: §8.4). Two separate OE constructions have been suggested as the sources: *he wæs huntende* and *he wæs on huntunge*. Inasmuch as both came to use the same ending, that is, *hunting(e)* and the preposition of the latter was reduced from *on/an/in* to *a* and eventually to zero, the two coalesced. Yet in the North *-ing* and *-ande* remained distinct much longer even though the progressive was stronger there. In Scotland the two were kept separate because participle and gerund did not coalesce.

In early ME the frequency of the progressive was low. The *Polychronicon* (in English translation, 1387) has 5/100,000 words, which is fewer even than *Orosius* (OE; late ninth century) at a rate of 518/100,000. In the ME period "the use of the progressive is much higher in Northern texts than in midland or southern texts" (Fischer 1992: 251). Nevertheless, *Havelok* (c. 1300), a **Northern** text, has no examples of the progressive.[6] The use of the progressive with the perfect and after modals came in the fourteenth century; the future and the passive progressives did not emerge until much later, yet by the end of the ME period there was a clear increase and the progressive sky-rocketed at the beginning of the ModE period (Strang 1972: 207–208).

The perfect (link: Perfect(ive) aspect)

In OE the auxiliary of the perfect was *habben/hauen* or *ben*, but the former was ousting the latter. In *Havelok* we find both, for example *Quanne he havede this pleinte maked* "when he had made this complaint" (l. 134); *Quanne he weren alle set* "when they had all sat" (l. 162).[7]

---

6 The nearest thing to a progressive is the following: *Hwo hors ne havede, com gangande* "Who did not have a horse, came walking" (*Havelok*, l. 2287).

7 Although this is a Northern text, where *they* might be expected, *he* is used for both "he" and "they."

The original distinction between change-of-state and (some) intransitives with *ben* and *stative* verbs with *hauen* is hard to maintain strictly. The loss of *ben* is sometimes explained by the high functional load of *ben* (passive, progressive, plus perfect) (Fischer 1992: 260–261). In ME the placement of the past participle at the end is still common and continued until the sixteenth century. Even today speakers distinguish between *I have done it* and *I have it done*.

Habban allowed the speaker to place the verb in the final, most emphatic position, and this may be a decisive reason for using the perfect rather than the simple past (preterite). According to Mustanoja the perfect as a "compound tense form is longer and therefore more emphatic than the simple preterite . . . A more emphatic verb form is desirable for indicating the completion of an action which continues up to the moment of speaking than for expressing an action which clearly belongs to the past" (1960: 504). Fischer supports this with the observation that the perfect is more frequent in instructional and colloquial texts (as compared to narrative ones) and occurs mostly in the first and second persons. While speculative, this is not uninteresting. But why this happened precisely in ME is not clear though this might be a part of the general change in Germanic languages from morphological tense/mood/aspect verbal marking to a system with grammaticalized auxiliaries (Fischer 1992: 256ff).

Modal auxiliaries

There was a strong decline in the *subjunctive*, even in OE times as revealed by the coalescence of the subjunctive and indicative inflections mentioned above (4.2.3.1; Table 4.2). The reason for the increase in the modal instead of the subjunctive may have to do with this or with the need for more emphatic expression, which is more easily possible when the lexical verb follows the modal.

The modal verbs *shal, wil, may, mot(e), can*, and others were taking on morphological and syntactic features which distinguished them more and more from lexical verbs (link: Grammaticalization):

- the lack of non-finite forms – they do not have an infinitive or present or perfect participles;
- the lack of the possibility of taking an object;
- the lack of notional meaning;
- the dissociation of tense and time – past tense modals usually express tentativeness rather than past time;
- the retention of the bare infinitive as a complement; and
- the need of a second verb – gradually only fossilized expressions are possible without one, e.g. *I must away now, I can no longer tarry*.

Shal and *wil* (sometimes *mot(e)* "may") rapidly developed into future **markers**, even though *shal* was tinged with obligation and *wil* with volition (Fischer 1992: 315; 6.3.3.1; link: The modal auxiliaries).

Negation

OE negation was with *ne*, sometimes coupled with *nan, neþing, næfre*. In *Havelok* we find both double negation and single, compare *In gode burwes and therfram / Ne funden he non that dede hem sham / That he ne weren sone to sorwe brouth,* "In good towns and from there / they found none that shamed them / that they were not soon brought to sorrow" ll. 55ff). Emphatic negation used *ne* plus *naht* (< *nawiht* "nothing"). In the *Anglo-Saxon (Peterborough) Chronicle* (1154) *ne . . . naht* lies at about 17%; in *Ancrene Wisse* (c. 1230), about 40%. By late ME *naht* alone was the most frequent type of negation. The double form was common in early ME in declaratives, imperatives, and optatives (used for wishes), but *ne* occurred alone in interrogatives. *Naht* was more common when *ne* was cliticized, that is, added on to a verb, as in *nis* < *ne + is*). Since *ne* is an unstressed element, it disappeared in favor of emphatic *naht*, which is still stressed in ModE. But in ME two or more negated **indefinite pronouns** or adverbs were still normal. This means that the non-assertive *any*-forms still did not have the distribution we find today (Fischer 1992: 280–284) (link: Negation).

Concord (aka agreement)

One of the consequences of fixed word order may well be the use of singular *concord* with conjoined subjects, for example *Wherof supplant and tricherie / Engendered is* "Whereof guile and treachery **is** engendered" (Gower: ii.2840–2841), with a plural (conjoined) subject, but a singular verb. But, as Fischer points out, concord was "to some extent more loosely structured in Middle English than in Present-Day English," compare *þanne the Mynstrall begynnen to don here mynstralcye euerych in hire Instruments* "Then the minstrel began to do **their** minstralcy each with **their** instruments" (Mandev. (Tit) 155.16f), with a singular subject (*Mynstrall*) but a plural verb (*begynnen*) and plural anaphoric pronouns (*here*, *hire*) (sources qtd. in Fischer 1992: 364, 366).

A further result of more fixed word order was the loss of dative subjects. In the sentence *Him is lever* literally: "to/for him is preferable" a dummy subject is added (cf. ModE *it is preferable to him*) on the model of *þe kinge* (dative) *is lever*, where *þe kinge* is re-interpreted as nominative. From this we get ModE *The king/ He prefers*, even though numerous "dative" predicates remain, for example *it pleases me* (link: Concord).

The passive

OE could form a passive only from an accusative object, and this continued to be the main rule in ME. The following example from *Sir Gawain and the Green Knight*, a late fourteenth century Northwest Midlands poem, shows the correspondence between active subject and passive subject:

Text 4.7 *Sir Gawain and the Green Knight* (short excerpt)

þe tulk þat þe trammes of tresoun þer wroȝt,	the warrior who wrought there the trains of treason
Watz tried for his tricherie, þe trewest on erthe.	was tried for his treason, the truest on earth

(Fytte the First, ll. 3–4) Frederic Madden (ed.) (1839) *Syr Gawayne: A Collection of Ancient Romance-Poems.* London: Taylor)

In the first line the subject *tulk* "warrior" is the nominative subject of the active verb *wroȝt* "wrought, made"; in the conjoined sentence *tulk* remains the subject but the verb is now passive (*was tried*). This changed in ME to include passive subjects corresponding to dative or prepositional objects in active sentences, something which had not been possible in OE. One factor in this expansion was the gradual decrease in the use of the indefinite *man* ("one") construction. More crucial was the loss of the inflectional endings of nouns since it made it harder and harder to distinguish nominative from dative. As a result, a dative noun in subject position looked just like a nominative. Eventually this led to the use of nominative pronouns as subjects as in the following examples:

ȝef me is iluuvet mare þen an oþer . . . mare idon god oðer menske (*Ancrene Riwle*: 48b.2)
if someone is loved more than another . . . more good or honor (is) done (to him)

þa he wes þus ilete blod (*Ancrene Riwle*: 31a.8)
when he was thus let blood

Both *me* [= *man*] and *he* are nominative, but the verb *lete* "let" is normally associated with a dative object, literally "to let blood to or for someone" (sources qtd. in Denison 1993: 110).

4.2.3.2 The article system, demonstratives, and prepositions

Several things were involved in the reduction in inflections. There was now a single indefinite article which developed out of the unstressed numeral *oon* "one" to *a/o/an*. The split in the OE ***demonstrative*** paradigm resulted in a definite article, initially with singular *the* < OE *se* by analogy with the other *th*-forms and plural *tho*. A ***deictic*** system emerged from the other half of the split: *that* (plural *tho*, later *those*) took on the meaning of deictic distance in the twelfth century. The second of the two deictic ***determiners*** ([link: Demonstratives](#)) was generalized from *þis*, the nominative and accusative singular of the emphatic OE demonstrative, to which the plural adjectival ending *-e* was added giving us the *this/these* pair (Lass 1992: 2.9.1.2; [Link: Article system](#)).

Prepositions began to be employed more widely as the older functions of case retreated into the background. Consequently, their number, which was relatively small in OE, grew in the early ME period. Sources of new prepositions were both ON (new *fro*; increased use of *at* and *with*) and French (*countre, maugre, sans, save*; partly anglicized *during, excepting, touching*; calqued *notwithstanding* < OF/Latin *non obstant*; increased use of *at*) (cf. Mustanoja 1960: 348–349). *In* expands its scope, probably under the influence of Latin *in* and French *en*, encroaching on the territory of *on* (e.g. *on his dagum* becomes *in his days*). Several of the prepositions take over functions once carried by case alone. *Of* is increasingly used for the genitive. Functions of the dative such as the marking of the indirect object, in contrast, were now more often carried by the use of the prepositions *to* and *for* (cf. *Herkneth to me, gode men* from Text 4.6, l. 1); however, verbs with dative objects, ones such as OE *helpan* "help" or *folgian* "follow, obey," now took direct objects, that is, ones indistinguishable from accusative objects. The prepositional dative, that is, to give something **to** someone, still rare in continuation of the *Anglo-Saxon Chronicle*, grew to 10% of total in the thirteenth century. Verbs of Romance origin usually had the analytic *to*-construction (Fischer 1992: 379–380).

4.2.3.3 Personal pronouns

The major innovations in the third person pronouns (*she, they, their, them*) were traced in 3.2.3. Further important changes in the early ME period were the loss of dual *wit* and *ȝit* by the end of the twelfth century as well as the continuing amalgamation of the dative and accusative cases. In OE the two cases had already become increasingly identical in the first and second person (*mē, ūs* and *þē, ēōw*). Now third person singular masculine dative *him* displaced the older accusative *hine*, just as feminine singular dative *hire* displaced accusative *hīe* (see Table 4.3).

The new dative-accusative *him* was now distinct from neuter *hit*, the old accusative, which now displaced old dative neuter *him*. In the plural the dative (*hem* and in the North *them*) prevailed over the old accusative *hīe*. However, both masculine and neuter genitive singular remained identical *his* (not included in the table). The old genitives began to function as adjectives rather than pronouns. The new forms appeared both with and without {-n}, hence *my* and *mine*, *thy* and *thine* (link: Personal pronouns system).

The pronominal prop-word *(o)on* "one" (< *an* as with the indefinite article) is essentially new in the early ME period. Its possible sources are pronominal and anaphoric. In ME this use of *one* follows an adjective as in . . . *a moche felde, / so grete one neuer he behold* (Mannyng HS (Hrl) 3267–3268) ". . . a large field, so great a one he never had beheld." In the earliest examples *one* had personal reference, but within this period non-personal reference began to develop (cf. *He haues a wunde in þe side . . . / And he haues on þoru his arum . . .*, Havelok, ll. 1981–1983) (sources qtd. in Fischer 1992: 223–224).

Relative pronouns (link: Relative pronouns) too, undergo change. Animacy (as with *who ~ which*) was less relevant in OE, where grammatical gender was used. In ME *þat* spreading from the North to the South replaced *þe* almost everywhere except in the Southwest and in the western Midlands, where the Wessex tradition was still strong. In the thirteenth century *þat* was restrictive and non-restrictive, animate and inanimate. In reference to a clause *þat*, for example as a sentential relative, was gradually replaced by *what* in early ME.

The *wh*-relatives (*whom, whose, which*) date from early ME, but were rare in the twelfth and still infrequent in the thirteenth centuries. In *Havelok* we find *that*, but *hwo* "who" is frequently used as well, not only as an interrogative (*Hwo haves thee thus ille maked* "Who has treated you thus so ill?" l. 1956), but also as a relative (*That was the name Griffin Galle. / Hwo mouthe ageyn so mani stonde* ". . . Griffin Galle, who could stand against so many" ll. 2033–2034). They were only frequent from the fourteenth century on. One factor

Table 4.3 Case leveling in the early ME period

	case	OE	ME
masculine	dative	*him*	*him*
	accusative	*hine*	
feminine	dative	*hire*	*hire*
	accusative	*hīe*	
neuter	dative	*him*	*hit*
	accusative	*hit*	
plural (all persons)	dative	*hem* (North: *them*)	*hem* (North: *them*)
	accusative	*hīe*	

encouraging their adoption was the fact that *that* could not be used after prepositions. This may also be a reason why *who*, which as a subject form never followed a preposition, was late in being adopted. *Which* is animate or inanimate, *whom* and *whose* usually animate. An early example is *þat Jesu Crist wass witerrli / þat illke, off whamm prophetess / Haffdenn for lannge cwiddedd ær, /þat . . .* "That Jesus Christ was clearly the same [man] about whom prophets had for a long time said that . . ." (*Ormulum* 6994–6995 qtd in Fischer 1992: 296ff).

As with so much which is credited to French influence, "It is likely that Latin and French played a role here too. In most accounts, however, it is believed that this influence was only slight and that it strengthened rather than initiated a new trend" (ibid.: 299). It seems *wh*-forms entered "by way of the most complex styles of writing" – which speaks for French influence. But it is more likely that the *wh*-relative emerged because of an overlap with embedded interrogatives (ibid.: 300), as in ModE *Do you know who went?*, where *who* can equally plausibly be analyzed as a relative pronoun (*the person who . . .*) or as an interrogative (*Do you know: who went?*).

4.2.4 Vocabulary

Early ME underwent significant change due to the massive influx of new vocabulary, chiefly from French, but also from **Low Dutch**. In the late ME period Latin borrowings began to increase as one of the results of the Renaissance ([link: Renaissance](#)) (see 6.1.2). Many of the borrowings from ON took place earlier but only now showed up in the written language. Lexical borrowing from ON (see 3.2.1) may be illustrated by the following lines from the *Lay of Havelok the Dane* (legend of founding of Grimsby), which was written in the North Midlands before 1300:

> Bernard *stirt* (leaped) up, that was ful *big*,
> And *cast* a *brinie* (mail coat) on his *rig* (back).

> (Geipel 1971: 64)

According to Geipel the *Ormulum* (see Text 4.5) uses some 120 different words which come ultimately from ON (ibid.), for example *naþe* "grace" (cf. German *Gnade*) and phrasal verbs like *farenn forþ* and *ȝedenn forþ* "travel, go." Just how important ON influence was on the spread of the **phrasal verb** pattern ([link: Phrasal verb (pattern)](#)) is disputed. Blake (1996: 126) seems to suggest such an influence, but Thim (2008) speaks against it.

French borrowing, whose impact was "prolonged, varied and ultimately enormous" (Burnley 1992: 423), led to major restructuring of English vocabulary. Since much of the new ruling class spoke French while the common people continued to speak English, it was less words for everyday things and activities which entered the language than words the new masters were likely to use. In a famous passage from Scott's *Ivanhoe* between Wamba, the jester, and Gurth, the swineherd, Wamba points out the difference between swine in the field and pork on the manor table ([link: Scott's *Ivanhoe*](#)). Jespersen comments that the French were the fashion leaders of the Middle Ages, but that English words were retained for everyday occupations, for example *baker, miller, smith, weaver, saddler, shoemaker, wheelwright, fisherman, shepherd*, and so on (Jespersen 1955: §§91, 97). This illustrates the nature of the restructuring of vocabulary in which everyday things are most likely to be designated by words of Germanic origin whereas fashion, art and literature, and learning will be more likely to draw on words of French (or Latin) provenance. Based on Swadesh's 200-word list of basic vocabulary and "a 700-word non-cultural, non-regional diagnostic list," research by Kaufman shows that only 7% (in ModE) comes from French (Thomason and Kaufman 1988: 365). In contrast, French words were taken into English massively in the areas of law and administration as well as the military. The Church also provided numerous new additions. The influence of French was more of the Central than of the Norman variety, especially after 1204, when the kings of England lost Normandy (link: Norman and Central French borrowings). Typical early loans can be seen in the Table 4.4.

Borrowing had already taken place before the Conquest even though then and immediately afterwards it was not very rapid. There was a slight increase from 1150 to 1200 and then a more rapid increase from 1200 to 1250, when Anglo-French bilingualism was well developed, for bilingualism was a necessary pre-condition for borrowing. But then loans poured in (Strang 1970: 250), and this continued until the end of the fourteenth century. This ran strikingly parallel to the move to English by the upper classes after the loss of Normandy. As relations with France grew more tenuous, bilingualism declined. However, as people moved to English in more and more domains, they also carried with them the French words they were accustomed to using. Accretions came in the terms for finance, property and business, for building and household equipment, for law and social organization, religion, war, the arts, clothing and food, entertainment, hunting, animals, and science and medicine. It is chiefly nouns which were adopted, but fairly many verbs and adjectives and a few other forms were as well. Forty percent of all French borrowings first show up in writing between 1250 and 1400. All in all over 10,000 words were borrowed from French in the ME period (Baugh and Cable 2002: § 133).

Why were words borrowed? The motivation for adopting so much lay for one in the fact that the donor language had more prestige. While the English were more advanced than

Table 4.4 French loan words and their English equivalents

early French loans (religious terms and feudal titles)		French replacements (1200–1250) taken from Brut, a Southwestern text			
fulluhtere	baptist	*boc-runen*	letter	*here-marken*	pensiles "standards"
forecwedere	prophet	*æthe*	treasure	*ʒisles*	hostages
hlæfdige (lit. "bread kneader") ModE *lady*	dame	*munucclif* (lit. *monk* + *life*)	abbey	*friðe*	park
eald-modor	granddame	*munstre*	nunnery	*wisen*	atyr ("attire")
hlaford (lit. "bread warden") > ModE *lord*	sire	*milce*	grace	*bolle*	coupe ("cup")
mæʒester (Latin borrowing)	meister	*hoʒian*	aspire	*at-breac*	ascapede
halig ModE *holy*	seint	*heren*	serve	*husting* (< ON *hus* + *thing*)	conseil
æþeling	prince	*here-toga*	chieftain		

the Normans in everything except military matters such as castle-building at the time of the Conquest, is was from Central French that later borrowing came and "was indeed borrowing from a language of high culture into one of lower culture" (Strang 1970: 251). French as the vocabulary of power, rank, and status established a new evaluative function, "the projection of attitudes that are upper-class on to the words" (link: French cultural ascendancy). Yet not all the words designating rank were of French origin, as the following list illustrates (Germanic words in bold): **king**, **queen**, **lord**, **lady**, *duke, prince, squire,* **alderman**, **thane**, **earl**, **knight**, *gentle,* **churl**, *villain, peasant, vulgar, common, illiterate,* and **lewd** (Leith 1983: 80–82).

It would be slightly misleading to assume that only French and Latin fed the vocabulary of ME. Actually words from what is sometimes called **Low Dutch** (Flemish, **Dutch**, Low German) – all of which are very similar to English – contributed quite a few words to ME. Language contact is in this case not related to a particular happening or period, but was an on-going process. Large numbers of Flemings went to England over the years, including mercenaries, traders, and craftsmen (weavers). Among the borrowings – all told some 2500 words (including modern borrowings) – we find numerous items from, for example, the areas of textiles (*cambric, nap, duck*); shipping (*boom, bowsprit, commodore, deck, dock, freight, lighter, rover*); art (*easel, etching, landscape*); and money (*dollar, groat, guilder, mart*).

As a source of new vocabulary, borrowing, which Jespersen regarded as "undemocratic" (1955: 101), came to prevail over **word formation**. He defends the latter, compounds such as *heiemen* (Text 4.2, l. 4) and **derivations** like *tell–tale* (Text 4.6), because they are transparent while borrowed words are opaque and require more education, compare *mouth–oral* and *hear–auditory*. Certainly, borrowing was seldom motivated by **lexical gaps**, the idea that a needed word was missing. Actually, the mass of words borrowed were redundant. "While we have not abandoned this technique altogether, it is generally true to say that English has been particularly receptive to the possibility of absorbing foreign words; instead of making up new words, we borrow them" (Leith 1983: 62). Yet Leith's view seems to ignore the enormous amount of **compounding** and metaphor in English, both of which have been and still are highly productive. Although some older derivational **morphemes** fell out of use, for example {for-, to-, ge-}, other affixes continued to be productive. The latter include prefixes such as {over-, under-, up-, down-, out-} (Schröder 2008) and suffixes such as {-ness, -ful, -less, -ish}, which occur quite frequently. The specific effect of French in ME is clear from the suffixes in Table 4.6.

In addition, new prefixes were adopted into the language, for example {counter-, dis-, re-, trans-}, as were Latinate suffixes such as {-able, -ible, -ent, -al, -ous, -ive}. The presence of a large number of non-native words employing a different set of affixes and using different

Table 4.5 **Domains of French borrowings**

fashion	*gown, robe, cape, frock, petticoat,* etc.
art and literature	*art, painting, music, beauty, poet, romance, story,* etc.
learning	*medicine, physician, study, grammar, logic, geometry,* etc.
law and administration	*jury, verdict, sentence, fine, prison; govern, administer, crown, state, realm, royal, court, council, parliament,* etc.
military	*army, navy, battle, combat, siege, peace,* etc.
church	*sermon, sacrament, baptism, chaplain, parson, pastor, vicar*

Table 4.6 Romance (French) derivational morphemes (suffixes)

suffix	origin	meaning	example
{-ard} {-art}	OFr but of Germanic origin	"characterized by some action, quality, or thing"	*shreward* "like a shrew"
{-ery}	OFr {-ier/-er} + {-y/-ie}	"the art or practice of"	*husbandry* "practice of husbanding"
{-ous}	OFr {-ous/-eus/-eux} < Latin {-osus}	"abounding in"	*gluttonous*
{-ment}	OFr, < Latin {-mentum}	"denoting a concrete result"	*chastisement*

stress patterns has had a lasting effect on the morphology and phonology of English. However, it has not eradicated the deep-seated usage distinctions between Romance and Germanic lexical items, even though it has blurred the edges at a number of spots.

4.3 French influence on Middle English and the question of creolization

The massive influence of French on ME has led some linguists to suggest that the language underwent *creolization* (see 3.3) (link: Creolization). By the time of the Barons' Revolt (1258–1265) bilingualism had declined in favor of English monolingualism in the nobility. The final move to English started in 1204 and was largely complete by 1235. However, even before this there was little likelihood that large numbers of non-noble English-speakers would have learned French between 1066 and the early 1200s, and afterwards there was little need to do so. Even where French was strongest, in the Eastern Midlands, the reduction associated with *pidginization* and the subsequent grammatical innovation characteristic of creolization was missing.

The major problem in confronting the question of creolization is that there are few vernacular English texts between 900, the last reliable point of reference in the OE period, and 1200, when the vernacular is once again documented. What we see in 1200 is relatively little change vis-à-vis OE in the South; some Norse-influenced change in the Midlands; and a great deal of this in the North. There was superficial French influence everywhere, but especially in the South (Thomason and Kaufmann 1988: 312–313). Simplification was already in progress before the Conquest. When written English texts once again crop up, the earliest and seemingly most productive area of grammatical innovation was the North, as pointed out in 4.2. Yet little speaks for French influence there since borrowings from French were particularly meager in the area of vocabulary, which is where the greatest influence might be expected (ibid.: 313). For ME overall, we cannot overlook the disproportion between massive French influence on vocabulary, little and none on morphology and *syntax*, and only trivial influence on phonology (cf. Thomason and Kaufman: 307) (link: Language imposition).

Bailey and Maroldt's (1977) suggestion is that massive English borrowings into OFr by the upper class in medieval England produced Middle English. This means that they see ME as French with English *relexification* and a mass of French words retained. This seems ungrounded since the basic vocabulary of English stems from OE, and ME grammar is clearly a continuation of the grammar of OE. Furthermore, the usual context of creolization, which is the presence of many languages, is missing in England, where there were basically only two. Bilingualism seems to be a much more likely candidate when it comes to explaining linguistic change in ME than does creolization. And even so, "The English-speaking majority among the population of some ninety percent did not unlearn their English after the advent of French, nor did they intentionally modify its structures on the French pattern" (Görlach 1986: 337–338). The case seems rather to be that French speakers learned English – and their French suffered as a result, as was pointed out in 4.1.2.

4.4 English literature (link: ME literature)

There was no use of English in worldly writing that would have been read in court circles, and whatever might have been written by the lower orders has not been passed on. Indeed, English-language writing from about 1150 to 1250 was almost exclusively religious or didactic in nature. The more notable religious works include *Ancrene Wisse* (Rule for Anchoresses), the *Ayenbite of Inwyt* (Prick of Conscience), and the *Ormulum*.

Throughout the thirteenth and fourteenth centuries French served as the literary language of England and was generally written under the patronage of the Court. At the time when French was best understood by the upper classes, they drew upon continental French literature, which was supplemented by French poetry written in England. This led to the adoption of the French tradition of versification and the fall into disuse of the Anglo-Saxon traditions as reviewed in 2.5 and 3.5.2 and in part still maintained at the end of the twelfth century by Laȝamon from Worcestershire in his *Brut* (c. 1200). This is an alliterative work about Brutus of Troy, the mythical founder of Britain, and is based largely on the Anglo-Norman version produced by Wace. *Brut* makes use of fewer inflections, but more prepositions and numerous now archaic words such as *drihten* and *ofslean* (Blake 1996: 127; see also 4.2.4).

The Owl and the Nightingale shows English verse under French influence. This work, an exchange of recriminations between the two birds, is basically a debate in the form of a poem. It runs to 1794 lines written in rhyming couplets. It was probably composed between 1186 and 1216, but the author is unknown. The two manuscripts of it which have survived come from the second half of the thirteenth century. In the poem the narrator overhears one summer night an argument between a dour owl and a carefree nightingale. Rather than resort to physical violence the two agree to enter into a debate, which itself proceeds along the lines of a medieval scholastic disputation. Consequently, the poem draws on all the current rhetorical devices and goes into topics such as music, ethics, marriage and adultery, and much more. The lines quoted in Text 4.8 are the introduction. With the exception of only a few words this passage is relatively easy to understand, and, of course, it conforms to the metrical and rhyming conventions of French poetic writing.

> **Text 4.8** *The Owl and the Nightingale*
>
> | | |
> |---|---|
> | *Ich was in one sumere dale,* | I was in a summer(y) valley |
> | *in one suþe diȝele hale,* | In a very hidden corner |
> | *iherde ich holde grete tale* | I heard a great debate being held |
> | *an hule and one niȝtingale.* | An owl and a nightingale |
> | *þat plait was stif & starc & strong,* | Who were pleading firmly, severely, and strongly |
> | *sum wile softe & lud among;* | Sometimes softly and loudly in between |
>
> *suþe* "truly, very"; *diȝel* "secret"; *hale* "hole, nook, corner"
>
> (MS Cotton, http://quod.lib.umich.edu/cgi/t/text/text-idx?page=home)

The text shows the retention of the old **weak adjective endings** (e.g. *suþe, grete*) in attributive position though not when used predicatively (*stif, starc, strong, lud*). Furthermore, the indefinite article appears with the spelling both of the numeral *one*, from which it is derived, and the weakened form *an*. The past participle of the verb *iherde* "heard, listened to" is used with the perfective prefix {i-}.

4.5 Dialectal diversity in early ME

As in the preceding OE period Early ME had a variety of regional **dialects** which were probably difficult for people from different regional areas to understand. Indeed, the Midlands dialect was now distinctly divided into an East and a West Midlands type, due, in all likelihood, to the strong ON influence in the East, which was part of Danelaw. Now as much for political as for linguistic reasons the Northern area was differentiated into Northern (England) and Lowland Scots (Scotland). Due to the lack of a written standard, many documents in English reflected rather more than before the presumed variety of the areas in which they were composed.

There were differences not only between the major regions, but also within them. However, for the purposes of this book it is enough to give a general impression of broadly regional distinguishing features of pronunciation, vocabulary, and inflection. In the case of pronunciation there are a number of highly visible North–South distinctions that may be attributed to the influence of Old Norse, for example OE ā → Southern /ɔ:/ and eventually /o:/ as in *stone* vs. Northern /e:/ as in Scottish *stane*, or Southern /tʃ/(*chest*) vs. Northern /k/ (Scottish: *kist*). In addition to these points, initial fricative voicing /v-, ð-, z-/ was widespread in the South (as in Dutch), but not present in the North (as in Frisian). Even today these sounds are voiced in the English regional accents of the Southwest (e.g. in *Zomerzet* "Somerset"). A few of the voiced forms have been maintained in StE, for example *vixen* vs. *fox*.

In the area of inflections the South, the Midlands, and the North differ inasmuch as the North adopted the ON ending {-s} for the present plural indicative of verbs as in *we loves*

Map 4.3
ME dialect regions

(cf. *þere many thosand lesis þer lijf* "where many thousand **loses** their lives" several lines before the excerpt in Text 4.9 from *Cursor Mundi* below). The Midlands form was generalized from the subjunctive {-en} (*we loven*). The South maintained the older form {-eth} (*we loveth*). The three regions also differed in the form of the present participle (before {-ing} was introduced): Southern *lovinde*, Midlands *lovende*, and Northern *lovande*. The short excerpt in Text 4.9 is taken once again from *Cursor Mundi* as an illustration of some of the regional differences.

Text 4.9 Parallel excerpts from *Cursor Mundi*, Northern (Cotton) and Southern (Trinity) versions

Northern	Southern	ModE
Sanges sere of selcuth rime,	*Mony songes of dyuerse ryme*	Many a song of different rhyme,
Inglis, frankys, and latine,	*As englisshe frensshe & latyne*	In English, French, and Latin.
to rede and here Ilkon is prest,	*To rede & here mony are prest*	Each one to read and hear is pressed
þe thynges þat þem likes best.	*Of þinges þat hem likeþ best*	The things that please them all the best.

Glossary

sere "very much"   *selcuth* "diverse, different" or "strange, odd"

ilkon "each one"   *prest* "ready"

Pronunciation (through spelling)

Northern English has /a/ for OE ā, where **Southern English** has /ɔ/ (*sanges–songes*; also Southern: *mony*)

Northern <s>, probably /s/ for Southern <ssh> /ʃ/ (*Inglis–englisshe*; *frankys–frensshe*)

Spelling (with no consequences for pronunciation)

Northern English tends to <i> for Southern <y>, but compare l. 4 (*thynges–þinges*)

Northern has <th> twice and <þ> twice; Southern has only <þ>

Vocabulary

Northern *sere* "very much" (< ON *ser*) – Southern *mony*

Northern *selcuth* (native word < OE *seldcuð*) "diverse" – Southern *dyuerse* (borrowed from French)

Syntax

Like in l. 4 is the predicate in a relative clause introduced by *þat* "that"; the antecedent of *þat* is plural; hence *likes/likeþ* may be understood as plural as well. However, the third person singular form of the verb would look the same. *þem/hem* "them" is the dative object of *like* "to please (dative: someone)."

Northern *sanges sere* – Southern *mony songes*; the word order difference seems to depend on the item *sere*, which follows the noun it modifies all three times it occurs in the first 25 lines of *Cursor Mundi*

Northern *ilkon* < the Northern form of Southern *ælch* "each" + *ane* "one" – southern *mony*

Northern *þem* (ON influence) – Southern *hem* (OE) dat. sing. masc.

Northern *likes* (ON influence) – Southern *likeþ* (OE) 3rd person plural present tense

4.6 Summary

This chapter has dealt with the way the lack of a standard gave ME freedom to undergo change perhaps more quickly than would otherwise have been the case. Attention has been given to the gradual expansion of the functions of written English. The missing written standard also meant that regional forms of English were preserved that otherwise might not have found written expression at all. Overall the loss of inflections and the acquisition of extraordinarily many words from French made Middle English into a language which looked very different from Old English. All the same there is little evidence for the kind of radical change that would have been the case if French–English creolization of whatever sort had taken place. Indeed, the lack of evidence due to the relative dearth of texts from this period leaves many interesting questions open.

Further reading

Both Knowles and Leith are understandable and stimulating social-cultural histories. Hopper and Traugott as well as Thomason and Kaufman are linguistically more challenging and more suited to those with a more advanced linguistic background. They focus much more stringently on language change, the former looking at processes of grammaticalization (not only in English) and the latter looking at the nature of change between Old English and Middle English (as mentioned at the end of chapter 3).

Hopper, P.J. and E.C. Traugott (1993) *Grammaticalization*. Cambridge: CUP.
Knowles, G.O. (1997) *A Cultural History of the English Language*. London: Edward Arnold.
Leith, D. (1983) *A Social History of English*. London: Routledge.
Thomason, S.G. and T. Kaufman (1988) *Language Contact, Creolization, and Genetic Linguistics*. Berkeley: University of California Press.

CHAPTER FIVE

Middle English

The Emergence of Standard English (1350 – 1500)

Chapter Overview:

This chapter:

- reviews the turbulent events of the late fourteenth and fifteenth centuries – demographic developments, the Black Death, the Hundred Years' War, the Peasants' Revolt, and the Wars of the Roses – with special regard to their influence on the language;
- highlights a number of linguistically important developments – the translation of the Bible into the vernacular, the rise of London speech and Chancery English, and the introduction of the printing press;
- explores grammar and vocabulary change and the functional expansion of the emerging standard, including the increasing importance of authored literature;
- provides textual examples from Wycliffe, Paston, Bokenham, Chaucer, Barbour, Caxton, Trevisa, and Blind Harry to give the flavor of Middle English and illustrate its social, functional, and regional variety.

Text 5.1 John of Trevisa's translation of Higden's *Polychronicon* (1387, excerpt)

As hyt ys y-knowe houw meny maner people buth in this ylond, ther buth also of so meny people longages and tonges; notheles Walschmen and Scottes, that buth nowt y-melled with other nacions, holdeth wel ny here furste longage and speche, bote [yet] Scottes, that were som tyme confederate and [lived] with the Pictes, drawe somewhat after here speche. Bote the Flemmynges, that [live] in the west side of Wales, habbeth y-left here strange speche and speketh Saxonlych y-now. Also Englischmen, [though] he hadde fram the bygynnying thre maner speche, Southeron, Northeron, and Myddel speche (in the myddel of the lond), as he come of thre maner people of Germania, notheles, by commyxtion and mellyng furst with Danes and afterward with Normans, in menye the contray longage is apeyred, and som useth strange wlaffyng, chytheryng, harryng and garrying, grisbittyng.

5

(J.R. Lumby (ed.) (1879) *Polychronicon Ranulphi Higden Monachi Cestrensis: Together with the English Translations of John of Trevisa and of an Unknown Writer of the Fifteenth Century*, 7 vols. London: Longman, Green, vol. 1, 8–10)

Glossary

ylond (1) "island"	*here* (3, 4, 5) "their"	*wlaffyng* (9) "stammering"
buth (1, 2) 3rd p. plur. pres. tense of *be*	*y-now* (5) "enough"	*chytheryng* (9) "chattering"
nowt (2) "not"	*maner speche* (6) "manner of ~"	*harryng* (9) "snarling"
y-melled (2) "mixed" past participle	*mellyng* (8) "mixing"	*garrying* (9) "grating"
ny (3) "nigh, near"	*apreyed* (9) "impaired"	*grisbittyng* (9) "tooth-gnashing"

5.1 Political and social turmoil and demographic developments

Text 5.1 by Trevisa names the peoples who lived in the Great Britain of his times: Welsh, *Scots*, Flemings, English (*Southern*, *Northern*, and *Midlands*). The Welsh and the Scots spoke their own languages; the others spoke English, though notably Southern, Northern, and Midlands varieties. After a period of relative stability in the thirteenth century with population growth in England to unprecedented levels – estimated at 6 million or even as many as 7 million (Prestwich 2005; Smith 1991), the fourteenth century brought political and social turmoil and population losses. The Great Famine of 1315–1317 ([link: Great Famine](#)) led to malnutrition and weaker resistance to disease and a decline in the population by as much as 10%. This had as one of its results labor shortages and a lower level of agricultural productivity; and this tended to lead to a kind of vicious circle. The agricultural crisis was reinforced by the higher rents imposed on tenants by Edward III (1327–1377). Then at mid-century (1348 onwards) the first major incursion of the bubonic plague reached England. The results of the Plague, or Black Death ([link: Black Death](#)), as it is also known, were a drop in population size of anywhere between 20% and 50% of the English population ([link: Demographic change](#)). The decline continued until 1420, and numbers only began rising again in the late fifteenth century.

5.1.1 The Hundred Years' War and the Peasants' Revolt

A second major factor in this period was the dynastic conflict between the French and the English crown, most especially the Hundred Years' War (1337–1453)[1] ([link: Hundred Years' War](#)), a war which ran remarkably parallel to the Black Death. The war was in reality a series of conflicts with sometimes quite long periods of peace in between: the Edwardian War (1337–1360), the Caroline War (1369–1389), the Lancastrian War (1415–1429), and English reversals and French revival (1429–1453) under Joan of Arc (1412–1431). The upshot was the loss of almost all the holdings of England on the Continent. The *French* language had clearly been in decline in thirteenth century England (cf. 4.1.2). By the end of the Hundred Years' War and in part because of the nationalistic sentiments and resentments toward France that the war engendered, French was no longer a realistic option even among the English nobility, where it was increasingly artificial, as the often quoted lines from Chaucer's *Canterbury Tales* (see 5.4.2) attest:

> ## Text 5.2 Chaucer, *Canterbury Tales* (excerpt from the Prologue, ll. 124–126)
>
> *And Frensh she spak ful faire and fetisly,*
> *After the scole of Stratford atte Bowe,*
> *For Frensh of Paris was to hir unknowe.*
>
> (W.W. Skeat (ed.) (1912) *The Complete Works of Geoffrey Chaucer.* London: OUP)

This quotation confirms the provincial character of French in England. Such attitudes are one of the consequences of French cultural ascendancy, which helped French as a language to maintain its prestige: it was seen as an object of cultivation, representing now outdated chivalrous society in its best form. Consequently, French continued to be used by the

---

1 There was also considerable on-going conflict with Scotland, which the English crown was trying to annex.

educated and in high society but was a matter of culture and fashion rather than an economic or political necessity as it had once been. In the fifteenth century it virtually disappeared as a language of everyday communication.

The decline in population size was not without effects on English. The labor shortages gave the peasants a stronger bargaining position, which led not only to higher wages, but also to a weakening of the traditional ties to the manors. As the geographical mobility of more and more people increased, there was necessarily considerably more contact between the various regional forms of the language. The Hundred Years' War also contributed to mobility. In this case, perhaps more importantly, it was social in nature. Since there were considerable casualties in the higher feudal ranks – also due to the plague – the rise of commoners to positions of leadership and authority in public service was increasingly possible. Late in this period Henry VII (reign 1485–1509), for example, sought more and more often to fill offices with people (businessmen) from the growing middle class.

Henry VII's move signaled a significant change in attitude: a hundred years before, the king and the nobility had tried to resist change from below. The Peasants' Revolt (aka Tyler's Rebellion or the Great Rising) of 1381 (link: Peasants' Revolt) (Plate 5.1) is the clearest example of the resentment engendered by the opposing social and economic forces. The king (actually Chaucer's patron John of Gaunt, who was the regent for young King Richard II, reign 1377–1400) had introduced a poll tax in 1377 and again in 1379 to finance the war against France. Another poll tax in 1380 was perceived as unjust and much too high. This led to massive opposition to royal authority as some 100,000 peasants marched on London protesting corrupt officials and demanding better terms and conditions for labor. The rebels stormed the Tower of London, and executed the Lord Chancellor, the Archbishop of Canterbury, and the Lord Treasurer. The king made concessions, which in the end were not honored. All the same, this may be seen as the beginning of the end of serfdom in England, which would mean better wages and more freedom. This social upheaval was part of the rise of capitalism; it would contribute to the renewal of learning (the Renaissance; see 6.1.2), and it was manifest in a variety of movements of religious dissent.

5.1.2 The Wars of the Roses (1455–1485)

The political and social unrest of the fourteenth century continued after the end of the Hundred Years' War in the form of dynastic struggle between the House of York and the House of Lancaster (link: Wars of the Roses). The two sides differed only inasmuch as York was supported by the commercial classes in London and – in the case of Edward IV (1342–1383) – by Parliament. John of Gaunt (1340–1399), the Duke of Lancaster and virtual ruler of England under Richard II, gave some backing to Wycliffe (see below), perhaps because of the latter's criticism of Church interference in State matters (see 5.2.1.1) and hence providing some support for religious and language change, but exacerbated social unrest by introducing the unpopular poll tax. Whatever else might be said, the series of wars that go under this name sped up the weakening of feudal power and strengthened the merchant classes since the wars further thinned the ranks of the feudal nobility and facilitated in this way the easier rise of ambitious and able people from the middle ranks of society. When the conflict was settled under Henry VII, a Lancastrian and a Tudor, power was essentially centralized. From the point of view of the language, this meant that the standard which had begun to emerge in the early fourteenth century would continue with a firm base in the usage which had been crystallizing in the London area at least since Henry IV (reign 1399–1413), the first king since the OE period who was a native speaker of English.

5.1.3 Lollardy

At the same time as the Hundred Years' War and the subsequent Wars of the Roses England underwent a considerable amount of religious innovation which was not only an expression of social change, but also contributed to changing attitudes toward language. Most notable was the Lollard movement (link: Lollards). The chief concern of the Lollards was to initiate change in the Medieval Church. This meant, among other things, challenging the role of Latin, which as a language accessible to the few only was a means of control over the many, that is, the people. Lollardy was an important current starting in the fourteenth and continuing in the fifteenth centuries. It converged in the 1380s with the mass dissatisfaction that led to the Peasants' Revolt (5.1.1) and gained support from it.

The word *Lollard* may have been derived from the **Dutch** word *lollaert* "mumbler, mutterer," meant to be a contemptuous designation of people without Latin learning. The movement was concerned with ridding the Church of corruption and aimed at greater separation of Church and State, such as not allowing priests to fill secular offices. The Lollards also favored having lay priests and more participation in the church by the laity.

A major focal point in the movement was John Wycliffe's (1320s–1384) translation of the Bible into English (link: Wycliffe) (Plate 5.2) (see 5.2.1.2). Such a translation was resisted by the authorities, but indicated the presence of a growing reading public, which surely increased with the availability of an English version of the Bible. Indeed, Lollard English may be seen as one of the important strands which fed into the incipient written standard. The translation was completed in or around 1382, making it contemporaneous with the Peasants' Revolt and the late writing of Geoffrey Chaucer, that is, the *Canterbury Tales* (1385–1400) (see 5.4.2). Wycliffe's work may also be reflected in *Piers Plowman* (see 5.4).

5.2 The expansion of domains

In the late thirteenth and early fourteenth centuries English took over more and more functions once reserved for Latin or French. Latin had been the language of law and the State as well as of the Church. Statutes appeared in Latin till about 1300, then in French. Parliament used French till about 1423 for petitions, from 1485 on in English and French and only in English after 1489. The turning point seems to have been the reign of Henry V (1413–1422), perhaps because of pride in the victory over the French at Agincourt. English was again used officially, especially by the royal bureaucracy, after 1420 (cf. Knowles 1997: 54).

The middle class grew from the fourteenth century on as the number of manufacturers, traders, and merchants increased. They were not rural, but based in London and other towns. Although they were international in outlook, we find that the London guilds used

English (not Latin) for records from the 1380s on; in 1384 a municipal London proclamation appeared in English (ibid.: 52). The earliest known will in English comes in the year 1383. London brewers began using it in 1422, and from the 1430s on more and more towns and guilds adopted English. It seems to have been in general use by 1450. The earliest personal correspondence in English available today comes from the late fourteenth century, but the Paston letters (see Text 5.5) and Stonor correspondence (from 1420–1430) provide a wider basis for information about private usage.

5.2.1 The decline of Latin

Latin was the major non-English language in England in this period, especially as the use of French decreased. It was the written standard not only in England, of course, but throughout Western Christianity. As the preceding section has shown, its prominence in religion was being challenged, but it remained the language of record, for example for court documents; and it was the language of learned discourse. Yet in this period and the EModE period it lost its primacy in all of these areas. As Caxton wrote, "*For the mooste quantyte of the people vnderstonde not latyn ne frensshe here in this noble royame of englond.*"[2] Its cultivation was due to its prestige as the language of religion and learning.

5.2.1.1 *De heretico comburendo*

In 1401, under Henry IV, this law, "On the burning (at the stake) of heretics," prohibited the translation of the Bible into English. The Western (Catholic) Church had itself forbidden **vernacular** translations at the Synod of Toulouse (1229); however, this ban was widely ignored elsewhere, but not in England where the idea of independent reading was associated with translation and the Lollards. Heretics were said to undermine the conservative establishment by "setting up schools, writing books and wickedly instructing and informing the people" (Knowles 1997: 64). This can be understood the way Knowles has phrased it: "Someone reading the English translation was still given an interpretation, but by the translator rather than the priest. A further problem is that the reader could be misled by the meaning of everyday English words, and fail to grasp the exact meaning of the original" (ibid.: 72). While it was legitimate to hold open discussions of these questions, they were to be conducted in Latin. This was clearly a question of power (cf. ibid.: 64–71). The Lollards put the independently available Bible in English above the Church. Serious study of the Scriptures might challenge the oral tradition and teaching and hence the authority of the Church. It was not until the Act of Supremacy under Queen Elizabeth I in 1659 that *de heretico* was repealed.

5.2.1.2 *Translations of the Bible*

In actual fact, Bible translations had been and continued to be made. Examples from the OE period include Bede's translation of the Gospel of John (c. 735) and the Wessex

---

2 See "Preface" to *The Romances of Rouland and Vernagu, and Otuel* (Auchinleck Manuscript) in "Preliminary Remarks," A. Nicholson (ed.) Edinburgh: Alex. I. Awrie, 1845: xi.

translation of the gospels of about 990. Wycliffe's translation (1385) was followed by Tyndale's. The latter loosed an avalanche of translations:

- Matthew Bible (1537) with royal assent,
- Great Bible (1539), which the nobility could read aloud; which women and merchants could read silently for themselves; and which common people were not allowed to read at all,
- Geneva Bible (1557/60) with Calvinist marginal notes,
- Bishop's Bible (1568) authorized by Queen Elizabeth,
- Douay-Rheims (1582) Roman Catholic, and the
- King James (or Authorized) Version (1611) (link: English translations of the Bible).

The following text is taken from Wycliffe's translation of Genesis, to which three further versions of verse 3 have been added for the sake of comparison: the Latin Vulgate, an earlier Wycliffe translation, and the EModE King James Version (KJV) of 1611. One remarkable point in the early Wycliffe version is how closely the translation followed the *word order* of the Latin original. The verb form *is* of this version also follows Latin *est*, while the later Wycliffe is freer both in word order and in the use of *was* for *est*. In comparison the KJV is still freer. It does not retain the *subjunctive* and employs the existential *there*-construction, a structure which only became current in the course of the late ME period (cf. Strang 1970: 211).

Text 5.3 Excerpt from the Wycliffe translation of the Bible with a comparative example in four versions (link: Translations of the Bible) **(Plate 5.2)**

1 *In the bigynnyng God made of nouȝt heuene and erthe.*
2 *Forsothe the erthe was idel and voide, and derknessis weren on the face of depthe; and the Spiryt of the Lord was borun on the watris.*
3 *And God seide, Liȝt be maad, and liȝt was maad.*
4 *And God seiy the liȝt, that it was good, and he departide the liȝt fro derknessis; and he clepide the liȝt,*
5 *dai, and the derknessis, nyȝt. And the euentid and morwetid was maad, o daie.*

Verse 3:

Latin Vulgate:	*Dixitque Deus fiat lux*	*et facta est lux*
Early Wycliffe:	*And God seide, Be maad liȝt;*	*and maad is liȝt*
Later Wycliffe:	*And God seide, Liȝt be maad;*	*and liȝt was maad (see above)*
King James Version:	*And God said, Let there be light:*	*and there was light*

(Genesis 1:1–5, http://en.wikisource.org/wiki/Bible_(Wycliffe)/Genesis#Chapter_1)

The Wycliffe text can be understood by a ModE-speaking readership, but there are quite a number of unfamiliar-looking words. They reflect both differing pronunciations and different conventions of *spelling*. In a few cases the *syntax* is in need of comment.

Spelling

bigynnyng "beginning" (1): While <y> and <i> were used for different vowel sounds in OE, they had become free variants by this time. In Genesis 2:7 we find *brething* "breathing" with <-ing> but *lyuynge* "living" with <-ynge>. "*Therfor the Lord God formede man of the sliym of erthe, and brethide in to his face the brething of lijf; and man was maad in to a lyuynge soule.*

heuene "heaven" (1): <u> is used within a word where today either <u> or, as here, <v> would occur.

Pronunciation

nouȝt "nothing" (1): <ou> for /uː/; <ȝ>, for /x/

heuene, erthe "earth" (1), etc.: final <e> may or, more likely, may not be pronounced: note *made* (1) and *maad* (3), both presumably pronounced /maːd/. <e> at the beginning of *erthe* is /e/.

Forsothe "forsooth, actually" (2): <o> was /oː/

Vocabulary

of "out of" (1)

idel "worthless, inactive" (2)

seiy "saw" (4): < OE sēah

departeide "separated" (4)

fro "from" (4): a borrowing from ON

clepide "called, named" (4)

morwetid "morning-tide, morning time" (5)

o "a(n), one" (5)

Syntax

derknessis, watris (2, 4) ModE regards these as uncountable and has a singular

weren (2) still with the past plural ending in {-n}

borun (2) past participle of beran "bear; lie upon"

be (3) "may there be [light]" 3rd person singular subjunctive (optative)

5.2.2 The emergence of a new standard

At the beginning of the thirteenth century people from all over England were moving to London and bringing their widely divergent *dialects* with them. Some mythic London English did not just crystallize; rather, a long process of adjustment must have begun. In this situation people's thoughts turned increasingly to the question of standards. Factors that influenced their behavior – whether conscious or not – included *language contact*, social climbing, and education (Shaklee 1980: 41). In the context of the waning feudal system, the emerging middle class, increasing social mobility, the economic and political opportunity offered by the more and more powerful guilds, and the necessity that people understand the law moved English into the center of learned attention.

In the fourteenth century the area south of the Humber River in the East Midlands, where the Black Death had been less severe, was the major population center. This area was also the center of wool and grain exportation in the thirteenth and fourteenth centuries. In the fifteenth century Yorkshire led in woolens, the northern and western counties in wool, the East Midlands in grain, and London, Norfolk, Essex, and Devon in shipping. In the fifteenth century and continuing into the sixteenth the enclosures (link: Enclosures and urbanization) were beginning to push more and more people off the land. With the increasing, often involuntary mobility of the population (see also 5.1) more and more common people from the Midlands and the North went to London, where many of them eventually took on prominent positions and gave their forms of English a certain currency.

London also attracted more and more people from all parts of the country because it was the center of government and administration and of trade and commerce. At the time of the Black Death London was by far the largest city with a population of about 70,000, followed by Norwich (12,000) and York (10,000). London English was the result of the concentration of power and people in London even though standardization was not carried through in this period. It was less a standard than a national language (Blake 1996: 10), that is, an instrument of national identity and loyalty.

5.2.3 The rise of London English

The language of London gradually began to take on the force of a standard more and more. Within the city there were two central forces driving *standardization* (link: Standardization). The first was the spoken language of everyday life in which a certain degree of leveling or *koinéization* (link: Koinéization) was ensuring that London vernacular speech would no longer be a Southern variety, but more a Midlands one laced with numerous Northern features. The second force, known as *Chancery English* (link: Chancery English), was more a matter of the written language and was promoted by the government administration, the Chancery. The latter moved more quickly toward what would be Standard English while the former was slower to lose its ME features. The effects of both of these forces were made possible by the extremely fluid social situation in the fourteenth century, which started out with a rigidly structured society, but was changed by the population losses of the Plague and the Hundred Years' War. Increasingly more Midlanders and Northerners were prominent in the London city government. "Most of the northern forms seem to be working their way up from the bottom, probably moving up into the upper-class sociolect as speakers of the dialect move into the upper class" (Shaklee 1980: 58). The presence of Caxton's printing press in London, though late in this period (1476; see below 5.4.4), was also to contribute greatly to this London-based standardization. All of the following factors indicate changes in the economic and political centers of power and allow us to make conclusions about the language forms which were recognized as standard.

With the rise of the lower classes the status of English improved. In the towns and most especially in London a new English-speaking class grew up which was neither noble nor peasant in nature. Here English was adopted fully in the fourteenth century, as the opening lines of *Arthour and Merlin* (before 1325) illustrate (see Text 4.4). Teaching in English was introduced in the mid-fourteenth century and was the rule by 1385. English was once again used in the law courts of London (1356) and after 1362 in all the courts of the land since French was no longer widely used or understood, as the following text testifies.

Text 5.4 The Statute of Pleading (1362) (ModE version)

The King, desiring the good Governance and Tranquillity of his People, . . . , that all Pleas which shall be pleaded in [any] *of his Courts whatsoever, before any of his Justices whatsoever, or in his other Places, or before any of His other Ministers whatsoever, or in the Courts and Places of any other Lords whatsoever within the Realm, shall be pleaded, shewed, defended, answered, debated, and judged in the English Tongue, and that they be entered and inrolled in Latin, . . .*

(From Statute of Pleading, www.languageandlaw.org/TEXTS/STATS/PLEADING.HTM)

Latin was still prominent in scholarly writing and would be retained longest in this capacity. Note that Latin is explicitly named as the language of record in Text 5.4. There is virtually no learned writing in English until the EModE period (6.4.2).

5.2.4 London as a demographic and economic center

The East Midlands was geographically and linguistically well suited for the development of a standard not only because the Midlands are located in the middle but also because its language was not as extreme as that of the innovative North or as conservative as in the South: Midlands sounds and inflections were a kind of compromise. In addition, the East Midlands was not only the most populous but, in this agricultural age, the most prosperous area: almost a quarter of the English population was from Norfolk, Suffolk, and Lincolnshire in the period starting from the Norman Conquest and continuing for 300 years. In contrast, the South was simply smaller, and the North had the disadvantage of being hilly, as was the West. Furthermore, the universities in Oxford and Cambridge, located in the Midlands, were taking over intellectual leadership. The influence of Oxford usage, as seen in the writing of Wycliffe, is disputable. The dialect of Oxfordshire was, in addition, less clearly typical of the East Midlands and had a number of southern features. In any case the Wycliffe standard came into disrepute because of its connection with religious fanaticism (Samuels 1963; Blake 1996: 169–170). The most important influence on the development of StE seems to have been the language of the Chancery, which was used in official records and in the letters and papers of men of affairs.

The language used in London, but also that of the universities, was especially influential because many people from elsewhere who adopted it carried it back with them when they returned home, thus spreading it. The changes that London English underwent, be they Midland or Northern in origin, entered the city through the eastern counties. In any case London English was widely accepted as the written standard almost everywhere, though

Northern texts might still be recognized as such. Yet the spoken language must have varied considerably as one moved from region to region.

Among the changes attributable to the greater social mobility of the fourteenth and fifteenth centuries the *Great Vowel Shift* (GVS) is one of the most prominent. Although it is not clear exactly when this change began, it seems to have had its roots in the period this chapter looks at. Samuels points out that change is likely to be more rapid under conditions of contact due to migration, and that was clearly the case in London in the fourteenth and fifteenth centuries. Furthermore, he argues that the upper classes may have chosen to emphasize those variants of vowels which maintained the distinctions from the lower orders most effectively. Although he exemplifies this in regard to processes of change that took place after the ME period, it may fairly be assumed that the same forces for change were in effect in this period, in which London was expanding so rapidly and which was so potentially threatening to the upper classes (cf. Samuels 1972: 106–107, 132–133). The GVS will be treated in chapter 6.

5.2.5 *Wave theory* (link: Wave theory)

As particular speakers and their speech communities gained in power and prestige, the language variants they used were adopted in neighboring areas, spreading like waves around a stone thrown into a pond. This was to apply to London English and its influence on neighboring and eventually even very distant areas. At the same time London English was itself the result of regional population migration and of social contact and demarcation, as already pointed out.

5.3 Chancery English (Chancery Standard)

By the end of the ME period, which is set at 1500 in this book, the most prominent dialect was that of London, a major center of commerce. The strongest influence on this English was exerted by the Chancery. It contained characteristics of the emerging modern standard which stemmed from the Northern dialects: third person plural pronouns starting in *th-* (see 3.2.3); *adverbs* ending in *-ly* rather than Southern *-lich*. However, Southern *-eth* continued to be used in the third person singular and *be/ben* in the present tense plural; Midlands past participles ending in *-en*[3] were also to be found in it. London vernacular in contrast retained third person plural *her* and *hem* and the occasional *marker* of the past participle with *y-* (Shaklee 1980: 48–49).

5.3.1 New grammatical patterns: pronouns

The spread of *you* (singular) for *thou* cannot be ignored in this period. In Chaucer's time singular *you* was well established, as the following table of *second person pronoun usage* (link: Second person pronoun usage) in the *Canterbury Tales* reveals:

---

3 Later many were replaced by weak participles, but strong adjectival forms such as *cloven, graven, hewn, laden, molten, mown, misshapen, shaven, sodden* survived.

Table 5.1 Second person pronouns in the *Canterbury Tales*

thou-forms		you-forms singular		you-forms plural		impersonal you	
thou	743	*ye*	567	*ye*	290	singular	55
thee	308	*you*	377	*you*	251	plural	19
thy	683	*your*	492				

(Mazzon 2000a: 136)

The use of *you*-singular is due perhaps to French influence (upper class and bureaucrats), but this is presumably not the whole story, for "it cuts across some straightforward social distinctions, suggesting that the 'rules' for the choice of pronouns in switching could be as refined as in Shakespeare's time, even though not identical" (Mazzon 2000a: 137; see 6.3.4). French singular *vous*, the model for this change, was much more consistent than English singular *you*. For example, where *you*-singular is used for deities, they are pagan ones; the Christian God gets *thou*, at least introductorily, though a shift to *you* may follow – as a sign of respect as with lords and ladies. Family address has children giving a parent *you*-singular while children always get *thou* from parents (ibid.: 136ff). Note the use of *yow* by the writer of Text 5.5 in a letter to his brother. Over time singular-*you* came to be used between equals while someone who gave *thou* indicated "I am superior"; *thou* was less a marker of intimacy than an insult (Knowles 1997: 58). The rapid spread of singular *you* over the next two centuries may be credited to its use as a polite form, for "in all cases of doubt one would rather be polite than risk giving offence" (see 6.3.4; Strang 1970: 139) (**link: Modes of address**).

5.3.1.1 The pronoun one

In the fifteenth century indefinite *one* begins to appear, as in *euery chamber was walled and closed rounde aboute, and yet myghte **one** goo from **one** to a nother* (Caxton *Eneydos* 117: 17–19) (1st *one* = indefinite; 2nd *one* = anaphoric). But earlier examples can be seen as in the following fourteenth century example from *Gawain* (ll. 2201–2): *Quat! hit clattered in þe cliff, as hit cleue schulde, / As **one** vpon a gryndelston hade grounden a syþe* (Fischer 1992: 224). Here the influence of French *on*, which appears only as a subject, may reinforce the use of indefinite *one* in English, but since earliest instances show non-nominative case *one*, French was hardly the decisive factor. Note the gradual loss of indefinite *man* (also *men*, *me*) in ME. The motivation for this loss is not clear. Possibilities: similarity to *man* "man" and the problems of **agreement** and anaphoric reference may have caused this plus the availability of *you, they, we, people*, and so on as indefinite referents (ibid.: 225).

5.3.1.2 The relative pronoun

In sentential relative clauses *þat* was gradually replaced by *what* in early ME and then by *which* (Late ME). Constraints on non-restrictive *that* probably began in ME, but were essentially EModE. *Which* begins to replace *that* in the fifteenth century. Chaucer has 75% *that*; Caxton, a hundred years later, only 50% (ibid.: 297). Correspondence from the fifteenth century shows how the new forms were spreading (**link: Relative pronouns and clauses**).

5.3.2 Periphrastic structures

It was in the early ME period that the widespread beginnings of phrasal (periphrastic) structures could be found. These are combinations of two words which take over the function of a single word with an inflectional ending. The auxiliary *have* (also *be*) could be combined with the past participle in a periphrastic construction such as *the Flemmynges . . . habbeth y-left here strange speche* (Text 5.1, ll. 4–5), which was essentially the same in meaning as the past *the Flemmyngs . . . lefden . . .* The use of inflections is called synthetic, and the use of periphrasis is called analytical. The expansion in the use of the latter affected the progressive, the modal auxiliaries in place of the subjunctive, and periphrastic *do*. Periphrastic verbal expressions do, in fact, occur in OE, but the auxiliary status of, for example, *habban, beon, willan*, or *sculan* is hard to determine. In ME, however, the perfect and future developed rapidly as did the modal subjunctive. The progressive became more frequent by the end of the ME period. Periphrastic *do* began growing in use, but developed most strongly in the EModE period.

5.3.2.1 Periphrastic do (link: Auxiliary or periphrastic do)

Do had three uses in OE: (1) full or lexical verb; (2) pro-form or substitute *do* allowing a continuation of a report without having to repeat the same verb; and (3) causative *do*, especially with *that*-clauses, rarely with infinitives. The first remains a part of language and is of no further concern here. The second use of *do* is rare in this period. An example of it can be taken from the *Canterbury Tales*:

> This pardoner hadde heer as yellow as wex,
> But smothe it heng, as **dooth** a strike of flex;
>
> ("General Prologue," ll. 675–676)

Here *dooth* stands for *heng*, making a repetition of the original verb unnecessary. While this served the stylistic purposes of avoiding unwanted repetition, it also marks the course of *doon* toward becoming a grammaticalized form bleached of more specific meaning. A later passage from the *Canterbury Tales* shows a further stage in this process:

> **Do**, dame, telle forth youre tale, and that is best.
>
> ("Prologue to Wife of Bath's Tale," l. 853)

Here the verb *do* might be considered to stand in apposition to *telle*, but it could also be an early example of *do* as an auxiliary using a pattern which is found in the ModE emphatic use of the imperative, for example *Do tell us your story!* The third use was possibly established in analogy to causative OE *haten* "order, bid" and *leten* "allow, cause to do" on the model of French causative *faire* "make, do." It is illustrated in the following line from *Piers Plowman*: *And Gyle dooth hym to go* (l. 2212) "And Gyle ordered him to go." Causative *do* did not persist in the language, but it did help to establish the periphrastic *do* as a formal possibility. For more on *do* see link: The auxiliary *do*.

5.3.3 Word order changes (link: Typological change)

Word order changes continued throughout this period (see 2.3.3 and 4.2.3). Especially remarkable in this period is the gradual move from accusative object before the verb, as a common OE pattern, to accusative object after the verb, which comes to dominate by the end of the ME period.

Table 5.2 Change in verb – object word order

accusative object	1000	1200	1300	1400	1500
before verb	52.5%	52.7%	40+%	14.3%	1.87%
after verb	47.5%	46.3%	60-%	85.7%	98.13%

(Fries 1940, qtd. in Hopper and Traugott 1993: 60)

The impression given in the table should be relativized inasmuch as the percentages "conceal complex word order adjustments involving differences such as those between pronoun and noun, definite and indefinite NP, heavy and light NP, independent and dependent clause, and so forth" (Hopper and Traugott 1993: 60). Verb second position continues to show up in ME where it would not in ModE, but as Fischer observes, "By the fifteenth century it was mainly triggered when a *wh*-element or a negative element was the first constituent in the clause" (Fischer 1992: 375), which is basically the situation in ModE.

Of all the text excerpts used in this chapter, only Text 5.5, John Paston II, an upper-class businessman, writing to his brother in 1475 contains a clear case of the progressive (link: Progressive (aspect)) (l. 14). This may be attributed to the colloquial *style* in which the letter was written. The *Canterbury Tales* contains a further possible example, but its somewhat unusual word order – *Singinge he was, or floytinge, al the day* (l. 91) – by **topicalizing** the participles has a more adjectival than verbal effect.

Text 5.5 Correspondence: excerpt from a Paston letter (1485) (link: The Paston letters)

I prayed yow sende me som tydyngys suche as ye
heere, and howgh that my brother Edmonde doth,
for as for tydyngys heere, theere be but fewe saffe
that the assege lastyth stylle by the Duke of Burgoyn
affoore Nuse and the Emperore hathe besegyd also,   5
not ferre from thense, a castell and an other town in
lyke wise wherin the Dukys men been. And also the
Frenshe Kynge, men seye, is comyn nyghe to the
water off Somme wyth iiii sperysl and some men
trowe that he woll at the day off brekyng off trewse,   10

yow-ye: polite form used to his brother
how + that: a subordinator; *doth* for "is doing"
be: a subjunctive form

hathe: a Southern and Midlands form for *has*
  (also *doth* for *does*)
been: a Southern form for *are*
is: auxiliary for perfect with verb of motion

woll: modal verb (no inflectional ending)

> *or ellys byffoore, sette uppon the Dukys contreys heere.*
> *When I heere moore I shall sende yow moore tydyngys.*
> *The Kyngys Imbassatorys, Sir Thomas Mongomere and*
> *the Master off the Rollys, be comyng homwardys from*
> *Nuse, and as for me I thynke that I shold be seke but* 15
> *iff I see it.*
>
> *heere*: present for future in a temporal clause;
> *shall*: a future marker in the main clause
> *be comyng*: progressive aspect "are coming"
> *shold be*: modal auxiliary subjunctive

In the excerpt we see an interesting mixture of older forms – many of them typically Southern – with newer forms.

5.3.4 Vocabulary

5.3.4.1 Low Dutch

The major sources of ***borrowing*** into the lexicon of ME, as traced out in 4.2.4, remained active. Flemish, Dutch, and Low German words – all structurally similar to English – continued to be adopted, especially since a great many Flemings, including mercenaries and traders and craftsmen (weavers) went to England over the years. In the Peasants' Revolt (see Plate 5.1) their language seems to have betrayed them to rebels, who killed around 160 of them, probably chiefly for reasons of economic rivalry: "many fflemmyinges loste here heedes . . . and namely they that koude nat say Breede and Chese, But Case and Brode" (Kingsford 1905: 15).

5.3.4.2 French and Latin

Although quite a few ***Low Dutch*** words entered the language, it was the presence of an extraordinarily large number of French and Latin borrowings which had a major effect on the structure of English ***vocabulary***. Numerous native words dropped out of use as they were replaced by ***loan words***, but very often the old words continued to exist beside the new ones, a process which led to a differentiation of meaning. In Text 5.6 there is especially good evidence of the influence of French vocabulary. Here there is a large number of doublets such as *augmentacioun and encrees* (l. 2) which may once have had its justification in juxtaposing a French borrowing and a synonymous native Germanic word, thus easing comprehension. Jespersen points out that writers in, say, the thirteenth century used a French word with an English one next to it as an interpretation, for example *cherité, þet is luve* (*Ancrene Riwle*, 1225 qtd. in Jespersen 1905: §98). This was hardly the case anymore. Certainly, by Chaucer's time the reader would have been familiar with both members of a pair and they would serve to heighten the effect of the passage, for example in *honour and worship* or *olde and auncyent doctours* (ibid.). In other words, as in the text by Bokenham, doublets seem to be largely a stylistic device without any further function since both words might be of French origin, as in the initial example from l. 2. And, indeed, writers continue to use such ***binomials*** (link: Binomials) in ModE, as we see in *aid and abet* or *assault and battery*.

> ### Text 5.6 Bokenham on English and French (1440)
>
> *And þis corrupcioun of Englysshe men yn þer modre-tounge, begunne as I seyde with famylyar commixtion of Danys firste and of Normannys aftir, toke grete augmentacioun and encrees aftir þe commying of William conquerour by two thyngis. The firste was: by decre and ordynaunce of þe seide William conqueror children in gramer-scolis ageyns þe consuetude and þe custom of all oþer nacyons, here owne modre-tonge lafte and forsakyn, lernyd here Donet on Frenssh and to construyn yn Frenssh* 5
> *and to maken here Latyns on þe same wyse. The secounde cause was þat by the same decre lordis sonys and all nobyll and worthy mennys children were fyrste set to lyrnyn and speken Frensshe, or þan þey cowde spekyn Ynglyssh and þat all wrytyngis and endentyngis and all maner plees and contravercyes in courtis of þe lawe, and all maner reknygnis and countis yn howsoolde schulle be doon yn the same. And þis seeyinge, þe rurales, þat þey myghte semyn þe more worschipfull and honorable and þe* 10
> *redliere comyn to þe famyliarite of þe worthy and þe grete, leftyn hure modre tounge and labouryd to kunne spekyn Frenssh: and thus by processe of tyme barbariʒid thei in bothyn and spokyn neythyr good Frenssh nor good Englyssh.*

Text 5.6 contains thirty borrowings from French or Latin; in addition, there are fourteen doublets. Five of them consist of two French terms (see example l. 2); in five both members are Germanic in origin, for example *to lyrnyn and speken Frensshe* (7); the remaining four are mixed English–French, namely *nobyll and worthy* (7), *wrytyngis and endentyngis* (8), *reknygnis and countis* (9), and *worschipfull and honorable* (10). Jespersen (1905: §100) talks about:

> the differences that have developed in course of time between two synonyms when both have survived, one of them native, the other French. The former is always nearer the nation's heart than the latter, it has the strongest associations with everything primitive, fundamental, popular, while the French word is often more formal, more polite, more refined and has a less strong hold on the emotional side of life. A *cottage* is finer than a *hut*.

5.3.4.3 The structure of the vocabulary

Two remarks about the overall nature of the English vocabulary can be distilled from the large amount of borrowing which took place. The first is that a number of native Germanic words grew obsolete in this process, words such as *fulluhtere, forecwedere, ealdmodor, mæʒester,* and *æþeling* (see Table 4.4 in 4.2.4). Yet, as a second point, synonyms at different levels of style emerged and became characteristic of the stylistic differentiation at least in part possible in English. There are, for example, some cases of Germanic–French–classical triplets like *rise–mount–ascent*; *ask–question–interrogate*; *fast–firm–secure*;

fire–flame–conflagration; *holy–sacred–consecrated*; and *time–age–epoch*. "The difference in tone between the English and the French words is often slight; the Latin word is generally more bookish" (Baugh and Cable 1993, 2002: §144).

There seem to have been two main motives behind the widespread borrowing from French and later Latin. The first, implicit in what has been said up to now, lies in the fact that English had remained the language of the common people. In contrast French had higher prestige with the consequence that its use – or the use of French borrowings in English – distinguished the speaker from the common run of people. French supplied the terms for government and organization, cookery, and much else. Prestige also explains the large influx of Latinate words that came in the fifteenth century and continued in the EModE period (sixteenth century): "It can be no coincidence that writers throughout this period characterised English as 'rude' and lacking in eloquence" (Samuels 1972: 94).

Almost as significant as the French influence following the Norman Conquest was the increase in words of Latin origin. Although this process began in late medieval times, it was with the revival of learning in the Renaissance that classical borrowing really took off.

As positive as these new words were for the increased possibilities of expression they offered, they were also accompanied by controversy and were rejected in many cases. Besides enriching the language, they also made certain stylistic *registers* more inaccessible to the masses and so widened the educational gap between the classes. For many people the semantic relations between everyday words and the corresponding scholarly Latinate words were not immediately evident, but had to be learned. This continues to be the case today. That is, the association between a verb like *see* and the corresponding *adjective* *visible* ("able to be seen") must be established. While both of these words are well known, this is not always the case, as with pairs like *smell* and *olfactory*. Hence the designation of these non-Germanic items as *hard words* (see also 6.3.2) (link: Inkhorn and pretentious words). Jespersen for one regarded the presence of such items as "undemocratic" since they are opaque and require more education.

The second point is that the recipient language may have had *lexical gaps* (link: Lexical gaps). But people such as Jespersen consider the notion mistaken that English was missing the words it borrowed and that borrowing reflects inferiority in vocabulary and culture. The mass of words borrowed were redundant.

One consequence of the widespread adoption of *Romance language* words is the presence of a large number of non-native words employing a different set of affixes and using different stress patterns. This had a lasting effect on the morphology of English. However, it has not eradicated the fundamental distinction between Romance and Germanic lexical items, even though many Romance words are part of everyday vocabulary.

The addition of French vocabulary is all the more dramatic when considering that in 1066 there were only fifty French loan words recorded in English. By the end of the ME period 28.3% of the vocabulary was of French origin according to entries in the *Shorter Oxford English Dictionary* (first published in 1933 as a more concise version of the *OED*); 28.24% came from Latin; and 27% were Germanic (Finkenstaedt and Wolff 1973: 121–128). Of the French borrowings it is estimated that 20% entered English before 1450 and that these are among those with the highest rate of use (Bailey and Maroldt 1977: 32). A short example, which should not be overgeneralized, may illustrate the nature of the words from these three sources:

- Germanic: *mother, father, brother, sister, son, daughter*
- French: *aunt, uncle, niece, nephew*
- Latin: *maternity, paternalistic, fraternity, sorority, filial, avuncular.*

The more intimate relationships are of Germanic origin, the more distant ones, of French, while the more abstract qualities are Latin in origin (see also 5.3.2).

5.4 Literature

The period stretching from the middle of the fourteenth to the end of the fifteenth centuries shows increasing individualization in the areas of literature (link: ME literature). While there is still a great deal of writing such as *Sir Gawain and the Green Knight* by unidentified authors, we also have the literature of Chaucer, Langland, Wycliffe, Barbour, Trevisa, and Blind Harry. All of these are exemplified in this chapter or in a link to further texts with the hopes of making Middle English more familiar. There will also be a short look at a major revolution in the media: printing.

5.4.1 Continental literary models

In general the French tradition of meter and rhyme was adopted, but *Piers Plowman* and *Sir Gawain* do not follow French fashion. From 1250 there was a growing body of literature in English, which is concomitant with the spread of English among the upper classes. The types of literature that had previously appeared in French now appeared in English. The most popular type at this time was the romance, for example *Sir Gawain and the Green Knight* or *Morte d'Arthur*.

5.4.2 *The Canterbury Tales*

In what is the best-known piece of literature from the ME period Geoffrey Chaucer (1340–1400) (link: *Canterbury Tales* / Chaucer) produced a witty and perceptive picture of English society at the end of the fourteenth century. In *The Canterbury Tales* he introduces a group of pilgrims who are making their way on a five-day pilgrimage from Southwark, then near and now in London, to the grave of St. Thomas Becket outside Canterbury (link: Pilgrimages) (Plate 5.3). In the Prologue he portrays some thirty travelers who are to tell two stories each on the way there and two again on the way back. This motivates a collection of tales comparable to Bocaccio's *Decameron* but differing greatly in style and, most importantly, reflecting the diverse social origins of the pilgrims. The tales come from all over Europe and the Orient. There is usually a clear point or a moral, each tale ending with a proverb or some other "wisdom"; some come from the lives of the saints, but some are low fabliaux. Originality was not a goal, but rather the embellishment of the stories with the goal of instructing and entertaining. All but two are in verse.

Chaucer was in the king's service throughout his life and had ample opportunity to travel and observe people at home and abroad. Best of all he wrote with originality, freshness, and humor. As his best-known modern translator wrote, his tales reveal "moral and pious interest, qualified by an intense feeling for the romantic and by increasing touches of wit and personal observation" (Coghill 1952: 13–14). The Prologue is a "concise portrait of an entire nation, high and low, old and young, male and female, lay and clerical, learned and ignorant, rogue and righteous, land and sea, town and country; but without extremes" (ibid.: 15). Chaucer avoids predictability, writing in a didactic, argumentative, amusing style, now in a high and now in a low tone. The choice of characters allows him to show a highly stratified society, with nobles such as the knight, the "first estate," at the top. The "second estate," the clergy, is portrayed by the nun, the monk, the friar, and the parson. Commoners, the last of the three traditional estates, appear on different levels, a higher one in the figures of the squire, the wife of Bath, the physician, the merchant, the franklin, the yeoman; the middle with the pardoner, the summoner, the clerk, the reeve; and the lower with the miller, the cook, the plowman, and the shipman. Connected with this is a distinction between polite (courteous) and unrefined behavior. Chaucer was not averse to revealing the foibles and sins of the supposedly better, but showed genuine respect for the truly good (e.g. the parson).

The **doctour of phisyk** (the physician) can serve to introduce *The Canterbury Tales*. The passage quoted comes from "The Prologue" (ll. 411–428):

Text 5.7a *Canterbury Tales*, "The Prologue" (1385, excerpts)

With us ther was a Doctour of Phisyk
In al this world ne was ther noon him lyk
To speke of phisik and of surgerye;
For he was grounded in astronomye.
He kepte his pacient a ful greet del   415
In houres, by his magik naturel.
Wel coude he fortunen the ascendant
Of his images for his pacient.
He knew the cause of everich maladye,
Were it of hoot or cold, or moiste, or drye,   420
And where engendred, and of what humour;
He was a verrey parfit practisour.
The cause y-knowe, and of his harm the rote,
Anon he yaf the seke man his bote.
Ful redy hadde he his apothecaries,   425
To sende him drogges and his letuaries,
For ech of hem make other for to winne;
Hir frendschipe nas nat newe to beginne.

(W.W. Skeat (ed.) (1912) *The Complete Works of Geoffrey Chaucer.* London: OUP)

The language is relatively easy for a ModE reader to understand. Aside from the difficulties of the unfamiliar spelling we see double negatives (*ne . . . noon*, l. 412; *nas nat*, l. 428) and the {y-} prefix to the past participle, by this time growing rare, but convenient to supply a weakly stressed syllable as in l. 423. What is surely more difficult in such a text is the background knowledge of the intellectual world of the fourteenth century. The following points offer help in understanding the world of medieval medicine, in which treatment was by purging, blood-letting, sweating, and vomiting – all in order to restore the equilibrium of body liquids.

l. 411   *Doctour of Phisyk*: *Physic* meant the art of treatment with drugs or medications (as opposed to surgery).

l. 413   *surgerye*: The barber surgeon was one of the most common medical practitioners of the Middle Ages – generally charged with looking after soldiers. In this era, surgery was not conducted by physicians, but by barbers, who were looked down on by physicians.

l. 414   *astronomye*: This is a what we today call astrology ([link: Astrology](#)), reading the stars, calculating which celestial bodies are rising (ascendant) or falling (descendant) in order to determine what kind of influence on a person the skies have.

l. 416   *houres*: as for *horoscope*, the observation of the time of one's birth for astrological purposes.

l. 417   *ascendant* (see above).

l. 420   *hoot, cold, moiste, drye*: The humors (see l. 421) were associated with the seasons: autumn: cold-dry; winter: cold-wet; spring: warm-wet; and summer: warm-dry.

l. 421   *humour*: "liquid, fluid." The four liquids whose balance (temperament, complexion) were essential for good health (good humor/temper vs. bad humor/temper) ([link: Theory of the humors](#)).

l. 425   *apothecaries*: An apothecary sold ingredients and offered general medical advice and a range of services that are now performed solely by other specialist practitioners.

l. 426   *letuaries*: sweet medicines made with honey and sugar.

The image of the doctor can be contrasted with that of the friar or of the wife of Bath, where Chaucer's critical tone comes through. There is almost always a certain distance, seeming tolerance, and a bit of tongue-in-cheek satire. Chaucer makes fun of both for their sexually loose ways (even though the friar will have taken a vow of chastity); the "good wife" may not have been good in the sense of being virtuous.

Text 5.7b *Canterbury Tales*, "The Prologue" (1385, excerpts)

A Frere ther was, a wantown and a merye,
A limitour, a ful solempne man.
In alle the ordres foure is noon that can   210
So muche of daliaunce and fair langage.
He hadde maad ful many a mariage
Of younge wommen, at his owne cost.
Un-to his ordre he was a noble post.

. . .

> *A good Wyf was ther of bisyde Bathe,*   445
> *But she was som-del deef, and that was scathe.*
>
> . . .
>
> *She was a worthy womman al hir lyve,*
> *Housbondes at chirche-dore she hadde fyve,*   460
> *Withouten other companye in youthe;*
> *But therof nedeth nat to speke as nouthe.*
>
> . . .
>
> *She coude muche of wandring by the weye:*
> *Gat-tothed was she, soothly for to seye.*
> *Up-on an amblere esily she sat,*
> *Y-wimpled wel, and on hir heed an hat*   470
> *As brood as is a bokeler or a targe;*
> *A foot-mantel aboute hir hipes large.*
> *And on hir feet a paire of spores sharpe.*
> *In felawschip wel coude she laughe and carpe.*
> *Of remedyes of love she knew perchaunce,*   475
> *For she coude of that art the olde daunce.*
>
> (W.W. Skeat (ed.) (1912) *The Complete Works of Geoffrey Chaucer.* London: OUP)

Linguistic points

Note the words of ON origin in ll. 446 and 474.

l. 208   Much freer word order than in ModE, dictated perhaps by the meter and rhythm.

l. 210   The subject position would be filled in ModE: in all four orders there is no one that can . . .

              can: used without a following infinitive in the sense of "be able to do"

l. 446   *scathe*: "too bad, a shame"; < ON *skaðe*

l. 462   *nouthe*: "right now"; < *nūþā*

l. 467   *coude*: "was good at"; see l. 210

l. 471   *targe*: "shield" < OF *targe*, cf. ModE *target*

l. 474   *carpe*: "chat" < ON *karpa*

Cultural points

1. 209   *limitour*: a mendicant friar, whose area of begging was *limited*

l. 210   *ordres foure*: the four mendicant orders: Dominicans, Franciscans, Carmelites, Austin Friars

l. 211   *fair langage*: flattery

1.468   *gat-tothed*: "lecherous"

A specifically religious text, written shortly before *The Canterbury Tales*, is *Piers Plowman* by William Langland, a contemporary of Chaucer's. Langland's allegory also offers a prominent example of the continued use of alliteration rather than rhyme (link: *Piers Plowman*). The romance *Syr Gawayn and the Grene Knyȝt*, written by an anonymous author and representing the language of the northwest Midlands, also follows the alliterative tradition (link: *Sir Gawain*).

5.4.3 *The Brus* (link: *The Brus*)

One of the earliest works written in Scots, the first part of *The Brus* – up to the battle of Bannockburn (1314) – was completed in 1375 according to its author, John Barbour (1316/20–1395) and is an example of the adoption of French rhyme and octosyllabic meter. It is a heroic romance about Robert the Bruce, King of the Scots in the late thirteenth and early fourteenth centuries. Well known is the famous line: *A! Fredome is a noble thing!* (Book 1, l. 225). In reading the excerpt from *The Brus*, it should be pointed out that the letter <ß> is a ligature of long *es* <ʃ> and short *es* <s>. Thorn <þ> is still used regularly for <th>.

Text 5.8 John Barbour, *The Brus* (1375, excerpt)

Storyis to red ar delitabill,		It is delightful to read stories,
suppos that tha be nocht bot fabill.	*suppos* "if"; *be* is subjunctive	Even if they are nothing but fable,
Than suld storyis that suthfast wer,	<s> for Southern /ʃ/	Then should stories that are truthful,
And tha war said on gud maner,	*tha* "they" Northern < ON	If they were told in good manner,
Haf doubill plesans in hering.		Have double pleasure in hearing.
The fyrst plesans is þe carping,		The first pleasure is the talking,
And the tothir the suthfastnes		And the second the truthfulness,
That schawys the thing richt	<a> for Southern <o>; also	That shows the matter rightly, as it
as it wes	*na, haly*	was;
And suth thingis that ar likand	pres. participle in –*and*	And true things that are attractive
To manis hering ar plesand.	(Northern)	Till many hearing it are pleased.
Tharfor I wald fane set my will,	*wald* for Southern *wold* "would"	Therefore I would fain set my will,
Gif my wit micht suffis thartill,	*micht* for the subjunctive; *þar*:	If my wit might suffice for it,
To put in writ ane suthfast story,	/ɛ/ + /r/ becomes /a/	To put in writing a truthful story,
That it lest ay furth in memory,		That it last forever in memory,
Sa that na tym of lenth it let,	*let, ger* without {s} = subjunctive	So that no length of time may block it,
na ger it haly be forȝet.	*ger* "cause" (Northern)	Nor cause it wholly to be forgotten.

(J. Barbour (1856) *The Brus*. Aberdeen: Spalding Club)

5.4.4 Printing

The introduction of printing to Europe was a revolutionary development which had wide-reaching and long-lasting effects. Indeed, many people among those who had a stake in the power of their own literacy were suspicious of the social unrest that could result from increased access to knowledge and enlightenment on the part of the lower orders. This was similar to the fears Church and State had had a hundred years before in connection with the vernacular translation of the Bible in the framework of the Wycliffe movement and the Peasants' Revolt. The consequences of printing were, as we now know, enormous, though generally peaceable.

Printing using movable type was originally introduced to Europe by Johann Gutenberg and was well established early in the second half of the fifteenth century. William Caxton (1414/20(?)–1492) ([link: Caxton](#)) spent much of his early adulthood on the Continent. He learned the printing trade in Cologne and then set up as a printer in Bruges, where he printed books in Latin, French, and English. The first book to be printed in English was *Recuyell of the Historyes of Troye* in 1473. Soon after this in 1476 he moved to Westminster, now a part of London, where he published almost exclusively in English and enjoyed considerable success because he catered to a growing and increasingly influential public, which included not just nobles but an upper-class readership which was eager for writing in English. He brought out mainly classical works in translation such as *Eneydos* (the *Aeneid*); romances, for example Malory's *Morte d'Arthur* or Gower's *Confessio Amantis*; histories like the *Recuyell* mentioned above; and literature such as Chaucer's *Canterbury Tales*, but also liturgical works, school books, and books of etiquette.

When Caxton set up shop, the English language had undergone only the beginnings of the process of standardization. For the written language this was chiefly due to the Chancery Standard (see 5.3). Caxton reflects on the possible causes of the great variety to be found in English and illustrates the problem of diversity with his well-known story in the "Prologue" to *Eneydos* (Text 5.9) about a merchant from the north-central Midlands who, stranded on the Kent side of the Thames estuary, tried to buy some eggs from a local woman.

Text 5.9 William Caxton, "Prologue" to *Eneydos* (1490)

And certainly our language now vsed varyeth ferre from that whiche was vsed and spoken whan I was borne. For we Englysshe men ben borne vnder the domynacyon of the mone, whiche is neuer stedfaste but euer wauerynge, wexynge one season, and waneth and dyscreaseth another season. And that comyn Englysshe that is spoken in one shyre varyeth from a nother. . . . And specyally he axyed after eggys. And the good wyf answerde that she coude speke no frenshe. And the marchaunt was angry for he also coude speke no frenshe but wold haue hadde egges and she vnderstode hym not. And thenne at laste a nother sayd that he wolde haue eyren. Then the good wyf sayd that she vnderstood hym wel.

What is notable about this text is the misunderstanding caused by the rival words for eggs. The merchant used the form derived from ON, *eggys* or *egges*; the woman was only familiar with the Southern word *eyren*. Caxton alone, for all the influence he may have had, could not bring about the standardization and unity of usage that was to become more or less programmatic in the EModE period (see next chapter). Many contemporaries such as the London printer Richard Pynson ([link: Copyright law](#)), who drew on the Chancery Standard even more than Caxton, also contributed to this development.

5.5 Variation

While standardization was a growing, but not fully developed force in the late ME period, it did not change the fact of regional and social variation which was as strongly present as before. In the texts in section 5.4 we have had examples of Southern, of London-based, Midlands, and Scottish English. Here two further examples are added.

5.5.1 England

There seems to have been widespread awareness of regional differences. This is very clearly summed up in another well-known passage, the remarks by John Trevisa ([link: Trevisa](#)) on the linguistic state of the realm. Trevisa, a contemporary of Wycliffe's at Oxford and perhaps a contributor to his Bible translation, inserted his comments on English into his translation of Ranulf Higden's (1280–1363) *Polychronicon*,[4] a history of the world (Plate 5.4).

Text 5.10 John of Trevisa's *Polychronicon* (1387)

This apeyryng of the burth-tonge ys bycause of twey things. On ys for chyldern in scole, ayenes the usage and manere of al other nacions, buth compelled for to leve here owne longage, and for to construe here lessons and here things a Freynsch. . . .

. . . Hyt semeth a gret wondur houw Englysch, that ys the burth-tonge of Englysch-men and here oune longage and tonge, ys so dyvers of soun in this ylond. . . . for men of the est with men of the west, as hyt were undur the same party of heven, acoredeth more in sounying of speche than men of the north with men of the south; therefore hyt ys that Mercian, that buth men of myddel Engelond, as hyt were parteners of the endes, undurstondeth betre the side longages, Northeron and Southeron, than Northeron

5

---

4 *Ranuiphi Castrensis, cognomine Higdon, Polychronicon (sive Historia Polycratica) ab initio mundi usque ad mortem regis Edwardi III in septem libros dispositum*), went up to 1342/1344 and was continued by John of Malvern until 1357. Trevisa translated it in 1387, and Caxton published it in 1482.

and Southeron undurstondeth eyther other. Al the longage of the Northumbres, and specialych at York, ys so scharp, slyttyng and frotyng, and unschape, that we Southeron men may that longage unneth 10
undurstonde.

(J.R. Lumby (ed.) (1879) *Polychronicon Ranulphi Higden Monachi Cestrensis: Together with the English Translations of John of Trevisa and of an Unknown Writer of the Fifteenth Century,* 7 vols. London: Longman, Green, vol. 1, 8–10)

Glossary

apeyryng (1) "impairment"	*buth* (2, 7) "are"	*slyttyng* (10) "piercing"
ayenes (1) "against"	*a* (3) "in"	*frotying* (10) "abrasive"
here (2, 3) "their"	*ylond* (5) "island"	*unschape* (10) "misshapen"

Trevisa recognizes, coming as he did from Cornwall, where Cornish was spoken, that a large variety of languages were spoken in England, but what he emphasizes in this passage is that there is a broad division of the country into North, Middle (Mercian), and South. Furthermore, he emphasizes his sympathies with the Midlands, where the east and the west shared a great deal and understood the North and the South better than the latter understood each other. Trevisa's remark about Northern speech makes his attitude clear when he ends this excerpt with a disparaging remark on the sharp, shrill, grating and misshapen language of Northumbria, thus putting himself into what was to develop into a long tradition of disdain for whatever was not oriented toward London and the Southeast. For linguistic aspects of difference between the regions see 4.5.

5.5.2 Scotland (link: Early history of Scotland)

The English which developed in the Lowlands of Scotland, more accurately referred to as Scots, was an extension of Northumbrian. Even today the ***traditional dialects*** of the two areas share many features (see 8.2.7; 8.3.2), but the fact that an independent kingdom developed in Scotland led to the establishment of an independent variety of the language and an incipient standard.

The earliest period recognized is that of Early Scots, which runs roughly parallel to the ME period. Under the reign of King David I burghers (settlers) from Northumbria moved to the burghs (towns) of Scotland, including Berwick, Stirling, Dunfermline, Aberdeen, Perth, Scone, and Edinburgh. These settlements were linguistic beachheads of English in largely Gaelic-speaking Scotland. But as powerful and prestigious communities they eventually prevailed over Gaelic until all of the Lowlands was English (Scots) speaking by the end of this period. It is also within this time that the regional differentiation into Southern, Central, and Northern Scots took place and Scots itself began replacing Latin as the language of record.

Early Scots can be distinguished from ME in its somewhat different vocabulary, in which some items derived from OE were retained in Scots but not in English, for example *umbeset* "surround." Scots was also characterized by different borrowings from French, words like *vevaris* "provisions," or from Low Dutch, as with *howff* "courtyard."

Among the earliest Scots literature is John Barbour's *Brus* (see Text 5.8), but also the heroic narrative *Wallace* by Blind Harry about the fighter, The Wallace (link: Wallace), who defended Scotland against England. The poem is a long, heroic, and highly patriotic work that – in translation – has remained popular in Scotland. Together with the translation the text is readable. The spelling and vocabulary may cause difficulties, but the grammar is astonishingly similar to ModE.

Text 5.11 Blind Harry, *Wallace*, c. 1478

BUKE FYRST	First Book
OUR antecessowris, that we suld of reide,	Our ancestors, who we should read of,
And hald in mynde thar nobille worthi deid,	And hold in mind their noble worthy deeds,
We lat ourslide, throw werray sleuthfulnes;	We let pass by, through veritable slothfulness;
And castis ws euir til vthir besynes.	And continually occupy ourselves with other business.
Till honour ennymys is our haile entent,	To honor our enemies is our whole intention,
It has beyne seyne in thir tymys bywent;	It has been seen in bygone times;
Our ald ennemys cummyn of Saxonys blud,	Our old enemies came of Saxon blood,
That neuyr yeit to Scotland wald do gud,	Who never yet to Scotland would do good,
Bot euir on fors, and contrar haile thair will,	But necessarily and against their will,
Quhow gret kyndnes thar has beyne kyth thaim till.	How great kindness there has been revealed to them.
It is weyle knawyne on mony diuerss syde,	It is well known on diverse sides,
How thai haff wrocht in to thair mychty pryde,	How they have tried in their mighty pride,
To hald Scotlande at wndyr euirmar.	To hold Scotland down evermore.
Bot God abuff has maid thar mycht to par:	But God above has lessened their might:

(Blind Harry (1820), *Wallace*. Edinburgh: Constable & Blackwood)

5.6 Summary

Amidst religious and social conflict English continued to spread in this period. And the growth of London contributed to the process of standardization. Features of the South, the East, and the North can be found in the emerging standard, thus testifying to the demographic mobility of this period, motivated among other things by the labor shortages caused by the Plague and the Hundred Years' War, and the chances for economic and social advancement that grew up as a result. The Lollard movement was one consequence of demographic change; part of its program lay in the move against the monopoly of Latin in the Church. Wycliffe's translation of the Bible into English must be seen in this context. The type of English he used might have had greater influence on the standard if it had not been so strongly associated with religious radicalism. In the end it was the spoken English of London and the written English of the Chancery which exercised the greatest influence. Both were the result of dialect leveling (koinéization). Among the changes explored was the new use of second person pronouns, as *you* grew in prominence vis-à-vis *thou*, but also the beginnings of periphrastic *do*, word order changes, and the increasing use of the progressive form. Massive borrowing from French and Latin led to a restructuring of the vocabulary of English, contrasting everyday Germanic words with more learned ones. Literary production – now often independent of religion or dynastic motives – reached a first high point in Chaucer's *Canterbury Tales*. At the end of the period printing was introduced, and publishing in English was a response to growing English literacy. Both printing and the emergence of a reading public led to the accelerated development of a written standard without, however, restraining the regional varieties.

STUDY QUESTIONS

Social and cultural background

1. What was the social relationship between English and its neighbors French and Latin? That is, what type of contact did they have?
2. How "undemocratic" are the results of the massive import of Romance vocabulary?
3. What was the overall effect of the two languages on English?

Linguistic background

1. In Text 5.6 (Bokenham) there are over thirty words borrowed from French or Latin. List them. Which language supplies the larger number of loan words?
2. What proportion of English vocabulary is of Romance (classical and French) origin?
3. How have these borrowings influenced the derivational morphology of English?

Further reading

Shaklee couples social change more explicitly with linguistic change, focusing on the standardization process. Mazzon looks specifically at the usage of the second person pronouns in both Chaucer and Shakespeare. The literature by Hopper and Traugott, Knowles, Leith, and Thomason and Kaufman has already been mentioned in the further reading recommendations in chapters 3 and/or 4.

Hopper, P.J. and E.C. Traugott (1993) *Grammaticalization.* Cambridge: CUP.
Knowles, G.O. (1997) *A Cultural History of the English Language.* London: Edward Arnold.

Leith, D. (1983) *A Social History of English*. London: Routledge.

Mazzon, G. (2000) "Special Relations and Forms of Address in the *Canterbury Tales*," In: D. Kastovsky and A. Mettinger (eds.) *The History of English in a Social Context. A Contribution to Historical Sociolinguistics*. Berlin: Mouton de Gruyter, 2000, 135–167.

Shaklee, M. (1980) "The Rise of Standard English," In: T. Shopen and J. Williams (eds.) *Standards and Dialects in English*. Cambridge, Mass.; Winthrop, 33–62.

Thomason, S.G. and T. Kaufman (1988) *Language Contact, Creolization, and Genetic Linguistics*. Berkeley: University of California Press.

CHAPTER SIX

The Early Modern English period (1500 – 1700)

O, good my lord, no Latin; I am not such a truant since my coming, As not to know the language I have lived in: A strange tongue makes my cause more strange, suspicious; Pray, speak in English . . .
(Queen Katharine in Shakespeare, *Henry VIII*, Act I: Scene I)

Chapter Overview:

This chapter:

- introduces the Tudor dynasty which brought England a relatively long period of peace, prosperity, and economic and territorial expansion, thus facilitating the spread of Southern English;
- looks at the effects of printing, which became more widespread and reinforced the notion of a standard, as initiated in the late Middle English period with the rise of London and Chancery English;
- shows how religion caused violent dislocations and religious conflict beginning under the Tudors and coming to a head in Stuart England. This conflict was the result of fundamental socio-economic change and the need for a more rapid change in social structures;
- reviews major linguistic developments and exemplifies them in the domains of religion, especially the Bible in translation, and scientific writing. It also includes literary excerpts from Sidney, Milton, and Congreve.
- provides a final short look at regional differences.

6.1 The Early Modern English period

This period is a time of significant change in the language as it develops from Middle to Modern English. Although scholars give differing beginning and end dates for the period, there is fairly widespread consensus about a starting point around 1500, which is close to the introduction of printing in English (1476) or the beginning of the Tudor dynasty (1485). The period may be closed at 1700, though some prefer 1750 as an end date. In any case this period lies before the Industrial Revolution and the demographic changes it brought. From a dynastic point of view 1700 is close to the Act of Union (1707) and includes the literary exuberance of the Restoration and ends just before the appearance of the landmark magazines of Addison and Steele, *The Tatler* (1709) and *The Spectator* (1711–12). Within the period itself there were a number of monumental events which had an effect on the language: the Anglican–Protestant Reformation, the first colonial ventures (see chapter 7), the Puritan movement, the Civil War and Commonwealth, and the Restoration. Alongside the political and religious turbulence of these times there was also enormous social and cultural change as London grew in size and importance, as literacy spread, as the theater blossomed, and as Renaissance learning made its mark on the language.

6.1.1 Economic and demographic developments

This period saw the growth of a national market, which slowly began to replace local markets. Mercantilism was the predominant economic view in this period with its emphasis on the competition between countries (the up-coming nation-states) and the "wealth of nations." The production of wool and woolen goods was the major industry, as it had been throughout the preceding centuries. In 1560 grain overtook wool in profitability in England. The focus of commercial activity lay increasingly in the Southeast and in London, where a population mix consisting of people from the various regions came together with substantial consequences for the language.

Throughout – and beyond – this period land enclosures were carried out. They were, in effect, a privatization of the commons and part of the paradigmatic of change from subsistence to market agriculture, first in wool and later as modern agriculture. This was clearly beneficial for the better off. The rate of enclosure increased in the seventeenth century and contributed to the social unrest of the period with depopulation of villages, an increase in vagrancy, and even riots and protests as in the Newton Rebellion (link: Enclosures and urbanization) (1607) in Northamptonshire. The excess, dispossessed population contributed to the overall process of urbanization.

6.1.2 Reformation and Renaissance

The break with the papacy was initially an institutional act in which the king simply replaced the Pope as the head of the Church. In this "reform" the Crown profited from the confiscation of Church possessions. Yet below this political-administrative switch were religious movements of a more radical nature, especially Puritanism and Quakerism. The former was a reflection of the growing concerns of the middle class; the latter grew especially in the lower classes. Both were a part of the changing social structure of England and influenced attitudes toward and use of language.

The Elizabethan period marked the beginning of the Renaissance in England. This not only reflected a renewed interest in classical learning, it also stimulated a paradigmatic change in the way people viewed science, which was, under the influence of Bacon, to become more empirical. The period also marked the beginning of a literary boom that started at the end of the sixteenth and continued into the seventeenth century, including, for example Marlowe, Shakespeare, Jonson, Spenser, and Milton. As literacy spread, the significance of the press grew. Freedom of expression (within certain limits) was strongly defended by Milton. Massachusetts Bay colony introduced the first law providing for common schools for everyone (1647). In England Oxford developed into the university closer to the establishment while dissenters were more at home at Cambridge. The Royal Society, founded in 1660, was located in London and later in Oxford as well.

6.1.3 Political-dynastic developments

The Tutor dynasty was not always peaceful, but it did accomplish one extremely significant thing: it united England (and Wales) and ended English territorial ambitions in France.[1] The relative tranquility was important for economic stability and growth. Markets flourished as did trade. Succession was problematic after the death of Henry VIII (1491–1547): Edward VI (1537–53) was only nine when he became king and fourteen when he died. His successor, Mary I (1516–58), attempted to return England to the Roman Catholic Church and in doing so invited conflict. She was followed by Elizabeth I (reign 1558–1603), whose rule, while not free of intrigue, did establish a period of relative prosperity.

Elizabeth's successor, James VI (1566–1625), the Stuart king of Scotland, became James I of England in the union of the Scottish and English crowns. He showed no sympathy for dissenters and separatists, but did support the independence of the Church of England. Under his successor, Charles I (1600–49), especially due to the influence of Laud (1573–1645), Archbishop of Canterbury, religious controversy escalated, leading eventually to the Civil War (1642–51), in the course of which first Laud and then Charles I were executed.

6.1.4 The Puritans, the Civil War, and the Commonwealth

The English Civil War (1641–49), the Commonwealth (1649–53, 1659–60), and the Protectorate (1653–59) were ostensibly based on religious conflict, but were due to massive socio-economic change in English society. Two main parties, the Royalists (aristocracy) faced off against the Parliamentarians (middle class), who wanted to secure more democratic control through Parliament. This was a conflict set at the fault-line between the older feudal order and the emerging bourgeois forms of organization and the new middle-class values of life, liberty, and property. The disinherited, Brownists and Separatists, but others as well, made common cause with the middle class and had a remarkable influence on the Independents, pushing them toward religious toleration and republicanism. But by the

---

1 Calais, lost in 1558, was the last French territory held by England – if the Channel Islands are not counted.

1650s the Independents had become substantial people and the Puritans were hardly different from the Presbyterians. Consequently, new groupings of Anabaptists, Millenarians, and Quakers arose (link: Religious groups at the time of the English Civil War).

The consequences of the Commonwealth and Protectorate included a program promoting godliness, such as closing the theaters, laws against adultery, blasphemy, and [religious] enthusiasm. Cromwell's New Model Army, with financial backing from the City, defeated the forces of both Parliament and the Crown; it defeated the Scottish forces; and it conquered Ireland. This paved the way to union between England and Scotland and it cemented the subjection and colonization of Ireland under a Protestant Ascendancy.

Army leadership was largely in the hands of Levellers (link: Religious groups at the time of the English Civil War), thus giving it a political motivation, including universal male suffrage, a reform of electoral boundaries, supremacy of Parliament (thus weakening the power of the Lords and the Crown), religious freedom, and an end to imprisonment for debt.

6.1.5 Restoration England

In 1659 Oliver Cromwell's son Richard was deposed and the Rump (link: Rump) Parliament[2] was reconvened to include the MPs excluded in 1648. In 1660 the monarchy was restored under Charles II (1626–85) and the Long Parliament (1640–60) was ended (see Text 6.1). Despite Restoration deeper fundamental changes were not reversed, such as the continuing weakening of the power of the monarch and of the distinctions between the nobility, the gentry, and well-to-do merchant class. Religious acrimony did not disappear with the return of the Stuarts – indeed the Act of Conformity defined "us and them" more clearly than ever: *us* was the Church of English; *them*, the dissenters and the Roman Catholics. Yet this position was not tenable in the long run and soon virtual religious toleration was established. The question of a return to Catholicism was finally answered negatively when Catholic King James II (1633–1701) was replaced by his Protestant

daughter Mary and William of Orange in 1688 (link: The Glorious Revolution). His sister-in-law Anne, the daughter of James II, was the final Stuart monarch.

The diary of Samuel Pepys gives an eye witness account of the era. The excerpts in Text 6.1 include passages describing the execution of the regicides (October 13, 1660), the now reopened theaters (November 20), the return of High Church practices (July 8), and laxer life styles (September 4, 1660 and August 1, 1661). The Restoration ended (Puritan) antipathy toward foreign ideas. French ideas and social ideals as well as *French loan words* were once again *en vogue*. It was the age of the coffee-house and of *politeness*, which rejected both ordinary, colloquial, or provincial usage as well as the affected speech often ridiculed in Restoration comedy. Of course, it would be mistaken to believe that such ideas went far beyond a relatively restricted circle in London society. No doubt the boys quoted in the entry for February 7 were hardly representatives of polite ideals.

2 The now small Parliament consisted of Levellers but had not sat since 1653.

Text 6.1 Samuel Pepys, excerpts from his diary (1660ff)

1660

1 January. *Blessed* be *God, at the end of the last year I was in very good health, ... I lived in Axe Yard,[3] having my wife and servant Jane, and no more in family* then *us three. . . . The condition of the state was thus. Viz. the rump . . .* was *lately* returned *to sit again. . . . The new Common Council of the City* doth *speak very high; and* hath *sent to Monke their sword-bearer, to acquaint him with their desires for a free and full Parliament, which is at present the desires and the hopes and expectation of all.[4]*

7 February. *Boys* do *now* cry *"Kiss my Parliament!" instead of "Kiss my arse!" so great and general a contempt is the* Rump come *to among men, good and bad.*

8 July. To Whitehall to chapel, *where I got in with ease by going before the Lord Chancellor with Mr Kipps. Here I* heared *very good* musique, *the first time that I remember ever to have heard the organs and singing-men in surplices in my life.*

4 September. *To Axeyard to my house; where standing at the door, Mrs Diana comes by, whom I took into my house upstairs and there* did dally *with her a great while, and find that in Latin* nulla puella negat. *So home by water; and there sat up late, putting my papers in order and my money also, and teaching my wife her musique lesson, in which I take great pleasure.* So to bed.

13 October. *I went out to Charing Cross to see Major-Generall Harrison hanged, drawn, and quartered – which was done there – he looking cheerfully as any man could do in that condition. He was presently cut down and his head and his heart shown to the people, at which there* was *great shouts of joy. . . . Thus it was my chance to see the King beheaded at Whitehall and to see the first blood shed in revenge for the blood of the King at Charing Cross.*

20 November. *Mr Sheply and I to the new playhouse near* Lincolnes *Inn Fields (which was formerly Gibbons's tennis court), where the play of* Beggers' Bush *was newly begun. And so we went in and saw it.*

1661

4 May. Lords *Day. . . . Mr Holliard came to me and let me blood, about 16 ounces, I being exceedingly full of blood, and very good. I* begun *to be sick; but lying upon my back, I was presently well again and* did give *him 5s for his pains; and so we parted. And I to my chamber to write down my journall.*

---

3 North of what is today Downing Street.

4 Monke, head of the army in Scotland, supported a return to civil authority and was about to march on London. He demanded the return of the "moderate" members of Parliament excluded in 1648, and hence the likelihood of the return of the king.

> 1 August. *At the office all the afternoon, till evening to my chamber; where, God forgive me, I was sorry to hear that Sir W. Pens maid Betty was gone away yesterday, for I was in hopes to have had a bout with her before she had gone, she being very pretty. I have also a mind to my own wench, but I dare not, for feare she should prove honest and refuse and then tell my wife.*
>
> 1665 [the plague]
>
> 12 August. *The people die so, that now it seems they are fain to carry the dead to be buried by daylight, the nights not sufficing to do it in. And my Lord Mayor commands people to be within at 9 at night. . . .*
>
> (Pepys, S. (1978) R. Latham and W. Matthews (eds.) *The Diary of Samuel Pepys*. London: Bell & Hyman)

The excerpts from Pepys' diary reveal a great deal about the life and interests of well-situated gentlemen. The language is easily understandable though the spelling varies and some constructions are worth noting:

- the use of non-emphatic affirmative *do* (February 7, September 4, 1660 and May 4 1661) is not present-day usage;
- the *subjunctive*, *be* (January 1, 1660) and *forgive* (August 1, 1661), both fixed formulaic expressions;
- the perfect is formed with the auxiliary *be* when movement is involved: *was returned* (January 1, 1660), *is come* (February 7, 1660), and *was gone* (August 1, 1661; but *had gone* in the same entry);
- simple *die* is employed for what today would be progressive *are dying* (August 12, 1665);
- third person single present tense *hath* and *doth* are maintained (January 1, 1660);
- *heared* for *heard* (July 8, 1660); *begun* for *began* (May 4, 1661)
- no use of the apostrophe in the possessive: *Lincolnes* (November 20, 1660) and *Lords* (May 4, 1661);
- the use of an abbreviated *style* is apparent throughout, for example *To Whitehall to chapel* (July 8, 1660) or *So to bed* (September 4, 1660).

6.2 Early Modern English

6.2.1 Early Modern London

London grew from 50,000 inhabitants in 1500 to become the largest European city in 1700 at just under 600,000. This growth was largely dependent on migration from elsewhere in

England because the presence of endemic and epidemic disease in the city more than counterbalanced natural replacement. Estimates were that only 15% of the sixteenth and seventeenth century population of London were born there (Coleman and Salt 1992, qtd. in Nevalainen and Raumolin-Brunberg 2000: 291). Migration was powered by a rural push which included the enclosures and an urban pull due to high wages in London. It led to a centralization of politics and economics and to upheavals in the provincial economies, including agrarian change and urban crises (ibid.: 292).

6.2.2 *Koinéization*

From the point of view of language the degree of movement from the North was significant. In the span of years from 1485 to 1500 61% of the inflow was from there and 11% from the *Midlands*. However, by the period 1654–74 the share of migrants from the Midlands had increased to 45% (Wareing 1980, qtd. in ibid.: 293). The complex social structure that was supplanting the outdated Medieval model of social relations was "more often loose-knit" than in the countryside (ibid.: 295). This geographic mobility together with the relatively great social mobility of London promoted language change and leveling (ibid.: 297; Shaklee 1980: 48–59). Although the written standard differed from the spoken language of the capital, the two together provided two national models, a highly prescriptive one, *Standard English (StE)*, for writing and a colloquial one, which may be called *General English (GenE)* (cf. Wells 1982: 2ff), which is considerably less rigid. The latter was not the overt, publicly recognized standard, but the *covert norm* (link: Covert and overt norms) of group *solidarity* (link: Power and solidarity). It was GenE which would evolve into a supra-regional, nationwide covert standard. Both it and StE would eventually also be valid for Scotland, then Ireland, and then the English-using world beyond the British Isles (see also 5.3 and 7.2.1).

6.2.3 *Standardization*

Early Modern English underwent a considerable amount of standardizing. This had already begun with the development of written, *Chancery English* from 1430 on (see 5.3). As a result written English lost almost all of its regional features in the years after mid-century. The standardizing tendency was reinforced by the introduction of printing in English starting in 1476 (see 5.4.4). However, in the sense of its recognition and spread, there was no real standard until the sixteenth century, and then the consensus among those whose writing about the language has survived[5] agrees that the standard (esp. in regard to pronunciation) was *Southern* rather than *Northern* or Western and was to be found especially among the well-bred and well-educated in London. This would be the Court, the highest classes, the administration, and learned people, including those at the universities. It rules out speakers of regional *dialects* as well as what were called vulgar, effeminate, or affected speakers. The circle of those using the standard would, consequently, be socially limited and

---

5 This would comprise Hart (1530), Puttenham (1589), Coote (1597), Gil (1619, 1621), Butler (1633), Wallis (1653), Price (1665), Coles (1674), and Cooper (1685) in the sixteenth century – all mentioned in Dobson (1955).

regionally restricted, even though the variety of acceptable forms would most likely be relatively wide (Dobson 1955).

6.2.4 Latin

The pre-eminence of Latin as the language of record and, above all, of scholarship continued for some time (see 6.4.2) despite the efforts of Wycliffe and the Lollards to displace it at least in the domain of religion (see 5.1.3). In the fifteenth century English was not considered to have the fixity of morphological and syntactic form "that was desirable for a language meant to convey scientific and scholarly thought." Furthermore, this century was too much "a period of anarchy and cultural decay" (i.e. the War of the Roses) for English to develop in that direction (Söderlind 1998: 461).

Indeed, Latin experienced a revival in the English Renaissance (early sixteenth to early seventeenth centuries), which brought with it the rediscovery and use of classical (Ciceronian) rather than Medieval Latin for "all registers including various literary uses and forms, and the domains of law, scholarship, and science" (Görlach 1998: 10). Ironically, this highly respected standard was, in a sense, too inimitable to be seriously adopted. Rather, the spread of literacy and literary consciousness and improved economic conditions promoted English in the middle classes, who knew little or no Latin (Söderlind 1998: 462). It was no wonder that printers wanted to publish English-language books, for that was where their market was.

Although patriotic feeling, once directed against French, militated against Latin now, although the Puritans favored English over Latin, and although "some of the more fanatical sort looked upon Latin as the language of the Beast" (ibid.: 462, 467), Latin continued to be used on into the seventeenth century for learned writing, and its influence on vocabulary was extensive (see 6.3.2 and 6.4.2). Yet, little by little "English encroached more and more on this domain, and nobody any longer objected to this development" (ibid.: 462). By the time of the Restoration (1660), Latin was no longer the medium of instruction in the grammar schools nor was it used more than exceptionally in scholarly writing (Görlach 1998: 10).

6.2.5 *Typology*

A typological perspective on the changes which EModE was undergoing necessarily puts stress on the long-term underlying currents which "the language" was subject to. This is a part of the shift from the largely synthetic to an essentially analytic language mentioned in connection with changes in OE and ME, but it goes beyond them. In addition to the extensive replacement of inflection by more rigid *word order* (see 3.2.3, 3.3.2, 4.2.3, 4.3, and 5.3.3), there is a basic shift from the traditional gender system to one based on the feature [±human]. This led to a loss of the old masculine–feminine–neuter distinction and the establishment of a personal–non-personal one, as shows up in the new distinction between *who* and *which* or between *somebody* and *something*. From a purely linguistic perspective it is only possible to confirm these changes and to attribute them to some underlying and somewhat mystic (or mystifying) force of drift (link: Linguistic drift). *Language contact* (including dialect contact) made changes more likely because contact established a set of alternatives (variants) which speakers could choose from either in the process of standardization or as an expression of social class, speaker gender, and so on. The presence of contact does not solve the ultimate conundrum behind change, but it does emphasize human agency, which may be either conscious (change from above) or sub-conscious (change from below). It is powered by ***accommodation*** (or non-accommodation), that is, by identification with a group (solidarity) or with prestige (power) (link: Socio-linguist aspects of change).

In a situation like the one which existed in London in the late Middle Ages and the Early Modern period traditional ties of community solidarity had weakened, and the fluid social structure led to new ways of signaling belonging, which included choices between alternative ways of using the language. As research on linguistic variables has shown, almost any linguistic feature can serve as a ***marker*** of identity. The fact that it is necessary to stress *any* reveals how little we can say about drift. Change can zigzag; it can move in a particular direction, but then undergo a reversal. One particular case was the introduction of *do*-periphrasis in non-emphatic affirmative sentences in the EModE period.[6] This was then extended to other contexts such as negation. And then it was reversed in affirmative sentences (see 6.3.3.1 for discussion and examples).

The fifteenth century saw the following developments which show the effects of interregional influence:

- Northerners introduced the verb inflection {-s} into the language of London which would gradually displace Southern {-th} (see below).
- The North was also the source of relative *the which*, as exemplified in the following quotation from Bunyan's *The Pilgrim's Progress*: *We indeed came both together until we came to the Slough of Despond, into **the which** we also suddenly fell* (1677/78: Second Stage). This variant, which was not used by Bunyan everywhere, did not become part of the standard.
- London itself seems to have been the motor for the diffusion of further innovations such as the generalization of ***nominative you*** for original nominative *ye* in the sixteenth century. Bunyan, linguistically conservative and probably highly influenced by the King James Version of the Bible, used this with moderation, but see the following example: *if that you breed so fast, I'll put **you** by **yourselves*** (Bunyan: Author's Apology).
- *You* also replaced *thou* as a singular form and the two could even be mixed, as in *Keep that light in **your** eye, and go up directly thereto, so shalt **thou** see the gate* (Bunyan: First Stage).

Other innovations which seem to have originated in London under the "accelerating effect" of the Civil War were:

- the new neuter possessive form *its* (cf. Raumolin-Brunberg 1998), illustrated as follows from Bunyan: [the slough] *doth much spew out **its** filth* (First Stage); neuter *his* is no longer used in Bunyan, but he does employ the circumlocution *of it*; cf. *Christian saw the picture* [of] *a very grave person hang up against the wall; and this was the fashion **of it*** (Bunyan: Second Stage);

6 Periphrastic *do* may ultimately be due to Celtic–English language contact in the Southwest of England (Filppula et al. 2008: §2.2.4).

- the prop-word *one*, as in *Piety: Why, did you hear him tell his dream? / Christian: Yes, and a dreadful one it was . . .*) (Bunyan: Third Stage); and
- {-body} compounds, which grew at the expense both of {-man, -one} and of simple pronouns like *none* and *any*, for example, *Christian: What, did your neighbors talk so? / Faithful: Yes, it was for a while in every body's mouth* (Bunyan: Fifth Stage, but a unique example in *Pilgrim's Progress*) and *Is there any hope?* (First Stage).

These innovations spread from London to East Anglia and then to the North (Nevalainen and Raumolin-Brunberg 2000: 324ff).

6.3 Regulation and codification

English did not just replace Latin; it could only do so after it had undergone a development in style and vocabulary. This seems to have been connected with ideas of regulation. Consequently, *prescriptivism* took on greater force, especially after 1660:

> The Restoration period longed for prescription. It is perhaps oversimplifying things to contrast Elizabethan licentiousness and experiment with Restoration longing for regularization. After all, the Elizabethans had been busy regularizing what to them was most urgent, the orthography, and their controversy over loan-words had prepared the way for a consensus of enlightened opinion on this question. For accidence and syntax, they had not cared so much.
>
> (Söderlind 1998: 472)

That was to change as free variation (as with *that* vs. *who*), double negation, double comparison, and *pleonastic do* attracted the criticism of a whole generation of prescriptive grammarians.

6.3.1 Spelling and pronunciation

6.3.1.1 Spelling

What is characteristic about **orthography** in the EModE period is that it underwent a high degree of regulation in the hands of the printers. For modern eyes sixteenth and seventeenth century **spelling** seems strange and irregular at times. On the whole, however, there was a great deal of agreement coupled with a fair amount of toleration of alternative spellings. The **alphabet** no longer used letters unfamiliar to present-day readers of English even though <y> sometimes served as a replacement for earlier <þ> (see Text 6.3, where *ye* stands for both *the* and *thee*). <v> and <u> are usually positional variants of each other. Initial <v> stands not only where ModE has <v> as in *vallies* but also where it has <u> as in *Vranias*; medial <u> appears in both *huntresse* and *loue* (see Text 6.6). The letter <j> is still rare at the beginning of the period; instead <i> is used for both the vowel (*him*) and the consonant (*Iesus*). Furthermore, we often find <y> where ModE has <i>: Text 6.3 has both *hys* and *his*.

In addition, from the mid-seventeenth to the mid-eighteenth centuries capitalization of the most prominent words, especially nouns (cf. modern German) was widely practiced and lingered on, at least in letter-writing, until the end of the eighteenth (Osselton 1998a: 459). For a closer look at seventeenth century spelling see link: Text 6.14 + exercise.

Public spelling was determined by printers, who failed to make the adjustments which would have brought English orthography more closely into line with the traditional values of the letters in the Latin alphabet. Quite the contrary, respect for learning and a recognition of the etymologies of numerous words led to changes which made their spellings more Latin-like, for example *dette* became *debt* (< Latin *debitus*), *amonest* became *admonish* (< *admonire*), *vittles* became *victuals* (< *victualia*) (cf. Blake 1996: 203–204). Not only did the older and the newly introduced spellings often exist side by side, private spelling practices also often contained archaic and idiosyncratic forms which even such luminaries as Dr. Johnson practiced. Although known for "fixing" the standard, Johnson deviated considerably from it in his letter-writing orthography. The spelling used in letter-writing is characterized by the following points (Osselton 1998b: 40ff):

(i)   contractions, for example &, *w^{ch}*, *y^m*, *lic^{ce}*, *punishmt*, *tho*, *thro*, *thot*, etc. (from letters of Addison, first decade of eighteenth century); some went back to medieval manuscripts; but the practice continues today (see 13.3.1.1). Contractions reached their peak in the early eighteenth century;

(ii) phonetic spellings, for example *don't*, *I'll*, *'twill*; possibly as markers of style;

(iii) retention of older spellings, for example *diner* for *dinner* (Johnson); *cutt* (Pope), especially the diversity in the spelling of past tense and past participle forms ending in {-ed}, for example *saved*, *sav'd*, *save'd*, *sav d*; *lackd*, *lackt*, *lack't*.

6.3.1.2 The Great Vowel Shift (GVS)

The GVS, which brought significant change to pronunciation, is a ***chain shift*** involving the long vowels of ME. It is not fully clear just when this shift began though it is generally assumed to have begun in the ME period (Lass 1999: 72–73; Bailey and Maroldt 1977: 31; see 5.2.4). However, the full extent of the shift is best located in the EModE period. This may be assumed on the basis of the mismatch between spelling and pronunciation which came about in the course of the shift. This conclusion depends on the existence of a sound-to-spelling relationship that is largely congruent with the Continental phonetic values of the vowel-letters. English spelling was generally fixed by the early sixteenth century and represents the stage of pronunciation reached at or before that time, but this no longer applied by the end of the EModE period. As Figure 6.1 indicates, the GVS was not a single change involving only one sound, but a whole set of related changes. Furthermore, there are two distinct shifts since the back vowels changed differently in the South and Midlands than in the North and Scotland. Seen systematically, the high vowels /iː/ and /uː/ ***diphthongized***, thus moving toward the center to become [əɪ] and [əʊ] and eventually developing into ModE /aɪ/ and /aʊ/. *Time–time* /tiːmə/ became /təɪm/ and *fūl–foul* /fuːl/ became /fəʊl/. The now unoccupied articulatory space for a high front and back ***monophthong*** would attract the next lower front and back vowels, /eː/ and /oː/, which would then move upward (*teem* and *fool*). The same pull-attraction would be repeated as /ɛː/ and /ɔː/ moved upward to realization as /eː/ and /oː/ (*team* and *foal*). A final member of the chain, low front /aː/, would move to /ɛː/, compare *tame*. A second socially more plausible scenario attributes initiation of the shift to the fact that London English originally had four long front vowels, as in Figure 6.1. The lower classes in London were merging *meat* /ɛː/ and *meet* /eː/ into the higher vowel /eː/. The socially higher standing may then have raised their /eː/ toward /iː/ and their /oː/ toward /uː/, possibly following the model of French, which was also raising these vowels. But in any case the effect was to set themselves off from the lower orders (Fennell 2001: 160–161). In addition, newcomers in London such as the East Anglian cloth-traders migrating to London in the fourteenth and fifteenth centuries had only three long front vowels: they did not distinguish /ɛː/ and /eː/. In their move to accommodate to London speech they would have raised and differentiated their mid-vowel, making London /ɛː/ into /eː/ and London /eː/ into /iː/ (Blake 1996: 210–211).

The GVS was essentially complete in the form indicated in Figure 6.1 by about 1600. However, changes in the resulting vowels and diphthongs have continued into the present and are sketched out in 8.2.5.6, 10.3.3, and 11.3.1. In the North and in Scotland the movement of /oː/ to the front ensured that /uː/ would not be under pressure to diphthongize as was the case further south, hence the familiar Northern and Scottish forms *aboot* and *hoose*. It also helps us to understand why *good* is pronounced in such a variety of ways in Scotland: rounded *geud* /gøːd/ (Angus) and /gyːd/ *guid* (Glasgow), but unrounded /giːd/ *geed* (Black Isle) and *gade* /geːd/ (Fife) (McClure 1980: 30).

6.3.1.3 The short vowel system

The short vowel system remained, in contrast, relatively stable with only relatively small shifts in articulatory space. /i/ is as in *pit*; /e/ ~ /ɛ/ as in *pet*; /a/ ~ /æ/ as in *pat*; /u/ as in *put*; /o/ ~ /ɔ/ ~ /ɒ/ as in *pot* (see Table 6.1).

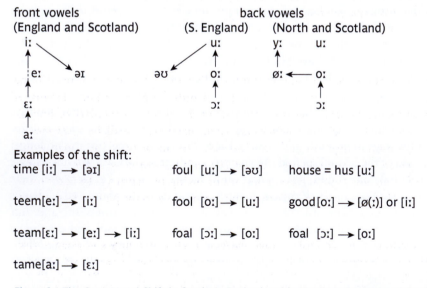

```
front vowels                          back vowels
(England and Scotland)    (S. England)    (North and Scotland)
   iː                          uː          yː      uː

   eː        əɪ         əʊ     oː          øː ←── oː

   ɛː                          ɔː                 ɔː

   aː
```

Examples of the shift:

time [iː] → [əɪ]	foul [uː] → [əʊ]	house = hus [uː]
teem [eː] → [iː]	fool [oː] → [uː]	good [oː] → [ø(ː)] or [iː]
team [ɛː] → [eː] → [iː]	foal [ɔː] → [oː]	foal [ɔː] → [oː]
tame [aː] → [ɛː]		

Figure 6.1 The Great Vowel Shift in Southern England and in Northern England and Scotland (adapted from Wells 1982: 185, 186)

Table 6.1 Short vowel system

	1400		1550		1650	
high	i	u	i	u	i	u
high-mid	e	o				
low-mid			ɛ	ɔ	ɛ	
low	a		a		æ	ɒ

(Lass 2000: 223)

6.3.1.4 Consonants

The consonant inventory of English changed in this period through the establishment of /ŋ/ (*sung*) and /ʒ/ (*vision*) as phonemes. Throughout OE and ME [ŋ] had been an *allophone* of /n/ which assimilated to a velar place of articulation when followed by /k/ (*think*) or /g/ (*thing*). The loss of voiced stops (b, d, g) after a *nasal* was a combinatory (*phonotactic*, see link: Phonotactics) restriction on final /-mb/, /-nd/, and /-ŋg/: *lamb* →/læm/, *land* →/læn/,[7] *rang* →/ræn/. This led in the case of /-ŋg/ to new oppositions which were dependent on /ŋ/ by itself and was now distinct from /n/ as in the *minimal pair* (link: Minimal pair) ModE *sun* vs. *sung*. A further phoneme which was lost or replaced by /f/ was /x/, as in *right* or *tough*.[8] The new *fricative* /ʒ/ was the result of *palatalization* of the combination /z/ + /j/ or /ɪ/ in an unstressed syllable. *Vision* /vizjən/ became /viʒən/ (see 8.2.5.1 and 10.3.3; link: Palatalization). This process was reinforced since it established system symmetry with /ʃ/ (Samuels 1972: 34), giving English four pairs of voiceless–voiced fricatives (f–v, θ–ð, s–z and ʃ–ʒ). Other changes in the acceptable combinations of sounds led to a reduction of the initial clusters /wr-/ (*write*), /gn-/ (*gnash*), and /kn-/ (*know*) to their the second element. The result was pairs of homophones such as *write–rite* – and with the loss of /x/ – *right*; *gnash–Nash*; and *know–no*.

6.3.2 Vocabulary and meaning

Lexical *borrowing* was especially strong in the EModE period. Sources continued to be French and *Dutch*, but most notable were the loan words from the classical languages (6.4.2). Many of the new borrowings were not part of the general vocabulary of English but of specific fields such as science (*commensurable* or *quadrable*), medicine (*paregoric* or *sporadic*), or religion (*quadragesima* or *latitudinarian*). The majority of Latin loan words were, however, general, for example, *immaturity, invitation, parental, relaxation, relevant*, or *susceptible* (cf. Rissanen 1998 for examples of borrowing by century). In addition to borrowing, the vocabulary continued to expand by means of word formation. In the latter

---

7 Loss of /d/ is incomplete. /d/ is articulated in careful pronunciations, but frequently lost in allegro (= rapid) delivery. Speakers of some dialects, for example Scots or African American English, regularly lose this /d/.

8 Some regional dialects, especially those of Lowlands Scots have retained /x/. In 1.2.1 it was indicated that /h/ and /x/ may actually be regarded as distributional allophones of each other: /h/ occurs exclusively before a vowel (in OE also before a sonorant /n, r, l, w/). /x/ occurred before a consonant (*right*) or in final position (*though*).

half of the sixteenth and early seventeenth centuries there was a backlash against the large number of borrowings, pejoratively termed "*inkhorn terms*" (link: Inkhorn terms) and often regarded as obscure, affected, or pompous. In the case of the purists resistance took the form of a more or less strong move to use words with Germanic roots in the place of words of classical origin (cf. Barber 1976: chap. 4; see 6.4.2 for examples).

Many people considered such words to be pretentious and/or obscure, and present-day users of English will agree in the cases in which the words objected to have not come into common use, for example *obtestate* "to call upon as a witness" or *expend* "to weigh mentally, to ponder." However, such now common words as *native, fertile,* or *verbosity* were also once the subject of ridicule. Opposition to "unnecessary" foreign borrowings and to what are

often called "*hard words*" (link: Hard words) continues into our own times.

Changes in meaning took place in a variety of ways. For one, the number of members in a semantic field might change thus causing a shift in the meaning of the individual members of the field. For example, a term such as the military rank *ensign* meant one thing in the sixteenth century when it was number five in an eight-rank system – embedded between *common/private soldier, corporal, sergeant* below it and *lieutenant, captain, colonel/coronel,* and *general* above. In the nineteenth century, however, it was number eleven in a system of sixteen ranks (ibid.: 143ff). Besides change in semantic field relations, the meaning of any given word may undergo broadening or narrowing. The word *secure,* for example, has lost one of its earlier meanings, namely "carefree, overconfident," thus making the Ghost's speech in *Hamlet* I:5 difficult for a present-day reader to understand: In the passage "*Sleeping within mine Orchard, / My custome alwayes in the afternoone; / Vpon my secure hower thy Vncle stole / With iuyce of cursed Hebenon* [a not further identified poison] *in a Violl,*" the hour was carefree rather than safe (ibid.: 148). Change may also involve amelioration, the taking on of a more positive meaning, or pejoration, a more negative one. Among his many examples, Barber, whose treatment is well worth reading, gives *enthusiasm,* now quite positive, but once a negative designation for religious zealotry and *ringleader,* now negative, but simply neutral "leader, head" in EModE (ibid.: 153).

6.3.3 Grammar and morphology

The EModE period saw a number of important general developments in the area of grammar, a few of which will be reviewed in this section.

6.3.3.1 The verb

Inflections weakened inasmuch as there was continued loss of *strong verbs* which developed into weak ones, some of which were in the long run not accepted as standard, for example, *catched* or *teached*. In other cases a strong and a weak form coexisted and still do: *swoll/swelled* or *dove/dived*. There was sometimes a great deal of uncertainty about the past tense form as with *write,* which could be *wrote, wrate,* or *writ*.

Third person {-s} vs. {-(e)th} is a further inflectional point. This distinction is one of the most noticeable in this period, and it may be used as evidence of the influence of *Northern* on *Southern English*. In ME Northerners used the ending {-s} where Southerners

used {-(e)th}. In each case the respective inflection could be used in both the third person singular present tense as well as in the whole of the plural (link: Plural {-s} and {-(e)th} in EModE).[9] While zero became normal in the plural, in the third person singular present tense there was no such move, and the two forms were in competition with each other both in colloquial London speech and in the written language. In the early sixteenth century {-s} was probably the informal variant while {-(e)th} was neutral or formal; it was, for example, favored by the Chancery and by printers at the beginning of the sixteenth century (Nevalainen and Raumolin-Brunberg 2000: 311). The KJV of the Bible (1611) regularly uses {-th}, and {-th} lingered on into the seventeenth century, especially for "lofty" and "stately" prose (Bambas 1998: 68) as in Bunyan's *The Pilgrim's Progress* in the 1670s:

Text 6.2 Bunyan, *The Pilgrim's Progress*: First Stage (1677/78)

The man that met thee is one Worldly Wiseman, and rightly is he so called; partly because he savoreth only the doctrine of this world . . . (therefore he always goes to the town of Morality to church) and partly because he loveth that doctrine best, for it saveth him best from the cross, . . .

By end of the sixteenth century (1580–99) {-s} was at a level of about 45% in London, a level reached in East Anglia only in the period 1620–39 (Nevalainen and Raumolin-Brunberg 2000: 311). The ratio was about one {-th} to every two instances of {-s} in selected prose by Queen Elizabeth I, though not for the verbs *have* and *do*, where *hath* (90%) and *doth* (100%) continued to dominate (Lass 1999: 163). In any case there was a great deal of variation from one writer to another or even between works by the same author: Lily's *Euphues* (1579–81) has 3% {-s}; his *Woman of the Moone* (1584) has 85% {-s}. Sydney's *Apology for Poetrie* (1595): 14%, Queen Elizabeth I's letters: 75% (data from Franz 1939 qtd in Bambas 1998: 65). Yet even where *-th* continued to be written it was less and less certain by the mid-seventeenth century whether the pronunciation was /θ/ or /s-z/.

Do-*periphrasis* is the most dramatic development in the grammar of EModE. As stated in 5.3.2.1 the structure could be found in ME. In EModE, however, it took on a new trajectory. The causative use of *do* disappeared and instead we find *do* as an auxiliary in affirmative and negative declarative and interrogatory sentences. The frequency of verbs with auxiliary *do* as a percentage of all verbs which *do* could appear with is less than 10% throughout the fifteenth century. In the sixteenth century there is a dramatic increase and by around 1700 the situation we know from present-day English had been reached. In affirmative statements *do* is now reserved for emphatic use (cf. Ellegård 1953), even though the upper class retained negation and interrogation without *do*-periphrasis in formal speech longer than was the case in colloquial language (cf. Tieken-Boon van Ostade 1998). Furthermore, a number of verbs, for example *know* and *doubt*, were slower in adapting to *do*-periphrasis. Table 6.2 shows approximate frequencies for affirmative declaratives (*that*

---

9 The ME Midlands plural ending was originally {-en}, which underwent first /n/-deletion when unstressed; this left {-e}, pronounced /ə/, which was regularly deleted leaving zero.

Table 6.2 Frequency of *do*-periphrasis in a restricted corpus (approximate percentages)

period	affirmative statement	negative statement	affirmative question	negative question
1400–1425	0%	0%	0%	12%
1425–1475	0.5%	2%	5%	8%
1475–1500	2%	5%	7%	12%
1500–1525	2%	8%	23%	59%
1525–1535	3%	11%	35%	60%
1535–1550	8%	28%	43%	75%
1550–1575	10%	38%	56%	85%
1575–1600	7%	24%	40%	65%
1600–1625	4%	37%	68%	94%
1625–1650	3%	32%	83%	84%
1650–1700	2%	45%	79%	92%

(after Ellegård 1953: 162)

slough is the beginning of the sorrows that **do** *attend those that go on in that way*, Bunyan: First Stage), negative declaratives (*Truly, said Christian, I do not know*, ibid.) and interrogatory sentences (*Do you see yonder wicket-gate?* ibid.).

The big question is why this developed. In the case of negation the adoption of *do* was a way of preserving the negative-first principle. The *ne* negator as in *In al this world* **ne** *was ther noon* (*ne + an*) *him lyk* (Chaucer "Prologue" [Doctour of Phisyk]) was also commonly reinforced by following emphatic *not* (< *nawiht*) as in *But he* **ne** *lefte* **nat** (Chaucer "Prologue" [Persoun]). This double negative shows that the current StE stricture against ***multiple negation*** did not always count. It was only in the EModE period that its occurrence began to decline, at least in the standard language. When weakly stressed *ne* was dropped, this left the negator after the verb it negated, for example *I go not*. With the introduction of *do, not* could follow it and still precede the lexical verb, for example *I do not go*, thus preserving the negative-first principle (cf. Mazzon 1994). In the case of affirmative statements a variety of reasons for periphrastic *do* have been advanced, such as to distinguish verbs with identical present and past tense forms, for example *cast, put, set* as in *I do/did set . . .*; to avoid ***consonant clusters*** in the second person singular forms (e.g. *jumpedest, illuminateth*); or to add emphasis or a tone of seriousness to a statement (*I do solemnly swear . . .*). Expansion of the form was rapid in this period when the morpho-phonology of the verb was changing drastically, but it was retained in the long run only where it was functional, namely in questions, negations, and emphatic affirmation (ibid.: 217).

The periphrastic expression of aspect, voice, and tense

The ***progressive*** was used much more frequently in EModE than it had been previously, but by no means as widely as in present-day English. Where Bunyan writes *why standest thou still?* ModE usage would have *why are you standing still?* The passive was now formed with *have* (and *get*) as in *If they had any parte of their liberties withdrawne* (OED: *have* 18 (1568) q.v.). This was helpful in making an indirect object (*they*) the subject of the passive construction. The ***perfect*** is still commonly formed with either *have* or *be*, the latter with intransitive verbs, especially ones of movement, and verbs of change of state (see examples in Text 6.1). The shift to *have* may have helped distinguish between perfects and passives, for example, the ambiguous *it was grown*.

The subjunctive and the modal verbs

The system of modal verbs was undergoing changes in this period, which are still in progress (see 8.2.3.1). The motivation for the new meanings and functions lay, as already mentioned (4.2.3.1), in the loss of the distinctive endings, in this case, subjunctive inflections. Consequently, the subjunctive continued to be used where distinctive forms survived, namely as present tense *be* and past tense *were* (all persons) and in the second and third persons singular present tense with no ending, for example *Blessed be God* (Text 6.1 [January 1]) or *Mr. Worldly Wiseman: I would advise thee, then, that thou with all speed **get** thyself rid of thy burden,* Bunyan: First Stage). At least some of the distinction between indicative and subjunctive, namely the expression of the hypothetical, was taken over by the modals. This is, of course, also a part of the general move toward periphrastic (analytic) constructions. The older, presumably more or less original meanings of modals were obligation (*must, shall*), volition (*will*), and ability, knowledge, power (*can*) ([link: Deontic and dynamic modality](#)). With the change in paradigm the past tense forms *should, would,* and *could,* as indications of tentativeness, were increasingly used where once the subjunctive had expressed possibility or probability ([link: Epistemic modality](#)). At the same time the system of ***semi-modals*** such as *have to, want to, be going to,* and *be able to,* which have past tenses, infinitive and participle forms, were further elaborated and took over many of the original meanings of the modals ([link: The semi-modals](#)). *Must,* an originally past tense form whose present tense form *mot* was lost in the sixteenth century, did not participate in this move to tentativeness. *May* can now be used in wishes instead of the subjunctive as in *"A god rewarde you," quoth this roge; "and in heauen may you finde it"* (Harman qtd. in Rissanen 1999: 229), where *rewarde* is subjunctive, but *may you finde it* is modal.

This section focuses, in closing, on the use of the modals *shall* and *will* to express the future and on the principal semi-modal of the future, *be going to.* The two modals developed into true auxiliaries only in the EModE period. Before this they retained a great deal of the original meanings: for *shall* this was obligation (and *should* often still expresses this) and for *will* it was volition. The shift of *shall* from **modality** to future marker may be partly the result of Wycliffe's use of *shall* to translate the Latin future tense. With *will* the predictive meaning seems to have developed more naturally as a kind of outgrowth of volition: "What I want (= volition) is what will be (= prediction)." The former was associated with the written, the latter, with the spoken language (cf. Rissanen 1999: 211).

Assuming all of this, the pattern of use of *shall* and *will* in EModE still needs some comment: why was it that by the early seventeenth century *shall* was so strongly associated with the first person and *will* with the second and third persons in statements? The original volitional meaning of *will* would have hindered its use in the second and third persons because it is unusual to attribute volition to others; this would have promoted the predictive function of *will.* For the first-person speaker the opposite is the case: people do not impose an obligation on themselves; rather, they express an intention. The reverse is the use of first person *will* for a promise or threat and second and third person *shall* for a command or threat (ibid.). Corpus studies have, however, not completely substantiated this explanation (ibid.: 212), for which reason it is often – especially for speakers who do not come from southern England – viewed as a somewhat arbitrary prescriptive rule.

In this period a further means of expressing the future began to develop: *be going to*. The earliest generally recognized example is *Therfore while thys onhappy sowle by the vytoryse pompys of her enmyes was goyng to be broughte into helle for the synne and onleful lustys of her body* from 1482 (*The Revelation to the Monk of Evesham*: 43). Since the main verb *broughte* expresses movement, the idea of movement is less prominent in *goyng*. Instead the notion of purpose, and therefore futurity, is promoted (Danchev and Kytö 1998: 148). This is a natural step in the process of **grammaticalization**: a central meaning (here: movement) becomes less prominent and an associated meaning (here: intention, futurity) becomes salient. Although this example is very early and may not be a true case of grammaticalized *be going to*, the construction seems to have become part of the grammar by the mid-seventeenth century (ibid.: 158). As intuitive as the process of meaning transfer by association ([link: Abduction](#)) is, the question still remains as to why grammaticalization of *be going to* took place at this point in the history of English and not earlier or later. One plausible but unproven explanation might be the existence of a similar future construction in French (*aller de faire quelque chose*) which would have been **calqued** (translated word for word) onto English. Not only was French widely known and spoken, it was also widely translated into English in the Late ME and EModE periods. This could have supplied the necessary impetus for its adoption and further development in English (ibid.: 157). By the second half of the seventeenth century the main verbs *go* and *come* were being used in this construction, which is an indication that the original meaning of *go* had bleached out and been generalized to the new meaning of intention and futurity.

6.3.3.2 The nominal phrase

Nouns underwent relatively little change as we move from ME to EModE aside from the tendency to introduce the {-s} plural for nouns with a previously unmarked (zero) plural. The <f>–<v> alternation as with *wife–wives* was also generally accepted. The genitive singular continued to be used sometimes with and sometimes without an apostrophe. In the sixteenth century the genitive {-s} as in *Gods blessing* and the *of*-genitive as in *the blessing of God* are supplemented by the construction *God his blessing*. The latter was a misinterpretation of the genitive ending as unstressed *his* (= *'is*) and was occasionally extended to *her*, giving us *Venus her shell* for *Venus' shell* (Blake 1996: 218). In the personal pronoun system *his*, which had been both masculine and neuter in reference, was restricted to the masculine; and neuter possession was expressed by *of it*, *thereof*, or the new pronoun *its*, which was formed in analogy to the genitive {-s} (cf. Nevalainen and Raumolin-Brunberg 1998). In Bunyan's work, which makes no further use of neuter *his*, we find expressions such as *upon the top **thereof**; . . . the wall; and this was the fashion **of it***; and *Every tub must stand on **its** own bottom* (all from Second Stage).

The **demonstrative** system had a three-way contrast between *this/these* (near the speaker), *that/those* (near the hearer), and *yon(der)* distant from both. The distinction was not always carefully maintained, and the third member began to fade except in regional dialects. It is known, of course, to readers of Shakespeare, who are familiar with such lines as *But soft! what light through yonder window breaks* (*Romeo and Juliet* II.2) or *Yon(d) Cassius has a lean and hungry look* (*Julius Caesar* I.2).

The attribution of *who* to animate human antecedents and *which* to all others was beginning to be the rule, but again phrases such as the following from the Lord's Prayer are widely familiar: *Our Father **which** art in Heaven*.[10] The slowness of this change is credited to the fact that *who(m)* was first accepted in less prominent positions as object and only later in focal position as subject.

Adjective comparison shows a strong move toward the analytic form with *more* and *most*, a tendency which continues today. Forms such as *learneder* were replaced by *more learned*. Double comparatives and superlatives could still be found frequently, as in *Julius Caesar*, where Antony says of Brutus, who was one of Caesar's assassins: *This was the most unkindest cut of all* (III.2). They would be growing less common with time.

6.3.3.3 The sentence (word order)

Subject–verb is the dominant pattern of word order in affirmative declaratives in EModE. Other patterns still occur, but they are relatively rare, as in *Then was Christian glad and lightsome, . . .* (Bunyan: Third Stage). It seems that an initial **adverb**, as in this case, is the most likely element to trigger verb–subject inversion. In interrogatives without *do*-periphrasis there is, of course, also verb–subject order, for example *. . . why standest thou still ?* (Bunyan: First Stage).

6.3.4 Pragmatics: second person address, titles

The preceding example is only one of many in this chapter which show the retention of second person singular *thou/thee*. The two (nominative/accusative) forms of address, *thou/thee* and *ye/you*, had long coexisted (cf. 5.3.1, *The Canterbury Tales*), but by about 1600 *thou* was becoming a somewhat exceptional form. Bruti sees the choice between the two as guided by two criteria: (1) social distance and (2) emotional attitude (see Figure 6.2); for an illustration see link: Shakespearean texts.

By the end of the EModE period *you* was the dominant second person pronoun, singular and plural. Some of the dialects of Britain retained reflexes of *thou*, but they seem to be

Social distance		
inferiors	equals	superiors
Thou ◄────────────	You/Thou ────────────	► You

Emotional attitude		
anger/contempt	indifference/neutrality	familiarity/intimacy
Thou ────────────────	You ────────────	► Thou

Figure 6.2 Criteria for the choice between *thou* and *you*
(Bruti 2000: 35)

---

10 Note the continuation with its subjunctive forms: *. . . hallowed **be** [subjunctive] thy Name. Thy Kingdom come [subjunctive]. Thy will **be** done in earth as it is in heaven.*

generally recessive. The choice of the Quakers to address everyone in the singular with the *thou*-form was basically a way of making a political statement. It was, in Barber's words "a subversive gesture, a refusal to recognize the authority of secular jurisdiction" (1976: 211).

As the discussion of *thou* vs. *you* shows, in the Elizabethan period people constantly placed others in the social hierarchy. There was a hierarchy in which the nobility was addressed as *Lord* or *Lady*; the gentility as *Sir* or *Dame* with an alternative of *Mr.* and *Mrs.* for the professions; yeomen and their wives as *Goodman* or *Goodwife*; while craftsmen and laborers were not accorded any title (Nevalainen 1994: 318). "Thus, titles, occupational terms like *parson* or *cook*, generic terms like *man, woman,* and *gentleman,* even terms of relationship like *husband* and *wife* (used freely between spouses on good terms) were frequently used in direct address; and if one of these was not appropriate or available, a vague word like *neighbour* was even used," and condescension was expressed by using *fellow* (Leith 1983: 82–83).

6.4 Religious and scientific prose and belles lettres

EModE varied enormously according to field, formality, text type, and written vs. spoken use, though the last is difficult to ascertain with any certainty (link: **Register**). And of course the regional origins and educational background of the user were also significant. A look at the two areas of religious and scientific writing as well as at several examples of imaginative literature can help to provide a wider view of variation within the standard written language (see 6.5 on regional differences).

6.4.1 Religious writing: translations of the Bible

The major text in the sphere of religion, and in this period a very contentious subject, was the Bible in English. The introduction of a ***vernacular*** translation had been a major goal of reformers such as the Lollards; and Wycliffe's translation was a milestone in this process (see 5.1.3 and 5.2). Nevertheless, both Church and State insisted on Latin. In the early sixteenth century, however, Continental developments, specifically the Lutheran Reformation in Germany, could no longer be ignored, and both Lutheran ways of thinking and the subversive writing associated with the Reformation were finding a sizable following in England. Exposure to Luther's German translation of the Bible inspired William Tyndale to do the same for English. Since the Church did not adopt his position, he moved to the Continent, where he successfully completed a translation of the New Testament in 1524 and saw it published in Worms, Germany in 1526. He personally never finished this project before being captured and executed (in Belgium) in 1536 on orders from Henry VIII. Yet his translation was smuggled into England and read there.

Tyndale's work was different from previous translations because it was based on the Greek and Hebrew texts and not their Latin translation. Furthermore, its eventual dissemination was much wider because of printing. Most of all, it was extremely influential for all the important translations to follow (link: **English translations of the Bible**). We can see this by looking at Tyndale's translation of Matthew 1: 18ff and comparing it line by line with the King James (or Authorized) Version of 1611. The two differ very little, chiefly in the choice of vocabulary, for example *betrouthed/espoused* (in verse 18) and *perfect/just, loth/not willing, secretely/privily* (in 19). Note the use of <y> in the Tyndale version as a replacement for ME <þ>: *ye* in 18 and the first two times in 20 is "the"; but it is "thee" the second two times in 20 since the two spellings (<the> and <thee>) are not differentiated here. Interestingly, Tyndale's use of *ye* ("thee") in 20 (*Ioseph ye sonne of David feare not*) is a case of an accusative replacing the nominative in much the same manner as *you* (accusative) was also replacing *ye* in the second person plural ([link: Nominative *you*]). The KJV reverses this and "correctly" uses *thou* in 20.

Text 6.3 Matthew 1: 18–21 as translated by Tyndale (1526) (in italics) and in the KJV (1611)

18   *The byrthe of Iesus Christ was on thys wyse.*   *When hys mother Mary was betrouthed to Ioseph*
    Now the birth of Jesus Christ was on this wise: When as his mother Mary was espoused to Joseph

    before they came to dwell to gedder she was fou[n]*de with chylde by ye holy goost.*
    before they came together,   she was found with child of the Holy Ghost.

19   *The*[n] *Ioseph her husbande beinge a perfect ma*[n] *and loth to make an ensample of hir*
    Then Joseph her husband, being a just man,   and not willing to make her a publick example,

    was mynded to put her awaye secretely.
    was minded to put her away privily.

20   *Whill he thus thought behold ye angell of ye Lorde appered vnto him in a dreame saynge:*
    But while he thought on these things, behold, the angel of the Lord appeared unto him in a dream, saying,

    Ioseph ye sonne of David feare not to take vnto ye   *Mary thy wyfe. For that which is coceaved in her*
    Joseph, thou son of David, fear not to take unto thee Mary thy wife: for that which is conceived in her

    is of the holy goost.
    is of the Holy Ghost.

21   *She shall brynge forthe a sonne and thou shalt call his name Iesus. For he shall save his peple from*
    And she shall bring forth a son, and thou shalt call his name JESUS: for he shall save his people from

    their synnes.
    their sins.

(Tyndale, www.studylight.org)

Even before Tyndale was executed, Henry VIII initiated, in 1534, the Anglican Reformation, the separation of the Church of England from the Roman Catholic Church, and saw it completed by an act of Parliament in 1536. In 1549 Thomas Cranmer's *Book of Common Prayer*, a centerpiece of Anglicanism, was completed in a first version and revised in 1552. A new version came out a hundred years later in the Restoration in 1662. A look at the liturgical prose of 1552 in comparison with 1662 shows that religious writing of this kind – here dictated consciously from above – remained linguistically conservative in regard to a number of grammatical points while moving with the times in other points. Note, however, that the results are dependent on the type of text. When biblical passages are quoted, then in 1552 we find the usage of the Great Bible (1539) or in 1662 that of the conservative KJV (1611). Elsewhere in the *Book of Common Prayer* we find the results listed in Table 6.3, which are not absolute, but represent general tendencies.

Learned as opposed to natural change is conscious change from above. Natural change, as less conscious, appears in less prominent contexts (Nevalainen 1998: 166). It would seem that the use of {-th} and the case and number distinctions in the second person personal pronouns were points high in people's awareness and were consciously imposed from above while the switch from *which* to *who* generally came from below the level of awareness and entered at less intrusive places in the sentence (see ibid. for discussion). In the case of the replacement of Southern *be* (*they be*) by Northern *are* (*they are*) the change reflected the almost complete replacement of *be* with *are* which had meanwhile taken placed in all but the most isolated places in the South(west). Furthermore, the two shifts (to *are* and to *who*) are stronger in passages intended for oral presentation while *be* and *which* tend to occur is passages meant for silent reading (ibid.: 184ff).

6.4.2 Scientific writing

The trend at the middle of the sixteenth century was against free borrowing of new words from foreign languages (as we see in the work of Cheke, Ascham, Wilson, etc.). Within the area of science some scholars such as Ralph Lever (*The Arte of Reason, rightly termed, Witcraft*, 1573) suggested not only such English-based words as *witcraft*, but also *forespeach* "preface or foreword," or *backset* "a thing that must be set after," namely a predicate, *saywhat* "definition," *yeasay* "affirmation," and *endsay* "conclusion" (Lever, ibid.: sigs. *5^v–*7^r). But science did not go his way. Science writers did not use Latin merely to lend their prose elegance, but to achieve a style both simple and clear. Yet unlike the biblical translators, who had the same aim, there was seldom a native equivalent. Consequently,

Table 6.3 Comparative grammatical features in the *Book of Common Prayer* 1552 and 1662

feature	1552	1662
3rd person singular ending	mixed {-th} and {-s}	reversion to {-th}
2nd person singular personal pronoun	*thou/thee* but some *ye/you*	largely a return to *thou/thee*
nominative *ye/you*	both *ye* and *you*	largely a return to *ye*
nominative *which/who* with human reference	56 *who* vs. 129 *which*	172 *who* vs. 13 *which*
present tense plural *be/are*	52 *are* vs. 105 *be*	125 *are* vs. 32 *be*

(Nevalainen 1998)

they turned regularly to Latin and Greek neologisms, which they usually anglicized in form. This allowed scholars to write in English, yet not to give up completely the internationally familiar terms (Johnson 1998: 262–263).

In popular science writing the authors had to make the Latinized vocabulary clear. One solution was to offer a gloss, as in the following examples from Bartholomew Traheron's *The most excellent worckes of Chirurgery made and set forth by maister John Vigon*, 1543:

"Paroxismos is the access, invasion, and firstcoming of a fever. It is derived of paroxino which in Greek signifieth to sharpen, to stir up, etc."

"Undimina is a barbarous term, in Greek it is called oedema, in Latin tumor. for it is soft swelling without pain."

(qtd. in Johnson 1998: 268)

A second way was to couple a new term with an old, approximately synonymous word, as we can see in Reginald Pecock: *appetites or lusts*; *accidents or fallings*; *nextness or immediation* (Johnson 1998: 268; see 5.3.4.2).

Two texts from the sixteenth century, both dealing with astronomy, show the significant paradigmatic change in science writing which took place after 1530. The period before this date, represented here by Text 6.4a, Robert Copland's translation of *Le Compost et Kalendrier des bergiers*, in English *Kalender of Shepardes* (1508), is typical of the scientific prose of the earlier period. It is characterized by the writer's lack of scientific competence. After 1530, and especially as in Recorde in Text 6.4b, the quality of scientific prose is much improved though not modern.

Text 6.4a Robert Copland, *Kalender of Shepardes* (1508)

Some moving been ["are"] of the skies and planets that excedeth the understanding of Shepherds, as the moving of the firmament: in the which been the stars against the first mobile in an hundred year one degree, and the moving of the planets in their epicycles, of the which how well the Shepherds be not ignorant of all, yet they make no mention here, for it sufficeth them only of two. Whereof the one is from orient into the occident above the earth, and from occident in the orient under it, that is called the diurnal moving, that is to say that it maketh from day to day xxiiii. hours, by the which moving the .ix. sky that is the first mobile draweth after, and maketh the other skies to turn that been under it.

(Copland, from 1518 edition, sigs. I7^r–I7^v; expanded contractions and modernized spelling, qtd. in Johnson 1998: 258)

> ### Text 6.4b Robert Recorde, *The Castle of Knowledge* (1556)
>
> *At the first beginning of the world, when this art was unknown, men marked the rising of the Sun and the Moon, and other notable stars, as the Brood-hen, which is called of many men the Seven stars, and other like: and perceiving them to rise always about the East, and so to ascend by little and little to the South, from whence they did descend again softly to the West, where they did continually set: and the next day again they perceived them to begin their accustomed course, and so continued like as before: wherein although they saw some diversity, yet they perceived that diversity to be uniform, and after a year to return to the old state again. By this occasion they began to imagine that this matter of moving could not be but in a round and circular form, and also in a round and circular body.*
>
> (Recorde, London 1556: 101, qtd. in Johnson 1998: 258–259)

In the following years modern science continued to develop, one of the consequences of which was the founding of the Royal Society in 1660/62. Its earliest members, including John Wilkins, Robert Hooke, Christopher Wren, John Evelyn, and Robert Boyle, promoted all branches of knowledge. The Society indicated an interest in English in naming a committee of twenty-two including Dryden and Evelyn to make suggestions for the improvement of the language. While an academy was not ever founded, Evelyn (1620–1706) formulated an impressive program, comprising "a dictionary, a grammar, a spelling reform, lists of technical terms and dialect words, translations of ancient and modern writers, and works to be published by members themselves to serve as models for good writing" (Söderlind 1998: 473). Early on, the Royal Society endorsed short, factual writing without prefaces, apologies, or rhetorical flourishes for its reports. By the end of the seventeenth century this style had become increasingly common (ibid.: 468). Despite the move to English some writing would continue to appear in Latin, for example in the work of Isaac Newton (1642–1727), president of the Royal Society from 1703 till his death. His *Principia* (1687) was written in Latin, but *Opticks* (1704) was in English (Latin translation in 1706). Text 6.5, describing experiment no. 8, is taken from this book.

> ### Text 6.5 Isaac Newton, *Opticks* (1704)
>
> *Exper. 8 . . . The Book and Lens being made fast, I noted the Place where the Paper was, when the Letters of the Book, illuminated by the fullest red Light of the solar Image falling upon it, did cast their Species* ["image"] *on that Paper most distinctly: and then I stay'd till the Motion of the Sun, and consequent Motion of his Image on the book,*

all the Colours from that red to the middle of the blue pass'd over those Letters; and 5
when those Letters were illuminated by that blue, I noted again the place of the
Paper when they cast their Species most distinctly upon it: and I found that this last
place of the Paper was nearer to the Lens than its former place by about two Inches
and an half, or two and three quarters. So much sooner therefore did the Light
in the violet end of the Image by a greater Refraction converge and meet, than the 10
Light in the red end. But in trying this the Chamber was as dark as I could make it.
For if these Colours be diluted and weakened by the Mixture of any adventitious
Light, the distance between the Places of the Paper will not be so great. . . . And
were the Colours still more full, I question not but that the distance would be
considerably greater. 15

(D. Burnley (ed.) (1992) *The History of the English Language. A Source Book*. London:
Longman, 270)

Although the text is immediately understandable, several points deserve comment. One of
them is the use of sentence-internal capitalization, especially for nouns (in blue in l. 1). This
practice increased throughout the seventeenth century and reached a high point about the
time Newton's text was written, but in the eighteenth century it receded once again. The
use of periphrastic *do* is still not congruent with present-day practice. In the third line we
find *do* in a non-emphatic affirmative sentence, but in line 13 we find a negation without
do. In l. 4 *sun* is referred to with the possessive *his* (long maintained for reference to the sun
in literature), but *paper* is referred to by the new possessive *its* (l. 8). The auxiliary–subject
inversion in l. 9 would still be observed in ModE, as would the somewhat old-fashioned *if-*
less inversion in the conditional clause in l. 14. Subjunctive *be* in the conditional clause in
l. 12 has meanwhile dropped out of use.

6.4.3 EModE literature

It is tempting to offer samples of all the great writers of the EModE period, but this is
obviously not feasible. The website which accompanies this book, however, makes a number
of samples – often with suggested exercises – available. Assuming that Shakespeare (Plate
6.1) is the most familiar writer from this period, no lengthy texts by him are included here,
nor is anything about Elizabethan theater ([link: Elizabethan theater]). Instead there are
excerpts from Sidney, Milton, and Congreve. Language examples from Bunyan (Plate 6.2)
and Shakespeare have been used at various points in the chapter.

Sir Philip Sidney (1554–86) is best remembered for his *Arcadia*, a romance little read
today which he wrote for his sister Mary while living with her while he was in disfavor at
the Court. Despite the lines quoted here, *Arcadia* is a prose composition. It is extravagant
in style and touches on countless subjects in a fanciful way. It is quoted here as an interesting
example of polished sixteenth century English.

COMPANION @ WEBSITE

Text 6.6 Sir Philip Sidney, *Arcadia* (1580s; published 1590)

But Basilius *to entermixe with these light notes of libertie,*
some sadder tune, set to the key of his own passion, not seeing
there Strephon *or* Klaius, *(who called thence by* Vranias *letter,*
were both gone to continue their suite, like two true runners,
both employing their best speed, but not one hindring the
other) he called to one Lamō *of their acquaintance, and willed*
him to sing some one of their songs; which he redily performed
in this doble Sestine.

    <en-> for <in->; final <–ie>

    initial <v> for ModE <u>
    auxiliary *be* with verbs of
5   motion
    (ō) for <o> followed by <n>

Strephon. *You Gote-heard Gods, that loue the grassie mountaines,*
        You Nimphes that haunt the springs in pleasant vallies,
        You Satyrs ioyde with free and quiet forrests,
        Vouchsafe your silent eares to playning musique,
        Which to my woes giues still an early morning:
        And drawes the dolor on till wery euening.

    medial <u> for ModE <v>
10 initial <v> for ModE <v>;
    <i> for <j>
    free variation of <i> and <y>,
    cf. l. 19; usual 3rd person
    {-s}, cf. ll. 18, 20

Klaius. *O* Mercurie, *foregoer to the euening,*
     O heauenlie huntresse of the sauage mountaines,
     O louelie starre, entitled of the morning,
     While that my voice doth fill these wofull vallies,
     Vouchsafe your silent eares to plaining musique,
     Which oft hath Echo *tir'd in secrete forrests.*

15 "precursor"
    medial <u> for ModE <u>
    mercury is the morning star
    subordinate conjunction + *that*;
    simple (*doth fill*) for progressive
20 3rd person {-th} retained with
    do and *have*, cf. ll. 18, 20

. . .

Strephon. *Me seemes I see the high and stately mountaines,*
        Transforme themselues to lowe deiected vallies:
        Me seemes I heare in these ill-changed forrests,
        The Nightengales doo learne of Owles their musique:
        Me seemes I feele the comfort of the morning
        Turnde to the mortall serene of an euening.

    dative subject "It seems to me"

    non-emphatic affirmative *do*,
25 cf. 18, 31, 33, 34

. . .

Strephon. *These mountaines witnesse shall, so shall these vallies,*

    future *shall*

Klaius. *These forrests eke, made wretched by our musique,*
     Our morning hymne is this, and song at euening.

    "also"

. . .

Zelmane. *If mine eyes can speake to doo harty errande,*
       Or mine eyes language she doo hap to iudge of,
       So that eyes message be of her receaued,

30 *mine* + following vowel cf. *my*
    + consonant, cf. ll. 13, 18
    no possessive apostrophe;
    subjunctive *be*; cf. l. 35

> *Hope we do liue yet.*
>
> . . .
>
> | | |
> |---|---|
> | *Yet dying, and dead, doo we sing her honour;* | subject–verb inversion after an |
> | *So become our tombes monuments of her praise;*   35 | initial adverb |
> | *So becomes our losse the triumph of her gayne;* | |
> | *Hers be the glory.* | subjunctive *be* for a wish |

(A.E. Farnham (ed.) (1969) *A Sourcebook in the History of English*. New York: Holt, Rinehart and Winston, 107–109)

John Milton (1608–74), one of England's greatest poets, was a free thinker in terms of liberty of conscience and a man of great tolerance. He was associated with the dissenters and was a supporter of the Parliamentary party during the Civil War and the Commonwealth. Yet he did not hesitate to criticize the lack of tolerance and of openness of the Parliamentarians (link: Excerpts from *Areopagitica*) (Plate 6.3). Milton is best known as the author of *Paradise Lost* (1667), an epic poem recounting the divine history of the world on two levels, that of the celestial conflict between God and Lucifer and that of the domestic world of mankind, Adam and Eve. The following lines about Lucifer's rebellion against God come from the Prologue.

Text 6.7 Milton, *Paradise Lost* (1667)

Who first seduc'd them to that fowl revolt?
Th' infernal Serpent; he it was, whose guile
Stird up with Envy and Revenge, deceiv'd   35
The Mother of Mankinde, what time his Pride
Had cast him out from Heav'n, with all his Host
Of Rebel Angels, by whose aid, aspiring
To set himself in Glory above his Peers,
He trusted to have equal'd the most High,   40
If he oppos'd, and with ambitious aim
Against the Throne and Monarchy of God
Rais'd impious War in Heav'n and Battel proud
With vain attempt. Him the Almighty Power
Hurld headlong flaming from th' Ethereal Skie   45
With hideous ruine and combustion down
To bottomless perdition, there to dwell
In Adamantine Chains and penal Fire,
Who durst defie th' Omnipotent to Arms.

(www.dartmouth.edu/~milton/reading_room/pl/book_1/)

Very obviously the spelling conventions of this excerpt are different from today's. Apostrophes, which were not yet common in the ME period – and missing from Pepys' writing (Text 6.1) – are widely used to indicate elided syllables, for example *Heav'n* (37), contractions like *th' Ethereal* (45), or past tense forms such as *seduc'd* (33). Yet *Stird* (35) and *Hurld* (45) do without the apostrophe. A final <e> (not pronounced) appears in *Mankinde* (36) and *ruine* (46); <-ie> is used where present convention has <-y> in *Skie* (45) and *defie* (49); and *Battel* (43) does not follow modern spelling. Yet this is no real obstacle to reading the text. The grammar of the poem is close to that of ModE. There are a few constructions which are somewhat unusual, but not impossible in ModE, for example the word order in *he it was* (34) and *Him the Almighty Power / Hurld headlong flaming . . .* (44–45). The words *what time* (36) would today be expressed by *when*, and *oppos'd* (41) would not be used without a direct object. The real difficulties such a text may cause are of a different nature: the meandering **syntax** of the two sentences which run from the second half of l. 34 to the end of the excerpt are convoluted beyond easy understanding. But even in Milton's own times this is vastly different from what we see in *Pilgrim's Progress* and was surely part of the artfulness of his poetry. Add to this the referential opacity of *infernal Serpent* (of the Garden of Eden), the *Mother of Mankinde* (Eve), *Rebel Angels* (Lucifer and his band) and the result is a text which many ModE speakers have to struggle with.

Restoration literature was very wide ranging, including Milton and highly religious Bunyan, but also Behn, Butler, Congreve, and Dryden. Although much of the writing of this period is a continuation of earlier traditions, a great deal of emphasis lay on the theater and on comedy (link: Restoration comedy). This is very likely the case because the strict public morals of the Commonwealth had led to the closing of the theaters. With their reopening there was a grand renewal of English drama, now colored by influences and tastes picked up by the stay of much of the Court including Charles II in France during the Interregnum. Restoration comedy is well known for its openness to sexuality, which appealed not only to the nobility and their servants, but to many people from the middle class as well. The contrast to the work of both Milton and Bunyan could hardly be greater. Text 6.8 is a short excerpt from William Congreve's (1679–1729) comedy, *The Way of the World*. The scene is set in a chocolate-house, a meeting place of urbane society. The conversation between Mirabell and Fainall revolves almost totally around the intrigues of love and its conquests. Many of the names are remarkably reminiscent of Bunyan's allegorical names: Mirabell "admirer of the beautiful"; Fainall "desirous of everything," Petulant, and Witwoud "wants to know." Other such names include Wishfort, Waitwell, Foible, and Mincing.

Text 6.8 William Congreve, *The Way of the World* (1700)

MIRA. I did as much as man could, with any reasonable conscience; I proceeded to the very last act of flattery with her, and was guilty of a song in her commendation. Nay, I got a friend to put her into a lampoon, and compliment her with the imputation of an affair with a young fellow, which I carried so far, that I told her the malicious town took notice that she was grown fat of a sudden; and when she lay in of a dropsy, persuaded her she was reported to be in labour. The devil's in't, if an old woman is to be flattered further, unless a man should endeavour downright personally to debauch her: and that my virtue forbade me. But for the discovery of this amour, I am indebted to your friend, or your wife's friend, Mrs. Marwood.

FAIN. What should provoke her to be your enemy, unless she has made you advances which you have slighted? Women do not easily forgive omissions of that nature.

MIRA. She was always civil to me, till of late. I confess I am not one of those coxcombs who are apt to interpret a woman's good manners to her prejudice, and think that she who does not refuse 'em everything can refuse 'em nothing.

FAIN. You are a gallant man, Mirabell; and though you may have cruelty enough not to satisfy a lady's longing, you have too much generosity not to be tender of her honour. Yet you speak with an indifference which seems to be affected, and confesses you are conscious of a negligence.

MIRA. You pursue the argument with a distrust that seems to be unaffected, and confesses you are conscious of a concern for which the lady is more indebted to you than is your wife.

FAIN. Fie, fie, friend, if you grow censorious I must leave you: — I'll look upon the gamesters in the next room.

MIRA. Who are they?

FAIN. Petulant and Witwoud.

(www.gutenberg.org/ebooks/1292)

The Congreve text is easier to follow than the one from Milton. The only difficulties come from words no longer familiar, ones like *dropsie* "edema," *coxcomb* "conceited fool," *fie* an expression of disapproval, or the unnecessary French borrowing *amour* "love." The use of *confesses* "gives evidence of" would hardly be used with a non-human subject in ModE. Otherwise, the text is straightforward and a good example of the superficial ideals of a small set of London socialites.

6.5 Variation: South and North

The fundamental division remained the South–North divide, but with the gradual acceptance and spread of the written standard evidence of regional differences is relatively meager. For the **stereotyped** use of dialect see <u>link: Shakespeare *Henry V*</u>. The two short passages given here may illustrate South and North (here: Scottish), but the contrast between them and the standard is mostly in the spelling, seldom in vocabulary, and virtually never in grammar. This first is an extract from the diary (1550–63) of Henry Machyn, a London merchant.

Text 6.9 From H. Machyn's diary (1550–63)

The xxv day of Marche, the wyche was owre lade [day] ther was as gret justes as youe have sene at the tylt at Vestmynster; . . .

*The xiiij day of Aprell, the wyche was [Ester day] at sant Margett parryche at Westmynster . . . one of the menysters a prest of the ab[bay] dyd helpe hym that was the menyster [to] the pepull who wher reseyvyng of the blessyd sacrement of . . . Jhesus   5
Cryst, ther cam into the churche a man that was a monke of Elly, the wyche was marryed to a wyff; the sam day ther that same man sayd to the menyster, What doyst thow fyff them? and as sone as he had spokyn he druw his wod-knyffe, and hyt the prest on the hed and struck hym a grett blowe, and after ran after hym and struck him on the hand, and cloyffe ys hand a grett way and after on the harme a grett   10
wond; and ther was scyche a cry and showtt as has not byne; and after he was taken and cared to presun, and after examynyd wher-for he dyd ytt.*

(D. Burnley (ed.) (1992) *The History of the English Language. A Source Book*. London: Longman, 209–210)

This particular selection has been chosen to show the spelling of *Westminster* with an initial <v> (l. 2) and with <w> (4), which may reflect London pronunciation, in which the two are in some sort of variation. Initial <h> is widely used, but not in *ys* (10). The **hyper-correction** of *harme* (10), in contrast, shows the unstable status of /h/. Several words (*Aprell, menysters, prest, presun*) have <e> where present-day spelling has <i(e)>; this may reflect a phonetically opener realization of the short KIT-vowel[11] in London pronunciation. The **relative pronouns** are still highly variable: *the wyche* (1, 3, 6), *that* (4), *who* (5), all with no apparent reason. *Do*-periphrasis appears in a non-emphatic affirmative sentence (4). Second person singular *thou* is clearly current (8). The vocabulary is unexceptionable except for *fyff* (8), possibly from *fife* or *Fife* and meaning "hoodwink," and *cloyffe* (10), possibly from *cleave*. Both words seem more at home in the North or Scotland than in London.

The second selection is from the Preface to King James' book on writing poetry (1584). The text uses the Scottish spelling <quh> for Southern <wh>; initial /j/ appears as <z> as in *ze* "ye." {-ed} appears as <-it>, reflecting Scottish pronunciation. Many of the vowel realizations are obviously Northern, *quha, knawledge, ane* (without initial /w/), *sa, baith,*

---

11 The concept of lexical sets, for example, words with the vowel of *kit*, will be elaborated in 8.2.4.

sindry, and *twa*, where Southern forms would have a back vowel. We find *sould* with <s-> not <sh->. The inflection <-is> occurs where StE has <-(e)s>. **Concord** has a plural subject (*thais quha hes*; *men hes*) with a singular verb (*hes*). Individual words which are not familiar to speakers of the Southern standard are *quhilk* "which," *cautelis* "cautions," *sen* "since."

Text 6.10 King James VI, *Reulis and Cautelis* (1584)

The cause why (docile Reader) I have not dedicat this short treatise to any particular person is, (as commounly work is us is to be) is, that I esteme all thais quha hes already some beginning of knawledge, with ane earnest desyre to atteyne to farther, alyke meit for the reading of this worke, or any uther, quhilk may help thame to the atteining to thair foirsaid desyre. Bot as to this work, quhilk is intitulit, The Reulis and cautelis to be observit & eschewit in Scottis Poesie, ze may marvell paraventure, quhairfore I sould have writtin in that mater, sen sa mony learnet men, baith of auld and of late hes already written thairof in dyvers and sindry languages: I answer, That nochtwithstanding, I have lykeway is writtin of it, for twa caussis: . . .

(*King James VI and I. Selected Writings*) (2003) N. Rhodes, J. Richards, and J. Marshall (eds.). Aldershot: Ashgate.

6.6 Summary

This chapter has reviewed the major social, political, cultural, and demographic changes in sixteenth and seventeenth century England and has linked these to the history of the language. In this the role of London continued to be of central importance. EModE has been characterized both from an external point of view, especially in competition with Latin, which it gradually displaced as the standard written language. Important internal changes such as the Great Vowel Shift, extensive lexical borrowing from Latin, the spread of *do*-periphrasis, and the leveling of the second person pronoun from a mix of *thou* and *you* to *you* alone have supplied major examples of change in this period. A selection of textual excerpts has served to illustrate stylistic and regional variety in the language.

STUDY QUESTIONS

Social and cultural background

1. What were the major push- and pull-factors in the movement of people to London?
2. Comment on some of the effects of the English Civil War on society and language.
3. Focusing on the fields of religion and science discuss how the relationship between Latin and English changed within this period.

Linguistic background

1. How did patterns of population movement affect London English in this period?
2. What areas (spelling, pronunciation, vocabulary, grammar) were most strongly affected by the process of standardization in this period? What justifies your conclusions?
3. What kind of social relationship does the usage of singular *you* and *thou* reflect in Elizabethan society?
4. How did the changing population structure of London influence the GVS?
5. How did science writing deal with the problem of lack of terms for the various scientific disciplines? How does this fit in with the phenomenon of "inkhorn terms"?

Further reading

Barber is a very readable book-length treatment of EModE. It contains plentiful examples, but is not overloaded with detail. Rydén et al. is a collection of articles on a variety of linguistic aspects of EModE. Sim offers a more recent social and cultural portrait of the Tudor period (fashion, festivals, religion, reading, theater, sports). Hill traces the ideas behind the Civil War.

Barber, C. (1997 [1976]) *Early Modern English*, rev. ed. Edinburgh: Edinburgh UP.
Hill, C. (1972) *The World Turned Upside Down. Radical Ideas during the English Revolution.* Harmondsworth: Penguin.
Rydén, M., I. Tieken-Boon van Ostade, and M. Kytö (eds.) (1998) *A Reader in Early Modern English*. Frankfurt: Peter Lang.
Sim, A. (2009) *Pleasures and Pastimes in Tudor England*. Stroud: History Press.

CHAPTER SEVEN

The spread of English (since the late sixteenth century)

And who in time knows wither we may vent
The treasure of our tongue, to what strange shores
This gaine of our best glorie shal be sent,
T'inrich vnknowing Nations with our stores?
Which worlds in th'yet vnformed Occident
May come refin'd with th'accents that are ours.

(Samuel Daniel *Musophilis*, 1599)

Chapter Overview:

This chapter:

- begins with an account of changes in European society in the early modern period as background to the overseas expansion of English;
- reviews the subsequent establishment of new centers of linguistic diffusion;
- shows the establishment of General English (GenE) in contrast to the traditional dialects;
- observes the transplantation of English under the conditions of emigration and immigration as well as language imposition;
- mentions the effects of social change on language in the course of widespread education and urbanization;
- looks at the linguistic correlates of spread such as bilingualism, code-switching, and borrowing. This is done for English as a native language (ENL), as a second language (ESL), as English pidgins and creoles, and as a foreign language (EFL).

7.1 Social-historical background

English was spoken by about 4 million people inhabiting a large but peripheral island off the coast of continental Europe in or around the year 1600. Today English is spoken by sometimes larger and sometimes smaller groups of people on all the inhabited continents of our earth. Just how many people this amounts to is a matter of quite a bit of controversy, but realistic estimates of the *number of speakers* of English as a first or *native language* lies at somewhat over 360 million (for more on calculations and sources see <u>link: The numbers</u>). To begin with, let us remind ourselves of the political, social, economic, and, of course, linguistic situation in Europe and particularly in Britain in the seventeenth century.

By 1600 the dawn of a new age had broken over Western Europe or, indeed, a multiplicity of new ages. There had been a revival of learning, the Renaissance. There had been a new religious upheaval, the Reformation. There had been a series of exploratory voyages which were opening a new world far beyond Europe in the Age of Discovery. And there had been the beginnings of the Commercial Revolution with its radical capitalistic change in production and trade, initially under the label of mercantilism. All of these had the effect of moving Britain from the periphery of Europe to the center of the new Atlantic world in which England, in particular, was to be one of the most important actors. In the preceding chapters there has been ample opportunity to go into the effects on society and on the English language of both the Renaissance and the numerous religious movements, including the Reformation. There has, however, been only a hint at the effects of the Age of Discovery and the new economic forces.

7.1.1 The Age of Discovery

In the mid-fifteenth century European navigators had begun to venture beyond their home continent under Henry the Navigator, the Portuguese king who financed voyages along the Atlantic coast of Africa. The exchange of goods that followed included African slaves and, consequently, marked the start of what was to be a long and extremely tortuous relationship between Africa, Europe, and America. In 1492, at the end of the fifteenth century, came the first voyage of Columbus, who, under the Spanish flag, is credited with the European discovery of America. From this point on, first the Spanish, then the Portuguese, the French, the Dutch, and the English supported voyages of discovery and exploitation. The two Iberian countries concentrated their efforts in what is now known as Latin America. France and England were more prominently engaged in the North Atlantic, where ships under their flags fished and traded with the Native Americans (see 10.1 and 10.1.1). Text 7.1 by Richard Hakluyt outlines what, from an English point of view, were the main motivations for establishing plantations, that is settlements, in the Americas. Hakluyt's work was addressed to Sir Walter Raleigh, who had just sponsored the first, ill-fated English settlement in North America at Roanoke Island on the present-day North Carolina coast. The text contains a multitude of reasons for getting involved in the European race for colonies. Those given here are a selection from among the twenty-one which Hakluyt enumerated – and each of which was the subject of a separate chapter. There are four major criteria: religious, political, economic, and technical-geographic. A close reading of the text is a bit difficult because of the spelling, which not only differs from present-day practice, but is also inconsistent in itself (<u>link: Exercise on text 7.1</u>).

Text 7.1 Richard Hakluyt, *Discourse of Western Planting* (1584)

A particular discourse concerning the greate necessitie and manifold comodyties that are like to growe to this Realme of Englande by the Westerne discoveries lately attempted, Written in the yere 1584. by Richarde Hackluyt of Oxforde at the requeste and direction of the righte worshipfull Mr Walter Raghly nowe Knight, before the comynge home of his Twoo Barkes: and is devided into xxj chapters, the titles whereof followe in the nexte leafe.

1. *That this westerne discoverie will be greately for thinlargement of the gospel of Christe whereunto the Princes of the refourmed religion are chefely bounde amongst whome her ma^{tie} ys principall.*

2. *That all other englishe Trades are growen beggerly or daungerous, especially in all the king of Spayne his Domynions, where our men are driven to flinge their Bibles and prayer Bokes into the sea, and to forsweare and renounce their religion and conscience and consequently theyr obedience to her Matie.*

3. *That this westerne voyadge will yelde unto us all the commodities of Europe, Affrica, and Asia, as far as wee were wonte to travell, and supply the wants of all our decayed trades.*

4. *That this enterprise will be for the manifold imploymente of members of idle men, and for bredinge of many sufficient, and for utterance of the great quantitie of the commodities of our Realme.*

5. *That this voyage will be a great bridle to the Indies of the kinge of Spaine and a meane that wee may arreste at our pleasure for the space of tenne weekes or three monethes every yere, one or twoo hundred saile of his subjectes shippes at the fysshinge in Newfounde lande.*

12. *That the passage in this voyadge is easie and shorte, that it cutteth not nere the trade of any other mightie Princes, nor nere their Contries, that it is to be perfourmed at all tymes of the yere, and nedeth but one kinde of winde, that Ireland beinge full of goodd havens on the southe and west sides, is the nerest parte of Europe to yt, wth by this trade shall be in more securitie, and the sooner drawen to more Civilitie.*

15. *That spedie plantinge in divers fitt places is moste necessarie upon these luckye westerne discoveries for feare of the daunger of being prevented by other nations wth have the like intentions, wth the order thereof and other reasons therwth all alleaged.*

17. *That by these Colonies the Northwest passage to Cathaio and china may easely quickly and perfectly be searched oute aswell by river and overlande, as by sea, for proofe whereof here are quoted and alleaged divers rare Testymonies oute of the three volumes of voyadges gathered by Ramusius and other grave authors.*

(J.E. Illick (ed.) (1970) *America & England, 1558–1776.* N.Y.: Meredith, 4–6)

While the Spanish and Portuguese quickly took military possession of the areas that were to be their American empires, both the English and the French were slower in doing this: the English established a permanent colony at Jamestown, Virginia in 1607 and *Newfoundland* in 1610 and the French at Port-Royal in 1605 and Québec in 1608. From this point on, the course of colonization differed considerably. Canada remained fairly sparsely populated while numerous settlements began springing up in what was to be British North America, most notably in *New England* and in Virginia (see chapter 10). Eventually, the English intruded in the Caribbean, taking possession of a number of islands, most notably Barbados (1625, 1627) and Jamaica, which changed from Spanish to English hands in 1655 (see chapter 9).

7.1.2 Mercantilism and territorial expansion

All of the European possessions in the Americas, as elsewhere, were a part of the system of mercantilism, which sought national-imperial self-sufficiency by tying the colonial producers of staples to the homeland-metropolis via trade. Out of the mercantilism of early colonial expansion grew an imperial system which first expanded "internally" within the British Isles, especially in the conquest of Ireland, and then throughout the world. England – eventually to become the United Kingdom – got wood, including ship masts, furs, fish, sugar, tobacco, and later cotton from its empire, supplied its American colonies with slaves, and marketed its finished goods there as well.

All the while Britain exported its surplus, usually English-speaking, population (there were some speakers of Gaelic and Welsh as well) to its colonial holdings. In North America – later also in Australia, South Africa, and New Zealand – they were settlers; in the Caribbean – later also in Papua, Queensland, and *East Africa* – they were plantation owners and overseers; in *West Africa* – later also in *South* and *Southeast Asia* – they were traders. The often extremely different demographic make-up of this colonial empire explains much, but not everything, about the present linguistic status of English in the countries affected, as the following chapters will show.

Each of the settler territories became a new center of expansion into its particular periphery. By the nineteenth century one of the original offshoots of English expansionism, the United States, had arrived at a state in which it, too, could begin to create its own empire (link: US territorial expansion). This initially took the form of "internal" expansion in

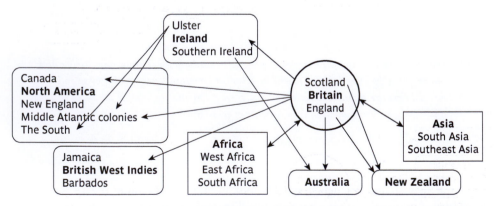

Figure 7.1 The spread of English from Britain (single-headed arrow: population movements; double-headed arrow: chiefly colonial administration) (link: Dates for the various movements). For maps see the individual chapters.

which the territorial basis of the United States expanded westward through North America to the Pacific coast and eventually northward to Alaska and beyond North America to Hawaii, Puerto Rico, the Philippines, and a number of smaller territories. Furthermore, the United States has claimed leadership in the Americas continuously for nearly 200 years. As with Britain, the motivations were mainly economic and political, but it became common practice by the end of the nineteenth century to justify expansion in the name of the spread of religion and civilization (link: The US religious and civilizing mission). Canada reached the stage of "internal" expansion across the continent parallel to the US, but it did not establish an empire outside of North America, perhaps because Canada was still a part of the British Empire.

In the Caribbean Jamaican influence can still be seen along the coast of Central America, where laborers (were) moved to exploit natural resources such as wood in Bluefields, the Corn Islands, and Belize. These people, who were speakers of Jamaican Creole (JC), were often slaves in the early period, but were later free laborers, as in the case of Puerto Limón, where they were employed in railroad building. Australia expanded to fill out its present-day borders, effectively making the whole continent English-speaking. It also exercised considerable influence on New Zealand, and extended its economic control to many of the neighboring island territories such as the Solomon Islands, Fiji, and Papua New Guinea just as South Africa did in regard to Nambia, Zimbabwe, Lesotho, and Malawi.

What we see, then, is economically and demographically motivated expansion and closely related to it, a geographical spread of English to a unique extent. While the other major European colonial powers, Spain, Portugal, France, and The Netherlands, also

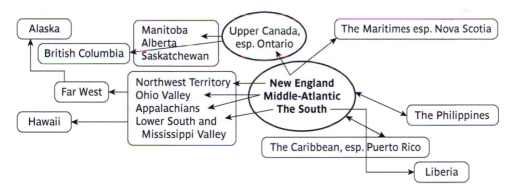

Figure 7.2 The spread of English in and from America (single-headed arrow: population movements; double-headed arrow: chiefly colonial administration) (link: Dates for the various movements). For maps see the individual chapters.

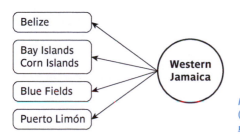

Figure 7.3 The spread of English from Jamaica (population movements) (link: Dates for the various movements). For maps see the individual chapters.

acquired colonial empires, they differed because they did not establish settler communities which repeated the process of expansion to the degree that Britain did. In the case of Russia there was "merely" what is most frequently seen as "internal" expansion eastward. And the late-comers to the field, Germany, Italy, and Japan, were able to acquire relatively few and less desirable territories and were knocked out of the game at the latest by losing World War I (Germany) or World War II (Japan, Italy). The relevant developments will be spelled out in more detail in the chapters that follow.

7.2 Language policy

Throughout the history of English both the geographic spread of its speakers and the role of the government or other powerful institutions in the shaping and status of the language have become evident again and again. Before its extension beyond England and the Scottish Lowlands, the use of the language as an everyday medium of communication depended very much on the settlement patterns of the Saxons. With the introduction of literacy and learning, centers of cultural power and prestige began to develop, and they tended to exert relatively great influence on *language attitudes* among the more educated. In principle, the founding of monasteries and the program of translation into and writing in English initiated by King Alfred is an early, important example of language policy in regard to English, one which effectively established the West Saxon variety and system of *spelling* as the OE written standard (cf. 3.4–5). In addition, this move effectively distanced it from Old Norse, which was restricted almost exclusively to the spoken medium.

In the ME period there was first a switch from English to Latin and French as the languages of the state and/or of learning, a move which largely divorced English from use in the written domain. This, as well as the subsequent move back to English, were matters of language policy. When English had once again come into use in the government, the varieties used in London gained greatly in prestige because of their association with the State and other institutions in the domains of commerce, printing, religion, and eventually education; consequently, they gradually took on the status of a standard (cf. chapters 5 and 6).

The social and political forces which were instrumental in shaping English in the period of spread may be partially explained by looking at two rather contrary currents: tradition and modernization. The former has to do with the more sedentary population in the predominately rural areas, what Samuels refers to as "conservative peripheral areas" (1972: 133). Here the *traditional dialects*, while not unchanging, developed relatively independently of the changes in the modernizing part of society. The relative lack of cultural and linguistic contact and mixing provided for greater stability and slower change, something which is typical of more isolated communities. The latter current, modernization, found its expression in the newly forming urban communities whose population consisted of people from all the dialect areas of England. They were "innovating central areas" (ibid.) characterized by contact. This led to greater social and linguistic instability and therefore to the emergence of new forms and structural leveling.

Language policy was a central part of the latter process, but not its only element. The State and such important institutions as the Church, the ever more indispensible schools and universities, and the growing – and increasingly ungovernable – publishing sector pursued a sometimes clearly formulated and sometimes more or less implicit program which selected and promoted a particular variety of English. This new variety was transmitted most prominently in educational contexts, which very often meant in the form of writing. While the grammar schools saw it as their brief to teach the classical languages, Greek and, above all, Latin, the medium of instruction was English. Printing, as we saw in chapter 5, was increasingly geared to the reading public, and that public read English and not Latin. The overall trajectory amounted to the extension of the standard language to more and more domains. Yet, as we have seen in chapter 6, this "program" had neither uniform nor uncontroversial goals as far as *codification* was concerned. On the one hand, StE emerged (chapter 5), but the contact between and mixing of people speaking different dialectal forms of English was multi-focused and non-institutionalized, and this led, on the other hand, to the parallel emergence of *non-standard GenE*. Despite the obvious lack of agreement between standard and non-standard on numerous points the overall result is remarkably uniform: the two together make up what with a great deal of justification may be called *General English (GenE)*.

7.3 The emergence of General English (GenE)

There is much more that is common to StE and non-standard GenE than distinguishes them. GenE without the modification "non-standard" covers both. It is a broad concept which may conveniently be used to refer to those varieties of English which are not traditional dialects nor English creoles. There are two poles to GenE. At the one end we find the highly standardized variety called StE, which is specifically prescribed for published writing and more formal situations of public discourse. At the other end there is the more colloquial type, which includes a great deal of non-standard English, but not just any kind of non-standard. What is non-standard in the framework of GenE follows a large "canon" of grammatical items which are found all over the ENL world, but do not belong to StE. These non-standard components of GenE are similar enough to be readily comprehensible to other speakers of GenE anywhere. Typical items are ones such as third person singular present tense *don't*; the use of *ain't* for the negation of present tense *be* and *have*; *multiple negation*; non-standard verb forms like past tense *knowed* or *seen*; pleonastic (repeated) subjects like *my sister she . . .*; conjoined pronominal subjects in the object case, for example *me and him went*, and many more. Despite the length of the list, the two poles share most of their grammar, and their vocabulary and phonology as well. This cannot be said of the traditional dialects or the English creoles. It is only the "fine distinctions" which separate the two poles of GenE. Linguistically the differences are relatively insignificant; socially they are highly charged. StE is associated with the *overt norms*; non-standard GenE with *covert norms*. The former is **power-oriented**; the latter carries *solidarity*.

Both poles were involved in similar processes of norm establishment. In the long run, there was widespread agreement on the vocabulary used and on the central *grammatical categories*. This agreement arose and spread, most likely due to *koinéization* (link: *Koinéization*). In spite of everything shared, the basic dichotomy between StE and non-standard GenE have remained socially and linguistically significant. The former, StE, was increasingly used in published writing and, arguably in speech (cf. Cheshire 1999). But in everyday spoken communication all over the English-speaking world non-standard forms are omnipresent. In addition, the local, regional, and **national varieties** are spoken with their respective pronunciations. The most important point is that phonetic de-coding is basically easy. In most cases speakers with even very different GenE pronunciations understand each other after a relatively short period of adjustment because there is a large degree of phonological agreement within GenE. The non-standard grammatical variants are, in the end, not a barrier to understanding, even if they are not actively used by everyone. You may or may not use double negatives and third person singular *don't* as in *It don't look like nothing's gonna happen*, but you are hardly likely to misinterpret this sentence.[1] It is instructive to look at some of the ways in which GenE and one or the other traditional dialect have diverged in their development. This will be done by looking at two representative traditional dialects.

7.3.1 Grammatical *gender* (link: Gender) in GenE and in traditional dialects

Evidence from West Country and Newfoundland dialects reveal how differently traditional non-standard forms have developed in comparison with their modern GenE counterparts. The latter today has only remnants of gender marking. A few instances of lexical gender marking of the {-er/-or} vs. {-ess} type are used sporadically, but the feminine suffix is largely optional (cf. *actor–actress*; *waiter–waitress*). In the pronoun system there is a human vs. non-human distinction as seen in the **relative pronouns** *who* vs. *which*. Within the human category a male vs. female distinction is made in the third person singular of the personal pronouns with masculine *he*, feminine *she*, and neuter *it* generally according to natural gender (= sex) (link: Personal pronoun systems of English). In addition to this, GenE recognizes some special cases such as feminine reference, mostly on the part of men, to cars, boats, and so on. So there is nothing strange about getting gas in North America and saying *fill'er up*.

In English West Country dialect a very different system has been maintained in which every object which has a shape of its own (dead or alive) is either masculine or feminine; nearly always the former, for example *pitcher, tool, book, house, coat, cat, letter* = *he*. In contrast, *it* is impersonal or abstract, used to express an action or a noun of the undefined sort, such as *water, snow, air, weather, hay, beer*. This is a basic **count vs. mass** distinction (link: Count and mass nouns) and may be traceable to Proto-Indo-European, where animate was masculine with the subcategory feminine for female humans and both stood in contrast to inanimate, which was neuter (Wagner 2004a: 481–482). In the West Country as well as Newfoundland, which was largely settled by people from the English *Southwest*, we find this system. The Survey of English Dialects (SED) contains the following examples:

ˈjuː gɒd ə ˈbʌɪɫ ˈpʊd ə ˈbɒdɫ ʌp tuː ən ən stiːm ən
"you got a boil, put a bottle up to it and steam it"; *bottle* referred to as *ən* < OE *hine* (masc. sg. acc.)

---

1 For the reader who is uncertain, this sentence might be paraphrased in StE as *It appears as if nothing is going to happen*.

aːv ˈlɔːs ən iː ˈvaːɫd d̠ɾuː mɪ ˈpɒkət
"I've lost it [a knife]; it fell thru my pocket"; *knife* referred to as nom. and as acc. *(h)ine* and nom. *(h)e*

ðat də kiːp ˈiː daʊn
"that keeps (h)e [a cart] down"; replacement of object case *him* with subject case *he* (ibid.: 482–483)

The final example also demonstrates *case leveling* ([link: Pronoun case leveling](link)), which occurred in GenE, where object form *you* replaced subject form *ye*. In addition, it supplies us with an example of the auxiliary *do* /də/ used to mark *habitual aspect* ([link: Habitual aspect](link)), not GenE(!), here in the sense that something always keeps the cart down.

More recent material from the West Country and from Newfoundland shows a system with more mixing, where *it* is often used instead of *en* in object position while *he* is retained as a subject: compare *when I saw the plough nobody valued **it**, if **he** had been kept dry **he** would have been good now* (Somerset) and *Oh yes **he** [a certificate] had to go in wid **it** [application for old age pension] see, **he** had to go in wid **en**, now **he** won't be, come back no more 'fore I gets 70, if I lives till dat* (Newfoundland) (ibid.: 490ff). This Newfoundland example shows dialect mixing, as we clearly see in the parallel use of *wid it* and *wid en*. Furthermore, the use of non-third person *present tense {-s}*, a further traditional dialect usage shows up here as well (see 7.2.3).

7.3.2 The present tense verb inflection {-s}

The use of non-third person {-s} is not unknown in GenE, but tends to be restricted to such relatively fixed uses as A: *Says who?* B: *Says I*.

"This is something he has to do."
"Says you?"
"Says him."

(L. Barclay. *No Time for Goodbye*. London: Orion, 2008, 358)

Cheshire (1979: 52) remarks on the variable use of present tense {-s} – as seen in examples like *I knows how to handle teddy boys*; *You knows my sister, the one who's small*; or *They calls me all the names under the sun, don't they?* – in the *vernacular* English of Reading, England, which resembles that of the English Southwest. She remarks that this is a usage which must once have been much more widespread. Accordingly the auxiliary *do* was invariably *do*, for example *She cadges, she do* (ibid.: 54), and the past of the auxiliary was *did*, while the lexical verb *do* was invariably *dos* /duːz/ in the present tense, as in *we does things at school* . . . (ibid.: 52) and *done* in the past, for example *Well, he never done it, did he?* (ibid.: 57). In Cheshire's study the effect of the gender of the speaker is emphasized: "tough" young people, especially boys who were associated with the vernacular culture, were more likely to use the traditional forms: "vernacular speech in adolescents is controlled by the norms of the vernacular culture, as embodied in the behaviour of the peer group" (ibid.: 63). Now while this pattern, which also distinguishes lexical *has* from auxiliary *have*, is distinctly different from GenE, it is not so strange as to make comprehension overly difficult. In fact, in the case of auxiliary *do*, negative third person singular *don't* is widespread wherever GenE is spoken. In findings like those illustrated by these studies we see the effect of covert norms on both non-standard traditional dialect and non-standard GenE usage.

The interesting point in the context of this chapter is that the kind of English which was exported as the language spread was the General English that had become established in the Southeast of England, most especially in London. The transplantation of forms such as those from the English Southwest was definitely less common. GenE was the result of both *overt* and *covert processes* (link: Covert and overt norms). The emerging grammatical system of GenE seems to have been widely adopted in the public sphere, be it government, schools, the Church, publishing, or the commercial sector. It had verb forms, pronouns, noun inflections, prepositions, *adverb* and *adjective* forms, and *word order* which differed, if at all, only in matters of detail in its non-standard as opposed to its standard forms. The more widely diverging systems as seen in the gender categories of the West Country or those second person singular personal pronouns which retained a distinct singular form such as *thou* (see chapter 6), are not part of the new GenE.

7.4 Transplantation

English as a Native Language (ENL) has been carried overseas from Britain and established in new ENL communities, most prominently in Ireland, North America, the Caribbean, South Africa, Singapore, Australia, and New Zealand. In far more countries in *West*, *East*, and *Southern Africa*, in South and Southeast Asia, and in the Western Pacific English has been adopted (or imposed) as a Second Language (ESL) and in some, including the Caribbean, as a pidgin or a creole. This movement outwards has reinforced the increasing spread of *English as a Foreign Language (EFL)*. There are numerous differences between and within these three categories of countries. In some cases new regional or national standards have arisen; in other cases external norms, usually those of England or the United States, continue to be the source of the norms. In this section and in 7.5 some of the most salient general points will be presented, but the treatment of regional standards will be reserved for the appropriate chapters.

7.4.1 Emigration, immigration, and imposition

Emigrants came from all over England as well as from Scotland and Ireland, but there seem to have been two important biases in the self-selection of the people leaving. One of these was rooted in the turbulence of seventeenth century England in which the suppression of the religious dissenters encouraged many of them to turn their backs on the country. The early dissenters, up to the English Civil War, may be characterized as part of the new middle class and were, consequently, better educated than average. This would ensure that they were familiar with the emerging (written) standard. With the outbreak of the Civil War, new religious and social protesters appeared who were generally poorer and less well educated, but who had been uprooted from traditional rural life and were becoming a part of the developing urban proletarian classes. These people were less affected by the new written standard, but they were clearly changing by giving up their more particularly regional forms of speech in favor of the new spoken urban varieties, most especially that of London, which were to become GenE.

The kind of English which was transferred overseas by British and Irish settlers was based on the two traditions within GenE. Early movement to North America was influenced by the better-educated Separatists and Puritans in New England and by the genteel classes that were to become the planters of Virginia and the Carolinas. New waves of migrants from London and the Home Counties, the North of England, from Scotland, and from Ulster were largely speakers of non-standard GenE. With the transportation to the penal colonies of Australia, there was a similar division: the officers who administered the settlements were closer to StE while the transported prisoners were the carriers of the non-standard. In South Africa there was an initial influx of military officers, administrators, schoolmasters, and parsons and in 1820 of middle-class British. Consequently, there is little regional influence from Britain "other than the lower-middle or lower-class speech of the Home Counties" (Lanham 1996: 20). In New Zealand the settlers came from both the United Kingdom and from Australia.

In those countries such as Nigeria and the Philippines, where British or American colonial control was established, but where relatively few European or American native speakers of English settled, the usual language of administration was English. Inasmuch as it was taught in the schools, it was StE. However, there was also a parallel emergence of *English pidgins* and *creoles* in many of these countries (see 7.5.4). In the post-colonial period, independence did not bring about abrupt change.[2] English continued to be used, but what was once imposed by imperial domination has in the neo-neo-colonial period mutated to self-imposition. In most of these countries English is a Second Language, but it is, in the meantime, the native or primary, that is, most frequently used, language in the Anglophone Caribbean and in Singapore.

The reasons given for retaining or fully adopting English include at least the following points:

- English is a world language / library language / language of wider communication.
- English is neutral vis-à-vis competing indigenous languages, hence promoting national unity.
- English is a fully developed language while the indigenous languages would demand too many resources to be suitably modernized.

This view should not blind us to the disadvantages which also ensue, as summed up in the following points:

- The use of English implants a code and a content which empowers the North by continuing its domination (exploitation, penetration, fragmentation, and marginalization) of the South; the development of the indigenous languages would combat the hegemony of the North.

---

2 Much the same sort of heritage can be traced in the former French, Spanish, and Portuguese colonies.

- Many indigenous languages are threatened in their very existence; their demise would entail a loss of invaluable and irreplaceable traditions.
- The use of English damages the self-esteem of indigenous communities, who suffer inestimable damage in status and prestige.

Each of these points can be and have been elaborated in a variety of ways, but they all have to do with what is, in the end, "*linguistic imperialism*" (cf. Phillipson 1992). The words of Gilbert Ansre summarize this "linguistic imperialism" very pointedly. It is

> [t]he phenomenon in which the minds and lives of the speakers of a language are dominated by another language to the point where they believe that they can and should use only that foreign language when it comes to transactions dealing with the more advanced aspects of life such as education, philosophy, literature, governments, the administration of justice, etc. . . . Linguistic imperialism has a subtle way of warping the minds, attitudes, and aspirations of even the most noble in a society and of preventing him from appreciating and realizing the full potentialities of the indigenous languages.
> (qtd. in ibid.: 56)

The positions represented above cannot be fully reconciled with each other. Both "sides" have their merits. The ways in which ESL societies are developing shows that many "solutions" are possible and that none is a priori correct. In chapter 12 the role and some of the features of ESL will be presented.

7.4.2 Education and urbanization

In the last two hundred years the traditional ENL countries Britain and Ireland, the United States and Canada, Australia, New Zealand, and South Africa have undergone the same pan-European processes of the spread of literacy and the urbanization of society. The first of these developments has brought about a mass reading public on a scale unheard of before, especially with the introduction of cheaper wood-pulp paper and the rotary press in the nineteenth century. As a result, more and more people came into contact with the kind of written English which is widely associated with StE even though it was the less formal English of the popular press that most people consumed. The second development, urbanization, brought people with varying linguistic and cultural backgrounds together, both ENL speakers of often very different regional varieties as well as indigenous and immigrant people with non-English language backgrounds. Wherever the immigrants went there was a different mix. This has resulted in a number of different but closely related standards, as we will see in the following chapters.

7.5 Linguistic correlates of European expansion

English around the world is to a great extent mutually intelligible to its native and *primary language* users. Yet the kind of English these speakers use is far from uniform. We need to ask ourselves what aspects are similar more or less everywhere and why this is so. Of course, the reverse is also true: what is different and why? The goal of this section is to introduce important relevant factors. We will do this by first making some general observations and then looking one after the other at ENL, including English as a primary language, then at ESL speakers, at pidgin and creole English communities, and finally at EFL users. In chapter 13 we will extend this view by adding what is now sometimes called *English as a Lingua Franca (ELF)* or English as an International Language (EIL).

7.5.1 Change during the period of spread

In the history of English as we have been looking at it in the previous chapters we have seen processes of internal change influenced by contact, especially contact which can "destabilize" a *speech community* and hasten processes of change already taking place. While Old English–Old Norse and Old English–Old French contact were both motors for far-reaching change, it is unlikely that *creolization* (link: Creolization) took place. As we will see in chapter 9, catastrophic destabilization provides the "best" conditions for *pidginization* and creolization, and this was not so in either case.

We have seen the Anglo-Saxon imposition of OE and the suppression or displacement of the Celtic languages OE was in contact with, which was so great that we have no evidence of what Pictish (see Plate 1.2), a Celtic language spoken in the north of Britain, even looked like. In the further spread of English we will encounter further examples of *language imposition* and *language loss* (link: Language imposition, shift, loss, and death), but also cases of long periods of stable contact which have led to *bilingualism* and the areal spread of features of *syntax*, morphology, phonetology, and lexis.

Just as the influence of *Norman French* and Latin on the vocabulary of English has been emphasized, so *borrowing* will continue to offer the major evidence of continuing *language contact* with numerous further languages. This will be evident in *loan words,* loan blends, phenomenon creation, and *loan translations (calques)* (link: Borrowing), but will not be so drastic as to lead to new processes of word formation or to a major restructuring of the vocabulary like that initiated by French–English contact and the renewed impact of Latin in the Renaissance. Change has also been stimulated by contact between speakers of varying regional forms of English (koinéization) as well as by features introduced by bilingual speakers (language shift) (link: Generation model; link: Language imposition, shift, loss, and death). Language change under the influence of speakers of non-English traditional languages shows the effect of the *substrate languages* (link: Substrate languages). Change has been not only lexical, but also pragmatic-semantic, grammatical, and phonetic-phonological.[3]

With the significant exception of English pidgins and creoles, syntactic change has been unspectacular in the last four hundred years, but by no means absent. While major changes in inflection or in word order have not taken place, the process of *grammaticalization* (link: Grammaticalization) has continued. This can be seen especially in the verb system of English, where the loss of strong (i.e. irregular) verbs has continued, where the progressive form was extended to the passive, where the *subjunctive* (link: Modality; link: Subjunctive) became increasingly rare, where periphrastic *do* was finally limited to the usage

3 Differences in pronunciation will be largely postponed to the following chapters.

it has today in StE, where new *periphrastic be going to* (link: Periphrastic *be going to*) became current, and where there has been continuing adjustment of the system of *modal auxiliaries* and *semi-modal verbs* (link: Modality), including the use of polite *should* and *would* (for wishes). Furthermore, *prescriptivism* banned the use of *double modals* (link: Double modals) and *multiple negation* (link: Multiple negation). The pronoun system of StE took on its current form relatively early in this period with the final loss of *thou–thy/thine–thee* and *ye* as well as the replacement of neuter singular possessive *his* with *its*. The *deictic* (link: Demonstratives) pronoun and *determiner* system lost the *yon* and *yonder* member, thus changing from a three-way to a two-way distinction. The ModE distinction between *relative who* and *which* (link: Relative pronouns) was confirmed, as was the present-day expression of the comparative and superlative with {-er} and {more} and with {-est} and {most} (see 6.3.3.2).

While the shifts in *second person pronoun usage* have often been seen as evidence of a kind of democratic leveling in society, there was also a further development in the direction of more rigorously class-based distinctions. So-called "good" language was associated more and more with "proper" social attitudes and "correct" social behavior, and this was increasingly connected with London and the upper middle and upper classes, where there was a growing wish to acquire a polished pronunciation, which could be attained through education. Concomitant with this was the (now known to be mistaken) association of writing with *correctness* and spoken language with sloppy usage. The centrality of writing was closely connected with the spread of literacy, and to this belongs the influence of French and Latin on spelling.

As with both official and de facto language policy in post-Conquest England, various sorts of *language policy* and *language planning* (link: Language planning and language policy) have been highly significant in the encounter of English-speaking people, often in positions of economic power and administrative influence, on speakers of other languages. The functional expansion of English has varied and continues to vary considerably between ENL and ESL countries. Yet while colonial and post-colonial power structures have had a strong effect on the spread of English, other, more local forces have also been involved. These local forces are increasingly leading to the establishment of new regional and national standards in which what once might have been regarded as non-standard and even as an error is now regarded as fully acceptable. Other forces which have also contributed both to the spread of the language and to change within it include covert as well as overt prestige and the various types of motivation which lie behind language *accommodation* (link: Accommodation), be it in the direction of convergence or of *divergence*.

Overall, a variety of approaches continue to play a role. Among them we find (a) the family tree model, (b) geographical spread, whether in a wave, a jump, or an areal model, and (c) social factors like power and solidarity, which affect spread and what variants are spread, whether based on aspects of social identity such as gender, ethnicity, education/class, or local social networks. Change continues to be motivated by such forces as (a) linguistic universals or (b) language contact, bilingualism, and *code-switching*; lexical and semantic gaps and borrowing; as well as social and communication accommodation and *hyper-correction*. Furthermore, changes conform to phenomena such as assimilation and speech economy, *phonotactic* regularization, grammatical and phonological reanalysis, analogical and system-induced change, and *chain shift* mechanisms. All these topics will come up in the following chapters.

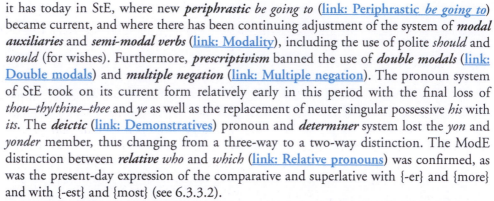

7.5.2 Communities of native and primary language users

Inasmuch as overseas territories were settled by monolingual English speakers, the new groups were basically continuations of the speech communities that remained in Britain. Since a native language is generally the one a person learns as a child, there is no difficulty in calling the language of these people precisely this: a native language. The real problem of definition comes in the case of bi- or multilingual societies. For some speakers in such communities it may be hard to label one or the other language as native – and indeed it may not be worth the trouble to do so. We can simply assume that some bilinguals are relatively balanced in their degree of competence and ease of communication in both languages even though there are almost always differences by area or domain. This means that even highly balanced bilinguals may prefer one language for, say, the domains of sports or work and the other, for religion or family. What is perhaps most important is to discern whether a person's English is dominant enough in at least a few domains to be understood as a primary language. This language may be distinguished by being the one most frequently used – be it as a native, a second, or a foreign language.

In the settlement phase of North America, Australia, South Africa, and New Zealand native and primary language users were in the majority, but the kinds of English which they brought with them often differed to begin with, and the physical and social situation in their new home was significantly different from back home. Both of these aspects led to changes in their English.

The mixing of people from different dialect regions in Britain had the effect of evening out differences. This is a process known as leveling or **koinéization**.[4] If native speakers, who in the period of colonial settlement were often farmers, used the **Northern** form (*hay*) *stack*, the Southwestern *mow*, or if the people in between used the word *rick* for what was essentially the same referent, theoretically all three could continue to be employed alongside each other. But it is more likely that people will eventually opt for only one of them. In this case all three happen to still be in use in Australia and North America, but evidently *stack* predominates since only it shows up in such non-farm contexts as the widely used **idiom** *like looking for a needle in a haystack*. Also common to the process of leveling is usage in the context of national broadcasting, domestic marketplaces, and advertising. While *clabber, Dutch cheese, smearcase,* and *cottage cheese* may once have competed with each other in the US, national advertising and marketing has settled the case in favor of *cottage cheese*. The development of new national markets and widespread consumer societies has been a significant factor in the emergence of regional and national language communities. It has been said that in 1903 "Waltzing Matilda" (see Text 7.2) was adopted by the Billy Tea company for national advertising, thus helping to establish the song's language and ideology throughout Australia.

Borrowing and **word formation** make up the second set of factors that have led to divergence in the vocabulary of the varieties of English used throughout the world. Both are widely practiced and fundamentally identical processes, but, of course, the items borrowed and the new words created differ by country. This is a consequence of the dissimilar natural and social conditions of the various places the language is used in and of the differing languages with which the speakers of English were and are in contact.

---

4 Koinéization is the making of a *koiné*, literally a common or shared language. The term derives from the Greek word *koiné*, meaning "common" and referred originally to the variety of Greek which became the lingua franca of the Hellenistic period (cf. Thomson qtd. in Siegel 1993: 5). See also 10.2.2.

We noted that OE depended especially strongly on native processes of *word formation* (link: Word formation processes) while ME borrowed lexical items much more freely. In the process of the spread of English throughout the world there has been considerable use of both sources of new vocabulary. One tendency that might be pointed out is that the English spoken in predominantly ESL societies is – probably because of the prevalence of bilingualism – generally more likely to resort to borrowing (link: Borrowing). Although not dependent on bilingualism, the incidence of massive borrowing indicates that it tends to follow periods of widespread bilingualism, as we have observed in regard to both OE and ME. This was the case *after* the Viking invasions, when the integration of the Norse-speaking communities was occurring. Likewise, the major evidence for French borrowings comes from the period *after* 1204, when the landowning classes had to decide for either Normandy or England and bilingualism began to decline.

Loan words may be borrowed directly, conforming sometimes more and sometimes less to the phonological patterns of the language of origin as opposed to English pronunciation patterns. Among other things, mixed compounds (loan blends) come about, in which one part of the new word is English and the other part borrowed. In other cases we have calques or loan translations, in which a foreign word is translated into English element by element. In addition, the semantics of the word in English may diverge to a greater or a lesser extent from the original semantics. Let us look at some examples.

First, there is the question of frequency of occurrence. While Australian English is characterized by a large number of typically or even specifically AusE words, their presence in any extended example of Australian StE is rather skimpy and scattered. In one Australian novel (*True History of the Kelly Gang* by Peter Carey, first published 2000) we find more than the usual incidence of specifically Australian words, probably because it is in the interest of the author to generate a genuine-sounding historical Australian atmosphere. One of them is the loan word *currawong* (Carey 2002: 133) for a black, white, and grayish bird (also a kind of tree, but not in this context). The word comes from *garrawang*, a word in the Yagara language, but it has obviously undergone a certain amount of phonological change (see also Text 7.2 *billabong, coolibah*). Loan translations were impossible to find in this novel. And even literary examples of loan blends are rare in this source. A fifty-page search of Carey yielded only *kangaroo dogs* "dogs bred to hunt kangaroos" (140). South African English (SAfE) contains, in contrast, numerous loan translations, which stem most commonly from **Afrikaans**, a sister language of English, for example *Kaapstad*, which is translated directly as *Cape Town*, or *outspan*, a literal translations of *uitspan* "unbridle or unyoke," whereby {-span} remains untranslated. However, writing in an ESL society such as Nigeria or India may differ in significant ways (see 7.4.3).

Word formation using so-called native elements, that is, **morphemes** which are firmly rooted in the language, is a major source of new vocabulary. In Carey the reader happens onto *bushranger* "bandit in the wilds" (115) and *bushmanship* "ability to fend for oneself in the wilds" (117). Text 7.2 is a *bush ballad*, a kind of back country folk song. Other compounds include *cockatoo fence* "farm fence" (126) from the name of Cockatoo Island, a penal settlement, and originally from the word for the bird taken from Dutch *kaketoe*, which borrowed it from Malay *kakatua*. **Shortenings** such as *phiz* (ibid.: 113) "face," from *physiognomy* are not highly common and will probably be understood in the context of their use.

Words from British and Irish regional dialects are a further source of AusE vocabulary. Examples include *barrack* "shout, cheer, egg on" (147), *chook* "chicken" (108), and *skerrick* "little bit" (117) (see also Text 7.2 *swag*, *billy*). This source of vocabulary cannot be ruled out in ESL societies, but is highly unlikely since the major language input has been by way of the schools and is therefore StE.

Semantic change, especially broadening and narrowing, is also affected, as where *mob* (110) has the additional meaning of "flock (of sheep)" – hence broadening – (see also Text 7.2: *waltzing*) or *shag* (114) "have sex" (also BrE) – presumably a narrowing (see also Text 7.2 *squatter*).

Text 7.2 "Waltzing Matilda" (1887)

"Waltzing Matilda"
Banjo Patterson (Christina Macpherson manuscript)

Oh there once was a swagman camped in the billabong
Under the shade of a Coolibah tree
And he sang as he looked at the old billy boiling
Who'll come a'waltzing Matilda with me

Refrain:
Who'll come a'waltzing Matilda my darling
Who'll come a'waltzing Matilda with me
Waltzing Matilda and leading a waterbag
Who'll come a'waltzing Matilda with me

Down came a jumbuck to drink at the billabong
Up jumped the swagman and grabbed him with glee
And he said as he put him away in the tucker bag
"You'll come a'waltzing Matilda with me"   + Refrain

Down came the squatter a'riding his thoroughbred
Down came policemen, one, two and three,
"Whose is the jumbuck you've got in the tuckerbag?
You'll come a'waltzing Matilda with me."   + Refrain

But the swagman he up and he jumped in the water-hole
Drowning himself by the coolabah tree
And his ghost may be heard as it sings by the billabong
Who'll come a'waltzing Matilda with me.   + Refrain

waltzing "traveling on foot" slang
matilda "bag, swag" colloquial
swagman "itinerant worker" compound of Brit. dialect *swag* "bed-roll" + *man*
billabong "waterhole" < Wiradjuri *bila* "river" + *bong*
coolibah "kind of eucalyptus" < Yuwaaliyaay *gulabaa*
billy "can for boiling water" < Scot. dialect *bally*
a-waltzing a-prefixing: earlier stage in the development of the progressive (see 4.2.3.1; 5.1; 8.2.5.7; Text 10.3)

jumbuck "semi-wild sheep" < Aus. pidgin
jump up (?)
tucker "food" British slang

squatter "a prosperous farmer"

(www.nla.gov.au/epubs/waltzingmatilda/index.php?p=three_versions)

Besides the innovations in vocabulary, as just illustrated, local pronunciations began to emerge which resembled the speech of the major immigrant groups. This includes, for example, the *rhoticity* of much of American speech, which derives in large part from the settlers from Ulster and, possibly, the English West Country, and Australian pronunciation, which is clearly a reflection of the vowel shifts of Cockney.

Grammatical forms are everywhere fairly similar if we restrict our view to the standard language of the new territories. However, as might be expected, features now considered non-standard in BrE sometimes "worked their way up," forms such as the standard AmE past participle *gotten*. In SAE the contact-influenced construction *busy* (< Afrikaans *besig*) + V-*ing* for non-action verbs as in *busy waiting* will come across as strange elsewhere (11.2.2).

Also amenable to contact-influenced change are various *pragmatic idioms* (link: Pragmatic idioms). An example is *kia-ora* from Māori, sometimes used in New Zealand English (NZE) as a greeting or to wish someone well. *Discourse particles* (link: Discourse particles) are another example from the area of *pragmatics*. The use of *no* to introduce statements has been adopted from Afrikaans in some forms of SAfE (11.4.6), where it functions somewhat like English *well*, for example *No, that'll be fine. We can do that easily for you*. Further discussion of these and other points can be found in the following chapters.

7.5.3 ESL speaker communities

In communities where English is a second language most types of word formation and borrowing occur as they do in ENL countries. In addition, *L1*-influenced pronunciation and grammatical structures specific to ESL may be found. East and West African English tend to use a *vowel system* highly reduced in comparison to ENL varieties. East African English may have as few as five vowels, which means that long /iː/ and short /ɪ/ are not distinguished; nor are /eɪ/ and /e/; or /æ/, /ɑː/, /ɜː/, and /ʌ/; or /ɒ/, /ɔː/, and /əʊ/; or /uː/ and /ʊ/ (Angogo and Hancock 1980: 75; see 12.3.1). One of the best known examples of a grammatical difference is the frequent leveling of grammatical *tag questions* (*isn't he, aren't we, can't they*, etc.) to a single form: *isn't it?* (12.3.2; 12.4.4.2).

Strategies of communication different from those familiar to native speakers may be used. For example, *modes of address* and expressions of *politeness* sometimes come across as more formal than the often highly informal usage of many native speakers. The use of titles when addressing a person to whom respect is due is likely to persist longer where the L1 demands this. At one point the narrator in Chimamanda Ngozi Adichie's *Purple Hibiscus* (first published 2004) greets a bishop by saying, "Good afternoon, sir, *nno*," formal (*good afternoon*) and respectful (*sir*) with the Igbo word *nno* for "welcome" (2005: 94). This is a literary example aimed at an English-speaking readership which may not be familiar with Nigerian life and customs, and this is perhaps reason enough to use Igbo vocabulary frequently. However that may be, second language use of this sort is indicative of the type of language mixing which is commonly found among bilinguals.

Because so many languages are used in ESL countries such as Nigeria, *bilingualism* and multilingualism are a normal and necessary part of everyday life. Very often *code-switching* is a function of the situation speakers find themselves in, where the principle is to accommodate through language choice to as many people as possible. The default language in any given situation may, by silent, mutual agreement, be fairly clearly established or, in any case, quickly negotiated. Since StE is hardly ever a native language in Nigeria, it is unlikely to be the language of choice in more familiar situations. It may, however, be a primary language in domains such as work, education, and some types of public administration. We see some evidence of this in a passage from the domain of religion in Adichie's novel, where we read:

> Papa changed his accent when he spoke, sounding British, just as he did when he spoke to Father Benedict. He was gracious, in the eager-to-please way that he always assumed with the religious, especially with the white religious.
>
> (2005: 46)

The father, who had studied in Britain, uses English with his family and is able to switch *accents* by situation or for stylistic purposes. In a second passage from the same novel we see how code-switching in a context of bilingualism can be used:

Text 7.3 Igbo borrowing in English

Every time Aunty Ifeoma spoke to Papa, my heart stopped, then started again in a hurry. It was the flippant tone; she did not seem to recognize that it was Papa, that he was different, special. I wanted to reach out and press her lips shut and get some of that shiny bronze on my fingers.

"Where do you want to take them [the narrator and her brother]?" Papa asked, standing by the door.

"Just to look around."

"Sightseeing?" Papa asked. He spoke English, while Aunty Ifeoma spoke Igbo.

"Eugene, let the children come out with us!" Aunty Ifeoma sounded irritated; her voice was slightly raised. "Is it not Christmas that we are celebrating, eh? . . ."

. . . "Okay. They can go with you, but you know I do not want my children near anything ungodly. If you drive past mmuo, keep your windows up."

"I have heard you, Eugene," Aunty Ifeoma said, with exaggerated formality.

(C.N. Adichie (2005) *Purple Hibiscus.* London: Harper Perennial, 77–78)

In this passage we read English, but must imagine Auntie Ifeoma's words in Igbo. In the context of the novel, Ifeoma, a well-educated university lecturer, seems to choose Igbo in order to counter her English-speaking brother Eugene, a successful and wealthy entrepreneur. But even Eugene uses the Igbo word *mmuo* "spirit mask" for something not easily expressed in English. Ifeoma represents a freer, less constrained attitude toward life and recognition of the values of tradition and family. Eugene is a strict Christian who practices charity toward the less well-off, but is authoritarian and brutal within his immediate family. Language comes to symbolize this, as even the names – European Eugene and African Ifeoma – help to transmit the dilemma of the young first person narrator caught between these two forces.

7.5.4 Pidgin and creole communities

A final aspect of some ESL countries, especially in West Africa, is the use of a completely different tradition of English, namely Pidgin English. English pidgins and creoles are a group of often closely related languages that originated as *trade languages* along the coast of West Africa and which were later carried to other parts of the colonial world. In West Africa pidgins have remained largely non-native languages. This means that they are not the first language of anyone. Instead they function as *lingua francas*, which means that they are used as a means of communication among people who do not speak the native languages of their communication partners. While the pidgin allows communication between these people, it is frequently so reduced in its linguistic repertoire that it is not conducive to elaborated or highly differentiated exchanges. Consequently, a pidgin is used in only a restricted number of social functions and in only a few domains. In Nigeria pidgin is employed especially often in market situations. In a final passage from Adichie we can observe the use of Nigerian Pidgin English (NPE). Police officers have come to search Ifeoma's house during student protests:

Text 7.4 Code-switching into NPE

She opened the door only a crack, but two wide hands reached in and forced the door ajar. . . .

"What is it? Who are you?" Aunty Ifeoma asked.
"We are here to search your house. We're looking for documents designed to sabotage the peace of the university. . . ."
"Who sent you here?" Aunt Ifeoma asked.
"We are from the special security unit in Port Harcourt."
"Do you have any papers to show me? You cannot just walk into my house."
"Look at this yeye woman [mother] *oh! I said we are from the special security unit!" the tribal marks curved even more on the man's face as he frowned and pushed Aunty Ifeoma aside.*

"How you go just come enter like dis? Wetin be dis?" Obiora [Ifeoma's son and the slightly older cousin of the narrator] *said, rising, the fear in his eyes not quite shielded by the brazen manliness in his pidgin English.*

(C.N. Adichie (2005) *Purple Hibiscus.* London: Harper Perennial, 230–231)

This passage shows the use of NPE for communication between people who may not share a common *autochthonous* Nigerian language, but as the exchange between Ifeoma and the men makes obvious, they all do speak English. Nevertheless, Obiora chooses to use NPE, and the comment in the text makes it clear that pidgin is a stronger, more manly language and therefore, in Obiora's eyes, more suitable for a confrontation.

In the Caribbean (see chapter 9) we find creoles rather than pidgins, because everywhere the original pidgins have been succeeded by creoles. These are the native languages of whole communities of speakers. As such they are used in the full repertoire of communicative functions and in an expanded number of *domains* and *registers*. A short passage from Andrea Levy's novel *Small Island* (2004) gives us a sample. The narrator is Hortense, who is a school girl in the passage quoted; Miss Jewel is her aunt:

Text 7.5 Code-switching between English and Jamaican Creole

Miss Jewel called me every day after school, "Miss Hortense, di boy gone, come help me nuh."
Her colossal leather-worn hands squeezed waterfalls from washing. Her breasts wobbled: two
fallen fruit trapped by the waistband of her skirt. Her legs bowed.

"Miss Jewel," I asked, "why your legs stick out so?"

She solemn, sucked her teeth and said, "Me nuh know, Miss Hortense. When me mudda
did pregnant dem she smaddy obeah'er. A likkle spell yah no." And she sang as she washed.
"'Mr Roberts wash him sock at night. And sidung pon de ground.'"

"No, Miss Jewel," I told her, "you are singing the wrong words. It is 'While shepherds
watched their flock by night'."

"Weh you mean shepherd, Miss Hortense?"

"A shepherd is a man who looks after sheep."

"Sheep? Dem nuh have none ah dat in Jamaica?"

"No, it is England where the shepherd is, Miss Jewel."

"Oh, Hengland. Ah deh so de Lawd born ah Hengland?"

(A. Levy (2004) *Small Island*. London: Review, 42–43)

In the Pacific we find both pidgins and creoles. Exemplary is ***Tok Pisin***, the language most widely spoken in Papua New Guinea. For more and more people in the urban areas it is the native language despite the name Tok Pisin, which comes from English *talk pidgin*. In more rural, highly polyglot areas of the country it is still a pidgin and serves as a lingua franca. See Text 9.4.

7.5.5 Foreign language speaker communities

The spread of English also includes the significant increase in the teaching and learning of English as a Foreign Language (EFL). The development of this aspect of spread most likely runs parallel to the rise of first Britain and then the United States as the major global players from the late eighteenth century on. With the defeat of the Spanish Armada England was relatively free to move into overseas territories. With the victory over France at the end of the Seven Years' War / French and Indian War in 1763 British imperial power was secure. And just as the Empire was beginning to decline in the period following World War I, American power began to take on a global aspect.[5] English was not a prominent foreign

---

5 American isolationism finally ended with the military engagement of the United States in World War II.

language, and certainly not a competitor of first Latin and then French – which were taught as the primary foreign languages in European schools – until relatively late. However, the choice of English as a foreign language grew enormously in the course of the twentieth century, and there are now estimated to be as many as 750 million EFL speakers.

EFL may be learned under conditions of formal instruction, for example at school, or by being exposed to the language while spending time in a country where it is spoken, for example the English spoken by an undocumented Chicana working as a nanny in a Manhattan home. EFL has a full linguistic repertoire and may potentially be used in as full a range of registers, *styles*, and domains as any L1. In general, ENL or ESL competence is the EFL norm even though the degree of attainment may fall short of this. Such stages of imperfect learning are sometimes referred to as *interlanguage* (link: Interlanguage, learner's language), and they are characterized by what native speakers are likely to think of as errors. However that may be, for many learners the opportunities to use the language will be restricted and may, especially for those who learned the language in school and seldom if ever used it, eventually undergo a process of *attrition* (link: Attrition). Where the language is used for communication it may develop into a lingua franca of sorts, which implies that it is used in more or less limited situations and that the functions it fulfills are reduced vis-à-vis an L1. Some of the linguistic features of this English are listed in the following:

- no third person singular present time {-s}
- interchangeability of relative *who* and *which*
- use of a preposition where L1 English has none, for example *to discuss **about** something*
- verb complement forms such as *want that they respond*.

For more on English as a Lingua Franca (ELF), aka English as an International Language (EIL) see chapter 13.

7.6 Summary

In general, there has been behind the spread of English a *unifying* force in the guise of GenE, which has come to be used by more and more speakers. All the same, this is not a *uniform* variety even though it is a variety which is widely comprehensible throughout the English-speaking world. The differences within GenE which people are most aware of can be described in two dimensions. One indicates the regional and national varieties of English, varieties which include ENL, ESL, and EFL. Kachru's concentric circles (see Figure 7.4) are an early attempt to describe the relationship between ENL, which is his inner circle; ESL, which is the extended (or outer) circle; and EFL, the expanding circle. In Figure 7.5 these distinctions are projected onto the horizontal axis. The ENL varieties are closest to the center and the intersection with the vertical axis, and the ESL and EFL varieties further out. Most distant are the English pidgins and creoles, which are peripheral in the sense that they represent more or less independent linguistic systems, yet ones historically, socially, and linguistically related to English. The vertical axis has a highly disputed, but nonetheless widely recognized pole represented by StE and an opposite pole which stands for the non-

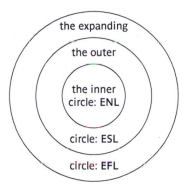

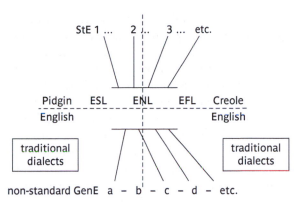

Figure 7.4 An external view of English (after Kachru 1985)

Figure 7.5 A two-dimensional model of English showing status variation (ENL, ESL, EFL, Pidgin and Creole English) as well as GenE and traditional dialects

standard forms of GenE. In Figure 7.5 both ends are shown as diverging in a series of diagonal lines to indicate, at the upper end, the existence of various regional and national standards. The StE lines correspond in extent to the series ESL–ENL–EFL on the horizontal axis. At the lower end, the non-standard GenE lines also diverge as they show more or less affinity to the linguistic features of the traditional dialects. The latter are, however, outside of the range of GenE. The higher the position of a variety on the vertical dimension, the greater the overt social prestige and the education associated with it. The farther down one moves, the greater the stylistic variation and the stronger the dimension of covert prestige.

All of these complicated relationships are, in the end, the result of the extremely diverse conditions which have accompanied the spread of English from its insular British origins to the many places and situations where it is found today and which will be explored in more detail in the following chapters.

STUDY QUESTIONS

Social and cultural background

1. How justified is the label "linguistic imperialism" in regard to the spread of English?
2. How have urbanization and changes in level of education affected English?
3. What centers have been active in the diffusion of English to the periphery? How do they differ from each other?

Linguistic background

1. What justifies the grouping of both standard and non-standard under the label GenE? Do you agree with this approach?
2. This chapter does not use an approach which divides World English into a British and an American branch (as Strevens 1992, for example, does). What are the advantages and disadvantages of such a British–American division?
3. The concept of "Native Language" is sometimes difficult to apply. Name an instance where you feel it is clear and one in which it is doubtful.
4. Give examples of how language contact has led to regional differences in English.

Further reading

Jenkins' book is very student-oriented and can stimulate awareness of many of the important questions connected with the spread of English; it can also irritate the reader because of its sometimes facile treatment of these questions. Bex and Watts have compiled a useful collection of contributions on a variety of aspects of StE. McArthur takes a synchronic, non-monolithic perspective on English in the world. Kachru is a veteran proponent of a less parochial view of English. Mesthrie and Bhatt provide an introduction to many of the linguistic aspects of varieties of English around the world. Schneider gives a comprehensive overview. Phillipson's chapter three, "Linguistic Imperialism: Theoretical Foundations," is especially thought provoking. Schneider looks individually at sixteen different post-colonial Englishes and includes a full chapter on English in the US.

Bex, T. and R. Watts, (eds.) (1999) *Standard English: The Widening Debate*. London: Routledge.

Jenkins, J. (2009a) *World Englishes. A Resource Book for Students*. 2nd ed. London: Routledge.

Kachru, B.B. (ed.) (1992) *The Other Tongue: English across Cultures*. 2nd ed. Urbana: University of Illinois Press.

McArthur, A. (1998) *The English Languages*. Cambridge: CUP.

Mesthrie, R. and R. Bhatt (2008) *World Englishes: The Study of New Linguistic Varieties*. Cambridge: CUP.

Phillipson, R. (1992) *Linguistic Imperialism*. Oxford: OUP.

Schneider, E. (2003) *Postcolonial Englishes: Varieties around the World*. Cambridge: CUP.

CHAPTER EIGHT

English in Great Britain and Ireland (since 1700)

CONTENTS

The English have no respect for their language, and will not teach their children to speak it. They spell it so abominably that no man can teach himself what it sounds like. It is impossible for an Englishman to open his mouth without making some other Englishman hate or despise him.
(G.B. Shaw "Preface" to *Pygmalion*, 1912)

Chapter Overview:

This chapter

- reviews the most important developments in Britain and Ireland;
- looks at England and Wales to demonstrate the codification aspects of standardization;
- reviews changes in vocabulary and also grammar and grammaticalization;
- explains how the pronunciations of different varieties may be approached as an introduction to the results of mergers, splits, and further chain shifting;
- follows with a section each on the standard and traditional dialects of Scotland and on standard and vernacular Irish English with special attention to grammatical aspect in the vernacular;
- finally discusses changes in urban English especially with regard to immigration. Two examples are given: Black British English and Chinese–English code switching.

8.1 Social and historical developments in Britain and Ireland

The three hundred years or so which this chapter traces have brought numerous changes, but the one thing which has not changed is variation in the language. Shaw's words are exaggerated, but they do testify to one thing this chapter will demonstrate: The English language in Britain and Ireland is anything but uniform. Furthermore, its variety is not about to go away. People identify with *their* language, be it a **traditional dialect**, an urban *vernacular*, English formed by an immigrant heritage, a national (English, Scottish, Irish, Welsh) variety, or **Standard English**. But before turning to the language, the chapter begins with a brief account of some of the important happenings in the areas of demography, transportation, industrialization, urbanization, education, and the media, always with an eye to their effect on the English language.

8.1.1 Political union

The Act of Union (1707) created the United Kingdom and can, coincidentally, pretty much serve as the starting point of the Modern English (ModE) period. The UK as it was initially created was still "unfinished" inasmuch as Ireland was still to be added by the second Act of Union, effective from 1801 on. Another hundred plus years later Ireland left the United Kingdom to become the Irish Free State (1922) within the framework of the British Commonwealth, and then in 1949 the Republic of Ireland was created outside of the Commonwealth. Both are now members of the European Union. For more on **political-social change** see link: Political change.

8.1.2 Demographic developments

These include a continuation of urbanization due to further enclosures (link: Enclosures) as a push-factor and to incipient industrialization as a pull-factor. Since the movement to the towns and cities was more rapid than the jobs available, a new impoverished urban class emerged which was perceived by the establishment as a threat which could not be dealt with by relying on the traditional poorhouse solutions. The answer to what was seen as over-population lay in resettling large numbers of people in the colonial territories (see 11.1). In the sixteenth and seventeenth centuries the southeastern part of Ireland was settled by people from the English **Southwest** while the North was settled by Scots (see 8.4). In both cases the native Irish were driven from their lands and forced to move to the west; some were even sent to Barbados as slaves.

8.1.3 London and other urban centers

The linguistic role of London cannot be exaggerated. Most migration was directed there. Indeed, the London area would have suffered considerable depopulation between 1700 and 1780, had it not been for the enormous movement of people from the countryside to London (Hobsbawm 1990: 43). But this was, for many, only the gateway to further movement to North America (chapter 10) and later to the Southern Hemisphere (chapter 11). All in all 69% of the natural population increase of England between the beginning of the Civil War (1642) (link: English Civil War) and the close of the seventeenth century emigrated to America. The movement of people leaving Britain, mostly for North America, continued into the eighteenth century. Estimates put the figure of emigrants at 20% of natural increase (Bailyn 1988: 40) (link: European expansion and the concept of the frontier). This movement first to London and then on to other parts of the world offers an important explanation for the relative uniformity of GenE throughout the world. It can reasonably be conjectured that these people – the more mobile and perhaps more ambitious part of the population – were probably ready to give up the more parochial features of their traditional dialect in favor of London English as they began to identify more strongly with London groups.

8.1.4 The Industrial Revolution (link: Industrial Revolution) and the transportation revolution (link: Transportation revolution)

These were among the most significant social changes of the eighteenth and nineteenth centuries. Partly as a prerequisite for and partly as an effect of industrialization there were fundamental changes in transportation. First, in the period after 1750 there was the estab-lishment of turnpikes, then canals, and finally railroads. Among their consequences was the development of regional and supra-regional markets and, concomitant with this, greater labor force mobility in a money rather than barter economy with the potential for consump-tion. It hardly seems necessary to point out that this led to a weakening of the rural traditional dialects and an upsurge of new urban varieties in the process of *dialect leveling* or *koinéization* (link: *Koinéization*).

As industrialization continued, new centers in the Northeast (mining) and in the Western *Midlands* (textiles in Manchester and Birmingham and commerce in Liverpool) began to emerge. Immigration of labor from "abroad" also ensured further language and dialect contact as Irish workers found jobs in the major projects of canal building in the eighteenth and nineteenth centuries and then in the building of the railways. Enclaves of Irish came into being, especially in Liverpool.[1] Despite linguistic leveling the general distinctions were retained between the North (now divided more clearly than ever between the English North and Scotland), the East Midlands and the now industrializing West Midlands, and the South. The emergence of a new, mostly working-class, urban population in the North in the nineteenth century was accompanied by a literature of its own. Pamphlets, broadsides, and almanacs showed local consciousness and pride in vernacular culture and language. As the novels of Elizabeth Gaskell demonstrate (link: Working-class literature), language – be it traditional dialect or working-class *koiné* – was a *marker* of class solidarity (cf. Wales 2002: 57ff).

8.1.5 Education and the mass media

Urbanization led to higher rates of literacy, so that by the 1840s the majority of the population could probably read and write. This was accomplished a full generation before the enactment of the Elementary School Act (1870) and was the result of private initiative and of Dame Schools (link: Education in Britain; Elementary School Act). Widespread literacy led to an expanding publishing market, especially one geared to cheap books and newspapers with high entertainment value. Technological improvements, such as cheap wood-pulp paper and the rotary press, contributed to a reduction in printing costs; and rapid rail transportation lowered the costs of distribution.

Since the late twentieth century one potentially significant development in the area of language has been the movements for political devolution and/or independence in Scotland and Wales, with so far little effect on the English language. There has been no broad

---

1 Similar concentration could also be found in a number of larger American cities such as Boston and New York. The Irish contribution to Australian immigration was also significant.

movement to raise Scots to a national language in Scotland, but Scottish Gaelic and Welsh have attracted more attention. More relevant to linguistic change has been the significant increase in immigration. English remains the default language in public encounters both in the United Kingdom, where it coexists with officially recognized Welsh, and in the Republic of Ireland, where Irish Gaelic has official status. English also shares private space with a long list of immigrant languages whose numerical leaders are (in this order) Punjabi, Bengali, Saraiki, Urdu, Sylheti, Cantonese, Greek, Italian, Black British English/Creole, Gujarati, and Kashmiri.

8.2 England and Wales

8.2.1 The Standard, language policy, and attitudes toward StE

In the eighteenth century StE existed as a monument to the new unity of the nation after the Civil War and the Glorious Revolution (link: Glorious Revolution). It plastered over continuing ethnic, religious, and class division and was essentially the product of the upper orders of society in the Georgian Age. On the one hand, StE ensured that the innovations of the EModE period were maintained, for example:

- the conclusive move from third person singular {-th} to {-s};
- the completion of the switch to second person singular (subject and object) *you*;
- third person possessive neuter *its*;
- present tense plural *are* for earlier (Southern) *been*;
- the expansion of the progressive;
- the use of relative *who* for persons and *which* elsewhere;
- the relegation of double negation and double comparison to the non-standard language;
- reduction of the *subjunctive*;
- restriction of the perfect auxiliary to *have*;
- reduction of the *demonstrative* system from a three-term to a two-term system;
- adoption of standardized *spelling* and punctuation.

On the other hand, it more or less institutionalized a new division in society (see following).

8.2.1.1 Standard English and prescriptivism.

In the eighteenth century standard languages were part of the ideological work of nationalism. Only in recent times had England, Ireland, Scotland, and Wales set about establishing their own languages (Joseph 2004: 94). We need to remember, as Hobsbawm points out, that a national language is "a discursive construction," the attempt "to devise a standardized idiom out of a multiplicity of actually spoken idioms, which are downgraded to dialects" (1990: 51).

Originally, StE, as the emerging national language of the UK, was "the property of nationalist intellectuals rather than of ordinary users," but with widespread education this ceased and: "The linguistic ideology then becomes common national property, at least as likely to find firm belief among the working classes who do not control it as among the upper classes who do" (Joseph 2004: 121). In Victorian England, when the white-collar class masked class in a nationalistic guise "in their obsession with 'speaking properly' as a mark of respectability, they were contributing to the linguistic construction of their nation" (ibid.: 122).

The expectation that the standard should be learned and used by everyone led in two problematic directions. One was the readiness to extend English to speakers of other languages, most especially Welsh, which was systematically suppressed until relatively recently. The second was the misapprehension that the use of StE correlated with intelligence. Just because children from the higher strata of society were more successful in school and also spoke varieties of English relatively closer to the standard did not justify associating intelligence with StE (and a "proper" *accent*: see 8.2.4). It only indicated that class privilege virtually guarantees scholastic success. Initially StE was a feature which could relatively confidently be associated with a good education regardless of native intelligence. The converse (non-standard English = poor education) may have once had some grounding in fact, but it certainly had nothing to do with intelligence, and today a good education, while encouraging a mastery of StE, no longer signifies what it may once have done.

8.2.1.2 Codification

The seventeenth and eighteenth centuries contributed enormously to the process of *codification*. This was a largely prescriptivist project whose aims were to purify and fix the language, and it affected pronunciation, grammar, spelling, and vocabulary. There was a widespread feeling that good grammar and good morals were closely connected. This shows that power lay at the center of the process of *standardization*, where an elite was most likely to impose its language and manners as a whole.

An important part of the move toward standardization was the desire of many of the more learned to fix the language in its ideal state. For these purposes Swift proposed the establishment of an academy on the model of the *Académie française* in France or the Italian *Accademici della Crusca*. This never came about, but individual grammarians played an important role in setting the standard.

Initially grammarians were still relatively open to regional forms. By end of the seventeenth century regionalisms were seen as "incorrect"; and grammarians "were prescribing the correct language for getting ahead in London society, and standard English had risen to consciousness" (Shaklee 1980: 60). As the language grew more complex and the possibilities for making stylistic distinctions increased, the number of people who aspired to use the new standard grew as well, and there was an enormous need to know just what it consisted of, hence the advent of *grammars*, books on orthoepy (the study of correct pronunciation) (link: Codification), and *dictionaries*.

The best known of the early dictionaries is Samuel Johnson's monumental *Dictionary of the English Language* (1755; Plate 8.1), which stands at the beginning of a long tradition of lexicography that would include the incomparable twelve-volume historical *Oxford English Dictionary* (1928; plus supplements; now in an internet edition) as well as hundreds and hundreds of further general and specialized dictionaries.

Samuel Johnson perceived a need for order and rules in the language. Variety was seen as negative; instead, "purity" was to be achieved. To accomplish this Johnson relied on an appeal to experience and analogy, and drew on the authority of writers of reputation. These were neither to be as old as Chaucer nor more recent than the Civil War, which lay a hundred years before. Text 8.1 is a short excerpt from his Preface, in which he sketches out some of his criteria. Before reading it, note that in the typography of the period non-final <s> appears as a so-called long <ſ>.

Text 8.1 S. Johnson, Preface to *A Dictionary of the English Language* (1755)

When I took the firſt ſurvey of my undertaking, I found our ſpeech copious without order, and energetick without rules: wherever I turned my view, there was perplexity to be diſentangled, and confuſion to be regulated; choice was to be made out of boundleſs variety, without any eſtabliſhed principle of ſelection; adulterations were to be detected, without a ſettled teſt of purity; and modes of expreſſion to be rejected or received, 5
without the ſuffrages of any writers of claſſical reputation or acknowledged authority. Having therefore no aſſiſtance but from general grammar, I applied myſelf to the peruſal of our writers; and noting whatever might be of uſe to aſcertain or illuſtrate any word or phraſe, accumulated in time the materials of a dictionary, which, by degrees, I reduced to method, eſtabliſhing to myſelf, in the progreſs of the work, 10
ſuch rules as experience and analogy ſuggeſted to me; experience, which practice and obſervation were continually increaſing; and analogy, which, though in ſome words obſcure, was evident in others.
So far have I been from any care to grace my pages with modern decorations, that I have ſtudiouſly endeavoured to collect examples and authorities from the writers 15
before the reſtoration, whoſe works I regard as the wells of Engliſh undefiled, *as the pure ſources of genuine diction. Our language, for almoſt a century, has, by the concurrence of many cauſes, been gradually departing from its original* Teutonick *character, and deviating towards a* Gallick *ſtructure and phraſeology, from which it*
ought to be our endeavour to recal it, by making our ancient volumes the ground- 20
work of ſtile, admitting among the additions of later times, only ſuch as may ſupply real deficiencies, ſuch as are readily adopted by the genius of our tongue, and incorporate eaſily with our native idioms.

(www.gutenberg.org/dirs/etext04/pengl10.txt)

Needless to say, current conceptions of the source of suitable words ([link: Criteria of correctness](#)) are quite different from Johnson's. In writing, for example, that *Commerce . . . corrupts the language* he was ignoring the fact that English had always drawn freely on foreign words and **idioms**. Furthermore, Johnson was unwilling to give the task of lexicography to an academy (*If an academy ſhould be eſtabliſhed for the cultivation of our ſtile, which I, who can never wiſh to ſee dependance multiplied, hope the ſpirit of Engliſh liberty will hinder or deſtroy, . . .*). Instead, he took on the task himself, and he was astonishingly good at it. In writing his *Dictionary* he revealed his subjectivity from time to time, but also showed that he could maintain a certain amount of self-distance:

> ### Text 8.2 Definitions from Johnson's dictionary
>
> *Tory: (A cant term, derived, I suppose, from an Irish word signifying a savage.) One who adheres to the antient constitution of the state, and the apostolical hierarchy of the church of England, opposed to a whig.*
>
> *Oats: A grain, which in England is generally given to horses, but in Scotland supports the people.*
>
> *Lexico'grapher: A writer of dictionaries; a harmless drudge, that busies himself in tracing the original, and detailing the signification of words.*
>
> (from: *Johnson's Dictionary. A Modern Selection* (1982) E.L. McAdam and G. Milne (eds.) London: Papermac)

8.2.2 Vocabulary

The expansion of vocabulary in this period has been similar to the additions of vocabulary in other varieties in the sense that linguistic and cultural contact led to the adoption of new words and expressions. This was due to the influence of the colonies and colonial goods and, somewhat later, to immigrants from abroad. Typically new objects, especially plants, animals, and topography, and new acts, for example clearing, cultivating, and settling the land and institutional innovations, guaranteed the acquisition of new words and expressions. For examples see 9.3.2; 9.5.3; 10.1.3; 10.2.3; 11.4; 12.3.2; 12.4.4; 12.4.5.3).

The differentiation of vocabulary according to class, gender, ethnicity, age, and region continues to be an important factor in language change. Only one example will be given to illustrate the type of distinctions involved: the class-oriented ones which the speakers of the language love to indulge in. That is, what is posh or upper class (U) and what in not (Non-U). This was initiated many years ago in Ross (1954) and continued in Wales (1994). According to Wales (1994: 7) U/Non-U usage is *America/the states*; *cake/pastry*; *helping/ portion*; *pudding/sweet, dessert*; *scent/perfume*; *sick/ill*; *table napkin/serviette*; and *spectacles/ glasses*. The **adjective** *appalling* is supposedly U, as are *absolutely* and *brill*.

8.2.3 Grammatical developments

From the point of view of standard grammar, little has happened since 1700 (cf. 8.2.1). Chief of among the developments is the completion of the *TMA* (tense–modality–aspect) paradigm, such as the extension of the progressive to the passive. Where once such forms as *the house was building* were common, today they are rare and are considered non-standard for *the house is being built*. Overall the progressive form occurs more frequently in ModE than it did in EModE, and is apparently still extending its scope (cf. 11.2.1.1).

The modal auxiliaries continued to expand thus reducing the subjunctive even further. The modals themselves had undergone so much restriction that a renewed modal system has begun to emerge. The actual changes in the system involve processes of both grammaticalization and *lexicalization*.

There are a number of recent developments in ModE which can be seen as cases of grammaticalization. They seem to be generated in the vernacular, that is, distant from pressure to be correct. Among these processes we may count the phonetic amalgamation of the semi-modals such as *going to → gonna* or *supposed to → supposta*. Furthermore, there is the development of the new preterite-present verb *got*, and the development of grammatical *lets*, *lemme*, and *there's* (link: **Grammaticalization and lexicalization**). Although some aspects of these changes are specifically American, they will be dealt with in this chapter.

8.2.3.1 The development of the modal verb

From a formal point of view, the modal verbs are intimately connected with the older Germanic emergence of **preterite-present verbs** (link: *Preterite-present verbs*), all of which do not have the third person singular present tense inflection {-s}. The present tense forms of these verbs were originally past tense forms (preterites) and thus had no such ending. This lies behind the class of traditional modal auxiliaries *may, must, can, will, shall*,[2] which do not have a third person singular {-s} inflection. More recently the **NICE** features, which are concerned chiefly with the lack of the use of periphrastic *do*, have come to apply to all the auxiliaries, that is, the primary auxiliaries, *be, have,* and *do* and the modal auxiliaries, but not to lexical verbs:

N   direct Negation (*should > shouldn't*)
I   Inversion in questions (*I will > Will I?*)
C   Code or reduced forms (*I may go > so may you*, i.e. without repeating the main verb *go*)
E   Emphatic affirmation (*Must we run? Yes, we múst*)

(Coates 1983: 4)

Four of the five modal verbs listed have "new" past tenses; all the same, they do not have non-finite forms, that is, there is no infinitive, no present participle, and no past participle. The traditional modals are also characterized by the absence of *to* before the following infinitive. The semantic criteria for modality are extremely varied but center on the opinion or attitude of the speaker (cf. Lyons 1977: 452; Palmer 2001: 2) or a speaker's judgment of the likelihood of a proposition being true (Quirk et al. 1985: 219). Modality as such can be expressed in a variety of ways, such as lexically with **adverbs** like *possibly* or *probably*. But the modal auxiliaries are special from a formal point of view, for they represent grammaticalized modality in English. More recent developments have led to what may be seen as a new wave of grammaticalization and a new groups of **semi-modals**.[3] These verbs not only carry meaning much like the traditional modals, but also fill some of the semantic gaps in the traditional modal system, such as that caused by the **bleaching out** of usages such as the volitional meaning of *will*.

---

2 Further modals are also recognized, most commonly *ought (to), need, dare,* and *used to*. See further discussion below.
3 The term semi-modal is from Palmer (1988); Coates (1983) uses quasi-modal, and Joos (1968), quasi-auxiliary.

The major argument for the existence of this new class is *to*-amalgamation. Several of the semi-modals are characterized by frequent amalgamation of the marker *to* with the preceding element in the semi-modal. This is coupled with considerable phonological restructuring such as vowel reduction to **schwa** and consonant shortening as in *oughta*, *gotta*, and *hadda*, which are pronounced with a single, rather than a double (i.e. long) /t/ or /d/. The latter is especially noticeable in AmE, because a true geminate (double) or long [tː] (not a spelling one) cannot be flapped whereas a single or short [t] will be flapped if followed by an unstressed syllable. In other words, *gotta* is flapped [gɑ:ɖə] while *go to (town)* is unflapped [gɑ:tːʊ]. Such **assimilation** also occurs in *hafta*, *hasta*, *usta*, and *supposta*, in which the original final voiced element of the verb has been de-voiced to match the /t/ of *to*. In the case of *wanna* post-nasal /t/ has been lost as is typical in the environment of a **nasal** plus an unstressed syllable in AmE (cf. *winter* [wɪnər]; see 10.3.3).

Support for the assumption that this is grammaticalization comes from the role these new (semi-)modals play in the types of modality in English. Three types are readily recognized: deontic, epistemic, and dynamic. A fourth, evidential, seems to be emerging. Each has a strong and a weak pole.

- **Deontic modality:** obligation (strong) and permission (weak). The status of the semi-modals gains support from the fact that the expression of the past is usually made using a periphrastic form (*be obliged*, *be allowed*) or an amalgamated form (*hafta*, *hasta*, *gotta*), for example *you may use my car: you **were allowed** to use . . .*; *they must pay the bill: they **had to** (**hadda**) pay the bill*.
- **Epistemic modality:** logical necessity (strong) and logical possibility (weak). Here the expression of the past is by means of perfect infinitives, for example *this must be correct: this must **have been** correct*; *it may sound strange: it may **have sounded** strange*. The amalgamated forms crop up as options, for example *you gotta be kidding*, even past: *you gotta have been kidding*.
- **Dynamic modality:** volition (strong) and ability (weak). Only with dynamic modality is the expression of the past with the morphological past of the traditional modal possible: *he can't translate this: he **couldn't** translate this*; *she won't help him: she **wouldn't** help him*; also *gonna* as in *they're gonna go soon: they **were gonna** go soon*. New amalgamated *wanna* (volition) and *gonna* (intention and "strong" future) fill in the gap left by the now rare use of *will* for volition.
- **Evidential modality** (emerging): factual (strong) and hearsay or quotative (weak) modality. The expression of the past is made with the perfect infinitive, with the morphological past of the modal expression, or with both simultaneously: *he's supposta be nice: he **was** supposta be nice / he is supposta **have been** nice / he **was** supposta **have been** nice* (for more detail see link: Modality).
- **Habitual *usta*** is de-grammaticalizing inasmuch as it now occurs virtually always with *do* in questions and negations. It has turned from a traditional to an amalgamated form. It is one of the few grammaticalized modals of habituality in StE.

8.2.4 Pronunciation and the emergence of Received Pronunciation (RP)

In the mid-nineteenth century a remarkably unitary pronunciation emerged among the boys at the elite private boarding schools of England. This accent was connected with the

power and prestige of the upper-class people who spoke it, thus taking on associations of competence and status. From the beginning of radio broadcasting in the 1920s and up until the late twentieth century it was the voice of the BBC. *RP* is, consequently, something of a class accent and is emulated by some and rejected by others for this reason. Its development and status have, however, been so prominent that it often serves as a *reference accent* (link: Reference accents) when talking about accents of English wherever they may be used. Today a modified regional form sometimes called *Estuary English* (link: Estuary English) is displacing it in some areas (see 8.5.2).

There are four more or less systematic ways of *comparing pronunciation* (link: Comparing pronunciation) both across time and across the globe:

- the **phonetic realization** of any given phoneme, for example /l/ as clear [l] or dark [ɫ];
- differences in the **phonemic system**, as when /w/ (as in *wear*) and /hw/ (or /ʍ/) (as in *where*) are distinct in Scottish English while in RP or GenAm they usually are not;
- the distribution of phonemes in standardized **lexical sets** of words such as the BATH words which have [ɑː] in RP but [a] or [æ] in the North;
- *phonotactic* **restrictions** on where phonemes may occur (see the following).

8.2.5 Phonotactic change

Among the numerous points which could be presented here the following are perhaps the most widely known. For the consonants they revolve around yod, that is, /j/, T, and L. In addition, we will return briefly to vowel *chain shifts* and give an example each of a vowel split and a vowel *merger*.

8.2.5.1 Rule ordering

Feeding and *bleeding* are two processes which help us to establish a better understanding of changes. One of the consequences of feeding is that a new rule will apply to more words. An example would be the addition of *intrusive /r/* to the **linking-/r/** rule. According to the latter a final orthographic <r> in a *non-rhotic accent* is pronounced if the following word begins with a vowel and no pause occurs between the two. In RP, for instance, *mar* by itself is /mɑː/, but becomes /mɑːrɪt/ in *Don't mar it*. The conditions for linking-r are (among other things) a final /ɑː/, /ɔː/, or /ə/, and this comes to apply to other words with these final sounds, but no final <r>. That is, there has been feeding, which results in the pronunciation of /r/ in *saw it* /sɔːrɪt/.

The opposite effect, bleeding, can be illustrated with the example of *yod-dropping* and *palatalization.* Early on yod before /uː/ was lost, for example, after /tʃ/, /r/, and consonant + /l/ (/bl-, fl-, gl-/) (*chew, juice, rude, crew, grew, flue, flew, glue*). In East Anglia all incidences of post-consonantal /juː/ became /uː/ (*few, music, cube, Hugh*) while other accents, especially GenAm, lost /j/ only after alveolars (/θ, s, z, l, n, t, d/) as in *enthusiasm, sue, resume, lewd, new, tune, due*). Palatalization applied to /s, z, t, d/, which developed into /ʃ, ʒ, tʃ, dʒ/ wherever they were followed by high front /i/ or /j/ preceding a weak syllable,[4] as in

---

4 There are cases in which palatalization occurred even with a following stressed syllable, for example *sure, sugar*.

s + j > ʃ   *nation, issue*
z + j > ʒ   *vision, Asian, Tunisian, azure, pleasure*
t + j > tʃ   *virtue, nature*
d + j > dʒ   *adventure, education.*

The spelling reflects the earlier unpalatalized pronunciation. Now see how rule ordering and bleeding affect each other. In a variety in which the yod (/j/) before a /uː/ is lost the fusion just described cannot take place. This is a case of bleeding, since there is a loss of words to which the conditions of change apply: compare *mature* /mətuːr/ (bleeding) vs. /mətʃuːr/ (no bleeding).

8.2.5.2 Intervocalic T and Glottaling (link: T-flapping; link: Post-nasal T; link: T-loss and glottal stops; link: Glottaling)

These are two current shifts in the phonotactics of T. In GenAm (and the North of England, Dublin, Australia, Cockney and even casual RP) original /t/ if preceded by a vowel, /r/, or /l/ and followed by an unstressed vowel (including syllabic [l̩] or [r̩]) is voiced and tapped. This is often perceived as a /d/, for example *latter = ladder*. In urban Britain original /t/ in the same environment may become the glottal ***stop*** [ʔ], cf. /læʔə/. Glottaling, as it is called, is spreading to the other voiceless stops as in [tɒʔl̩] (*topple*) or /rɪʔɪ/ (*Ricky*).

8.2.5.3 L-Vocalization (link: L-vocalization)

This is typical of working class London speech, but also found in the American South and in New Zealand, and is similar to ***R-Dropping***. A dark [ɫ], which is accompanied by vocalic [ʊ] is articulated with the tongue making contact with the roof of the mouth. If tongue contact is not made, what remains is vocalic [ɫ] or [ʊ]. *Milk* is now no longer /mɪlk/ but [mɪʊk]. This is leading to a whole new series of ***diphthongs***, for example [ɪʊ], [ɔʊ] (*balk*), [aɪʊ] (*bile*), [eʊ] (*belt*), etc.

8.2.5.4 Splits: the **TRAP–BATH** Split

Here the members of one "set" of words divides into two sets distinguished by a phonemically different pronunciation. Such changes in the phonemic system are especially noticeable among the vowels. In EModE /æ(ː)/ became first long before voiceless ***fricatives*** (except /ʃ/) or nasals, as in *staff, laugh, craft, after*; *path, bath*; *pass, last, clasp, ask*; *dance, grant, branch, demand*; and *example*. Then /aː/ underwent ***backing*** to /ɑː/, but in a very uneven fashion (link: TRAP–BATH split). Consequently exceptions abound: *gaff, math, aster, asp, gasket, romance, rant, mansion, stand, ample.*

8.2.5.5 Mergers (link: Mergers)

The ***THOUGHT NORTH FORCE Merger*** led to a convergence with the same vowel in these three lexical sets and proceeded as in Table 8.1. The main stations were vowel lengthening before /r/, the breaking of long /oː/, the raising of /ɒ/ to /ɔː/, R-Dropping, and diphthong smoothing.

Table 8.1 The FORCE mergers

	THOUGHT	*NORTH*	*FORCE*
EModE	ɒː	ɒr	oːr
Pre-R lengthening	—	ɒːr	—
Pre-R breaking and laxing	—	—	ɔər
Phonetic shift	ɔː	ɔːr	—
R-dropping	—	ɔː	ɔə
1ˢᵗ FORCE Merger (smoothing)	—	—	ɔː
Mod RP	ɔː	ɔː	ɔː

This merger is complete except "in some provincial, Celtic, West Indian, and American accents" (Wells 1982: 236). In a second FORCE Merger all the /ʊə/ centering diphthongs, as in *your, poor, moor*, and so on **monophthongize** and open to /ɔː/, for example *sure = shore*. This shift is in progress and its results are uneven.

8.2.5.6 Chain-shifts: the Southern Shift

It is radical rotations of vowel systems, and not differences of inventory, that account for the greatest differences between vowel systems and for problems of cross-dialectal comprehension. In these rotations, whole sets of vowels reverse their relative positions to each other; phones that represent one phoneme in one dialect represent an entirely different phoneme in another.

(Labov 1991: 3; see link: General principles of chain shifting)

The GVS (6.3.1.2) did not just happen and stop. Although the standard language and RP, the standard accent associated with it in England, have acted as brakes on further change, it has continued in the vernaculars, especially Cockney (see Figure 8.1). Variations on the **Southern Shift** are to be found in southern England, Australia, New Zealand, South Africa, and parts of the US (see 10.3.3; 11.3.1). To illustrate Cockney we move now to London English.

8.2.5.7 London speech

The London vernacular, most especially Cockney, was used in an often highly stereotypical fashion in the mouth of Sam Weller, one of the characters in Dickens' *Pickwick Papers* (1837; Plate 8.2). The following excerpt illustrates a few of the pronunciation (blue) and grammatical (blue italics) features attributed to this variety. Sam Weller, Mr. Pickwick's servant, has gone to visit his "mother-in-law" (= step-mother) at the pub she and Sam's

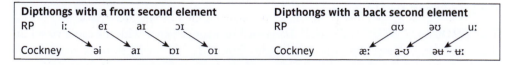

Figure 8.1 Continuation of the GVS: Cockney in comparison with RP

father run in Dorking. She is sitting at the fire with Mr. Stiggins, a vice-shepherd (assistant pastor) and free-loader. Stiggins (and Mrs. Weller) have been collecting money for "our noble society for providing the infant negroes in the West Indies with flannel waistcoats and moral pocket-handkerchiefs." Sam doesn't understand what the latter are.

Text 8.3 Nineteenth century London English: "Samuel Weller Makes a Pilgrimage to Dorking and Beholds his Mother-in-law"

"What's a moral pocket-ankercher?" said Sam; "I never see one o' the articles o' furniter."

"Those which combine amusement with instruction, my young friend," replied Mr. Stiggins, "blending select tales with wood-cuts."

[Eventually, Sam's father shows up:]   5

"What, Sammy!" exclaimed the father.

"What, old Nobs!" ejaculated the son. And they shook hands heartily. . . .

"It cert'nly seems a queer start to send out pocket-'ankerchers to people as don't know the use on 'em," observed Sam.

"They're alvays a-doin' some gammon of that sort, Sammy," replied his father.   10
"T'other Sunday I wos walkin' up the road, wen who should I see, a-standin' at a chapel door, with a blue soup-plate in her hand, but your mother-in-law. I werily believe there was change for a couple o' suv'rins in it, then, Sammy, all in ha'pence; . . . What d'ye think it was all for?"

"For another tea-drinkin', perhaps," said Sam.   15

"Not a bit on it," replied the father; "for the shepherd's water-rate, Sammy."

"The shepherd's water-rate!" said Sam.

"Ay," replied Mr. Weller, "there was three quarters owin', and the shepherd hadn't paid a farden, not he – perhaps it might be on account that the water warn't o' much use to him, for it's wery little o' that tap he drinks, Sammy, wery; he knows a trick   20
worth a good half-dozen of that, he does. Hows'ever, it warn't paid, and so they cuts the water off. . . . Upon this, the women calls a meetin' sings a hymn, wotes your mother-in-law into the chair, wolunteers a collection next Sunday, and hands it all over to the shepherd. And if he ain't got enough out on 'em, Sammy, to make him free of the water company for life," said Mr. Weller, in conclusion, "I'm one   25
Dutchman, and you're another, and that's all about it." . . .

"The worst o' these here shepherds is, my boy, that they reg'larly turns the heads of all the young ladies, about here. Lord bless their little hearts, they thinks it's all right, and don't know no better; but they're the wictims o' gammon, Samivel, they're the wictims of gammon."   30

(Charles Dickens, *The Pickwick Papers*. 3rd ed. London: Collins, 1953 [1837], chap. 27, 373–377)

Pronunciation:

ankercher: aitch-dropping (l. 1)

furniter: yod-dropping; no palatalization (l. 2)

wos: ɒ-raising before fricatives (l. 11)

wen: aitch-dropping; /hw/ to /w/ (l. 11)

werily: /v/ to /w/ (stereotypical Cockney) (l. 12)

suv'rins: **eye dialect** ([link: Eye dialect](#)) for *sovereign* (l. 13)

farden: /d/ for /ð/; but not /v/! (l. 19)

warn't: singular *were*; pre-**NURSE Merger** (of /ɜː/ and /ɑː/) ([link: Pre-Nurse merger](#)) (l. 19)

Samivel: /w/ to /v/ (stereotypical) (l. 29)

Grammar:

never: general negator (8.3.2.2) (l. 1)

see: leveled for *saw* (l. 1)

as: non-standard relative pronoun (l. 8)

on: non-standard for *of* (l. 9)

're a-doin: older progressive (< *on/at doing*) (l. 10)

they cuts: third person plural pronoun + verb with {-s} (l. 21)

the women calls: third person plur. noun subject + verb with {-s} (l. 22)

ain't: generalized negative of *be* and *have* (present tense) (l. 24)

these here: emphatic deictic form (l. 27)

don't know no: double negative (l. 29)

Wells points out that Dickens' Cockney was a literary *stereotype*, especially the switching of /v/ for /w/ and vice versa. If, as Wells says, Dickens' Cockney "was seriously out-of-date at the time he wrote," (Wells 1982: 333) this does not mean it never was the case (see Text 6.9).

8.2.6 Spelling conventions

In Modern English, spelling conventions are only gradually different from those of the EModE period. Among the uniformly accepted changes we find the move to use lower case letters for all but proper nouns, adjectives, and verbs (e.g. *Britain, Welsh, Anglicize*). The "long" <ſ>, as in <ſpeech> (see Text 8.1), disappeared, as did the <k> at the ends of words like *Teutonick* (Text 8.1, l. 18). Nevertheless, there have been a variety of movements to further reform English *orthography*. The usual basis for such suggestions has been to come as close as possible to a one-to-one relationship between each phoneme of the language and the letter or combination of letters employed to represent it. In other words, with the exception of a few shorthand systems of writing, for example Pitman shorthand, the alphabetic principle has been maintained. And in most cases the roman *alphabet* has been used, but again there have been exceptions such as Lodwick's universal alphabet (Abercrombie 1965: 51; see Figure 8.2).

The roman alphabet has, however, been modified to ensure greater consistency, as in the "New Spelling" by the Simplified Spelling Society of Great Britain, which is illustrated in the following rendering of the beginning of Lincoln's "Gettysburg Address":

> ### Text 8.4 Lincoln's Gettysburg Address (excerpt) in the New Spelling
>
> *But in a larjer sens, we kanot dedikaet – we kanot konsekraet – we kanot haloe – dhis ground.*
> *Dhe braev men, living and ded, huu strugld heer, hav konsekraeted it far abuv our puur pouer*
> *to ad or detrakt.*
>
> (P. MacCarthy (1972) "Criteria for a New Orthography for English," In: *Talking of Speaking:*
> *Papers in Applied Phonetics.* Oxford: OUP, 71)
>
> Conventional spelling:
> But in a larger sense, we cannot dedicate, we cannot consecrate, we cannot hallow this ground.
> The brave men, living and dead, who struggled here, have consecrated it far above our poor
> power to add or detract.

What has been undertaken in Text 8.4 is, for example, to use only <k> for /k/ and to spell all instances of /k/ with <k>: *kanot, konsekraet, detrakt*. /dʒ/ is always <j> as in *larjer*. /θ/ remains <th> (not shown), but /ð/ is spelled as <dh>, as in *dhis* "this"; final silent <e> is dropped as in *sens*. The <e> is sufficient to render /e/ and is consequently also used in <ded> for standard <dead>. In *konsekraet* the use of <ae> for /eɪ/ ensures the proper vowel quality, as do <ee> for /iː/, <uu> for /uː/, or <ou> for /aʊ/. In other words the basic phonetic principle of English orthography is extended.

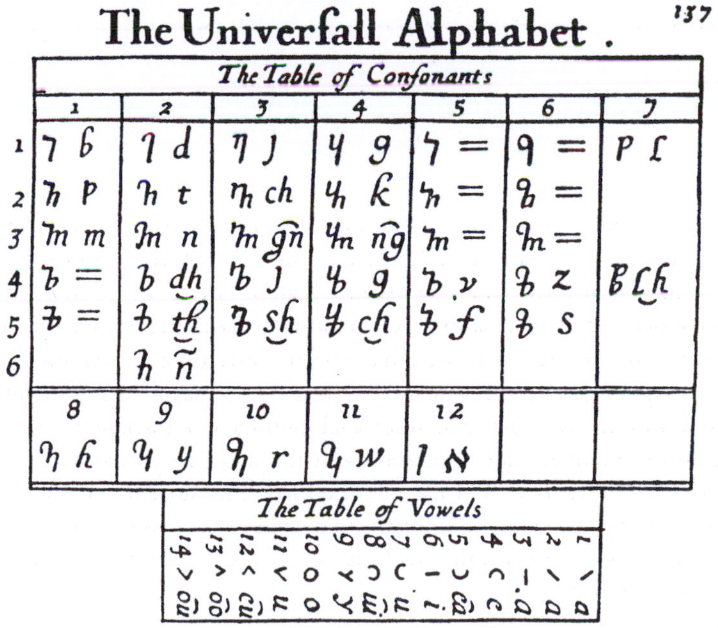

Figure 8.2 Lodwick's Universal Alphabet
(Abercrombie 1965: 51)

Standard English spelling – be it British or American – continues to give general preference to etymological spellings, which help to increase inter-linguistic intelligibility, and it retains "silent" letters such as the <r> in words like <car> or <card> thus allowing a more universal acceptance of spelling, in this case between rhotic and non-rhotic accents. For priniciples involved in AmE–BrE spelling differences see 10.3.2; link: Spelling reforms.

8.2.6.1 Traditions and conventions of Scots spelling

The traditions and conventions of Scots spelling are largely those of StE spelling, but are extended to a number of specifically Scottish conventions such as <ui> for fronted /(j)y/; <ae> for /eː/. The spelling is more or less connected to a word's phonemic realization but leaves leeway for varying regional realizations as with <ui> in *guid* "good," which can be /ø/ (Angus), /wiː/ (Northeast), /eː/ (Fife), /y/ (Glasgow), or /iː/ (Black Isle) (McClure 1980: 30).

Text 8.5 Text in one suggested spelling for Scots

The Scots Leid Associe (kent in Inglis as the Scots Language Society) is a bodie that warks for the furdal [support, furthering] o the Scots leid in "leiterature, drama, the media, education an ilka day uiss [everyday use]." It wis foundit in 1972, an haes about 350 memmers the nou.

The SLA sets furth a bi-annual journal, Lallans, that's nou a 144-page magazine wi prose, musardrie [poetry], reviews, news etc. aw in Scots. It's furthest [supported, furthered] wi help by the Scottish Arts Council. Lallans is postit free tae memmers o the SLA, an it is estimate that it haes a readership o about a thousan, syne [since] copies is also postit tae libraries an siclike.

(http://sco.wikipedia.org/wiki/Scots_Leid_Associe)

8.2.7 Regional English

With the spread of elementary and then secondary education the marginalization of the traditional dialects was reinforced. They were increasingly associated with poor education and lack of sophistication while the schools and the standard language that the schools promoted were seen as a route to greater vocational opportunity. As a result, StE – clearly established within the tradition of writing and as the social institution of symbolic power – gained in overt prestige. Yet the traditional dialects were not about to go away as they continued to be a mainstay of local and regional identity and a symbol of *solidarity*. As such the non-standard forms transmitted through them carried considerable covert prestige. In the following our attention turns to a variety of local features.

8.2.7.1 Shared features

A number of non-standard grammatical features are common to various regions in England and beyond. A few will be recounted here.

The principal parts of the irregular (strong) verbs

These have frequently been leveled. This is a continuation of the simplification which set in much earlier (see 4.2.3.1; link: Reduction of strong verb classes), but which proceeded unevenly in the various regions and in StE, as the following selection of items shows:

- The past participle takes the form of the past: *speak–spoke–spoke*; *break–broke–broke* (SW England, Ireland, and North); *bite–bit–bit*; *fall–fell–fell*; *take–took–took*; *write–wrote–wrote* (North); *go–went–went* (North, Scotland, and Ireland).
- The past takes the form of the past participle: *come–come–come*; *do–done–done*; *see–seen–seen* (SW; Scotland; Ireland).
- Past and past participle are exchanged: *see–seen–saw* (Scotland).
- Past and past participle may become semi-regular: *take–tooked–tooked*; *steal–stoled–stoled* (SW England); *bring–brung–brung* (East Anglia, Scotland); or regular: *see–seed–seed*; *give–gived–gived*; *blow–blowed–blowed*; *hurt–hurted–hurted* (SW England); *know–knowed–knowed* (SW and East Anglia); *catch–catched–catched*; *draw–drawed–drawed* (East Anglia); *sell–sellt–sellt*; *tell–tellt–tellt* (North and Scotland).
- Regular forms may also become irregular: *creep–crope–crope*; *scrape–scrope–scrope* (SW); *shriek–shrunk–shrunk*; *wrap–wrop–wrop* (East Anglia).

(Wagner 2004b: 170 for SW England; Trudgill 2004: 143–144 for East Anglia; Beal 2004: 115–116 for the North; Miller 2004: 48 for Scotland = Central Scots; Winford 2009: 211 for Ireland)

Adverbs and adjectives

The adjective form is frequently used rather than the adverb in {-ly} as in *she were main strict* or *real good furniture* (Wagner 2004b: 167; also in the SW, the North, Scotland, and overseas varieties). Pleonastic comparatives and superlatives occur widely, for example SW *more fitter, most loveliest* (Beal 2004: 121).

Multiple negation

Multiple negation as in *He couldn't get a job nowhere* and the use of *never* as a general **past negator**, as in *I never eat no dinner* (single instance) is widely shared (examples from Beal 2004: 125–126).

Existential (aka expletive) *there*

This regularly has the singular (*There's more women coming into bus driving*) among working-class speakers. How widely – or with what restrictions – it applies varies. In Tyneside English, for example, it applies with lexical verbs, but not with *be* (cf. Tagliamonte 2009).

Infinitive marker

The use of vernacular *for to* to introduce purpose clauses, for example IrE *And there was always one man selected for to make the tea* (Filppula 2004: 85–86), also occurs in the North, the SW, Wales, and overseas varieties.

Pronoun exchange

Pronoun exchange, in which *case* is reversed, is widespread (SW, Wales, East Anglia, the North). This refers to the use of the subject pronoun for the object: *They always called I "Willie," see; you couldn't put she* [a horse] *in a putt.* The converse is also possible, compare *'er's shakin' up seventy; . . . what did 'em call it?; Us don' think naught about things like that.* Subject forms are much more common as objects than the other way around (55% to 20%) (Wagner 2004b: 158). In the North second person *thou/thee* often shows up as leveled *tha* in traditional dialects (see Text 8.7), but not north of the Tyne or in Northumberland (Beal 2004: 118). Today pronoun exchange is generally receding (link: Personal pronoun systems).

Zero plural marking

Zero plural marking of nouns after numerals is common (cf. Text 8.9).

The following two sections single out the South(west) and the North (as we have done in the previous chapters) in order to show some of the features of traditional dialect.

8.2.7.2 The Southwest

The Southwest is relatively conservative, retaining quite a number of older traditional features of the language. It has had considerable influence on vernacular Welsh English (link: Vernacular Welsh English), which has developed in a way similar to the Southwest (Penhallurick 2004).

Periphrastic *do*

There is continued use of non-emphatic affirmative *do*; most often it is used to express habituality – and as a tense carrier in affirmative sentences. It is often uninflected: that is, there is no {-s} in the third person singular present tense auxiliary *do*. In contrast, although it is recessive, lexical *do* may still take {-s} in all persons (Wagner 2004b: 169, 171; cf. 7.2.3). In the South(west), but also in East Anglia, the past tense of lexical *do* may be *done* while the past of auxiliary *do* is *did*: *you done it, did you?* (Trudgill 2004: 143–144).

Pronouns

Pronouns are extremely divergent from standard usage. Pronoun gender is different than StE. Count nouns are masculine or feminine; *mass nouns* are neuter. This is still strong in the far west, but receding in Somerset (see discussion and examples in 7.2.2). *Reflexive pronouns*, as elsewhere in the non-standard language, include *hisself, theirselves*; sometimes unmarked plurals, for example *ourself, theirself, yourself*. The relative markers *what* and sometimes *as* occur in addition to *who, which*, and *that*. Zero restrictive relative is common (Wagner 2004b: 157–166).

The definite article

This is overused in comparison to StE, but quite in line with the North, Scotland, and Ireland (ibid.: 155). Demonstrative pronouns are differently distinguished, like StE with close and distant, singular and plural, but also with a distinction between count and mass nouns (see Table 8.2). Here pronoun *case leveling* can still be seen in the now rare use of non-standard *they* for equally non-standard, but general *them*, for example *Well, like think one what's in there now, her, for killing all they women* (ibid.: 164).

Table 8.2 Demonstratives in Southwest English (from Wagner 2004b: 163)

deixis	number	count	mass	StE
close	singular	*these / thick*	*this* (*here*)	*this*
	plural	*these* (*here*)		*these*
distant	singular	*thick, thicky* (*there*)	*that* (*there*)	*that*
	plural	*they, them there*		*those*

Text 8.6 Southwest (Devon, Somerset): R.D. Blackmore, *Lorna Doone* (1869)

"Us may tich of her now, I rackon," said Betty in her most jealous way: "Annie, tak her by the head, and I'll tak her by the toesen. No taime to stand here like girt gawks. Don'ee tak on zo, missus. There be vainer vish in the zea – Lor, but her be a booty!"

(R.D. Blackmore, *Lorna Doone*. 1869, chap. 44)

Text 8.6 gives examples of the use of pronoun exchange (*us*, *her* as subjects), an irregular non-standard plural (*toesen*), and present tense indicative *be*. The spelling indicates a different set of vowels (*tich* "touch"; *rackon* "reckon"; *tak* "take"; *taime* "time"), yod-dropping (*booty* "beauty"), and the use of voiced initial fricatives (*zo* "so"; *zea* "sea"; and *vish* "fish"). A *gawk* is an awkward person, a fool, a simpleton; and *girt* means "stricken."

8.2.7.3 The North

The North is clearly different from the South, but the linguistic dividing lines (**isoglosses**) vary considerably from item to item, some clearly intruding on the Midlands. A part of the variation may be accounted for by the uneven patterns of immigration in the eighteenth and nineteenth centuries, when many Irish moved into the Liverpool, Manchester, and Newcastle areas. The North consists "of shifting boundaries and ideological oppositions, of conflicting cultural and mental landscapes and stereotypes" (Wales 2002: 46), but the kernel area is Northumberland, Durham, Cumberland, Westmorland, Lancashire, and Yorkshire, north, namely, of the Humber and Mersey Rivers. This treatment will be restricted to the FOOT–STRUT split, the Northern Subject Rule, and a few short incidental remarks.

The *FOOT–STRUT Split* (link: FOOT–STRUT Split)

One of the key North–South markers, the split has taken place chiefly in the South and parts of Ireland. In it ME short /u/ became opener + unrounded /ʌ/ in most words and ME short /u/ was retained as /ʊ/ in others, chiefly after labials: *foot, full, put, pulpit, butcher, bush* (exceptions: *fun, vulture, mud, putt, buck*) and where there is rounding as associated with /ʃ/, for example *sure, sugar, cushion*. New words with /ʊ/ arose out of ones with ME /oː/ via shortening and raising: *good, look, book*, thus creating **minimal pairs** like *look-luck*. In the North /ʊ/ remained and *look* and *luck* became homophones.

Table 8.3 The FOOT–STRUT Split

	mood	*blood*	*good*	*cut*	*put*
In the South:					
ME	oː	oː	oː	u	u
GVS	uː	uː	uː	–	–
shortening (early)	–	u	–	–	–
phonetic shift	–	ʊ	–	ʊ	ʊ
FOOT–STRUT	–	ɣ	–	ɣ	ʊ
shortening (late)	–	–	ʊ	–	–
phonetic shift	–	ʌ	–	ʌ	–
current result	uː	ʌ	ʊ	ʌ	ʊ
In the North:					
as in the South:	uː	ʊ	ʊ		
but no split:				ʊ	ʊ

(Wells 1982: 199)

The *Northern Subject Rule* (link: Northern Subject Rule)

A prominent feature of vernacular grammar, this describes how "the verbal *-s* suffix can be used with plural noun subjects as well as with demonstrative pronoun subjects, but not with a plural personal pronoun, unless there are some other sentence elements between the subject and the verb" (Filppula 2004: 88). Examples go back as far as the thirteenth and fourteenth centuries, for example, *The burds cums and paecks them but They cum an' teake them* (thirteenth century Scots) or *Fuok at cums unbudden, syts unsaer'd* (fourteenth century Northumbrian) (qtd. from Poplack et al. 2002: 107). The rule applies unevenly, for example, in York positive *be* follows the rule, but negative *be* does not: *I was, weren't I?* (Beal 2004: 122).

Pronouns (link: Northern vernacular pronoun use)

The following text demonstrates the use of the second person singular personal pronoun *tha* (*thou*) and *thee*. When *tha* is the subject there is no special verb inflection, that is, no {-st}. Other notable items are *owt* "anything" and *summat* "something."

> ### Text 8.7 Northern English (Yorkshire): B. Hines, *Kes* (1968)
>
> *"Where's tha been, Casper?" Billy just smiled and mingled, and moved alongside Tibbut.*
> *"Seen our Jud?"*
> *"Hey up, where's tha been? They've been looking all over for thee."* . . .
> *"What for? I haven't done owt."*
> *"Youth Employment. Tha should have gone for thi interview last lesson."*
> *"Seen our Jud? . . . Did he say owt?"*
> *"Just asked where tha wa' that's all. What did tha run away for when tha saw him?"* . . .
> *What's up, is he after thi for summat?"*
>
> (Barry Hines, *Kes*. Harmondsworth: Penguin, 1969, 134)

Article

The definite *article* is more widely used than in StE, and it is often reduced: *the* → θ → t → ʔ → zero when unstressed. In contrast, there is some loss of the indefinite article. It is, however, possible with *one* (and no intervening adjective): *I'll have a one*. Demonstrative *thae* ("those") occurs, but *them* is more frequent. There is also some use of *yon/yonder*; emphatic *this here* and *that there*.

Modals

Modals are used much as in Scots, that is, *may, shall*, and *ought* are rare; *must* is epistemic only (Beal 2004: 126). **Double modals** are possible in Tyneside and Northumberland, but only with *can/could* as the second verb: *might could, mustn't could; wouldn't could've; would could* (ibid.: 128). Modal-like *need* and *want* are followed by the past participle, as in *my hair needs cut; that referee wants shot*.

8.3 Scotland

8.3.1 Language shift

The Lowlands of Scotland have been an English-speaking area since the Anglo-Saxon invasions, and this book has repeatedly gone into some of the developments in Scottish English. As in England, urbanization and immigration (often from England) have led to a gradual expansion of the areas where English is the major home language. The Highlands and the Islands, in contrast, were long the home of Gaelic speakers. Without major urban centers these areas came to be on the sidelines and eventually the Highlanders and most of the Islanders switched to English. The kind of language they adopted was, however, not the Scots of the Lowlands,[5] but StE as introduced chiefly by school teachers. This meant that Highland English was more in the English than the Scots tradition.

8.3.2 The Lowlands

The Lowlands are divided linguistically into Central, Northern, and Southern, but all of the traditional dialects of this area are generally referred to as Broad Scots. The well-known poem by Robert Burns, "Address to a Haggis," is a good starting point for a short look at the history of Scots (Text 8.8, overleaf).

This text contains a number of relevant points. First of all, there are a number of unfamiliar words and spellings. These have been glossed below. In their morphology and *syntax* they are closely related to Northern English with which they once formed the single kingdom of Bernicia and later Northumbria. As elsewhere, inflectional morphology in Scots was gradually leveled even though perhaps more older forms survived in some of the rural dialects of Scotland than elsewhere.

---

5 Not so in the Orkney and the Shetland Islands, which became Scottish in the fifteenth century and were eventually settled by speakers of Scots.

> ### Text 8.8 Lowland Scots: R. Burns, "Address to a Haggis" (1786)
>
> | | |
> |---|---|
> | *Fair fa' your honest, sonsie face,* | Fair dappled your honest, happy face, |
> | *Great chieftain o' the pudding-race!* | Great chieftain of the pudding race! |
> | *Aboon them a' ye tak your place,* | Above them all you take your place, |
> | *Painch, tripe, or thairm:* | Paunch, tripe, or intestines: |
> | *Weel are ye wordy o' a grace* | Well are you worthy of all grace |
> | *As lang's my arm* | As long as my arm. |
>
> (from: R. Burns. *Poems and Songs*. London: Collins, 1955)

Glossary

fa' "dappled"	*a'* "all"	*thairm* "intestine, gut"
sonsie "comely"	*ye* "you"	*weel* "well"
o' "of"	*tak* "take"	*wordy* "worthy"
aboon "over, above"	*painch* "paunch"	*lang's* "long as"

8.3.2.1 Grammar: morphology

The Lowlands like England itself went through an extended process of inflectional loss (Miller 2004: 49; see 8.2.7.1). The role which analogy plays in language change became especially clear as more and more once irregular plural nouns such as *eye–een; shoe–shin* changed to regular plurals (*eyes, shoes*). *Voicing* change has been eliminated in nouns ending in /f/ in the singular, for example *wifes, knifes*, and so on. The missing distinction between second person singular and plural pronouns has been amended by adding a new plural form: *yous/youse/yins*. {-s} has been added to *mines* in analogy to *ours, yours, hers*, and the forms *theirselves* and *hisself* have brought these reflexive pronouns here, as elsewhere, closer to *myself, yourself*/-ves, and *ourselves*. Number in nouns is unmarked after numerals (*two stone, two foot*), as is also the case elsewhere. In accord with the Northern Subject Rule plural subject nouns take *is* and *was* (ibid.: 48ff).

8.3.2.2 Grammar: syntax

Negation

Negation of the verb is carried out using *no, not,* or *nae,* and *-n't*, for example *she's no phoned yet; she'll no be coming to the party; I've no seen him the day. Nae* is added to modal verbs (*cannae*) and the auxiliary *do* (*didnae*), and *never* may negate singular events, as elsewhere (ibid.: 50–51).

Tense and aspect

The tense and aspect system of Scots is generally similar to that of the North of England. The progressive is used with statives like *understand, like, want, intend,* and both the past and the perfect are possible for recently completed events. As in Northern England, *need* may take a past participle as a complement, for example *I need the car repaired; she needs collected at four o'clock.* (ibid.: 54ff).

Conditionals

Conditionals commonly have *would* in the *if*-clause, for example *If she would come to see things for herself; If she would have come,* and contrafactuals may have a doubling of the auxiliary *have*, for example *I reckon I wouldnae have been able to dae it if I **hadnae 've** been able to read music* (ibid.: 57).

Reflexives

Reflexives are used in non-reflexive contexts, for example *Myself and Andy changed and ran onto the pitch* (ibid.: 60).

Modal verbs

Modal verbs are significantly different in use than in StE. As in IrE *shall* and *ought* are seldom, if ever, used. Even a promise like *You will have the money tomorrow* makes do without *shall*, as does the interrogative *Will I open the window? Must* and *mustn't* are epistemic only. Double modals are common, for example *will can; might could; might can; would could.* Modals may occur after *to*, for example *I'd like to could do that* (ibid.: 52ff).

8.3.2.3 Scots pronunciation

Scots pronunciation shows up in the presence of the phonemes /hw/ (*what, where*) and (in some local varieties) /x/, as in *daughter* /dɔːxter/. Unusual **consonant clusters** like initial /kn-/ (*knee*) or /vr-/ (*write*) occur; and Scots is rhotic. The use of monophthongal /uː/ in words like *aboot, hoose,* and fronted /ø/ or /y/ in *good, moon, stool* goes back to the different trajectory of the GVS in the North and Scotland (see 6.3.1.2). Front /eː/ *hame* "home," *bane* "bone," and so on is monophthongal. Length is not phonemic in Scots (but see link: Aitken's Law).

8.3.2.4 Vocabulary

Differences may be illustrated by the following text as glossed below.

Text 8.9 Scots Leid: Aboot William Loughton Lorimer (2009)

The Translate
Lorimer haed aye been interestit in the Scots leid (syne he wis a bairn o nine year auld he haed written doun Scots wirds an eedioms) an his kennin o the strauchles o minority leids that he got frae his readins o the neutral press durin the Weir led him tae feel that something needit daein tae rescue the Scots leid. He becam convinced, that gin Scots wis tae be ruised up frae the laich status that it haed fawen tae, it needit twa main things first: I) a guid modren dictionar an II) a guid modren translate o The New Testament 5

> *that maist weel-read fowk an mony ithers wad be fameeliar wi. Sometime aboot September 1945, he decidit tae yoke tae on pittin The New Testament ower intil Scots. Bein an unco dab-haund wi leids, he read throu mony translates o New Testament beuks . . .* 10
>
> *His first drauchts wis begoued in 1957, an bi early 1961 he stairtit wark on The Gospels that teuk him twa year an three month tae feenish the first drauchts o. The last o the first drauchts (that seems tae hae been Hebrews) wis feenished on the 10t o October 1965. It haed sae faur taen him aicht year tae pit the hail New Testament ower intil Scots.*
>
> (http://sco.wikipedia.org/wiki/William_Laughton_Lorimer)

Glossary

aye (1) /eɪ/ "always"

leid (1) /lid/ "language"

syne (1) /səin/ "since"

bairn (1) "child"

kennin (2) "recognition"

strauchle (2)/straːxl/ "struggle"

gin (4) "if"

laich (5)/lex/ "low"

yoke tae (8) "begin work"

pit (8) "put, i.e. translate"

unco (9) /ˈʌŋkə/ "very"

draucht (11) /draːxt/ "draft"

begoued (11)/bɪgud/ "begun"

aicht (14)/ext, eçt/ "eight(h)"

Aside from the vocabulary and spellings with their associated pronunciations the text is easy to read. There is little in the grammar that diverges from StE. Note, however, the lack of a plural ending on *year* (ll. 1, 11, 13) and *month* (l. 10) following a numeral.

8.4 Ireland

English was spoken in some parts of Ireland (especially the southeast) for a considerable period after the Normans, the English, and the Scots invaded the island in various waves and campaigns starting in 1167. These English-speaking invaders were eventually completely re-Gaelicized. However, under the Tudors Ireland was once again invaded and colonized by settlers from Britain. Between 1500 and 1700 settlers arrived in southern Ireland from the South and southwest Midlands and in Ulster from the North and Scotland. Most of these newcomers spoke the one or the other variety of non-standard EModE. The conquest was completed by Cromwell's forces in 1649, in the course of which the Irish were commonly driven off the land and forced to move further to the west. English came to be the language of power and dominion, and little by little use of Gaelic began to recede. In the first half of the nineteenth century a massive move from Gaelic to English set in, often initiated by parents who wished to give their children the chance for a better future in England, America, or Australia, where many of them were to immigrate.

In the course of the eighteenth and nineteenth centuries a number of new forms emerged in IrE due largely to the rapid replacement of Irish by English and "not the least because of the introduction of compulsory schooling. This favoured substratal influences, especially since the teachers were themselves bilingual" (Fritz 2006: 298). The rapid shift meant that English was spoken by many people who had an incomplete command of the language. In expanding the use of the language to all the domains of everyday life speakers drew on the resources of Gaelic. This meant that there would be lexical *borrowing* from Gaelic, but, even more significantly, the pronunciation of English in Ireland was to show Gaelic features. In addition, its grammar revealed the influence not only of the contact varieties of English from the English Southwest or of Scotland, but also of the Irish substratum, as will be pointed out in 8.4.2.

8.4.1 Standard Irish English

Standard Irish English is very close to the Standard English of England and has contributed to English *loan words* from Gaelic, such as *clan* (< Gaelic *clann* "a group of people with common ancestors, a large family") or *whiskey* (< Gaelic *uisge beatha*, "water of life") (Hansen 1996: 91). IrE is characterized by idioms and expressions which are translations of Irish turns of speech. In this sense the points of the compass may be *above* (north), *below* (south), *back* (west) and *over* (east) (Barry 1984: 109). The standard pronunciation is phonologically close to RP. While the grammar of standard IrE is essentially the same as that of other varieties, rural and working-class vernaculars are often dramatically different.

8.4.2 The vernacular

The *divergence* of the vernaculars from StE is credited to a variety of factors, chiefly conservatism as seen in retentions from earlier English, dialect contact (especially from Scotland in the North), substratum Irish influence, best preserved in rural varieties near Irish-speaking areas, and features of second language acquisition due to rapid shift to English in the early nineteenth century (Filppula 2004: 73). This is less visible in morphology than in syntax – most especially the TMA system.

8.4.2.1 Tense, aspect, and the verb in IrE

Tense

Tense – present, past, and future – is modeled on English. The morphology of the verb also includes the use of the {-s} inflection for both singular and plural third person subjects in the present tense and may be part of the Northern Subject Rule traceable back to Middle Scots (and earlier) (see 8.2.7.3). In the South the singular may occur with personal pronouns as well as noun subjects, for example *when they was about three months old, or four, like* or *we keeps about ten cows that way, you know*, which is typical of southern England (Filppula 2004: 89–90).

Perfect aspect

In IrE this is more finely differentiated than in StE – frequently, but not always as the result of substratum influence (see Table 8.4). "It may be the case that, as Bliss (1984: 143) has claimed, 'Southern Hiberno English has precisely the same range of tenses [and aspects] as

Table 8.4 Perfect aspect in IrE

type	example	interpretation	status
indefinite anterior perfect	*I never went till it* [car race] *yet.* *I didn't hear him playing with years and years.*	experiential perfect but used with the past tense form	standard colloquial
after perfect, aka hot-news perfect	*You're after ruinin' me.*	relatively recent past; modeled on Irish, but word order as in English	stereotypically IrE; avoided in educated speech
medial-object perfect	*I have it forgot.* *Mary, I have your match made.*	focus on result; typically dynamic verbs; English and Irish models	recessive
be-perfect	*they are gone idle over it.* *And there was a big ash-tree growing there one time, and it is, it is, it is withered and fade' away now.*	intransitive counterpart of preceding used with change of state (*die*) or motion (*come, go, leave*); Irish + English models	recessive
extended-now perfect	*I'm in here about four months.* *We're living here seventeen years.*	continuative; Irish and English models	standard colloquial
standard *have* perfect	*we haven't seen one for years*	for all of above	more careful, educated usage

(Filppula 2004: 74ff; Fritz 2006: 291; Siemund 2004: 405ff; Winford 2009: 212–213)

Irish has, but the forms are built up of English material'" (Winford 2009: 214). The types of perfect aspect listed in Table 8.4 can be distinguished.

Progressive aspect

As in other varieties of Celtic-influenced English in Scotland, the Hebrides, and Wales, progressive aspect is used more widely than in StE and other non-standard Englishes, for example with verbs of emotion as in *And everybody was wanting to see* (Siemund 2004: 405) or verbs of state as in *they were belonging; the river is flowing into the Atlantic* (cf. Filppula 2004: 77–78). Occurrences such as *she is at the milking of the cow* (Siemund 2004: 405) probably go back to older forms of the English progressive (Winford 2009).

Habitual aspect

Habitual aspect is expressed in two relatively distinct ways. The first is habitual *do* as in *Two lorries of them* [peat] *now in the year we do burn* (Siemund 2004: 405) or the following longer nineteenth century quotation, which contrasts the habitual with the emphatic use of periphrastic *do*:

Text 8.10 Nineteenth century IrE (vernacular correspondence)

But Dear Joseph when you do write [emphatic] *you mite say some thing to William as some like to be mentioned by Name for he is very Kind to Mary Ann. But your Bother in Law does think* [habitual] *that as you have no Brothers or Sisters in Ireland but Mary Ann and him.*

(Fritz 2006: 295)

This *do*-form seems to have developed from seventeenth century Southwest English periphrastic *do*, which was reanalyzed as habitual and reinforced by the existence of a distinct habitual category in Irish (Winford 2009). The second is habitual *be*, as in *I am Surprised that Michael does not be enquiring after me* (Fritz 2006: 296) or *there be's a lot of people at . . .*, where earlier finite *be* (for *are*) presumably also came from the English Southwest (Winford 2009: 211). The verb *be* can be differentiated in the following ways:

- **simple copula**: *She's here now*
- **habitual**: *She be's here often*
- **habitual progressive**: *They do be fightin' among other.*

Habitual progressive aspect as in *they do be shooting there* is very typical of IrE. The use of *do* as in *They does be lonesome by night* is more typical of Southern IrE while *She be's going* or *you be's bored* is Northern (Filppula 2004: 78).

Further points concerning the verb

These are often shared with other non-standard vernaculars. *Multiple negation*, as in *Och, I don't know just, they're just not the same, nor never will be like the old people* is widespread in IrE as it is almost everywhere. The same applies to failure of negative attraction, where the negation of *anyone goes* is not *no one goes*, but *anyone doesn't go*, which is heard in the North and the South of Ireland, but also in Britain (ibid.: 82). As in Scotland the **modal auxiliaries** *shall* and *ought* are rarely used except in writing. This leads to the well-known use of *will* instead of more general *shall* in questions such as *Will I sing you a song?* (ibid.: 80).

Some shadow pronouns occur, as in *there's a man that **his** wife leaves him whenever she pleases*, which here is partially motivated by the need for a possessive. This usage is a possible instance of substratum influence since it is found in Welsh and Scottish English as well (ibid.: 85). Speakers avoid the *wh*-relative in favor of *that*, zero (also as a subject in restrictive relative clauses, e.g. *there's older people __ tell me that they were . . .*, and *and*, as in *There was this man **and he** (= who/that) lived. . . .* In the North *at* and *ats* is also used, which is either a form borrowed originally from ON or a contraction of *that* and *thats* (ibid.: 84).

A type of subordination particular to IrE (and Scots) is the addition of an *and*-clause, as in *'Twas in harvest time and the weather bad*; *I only thought of him there and I cooking my dinner* (ibid.: 87). Prepositional expressions are often parallel to Irish: *One year then he* [a fox] *took the half of them* [hens] *on me* and may also be substratal in origin. This is also the case with some focus structures such as the clefting of adverbs and verbs: *It's badly she'd do it now* and *It's looking for more land a lot of them are* (ibid.: 96–97).

8.4.2.2 Determiners and pronouns

The definite article is used more widely in IrE as also in ScE and WelshE, especially for languages (*the Irish*), disciplines (*the maths*), physical sensation (*the hunger*), diseases (*the measles*), social institutions (*the school*), quantifying expression (*the most/both of them*), festive days (*the St. Stephen's Day*), plural generics (*the goats*), non-count abstract and concrete mass nouns (*the coffee*), body parts (*took the head off him*), geographical areas (*the County Wicklow*) (ibid.: 90ff). The sources of this may be older English and substratum influence. The demonstrative *them* is used attributively as in *them houses* or by itself, for example *Them was cornstalks*. The personal pronoun of the second person plural is, as elsewhere, *yous/youse/yez/yiz* (ibid.: 92). And, finally, there is the now spreading non-reflexive use of reflexives: *Seeing that they are elected by ourselves, and represent us, . . .* (Fritz 2006: 286), which is attributed to older English and the substrate (Filppula 2004: 93).

8.4.3 The pronunciation of IrE

Pronunciation differs between South and North. While the South readily realizes <th> as [t̪] or [d̪], these phonemes are [θ] and [ð] in the North. T-voicing as in *water*, is spreading in Belfast and Dublin among young people (Wells 1982: 430, 445) while the South has a distinct slit fricative which can be traced back to lenition in Gaelic. Hence the <t> in a word like *water* or *bottom* has a slit fricative – and in extreme cases /h/ (ibid.: 428ff). The North and the South agree in both being firmly rhotic, but they differ in the way /l/ is realized – in the South as a clear [l] everywhere, even though [ɫ] is on the increase; the North has both but with [ɫ] more common in Belfast (ibid.: 431–432, 446). An /h/, sometimes realized postvocalically as /x/, may be retained, above all in names, for example *Haughey* /ˈhɒhiː/ or *McGrath* /məˈɡræh/ or in Irish words such as *Taoiseach* "Prime Minister" /ˈtiːʃəx/ (ibid.: 433). A final remark on the effect of the Irish substrate is the realization of <s> and <z> as non-palatal /s/ and /z/ or as palatal /ʃ/ and /ʒ/. Palatalization is triggered by a following palatal (/t, d, ʃ, ʒ, n, l/) if one of these is the last member of a consonant cluster. The result is that *slow*, *snow*, and *stop* are [ʃloː], [ʃnoː], and [ʃtɑp]; and *puzzle* is [ˈpʊʒl] (Bliss 1984: 138–139).

8.5 Urban varieties

The urban varieties of English are the strongholds of **non-standard GenE**. Although there are differences between the major centers, they also share quite a few features, as do the traditional dialects. They – ones like Glasgow–Edinburgh, Newcastle–Durham, Liverpool–Manchester, Birmingham, Bristol, Norwich, Belfast, Dublin, and, of course, London (see 8.2.5.7) – have a strong influence on the surrounding countryside. What distinguishes them today from the situation in the eighteenth and nineteenth centuries is the fact that immigration from the Commonwealth, but also from elsewhere, has injected new impulses into the language and culture of these cities. In addition, the London conurbation seems to be developing a new koiné, popularly called Estuary English (8.5.2).

Urban language surveys have not only provided a great deal of systematic, empirical data; they have also helped to advance insights into how people identify themselves linguistically – often according class, gender, ethnicity, or age – and into some of the roles which language plays in modern urban society. Frequent results have indicated that middle-class women are most often leaders in change toward the overt (standard) norm; working-class men are most often the initiators of changes toward the covert (local) norm. Stigmatized pronunciations, for instance, correlate highly with speech style, though what counts as stigmatized may vary considerably from place to place in the Anglophone world.

8.5.1 Vernacular Grammar

Non-standard urban grammatical features are often shared over a wide geographic range (nationally and internationally) and have been viewed in this book as a part of GenE (see 7.2.1). This chapter has reported extensively on shared regional grammatical differences, many of which appear in the urban varieties, but the latter seem to have adopted few of the more specifically traditional grammatical features.

8.5.2 Estuary English (= London Regional RP)

Estuary English is a koineized form of English that seems to be developing in London and its vicinity (the Thames Estuary and the lower Thames valley, i.e. Essex and northern Kent). It shares the less stigmatized features of Cockney and may be on its way to becoming a serious rival to RP as the pronunciation norm in Britain. The spread of some of its features to cities far removed from the London area (e.g. Bristol, Hull, Liverpool, Manchester, Glasgow) would support this. It also is less stigmatized as posh and therefore more acceptable for the "upwardly mobile speakers of local dialect" (Cruttenden 2001: 81). Like Cockney, Estuary English includes:

- a move of FACE to [aɪ] and PRICE to [ɑɪ]
- *L-vocalization*, e.g. *Paul* = *paw*
- the palatalization of initial /tj-/ and /dj-/, *Tuesday* as *Chewsday*
- the loss of /j/ in words like *new* (= *noo*), etc.
- increasing replacement of /t/ by [ʔ], especially before a consonant and in final position (e.g. *not that* as /nɒʔˈðæʔ/).

It differs from Cockney, however, in not having:

- *H-dropping* or
- the replacement of /θ, ð/ by /f, v/.

In contrast to Cockney:

- the realization of /r/ in Estuary English may be the velar approximate [ɰ] and
- /s/ may be rendered as /ʃ/ at the beginning of consonant clusters, for example /stuːdənt/, /stɒp/ and /əbˈstrʌkt/ become [ʃtuːdənt], [ʃtɒp] and [əbˈʃtrʌkt] (ibid.: 88).

8.5.3 British Black English

Since the early 1960s the ethnic make-up of most British cities has changed enormously. High levels of ethnically non-European immigration from Commonwealth countries have produced a "multicultural Britain." These immigrants and their children may not want to become linguistic replicas of the English people around them, but economic integration requires a command of GenE. This means that there are two forces pulling on them. One, the overt norm, is toward GenE, be it StE or the local vernacular. In the case of the descendants of black Britons from the Caribbean, the other force, the covert norm, is pulling them toward the *ethnic variety* or "patwa," sometimes called London Jamaican. The latter is a koineized form of West Indian Creole used by second and later generation British Blacks. It resembles Jamaican Creole but differs from it in avoiding many of the more **basilect** creole forms (cf. Sutcliffe 1984: 220–229; see also chapter 9). Most of these people regularly speak the English vernacular of their region and the patwa only on certain occasions (link: Code-switching). In regard to young London Blacks Sebba writes:

> most of them are, first and foremost, speakers of London English. Among women nearly all conversation seems to be carried on in London English except in certain, reasonably well defined, circumstances, when Creole is used. Among males the situation is different . . . In formal situations, such as at school and when white people are present, London English is likely to be used.
>
> (1986: 151)

Sebba suggests that "code-switching is used as a strategic and narrative device, as well as an additional resource for conveying affective meaning, i.e. for giving information about the attitude or state of mind of the speaker." A switch may serve to show solidarity or distance, to mark off speech acts, to report speech, to frame a narrative , or to create a black narrative persona (ibid.: 163–167). The differences between London English and London Jamaican are small, sometimes encoded in the tone of voice, which has not been further defined (ibid.: 152). A particularly indicative syntactic item is the use of *se* after verbs of speech and cognition in the same function as English *that* (*A all white jury found out se 'e was guilty*).

8.5.4 Chinese – English Code-Switching

Chinese immigrants to the UK are the third largest such group (after those from the Caribbean and from **South Asia**). Their linguistic background is diverse, but in some areas such as Tyneside as many as 80% have Cantonese as their heritage language (Wei 1998: 160). As in other immigrant communities (see also 10.4.2) a switch to ENL comes by the third generation (ibid.: 162). Inter-generational **code-switching** is common, as the following interchange illustrates:

Text 8.11 Chinese – English code-switching

Mother:	*Nay sik mut-ye a?* ("What do you want to eat?")
Child:	JUST APPLES.
Mother:	JUST JUST APPLES? *Dimgai m sik* YOGHURT *a?* ("Why not have some yoghurt?")

(ibid.: 155)

Members of the *speech community* vary from first-generation monolingual Cantonese speakers to more or less balanced bilinguals to younger members who have only minimal knowledge of the heritage language (ibid.: 171ff).

8.6 Summary

This chapter has approached the variety of English in Great Britain and Ireland first by looking at political, demographic, and social change. This was followed by a longer look at the influence of the expansion of education, especially because of its association with language standardization. Particular attention was paid to the role of dictionaries in the framework of codification. A short treatment of change in vocabulary was followed by a more expansive discussion of grammatical change and grammaticalization with a particular focus on more recent and still on-going developments in the modal verb system. Pronunciation was also extensively treated with observations on RP and later remarks on Estuary English. A variety of phonological developments including splits, mergers, and shifts were introduced. Spelling was touched on, especially approaches and attitudes toward spelling reform. A wide review of regional English rounded out the section on England and Wales. The section on the standard and the traditional dialects of Scotland was followed with a review of standard and vernacular Irish English with special attention devoted to the dual influences of settlement from Britain and the substrate on verbal aspect. The final discussion points out the diversity in urban English, due especially to immigration.

STUDY QUESTIONS

Social and cultural background

1. In the late Modern English period new linguistic centers besides London developed. What were they and why did they become prominent?
2. What effects did the increase in general literacy in the nineteenth century have on English?
3. It has been argued that StE is a "class-based" (Williams 1983) standard. What might justify this position? What speaks against it?

Linguistic background

1. Explain what is meant by grammaticalization using the example of *supposta*. What justifies this spelling?

2. What evidence supports the assumption of evidential modality as an emerging grammatical category?

3. Imagine the pronunciation /ɔːrɪstɔːrɪkəl/ for the words *or historical*. How did the first /r/ get there?

4. List the major pros and cons of spelling reform and use examples to illustrate what you mean.

5. What explanations help to justify the preservation of /ʊ/ as in *butch* or *sure* instead of /ʌ/ as in *come* or *cuss* in the FOOT–STRUT split?

6. The highly differentiated system of perfect aspect in IrE may be explained as due to the traditions of settlers from Britain or as due to the substrate. What speaks for one and what for the other source?

Further reading

Each of the following titles addresses a single aspect of the material treated in this chapter, but does so in a very accessible fashion. Abercrombie, though outdated inasmuch as RP has changed in its relative status, establishes a useful perspective on accent in England. Joseph discusses the identitarian role of language. MacCarthy does just what his title promises and would be helpful in answering question 4 on the linguistic background of spelling reform. Siemund looks at the problem of origins (as in question 6 above). Hopper and Traugott give an excellent overview of grammaticalization with interesting examples not limited to English. Wales explores the traditions of Northern English, and Wells offers useful historical information on changes in pronunciation, especially in volume one.

Abercrombie, D. (1965) "R.P. and Local Accent," In: D. Abercrombie *Studies in Phonetics and Linguistics*. Oxford: OUP, 10–15.

Hopper, P.J. and E.C. Traugott (1993) *Grammaticalization*. Cambridge: CUP.

Joseph, J.E. (2004) *Language and Identity. National, Ethnic, Religious*. Houndmills: Palgrave.

MacCarthy, P. (1972) "Criteria for a New Orthography for English," In: *Talking of Speaking: Selected Papers*. Oxford: OUP, 55–71.

Siemund, Peter (2004) "Substrate, Superstrate and Universals: Perfect Constructions in Irish English," In: B. Kortmann (ed.) *Dialectology Meets Typology. Dialect Grammar from a Cross-Linguistic Perspective*. Berlin: Mouton de Gruyter, 401–434.

Wales, K. (2002) "'North of Watford Gap.' A Cultural History of Northern English (from 1700)," In: R. Watts and P. Trudgill (eds.) *Alternative Histories of English*. London: Routledge, 45–66.

Wells, J.C. (1982) *Accents of English*. Cambridge: CUP.

CHAPTER NINE

English pidgins, English creoles, and English (since the early seventeenth century)

But is it not notorious to the whole World, that the Business of Planting in our British Colonies, as well as in the French, is carried on by the Labour of Negroes, imported thither from Africa? Are we not indebted to that valuable People, the Africans, for our Sugars, Tobaccoes, Rice, Rum, and all other Plantation Produce?

("In Defense of the Slave Trade," England, 1745, probably by Malachy Postlethwayt, qtd. in L.H. Fishel and B. Quarles *The Black American*, 3ʳᵈ ed. Glenview: Scott, Foresman, 1976: 16)

Chapter Overview:

This chapter:

- traces the spread of English to those parts of the colonial world where the relationship between English colonizers and traders and the colonized people was marked by early conquest and exploitation;
- shows this process as a history of economic, social and cultural domination resulting in language change;
- describes the introduction of pidgins and creoles, and deals extensively with the origin of creoles as a major instance of change;
- finally shows several textual examples.

9.1 European expansion and the slave trade

John Hawkins (1532–95) is seen by many as the creator of the modern British Royal Navy, something to which he devoted the second half of his career (1570–95). It is, however, the first part of his career for which he plays a role in the context of this chapter. In 1562, 1564, and 1567 John Hawkins, as a privateer, commanded three prominent voyages as part of the notorious triangular trade: the first leg to Africa, the second – and middle – leg (hence the "*middle passage*"; <u>link: The mechanics of the slave trade and the Middle Passage</u>; Plate 9.1) from Africa to the Americas, and the final one the return voyage to England. On the first voyage he carried 300 slaves from Africa to the Caribbean, on the second and the third, 400 each time, always with the promise of a high return for his backers. Hawkins was not the first Englishman to engage in the slave trade, and by no means the last, but he was to first to do so with system. All in all, men like Hawkins, most of them British, Portuguese, Dutch, Spanish, French, and, later, American, were responsible for carrying some 11 million Africans to the New World, thus depopulating many territories, weakening social structures, and throwing African development back by whole generations.

The massive colonial and imperial intrusion in *West Africa* had far-reaching linguistic consequences. The people enslaved and transported to the Caribbean were thrust into a situation in which they could make little or no use of their *native languages*. This was frequently a programmatic point among the slavers, who deliberately and systematically put people with different linguistic backgrounds (West Africa is a very polyglot region) together, thus ensuring that the consequent lack of communication would be a major hindrance to any attempts at rebellion. This practice was continued on New World plantations as well. Since, however, communication was a necessity, both between the slavers and their victims and among the enslaved themselves, a make-shift type of language emerged in which both sides, slave and slaver, used the grammatical structures of their native languages. In addition, the slaves used vocabulary borrowed from the language of the slave masters, that is, English, Portuguese, *Dutch*, *Spanish*, or *French*. In this way reduced contact languages, pidgins and later creoles came into existence. These languages were also used for trading purposes in Africa, hence the term trade language. Today Pidgin English, a lingua franca which has been passed on over the generations, is still widely used as a market language in much of coastal West Africa (see 9.3 for explanation of the terms introduced).

By the mid-fifteenth century, Spain and Portugal were trading with Africa in nuts, fruits, olive oil, gold, and slaves; by 1460 700–800 slaves were brought annually to Portugal; and by the end of the century there was a mad scramble for a monopoly in this trade, which the slave-traders tried to justify by emphasizing that they were Christians, while the slaves were not. In Europe there was little future for slavery because of the large impoverished European work force, which was increasingly being dislocated from the countryside and moving into the cities. In the Americas, after European discovery and conquest, there was, in contrast, a market for slaves. Indians had proved inappropriate labor because of their susceptibility to Old World diseases and their economic background – which in contrast to the African Gardener Culture (<u>link: African Gardener Culture</u>) was not suited to the disciplined regime of plantation life. Attempts to use European labor: indentured servants, prisoners, kidnapped women, children, and drunkards failed. They resisted all attempts to treat them as slaves by, for example suing or running away. Africans, on the other hand, could be purchased and held as permanent labor; they were not Christians and so could be rigorously disciplined; and they were present in seemingly inexhaustible supply. If they tried to escape, they could easily be identified and recaptured because of their skin color (Franklin 1980: 34–35).

9.1.1 The major slave-trading powers (link: The major slave-trading powers)

The slave trade was a source of wealth; and most of the slaves went to the West Indies, where by 1540 10,000 slaves were imported annually. Initially, the Portuguese controlled the trade, but the Dutch, who were more interested in the trade in slaves than in acquiring territories, took it from them in the 1630s and 1640s and dominated it throughout the seventeenth century. As the French developed an interest in slaving they entered the slave trade in the seventeenth century, establishing bases on the River Senegal about 1630 and founding colonies in the Lesser Antilles and later Guiana (1660s), Haiti and Louisiana (early 1680s).

It was the English who came to dominate the trade, but not until the Restoration (link: The Restoration). From 1672 until 1788 the slave trade was a cornerstone of English economic life. There had been earlier attempts on Britain's (England's) part: John Hawkins (see the introductory paragraph above), instructing his crews "to serve God daily" and "to love one another" (Faulkner and Kepler 1950: 11), set out under Elizabeth to secure African slaves. Forts were established early in the seventeenth century in Gambia (1618) and the Gold Coast (Ghana, 1631); by the end of the century, the off-shore islands around Sierra Leone had been settled by English privateers mixed with Africans. In America permanent colonies were established in the Lesser Antilles in 1625, briefly in Suriname (1651–66) and on Jamaica, which was taken from the Spanish in 1655; and, of course, there was the North American mainland from 1607 on and the first African laborers in Virginia from 1619 on.

9.1.2 The mechanics of the slave trade

Bases of operation were set up as well-guarded posts or "factories" on the coast. European goods were shipped in: cotton textiles; brass, pewter utensils; ivory boxes of beads of all sizes and shapes; guns, gunpowder; whiskey, brandy, rum; and a variety of foodstuffs. The ship *King Solomon*, for example, brought in £4250 worth of goods in 1720.[1] At the posts there were factors (slave traders, hence "factories") who procured slaves (Plate 9.1). Prices varied, but in the middle of the eighteenth century, a healthy young man brought £20. To fill a large vessel of about 500 it was often necessary to scour the interior or to make stops at several places. As a result the slaves often did not share an African language. Slaves often resisted sale and transport. Once captured, they had to be chained to prevent them from escaping. Many tried to jump overboard or committed suicide in some other way to escape slavery. But for the slaver it was worth it: profits of 100% were not uncommon.

---

1 This would today be £586,547 according to the retail price index and £6,768,233 according to average earnings (cf. Officer 2009). Franklin 1980 (chapter 3) is still an excellent source for the slave trade. But see also Tibbles 1994.

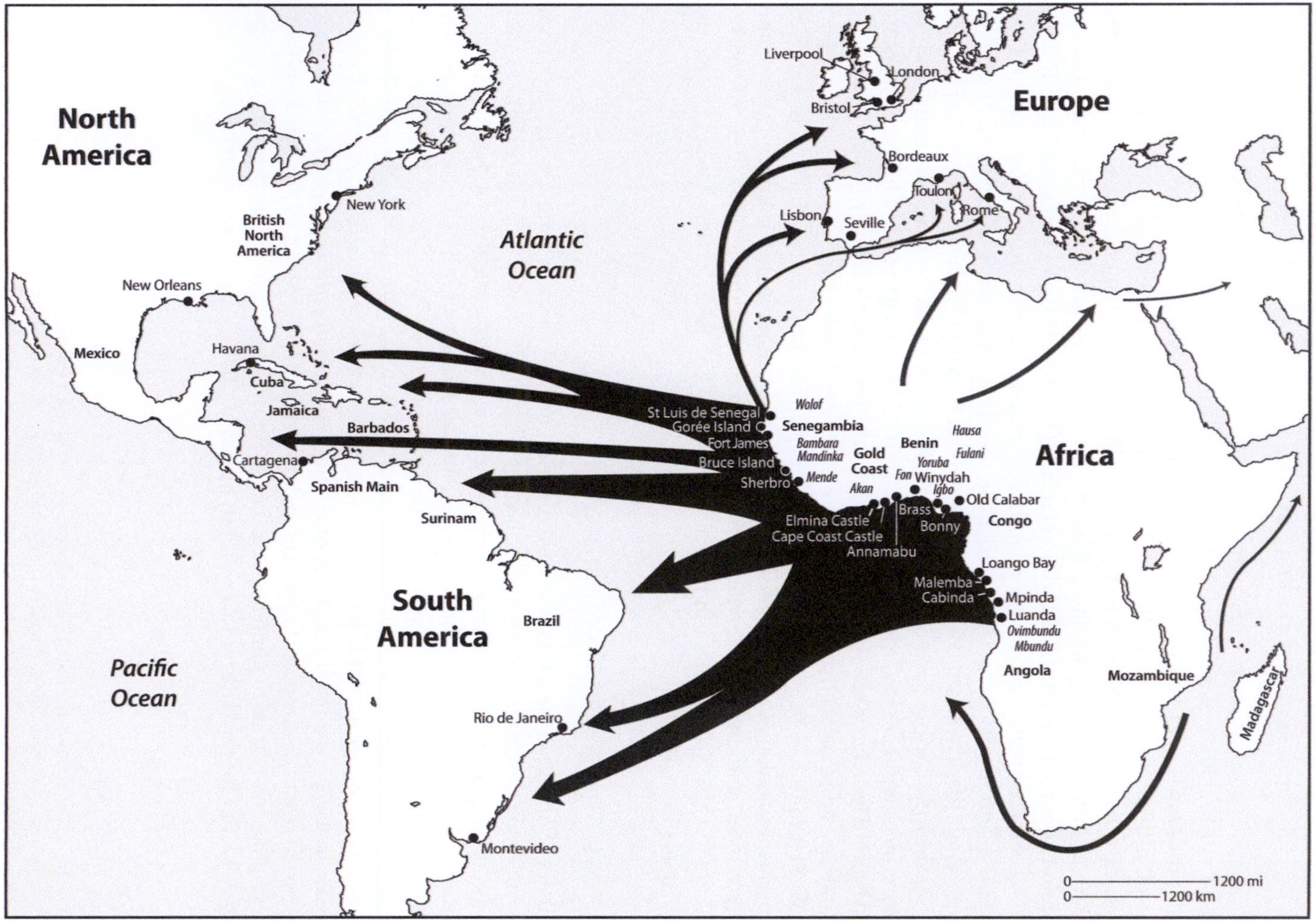

Map 9.1
The African slave trade

Plate 1.1 Britannia et Hibernia (second century). Ptolemy (Claudius Ptolemaeus), Roman citizen and Egyptian mathematician, astronomer, geographer, and astrologist. The World Map is based on his *Geography* (c. 150 CE), but is not original to it. This section shows the Continent (Belgium, Magna Germania, and the Rhine and Elbe rivers) on the right. Across the North Sea (Oceanus Germanicus) are Britain (Albion Insula Britanica) and Ireland (Ibernia Insula). See 1.5.1.

Plate 1.2 Serpent Stone (seventh–eighth century). A Pictish stone engraving located near Aberlemno, Angus, Scotland. The meaning/intention of the symbols (serpent, double disc, Z, mirror, and comb) is not known. See 1.5.2.

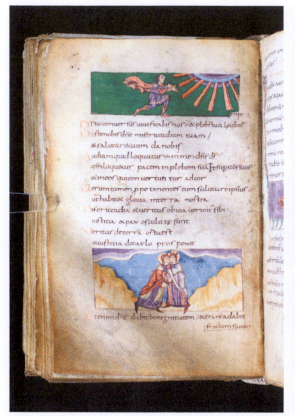

Plate 2.1 Mercy and Truth (ninth century). An illumination and an example of Carolingian minuscule script, Psalm 85:10 (in Latin), cf. ll. 9 –10: *Misericordia & veritas obviaverunt sibi: justicia & pax osculatae sunt* "Mercy and truth are met together; righteousness and peace have kissed each other." See 2.4. *Stuttgarter Psalter*, bibl. fol. 23. Württembergische Landesbibliothek, Stuttgart.

Plate 2.2 Medieval Church Music (late thirteenth century). Italian manuscript of a Gregorian chant or antiphonal. The Latin text reads, *Rex pacificus magnificatus e*[*st*] *cuius vultum desiderat universa terra P*[*roper*] *Dixit d*[*omi*]*n*[*u*]*s Antiph*[*on*]*a* "The King of Peace is almighty all the earth seeks his countenance – Proper. The lord said – Antiphon." See 2.4.

Plate 2.3 Runic Pin (650–850). This Anglo-Saxon disc-headed pin comes from Malton, North Yorkshire. It is engraved with the first seven or eight letters of the *futhorc*, the runic alphabet: ᚠᚢᚦᚩᚱᚳ plus ᛄᛚᚪᚫᛟ (F-U-TH-O-R-C + 3-L-A-Æ-O). See 2.4 and Figures 2.1 and 2.2.

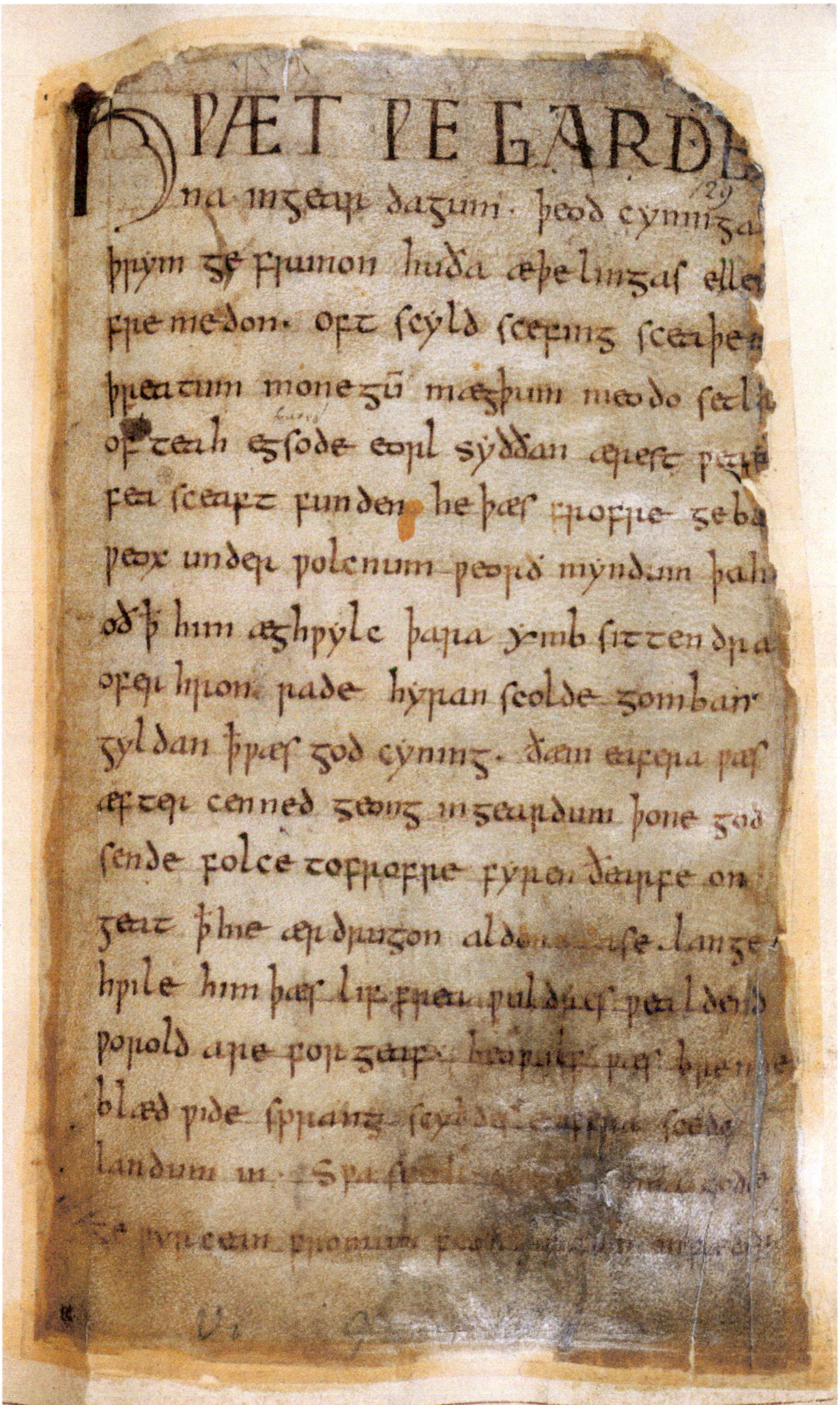

Plate 2.4 *Beowulf* (c. 1000). First page of the poem *"Hwæt! Wé Gárdena . . ."* See 2.5.1.

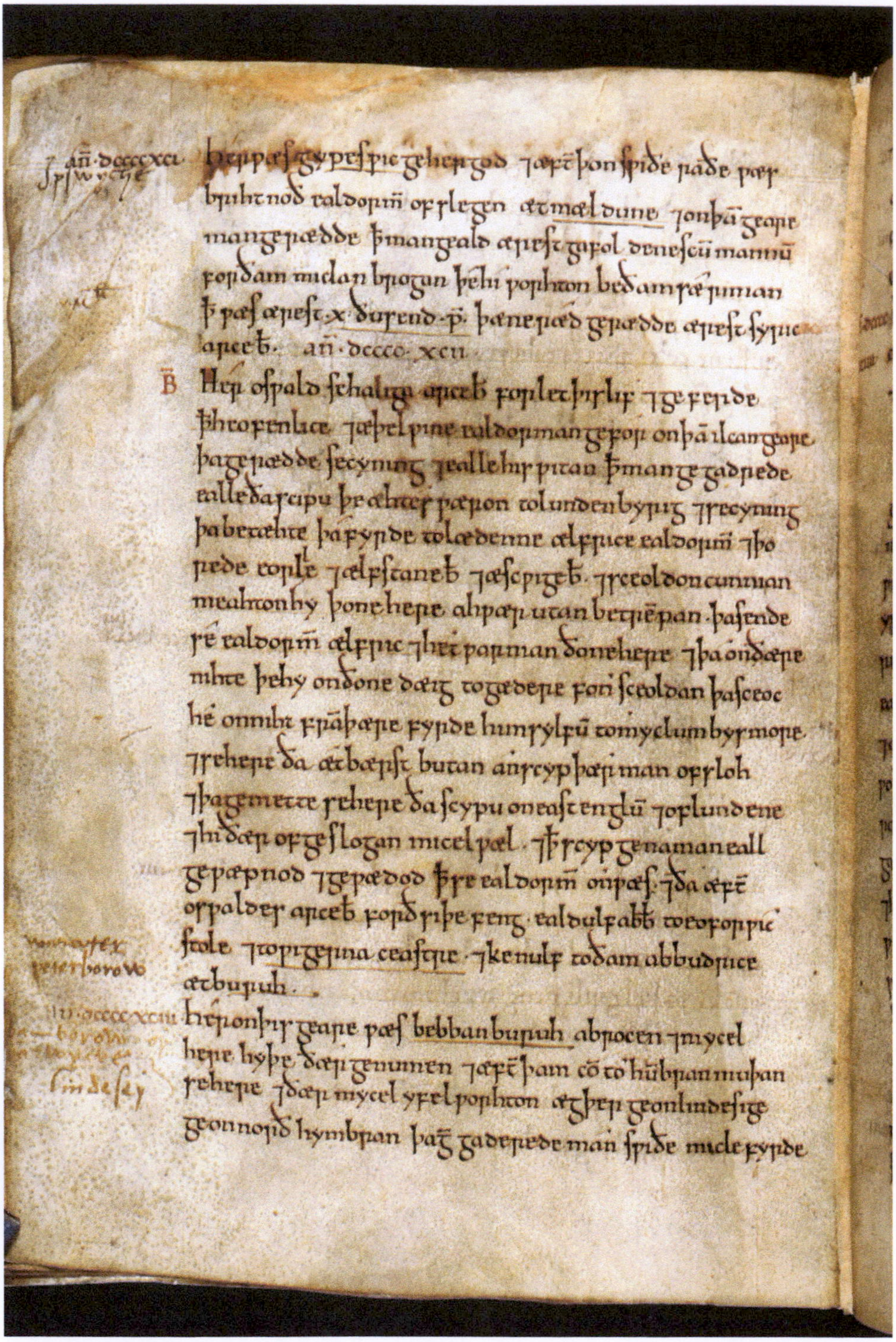

Plate 3.1 *Anglo-Saxon Chronicle* (copied in mid-eleventh century). A page from the record for the years 991 (end) 992, and 993 (beginning). See 3.1.1; also 2.2; 2.5; 2.5.3; 3.1.2; 3.4; 4.1.1.

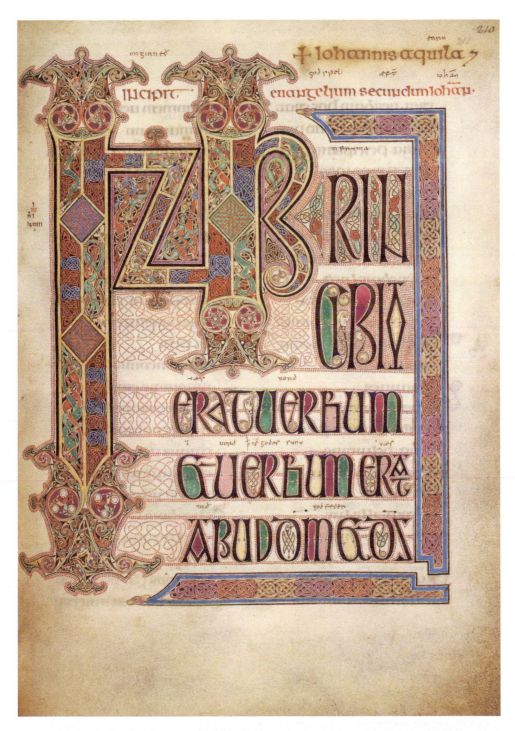

Plate 3.2 Book of Lindisfarne (c. 720). Gospels in insular script with illuminations; here: John 1:1. An OE interlinear translation was added in the tenth century. Note at the top: *incipit euangelium*, under which we find *onȝinneð (odspel* "beginneth (the) gospel" (*ȝod* + *spel* lit. "good story, news"). See 3.1.1.

Plate 4.1 **William the Conqueror** (eleventh century). Bayeux tapestry with the Latin text shown, [HI]C WILLELM DUX IN MAGNO [NAVIGIO MARE TRANSIVIT] "Here William the duke crossed the sea in a large boat." See 4.1.

Plate 4.2 **Death of King Harold** (eleventh century). Bayeux tapestry with the Latin text shown, HIC HAROLD REX INTERFECTUS EST "Here King Harold is killed." See 4.1.

Plate 5.1 The Peasants' Revolt
(c. 1385–1400). A depiction of the end of the 1381 peasants' revolt showing London mayor, Walworth, killing Wat Tyler. There are two images of Richard II. One looks on the killing while the other is talking to the peasants. See 5.1.1 and 5.3.4.1. British Library Royal MS 18.

Plate 5.2 Wycliffe
(late fourteenth century). Gospel of St John, 1:1ff (starting in the lower half of the page): *In þe bigynyng wš þe word 7 þe word was at god / 7 god wš þe word / þis was in þi begynyge at got / Alle þīgis weren maad bi hī: 7 wiþ.* See 5.1.3 and 5.2.1.2.

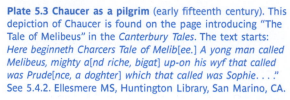

Plate 5.3 Chaucer as a pilgrim (early fifteenth century). This depiction of Chaucer is found on the page introducing "The Tale of Melibeus" in the *Canterbury Tales*. The text starts: *Here beginneth Charcers Tale of Melib[ee.] A yong man called Melibeus, mighty a[nd riche, bigat] up-on his wyf that called was Prude[nce, a doghter] which that called was Sophie. . . ."* See 5.4.2. Ellesmere MS, Huntington Library, San Marino, CA.

Plate 5.4 World map (late fourteenth century). Appeared in Ranulf Higden's *Polychronicon* of 1342 or 1344, but added later. The map (46 x 34 cm) shows the Red Sea in the upper right; Jerusalem is the red area in the center, while Britain is the red area at the bottom. In the left center we find Noah's Ark, and the whole is surrounded by the twelve winds. See 5.5.1. British Library.

Plate 6.1 Shakespeare, The First Folio (1623). The frontispiece of the collection of 36 of Shakespeare's plays with a poem addressed to the reader by B.I. (probably Ben Jonson). See 6.3.4.

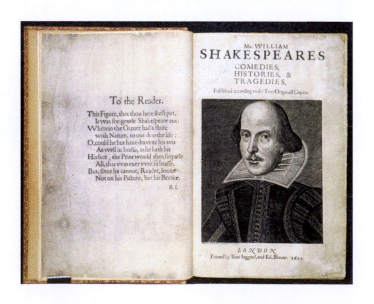

Plate 6.2 Bunyan, *The Pilgrim's Progress* (1683 [1677–78]). The cover of an early edition of Bunyan's influential Christian allegory. As suggested by the extended title, the journey of the pilgrim Christian to the Celestial City in what appears (a similitude) to be a dream. See 6.4.3; also 6.2.5 and 6.3.3.1–3.

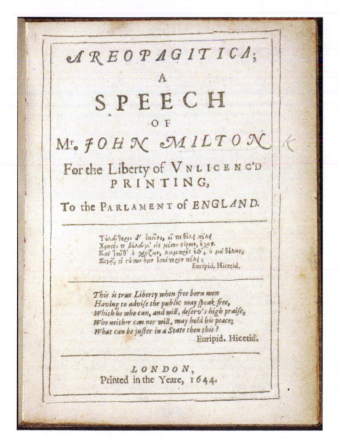

Plate 6.3 Milton, *Areopagitica* (1644). The cover of Milton's impassioned pamphlet arguing for freedom of expression. See 6.4.3.

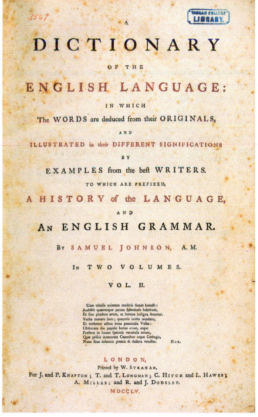

Plate 8.1 Johnson's dictionary (1755). The cover of the first edition. See 8.2.1.2.

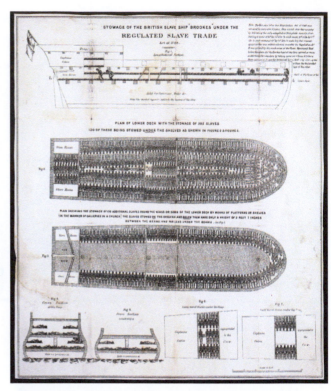

Plate 8.2 Dickens' Sam Weller (1833). The servant of Mr. Pickwick in Dicken's *Pickwick Papers*. Weller is an early stereotyped character in the Cockney tradition, whose language Weller represents as indicated in the ditty, where we find unpalatalized pronunciation of *fort'uns* /fɔːtuːnz/; *we eats*; coalescence of /ɔɪ/ with /aɪ/ *biled* for *boiled*; /v/ for /w/ as in *ven* and *ve*. See 8.2.5.7.

Plate 9.1 The Middle Passage (after 1788). The first leg of the triangular trade was from England to Africa; the second – and middle – leg from Africa to the Americas; and its final one the return voyage to England. The plan depicted was for the ship *Brookes* to carry the maximum number of slaves according to the Regulation Act of 1788, which allowed 6′ × 1′4″ per adult male slave; 5′10″ × 1′4″ per adult female slave; and 5′ × 1′2″ per boy. See 9.1 and 9.1.2.

Plate 9.2 Jamaican Creole Alphabet (current). Spelling based on Cassidy's *Dictionary of Jamaican English* (2nd ed. Cambridge: CUP, 1980), here as used in primary schools in Jamaica. Some people spell "Jamaican" as *Jumiekan*, others as *Jamiekan*. See 9.5.5.1. Source: www.phon.ucl.ac.uk/home/wells/blog0808a.htm.

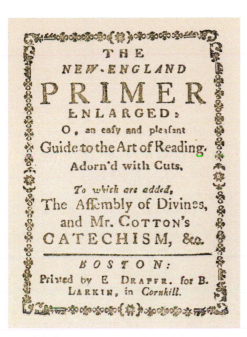

THE
NEW-ENGLAND
PRIMER
ENLARGED:
O, an eafy and pleafant
Guide to the Art of Reading.
Adorn'd with Cuts.

To which are added,
The Affembly of Divines,
and Mr. COTTON's
CATECHISM, &c.

BOSTON:
Printed by E. DRAPER, for B.
LARKIN, in Cornhill.

Plate 10.1 ***The New England Primer*** (1690). Literacy and religion were closely related in Puritan New England, as can be seen from the cover. See 10.2.1.

To all to whom these presents shall come greeting
I Robert Buchan of the town of Gorham County of Ontario
And state of N. York do hereby for myself my heirs Executors and
administrators Manumit and set free a Negro woman slave
named Bettee or Betsey aged about seventy years belonging
to the subscriber the above certificate of Manumission
is at the request and solicitation of the negro woman —
Witness my hand this 29th day of september 1821. —
Witness Robert Buchan
John Buchan
Recorded September the 30th 1821.

Highway Minutes (1798
First Book of Records Eastown

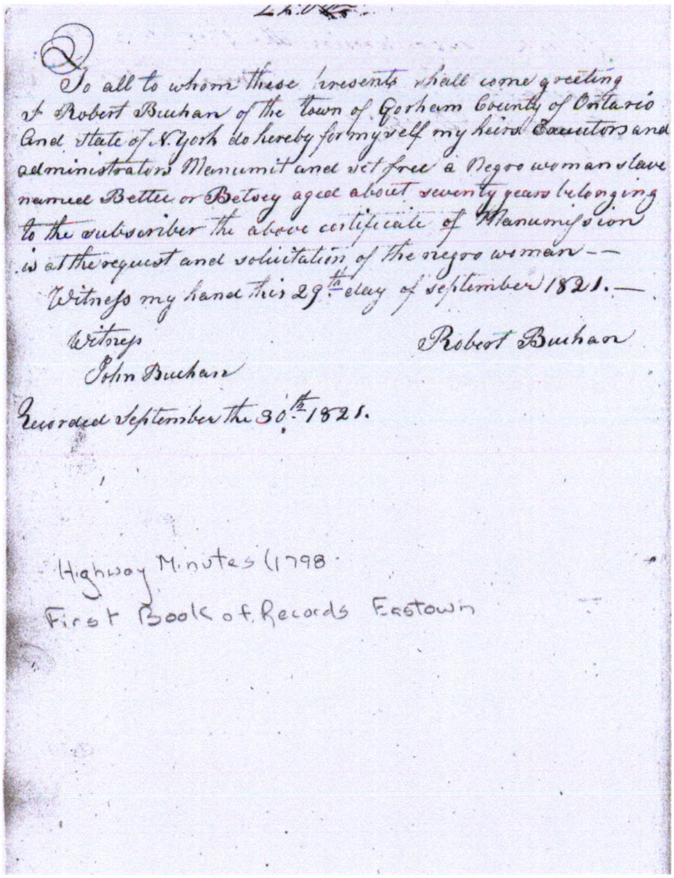

Plate 10.2 Manumission paper (1821). Issued in New York state: "To all to whom these presents shall come greeting I Robert Buchan of the town of Gorham County of Ontario and state of N. York do hereby for myself, my heirs, executors and administrators Manumit and set free a Negro woman slave named Bettee or Betsy aged about seventy years belonging to the subscriber the above certificate of Manumission is at the request and solicitation of the negro woman – Witness my hanse this 29th day of september 1821. Witness – John Buchan Robert Buchan Recorded September the 30th 1821." See 10.2.4.

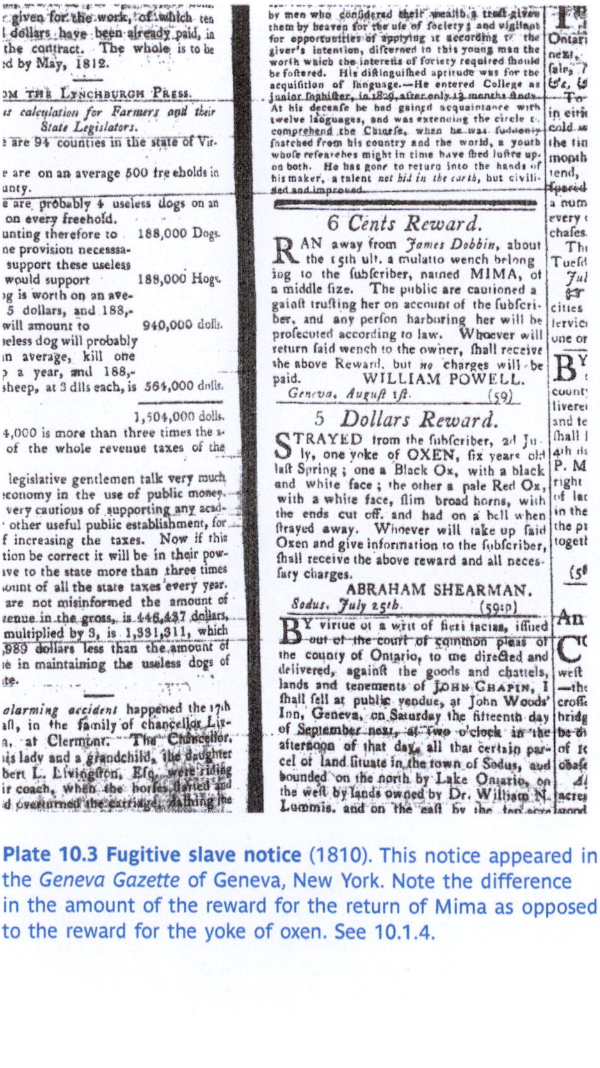

given for the work, of which ten
dollars have been already paid, in
the contract. The whole is to be
ed by May, 1812.

OM THE LYNCHBURGH PRESS.

calculation for Farmers and their
State Legislators.

are 94 counties in the state of Vir-

are on an average 500 freeholds in
unty.

are probably 4 useless dogs on an
on every freehold.
unting therefore to 188,000 Dogs.
ne provision necessa-
support these useless
would support 188,000 Hogs.
g is worth on an ave-
5 dollars, and 188,-
will amount to 940,000 dolls.
eless dog will probably
n average, kill one
a year, and 188,-
sheep, at 3 dlls each, is 564,000 dolls.

1,504,000 dolls.

4,000 is more than three times the a-
of the whole revenue taxes of the

legislative gentlemen talk very much
economy in the use of public money.
very cautious of supporting any acad-
other useful public establishment, for
f increasing the taxes. Now if this
tion be correct it will be in their pow-
ve to the state more than three times
ount of all the state taxes every year.
are not misinformed the amount of
enue in the gross, is 446,437 dollars,
multiplied by 3, is 1,331,311, which
989 dollars less than the amount of
e in maintaining the useless dogs of
te.

alarming accident happened the 17th
ft, in the family of chancellor Liv-
n, at Clermont. The Chancellor,
is lady and a grandchild, the daughter
bert L. Livingston, Esq. were riding
ir coach, when the horses started and
d overturned the carriage, dashing the

by men who considered their wealth a trust given
them by heaven for the use of society; and vigilant
for opportunities of applying it according to the
giver's intention, discerned in this young man the
worth which the interests of society required should
be fostered. His distinguished aptitude was for the
acquisition of language.—He entered College as
junior sophister, in 1829, after only 13 months study.
At his decease he had gained acquaintance with
twelve languages, and was extending the circle to
comprehend the Chinese, when he was suddenly
snatched from his country and the world, a youth
whose researches might in time have shed lustre upon both. He has gone to return into the hands of
his maker, a talent not hid in the earth, but civili-
zed and improved.

6 Cents Reward.

RAN away from James Dobbin, about the 15th ult. a mulatto wench belonging to the subscriber, named MIMA, of a middle size. The public are cautioned against trusting her on account of the subscriber, and any person harboring her will be prosecuted according to law. Whoever will return said wench to the owner, shall receive the above Reward, but no charges will be paid.

WILLIAM POWELL.

Geneva, August 1st. (59)

5 Dollars Reward.

STRAYED from the subscriber, 2d July, one yoke of OXEN, six years old last Spring; one a Black Ox, with a black and white face; the other a pale Red Ox, with a white face, slim broad horns, with the ends cut off, and had on a bell when strayed away. Whoever will take up said Oxen and give information to the subscriber, shall receive the above reward and all necessary charges.

ABRAHAM SHEARMAN.

Sodus, July 25th. (59:p)

BY virtue of a writ of fieri facias, issued out of the court of common pleas of the county of Ontario, to me directed and delivered, against the goods and chattels, lands and tenements of JOHN GHAPIN, I shall sell at public vendue, at John Woods' Inn, Geneva, on Saturday the fifteenth day of September next, at two o'clock in the afternoon of that day, all that certain parcel of land situate in the town of Sodus, and bounded on the north by Lake Ontario, on the west by lands owned by Dr. William N. Lummis, and on the east by the ten acre

Ontari
next,
sale, T
&c. &
To
in citi
cold
the tin
month
tend,
spared
a num
every
chases.
The
Tuesd
Jul
cities
servic
one or
BY
count
livere
and te
shall
4th d
P. M
right
of lar
in the
the pr
togeth
(5
An
C
west
—th
cross
bridg
be di
of it
obase
acres
agond

Plate 10.3 Fugitive slave notice (1810). This notice appeared in the *Geneva Gazette* of Geneva, New York. Note the difference in the amount of the reward for the return of Mima as opposed to the reward for the yoke of oxen. See 10.1.4.

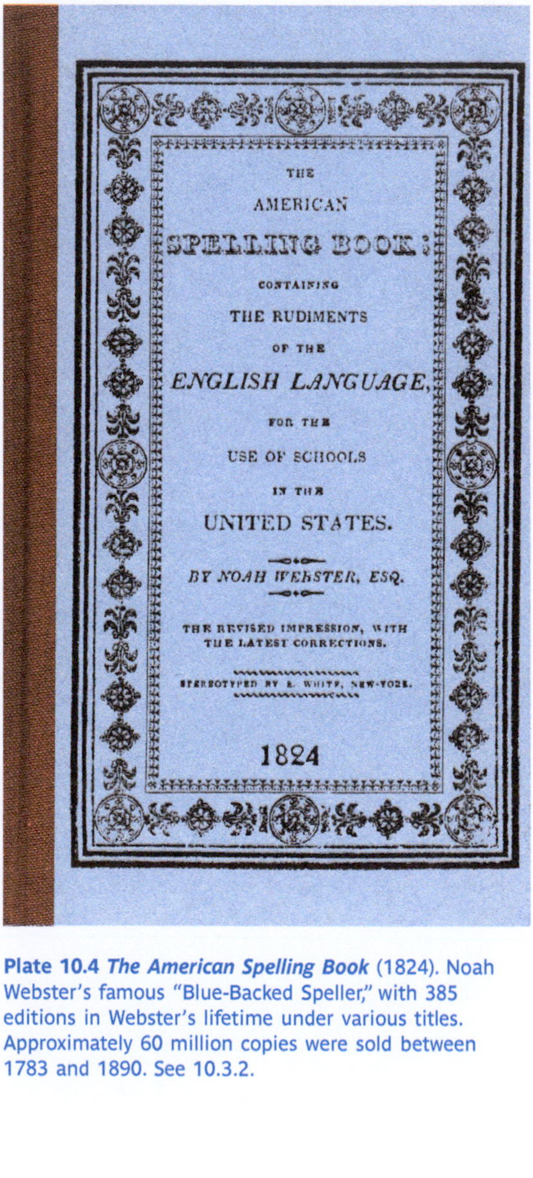

Plate 10.4 ***The American Spelling Book*** (1824). Noah Webster's famous "Blue-Backed Speller," with 385 editions in Webster's lifetime under various titles. Approximately 60 million copies were sold between 1783 and 1890. See 10.3.2.

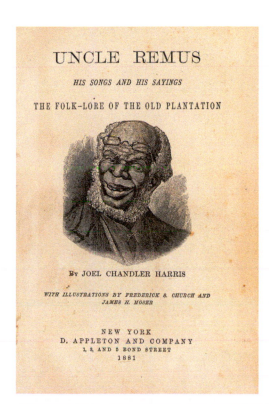

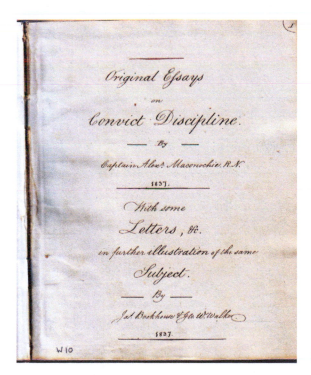

Plate 10.5 Harris' Uncle Remus
(1881). Animal folk tales re-told by
a white Southerner in African
American dialect with a minimal
StE frame. See 10.4.3.

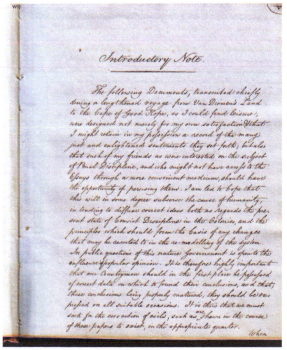

Plate 11.1 Convict discipline (1837). A handwritten account of the inhumanity of the penal system by Captain Alexander Maconochie. See 11.1.1.

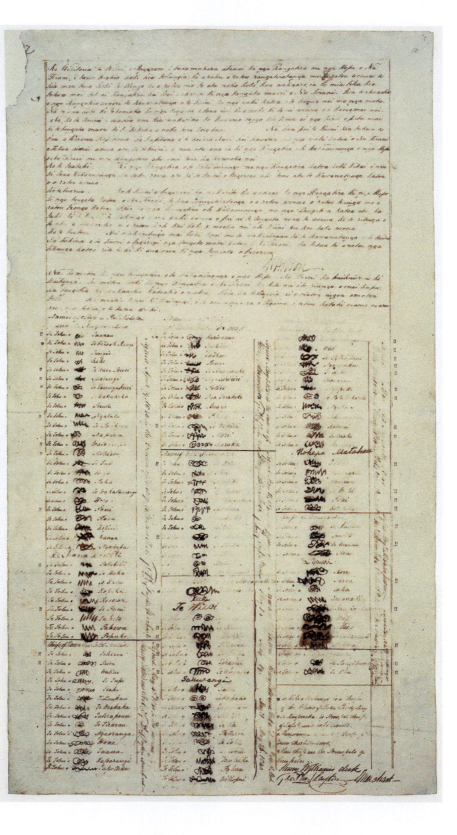

Plate 11.2 Treaty of Waitangi / Te Tiriti o Waitangi (1840). The English version of the Treaty begins as follows: "Her Majesty Victoria Queen of the United Kingdom of Great Britain and Ireland regarding with Her Royal Favour the Native Chiefs and Tribes of New Zealand and anxious to protect their just Rights and Property and to secure to them the enjoyment of Peace and Good Order has deemed it necessary in consequence of the great number of Her Majesty's Subjects who have already settled in New Zealand and the rapid extension of Emigration both from Europe and Australia which is still in progress to constitute and appoint a functionary properly authorised to treat with the Aborigines of New Zealand for the recognition of Her Majesty's Sovereign authority over the whole or any part of those islands. . . ." See 11.1.5.

Plate 11.3 South African road sign (current). In SAfrE *robot* is the term used for "traffic light" elsewhere. See 11.4.

Plate 11.4 New Zealand road sign (current). The names on the sign commemorate the two main linguistic traditions of New Zealand, English and Māori. See 11.4.2.

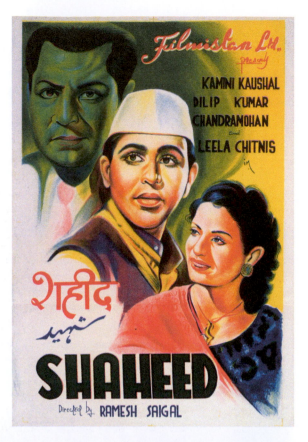

Plate 12.1 Bollywood film poster
(1948). This poster features both
English and Hindi, thus ensuring wider
appeal than a monolingual poster
would have. See 12.1.4.

Plate 12.2 Multilingual sign in Singapore (current). The four official languages of Singapore (English,
Malay, Chinese, and Tamil) appear on many signs, as they do here. See 12.2.2.

Table 9.1 The slave trade

	Dunbar (in Franklin 1980)	Curtin (1969)
16th century:	900,000	241,400
17th century:	2,750,000	1,341,100
18th century (till 1810)	7,000,000	6,051,700
19th century (from 1810):	4,000,000	1,898,400

9.1.2.1 Numbers and periods

In the eleven years from 1783 to 1793 Liverpool merchants alone moved 303,737 slaves to America. One conservative estimate (Dunbar, 1861, qtd. in Franklin 1980: 42) of the extent of the slave trade is given in Table 9.1 together with Curtin's more modern calculation.

Millions of people were expatriated from their African homes in less than four centuries in one of the most far-reaching and drastic social revolutions in the annals of history (Franklin 1980: 59). The European shippers took the best, healthiest, youngest, largest, ablest, most culturally advanced, leaving the impotent, stultified, and overwhelmed. In this way Europeans promoted the destruction of Africa. In the fifteenth century Africa was not far distant from Europe in development; European trade brought social and economic decline, ending in nineteenth century colonialism (see 12.1).

9.1.3 Plantation conditions and demographics

European factory workers were in a position structurally parallel to that occupied by the enslaved laborers of the New World, but the conditions of slavery were more extreme than the worst we know of in Europe. Take the death rate, for example. In St. Vincent in one year there were:

2656 slave births and 4205 slave deaths.

On one Jamaican plantation more than one half of the children died in infancy or by miscarriage, from diseases, and due to poor food. Owners thought it cheaper to buy than to breed new labor. Slaves were economic requisites, enhancing the wealth, power, and prestige of European countries. "There were few evidences of humanitarianism on the plantations of the West Indies" (Franklin 1980: 63).

Slavery in the Western world lasted four centuries, beginning in 1501 and finally abolished in Brazil in 1888. It concentrated the blacks of the New World heavily in the Antilles, coastal Latin America (mostly the Caribbean and Atlantic coasts), and the South of the United States. In 1950, 95% of the blacks and mulattoes in Central America were on the Antilles islands.

9.2 Language contact

Under the conditions of plantation labor the polyglot slave population was forced to wholly abandon its languages. Usually this proceeded in two steps: *pidginization* (link: Pidginization) and then *creolization* (link: Creolization). Both of these processes represent reactions to the radically changed social situation of their speakers and stand in stark contrast to the relatively slow development of English that we have been observing in the previous chapters. In its homeland English developed over a period of centuries from the varieties of Old, Middle, and Early Modern English to those of today, all of which may be attributed largely to the effects of social, political, cultural, and spatial separation, often reinforced by contact with other languages. The emerging pidgins and creoles of the sixteenth to nineteenth centuries, in contrast, were the results of catastrophic scenarios instigated within the plantation system in the Americas and elsewhere.

Two differing social situations characterized by two very different types of *language contact* were implicated in this linguistic development: (1) The fort situation, typical of, for example, West Africa. Here an outside group such as the English penetrated a multi-lingual area and imposed its language for the purposes of trade on the native population. Eventually, a process of *tertiary hybridization* (link: Tertiary hybridization) began in which the new pidginized language was adopted for use among different native groups. (2) The plantation situation was typical of the Caribbean and the Pacific areas, in which the dominant outside group transported people from their homeland to a new area overseas.

Indigenous people in fort situations become Europeanized to varying degrees. The female native partners/wives of the European men would presumably have learned the L2 well. Under fort circumstances the European language model diluted quickly as it was used for communication by clients and dependents and tertiarily by these in multilingual trade contacts within the native communities. While some Europeans will have learned non-European languages in the fort situation, hardly any will have done so in the plantation situation. On plantations the non-Europeans soon outnumbered the Europeans, thus lessening the laborers' contact with the *superstrate* language and creating poor conditions for learning the superstrate language well (cf. Bickerton 1988: 269–270).

9.2.1 The spread of English pidgins and creoles

Not every pidgin or creole with English as its major source of vocabulary is of interest in the context of this book. Some creoles whose vocabulary comes chiefly from English have little present-day connection to English. This is most obvious in the case of *Sranan*, the most widespread creole in Suriname, spoken by about 80% of the population (and the first language of approximately a quarter of the Suriname population).

In a number of countries an English creole, usually a low-prestige language, stands in a relationship to StE as (one of) the official language(s). That is the case in many of the territories of the Caribbean. *English pidgins* are prominent in West Africa (Cameroon, Gambia, Ghana, Liberia, Nigeria, and Sierra Leone – all former fort situations; see chapter 12). In each of these West African countries StE is an official language, but not one widely spoken as a home language, and the low-prestige form of English is a pidgin rather than a creole. The third major area in which English pidgins and creoles are to be found is the Pacific – with both fort and plantation type situations, though with a history of contract labor rather than slavery. Most prominent is *Tok Pisin* (Papua New Guinea) (link: Pidgin and creole English).

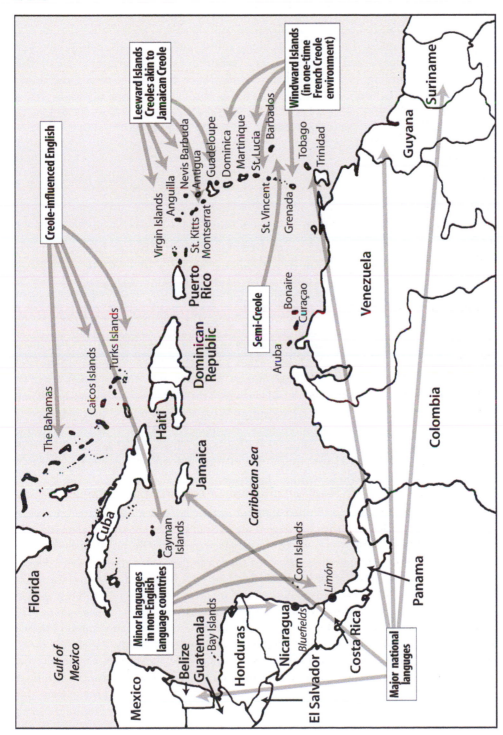

Map 9.2
Caribbean creoles

Florida

Gulf of
Mexico

The Bahamas

Caicos Islands

Turks Islands

Creole-influenced English

Mexico

Cuba

Belize
Guatemala
Bay Islands
Honduras
Nicaragua
Bluefields
El Salvador
Costa Rica

Minor languages
in non-English
language countries

Cayman
Islands

Jamaica

Corn Islands

Limón

Panama

Caribbean Sea

Haiti

Dominican
Republic

Puerto
Rico

Virgin Islands

Anguilla
Nevis Barbuda
St. Kitts Antigua
Montserrat Guadeloupe
Dominica
Martinique
St. Lucia
Barbados

Leeward Islands
Creoles akin to
Jamaican Creole

St. Vincent
Grenada

Tobago
Trinidad

Windward Islands
(in one-time
French Creole
environment)

Semi-Creole

Aruba
Bonaire
Curaçao

Venezuela

Colombia

Major national
languges

Guyana

Suriname

9.2.2 Cultural survivals

The transfer of peoples does not necessarily mean the transfer of cultures. The question arises as to how much of their African identity the tremendously suppressed slaves of the New World were able to keep. The details varied considerably in the various colonies, but, in general, such homeland institutions as kings, courts, guilds, markets, cult-groups, and armies were not transplanted. Despite occasional exceptions social institutions were snuffed out under the grinding, grueling plantation work. What did survive were those things closest to a person's behavior and feeling: parts or aspects of language, oral traditions, verbal values, music and performance styles, dance and kinesthetics such as ways of walking or laughing, religion, and perhaps some elements of family structure.

9.3 Pidgins

A pidgin is a type of language which has evolved in the context of contact between speakers of several different languages. Historically this has been chiefly in the context of trade or plantation labor. In this sense it is a *contact language* (link: Contact language). It may be a temporary, make-shift means of communication or it may be a more or less permanent and relatively fixed language system. Because it is used in a restricted set of circumstances, it is often referred to as a *marginal language* (link: Marginal language). In any case what is important is that it is not the native language of any of the speakers or groups of speakers: it is a non-native language. It nevertheless makes use of words, sounds, constructions, and strategies of communication which it may borrow from any of the native languages of its speakers as well as the dominant colonial language. This has led to these languages being called mixed languages (link: Hybrid languages). What is borrowed is usually reduced vis-à-vis the original languages. Furthermore, reduction applies to both the systematic linguistic aspects of language and the range of use of the language. That is, pidgins are employed in fewer situations and allow for less stylistic differentiation. For this reason they are justifiably termed *reduced languages* (link: Reduced language).

In summary, a pidgin is a reduced, impoverished language which is no one's native language and which is used for limited communication in situations of contact between people who do not share a native language. Linguistically, it may consist of elements of a wide variety of native languages; however, the language spoken by the people with the most prestige and/or power supply the majority of the vocabulary. This allows a great deal of variety. Some pidgins are relatively make-shift; others have been used over several generations. The former reflect the native languages of its users more strongly and are termed *jargons* (link: Jargon) by Mühlhäusler (1986a). Pidgins passed on from generation to generation are likely to be much more systematically structured and even contain internal means for the *derivation* of new words, relatively sophisticated *syntax*, and an expanded phonology (termed stabilized and expanded pidgins by Mühlhäusler). Obviously, the definition of a pidgin has to take into account linguistic, social, and historical factors. A pidgin differs from other related language types: A *lingua franca* (link: Lingua franca) is a reduced, simplified form of an existing native language used for communication in limited situations with non-native participants (and possibly some native ones); both creoles

Table 9.2 Pidgins distinguished from related terms

	contact	*marginal*	*mixed*	*non-native*	*reduced*
trade jargon	yes	yes	yes	yes	yes
pidgin	yes	yes	yes	yes	yes/no
lingua franca	yes	yes	no	yes/no	yes
koiné	yes	no	yes	no	yes/no
dialect	no	yes/no	no	no	no
creole	no	no	no	no	no

and extended pidgins can be used as lingua francas, as can GenE itself; a **koiné** (link: Koinéization) is a form of a language which has evolved as the long-term product of contact between speakers of differing (regional) varieties of a single language; a **dialect** (link: Dialect) is a variety of a language which differs from other varieties of the "same" language due to such features of its speakers as region, age, gender, ethnicity, class, religion, and so on; and a creole is a native language like any other, but one with a special history, usually rooted in a pidgin.

9.3.1 Examples of Pidgin English

If pidgins are, indeed, mixed languages and non-native ones at that, how is it that we can refer to them as *English* at all? The following are some examples (all Hawaiian Pidgin English (HPE) from Bickerton 1981). As in earlier chapters the original text is given in the first line, a literal word-by-word translation in the second, and a free Modern English translation in the third. Note that the HPE spelling is semi-phonemic:

difren belifs dei get, sam gaiz
different beliefs they get, some guys
"Some guys have different beliefs" [word order in HPE differs from GenE] (21)

haus, haus ai stei go in, jaepan taim
house, house I stay go in, Japan time
"When I lived in Japan I stayed inside the house" [no tense; time marked adverbially] (27)

go tak tu fala go hapai dis wan
go take two fellow go carry this one
"Take two men and carry this away" [*go* used as a **marker** of the imperative] (31)

Obviously the syntax of these HPE examples is not English, and the morphology is only partially so. We cannot say much about the pronunciation. What we can discern is that the vocabulary is more or less English. In fact, in the examples given above only the single word *hapai* is clearly not English. It is chiefly because the vocabulary comes to such a large extent from English that a pidgin may be called Pidgin *English*. In such cases English is the **lexifier** language (link: Lexifier). The phonology, morphology, and syntax of such a pidgin are not fixed; rather, they may reflect the native languages of its various users. In contrast, in well-established or extended and stabilized pidgins (link: Pidginization) phonology and syntax as well as lexis are relatively more fixed and shared within the larger community. The lexifier

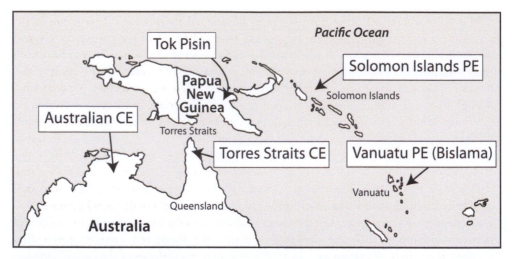

Map 9.3 Pacific pidgins and creoles

language, which is the language of the economically or militarily more powerful and more prestigious, is generally called the *superstrate* language (link: Superstrate language); its contributions are fairly obvious because it supplies most of the vocabulary used. In contrast, the native languages of the less powerful are referred to as *substrate languages* (link: Substrate languages); their influence is less obvious, but arguably present in phonology and communicative structures, less so in syntax, in morphology, and, of course, in lexis.

9.3.2 Lexicon and word formation

Make-shift pidgins (jargons) are characterized by their limited vocabulary, which in turn means that fewer words will have to carry relatively more functions/meaning. Tok Pisin (TP), for example, though an extended pidgin, has two prepositions, *long* (for spatial relations) and *bilong* (for possession or association), while GenE has several hundred. In the place of more precise lexical items such pidgins are likely to depend more on circumlocution. TP uses *gras* (< English *grass*) for various bunches of long stringy things: *gras bilong hed* ("hair") vs. *gras bilong fes* ("beard"). The following table shows the major sources of vocabulary *borrowing* in three *stable pidgins* in the Pacific area.

In general a tendency has been noted for the kind of words borrowed to have a higher share of archaic and regional items than is the case in GenE. Furthermore, we find reanalysis of *morpheme* boundaries, substratum *calques*, *semantic shifts*, and *reduplication* (see below, this section).

Table 9.3 Sources of vocabulary in three Pacific pidgins with an English lexifier

Bislama:	90% English	5% indigenous	3% French
Tok Pisin:	77% English	16% indigenous	7% German (etc.)
Solomon Pijin:	89% English	6% indigenous	5% other

(Mühlhäusler 1986a: 198)

Pidgins (and creoles) often do not retain the original morphological structure of the lexifier. This means that inflections (e.g. for the plural of nouns or the past tense of verbs) are not borrowed together with the word. Instead one single form may be used for both present and past, as in the example above of *stei*, which is used where there would be *stayed* in GenE. Furthermore, there are a number of cases in which the distinction between what in English are two different words is not maintained. For example, in TP, *tudir* < English *too dear* means simply "expensive." In this way the English morphological structure (a sequence of the two morphemes, {too} and {dear}) is ***reanalyzed*** (link: Grammaticalization) as a single, indivisible morpheme {tudir}. The same applies to *lego* < *let go*, which has become a single word meaning "let go"; and *sekan* < *shake hands*, meaning "make peace" (examples from Mühlhäusler 1986a: 167). Internal resources for adding to the vocabulary by the process of word formation are seldom found in a pidgin though they begin to develop in creoles.

Borrowing may also ignore the semantic, syntactic, and stylistic constraints (link: Style) of the donor language. In TP, a stable pidgin, the stylistically neutral word for "rear end" is *as* (< English *arse*). Furthermore, *as* undergoes semantic broadening (link: Semantic broadening) and comes to mean "origin" or "cause" as well (ibid.: 168). The syntactic class of a word may also be different than in the lexifier, as when TP *tasol* (< *that's all*) is used as the conjunction "but" (ibid.). Of course, when the pidgin is used (at the low-prestige end) in a given society together with StE (at the high end), the long-term influence of StE norms, including those of social acceptability, is likely to be fairly strong.

The use of Pidgin (or Creole) English against the background of a society with non-European traditions may also lead to a restructuring of some lexical fields, as can be seen in the case of ***kinship terms*** (link: Kinship terms). Here TP has *papa* and *mama* much as used in GenE. However, the important distinction between a paternal uncle (*smolpapa*) and paternal aunt (*smolmama*), on the one hand, and a maternal uncle or aunt (undifferentiated *kandare*), on the other, must be maintained. Furthermore, not only is a single word used for both a grandparent and a grandchild (undifferentiated for gender: *tumbuna*), there is also only one word for both a brother's brother and for a sister's sister (*brata*), and a different one for a brother's sister and a sister's brother (*susa*) (Mühlhäusler 1986a: 169; see Table 9.4).

A further type of borrowing that is often pointed out is the ***calque*** or ***loan translation*** (link: Loan translation), in which the elements of, for example, a substrate language are translated into the lexifier language, English. This gives us *big áy* for "greedy" or *stròng-héd* for "stubborn" in Nigerian PE. Further examples are American Indian PE and the putative calques *warpath, paleface, firewater, peace pipe*; also Chinese PE *no can do* "something is impossible to do" (ibid.: 194–195).

Table 9.4 Kinship terms in Tok Pisin

English	Tok Pisin	English	Tok Pisin	English	Tok Pisin
mother	*mama*	maternal aunt or uncle	*kandare*	paternal aunt	*smolmama*
father	*papa*			paternal uncle	*smolpapa*
same-sex sibling	*brata*	opposite-sex sibling	*susa*	grandparent or grandchild	*tumbuna*

A process not dependent on borrowing alone is ***reduplication*** (link: Reduplication), which may occur without the influence of the substratum. In pidgins it occurs in order to signal a variety of distinctions in meaning, such as the plural or a large quantity of what the non-reduplicated noun designates (West African PE *dók-dók* "dogs"), repetition and continuity of action (*tók-tók* "constant talk"), indivisibility (*kwíkwík* "quickly"), or intensification (*bík-bík* "very big") (Schneider 1967).

Lexical distinctions can also be made by using regular derivational processes, at least in older, stabilized pidgins. The English word *find* shows up in TP as the root {pain} (pronounced like "pine"). It takes this form because the substrate languages do not have the phoneme /f/ and therefore replace it with a /p/. Furthermore, as in many pidgins and creoles as well as many non-standard forms of GenE, final ***consonant clusters*** (link: Consonant clusters) (combinations of one or more consonants) such as /-nd/ are simplified to /n/. Since *pain* is a transitive verb, it regularly takes the final syllable {-im}, which marks transitivity. By itself it means "search." When the action of searching is successful (that is, finding), this is marked by adding the word "finish," a "completive aspectual marker," which in TP is, phonetically, *pinis* (/f/ > /p/; /ʃ/ > /s/). Thus we find here the following pairs:

painim / *painim pinis*	search / find
boilim / *boilim pinis*	boil / sterilize
promis / *promis pinis*	promise / keep a promise

(Mühlhäusler 1986a: 171)

(For more examples see link: Word formation in Tok Pisin.)

9.3.3 Syntax

The grammatical structure of pidgins varies considerably depending on whether the pidgin is new and relatively make-shift or whether it has existed long enough to become stabilized and expand. The examples given in 9.3.1 represent the make-shift pole, in which the native languages of the speakers provide most of the grammatical input.[2] TP represents the other end of the pole. It has a history of well over 100 years, and it is currently undergoing the process of creolization (see 9.4.1). As a result its grammar is relatively complex. Following are a few examples of the system of TP.

Let us start by looking at the system of ***personal pronouns*** (link: Personal pronouns), as we have so far done in most of the chapters. Note that no gender distinctions in the third person singular are made (see Table 9.5).

While early pidgins often have no systematic means of indicating tense, ***aspect***, and number and rely on the context, these categories begin to appear as pidgins stabilize and then expand. One of these grammatical markers was introduced to TP by plantation workers returning from Samoa (and speaking Samoan Plantation PE) around 1900. It is the affixation of the English word *fellow* (in TP: *-pela*) to mark monosyllabic attributive adjectives, for example *smolpela dokta* "little doctor, i.e. medical orderly," or to mark first and second person pronouns as plural, for example *mi* "I" vs. *mipela* "we"; *yu* "you

2 It has been argued that pidgin formation may also be guided by universal principles (see 9.5.4).

Table 9.5 The personal pronouns of Tok Pisin (stabilization stage)[3]

person	singular	plural
1st	mi "I, my, me"	mi-pela "we, our, us"
2nd	yu "you, your"	yu-pela "you all, you all's"
3rd	em "he/she/it, his/her/its, him/her/it"	em ol "they, their, them"

(Mühlhäusler 1986a: 159)

(singular)" vs. *yupela* "you (plural)" (Mühlhäusler 1986a: 153–154). In both cases this is a good example of grammatical reanalysis. The Samoan use of *fellow* (*pela* or *fela*) was variable in word order, coming sometimes before and sometimes after a noun or adjective and carrying, in greater or lesser fashion, the meaning "thing." In TP it was reanalyzed, that is, grammaticalized, in the sense indicated at the beginning of this paragraph.

TP also gradually introduced tense markers such as the future marker *baimbai* (short form: *bai*) < English *by and by*:

em bai go long maket
she will go to market

(Mühlhäusler 1986a: 186)

Furthermore, what was originally the pronoun for the third person singular (*he, she, it*), namely *i*, became a marker indicating that the next element in the sentence was the verb (or predicate):

em	*i*		*tok se*	*papa*	*i*		*gat sik*

he PREDICATE MARKER say that the father PRED. MARKER got sick
"he said that the father was sick"

(ibid.: 189)

As a final syntactic point let us look at how relative clauses are formed, another point we have been following up in the various stages of the language we have looked at. Quite a number of English-lexifier pidgins have the relative element *we* (< *where*), pronounced /weː/. Mühlhäusler lists West African PE, Bislama, Solomon Islands PE, TP, Queensland Kanaka English, Krio, Torres Strait Broken, and Northern Territory Kriol. In each case the emergence of the relative pronoun may well be an independent development rather than a case of a historical relationship. For example, when *we* showed up in TP (early 1970s), TP itself had lost any contact with German West Africa, the locale of its presumed source. The development of *we* seems to have spread from place (*ples we*) to time (*taim we*) to animates (*man we*) and finally to inanimate things (*samthing we*), whereby each construction represents a case of reanalysis (Mühlhäusler 1986a: 189–190). In a later step TP speakers moved

---

3 In recent Tok Pisin we find a more elaborated pronoun system in which the first person plural has been differentiated into an exclusive first person plural (*mípela*) "speaker and one or more others, but not the addressee" and an inclusive first person plural (*yumi*) "speaker and addressee(s)"; third person plural is now simply *ol*.

in the direction of the lexifier language and introduced the relativizer *husat* "who," originally an interrogative ("who?") adapted as a kind of loan translation from English and used in written TP (for example, in translations).[4] In TP *husat* first applied to people (as does English *who*), for example *Mister Paul Langro husat i bin askim . . .* ("Mr. Paul Langro who asked . . ."), but then was extended to things as well, for example *insait long biktaun bilong PNG husat i gat haus bet* ("in the cities of PNG which have betting shops") (ibid.: 245–246).

9.3.4 Pronunciation

This remains the least stable linguistic level in pidgins. In early pidgins, the inventory of sounds is limited, and sounds unusual in the world's languages are seldom retained (/x/, /ð/, θ/, /ʃ/, /ʒ/). A five-vowel system (/i – e – a – o – u/) is frequent, and vowel length differences are often lost. Substratum influence is generally notable, especially in the jargon stage, but it subsides under stabilization. The lack of a distinction in TP between /s/, /ʃ/, and /tʃ/ (all realized as /s/) can lead to ambiguity. For example *sip* can be English *ship, jib, jeep, sieve*, or *chief* (together with the lack of a long–short vowel distinction, final de-voicing, and the realization of /f/ as /p/). Likewise *pis* represents *beach, beads, fish, peach, piss, feast*, and *peace*. This explains the misunderstanding on the part of a Member of the House of Assembly in Port Moresby who is reported to have said, "les long toktok long sit nating," intending to say, "tired of talking to empty seats." Unfortunately, this was wrongly translated as "tired of talking to a bunch of shits." It would have been better if he had used the established term *sia* "seat" (Mühlhäusler 1986b: 561).

In the expansion phase there is an increase in vowels, for example the five-vowel system develops into a seven-, ten- or even twelve-vowel system. Many of the new distinctions come from the lexifier language, but possibly also from substrate languages or ***adstrate*** languages (outside ones, neither the superstrate (lexifier) nor one of the substrate languages). More marginal consonants are added, allowing further distinctions; additions may be phonologically non-English as with Nigerian PE /gb/, /kp/, and /ɲ/. Phonological rules also begin to emerge: (1) ***phonotactic*** restrictions change and (2) deletion, permutation, or addition of the base forms becomes possible. For example, consonant clusters are allowed: where earlier we had *pún* we may now find *spún* "spoon"; *sipik* becomes *spik* "speak" (NigPE). TP had *tiret* or *sitiret* for present-day *stret* "straight." TP also now has unstressed syllables (e.g. /pəla/ for earlier /pela/); earlier word initial pre-nasalization is lost, as with /mb-, nd-, [ŋ]g/, or regarded as a marker of social backwardness. Stylistic variation such as imitating older pronunciations to make fun of a (rural) mentality may occur.

9.4 Creoles

Conventionally creoles are described as nativized pidgins, that is, languages which have been adopted by children growing up in environments where a pidgin is their primary input language and therefore becomes their native language. In the process of becoming a native

---

4 It is interesting that this runs parallel to the introduction of relative *who* from interrogative *who?* in early ME, possibly under the influence of French *qui* (see 4.2.3).

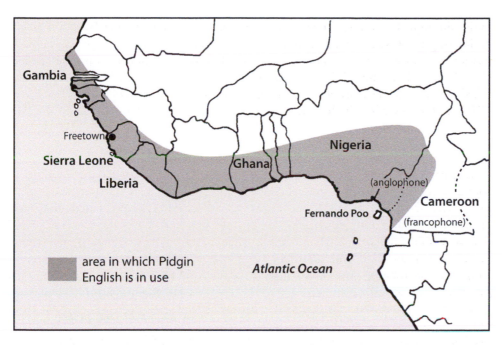

Map 9.4 West African Pidgin English

or a ***primary language***, a pidgin changes in its nature. It does not remain reduced.[5] Rather, it expands, lexically, syntactically, and morphologically. Its expansion includes the number and quality of the contexts in which it is used; it gains in stylistic differentiation, often finding expression in written texts, perhaps eventually becoming standardized. As a result it can no longer be regarded as marginal. The mixing that went into the pidgin and the contact that characterized its genesis are now only historical, and for this reason cannot be seen as definitive synchronic (link: Synchronic and diachronic description) features.

9.4.1 Creolization

Despite all that has been written about the process of creolization, very much still remains vague. Does, for example, creolization necessarily presuppose the prior existence of a pidgin? Some such as Bickerton (1988: 278), for example, sees one possible evolution of creoles in a reduction of the acrolect toward the pidgin stage with a loss of markers of case, gender, and number or of tense, modality, and aspect. In 9.5 we will go into this question in more detail.

9.4.2 Examples of English creoles

Illustration is first necessary so that we can understand better what we are dealing with. In the following examples the abbreviations in capital letters indicate functional markers, for example NEG "negator"; LOC "locative marker" (someone or something is somewhere); ANT "anterior, past marker"; EXIST "existential marker" (something exists); PROG

---

5 Of course, a pidgin need not remain reduced, as we have seen with numerous examples taken from stabilized and expanding pidgins.

"progressive marker"; FUT "future marker." The spelling in the example sentences follows varying conventions.

Guyanese Creole

mii no   noo wisaid   den de. yu noo ou laang   wii bin gat   a mashiin?
me NEG know what side they LOC you know how long   we ANT have that machine
I don't know where they are now.   Do you know how long we've had that machine?

it a wan naif	*ii a gu, ii a waak*
it EXIST one knife	he PROG go he PROG walk
There was a knife.	He was going along.

(Rickford 1987: 133, 130)

Hawaiian CE

ai no kea hu stei hant insai dea,	*ai gon hunt*
I NEG care who PROG hunt inside there	I FUT hunt
I don't care who's hunting in there,	I'm going to hunt
Jan bin go wok a haspital	*get wan wahini shi get wan data*
John ANT FUT work at hospital	EXIST one wahin she got one daughter
John would have worked at the hospital	There is a woman who has a daughter

(Bickerton 1981: 28, 55, 67)

Obviously, creoles are differently structured than GenE, and we would have no grounds for dealing with them if ones like those illustrated here did not stand in a continuum relationship to GenE.

9.4.3 The language *continuum* (link: Continuum)

Many English creoles are spoken in countries where English is the official language. Consequently, the creoles, which share a good bit of their vocabulary with English, are regarded as being forms of English, often, however, with pejorative designations, such as "broken" or "bastard" or "bad." This is the case in Jamaica and in Guyana.

9.4.3.1 The Creole continuum

The creole continuum in countries in which English is the official language and the majority of the population speaks either English or an English creole covers a variety of forms that lie between the two extremes of StE (the *acrolect*; link: Acrolect) and the broadest creole (the *basilect*; link: Basilect). The varieties in between are called *mesolects* (link: Mesolects). A continuum implies that "given two samples of Jamaican speech which differ substantially from one another, it is usually possible to find a third intermediate level in an additional sample. Thus it is not practicable to describe the system in terms of two or three or six or any other manageable number of discrete social dialects" (DeCamp 1971: 354).

mi a nyam   me a eat   me eatin'   I eatin'   I is eatin'   I am eating
basilect ◄——————————   mesolects   ——————► acrolect

(after Singh 2000: 74)

There may be a fundamental difference between the acrolect and all other varieties in the continuum, and this distinction may well be rooted in the feelings speakers have about any kind of divergence from the standard. Despite the increase in local pride in the creole, the general tendency has been toward the acrolect. Young speakers may have command of a far greater range within the continuum than older ones (Rickford 1987: 38).

A great deal of attention has been given to the question of the continuum, and there is a fair amount of controversy over whether or not such a thing really exists. The alternative is to see distinct or discrete varieties (say, two or even three). Where two distinct varieties exist, one will generally have more prestige and be the High or classical language. The other is the Low (demotic or vernacular) language. Such relationships are cases of *diglossia* (link: Diglossia). (If there are more than two languages or varieties involved this is triglossia or even polyglossia.) However, this does not seem to be the case where English creoles coexist with English. In these cases there is a "mixed" area in the continuum between acrolect and basilect. Furthermore, it is somewhat ordered since there is an *implicational relationship* (link: Implicational relations) between some of the items in the basilect and the acrolect. Table 9.6 illustrates this for Guyanese CE.

This means that if, for example, a creole speaker forms the progressive by combining *a* with the verb (*a* V as in *ii a gu* "he/she is going") that speaker will also have all the features which follow it in the implicational scale. Concretely, this means he or she will pronounce *this* as *dis* and *car* as /kjar/. The other way around, a speaker who produces *hiiz guing* ("he's going") instead of *ii a gu* will not produce anything above it in the list. Producing the more extreme creole form implies producing the less extreme ones. Speakers adapt to StE by "losing" the features from the top down in the table. However, movement is not in the direction of adaptation to the acrolect only. The standard itself is open to the adoption of creole elements, especially as speakers with a creole background move up in society and gain in prestige. Almost inevitably they will take some creole elements with them (cf. the role of mobility in the ME period as elaborated in chapter 5).

Just what determines what degree of creole a speaker will produce seems to be a fairly complicated equation involving education and social status, the given social situation (official or familiar) including solidarity, urbanity, age, ethnicity, and gender. Text 9.1 is a basilect Guyanese CE text produced by a young boy whose background was that of a field worker; Text 9.2 represents a mesolect and comes from a young girl whose father was a building contractor and who was going to secondary school in Georgetown, Guyana.

Not every creole feature can be listed in a table like 9.6. What is listed is a practical question, not a systematic one. This should be clear from the fact that the items in the list are a mixture of points of pronunciation, syntax, and vocabulary. Furthermore,

Table 9.6 Implicational relationships in Guyanese CE

basilect item	(explained as), if used,	implies		the use of what follows in the list	
wan	(as indefinite article)	>	*na* V	(pre-verbal negation)	>
dem	(as subject case pronoun)	>	*aa*	(low unrounded as in *all*)	>
V + 0	(as dynamic verb past)	>	*a* V	(as progressive)	>
d (for ð)	(as in *this*)	>	*ky*/*gy*	(as in *car, girl*)	

(Rickford 1987: 19)

implicational relations in Guyana look very different in Jamaica (DeCamp 1971 in Rickford 1987: 20):

> /d/ (as in *this*) > *t* (as in *thin*) > *pikni* (for *child*) > *no ben* (for *didn't*) > *nanny* (for *granny*) > *nyam* (for *eat*)

The question of ordered change which implicational relations suggest is complex and will not be explored here. If you are interested look at the link: Life-Cycle Theory.

9.4.3.2 Direction of change

The direction of change is frequently toward GenE. But clearly the direction is not fixed, nor is it uniform. ***Pronunciation change*** commonly proceeds by lexical diffusion rather than strict laws of sound change. This means that a phonological innovation triggered off by borrowing words with a "new" sound may be restricted to the borrowed material. However, the innovation may continue to expand until the change is "complete" in the sense that all the words with sounds that qualify for a particular change have actually changed. Sometimes, furthermore, innovations lead to forms which are neither basilectal nor acrolectal. This includes cases of rule generalization and ***hypercorrection***. TP, for example, is "restoring" medial consonant clusters and some final ones. Restoration, such as *bihain > bihaindim* or *poin > pointim*, where the acrolect has /d/ (*behind*) or /t/ (*point*) has led to hypercorrection, as in *kis* "catch" > *kistim* even though there is no /t/ in the lexifier. A second example is the influence of AusE, which leads to original TP /e/ being pronounced as /aɪ/, for example *nem > naim* "name." As a reaction against this there is a countermovement which changes original TP /aɪ/ to /e/, for example *laik > lek* or *kaikai > keke* (Mühlhäusler 1986a: 238–240).

9.5 Theories of origins

In this section we will review four approaches to how creoles come about. The interest in following up this question lies in the fact that there are so many structural similarities between creoles with European-language lexifiers throughout the world that many linguists feel a suitable explanation would contribute very much to our understanding of how languages evolve and continue to develop. Most of these theories set out to account for the many parallel, similar, or even identical forms which creoles have, but which do not show up in

Table 9.7 Putative European-language sources for verbal markers in various Caribbean creoles

	negation	anterior	progressive	existential
Sranan	no	(b)en	(d)e (< *there*)	de (< *there*)
Guyana CE	no	bin	a (< *on/at*?)	a/get
HCE	no	bin	stei (< *stay*)	get
Haitian CF	pa (< *pas*)	te (< *été*)	ap (< *après* or *au près*)	gê (< *j'ai*?)
Papiamentu	n (< *no*)	taba/a (< *estaba* /ya)	ta (< *está*)	tin (< *tener*)

the standard forms of their lexifier languages. In the following table Sranan, Guyana CE, and Hawaiian CE have English as their lexifier; Haitian CF has French, and Papiamentu has Spanish (possibly Portuguese). Despite the different lexifiers, the creoles themselves have fully parallel forms.

In the case of the negation marker each of the creoles has chosen one of the central words used in the lexifiers for negation. The anterior (or past time) marker is apparently derived from the past participle of the verb *be* in the lexifier (or in the case of Papiamentu from *ya* "already"). Progressive aspect, that is, an on-going action, is marked by a particle derived from a word for being at some place (English *there*, *at/on*, or *stay*, French *au près* or *après*, and Spanish *está* "be somewhere or in some condition"). The existential, finally, comes from a word for having something or being somewhere (as in StE *there is/are*). Other categories of the verb (completive, habitual, *irrealis*) have grammatical particles derived in a similarly parallel way from their lexifiers.

9.5.1 *Monogenesis* (link: Monogenesis)

This approach postulates one unique origin for all pidgins and creoles with a European-language lexifier. The proto-pidgin that they all ultimately come from is presumed to have had a Portuguese lexical base[6] and was supposedly widely used on the trade routes along the Atlantic coast of Africa, around the Cape of Good Hope, into the Indian Ocean, and on to China. As further Europeans entered the colonial trade they would have used the "same" pidgin, but replaced Portuguese words with Dutch, French, or English ones in a process called "*relexification*" (link: Relexification) (cf. Thompson 1961; Voorhoeve 1973). This theory is supported not only by the similar grammatical structure of all (or many) of the pidgins and creoles involved, but also by the "residue" of Portuguese words in, for example, English creoles, words such as *pickaninny* < Portuguese *pequeno, pequenino* "small (child)," *savvy* < *saber* "know," or *sampata* < *sapato* "sandal" (Cassidy 1971: 207ff).

This pidgin would have been extremely simple. Everything "inessential" would have been lost (no gender, no cases, no verb endings). The influence of the substrate languages shows up in the phonology or the use of an aspect-mode system instead of a tense system (Whinnom 1965: 519; Winford 2009), but the vast majority of the vocabulary is clearly from the superstrate language. In Whinnom's words: "If Portuguese pidgin particles survive in a pidgin or creole, this must surely be regarded as conclusive proof of Portuguese pidgin origin" (1965: 520).

Criticism

Relexification was theoretically at the pidgin stage, yet this stage predated many creole developments. How could it be that so many of these later developments were similar or parallel if the common source lay further back in history?

---

6 Some (esp. Whinnom 1965) suggest that this may have come from the Mediterranean *lingua franca* ("French language"; aka *Sabir*) used among sailors and traders and relexified with Portuguese words in the late fifteenth or early sixteenth century. This *lingua franca* is not to be confused with the same term used for a simplified language of wider communication (see 9.3).

9.5.2 *Polygenesis* (link: Polygenesis) or parallel development

This theory soon displaced the monogenetic one. It is based on two important points: (1) the presence of an African substrate and (2) the plantation situation under conditions of slavery. Indeed, the substrate seems to be central to much of the development of both pidgins and creoles, especially in the matter of vocabulary.

9.5.2.1 African lexical influence

Cultural uniformity existed in West Africa in the form of similarities in folklore, religion, kinship structures, music, as well as language. Linguistic similarity seems to go back to the Akan and Ewe language groups since early trading was concentrated in their area and Akan influence continued in the West Indies, for example Coromanti leadership in many early slave revolts (link: Slave revolts). In general, African religion, magic, music, superstition, forms of amusement survived in pure or in syncretized form (link: Syncretism). Obviously no African language survived more than two to three generations in the New World. But language influence is said to be present in underlying structures. Even some lexical items were retained – usually in the private sphere (Alleyne 1971: 175–176) or in communities of maroons (runaways) and in some secret religious societies (Holm 1988–89: 79–80). Turner (1949) shows numerous retentions in *Gullah* (a South Carolina creole), as does Cassidy (1971, 1980) for Jamaican Creole (JC). Both list about 250 items plus personal names and formulas in stories, songs, and prayers. Because of stigmatization many retentions were masked or reanalyzed, for example *bákra* ("white man"): Belizean CE *bakra* is associated with "back raw"; GC associated it with "back row" (where white prisoners had to sit in church); in Sranan *ba kra* is associated with "brother soul"; in Trinidad CE, ultimately under French influence, from "bas courant" (literally "low" + "common person").

9.5.2.2 African calques and reduplication

Calques or loan translations are words in which each part of the word is a translation of a West African expression, as in Bahamian *big-eye* or Haitian CF *gwo ze* (< French *gros œil* "big eye") on the model of Twi *ani bre* or Igbo *ana uku* all with the meaning "greedy" (Holm 1988–89: 86–88). On calquing and reduplication Holm says, "It seems likely that reduplication became a productive mechanism for word formation in the creoles via calquing on African models" (ibid.: 88). Cassidy traced numerous examples of reduplication in JC to African sources, including *putta-putta* "mud" from Twi *pctcpctc* "muddy" or Yoruba *pòtòpotò* or Baule *pòtopóto* "mud."

9.5.2.3 The plantation situation

Similarities in the plantation context in the Caribbean basin are also crucial. There seems to have been no wholesale attempt at learning the acrolect, but rather a massive incorporation of lexical items from the lexifier into the creole. This caused the morphological and syntactic systems to undergo a kind of restructuring that very much resembles simplification – somewhat like the case of English in contact with Old Norse and *Norman French*; see 3.3 and 4.3).

The personal pronoun systems of English creoles illustrate this inasmuch as they tended to preserve distinctions made in the substrate languages but not found in GenE (see link: Personal pronouns). We saw this above in TP (9.3.3); in Table 9.8a the distinction between inclusive and exclusive first person plural has been taken into the system. On the other hand, gender distinctions as found in the third person singular pronouns (*he, she, it*) of GenE are frequently neglected or adopted from the lexifier only at a late stage (cf. JC). The three examples in the tables below have been taken from the Pacific, West Africa, and the Americas. The Pacific creole, Table 9.8a (TP as given here is a late model and may be considered to be at the creole stage), differs from the others inasmuch as it includes ***dual*** and ***trial*** number and distinguishes between inclusive and exclusive in the non-singular, thus clearly reflecting the linguistic background of the native speech communities. Furthermore, the use of the morpheme {-pela} is specific to the Pacific area. The West African example (Table 9.8b, explicitly a pidgin) is distinguished by the use of some case distinctions. It and the American example share the use of second person *una*. The American (Caribbean) example, Table 9.8c, shows little evidence of case, which may be a reflection of extreme early simplification.

Table 9.8a Pacific example: the personal pronouns of Tok Pisin

	1st person inclusive	*1st person exclusive*	*2nd person*	*3rd person*
Singular	*mi*	—	*yu*	*em*
Dual	*yumitupela*	*mitupela*	*yutupela*	*tupela*
Trial	*yumitripela*	*mitripela*	*yutripela*	*tripela*
Plural	*yumi*	*mipela*	*yupela*	*ol*

Table 9.8b West African example: the personal pronouns of West African PE

	1st person	*2nd person*	*3rd person*
Nominative	*a*	*yu*	*i*
Possessive	*ma, mi*	*you, yu*	*im*
Object	*mi*	*yu*	*am*
Emphatic	*mi*	*yu*	*im*
Plural (all cases)	*wi*	*una*	*dem*

(Agheyisi 1971: 122, 127)

Table 9.8c American example: the personal pronouns of Jamaican Creole

	1st person	*2nd person*	*3rd person*
Singular	*mi*	*yu*	*i(m)*
Plural	*wi*	*unu*	*dem*

(Holm 1988–89: 201)

Criticism

Areal language similarities in West Africa may be more wishful thinking than linguistic reality.

9.5.3 The influence of the superstratum

The idea here is that the creoles might be traced back to the influence of dialectal or regional forms of English, to baby- or foreigner-talk, or to maritime jargons. These influences would then be sufficient to explain the differing forms of the English creoles vis-à-vis the standard language.

9.5.3.1 Regional dialects

Speakers of non-standard English moved in large enough numbers to the colonies (especially Barbados; see 9.5.5.1) to provide a model. This could then serve as an explanation for why *does* and *did* are used in the mesolects of, for example, Guyana and Jamaica, where many of the English small-holders moved after they were displaced in the move to sugar cultivation on large holdings in the late seventeenth century. This may explain the use of positive *does (doz)* and *did* to express habitual action (now archaic in StE; also not present in the basilect) (Bickerton 1988: 271). The influence of regional English may also be found in the lengthy word lists that have been compiled showing, for example, the presence of Scottish English words in JC/English (cf. Craig 1982). Note examples such as *krabit* (Miskito Coast) < ScotE *crabbed, crabbit* "ill-tempered." Archaic usage /pronunciation is also found, for example *bail* "boil" or *jain* "join" in Miskito Coast CE or *liard, criard* (with {-ard} agentive). Slang and vulgar GenE usage is common in many English-lexifier pidgins and creoles, for example *pis, switpis, pisbag, pisol* for *urine, diabetes, bladder, urethra* respectively.

Criticism

A problem regional and stylistic sources can bring with them is that at some point it becomes necessary to shop among an assortment of varieties in order to account for the creole forms. If this becomes too arbitrary, it is no longer credible.

9.5.3.2 Foreigner- and baby-talk

This input presupposes that Europeans simplified their speech when speaking to West Africans in the trading centers and to slaves on the plantations. Accordingly traders/masters would use their own language in a reduced fashion, for example, leaving out unnecessary endings. This would serve as the input for those learning the European language. Hence on top of the difficulties everyone has learning a foreign language would come that of not even having a genuine, full model.

Criticism

One criticism of this approach is that while it is true that there are some cultural conventions about the ways people simplify their native languages, there are only vague similarities in the way they do so.

9.5.3.3 Nautical jargons

Nautical jargons are sometimes presupposed to be the model for the various pidgins. This is based on the fact that the crews of the various trading ships were often polyglot and that the languages (or jargons) they used were mixtures involving items from a variety of sources. Clearly Miskito Coast CE *gyali < galley* "kitchen" or "cooking hut" is likely to be ultimately of nautical origin. (And, of course, one such language served as the basis of the monogenetic theory: Sabir; see footnote 6.)

Criticism

It is not clear whether any such jargon was fixed enough to have served as a widespread model, especially not with regard to the remarkable structural similarity between the various creoles. Most of the jargons seemed themselves to have been variable and/or unstable.

9.5.4 The effect of linguistic universals – the *bioprogram*

This approach argues that the reduction found in pidgins is reversed and that this expansion is a consequence of an innate "bioprogram." It is a genetically transmitted human language acquisition device which sets off the realization of a set of universal grammatical categories under certain circumstances such as ones where the non-European population quickly outnumbered the Europeans and therefore fewer European linguistic features were maintained. Children handle this situation very differently from adults because the latter already have a viable language while the former must *make* one (Bickerton 1988: 273). In order to do this people who have been raised in the environment of a pidgin use the available lexis and morphology. These principles can be observed more clearly in creoles which rather than developing over many, many decades (such as TP) emerge instead within a single generation. Such a creole can abandon "millennia of diachronic change" (ibid.: 274). From the perspective of this book this means that beside internal change and language contact the factor of linguistic universals may play a role in the history of a language.

In his work on Hawaiian PE Bickerton excludes the influence of the substrate languages (Hawaiian, Japanese, Chinese, Tagalog, Portuguese) and of the superstrate English since Hawaiian CE has structures which none of these have, for example its *TMA* system (link: TMA). Yet these same structures are shared with other historically unrelated creoles. The discussion here is not about vocabulary, which has clearly been borrowed, but grammatical structures.

Criticism

It has been pointed out that speakers of Cape Verde Creole were present in Hawaii in the nineteenth century; thus a link to historical West African creoles was present (Mühlhäusler 1986b: 225).

9.5.4.1 Universal grammatical categories

If the source language morphemes for "certain minimal functions" are lost, lexical forms will be adopted to fulfill them. Some of the categories assumed to belong to the bioprogram and the sources of the forms used to realize them are listed in Table 9.9:

Table 9.9 Superstrate sources of grammatical items

indefinite article	< superstrate word for "one"	definitive article	< superstrate demonstrative
anterior marker	< superstrate for past participle of the copula	pluralizer	< superstrate for 3rd plural pronoun
non-punctual marker	< superstrate for location	irrealis marker	< superstrate for "to go"
irrealis *complementizer*	< superstrate for "for"	completive marker	< superstrate for "to finish"
relative pronoun	< superstrate for "where"	pronouns, if invariant	< superstrate accusative

Universal principles of syntax together with lexical bits and pieces of related meaning lead to the realization of grammatical items in creole languages. If lost (during pidginization), these categories will reconstitute themselves presumably using "an unmarked set of grammatical options" (Bickerton 1988: 282). Following the lead in the other chapters, we will look specifically at TMA. For criticism see **link: Bioprogram**.

9.5.4.2 Relative sequence of TMA particles

Probably every creole realizes the categories of tense, modality, and aspect. What is especially remarkable is that combinations of two or more of these categories show up in the same relative order: tense before modality before aspect in pre-verbal position. "A majority of creoles, like HCE, express tense, modality, and aspect by means of three preverbal free morphemes. Placed (if they co-occur) in that order" (Bickerton 1981: 58). Voorhoeve has shown this for Sranan, the English-lexifer creole of Suriname.

Here are a few examples from both a well-established pidgin and from creoles (the simultaneous use of markers of tense, modality, and aspect is rare):

Table 9.10 The relative order of the TMA elements in Sranan

waka	"have walked" (completive present)	
e-waka	"is walking"	*e* = progressive marker (A)
sa-waka	"will walk"	*sa* = future or irrealis marker(< shall) (M)
ben waka	"walked"	*ben* = past marker (T)
ben-sa waka	"would have walked"	
ben-e waka	"was walking"	
ben-sa-e waka	"would have to keep walking"	
sa-e-waka	"will be walking"	

(Voorhoeve 1962: 38–40)

Table 9.11 Combinations of tense, modality, and aspect in relative sequence

variety	example + gloss	TMA	source
Gambian Krio:	*Una bin go sidɔn klos mi* You should have sat near me	T+M	(Holm 1988–89: 418)
Liberian English (settler variety):	*hi ha dɔn gɛ de wɔk* He had COMP got the work	T+M	(ibid.: 425)

Table 9.11 Continued

variety	example + gloss	TMA	source
Cameroon PE:	*dem bin di kohnggohsa plenty* They were chatting a lot	T+A	(ibid.: 432)
Belize CE:	*we mi de luk fu rowp wan taym* We were looking for rope one time	T+A	(ibid.: 479)
Guyanese CE:	*mina wok a kriyool* I was working in (a) creole (workgang)	T+A	(Rickford 1987: 145)

Criticism

Some Indian Ocean pidgins and creoles do not seem to follow this pattern.

9.5.5 History and textual examples

The short overview in this section serves to provide a general historical outline that will make some of the linguistic differences in the two major English creole areas, the Caribbean and the Pacific, clearer.

9.5.5.1 The Caribbean

This area may be divided into an eastern and a western part on the basis of linguistic differences. The Eastern Caribbean consists of Barbados, the Lesser Antilles (British Leeward Islands) in the north and the Windward Islands in the south, eastern Jamaica, and Guyana. The Western Caribbean consists of western Jamaica, the Caymans, the Caribbean coast of Central America, especially Belize, and a smaller few islands (see Map 9.2). Linguistically, the eastern areas are less deviant vis-à-vis StE than the west and Guyana (Le Page and DeCamp, qtd. in Holm 1988–89: 466). One set of distinctions is that the east has **monophthongs** while the west has corresponding **diphthongs** (cf. Table 9.12).

Table 9.12 East–west pronunciation differences in the Caribbean

East:	GC (cf. Text 9.1)	West:	JC (cf. Text 9.3)	RP-GenAm
/eː/	*reezaa* ("razor")	/ie/	*liedi* ("lady")	/eɪ/
/oː/	*rood* ("road")	/uo/	*úol* ("old")	/əʊ – oʊ/

In Table 9.13 on page 236 we see some of the differences in **pre-verbal markers**.

Barbados

In the eastern part of the West Indies, Barbados (present population: 252,000) was historically important. Its language influenced Suriname, Jamaica, and the Carolinas, among others. Barbados is a relatively flat island, very suitable for agriculture. It was discovered and claimed by the British in 1624 and settled from 1627 on. It became the

Table 9.13 Tense and aspect markers in four selected Caribbean basilect varieties

	Barbados	Guyana	Jamaica (East, West)	Belize
Anterior	did	bin	E: bin, (b)en, min W: min, men, wen	mi/me
Progressive	-in	a	E: (d)a W: de	de
Habitual	doz	a/doz/oz/z	unmarked	unmarked or de/da
Completive	–	don	don	don
Future	goin tu	go/gu (sa)	go or wi	wan/wahn

center of the Eastern Caribbean area. Originally it was settled by Scots, English, and Irish, and its speech was a conglomerate of regional non-standard speech. The settlers were mostly small free-holders and raised chiefly tobacco and corn. The population reached 37,000 by 1642, when the English Civil War cut off immigration. In the 1640s there was a switch to sugar, and many of the Europeans left as African slaves were imported for the hard work on the sugar plantations. Those who left went to Suriname, to Jamaica, to the Carolinas, and to the Leeward Islands. Meanwhile the number of slaves increased dramatically:

1645:   6000 slaves and 40,000 whites
1685:   46,000 slaves and 20,000 whites
1705:   12,000 whites
1750:   80% slaves.

According to Hancock (1980), the English of Barbados was never really creolized; rather, creole features were introduced on the basis of nineteenth century contacts between the islands. Cassidy (1980), in contrast, sees the sugar economy and disproportion of blacks to whites as having led to creolization, yet with rapid and complete decreolization. After emancipation in 1838 Barbados began to export its people and their language, Bajan. Many of them went as workers and administrators to Guyana, Trinidad, the Windwards, and Panama.

Guyana and Guyanese CE

Guyana was settled by Dutch planters and their slaves from 1618 on, but large numbers of British from Barbados and the Leewards began settling there with their slaves after the mid-eighteenth century. Large numbers of Asian Indians (over 200,000) came as indentured servants between the end of slavery in the British Empire in 1838 and World War I. Today the inland area is inhabited mostly by Amerindians (almost 5% of the total population) while the inhabitants of the coast are (in approximate figures) 3% European or Chinese in descent; 30%, African; 51%, Asian Indian; and 13% are mixed. There has been a certain amount of intergroup hostility, especially between the Asian Indian and the African parts of the population. Linguistically, the Indo-Guyanese group is more rural and uses the basilect more than the more urban Afro-Guyanese group (Rickford 1987: chap. 2).

The basilect is relatively far from GenE as compared to Trinidad (with a similar ethnic history). This has been explained (inconclusively) as the result of (1) eighteenth century creole Dutch influence, (2) the large number of new slaves imported in the early nineteenth century, or (3) the effect of contact with the late nineteenth century Asian Indian indentured servants (Holm 1988–89: 461–465).

The two following "eastern" Caribbean English Creole texts both come from recordings published in Rickford 1987. The first represents the basilect while the second is high mesolect. This gives us some sense of the enormous amount variation to be found. The use of a spelling system oriented along the lines of StE spelling would have made the close relationship to GenE much clearer, but it would mask the differences effectively present in the spoken language.

A note on the transcription of this and the following text: <ii> = /iː/, <oo> = /oʊ/; <o> = /ə/; <O> = /ɒ/; <ou> = /ʌʊ/; <oh> = /ɔː/; <aa> = /ɑː/; <uu> = /uː/

Text 9.1 Guyanese CE: basilect

dis   bina won maan. well   ii   a   piil   kookno – wan kookno – wi wan dol kotlaas. wel dis bina
There was a   man.   Well,   he was peeling coconuts – a coconut   – with a dull machete. Well, there was this

mongkii hii ga wan shaap reezaa. an ii se   at ou – hii a paas   a   rood an dis – ii se   at ou,
monkey He had a   sharp razor.   And he said [how] – he was going by on the road and this – he said [how],

"ongkl! yu waan dis reezo fu piil yu   kooknot?" wel di man   glaad, bikaaz hii noo dat ou   hii
"Uncle, you want this razor to peel your coco nut?" Well the man was glad   because he knew that/how his

kooknot na   – hee kotlish   na sharp. Wel ii – wen di mongkii len om, wen ii   don   piil
coconut wasn't – his machete wasn't sharp. Well he – when the monkey lent him, when he was finished peeling

am . . .
it . . .

(Rickford 1987: 130)

Text 9.2 Guyanese CE: high mesolect

wid ingglish, rait? ai fong maiself spenin   tuu moch ov di taim on mai esee,
With English,   right? I found myself spending too much of the time on my essay.

ai jos push   mai esee Ondoniit n it kom – wen ai wuz finish,   den ai went
I just pushed my essay underneath and it came – when I   was finished, then I   went

bak tu mai esee. in di mat,   ai defnaitlii kudn   finish. noobOdii finish di peepo.
back to my essay. In the math [exam], I definitely couldn't finish. Nobody   finished the paper.

Hee geev os haaf n ouwo ekschro, n wii kudn   finish.
He gave us half an hour extra,   and we couldn't finish.

(Rickford 1987: 170)

Jamaica and Jamaican Creole

The most central and influential English-speaking country in the Western Caribbean is Jamaica. Its present population of around 2.5 million, of whom well over 90% speak JC (or Patwa, as it is often called), makes it the largest Creole-speaking country (Plate 9.2). It was captured from Spain in 1655 and settled from Nevis, Suriname, and Barbados in the east and by a significant number of British and their slaves from Suriname in the west. With the growth of sugar cultivation, more and more slaves were needed:

1675:   9500 slaves and 7700 whites
1734:   86,000 slaves and 7700 whites (slaves = 92%)
1835:   450,000 blacks and 35,000 whites (93% to 7%).

There was immigration of some 36,000 from India between 1844 and 1917, of whom approximately two-thirds stayed. The maroons were a special group of run-away (< Spanish *cimarrón* "wild") slaves who long preserved especially conservative creole forms. Today the ethnic composition of the population is four-fifths of African origin; the remainder are mixed plus a small number of Asian Indian, European, and Chinese origin.

The Mosquito Coast of Central America including various islands off the coast contains a number of English-Creole communities whose origin lies with labor migration from Jamaica chiefly in the logging industry and for plantation work. The largest creole-speaking community is Belize, where English is the official language and Belize CE the first language of about one-third and the second language of most of the remaining population (see Holm 1986; 1988–89: chap. 10 for more detail).

Text 9.3 poses little difficulty in reading once you get used to the spelling.

Text 9.3 Jamaican Creole, "William Saves His Sweetheart"

nóu, a úol táim anánsi-in stúori, we gwáiŋ at nóu. nóu wants dér wáz, a úol wíč liedi lív, had wán són,
Now, a old-time Anancying story   we going at now. Now once there was a old   witch-lady live, had one son,
We're now going to tell a traditional Anancy story. Once upon a time there was an old witch, who had a son

niem av wiljəm. wíljəm wór ingjéj, tu a jóŋ   liedi, frám a néks úol wíč   sékšon hú waz hár mádar in láa.
name of William. William were engage to a young lady from a next old witch's section who was her mother-in-law.
whose name was William. He was engaged to a girl whose stepmother was from a different witches' clutch.

nóu dát gjól fáda, had dát gjól wid iz fós waif. an áfra di wáif disíis, hii iz mári a néks wúman,
Now that girl's father had that girl with his first wife. And after the wife decease, he is marry a next woman
Now that girl's father had had her with his first wife. And after that wife died, he married another woman

wíč   is a úol wíč   an dát wúman bí·er túu dáatez   bisáidz.
which is a old witch. And that woman bear two daughters besides.
who was an old witch. And that women bore him two more daughters.

(Hall 1966: 154)

9.5.5.2 Papua New Guinea (PNG)

New Guinea is the second largest island in the world (divided politically into two parts: the western half, Irian Jaya, a part of Indonesia, and the eastern part, independent PNG). It is one of the most linguistically diverse places on earth with up to a thousand different languages. With the intrusion of the European colonial powers in the nineteenth century two important developments were initiated: (1) economic opportunities began to become available, especially in the form of contract labor on the plantations of Samoa, Vanuatu, and Queensland, and (2) the isolation of the many language communities began to decline.

The linguistic consequences could be seen in PNG in the emergence of lingua francas. They were encouraged by the various colonial administrations (British–Australian and German). In the one case, we have to do with a native-based lingua franca, Police Motu, now renamed more positively **Hiri Motu** (allegedly from the Motu word *hiri* "a trading voyage"). In the other, we have languages with European lexifiers, French in New Caledonia, German in New Guinea, but, above all, English in Papua, in New Guinea, in New Britain, New Ireland, the Solomon Islands, Vanuatu (formerly the New Hebrides), Fiji, Samoa, and Australia.

Although the overall lines of development and influence are not fully clear, there seems to have been one major strand which spread out via Australia (Australian PE, Roper River Creole, Cape York Creole) and one that spread from the New Hebrides, the Solomon Islands, Queensland, and Fiji to Papua and New Guinea. Early work-force movement was associated with **New England** whalers and with the Melanesian sandalwood trade. This was followed by the trade with beach-la-mar, a sea slug prized in China as an ingredient in soups (the pidgin English of Vanuatu goes by the name derived from the slug: Bislama PE). From the 1860s on, contract labor on the cotton and sugar plantations of Queensland and Fiji and the copra plantations in Samoa became economically important. And work-force movement back and forth between PNG and the sugar cane plantations of Queensland and the beach-la-mar and pearling work in the Torres Straits led to the use of early Tok Pisin (TP) as a lingua franca by returning laborers. Consequently, TP, Bislama, and Solomon Islands Pidgin are closely related as a group to Torres Straits Creole. Today TP is spreading in PNG as a lingua franca and is increasingly felt to be the national language, widely used in working life and government administration. It is the primary language for tens of thousands of people and is beginning to creolize (see Holm 1988–89: 510–513, 526–538, 584–586). The following TP text is much harder to read than the Caribbean texts because of the large number of non-English grammatical structures (in blue; see grammatical comments following the text).

Text 9.4 "Masalai Wokim Tripela Ailan"

Stori   *i go olsem.*   *Bipo bipo tru*   *i gat* *wanpela* *masalai man. Em* *i draipela* *bun tru.*
The story goes like this. Really long, long ago, there was a demon.   He had really huge bones.

Nem bilong em Koran Rainge. Em *i lusim bus*   *na kamdaun long ples*   *ol* *i kolim Ais. . . .*
His name   was Koran Rainge. He left the forest and came down to the place everyone calls Ais.

Solwara i save pulimapim dispela riva. Tasol long taim bilong ren,
The sea could fill up   this river.   But when it rained,

bikpela tait bilong bus   i kamdaun na wara   i kol, i olsem ais. . . .
a big flood [tide] from the forest came down and the water was cold   like ice.

Orait. Masalai Koran Rainge i laik   pilai   liklik   na em i kisim   tamiok ston bilong em
Well, Masalai Koran Rainge   wanted to play a little, so he took [catch] his stone axe [tomahawk]

na i katim wanpela longpela ailan i go tripela hap. . . .
and cut   a   long   island into three parts [half].

Masalai   i subim ol   i go ausait longwe liklik long nambis, na i luk olsem wanpela riva i kamap.
The *masalai* shoved them outside a long way a little into the sea, and they looked like a river starts.

Tasol i no riva,   i solwara tasol.   Na tude ol bikpela sip i save kam insait long dispela rot tasol.
But it was not a river, it was just the sea [saltwater]. And today, the big ships can come inside this way [road].

Bihain long Masalai Koran Rainge i katim Ailan Aviglo pinis, . . .   Selseme Martina (i bin raitim)
After *Masalai* Koran Rainge   had cut Aviglo Island, . . .   Selseme Martina (wrote this)

(*Wantok* 418, May 22, 1982, 19)

Grammatical markers

i	before predicates (except 1st and 2nd person singular; passim)
-im	marker of transitive verbs (*Em i lusim bus* "he left the bush")
em	3rd person pronoun "he, his, him" (see preceding; also *nem bilong em* "his name"; also feminine)
i gat	existential "there is/are" (*i gat wanpela masalai man* "there was a man-demon")
pinis	completive marker (after the predicate; *i katim Ailan pinis* "had cut the island")
bin	past marker (pre-verbal: *i bin raitim* "wrote (this)")
save	modal of ability (*i save pulimapim* "could fill (it) up")
laik	"want to" (*i laik pilai liklik* "wanted to play a little")
-pela	marker of monosyllabic attributive adjectives (*bikpela* "big")
wanpela	singular article (*wanpela masalai man* "a demon")
no marker	adverb (*tru* "really")
ol	plural marker (*ol bikpela sip* "the big ships")

9.6 Summary

Colonialism and imperialism contributed not only to the spread of GenE, but also to the emergence of English pidgins and creoles. Many of these languages belong under the label "English" even though they are part of a separate historical development in which various regional and/or non-standard forms of English came into contact with non-European languages. The historical situation (slavery and colonial exploitation) is relatively well documented, but the mechanics of pidginization and creolization are hotly disputed. There was clearly linguistic input from both the substrate languages and from English as the lexifier, but a development independent of both these sources is likely to have been involved in which language universals (the bioprogram) played a role. Pidgins as non-native, reduced, marginal, and mixed contact languages are less well documented, but creoles (native, expanded, socially more central languages with a mixed history) are important varieties which often stand in a special continuum relationship to StE.

STUDY QUESTIONS

Social and cultural background

1. What is meant by the term "middle passage" and why is it called this?
2. What were the (supposed) advantages of the slave trade? Who profited from the slave trade?
3. Both Barbados and Guyana belong to the Eastern Caribbean, yet the two are linguistically very dissimilar. How might this be explained? How do the two compare demographically, that is, what is fundamentally different and what is similar in the two countries?
4. What kinds of contact were there between speakers of English and speakers of the local languages of (a) West Africa, (b) the Caribbean basin, and (c) the Pacific–New Guinea area?

Linguistic background

1. Are the so-called English pidgins and creoles really *English*? List the arguments which speak for and against seeing them as English and take balance in this question.
2. How do different societal traditions show their influence in the linguistic *system* of English creoles? Illustrate this using one example.
3. In the case of Guyanese Creole English Rickford includes the element *na*V (that is, negative *na* before the verb) in an implicational scale. If a speaker of GCE uses this construction, will he or she use the *a* + V (i.e. progressive *a* before the verb) as well? What does this tell us about the likelihood that the speaker will use *wan* as the indefinite article? Explain.
4. This chapter outlines a variety of approaches to the question of the origins of creoles. What speaks for the substrate concept and what for the universalist theory? Does each exclude the other? Explain why or why not.

Further reading

Franklin is a classical and a very clearly written history of African Americans with several highly readable chapters on the African background of these people and the mechanics of slavery and the slave trade. *Transatlantic Slavery* (Tibbles) supplements Franklin nicely on the slave trade from a British point of view. Holm (1986) follows the movement of slaves and free laborers – and their language – in the Caribbean basin and elsewhere. Among the numerous introductions to pidgins and creoles both Holm (2000) and Singh are reliable and readable. Mühlhäusler places his emphasis on the successive stages of development from trade jargon to pidgin, to extended pidgin, to creoles. In his work he draws especially strongly on the evidence from Tok Pisin while the others concentrate more on the Atlantic pidgins and creoles. Bickerton is the most prominent proponent of the bioprogram approach to the origins of creoles. His work deserves careful attention, especially since it ties creole studies strongly to other areas of linguistics such as first and second language acquisition, animal language, and the origins of human language as such.

Bickerton, D. (1988) "Creole Languages and the Bioprogram," In: F.J. Newmeyer (ed.) *Linguistics: The Cambridge Survey*. vol. 2, *Linguistic Theory: Extensions and Implications*. Cambridge: CUP, 268–284.

Franklin, J.H. (1980) *From Slavery to Freedom. A History of Negro Americans*, 5th ed. New York: Knopf.

Holm, J. (1986) "The Spread of English in the Caribbean Area," In: M. Görlach and J.A. Holm (eds.) *Focus on the Caribbean*. Amsterdam: Benjamins, 1–22.

Holm, J. (2000) *An Introduction to Pidgins and Creoles*. Cambridge: CUP.

Mühlhäusler, P. (1986) *Pidgin and Creole Linguistics*. Oxford: Basil Blackwell.

Singh, I. (2000) *Pidgins and Creoles. An Introduction*. London: Arnold.

Tibbles, A. (ed.) (1994) *Transatlantic Slavery. Against Human Dignity*. London: HMSO.

CHAPTER TEN

English in North America (since the early seventeenth century)

the good hand of God favored our beginnings. . . . In sweeping away great multitudes of the natives by the smallpox, a little before we went thither, that he might make room for us there.
(W. Bradford 1638, "New England's First Fruits," In: *Massachusetts Historical Society, Collections*, 1792. Cambridge, MA)

Chapter Overview:

This chapter:

- looks at the earliest evidence of English in North America and reviews Colonial English, including English – Native American language contact as well as the influence of contact with Dutch in New Amsterdam (New York) and with African American Pidgin English;
- examines the central question of koinéization (dialect leveling) of AmE;
- looks at standardization in the US during the period after US independence and concentrates strongly on pronunciation while giving a few examples of AmE vocabulary and grammar;
- presents non-standard GenE in America as well as regional forms (the South, the frontier, Canadian English) and the most prominent ethnic varieties (American Indian English, immigrant English, African American Vernacular English, and Chicano English).

10.1 The beginnings of English in North America

English has been in use in North America since the late sixteenth and early seventeenth centuries, when fishing vessels arrived at the Grand Banks off the coast of Nova Scotia to fish the cod to be found there in great abundance and where traders did business with the Indians (cf. Mann 2005: 47ff). Traders soon began going to the Chesapeake Bay area as well to trade for furs from the Native Americans. The crews of these ships were themselves often international (but European), which meant that in those cases where English was spoken on board, the language was far from the StE of England. What was spoken would very likely have been a mixture, possibly a leveling of varieties of regional English from England and Scotland (Wales and Ireland still had relatively few English speakers). Added to this would be English spoken as a foreign language (EFL) among the non-native crew members. This was then salted with *nautical jargon* (see 9.5.3). As prominent as this jargon may have been, there were probably as many varieties as there were ships, each representing a different mix of English.

10.1.1 Native American – English contact

All this notwithstanding, the early contacts of European sailors and traders with the Native Americans did leave behind two important traces. The first of these was disease, one of the most significant and tragic parts of what one author (Crosby 2003) calls the "Columbian Exchange." The second was the English language, which some of the Native Americans learned well enough to serve as interpreters in negotiations with the settlers who came soon after. It is not impossible that these early nautical varieties of English had a linguistic impact on the mainland of North America, though it would hardly have been a permanent one. The English of the seafarers was probably used in the early days in North America, but the continued influence of nautical jargon can only be seen somewhat indirectly, according to Dillard (e.g. 1980: 407), in the use of *American Indian Pidgin English* (link: American Indian Pidgin English) and in the pidgin and creole English spoken by African slaves (see 10.2.4 and 10.4.3). English was clearly around before colonization, but it was through the large number of settlers that the language became truly native to North America.

10.1.2 The Pilgrims and the Indians

The consequences of these two legacies can be seen quite concretely in the situation which the Pilgrim Separatists encountered when they arrived in Plymouth (Massachusetts) in 1620. Several years before their arrival an English expedition had landed there, taken a number of Indians as slaves, and left smallpox behind, which killed off over 90% of the Indian population, leaving the land empty. In the words of William Bradford (see chapter epigram) this was due to God's providence (see also Mann 2005: 55ff.) As for language, Bradford (speaking of his group in the third person) tells of the Pilgrims' contact with Native Americans in 1621:

Text 10.1 W. Bradford on contact with Native Americans (1621)

But about the 16. of March a certain Indian came bouldly amongst them, and spoke to them in broken English, which they could well understand, but marveled at it. At length they understood by discourse with him, that he was not of these parts, but belonged to

> *the eastrene parts, wher some English-ships came to ffish, with whom he was aquainted, and could name sundrie of them by their names, amongst whom he had got his language.*
>
> (W. Bradford (1912 [1620–1651]) *The History of Plymouth Plantation.* 2 vols. W.C. Ford (ed.) Boston: Massachusetts Historical Society, Book XIII)

The Indian mentioned was Samaset, and he provided the Pilgrims who had survived the first ***New England*** winter with information and, most importantly, introduced another Indian, Squanto (Tisquantum), to them. The latter spoke fluent English, having spent several years in England as a slave from 1605, but returned to America with Captain John Smith in 1612. He was recaptured and taken to England once again. His final return home in 1619 was only to find that his people (the Patuxet of the area where the Pilgrims had settled) had died in the smallpox epidemic. Squanto proved to be so helpful to the English that he has become a mythological figure in American history, understood as a sign of friendship between Native Americans and Europeans.

10.1.3 The influence of Native American languages on English

A great many Native American borrowings come from the eastern Indians, many of them from the Algonquian language family, to which the tribes of New England all belonged[1] as did many of the tribes further south and west. By the very nature of the contact situation – Europeans in a strange environment with unfamiliar plants, animals, and native people – words for new things would have to come from the one or the other of the two most important sources: (1) ***word formation*** (link: Word formation) using elements native to English or (2) ***borrowing*** (link: Borrowing) from an indigenous language. The first path led to compounds (link: Compounding) such as *black walnut* (in contrast to what in AmE is called the *English walnut*), *blackbird*, or *tableland*, and extensions of European English, using terms like *yew*, *robin*, or *bluff* to cover newly encountered flora, fauna, and topography. The second path leads us to Anglicized words borrowed from Indian languages. Marckwardt lists approximately fifty such items (1980: 30).

The words borrowed remind us of the list in 1.4.2 (Table 1.6) of words borrowed from Latin into the ***Germanic languages***. Overall, the significance of both sets of words for English as a whole is minimal though both do bear witness to the importance of contact in both cases.

---

1 The Algonquian family includes Abenaki Cree, Delaware, Massachuset, Narraganset, and Ojibwa along with more than twenty further languages (see Driver 1969: 43).

Table 10.1 Borrowings from eastern American Indian languages

Borrowing from the more easterly Algonquian language family:

- animal names: *chipmunk* (< Ojibwa *ačitamo·nˀ*), *moose* (< Algonquian *moos*), *muskrat* (< Algonquian-Massachuset *musquash*), *opossum* (< Algonquian), *raccoon* (< Algonquian *raugroughcun / arocoun*), *skunk* (< Abenaki *segañk8*), *terrapin* (< Algonquian-Delaware *tó·lpe·w*), *woodchuck* (< the Algonquian *ockqutchaun*);
- plant names: *hickory* (< Algonquian *pawcohiccora*), *persimmon* (< Algonquian *pessemin*), *pecan* (< Algonquian-Ojibwa *paka·n*), *squash* (< Narraganset *askútasquash*);
- foods *hominy* (< Algonquian *-homen*), *pemmican* (< Cree *pimihka·n*), *pone* (< Algonquian *appone*), *succotash* (< Narraganet *msickquatash*);
- words for aspects of native culture and society: *manitou* (< Ojibwa *manito·*), *powwow* (< Narraganset / Massachuset *powwaw / pauwau*), *sachem* (< Narraganset *sâchim*), *papoose* (< Narraganset *papoòs*), *squaw* (< Massachuset *squa / ussqua*), *moccasin* (< Algonquian *mockasin*), *tomahawk* (< Algonquian *tomahack*), *wigwam* (< Abebaki *wikəwɑm*).

10.2 *Colonial English*

The English language which the settlers carried along with them was, of course, that of England. The colonists surely brought various regional forms, but it is generally accepted that the largest number of those who arrived came from southern England. Baugh (1957) concludes – on the limited evidence of 1281 settlers in New England and 637 in Virginia for whom records exist for the time before 1700 – that New England was predominantly settled from the southeastern and southern counties of England (about 60%) as was Virginia (over 50%). Fisher's figures indicate that 20,000 Puritans came between 1629 and 1641, the largest part from Essex, Suffolk, Cambridgeshire, and East Anglia with fewer than 10% from London, and that 40,000 "Cavaliers" fled especially from London and Bristol during the Civil War and went to the Chesapeake area and Virginia (Fisher 2001: 60). The Middle Colonies of Pennsylvania, New Jersey, and Delaware probably had a much larger proportion from northern England, including 23,000 Quakers and Evangelicals from England, Wales, Germany, Holland, and France. Over 250,000 from northern England, the Scottish Lowlands, and especially Ulster settled in the back country (Baugh 1963: 108–109; Fisher 2001: 60). In each of the areas settled the nature of the language was set by speech patterns established by the first several generations.

Despite the varied regional origins of the English-speaking settlers in North America, there was relatively little difference in the English which British and Irish colonists spoke. Dialect geographers working within the Linguistic Atlas ([link: Linguistic Atlas of the United States and Canada](#)) of the United States and Canada have collected numerous regional differences within AmE, but they consist largely of incidental differences in vocabulary as well as a number of systematic differences in pronunciation. None of these, however, represent a barrier to mutual understanding. There is, rather, a basic similarity within AmE, and it can be credited to two factors: (1) the relatively high degree of education and respect for learning (especially in New England; see 10.2.1) and (2) the leveling or koinéization of varieties as they mixed in the new environment (see 10.2.2).

10.2.1 Learning and education in New England

The first and foremost purpose of education (link: Formal education in America) was to prepare people for their further life by ensuring that they had the necessary knowledge and proper attitudes. This was achieved chiefly in the family, where a trade or homemaking was learned. For the Puritans education was the major element of culture and society beyond religion itself. Indeed, the main motivation for establishing schools was to provide the people with access to reading and writing and hence to the Word of God (Plate 10.1). The Puritan population was, consequently, extraordinarily well educated. Practically all the ministers of the Puritan (later: Congregational) Church in the colonial period were college-educated. One out of 200 in the first years was a graduate of Cambridge, which means one in every forty households. Furthermore, common schools were instituted in 1642 (in Boston already in 1635) and legally mandated in 1647 as seen in the following law text:

Text 10.2 Early ModE Puritan legal text

It being one chiefe piect [project] *of yᵗ ould deluder, Satan, to keepe men from the knowledge of yᵉ Scriptures, as in formʳ times by keeping yᵐ in an unknowne tongue . . . It is therefore ordᵈed, yᵗ evʳy township in this iurisdiction, aftʳ yᵉ Lord hath increased yᵐ to yᵉ number of 50 householdʳˢ, shall then forthwiᵗʰ appoint one wᵗʰin their towne to teach all such children as shall resort to him to write & reade . . . & it is furthʳ ordered, yᵗ where any towne shall increase to yᵉ numbʳ of 100 families or householdʳˢ, they shall set up a graṁer schoole, yᵉ mʳ thereof being able to instruct youth so farr as they may be fited for yᵉ university. . . .*

(qtd. in P.R. Lucas (1984) *American Odyssey, 1607–1789*. Englewood Cliffs: Prentice-Hall, 117–118)

As a result the literacy rate in Massachusetts was high: 89–95% of (propertied) men; 42% of women (62% by century end). Sixty percent of the households contained books in Middlesex (Massachusetts) (and lending was widespread). University level education provided training for ministers. So important was this that within ten years of settlement in Massachusetts Bay, Harvard College was founded (1636).

The effects of learning and education on the language were twofold. First of all, where the level of education was high, as it was in New England, there was clearly a greater orientation toward the written word. This meant that the *relative* uniformity of English in early America was more a matter of grammar and vocabulary and less of pronunciation, and this is still today the essence of what is meant by StE, which shows a great deal of uniformity in its written form but a great deal of variation in its pronunciation. The second consequence of the early emphasis on education was the establishment of attitudes of correctness among the educated (or semi-educated), a perspective which continues very strongly in the twenty-first century, where people apologize for what they consider to be "bad grammar"

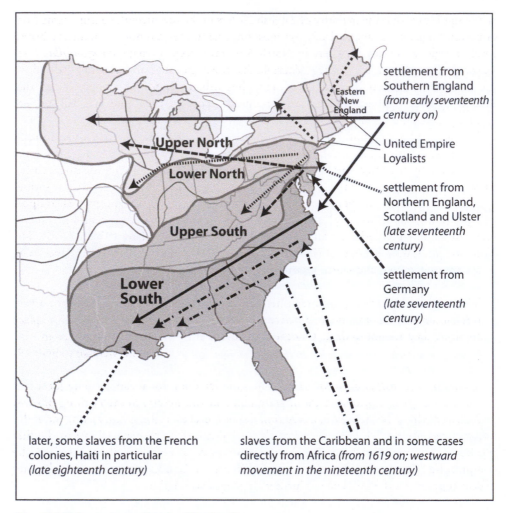

Map 10.1 Major sources and goals of immigration

(despite the fact that they, of course, use it). Outside of New England literacy was less widespread (or indeed, very low). Consequently, books and newspapers were rare in the American South (see 10.4.1).

10.2.2 *Koinéization* (link: Koinéization)[2]

Dillard entitled the second chapter of his *All-American English* (1975) "The American Koiné." This catches the important notion of dialect leveling, an extremely important development in the English language in America (and in other settler colonies as well). It is

2 The process in which a *koiné* emerges. The term derives from the Greek word *koiné*, meaning "common" and referred originally to the variety of Greek which became the *lingua franca* (link: Lingua franca) of the Hellenistic period (cf. Thomson qtd. in Siegel 1993: 5).

surely significant that the majority of English settlers in the seventeenth century came from Southern England (see above, 10.2). Yet most important, they did not maintain any British local or regional dialect anywhere in North America (except perhaps *Newfoundland*; see below 10.3.4). Indeed, it is entirely plausible that the beginnings of the koiné predated the move to America. Mobility in England, including urbanization, was already a factor that brought speakers of countless local varieties into contact with each other (cf. Bailyn 1988: esp. chap. 1), and that may have led to koinéization, especially in London.

It is not at all certain how a koiné becomes established. Some believe the variants shared by the most input dialects are the ones most likely to be adopted; others suggest that the variant used by the most speakers will be adopted; yet others feel "that demographical, social, cultural, occupational, and political factors – the social traits and status of various speakers and groups – outweigh linguistic factors in determining which elements compose a koiné" (Longmore 2007: 527). However that may be, numerous observers of the linguistic scene in Colonial America remarked on its uniformity (see Dillard 1975: 55–58). The words of John Witherspoon (1723–1794), a Scotsman who immigrated to America in 1769, are well known and worth repeating once more:

> The vulgar in America speak much better than the vulgar in Great Britain, for a very obvious reason, *viz.*, that being much more unsettled and moving frequently from place to place, they are not so liable to local peculiarities either in accent or phraseology.
>
> (qtd. in Mencken 1948: 19)

To recognize the koinéization of English in America does not mean to deny local and regional differences in pronunciation, grammar, and vocabulary, to say nothing of class, gender, and ethnic differences. Koinéization did not level everything in its path, and it did not occur overnight. More likely it stretched over at least three generations: in the first speakers accommodated to each other; the following generations then nativized the compromise forms. In looking at how AmE differs from BrE an important factor beyond dialect contact was the influence of further languages on English.

10.2.3 Colonial American English in contact with other European languages

In 1700 the population of the North American colonies was more than 200,000 (Indians not counted).[3] The settlers, mostly from England, Scotland, and Ireland, were concentrated chiefly in Massachusetts and Virginia (both with about 50,000). At the end of the colonial period in the United States the number had grown to about 2.5 million, of whom 20% were Africans (mostly slaves; link: European expansion and the slave trade). The population was surprisingly urban: Philadelphia with 40,000 and Boston with 25,000 were the second and third largest cities in the English-speaking world (but clearly far, far behind London). Charleston, South Carolina had 12,000, but Williamsburg, Virginia's largest "city," had a permanent year-round population of only 1500.

Yet despite the large numbers of people from Britain and Ireland and their descendants, other European settlers were also an important presence in colonial America. Approximately

---

3 By comparison late seventeenth century England had a population of 5 million, of whom 500,000 lived in London.

17% of the people living in New York and New Jersey were of Dutch origin; in Delaware (where there had been a short-lived Swedish colony, 1638–55) 9% were Swedish. Pennsylvania was heavily settled by Germans (approximately 30%) (Bailey 2004: 11), and throughout Canada and the Mississippi Valley the French were dominant, just as the Spanish were in Florida. The linguistic effect of the presence of the languages of these people is, however, remarkably small.

10.2.3.1 Dutch

Dutch contributed chiefly to the vocabulary and to a small extent to public culture. Among the words which entered AmE from Dutch we find the somewhat less well-known *cruller* (a kind of doughnut) and the ubiquitous *cookie*. Other food words include *cole slaw*, *pot cheese* (loan translation < *pot kees*) and *waffle*. The once very American word *boss* also comes from Dutch, as do *yacht*, *stoop* (the porch-like steps in front of urban houses), *snoop*, *spook*, *dope*, *dumb*, and maybe even *Yankee* (< *Jan Kees* "John Cheese" because of the Yankees', i.e. New Englanders', pale complexions – a disputed etymology; other explanations have been suggested). *Freebooter* is a **loan translation** (link: Loan translation) of Dutch *vrijbuiter*. In the same field of shipping ME already had borrowed widely from Dutch (see 4.2.4 and 5.3.4.1). Now, however, Americans added *scow* and overland transportation such as *span* (of horses) pulling a *sleigh* or the *caboose* on a train. More strictly cultural items include Saint Nicolas, better known as Santa Claus (both from the Dutch) and street names in New York, such as Wall St. (so named because of the Walloons who lived there) or Hell's Gate ("Bright Gate"). The various place-names ending in {-hook}(< *hoek*) such as Sandy Hook also come from Dutch. Further items, either regional or no longer current, were also borrowed into AmE (e.g. *patroon*, *hay barrack*, *boodle*, *erve* "small inheritance," *rolliche* "meat roulade," *olicook* "fat cake") (cf. Marckwardt 1980: 51ff).

10.2.3.2 German, French, and Spanish

These are the other important European languages which English speakers came into contact with in the colonial period, yet their influence was relatively negligible. This would change in the nineteenth and twentieth centuries.

10.2.4 The language of the African slaves

By the end of the colonial period the number of people of African descent in what became the United States had reached approximately one-fifth of the population. With probably only relatively few exceptions these people spoke the one or the other variety of English, depending very much on the nature of their relations with Euro-Americans. Slavery itself existed in all of the colonies, but there was also a small, slowly growing community of free African Americans (Plates 10.2 and 10.3). Among the slaves there were house servants, skilled craftsmen, and field laborers. This had consequences for the type of language spoken. Where contact was less intensive, it is very likely that a form of creole, if not, indeed, in some cases, pidgin English was common. Where contact was closer, de-creolized forms were in use, often very close to the usage of the white population.

10.2.4.1 African American Pidgin English and Plantation Creole

There is little direct evidence of Pidgin English in the North American colonies. In the very early period from 1620 to 1700 there are sporadic bits taken from the speech of slaves such as that of Tituba, a slave brought to Massachusetts from Barbados, who testified at the Salem witch trials (1692). The available evidence lists the following, recorded by one of the presiding judges at the trials, Justice Hathorne (an ancestor of Nathaniel Hawthorne): *I no hurt them at all; He tell me he God; They told me serve him* (Dillard 1973: 79).

10.3 Development of North American English after American independence

Overall, the same effects of education and the schools, the development of the reading public, and the effects of urbanization that we have seen in connection with Great Britain were also present in North America. The degree and tempo of the various developments may have differed, but the effect on the standard language was similar. Indeed, StE in Great Britain and Ireland and in North America (as indeed elsewhere in the world) is largely identical. Some of the points which differ will be elaborated on in the following sections.

10.3.1 Standard and non-standard English

Variations in AmE are not only regional, but also strongly social. On one side of a great divide lies cultured speech, which means the use of StE and the avoidance of **shibboleths** (link: shibboleths), that is, non-standard forms which members of the speech community are aware of and which sociolinguistics calls **markers**.[4] On the other side, there is non-standard GenE. The divide is evident in pronunciation, grammar, and vocabulary; and one single item may be enough to set the machinery of prejudice into action – a single *ain't*, an *ax* for *ask*, just a "leetle" Mexican accent (cf. Lippi-Green 2004). Part of the history of AmE includes a fair amount of prejudice and disinformation about what people consider to be *good* and *bad* language. The central formula is "language + *x*," whereby *x* may be gender, ethnicity, education, intelligence, urbanity, and dozens of other features. In the following a selection of these, "uneducated" and ethnic group usages, will be at the center of attention. Before looking at this we need to remember that what some people label as ignorance of the "rules" of English is, in most cases, merely a different set of rules than those of StE. Take, for example, the verb *ask/ax* as in *He axed me yesterday.* Wrong! many would cry. Well, slow down. *Ax* (for StE *ask*) is not so much wrong as merely a different historical development from earlier English. In OE the verb appeared as both *ascian* with /sk/ and *acsian*, where <-cs-> = /ks/, now spelled <x>. This is not to say that *ax* is acceptable where the standard is expected. Using it is not ignorance of English, but simply use of a venerable non-standard item.

---

4 Markers are variables speakers are aware of; *indicators* are ones which are below the level of consciousness (but observed by linguists); *stereotypes* are socially marked, consciously perceived speech items.

10.3.2 Standardization

The classical criteria of *standardization* ([link: Standardization](); also 5.2.2; 6.2.3; 8.2.1) were not all equally relevant in the American context. Selection and expansion were of minor importance, but *codification* and acceptance have been at the forefront of interest. The codified standard in America, like in Great Britain and Ireland, is independent of any single institution such as an academy, yet it would be mistaken to assume there was no authority. In fact, there has long been a conglomeration of self-appointed (or, indeed, self-anointed) experts – the authors and compilers of *grammars*, *dictionaries*, and *manuals of usage* ([link: Grammars; link: Dictionaries; link: Manuals of usage]()) – who represent authority in language. Very early on the single most imposing name within this tradition in the United States was Noah Webster (1758–1843), whose most influential books were *A Grammatical Institute of the English Language* (1783–85), consisting of three parts, a speller ([link: Spellers](); Plate 10.4) (1783), a grammar (1784), and a reader (1785), and his *American Dictionary of the English Language* (1828). Indeed, the dictionary has given his name legendary status, so much so that "Look it up in *Webster's*" – his name appears in the title of a variety of US dictionaries – bears witness to his authority.

10.3.2.1 Vocabulary

An important part of the national project of AmE has been to emphasize its independence from BrE. This has also led to a feeling of division between the United States and Anglophone Canada (see below 10.3.4). The title of H.L. Mencken's monumental book on English in the United States, *The American Language* (1919–63), offers testimony to this. Mencken's work emphasizes differences in vocabulary and meaning, especially in contrast to BrE. Much of what he compiled is quaint and vaguely interesting, but often simply trivial and dated. What he stresses in discussing Americanisms is the type of items concerned, namely words borrowed from other languages, words needed to accommodate American culture and institutions and (from a British point of view) provincialisms and archaisms as well as extensions and shifts of meaning (cf. Mencken 1963: 103–109).

There is ample material of the sort Mencken assembled, but the important perspective is that only the cultural-institutional items pose a really major problem of communication between *national varieties*. Such North American items include an endless list of names (*John Hancock, Paul Bunyan, Jim Crow, Sasquatch*), historical-geographic references (*Three Mile Island, Teapot Dome, the Qu'Appelle Treaty, the Beltway, Podunk*), institutions (*Bill 101, NBA, FDA, the Mounties*), traditional songs, music, and dances ("*Sweet Betsy from Pike,*" "*Roll, Jordan, Roll,*" "*The Virginia Reel*"), national customs (*trick-or-treat, Presidents Day, Levée*), and more. What is true in the United States and Canada is true of every country, and it is something we fully expect to encounter in an unfamiliar variety of English. This is an important part of the vocabulary of national languages; it is less the kind of thing you find in a dictionary and more what you use an encyclopedia to find out about.

AmE items are often recognized and understood, though not actively used in other varieties. And, of course, the same is true of the peculiarities of the other varieties, as well – an AmE speaker in conversation with a speaker of BrE may know what is meant by *draughts* but simply continue to use the AmE designation *checkers*. Why does this happen? One of the reasons is that this is the language of the speakers's speech community. In addition, the use of a given national item may be emblematic: it signifies; it labels the speakers as a member of a (national) speech community.

10.3.2.2 Spelling

The one aspect of the standard language which Webster is especially closely associated with is the reform of spelling, which he ardently supported and undertook step by step in his spelling book (which rivals McGuffey's six volumes of readers with sales of over 60 million by the 1960s; Plate 10.4). Much, but not all, of what he proposed was accepted and is now normal AmE usage.

These *spelling reforms* (link: Spelling reform) are not haphazard and unsystematic. Rather, we find the principles of:

- **simplification**: double letters (<waggon> → <wagon>; Latin spellings (<aesthetic> and <foetus> → <esthetic> and <fetus>), word endings (<catalogue> → <catalog>)
- **regularization**: all cases of <-our> become <-or> (<colour> → <color> and <-re> becomes <-er> (<centre> → <center>)
- **derivational uniformity**: noun–verb (both <practice>); noun–adjective (both <defense> and <defensive> have <s>)
- **reflection of pronunciation**: <z> or <s> as /z/ (<civilise> → <civilize>); <gh> in words like <through> or <night> may be simplified <thru> or <nite> in informal spellings thus coming closer to the pronunciation
- **stress indication**: doubling of the <l> indicates stress on the syllable ('traveled vs. re'belled)
- **pronunciation spellings**: *often* as /ɔːftən/ rather than traditional /ɔːfən/.

There are in addition a number of individual, unsystematic differences (<kerb> → <curb> or <cheque> → <check>). Today we also find nonce spellings, especially in advertising, ones such as <E-Z> ("easy," which works only for AmE, where the letter <z> is *zee* and not *zed*), <Xtra> or <Kwik>. Finally, it should be noted that AmE usage is not completely consistent; for example, we find <advertisement> with <s> and many people write <Saviour> (a reference to Jesus, hence capitalized) with <u> and <theatre> with <-re> as if the BrE spelling lent the word more standing.

Much of the variation in AmE lies in the greater willingness on the part of its users to accept the few modest reforms that have been suggested. Canadians seem to be of two minds about this with the consequence that we find far more variation between US and British spellings in CanE, and this may be one of the things which makes CanE specifically Canadian.

10.3.2.3 Grammar

StE does not have as much variation in this area as in morphology. Consequently, only few illustrative examples of differences will be listed. American speakers seem to be less strict about the adverbs which require the use of the present *perfect* (link: Perfect(ive) aspect) (*I already saw them* is fully acceptable); *have got* ("possess") differs in meaning from *have gotten* ("receive"); *have* is seldom used in negatives and questions without *do*; the frequency of use of particular **modal auxiliaries** (link: Modal auxiliaries) is often different; the reduced forms of the **semi-modals** (link: Semi-modals) such as *gonna*, *gotta*, and *wanna* are perhaps more commonly used. The mandative **subjunctive** (link: Subjunctive) (e.g. *important that someone go*) is more normal even in spoken standard AmE than in BrE. **Notional concord** (link: Concord, aka agreement) (e.g. *the team are ready*) is less frequent in AmE, but not uncommon. Finally, **copular verbs** (link: Copular verbs) may pattern differently in BrE and AmE (e.g. AmE *seems to be/looks like a fool* vs. BrE *seems/looks a fool*).

10.3.2.4 Morphology

Standard AmE has inherited a few different verb forms from those used in BrE. Well known are the following (in which the AmE form is hardly used in BrE (if at all), but not vice versa): **past tense** (link: Tense) *dove* (for *dived*); **past participle** (link: Principal parts) *gotten* (for *got*), *shaven* (for *shaved*), *proven* (for *proved*); past and past participle: a preference for {-ed} rather than {-t} as in *burned, dreamed, dwelled, kneeled, leaned, learned, spelled, spilled, spoiled* also *snuck* (for *sneaked*), *quit* (for *quitted*), *bet* (*betted*), *fit* (*fitted*).

Among the numerous differences in **prepositions** (link: Prepositions) here are a few. BrE frequently uses prepositions ending in –*st* where AmE has *amid, among, while*; compound prepositions that require *of* as the second element in standard BrE may do without it in AmE, for example *to go out the door*, but may take *of* in *alongside of, off of, opposite of*.

10.3.3 The pronunciation of AmE

The pronunciation which is most often recognized as the standard is frequently called *General American* (*GenAm*; link: GenAm), sometimes also Network Standard, probably so recognized because some version of it is spoken by the largest number of speakers of AmE and also because it is the pronunciation most widely used in broadcasting. Yet there is, in fact, no *universally* recognized standard of pronunciation.

10.3.3.1 Consonants (link: Consonants)

In this area there is little variation from region to region (but see below). Standard AmE has a system of twenty-four consonants, precisely the same ones as in *RP*. While the inventory is identical, there are numerous *phonotactic* differences and a differing functionality of [hw] and [ʔ]. Among the more important phonotactic points are:

- the *rhoticity* (link: Rhoticity) of GenAm (all three *r*'s are pronounced in *reporter*);
- the flapping (link: T-Flapping) of /t/ (= [ɖ]) in a voiced environment before an unstressed syllable (*latter = ladder*), a twentieth century development (MacMahon 1998: 486; see also 11.3.2);
- the loss of post-nasal /t/ (link: Post-nasal T) before unstressed syllables (*winter = winner*);
- the non-occurrence of /j/ (*yod-dropping*; link: Yod-dropping) after dental or alveolar consonants, that is, no /nj, tj, dj, sj, lj, θj/ in the same syllable (*new, tune, due, sue, lute, thew*); instead /n, t, d, s, l, θ/ occur alone or with *palatalization* (link: Palatalization) as in *educate* /edʒəkeɪt/.

The occurrence of the glottal stop (link: Glottal stop) [ʔ] in RP is increasing (a slow move in the direction of London speech) in such environments as represented by the <t>

in *not ever* or *see it*. A similar change cannot be observed in GenAm, where, however, [ʔ] is more common before stressed initial vowels (*ask Adam* [ʔæskʔædəm]. In both GenAm and RP [hw] is seldom used though perhaps not uncommon in emphatic speech.

10.3.3.2 Vowels (link: Vowels)

In the following we look first at one version of the early development in the pronunciation of AmE vowels, then at on-going shifts in three of the major (regional) systems of vowels in AmE. Taking Kökeritz's reconstruction of the Shakespearean pronunciation as a starting point Pilch (1955) showed the changes that the system used by Webster represent and how these, then, appear in ModAmE as shown in Table 10.2.

The major changes from Shakespeare (late sixteenth–early seventeenth centuries) to Webster (late eighteenth–early nineteenth) are:

- the **phonemicization** (link: phonemicization) of high central /ɨ/
- the phonemicization of short mid-back /o/
- the **monophthongization** (link: monophthongization) of /juː/ to /iː/ after /t, d, ʃ, j/ (*truth, duke, sure, your*)
- the continuation of the **GVS** (link: The Great Vowel Shift (GVS)) with the lowering of /ʌɪ/ to /aɪ/ and of /ʌu/ to /ɑʊ/.

The major changes from Webster's times to today (late twentieth–early twenty-first centuries) are:

- reversal of phonemicization of high central /ɨ/
- the dephonemicization of length in favor of phonetic quality, for example /i/ as /ɪ/ and /u/ as /ʊ/
- phonemicization of /ɜː/
- regionally differing **diphthongization** of /eː/ and /oː/ to /eɪ/ and /oʊ/
- varying loss of distinctions between low back /ɑ(ː)/, /ɔː/, and /ɒ/
- **backing** (link: Backing) of the first element of /ɔɪ/
- varying **fronting** (link: Fronting) of [u(ː)] to [ʉ(ː)]

Present-day AmE may be described as having a number of **vowel systems** in which different sets of changes are occurring. In fact, three different shifts seem to be in progress:

Table 10.2 The phonemes of English c. 1600 (Shakespeare), c. 1800 (Webster), and 2000

monoph-thongs	front			central			back			wide closing diphthongs			
	Sh	Web	Mod AmE	Sh	Web	Mod AmE	Sh	Web	Mod AmE	pre-GVS	Sh	Web	Mod AmE
high-long	iː	iː	iː		ɨː		uː	uː	uː/ʉː	iː	ʌɪ	ai	aɪ
high-short	i	i	ɪ				u	u	ʊ	uː	ʌu	au	ɑʊ
mid-long	eː	eː	eː/eɪ			ɜː	oː	oː	oː/oʊ	ɔi	ai	ɑi	ɔɪ
mid-short	e	e	e	ʌ	ʌ	ʌ			o				
low-long	æː	æː	æː/æ				ɑː	ɑː	ɑ/ɔː	iu	juː	juː/iː	juː/jʉː
low-short	æ	æ					ɑ	ɑ					

the Southern Vowel Shift, the Northern Cities Shift, and the Low Back Merger. Labov has characterized them and suggested how the principles that lie behind them may look (see General principles of chain shifting (link: Principles of vowel change). As a result of these principles there appear to be "two major types of English dialects, moving in diametrically opposite directions" (Labov 1991: 4). By adding in the effect of mergers we get a third major type. They are vaguely parallel to the North–Midland–South division (see Map 10.1), or even to the more traditional division in AmE into North, South, and West. What is characteristic of the shifts is that "phones that represent one phoneme in one dialect represent an entirely different phoneme in another" (ibid.: 3), for example *talk* in one accent sounds like *tuck* in another.

According to Labov's first principle tense or long vowels, which are peripheral, rise. For example, /æ/ (a phonologically short vowel) splits into two types in New York City: (1) long (before voiced consonants) and (2) short before voiceless ones:[5] [æː] vs. [æ] as in *bad* and *bat*. Then [æː] rises to [æːᵊ]. The first principle has been active for many hundreds of years in English (cf. the GVS; see 6.3.1.2). The second principle stands in contrast to this: *lax* or short vowels, that is, non-peripheral ones, fall (see Figure 10.1). The fifth principle is the mirror image of this: the change of high peripheral vowels to non-peripheral ones as the first element of diphthongs move back. To make up for the loss of peripheral vowels that results from this, new peripheral ones come into being according to the fourth principle, which says that low non-peripheral vowels become peripheral (ibid.: 10).

There are two pivot points in AmE. The first is the low front vowel /æ/, which has historically been unstable and has tended to rise (see above). The second is the unstable distinction between *long open o* and *short open o*, that is, /ɔː/ and /ɒ/. This has been resolved in two ways: either (1) [ɒ] is unrounded and lowered to [ɑː] and /ɔː/ is raised and over-rounded; or (2) the two *merge* (link: Mergers).

10.3.3.3 The Northern Cities Shift (link: Northern Cities Shift)

This shift applies from western New England and westward in the upper northern areas (NY, PA, OH, IN, IL, MI, WI), where we find:

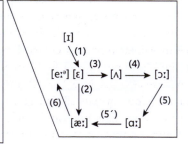

(1) non-peripheral [ɪ] falls to [ɛ];
(2) [ɛ] falls to [æː] (continue at (6)); or:
(3) [ɛ] moves to [ʌ] and
(4) [ʌ] backs to [ɔː];
(5) [ɔː] falls to peripheral [ɑː], which (5′) begins to front;
(6) peripheral [æː] rises to [eːᵊ] or higher
For example: (1) *tick = tech*; (2) *tech = tack*; (3) *tech = tuck*; (4) *tuck = talk*; (4) *talk = tock*; (5) *tock = tack*; (6) *tack/Ann = tin/Ian*.

Figure 10.1 The Northern Cities Shift

5 This is the result of phonetic lengthening in English before a pause or a voiced consonant as opposed to a short **allophone** before a voiceless consonant. The ultimate cause of this difference in length is not clear.

The Northern Cities Shift is unusual in English because it involves the short vowels, which historically have been stable. Furthermore, it is extremely complex. The larger the city, the more advanced the change.

10.3.3.4 The Southern Shift (link: Southern Shift)

This shift is to be found in the Southern Mountain region and the Upper and Lower South (different versions of it appear in southern England, Australia, New Zealand, and South Africa). In the Southern Shift we find that:

(1) /æ/ remains outside the US, while in America it splits into long, tensed [æː], which moves much as in the Northern Cities Shift, and short, lax [æ];
(2) long and short *o*, realized as ɔ(ː) and (ɑː), remain separate;
(3) [aɪ] monophthongizes to [ɑː] especially when followed by a pause or a voiced consonant;
(4) the back vowels are fronted, especially [uː] → [ʉː];
(5) the short front vowels become peripheral and move upward: [æ] → [æ̝̟], [ɛ] → [e̝̟], [ɪ] → [ɪ̝̟].

10.3.3.5 Low Back Merger (the third dialect) (link: Low Back Merger)

There are two centers for this change, Boston and Pittsburg. But it is found throughout the US and applies to Canada as well, though there is very little evidence of it in the South and it is diluted in the area of the Northern Cities Shift. This is a phenomenon essentially restricted to AmE (ibid.: 30). In it (1) /æ/ is relatively stable [æ] and (2) long and short *o* merge (*cot* = *caught*). It is progressing rapidly, and girls tend to be the leaders (cf. Labov 1972 on the role of lower middle-class women (link: Gender) as change leaders).

10.3.4 Canadian English

In the American Revolution (1775–83) the upper stratum in a number of areas, for example New York and the Eastern Shore (of Chesapeake Bay), were relatively strongly Loyalist. In the course of the internal struggle many prominent Tory landowners were dispossessed. All in all, the atmosphere was not congenial to them everywhere during and after the war. As a consequence an estimated 35,000 United Empire Loyalists (link: United Empire Loyalists) migrated to the Maritimes (especially Nova Scotia and New Brunswick) and another 5000 from Eastern Massachusetts, New York, Pennsylvania, and Maryland to Upper Canada, north of Lake Ontario (Countryman 1985: chap. 5; *History of Canada*). As a consequence of this the character of Canadian English (CanE) is not fundamentally different from AmE. Specifically CanE vocabulary contains no greater divergence than that of any of the other North American English regions.

This is not to underplay the important feeling of Canadian identity which many Anglophone speakers have. Pro-US attitudes correlate, for example, with more yod-dropping (as in *new*, *Tuesday*, *due*) and more frequent T-flapping (*latter* = *ladder*). In contrast, the letter <z> is *zed* (BrE) rather than *zee* (AmE) in a proportion of 3:1, which is the case for *chesterfield* (a Canadianism) vs. *sofa* as well. The perhaps best-known feature is

Canadian raising (link: Canadian raising), that is, the high diphthongs in *house* [hʌʊs] and *bite* [bʌɪt]. For those who produce them they occur before voiceless consonants, thus making the contrast between [bʌʊt] (*bout*) and [baʊd] (*bowed*). It is not clear whether this is an independent Canadian development or the maintenance of an older British distinction (Wells 1982: §§3.1.11). Furthermore, the leveling of the [aʊ] – [ʌʊ] distinction seems to be proceeding apace (but see Chambers and Hardwick 1986). These remarks apply above all to English speakers between Ontario and the Pacific.

10.3.4.1 The Maritimes

The situation east of francophone Quebec is more complex. This may be due to the settlement history of the Ottawa Valley, New Brunswick, Nova Scotia, and Prince Edward Island. Settlers came from Scotland and both northern and southern Ireland as well as from Kashubia, Poland, and Germany, and, of course, from the United States after the Revolution. The pronunciation is firmly rhotic, as the immigrant origins of the speakers might suggest.

10.3.4.2 Newfoundland

Newfoundland is a special case. The island was settled by people from Ireland and southwest England from 1583 on, and the province experienced little immigration until more recently. From the Southwest of England we get the voicing of initial /f/ and /s/ as Newfoundland /v/ and /z/. Clear [l] in all environments can be attributed to both southern Ireland and the English Southwest. But /t, d/ for /θ, ð/, [eː, oː] for /eɪ, oʊ/, and the occasional merger of /ɔɪ/ and /aɪ/ are more likely to be Irish in origin (cf. Chambers 1986). Elements of the traditional dialect of Southwestern England in Newfoundland have been discussed in 7.2.2.

10.4 Non-standard GenE

The non-standard is extremely widespread throughout the English-speaking world. Those of its forms which differ from StE may often be understood as archaisms and regularization. The non-standard forms are fully functional and systematic, but for whatever reasons were not selected when StE was codified. Throughout the following sections we will draw on literary texts written to depict non-standard GenE and regional and ethnic dialects. Text 10.3, from the early twentieth century, lies fully within the tradition of writing in the *American Vernacular* (link: American Vernacular), that is, the non-standard speech of the common people. Such writing, widespread in the nineteenth century and sometimes highly satirical, was usually good-naturedly condescending toward the uneducated. This is the case in Lardner's text. Though clearly exaggerated for its humorous effect, it gives an idea of some of the non-standard grammatical items (the numbers next to the words in blue correspond to the list which follows the text) and pronunciation.

Text 10.3 Non-standard General English: R. Lardner, "Three without, Doubled" (1917)

It was a Friday evenin' about three weeks ago when I come (4) home and found the Wife quaverin' with excitement.

"Who do you think called up?" she ast me. . . . "You couldn't never (7) guess," she says. . . . "It was Mrs. Messenger that's (8) husband owns this buildin' and the one at the corner, where they live at."

"Haven't you paid the rent," I says (5). . . .

"Well," she says, "I was just gettin' through with the lunch dishes and the phone rang."

"I bet you wondered who it was," says I.

"I thought it was Mrs. Hatch or somebody," says the Wife. "So I run (4) to the phone and it was Mrs. Messenger. So the first thing she says was to explain who she was – just like I didn't know. And the next thing she ast was did I play bridge."

"And what did you tell her?" says I.

"What do you think I'd tell her?" says the Missus. "I told her yes."

"Wasn't you (3) triflin' a little with the truth?" I ast her.

"Certainly not!" she says. . . . So then she ast me if my husband played bridge, too. And I told her yes, he did."

"What was the idear?" I says. "You know I didn't never (7) play it in my life." . . .

"Well, anyway, I told her you did," says the Missus. . . . "I got brains enough to know that Mrs. Messenger ain't (2) callin' me up and astin' me do we play bridge just because she's got a headache or feels lonesome or somethin'. . . .

(R. Lardner, *Gullible's Travels, Etc.* Chicago: University of Chicago Press, 1965 [1917], 115–118)

The following is a shortened list of non-standard features of GenE (for a longer text and more features, see link: Non-standard GenE). Numbers 2, 3, 4, 5, 7, and 8 occur in Text 10.3.

Non-standard verb forms:

1. **a-*prefixing*** (link: *A*-prefixing) represents a now archaic earlier stage (especially prominent in the sixteenth century) in the development of the progressive form, which first required a preposition before the gerund (e.g. *on doing something*); the preposition, weakened to unstressed /ə/, was prefixed to the verb. Over a period of time the prefix was dropped leaving us with the present-day form, for example *She's a-comin' round the mountain when she comes.*

2. *Ain't* (link: Ain't) is a contraction of both *be not* (*I, you, she, we, they* ***ain't*** *tired*) and *have not* (*I, you, she, we, they* ***ain't*** *done it*).
3. Generalized past tense *was* (*I, you, she, we, they* ***was*** *happy*); less often: *were* (*I, you, she, we, they* ***were*** *happy*).

4. Non-standard *principal parts* (link: Principal parts) (examples):

Table 10.3 Examples of non-standard principal parts

come	come	come	*She come back to me las' week.*
know	knowed	knowed	*If I a-knowed you was comin', I'd a-baked a cake.*
go	went	went	*I have went to college.*
give	give	given	*We give it to' em yesterday.*
do	done	done	*They done it last summer.*
see	seen (seed)	seen	*Nobody seen* (also: *seed*) *it.*
run	run	run	*So I run to the phone.*

5. Non-third person *present tense* {-s} (link: Present tense {-s}) in a narrative function: "*I bet you wondered who it was," says I.*
6. Third person present singular *don't* (link: Third person singular *don't*) (*He **don't** care what you say*).
7. *Multiple negation* (link: Multiple negation) (*She didn't do **nothing** to help solve **no** problems*); note that negation can be copied onto any or all indefinite elements.

Non-standard pronoun usage:

8. Use of *that* as a non-defining relative: *It was Mrs. Messenger **that's** husband owns this buildin'.*
9. Regularized *reflexive pronouns* (link: Reflexive pronouns): *myself, yourself, **hisself**, herself, itself, ourselves, yourselves, **theirselves.***
10. Regularized *possessive forms*: *mine, **yourn**, **hisn**, **hern**, **ourn**, **theirn**.*
11. Non-standard *relative pronouns*: *The fellow **as / what** went to see her was right smart.*
12. Zero subject relative in defining relative clauses: *The car ø went around that corner was real fast.*
13. *Demonstrative determiner*: ***Them** flowers is mighty purty.*

10.4.1 The *regionalization* (link: Regionalization) of AmE: the development of Southern AmE

It is not certain just how to interpret the many comments by British travelers in the American colonies/the United States which attest to what was perceived as great uniformity. Such comments may have been motivated by the *relative* uniformity in comparison to the very noticeable presence of distinct regional dialects in Great Britain. The reason for such comments may, however, have lain in a *real* uniformity. Certainly, American settlers did not retain more than a few distinctly British regional forms as AmE developed (Kretzschmar 2004: 42). It is remarkable that comments on the uniformity of AmE became rare by the early nineteenth century. It is doubtful that this was the result of a koinéization process in Great Britain which would have diminished the distinct regional forms in England and lessened the contrast to America. After all, most of the visitors who made the comments were far removed from the British working classes and their emerging koinés. One intriguing suggestion is that Southern regional English gradually emerged due to language contact, namely the influence of African American Vernacular English (AAVE) (link: African

American Vernacular English (AAVE)) on Southern AmE (Dillard esp. 1992: chap. 4). According to this the white population of the South (except for large landowners) was mobile and this speaks "against the direct transmission of British regional dialects to the South in regionally formulated patterns. The slaves, on the other hand, come closest to the kind of settled, tied-to-the-land peasantry upon which dialect zones have generally been based" (Dillard 1992: 102). Evidence for the influence of AAVE includes testimonies like these:

> One Thing they are very faulty in, with regard to their Children, which is, that when young they suffer them to prowl amongst the young Negroes, which insensibly causes them to imbibe their Manners and broken Speech.
>
> (G.L. Campbell in *The London Magazine*, 1746)

> Each child has its [slave] *Momma*, whose gestures and accent it will necessarily copy, for children we all know are imitative beings.
>
> (John Davis, 1799) (both qtd. ibid.: 95)

Rhoticity offers important support for this hypothesis. The Upper South (the southern *Appalachians*, Kentucky, eastern Tennessee, northern Alabama, and northern Arkansas with peripheral areas in southern Indiana and Illinois and most of Missouri, Oklahoma, and much of northeastern Texas) has no linking /r/ (link: linking -r and intrusive -r). The Lower South (Louisiana, Alabama, the Virginia Piedmont and eastern North Carolina, South Carolina, Georgia, and Florida) vacillates (McDavid and O'Cain 1980: 172, Map 157). As a result, McDavid and O'Cain see Southern usage as an American innovation. Gilbert (1984: 409–410) sees in this the influence of the English creoles (and pidgins) of the Caribbean and West Africa, which are non-rhotic. Dillard sees less historical influence from British dialects (which would mean selective retention) and finds it more likely that "the major difference in non-prevocalic /r/ distribution relates to the greater persistence, wider distribution and stronger influence of Black English Vernacular [AAVE] in the South. Just as often, on the other hand, more than one influence may well have been operative" (1992: 97). However that may be, such language contact can hardly explain the non-rhoticity of New England, where little African-influenced English was spoken. A more likely source would be the influence of newly non-rhotic accents of southern England

In any case, the popular distinction between North and South (in speech) was established by the time of the American Civil War (1861–65), but has little in the way of pronunciation *isoglosses* (link: Isogloss) to support it besides /griːsi/ (North) vs. /griːzi/ (South); however, the changes recounted above in the Southern Shift, to which we can add the merger of /ɛ/ and /ɪ/ before nasals (*pin = pen*, both /pɪn/) also speak for Southern regionalization. There is at least some vocabulary evidence: Northern *brook* vs. Southern *branch, run*; *reckon* for *guess*; and *tote* for *carry*. Among the syntactic differences we find *like* (conjunction) for *as* and the use of some modals in second auxiliary position as in *He **hadn't ought** to have went*, but both are widespread elsewhere as well.

There is a strong tradition which associates regionalization (and not just Southern regionalization) with settlement history and the British origins of the settlers. Scots-Irish (Ulster) influence is, for example, frequently cited for the Appalachian area, but what is more telling than the occasional evidence of Scottish influence is the distinct "population mixture" which led, in each colony, to "a range of speech habits out of which its own regional characteristic could eventually emerge" (Kretzschmar 2004: 42). Furthermore, while many of the old regionalisms recorded in the Linguistic Atlas of the United States and Canada are no longer relevant (who knows the old farming items and the terms for them originally elicited in the surveys?) new regionalisms continue to appear and to follow the old regional bounds.

10.4.2 Language of the frontier (link: The concept of the frontier)

The frontier – pronounced /frʌnˈtiːr/ in GenAm and not /ˈfrʌntɪə/ as in RP – is a central American mythical-ideological concept. It designates an area, not a line (as elsewhere); it is where wilderness and civilization meet; and it is not a stopping point or limit, but offers an opportunity to go on. It represented something new: "We may safely conclude that the Colonial koiné . . . was created by the migrant population of British Northerners, together with English, Welsh, Germans, and other immigrants who moved westward" (Fisher 2001: 84). And the people who moved onto the frontier have been characterized as democratic, boisterous, exploitative, mobile, unconventional, rude, and optimistic. This clearly involved a social (self-)selection of people, who, among other things, showed an often open disdain for learning and books. They rejected thought and careful planning in preference to action and success. The hero of the frontier, for example a figure like James Fenimore Cooper's Nattie Bumppo (alias Leatherstocking) rejects civilization; and concomitant to his down-to-earth-ness, Nattie speaks dialect (not the high language of the traditional literary hero). True, Cooper sometimes has him speak "classical" StE ("Who comes? . . . Who comes hither, among the beasts and dangers of the wilderness?" (Cooper, *The Last of the Mohicans*, 1826: chap. 4). But scattered throughout Cooper's books Natty uses such homely pronunciations as *'arth* (earth), *l'arn* (learn), *creatur'* (creature), *natur'* (nature), *ag'in* (again), *atween* (between), and *afore* (before). Leatherstocking is just one of the many mythological and prototypical figures which nineteenth century America produced. In the following we look at a few aspects of frontier life which may be regarded as important for language.

10.3.6.2 Newspapers, books, schools, and libraries

There was a widespread and testified thirst for news: one newspaper enterprise per 12,000 in 1840 in the West; in the Mississippi Valley about one third of the families subscribed to one or more papers. The West was important for the national book market; for example, an early winter shortened the "publishing season" (Billington 1974: 81). Sometimes even tiny towns had more than one bookstore. One in eleven of the total Ohio Valley population was attending school in 1840 and one in thirty-two in Kentucky, as compared to one in six in New York, Pennsylvania, and Massachusetts. There were eleven libraries in Kentucky in 1812 (one per 37,000) though proportionately more in Ohio and Indiana (ibid.: 88). Yet the West contributed to lasting American anti-intellectualism: "The West naturally attracted men of action and material ambition, rather than the studious and the contemplative" (ibid.: 89). In the Appalachian region the literacy rate in 1860 lay at 54% (in the North: 94%) (Fisher 2001: 84; see <u>link: Literature of the Old Southwest</u>).

10.3.6.3 Language in the West

This is characterized in popular literature such as that collected by Botkin (1983) by its non-standard grammar, its attempts to represent local-regional pronunciation and uncultivated usage in modified spelling, and its boastful, exaggerated, and somewhat anti-establishment tone. Indeed, it is this language more than any other which has earned the title "**The** *American Vulgate*" (link: American Vulgate). The following excerpt, an anonymous example of American frontier tall talk, illustrates some of these features.

Text 10.4 Frontier speech: "The Boast"

I was ridin along the Mississippi in my wagon, when I came acrost a feller floating down stream, settin in the starn of his boat fast asleep. Well, I hadn't had a fight for ten days; felt as tho' I should have to kiver myself up in a salt barrel, to keep so wolfy about the shoulders. So says I, hallo stranger, if you don't mind your boat will run off and leave you. So he looked up at me slantindicular, and I looked down on him slantindicular. He took out a chor of tobacco, and says he, I don't vallee you tantamount to that; and the varmant clapped his wings and crowed. I ris up, shuch my mane, croocked my neck, and nickered like a horse. He run his boat plump head foremost ashore. I stopped my wagon, and set my triggers. Mister, says he, I can whip my weight in wild cats, and ride straight thro' a crab apple orchard on a flash of lightning – clear meat axe disposition – the best man, if I an't, I wish I may be tetotaciously exfluncuated. So we come together; he was a pretty severe colt, but no part of a priming for me. I put it to him mighty droll – in ten minutes he yelled enough, and swore I was a ripstaver! Says I, an't I the yellow flower of the forest? And I'm all brimstone but the head, and that's aquafortis! Says he, stranger, you're a beauty, and if I only know'd your name, I'd vote for you next election. Says I, my name is Nimrod Wildfire – half horse, half alligator, and a touch of the airthquake – that's got the prettiest sister, fattest horse, and ugliest dog in the district, and can out run, out jump, throw down, drag out and whip any man in all Kentuck!

(from: W. Blair (1960 [1931]) *Native American Humor*. New York: Chandler, 281)

The linguistic features which this text reveals are only generally regional inasmuch as this may be seen as a fairly representative example of the English of the ***Old Southwest***. The Old Southwest is the section of the United States which was the geographic southwest before the trans-Mississippi addition of the Louisiana Purchase (1803). The region includes parts of Georgia, Alabama, Mississippi, Louisiana, Kentucky, and Tennessee as well as trans-Mississippi Texas and Arkansas. More to the point the linguistic features are social, representing a type of person, one often considered (by the (sub)urban middle class) to be rural (hicks), uneducated (ignoramuses), and unpolished (boors). The use of "grandiloquent" language, that is, high-sounding but otherwise non-existent words (*slantindicular*, *tetotaciously exfluncuated*) belongs to this tradition.

10.5 Ethnic variety within AmE

The homogenization of AmE across the regions has had the consequence that geographical differences, though present above all in pronunciation, are relatively small. In contrast, *ethnic* group (link: Ethnicity) membership is a more distinctive source of variation in AmE pronunciation. In the following we will consider American Indian English, immigrant English, AAVE, and Spanish-influenced English, all of which may be regarded as examples of ethnic varieties. The degree of difference between these groups varies considerably, and each of the four cases represents a different paradigm of change.

10.5.1 *American Indian English (AIE)* (link: American Indian English)

Indians often were and are multilingual, each language spoken functionally well-suited to its own cultural context. Earlier it was, for example, important to speak several languages "so that . . . guests who come to the community from other tribes can be made to feel at home more easily" (Leap 1981: 132–133). Yet after European contact, language became a target of missionaries, administrators, and educators because it was a prime carrier of culture. From the Indian point of view maintenance was important (1) because their languages were a part of their cultural heritage (daily life, personal interaction, political decision making, ceremonial responsibilities) and (2) because their languages expressed cultural traditions (like animacy: corn grows; people don't grow corn). These languages remind us that "no single language has a monopoly over truth, logic, or precision of expression" (ibid.: 133). There are still more than 200 native languages spoken in the US and Canada as compared with about 500 at the time of European discovery. Indian life (and hence language) was destroyed through deliberate genocide or more subtle processes such as "removal," the reservation system, and constant pressure to join the mainstream.

Whatever may be said about the features of "American Indian English," it is important to see that it is not unitary. Leap uses the plural American Indian *Englishes* to emphasize this point. For behind each variety lies an ancestral language which has an effect on the grammar and the rules of discourse of AIE (Mesthrie et al. 2000: 270). Leap goes so far as to say, "the ancestral language base underlying each Indian English variety gave its speakers ways to communicate in ancestral language terms even though they were talking to outsiders" (ibid.: 271) For example, "to speak Ute English is to speak the Ute language in a form which non-Indians will understand" (ibid.: 272). As with other ethnic varieties of AmE, AIE is closely related to the local, often non-standard forms of non-Indian English. Hence Ute Indians also speak Basin English, which is shared by Indians and non-Indians in northeastern Utah and which is sometimes referred to as "Cowboy English," phonetically [kboi+ıngls] in Ute pronunciation, and syllable structure (ibid.).

In this sense we must look at any generalizations about AIE with reservation. That said, Leap points out that many of the "long–short" contrasts such as /iː/–/ɪ/ or /eɪ/–/e/ are not always maintained, which means that the same vowel may be used in *his* and *he's*. Since some consonants of English do not have counterparts in the ancestral languages, for example /ð/ and /θ/, they will be realized with more familiar phonemes, such as /d/ and /t/ (Leap 1993: 45ff).

Possible grammatical differences include lack of plural or possessive inflections and the treatment of uncountable nouns as countable ones (e.g. *furnitures, homeworks*). Furthermore, the order of sentence elements may be different than in StE:

They ride bikes is what I see them do. (San Juan Tewa)
There are circle dance songs that we have. (Mescalero Apache)
What he is doing there is he announcing. (Lakota)

(ibid.: 77)

A further significant point is the use of imagery different from StE. A Navajo would not say, "I must go there," but something like: "It is only good that I shall go there." Or: "The horse is running for me," instead of "I make the horse run" (ibid.: 79–80). In addition, the use of silence is more common: AIE speakers may use up to three times longer periods of silence before they answer a question or say something in a discussion (ibid.: 87ff).

Since English is tied to American values and de facto officially promoted, the ability to speak English has been a prerequisite to many types of employment and better living. Native American children were once forced by US *language policy* (link: Language policy) to attend boarding schools, thus separating them from tribe, tradition, and traditional language. The result has been a loss of interest in Indian culture and languages, which are sometimes seen as primitive, as well as reluctance among young people to speak these languages for fear of making mistakes, yet this does not necessarily guarantee proficiency in StE.

10.5.2 Immigrant communities, bilingualism, code-switching, *language retention (shift/loss)* (link: Generation model)

Immigrant groups have long played an important and varying role in American identity (link: Identity). On the one hand, many Americans see themselves as a nation of immigrants and celebrate this. On the other hand, many Americans expect the newcomers to assimilate in what was once widely praised as a melting pot. The language situation of immigrant communities follows a relatively straightforward line: the first generation arrives with all its native heritage – religion, dress, cuisine, music, political traditions, work attitudes, gender and family roles, and language. Assimilation begins as these first arrivals seek to become full members of the new society. This is nicely illustrated in the following excerpt from Abraham Cahan's short story *Yekl* (1898). Yekl, who has changed his name to Jake, receives a visit from Mamie Fein with whom he had entered into an amorous relationship before his wife Gitl and his young son Yosselé – now called Joey – arrived from Europe to join him in the Lower East Side of New York City. Mamie, who had lent Jake money, has found out about his deceitful treatment of her, and pays him a visit in his apartment to demand her money back:

Text 10.5 Immigrant English (Yiddish)

. . . there was a knock at the door.
"Coom in!" Gitl hastened to say somewhat coquettishly, flourishing her proficiency in American manners, as she raised her head from the pot in her hands.
"Coom in!" repeated Joey.
The door flew open, and in came Mamie, preceded by a cloud of cologne odors. She was apparently dressed for some occasion of state, for she was powdered and straight-laced and

resplendent in a waist of blazing red, gaudily trimmed, and with puff sleeves, each wider than the vast expanse of white straw, surmounted with a whole forest of ostrich feathers, which adorned her head. One of her gloved hands held the huge hoop-shaped yellowish handle of a blue parasol.

"Good-evenin', Jake!" she said, with ostentatious vivacity.

"Good-evenin', Mamie!" Jake returned, jumping to his feet and violently reddening, as if suddenly pricked. "Mish Fein, my vife, Mish Fein!"

Miss Fein made a stately bow, primly biting her lip as she did so. Gitl, with the pot in her hands, stood staring sheepishly, at a loss what to do.

"Say 'I'm glyad to meech you,' " Jake urged her, confusedly.

The English phrase was more than Gitl could venture to echo.

She is still green," Jake apologized for her, in Yiddish.

"Never min', she will soon oysgreen herself," Mamie remarked, with patronizing affability.

. . .

"You mush vant your twenty-fife dollars," he [Jake] presently nerved himself up to say in English, breaking an awkward pause.

"I should cough!" Mamie rejoined.

"In a couple o' veeksh, Mamie, as sure as my name is Jake."

"In a couple o' veeks! No, sirree! I mus' have my money at oncet. I don' know vere you vill get it, dough. Vy, a married man!" – with a chuckle. "You got a – lot o' t'ings to pay for. You took de foinitsha by a custom peddler, ain' it? But what a – do I care? I vant my money. I voiked hard enough for it."

"Don' shpeak English. She'll t'ink I don' knu vot ve shpeakin'," he besought her . . .

"Vot d'I care vot she t'inks? She's your vife, ain't it? Vell, she mus' know ev'ryt'ing. dot's right! A husban' dass'n't hide not'ink from his vife!" – with another chuckle and another look of deadly sarcasm at Gitl "I can say de same in Jewish [Yiddish] – "

"Shurr-r up, Mamie!" he interrupted her, gaspingly.

(A. Cahan (1970 [1898]) *Yekl.* New York: Dover, chap. 5)

The central point of the whole story comes out here as elsewhere: what kind of identity do these immigrants wish to show: Jake and Mamie (but even the newly arrived Gitl and Joey) reveal that they are beginning to adapt to life in America, if indeed in differing degrees (Gitl and Joey's uncertain English; Mamie's grand-lady allures; Jake's fears of being "green"). Linguistically, we can point out the following:

- *bilingualism* (link: Bilingualism) is a central point;
- *code-switching* (link: Code-switching) (e.g. *oysgreen* "to stop being 'green'") is a regular feature of speech;
- a non-native (here Yiddish) accent as indicated by the spellings <d> and <t> for <th>; <v> for <w>; <shp> for <sp->; final <f> for <v> (*fife*) and /ŋk/ for /ŋ/ (*not'ink*), and the vowel quality of *coom* and *knu*;
- restriction in stylistic *register* (link: Style) (Mamie's formal dress vs. her informal greeting "*Good-evenin'*") combined with:

- non-native *idioms* (and possibly other *pragmatic* features (link: Pragmatics) of communication) such as "*I should cough,*" a Yiddish idiom rendered in English and meaning "I should care"; plus informal colloquial AmE "*No, sirree!*";

- local native non-standard features (*oncet* for *once*; *foinitsha* for *furniture*) or the flapped /t/ of *shurr-r up* (*shut up*).

Text 10.5 is exemplary of a situation in which first generation immigrants spoke English often highly marked by **first language (L1) interference** (link: Interference). One generation later only a small selection of Yiddish items would remain, perhaps enough to serve as **emblematic markers** (link: Emblematic markers) of a speaker's Yiddish roots, for the L1 was often replaced by English even as the home language. Consequently the retention rates of the heritage language as the home language regularly dropped to only somewhat over half in the second generation and to below 10% in the third (Waggoner 1988: 91ff) according to the *generation model* (link: Generation model). What was true for Yiddish as illustrated here is also true of most immigrant languages. The exception to the high rates of language loss lies with those languages which have a community-based population of speakers or which are reinforced by continuing immigration.

10.5.3 African American Vernacular English (AAVE)

By the nineteenth century AAVE was marked by pronunciation at once reminiscent of the Caribbean creoles (see chapter 9) and of white Southern English. It had grammatical features which corresponded not only to non-standard white vernacular forms but also to distinctively African American ones, including a scattering of Southern and African American lexical items. The following text, in which the pronunciation is indicated in the non-standard spelling, illustrates a number of these features. It is from one of the many dialect stories written by Joel Chandler Harris, a white Southerner (Plate 10.5). This particular selection uses two varieties of AAVE. The frame story, featuring the white child of the plantation owner, is in StE. The characters Uncle Remus and 'Tildy use stereotypical, literary nineteenth century Southern AAVE, and Daddy Jack uses a creolized variety, perhaps reminiscent of the *Gullah* Creole (link: Gullah) spoken on the Sea Islands of South Carolina and Georgia. Daddy Jack's pidgin-creole forms are in blue. A StE version is given in the right-hand column.

Text 10.6 Nineteenth century AAVE and Creole English: J.C. Harris, "Why the Alligator's Back is Rough" (excerpt)

The night after the violent flirtation between Daddy Jack and 'Tildy, the latter . . . took the child by the hand, and together they went to Uncle Remus's cabin. The old man was making a door-mat of shucks and grass and white-oak splits, and Daddy Jack was dozing in the corner.

"*W'at I tell you, Brer Jack?*" *said Uncle Remus, as 'Tildy came in.* "*Dat gal atter you, mon!*"	"What did I tell you, Brother Jack?" . . . "That girl is after you, man!"

"Fer de Lord sake, Unk' Remus, don't start dat ole nigger. I done promise Miss Sally dat I won't kill 'im, en I like ter be good ez my word; but ef he come foolin' longer me I'm des nat'ally gwine ter onj'int 'im. Now you year me say de word."

. . .

"For the Lord's sake, Uncle Remus, don't start that old nigger [talking]. I have promised Miss Sally that I won't kill him, and I like to be as good as my word; but if he comes fooling around me I'm just naturally going to unjoint him. Now you hear me say the word."

After a while the little boy grew restless, and presently he said: "Daddy Jack, you know you promised to tell me a story to-night."

"He wukkin' wid it now, honey," said Uncle Remus, soothingly. "Brer Jack," he continued, "wa'n't dey sump'n' n'er 'bout ole man Yalligater?"

"Hi!" exclaimed Daddy Jack, arousing himself, " 'e 'bout B'er 'Gater fer true. Oona no bin see da' B'er 'Gater?"

. . .

"Dem all sem," continued Daddy Jack. "Big mout', pop-eye, walk on 'e belly;

. . .

"One tam Dog is bin run B'er Rabbit, tel 'e do git tire; da' Dog is bin run 'im tel him ent mos' hab no bre't' in 'e body; 'e hide 'ese'f by de crik side.

. . .

"'Eh-eh! B'er 'Gater, I hab bin come 'pon trouble. Dog, 'e do run un-a run me. . . . I proud fer yeddy Dog bark, et 'e is bin fetch-a me trouble lak dem.' "

"He's working on it now, honey. . . . Brother Jack, wasn't there something or other about Old Man Alligator?"

"Hi! . . . It's about Brother Alligator, for sure. Have you all seen that Brother Alligator?"

"They're all the same,". . . .

"[He has] a big mouth, pop-eyes, walks on his belly;
. . .

"One time Dog was chasing Brother Rabbit till he was getting tired; then Dog was chasing him till he almost didn't have any breath in his body; he hid himself by the creek-side. . . .

"'Oh-oh, Brother Alligator, I have met with trouble. Dog's been chasing and chasing me. . . . I am proud to hear Dog bark, he's been making me trouble like that.' "

(J.C. Harris (1881) *Nights with Uncle Remus. Myths and Legends of the Old Plantation*. Boston: Houghton Mifflin, 141ff.)

Among the more noticeable features of AAVE we find the following (not an exhaustive list):

nineteenth century Southern AAVE ('Tildy, Uncle Remus)

nineteenth century AACE (Daddy Jack)

Pronunciation:
- elision of intervocalic /ð/ (*Brer* "brother"; *n'er* "nother")
- /d/ for /ð/ (*dat*)
- /j/ before initial vowels (*year* "hear"; *yalligator*)
- non-rhoticity (*wukkin'*)
- loss of final consonant (*ole* "old")

elision of /r/ and /ð/ (*B'er*)

/d/ for /ð/ (*dem*)

/j/ before initial vowel + enclitic *-y* (*yeddy* "hear")

[a] for /aɪ/ (*tam* "time"; *lak* "like")

loss of final consonant (*tire* "tired")

- loss of initial unstressed syllable (*'Tildy* "Matilde")
- *gwine*, "going"; *onj'int* "un-joint"
- unpalatalized (link: Palatalization) *nat'ally* and *des* /nætəlɪ/ and /des/

loss of initial unstressed syllable (*'bout*, *'Gater*)
/b/ or /ß/ for /v/ (*hab*)
–

Grammar:
- ***zero copula*** (link: Copula deletion), i.e. no use of the linking verb *be* (*Dat gal atter you, mon!*; *He wukkin' wid it now, honey*)

- progressive marker deletion (= zero copula) (*He wukkin' wid it now*)
- no ending, but juxtaposition to mark the possessive (*Lord sake*)

- –

- –

- perfective marker *done* (*I done promise Miss Sally*)
- no 3rd person sg. pres. tense {-s} (*ef he come*)

zero copula (*Dem all sem*)
infinitive marker *fer* (*I proud fer yeddy*)

progressive marker *do* (*'e do git* "he was getting") or *is* (*is bin run B'er Rabbit*)
3rd person singular pronoun *'e* "he, she, it" (all cases) (*'e 'bout B'er 'Gater fer true*; *'e belly, 'e bahk, 'e tail*)
3rd person plural *dem* "they" (*Dem all sem*)
2nd person plural pronoun *oona*
remote tense marker *bin* (*Oona no bin see . . .*)
pre-verbal negation *no* (*Oona no bin see. . .*)
past tense negative marker plus double negation (*ent mos' hab no bre't*)

In present-day AAVE the more strongly creole features as seen in the Harris text have disappeared, as have a number of the pronunciation features (elision of intervocalic /ð/; initial <y> /j/; /ɑ:/ for /æ/; /e/ for /eɪ/; *gwine*; /aɪ/ for /ɔɪ/; /b/ or /ß/ for /v/ (*hab*); unpalatalized /nætəlɪ/). Among the grammatical items once again the more creole forms (pre-verbal markers of negation, tense, and progressive aspect) do not occur. However, stressed auxiliary *bín* does serve as a remote marker (*They bín sittin' there* "They have been sitting there for a long time") and unstressed *done* continues to be used as a perfective marker (*They done done it* "They have finished doing it"), as does the zero copula. Furthermore, a new form, ***invariant*** be (link: Invariant *be*), is spreading as a marker of the ***habitual*** (link: Habitual aspect), for example *They be yellin' and stuff* ("They are always yelling and so on") (see Green 1998, 2004). The following short excerpt from Alice Walker's *The Color Purple* (1982) illustrates some of the grammatical features of contemporary AAVE (even though the story plays in the early twentieth century).

Text 10.7 Twentieth century African American Vernacular English

I was in town sitting on the wagon while Mr. —— was in the dry good store. I seen my baby girl. I knowed it was her. She look just like me and my daddy. Like more us then us is ourself.

> *She be tagging long hind a lady and they be dress just alike. They pass the wagon and I speak.*
> *The lady speak pleasant. My little girl she look up and sort of frown. She fretting over*
> *something. She got my eyes just like they is today. Like everything I seen, she seen, and she*
> *pondering it.*
>
> (A. Walker (1982) *The Color Purple*. New York: Pocket Books, 14)

A number of grammatical features are typical of general non-standard vernacular English (*I seen, I knowed*); similarly the use of an adjective for an adverb (*speak pleasant*), the **pleonastic subject** (*My little girl she*) ([link: Pleonastic subjects](#)), and the singular ending on *ourself*. The non-marking of the past or past participle (*She look, be dress, they pass, I speak, she frown*) are more of a problem. In the cases of *look, dress, pass,* and *frown* it is possible to see the lack of marking as a simple question of the loss of the final consonant of a potential **consonant cluster**, for example in *looked* /-kt/ → /k/; this is, however, not a possible interpretation with *speak* for *spoke*; and the occurrence of *was, seen,* and *got* indicates that some past tense forms are marked (see Fasold 1972: chap. 2). The lack of {-s} in *she look* is commonplace in AAVE (cf. ibid.: chap. 3), as is its use with non-third person singular subject (not present in Text 10.7), but where this use of {-s} comes from is unclear (a continuation of the historical loss of inflections in English or an independent development in AAVE, in the case of {-s}-loss or the adoption and retention of the **Northern Subject Rule** ([link: Northern Subject Rule](#)) in the case of "overuse"). Zero copula is common here as in the Harris text, but invariant *be*[6] (*She be tagging long* and *they be dress*) is an innovation. Its ultimate source may lie in the use of the habitual modal auxiliary *will*, as used in making predictions (*Boys will be boys; He'll be sitting there staring into space*). In AAVE /l/ is frequently deleted (or vocalized), which would give us *Boys be boys; He be sitting there staring into space*). Once established, this pattern could easily have developed into present-day AAVE invariant *be*.

10.5.3.1 The phonology of the AAVE vowel system

Until the time of World War I most African Americans lived in the South, and they shared a unitary vowel system with white Southerners. Evidence from recordings made of Southern blacks born in the nineteenth century (1840s and 1850s) shows a number of similarities to Caribbean creoles: no fronting of the back vowels /uː/ and /ʊ/ or the first element of /aʊ/ (as among white Southern speakers) and monophthongal /eː/ and /oː/ (whites: diphthongal). Gradually /eː/ and /oː/ began to diphthongize, but fronting did not take place; the change of /aɪ/ to a short glide or monophthongal /a/ before voiced **obstruents** (Daddy Jack's *tam* "time") and the raising of /æ/ appear as independent AAVE developments (/æ/-raising is still not a part of Southern white pronunciation) (Bailey and Thomas 1998: 97ff). As Bailey and Thomas write about Southern white English and AAVE: "Some of the

---

6 Fasold 1972 calls this "distributive *be*"; elsewhere other terms are also used, for example "habitual *be*" (Fought 2003).

differences reflect the unique origins of AAVE, but others reflect innovations in white speech that did not develop in AAVE or innovations in AAVE that never spread to white vernaculars" (ibid.: 104). Since non-fronting and /æ/-raising remain features of many African American speakers, even for people whose grammar and lexis are standard, "vowel differences provide many of the phonological cues that listeners use in ethnic identification" (ibid.: 105).

10.5.4 Spanish-influenced English, especially *Chicano English (CE)* (link: Chicano English)

CE is a term which may be applied to a wide variety of dialects spoken by people of Mexican origin in the United States. It may be virtually identical with local Anglo varieties or may be English spoken by immigrants with a high degree of first-language interference. The CE of Los Angeles is distinct from both California Anglo English and AAVE, with which it is in contact. Furthermore, there are no signs of its being abandoned by its speech community, for:

> It is an important cultural marker, a reminder of linguistic history, and a fertile field for the study of language contact phenomena and linguistic identity issues. . . . Chicano English can vary on a continuum from less to more standard and from less to more influence by other dialects, and it encompasses a wide range of stylistic options.
>
> (Fought 2003: 2–3)

Part of the linguistic history of CE lies in its pronunciation, more so than in its grammar or semantics (ibid.: 226), but it is *not* a non-native variety (with interference from Spanish). It may contain the occasional Spanish word as a kind of emblematic marker of ethnic identity (ibid.: 6). In order to better estimate (1) to what extent it is ethnic in nature and (2) how stable (i.e. not merely a matter of interference from Spanish) we will look at some of its features.

10.5.4.1 Pronunciation differences

CE differs from non-native Spanish-influenced English in the realization of consonants. As might be expected among speakers with an (American) Spanish background, dental [d̪, t̪] often replace /ð, θ/, and consonant cluster reduction is common, for example *least* as /lis/; *hardware* as /hawɚ/ (Fought 2003: 67ff). Yet: "the sound systems of native and non-native English speakers are actually quite different" (ibid.: 63). CE speakers (but not Spanish native speakers) have T-flapping, do not have an epenthetic /ə/ before initial /sp-/ ("*espent*"), and do not merge /b/ and /v/, use /dʒ/ for /j/ (*you = Jew*), or merge /æ/ and /ɑ/ or /e/ and /eɪ/ (ibid.: 83–86). The alternation of /tʃ/ and /ʃ/, though highly stigmatized, is a feature of CE (Peñalosa 1980: 37).

10.5.4.2 Vowels

In general, CE speakers have less vowel reduction than Anglo native-speakers, perhaps due to the syllable-timing of this accent, and stress patterns lie somewhere between Anglo English and Mexican Spanish norms (ibid.: 72, 76). While Spanish interference would suggest the replacement of short /ɪ/ by tense /i/, they are distinguished in CE, even though their lexical distribution is different than among Anglos (Fought 2003: 65).

Two very prominent shifts are /u/-fronting and /æ/-raising (see above 10.3.3). In CE /u/-fronting to [ʉ], as in *look*, is best described as a complex interaction of social features. For people with greater [ʉ]-fronting we find two or more of the features "female; middle class; non-gang member." People with two or more of the features "male; working class; gang member or affiliate" have less [ʉ]-fronting. This shows that identities are constructed in a complex fashion and are not dependent on single features such as class or gender (ibid.: 122ff, 139).

As for /æ/-backing and /æ/-raising, some speakers frequently do both; and all speakers have at least some raising while some never back. Raising is especially common before nasals (so is some backing). A preceding liquid also increases backing, and, finally, men raise more than women (ibid.: 127–128, 134).

10.5.4.3 Grammatical variation

Much less characteristic of CE than pronunciation, grammatical variation includes the dropping of the past and past participial ending {-D}, which may be as much a matter of pronunciation as of grammar (see 10.5.3). There is widespread use of multiple negation. One sample contained 323 negations from twenty-eight speakers with a rate of multiple negation of 41% or more (ibid.: 142).[7] The question in regard to historical development is whether this is due to the influence of Spanish, which regularly uses multiple negation (*A mí no me gusta **nada*** "I don't like nothing"), whether it is borrowed from non-standard GenE or AAVE, or whether it is an independent development within CE. Male speakers show more evidence of influence from AAVE in regard to multiple negation and also more instances of invariant *be*. In contrast, female speakers probably incorporate more features of Spanish and seem to have a more positive attitude toward Spanish (ibid.: 149).

10.5.4.4 Bilingualism

Bilingualism is clearly not a prerequisite for being a speaker of CE, research has shown that the Spanish retention rates resemble those of other immigrant languages, that is, a loss of bilingualism in the second generation and a third generation with little more than a passive proficiency in Spanish (see 10.5.2). This confirms the high prestige and economic advantages of being a competent speaker of English. Yet Spanish is associated with ethnic pride, whichs leads to the use, even in the case of speakers whose Spanish is not fully fluent, of emblematic code-switching, in which, for example, a person may refer not to her *godmother*, but to her *nina* (Silva-Corvalán 1994: 11; Peñalosa 1980: 49; Fought 2003: 158; see link: Language loss).

10.5.4.5 Language attitudes

Most language users sound like the people they like and spend time with. The following text illustrates this very nicely for a young boy of Chinese descent, who finds recognition

---

7 Wolfram (1974) reports 87.4% among Puerto Rican English speakers (quoted in Fought 2003: 142).

and self-esteem in his relation to an older man (Tío Hector) who gives him the love and attention he needs. Note that this text shows not just English–Spanish code-switching (Spanish or Spanish-influenced English in italics), but also the enormous influence of AAVE (in blue).

Text 10.8 Spanish–English code-switching

I told Tío Hector Pueblo what I was doing. . . . Hector had said that he was going to teach me "street," . . .

"I ready, Tío," I said. I flexed my right arm, showing him my new, developing bicep.

"Say, *soy listo*. Dat mean, 'I ready,'" he said. "Dat's a mighty fine muscle, my fren'," he added, nodding his head and pursing his lips in stern approval.

"*Soy listo, Tío*," I said. "Teach me secret kick?"

Instead, he taught me how to walk.

"*Joven*," he said, "you *walkando como un armadillo* dat go from four leg to two leg." . . .

"*Joven*, you gotta show some *prestigio*. You gotta roll yo' shoulder *back*. Now, put up yo' head, *tu cabeza*. Lif up high. Keep yo' back mo' straight. Don forget yo' shoulder. . . . *Jesus Cristo*, wha's wrong wif yo' body, *chico*? Now, you try, take step same time – " . . .

"*Cho*' anger, *niño*! *Enojado*! You pissed! All dese kids pound you, you *angry!* Even if yo' li'l body all shrivel' up an bent, no matta! Mean mug, dat's good. Now, you practice yo' anger face." . . .

"I wan rearn [Chinese interference: /r/ for /l/] secret kick," I said. . . .

"*Niño*, firs' you need a face. *Tu cara bonita*, it look so empty. Dat piss kids off, dey tink dey got no effec' on you.

"Yo' *cara*, *she* start more *fight* den no secret kick can finish, you get my meaning," he said. I thought he was talking about cars in his shop [Tío Hector runs a car repair shop].

"*Cara bonita*. Han'some face. Yo' han'some face, *niño. Hombre!* You so much work! I gotta teach *walkando*, yo' face, gotta teach yo' secret kick, gotta teach you *Español, también!*

"*Escucheme, joven*. You get big, someday, you 'member Hector Pueblo, *hokay?*" He smiled and rubbed my hair.

When I started taking formal Spanish language classes in junior high, I persisted in the belief that *walkando* was the correct idiomatic gerund for the infinitive *andar*, to walk.

"*Señor Losada*," I said. "*Yo aprendí Español cuando era un joven, y la palabra correcta es 'walkando.'*"

(G. Lee (1994) *China Boy*. New York: Plume, 180ff.)

Despite the openness that this text bears witness to, the reality of North America is different. Few language questions generate such widespread engagement as the presence of the large number of Spanish speakers in more and more areas. Although the generation model seems to apply and 98% of the US population is at least minimally fluent in English, many monolingual speakers of English are alarmed at what some see as the immanent take-over of

English-speaking America by Mexicans and other Latin Americans (the *reconquista*). This has activated a number of nativist movements such as English Only and US English (link: English Only and US English) and has led more and more states to pass laws making English their official language (see Wiley 2004). This goes very much against the strong traditions of tolerance in what is in essence a country of immigrants, only some of whom came from English-speaking countries.

10.6 Summary

North American English is a collection of varieties with a number of often very different historical roots. The English which first reached the continent was highly influenced by nautical jargons, but the English of the settler communities which followed from the early seventeenth century on reflected their contact with Native Americans and with settlers speaking other European languages, but was above all the product of the English the settlers had brought with them. Nevertheless, AmE developed differently due to koinéization. Yet in the course of time distinct regional varieties of AmE emerged, initially a North–South (New England–Virginia) split, to which a Midlands and Western area could soon be added. A further colonial influence on AmE was the English of the African slaves.

After independence a basic, probably long-standing split between the standard language and non-standard General English became ever more evident. Today regional distinctions remain important, especially in regard to pronunciation, and continue to evolve in the form of the vowel shifts chiefly centered around a number of cities and their surrounding regions. In addition, ethnic varieties are of importance even though immigrant varieties largely tend to follow the generation model of movement toward assimilation by the third generation, as we saw in the case of Jewish-Yiddish immigrants and, in tendency, among Spanish-language immigrants as well. The two "*autochthonous*" ethnic groups reviewed, American Indians and African Americans, still retain distinct language varieties, but with the important difference that while AIE is very fragmented in nature, AAVE is – despite its wide geographic distribution – surprisingly similar and has been developing features of its own independent of whatever sources may originally have fed into it.

STUDY QUESTIONS

Social and cultural background

1. Contrast the traditions represented by the Puritans and by frontiersmen.
2. What were the major sources of the population of New England, the Middle colonies, the Chesapeake Bay area, and the back country?
3. What were the significant class/status differences in the slave population? Explain why these distinctions were important.

4. Explain how the generation model works. How does it apply to American Indians, Chicanos, and Jewish immigrants?

Linguistic background

1. Characterize the kinds of words borrowed into AmE from the American Indian languages.
2. Explain what is meant by koinéization. What speaks for it and what against it (as a formative force in AmE)?
3. Characterize the effect of region on North American English. What is more characteristic of region, pronunciation or vocabulary?
4. Is Canadian English a regional variety of AmE or are AmE and CanE distinct varieties? Support your position with arguments.
5. Why do you think that spelling is often so emotional a topic? Think about American vs. British spelling (e.g. <curb> vs. <kerb>) and about correct vs. incorrect spellings (e.g. <attendance> vs. <attendence>).
6. Why is grammar such an emotional issue? Think about *dived* vs. *dove* or *She don't live here no more* vs. *She doesn't live here any more*. How important is understandability? How important is appropriateness to the social situation? Explain when the *She don't* sentence would be the wisest choice and when the *She doesn't* one would be.
7. How does language reflect ethnic identity? Make reference to bilingualism and code-switching.

Further reading

Chambers discusses the standard in regard to CanE. Crosby gives a fascinating account of the role of disease in destroying large portions of the Native American population. Finegan and Rickford contains contributions on a variety of aspects of AmE and includes Wolfram's overview of social variety in AmE. Fought is the best current study of Chicano English. Various aspects of AAVE are treated in the articles in Mufwene et al. Current vowel shifts in AmE are well described in Labov, but this is demanding reading for the uninitiated. For an excellent summary of social dialect in AmE see Wolfram.

Chambers, J.K. (1986) "Three Kinds of Standard in Canadian English," In: W.C. Lougheed (ed.) *In Search of a Standard in Canadian English*. Kingston: Queen's University, 1–15.
Crosby, A.W. (2003) *The Columbian Exchange. Biological and Cultural Consequences of 1492*. rev. ed. Westport: Praeger.
Finegan, E. and J.R. Rickford (eds.) (2004) *Language in the USA. Themes for the Twenty-first Century*. Cambridge: CUP.
Fought, C. (2003) *Chicano English in Context*. London; Palgrave/Macmillan.

Labov, W. (1991) "The Three Dialects of English," In: P. Eckert (ed.) *New Ways of Analyzing Sound Change*. San Diego: Academic Press, 1–44.

Mufwene, S.S., J. Rickford, G. Bailey, J. Baugh (eds.) (1998) *African-American English. Structure, History, and Use*. London. Routledge.

Wolfram, W. (2004) "Social Varieties of American English," In: E. Finegan and J.R. Rickford (eds.), 58–75.

CHAPTER ELEVEN

English in the ENL communities of the Southern Hemisphere (since 1788)

It is therefore ordered and adjudged by this Court, that you be transported upon the seas, beyond the seas, to such place as His Majesty, by the advice of His Privy Council, shall think fit to direct and appoint, for the term of your natural life.

(Court sentence for penal transportation, R. Hughes, *The Fatal Shore*. New York: Knopf, 1987: 129)

The very day we landed upon the Fatal Shore,
The planters stood around us, full twenty score or more;
They ranked us up like horses and sold us out of hand,
They chained us up to pull the plough, upon Van Diemen's Land

(Convict ballad, c. 1825–30)

Chapter Overview:

This chapter:

- explores three major ENL varieties: Australian English (AusE), South African English (SAfE), and New Zealand English (NZE);
- compares and contrasts the closely related settlement history and demographics of the three varieties;
- focuses on the changing character of the (linguistic) relationship between these countries and Britain by looking at a selection of linguistic features intended to emphasize both similarities and differences in the grammar and pronunciation of these national varieties;
- exemplifies further specific features of these three varieties in the areas of vocabulary and pragmatics;
- points out that internal regional, social, and ethnic differences in the three countries resemble each other only in the most general terms;
- considers the influence of the autochthonous languages of each country on English.

11.1 Social-historical background

The movement of large numbers of people from the British Isles to its Southern Hemisphere colonies was a part of a major outward extension of Europeans into overseas territories (see chapter 7). Europe was unique in the Modern World in being able to export its excess population into territories regarded as empty. One of the results of this is has been the Europeanization of vast parts of the extra-European world, including Australia, South Africa, and New Zealand, where the English language was transplanted along with the people (link: European expansion and the concept of the frontier).

11.1.1 The situation in Great Britain and Ireland

Even before the beginning of the Modern English period population movement was considerable in England and was eventually to affect Scotland, Wales, and Ireland as well. The motor behind this lay in the gradual move from a subsistence and barter economy to a supra-regional and international market on a monetary basis. This was characterized by the improved, expanding, and increasingly specialized production of goods. At first slowly and then more and more rapidly the rural population left the countryside for goals in the cities, in the case of England, especially London. A trickle of people emigrating from Britain had already begun in the seventeenth century and before, and soon gained in momentum. The first of many goals abroad was Ireland under the Tudors, the Stewarts, and Oliver Cromwell (see chapter 8). This emigration was extended to the Caribbean, especially Barbados (chapter 9), and then to North America (chapter 10).

Emigration to the three countries which are the subject of this chapter was a later development, starting only in 1788 with Australia. One of the consequences of this is that the people who left for these new territories were much more likely to be urban in character (cf. Gordon and Sudbury 2002: 68ff). Urbanization led many of those who left their rural settings to London and the newly industrializing cities of the Midlands and the North, where they made their new homes. For others these cities were only an intermediate station on the way abroad. Initially, many of these people, impoverished and driven into petty crime, were sentenced to forced transport to the penal colonies of New South Wales (1787–88), Tasmania (1803), Queensland (1824), and, briefly, Western Australia (1851) until this system was abolished in 1868 (Plate 11.1).[1] The objectives of penal transportation were summarized at the time as deterrence of crime, reform of the criminals, and coloniza-tion of the new territories, while ridding the homeland of unwanted population. Those who emigrated voluntarily shared a lot as far as their origins are concerned. The linguistic conse-quence of their route abroad by way of the cities of England, especially London, meant that the new Anglophone inhabitants of the Southern Hemisphere colonies were familiar with the urban *koinés* of England and would retain relatively little of their traditional, local dialects. And even where they did retain elements of the latter, the long-term influence of the regional vernaculars would be overall small.

---

1 Early on prisoners, perhaps as many as 50,000 to 60,000, were also transported to the North American colonies: New England, Georgia, and Virginia (see for example Defoe's novel *Moll Flanders*, 1722). After American independence a new goal was needed, hence Australia.

11.1.2 Goals of emigration and transportation

11.1.2.1 Australia

The Europeans arriving in Australia did not find an empty land, but one with a population of indigenous peoples numbering approximately 500,000 – plus or minus 200,000. These people spoke a diversity of languages, perhaps as many as 250 different ones, of which fewer than 20 are still spoken by the youngest generation of today's 550,000 indigenous Australians, who themselves make up only 2.7% of the population. The remaining Aboriginal languages are threatened by extinction in a society in which virtually everyone speaks English.

Approximately 165,000 prisoners were transported over a period of some eighty years (1788–1868). A far larger number of voluntary settlers were attracted to the new continent during the gold rush of 1851–71, and many of them will have reinforced the linguistic traits already established.[2] The English of the convicts was largely that of Southern England as over two-thirds of the prisoners were English (or Welsh); about a quarter were Irish. The largest number of prisoners probably spoke London English and may well be the source of the Cockney-like vowel shifts found in Broad Australian, which is spoken by 34% of Australian speakers according to Delbridge (1970: 19). The officer class,[3] which took charge of the administration of the penal colonies, was presumably one of the sources of what was to become either Cultivated Australian (11%) or General Australian (55%) (ibid.). In any case, AusE is largely urban Southern English in character.

With the move from a white-only policy of immigration which was in effect from 1901 till 1973 more and more immigrants to Australia are now arriving from countries other than the United Kingdom. Today between a fifth and a quarter of the population of around 24 million are foreign born. Over a million of these 6 million people come from the UK and nearly 500,000 from New Zealand. Other European countries, especially Italy, Greece, Germany, and The Netherlands, are the origin of approximately 1 million new Australians. About 220,000 come from South Africa, the US and Canada and over 650,000 from Asia. Australia is, as a result, a multilingual society in which almost everyone can speak English, even though some of the English spoken, especially in the sugar plantations of Queensland as well as among some of the non-urban Aboriginal Australians, is a creolized variety which diverges considerably from GenE (see 11.5.3).

11.1.2.2 South Africa

The Khoisan[4] peoples of *southern Africa* were subject to incursions from both the north and the south. From the north came the Bantu peoples, originally from *West Africa*, and

---

2 The major linguistic difference in comparison with North America lay in the higher number of immigrants in America coming directly from distinct regions such as East Anglia or Ulster without lengthy interludes in the cities. Early immigration to America also largely predated the loss of rhoticity and reflects a somewhat different continuation of the GVS.

3 Over 500 officers, marines, and their families were among the more than 1300 who arrived with the First Fleet in 1788. The actual number of officers was, however, miniscule.

4 Aka Hottentots (Khoikhoi) and Bushmen (San), names which are today regarded by many as derogatory.

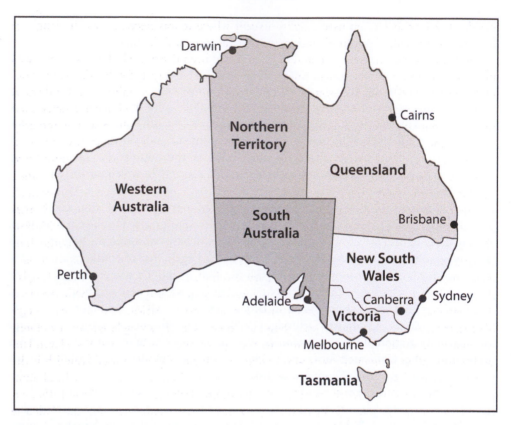

Map 11.1 Australia

from the sea came the Europeans, principally the Dutch, who colonized the Cape Town area from 1652 on. Among the Bantus it was especially the Zulus who later offered armed resistance to British and Afrikaner colonialism. The English language came with the British conquest of the Dutch colony between 1795 and 1806. In 1820 the first contingent of settlers from England, some 5000, including 1000 children, arrived in the Eastern Cape region. These people represented "a microcosm of nineteenth century Britain" minus the aristocracy (Gordon and Sudbury 2002: 73). Since half came from Middlesex and the Home Counties (ibid.) the language which prevailed was a rapidly koinéized type of Southern English which reflected the lower middle-class and lower-class speech of the London area. From that point on English was a distinct presence in South Africa. A second major period of British settlement lay between 1848 and 1862 in Natal. Here the social origins of the settlers were more clearly middle or upper middle class. Natal retained such social distinctions more rigidly and was also a more urban settlement than the Cape British. With this development two distinctive types of White South African English (WSAfE) were established: a Cape variety with little prestige and the Natal variety as something of a standard – generally oriented toward British StE and an RP accent. The people to be known as Black Africans and Coloureds as well as the laborers imported from India – approximately 150,000 between 1860 and 1911 (ibid.: 74) – together with the *Afrikaans*-speaking Boers and the British settlers were the majors inhabitants of nineteenth century South Africa. Few besides the British settlers used English except where it was necessary as the language imposed by the colonial administration and in education and the press.

From the 1870s on, after gold and diamonds had been discovered, there was increased immigration from Europe, though chiefly from Britain. New largely English-language cities in the north such as Johannesburg, which were centered around mining and industrial processing, grew up. The dominant position of the British and of the English language led to resentment and armed resistance on the part of the Afrikaners, which was temporarily settled in the Boer wars, the second of which (1899–1902) cemented British power and led to the establishment of the Union of South Africa (1909). The Union recognized two official languages, Afrikaans and English. The two stood in competition with each other, but together they effectively served to maintain white minority privilege and power in all spheres of life. Within the framework of the Union voting rights were restricted to Whites and the Cape Coloureds, but when the National Party took power in 1948, it withdrew voting rights from the Cape Coloureds and began to institute the policy of apartheid, or "separateness." Under the National Party an attempt was undertaken to make Afrikaans rather than English the language of secondary and higher education and to make English inaccessible to Black South Africans. Eventually, this policy failed as English was perceived as the language of education and opportunity for Black South Africans and as the language of resistance, espoused by the African National Congress, in the struggle against the repressive apartheid policies. With the complete opening of South Africa in 1994, eleven languages (out of an estimated twenty-five) were constitutionally recognized. English is the first language of over 8% of the South African population, thus coming behind Zulu (23.8%), Xhosa (17.6%), Afrikaans (13.3%), Northern Sotho (9.4%), and Tswana (8.2%), but before Sotho (7.9%), Tsonga (4.4%), Swati (2.7%), Venda (2.3%), and Ndebele (1.6%). What has emerged is justifiably termed "asymmetrical multilingualism" since English has not only retained its primacy in education, the economy, and government, but also remains relatively unmarked as an inter-ethnic means of communication and serves as the most general *lingua franca* in the country. Indeed, English is the medium of instruction in the vast majority of schools due to the low economic and educational value attributed to the Bantu languages. English, seen as an important key to information, learning, literature, and current affairs, is regarded as the means of access to job opportunities. Those without English may be barred from many such opportunities, and speakers with little or the "wrong" kind of English may be at a disadvantage. WSAfE continues to be the standard, and following the collapse of apartheid, children from "non-white" communities who attend (prestigious) schools which uphold WSAfE norms are increasingly adopting these norms into their own speech. At the less prestigious end of the spectrum, Broad WSAfE varieties tend to merge with second language Afrikaans English (generally the norm of White Afrikaners who are bilingual, or, in the Cape, with Cape Flats English, which is mainly associated with "Coloured" people (Bowerman 2004a: 935). On the other hand, Black South African English (BSAfE), an ESL variety, has emerged with its own linguistic features and is fulfilling an identitarian function in the Black South African community: "Black English is the established symbol of identity, solidarity and the aspirations of black South Africans" (Lanham 1996: 27; see also Branford 1996; see 12.1.2 for more on Black SAfE and English in the neighboring countries of South Africa).

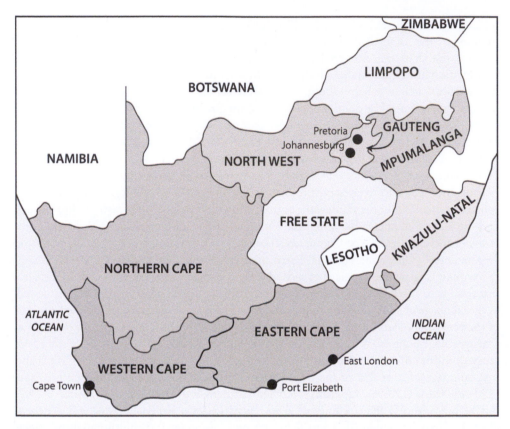

Map 11.2 South Africa

11.1.2.3 New Zealand

New Zealand was opened for settlement by the British in 1840, when the British Crown concluded the Treaty of Waitangi, signed by many (about 430), though not all, of the Māori chiefs of New Zealand (Plate 11.2). The presence of indigenous people makes New Zealand similar to both Australia and South Africa (as well as North America, of course), but the fact that the Māoris were united by a shared language made them quite different, as did the ordered nature suggested by the Treaty. In strong contrast to South Africa, where the African languages are vital, but similar to the Aboriginal languages in Australia, Māori is in decline. Its weakened status may be the reason it was declared an official language of the country in 1987. There has been state-financed television broadcasting in Māori since 2004. The language is spoken chiefly by Māoris, who make up just over 4% of the population, but less than 20% of them can still speak it (cf. Benton 1991: 187; figure updated).

The nature of the settlers is a further parallel to Australia since many of them came from New South Wales, thus establishing in New Zealand a variety of English only marginally different from AusE.[5] "Even now the similarities in pronunciation and older vocabulary

---

5 McKinnon (1997) gives, for settlement from 1840 to 1880: England 49%; Scotland 22%; Ireland 20%; Australia 7%.

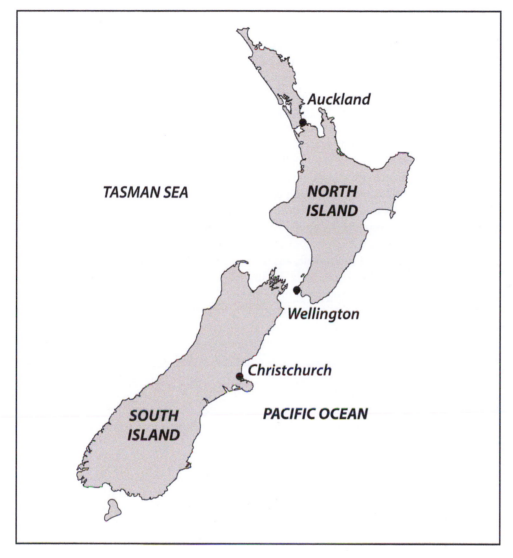

Map 11.3 New Zealand

suggest a single [AusE-NZE] dialect area with two major subdivisions" (Turner 1970: 85). In fact, before 1840 approximately 2000 English-speaking people were already living in New Zealand as whalers or as Christian missionaries, most of whom went there by way of Australia. Regular settlement had its sources in Australia and Britain, but without transported convicts. Between 1854 and 1870, and including the gold rush of 1861, 7239 arrived from Britain, of whom 30% were from Scotland, and 4523 from Australia (Gordon and Deverson 1985: 18). Today almost all of the approximately 4 million New Zealanders speak English, which is again similar to Australia – and very different from South Africa – and they sound *to outsiders* like Australians. New Zealand is 85% urban and here, too, similar to Australia with its urban population of over 90%. The figure for South Africa is less than 60%.

11.1.3 Standard and non-standard English in the Southern Hemisphere

The use of English was never really called into question in any of these territories, not even in South Africa, where English was not the numerically dominant language. The real question was what type of English would prevail. The source of the settlers, primarily Southern England and London, makes it clear that what this book has termed *General English* ([link: The emergence of non-standard General English](#)) would be the obvious choice. Yet, Southern English existed in two very distinct varieties, the StE of the higher social classes and the non-standard speech of the majority. The forces of standardization and prescriptivism, as seen in the English of the British Isles and North America in the seventeenth and eighteenth centuries, were a major factor in Australia, South Africa, and New Zealand as well. One of the main effects of the spread of the standard was the idea that anything besides it denoted inferiority, all the more so, the further the speakers were from England. The conservative SAfE accent, for example, still emulates RP despite the reality of the SAfE pronunciations of most speakers (Mazzon 2000b: 77). Eventually, however, the very distance to England was to ensure the adoption of elements of the covert norm as part of overt local standards. In any case, the new norms were seldom highly divergent from usage in the Southeast of England.

The new standards were sometimes justified by their users as features preserved from an older, purer form of English long since lost in England. The sense of a standard was also supported by the enormous relative uniformity of local usage over wide geographic territory (cf. ibid.: 76). Ancient complaints about the (largely fictive) loss of intelligibility brought forward in the cause of conservative norms were sometimes jettisoned as the strength of national identities prevailed. On the other hand, the roots of AusE in non-standard London English guaranteed there would continue to be struggles around less prestigious local AusE forms, such as Cockney greetings and swearwords and numerous vowel realizations. To some extent the national openness to new native norms joined forces with non-standard forms in the standardization process, thus giving legitimacy to what was once condemned – at least until the hegemony of the new national standard once again plastered over the everyday reality of divergent local usage.

Pronunciation is the most obvious marker of the overseas ENL varieties. Vocabulary follows, as speakers begin to identify *their* words with *their* culture and endow them with legitimacy in the form of dictionaries of national varieties. Acceptance is eased not only by the dictionaries, but by the presence of successful and widely recognized literature in the native idiom – and this is one reason why this book quotes from such writing. It is perhaps the grammar (morphology and syntax) which is slowest to adapt to local usage, most probably because it is here that the weight of the schools and of StE is felt most strongly. Middle-class norms seem to have been authority-based to a high extent among the Anglophone settlers of North America, South Africa, and Australasia.

11.2 Southern Hemisphere English: grammar

Both standard and non-standard English show remarkable similarities in Australia, South Africa, and New Zealand. "White South African English . . . differs little superficially from other first language varieties of English" (Bowerman 2004b: 948). "The morphology and syntax of Standard English in New Zealand do not differ categorically from those of standard British and American English" (Hundt et al. 2004: 560). Indeed, the standard may show divergence between AmE, AusE, BrE, NZE, and SAfE, but they are all "on the same scale," as Collins and Peters (2004: 593) have it.

11.2.1 Standard national Englishes

Every one of these national varieties has irregular verbs which have undergone different sorts and degrees of change in their *principal parts* (link: Reduction of strong verb forms). This is no different than what we observed earlier (see 3.3.2; 4.2.3.1; 6.3.3.1; 8.2.7.1; 10.4). In the end usage everywhere is indeed (1) variable, but (2) this is hardly of major significance since the variants overlap between varieties and nowhere do we come across unique verb forms unknown elsewhere. And as elsewhere a number of the leveled forms are regarded as non-standard, for example *seen* for *saw* or *done* for *did* (Mesthrie 2004a; Pawley 2004; Hundt et al. 2004; see Text 11.1: ll. 5, 14). Numerous grammatical points might be recounted here, for example:

- variation between or mixing of auxiliary and full verb morphology with *need* and *dare*: use of *do* or not in negation and questions; with or without the infinitive marker *to*;
- a different frequency of *shall*: much less common than in BrE; or of *must*: relatively rare in AusE and NZE, but especially frequent in SAfE (link: Modal auxiliaries);
- differences in subject–verb *concord* with collective noun subjects (*team*, *committee*, etc.) (link: Concord, aka agreement).

In this chapter only two cases with results typical of studies of morphology and syntax will be reviewed. They are the findings for the use of the progressive aspect and of the subjunctive.

11.2.1.1 The progressive

It has been observed that the *progressive* is used more widely in Southern Hemisphere ENL communities than in AmE and BrE. This includes the increasing use of the expanded form with stative predicates, especially, for example, of *will* + *be* + V*ing* in NZE, but the differences are statistical and not categorical, cf. Table 11.1, which shows the overall frequencies in six corpora.[6]

What these results indicate is that there has been an increase in the use of the progressive in BrE and AmE over a period of thirty years (columns 1 and 2) and, furthermore, that the higher use of the progressive in AusE and NZE is indicative of the "leading role" of these varieties in this expansion.

---

6 NZE in the Wellington Corpus (WCNZE, 1980s); AusE in the Australian Corpus of English (ACE, 1980s); BrE in the Lancaster-Oslo/Bergen Corpus (LOB, 1961) and thirty years later (1991) in the Freiburg-LOB Corpus (FLOB); AmE in the Brown Corpus (1961) and thirty years later (1992) in the Freiburg-Brown Corpus (Frown).

Table 11.1 Frequencies of progressive aspect in corpora of 1 million words

| LOB (1961) | 606 | Brown (1961) | 593 | WCNZE (1980s) | 802 |
| FLOB (1991) | 716 | Frown (1992) | 663 | ACE (1980s) | 789 |

(Hundt et al. 2004: 569)

11.2.1.2 The mandative subjunctive

The **mandative subjunctive** is marked by the lack of an ending in the present tense and is found after predicates such as *suggest, recommend, be important, be decisive*, and the like, for example *It is mandatory that she **reply** immediately / that she **be** here before the meeting starts* (link: Subjunctive). Here, too, there has been an increase is the use of the subjunctive, as the results in Table 11.2 show. In this case the leader is AmE; and BrE seems to be undergoing a remarkable shift. The results from NZE and AusE are remarkably high but do not tell us anything about change over time.

These two cases indicate very nicely what the general situation is like. All varieties of English are undergoing change, and in the process there is no clear bellwether variety. Furthermore, it is hardly possible to do more than speculate about the sources of change. Was the mandative subjunctive present throughout the history of Southern Hemisphere English or is its high rate of use the result of AmE influence? Or is there some other reason? Both exemplary cases are ones which involve the spread of distinctive forms and which may, therefore, be seen as moving against the general typological current of the leveling of distinctions.[7]

11.2.2 Southern Hemisphere non-standard GenE

Many of the non-standard grammatical forms recounted for the three Southern Hemisphere Englishes are shared not only among them, but with other non-standard varieties as well. Examples of this include:

- demonstrative *them* (see Text 11.1: l. 1; cf. esp. 8.2.1, 3, 8–9);
- the use of past existential *there* with *was* in all persons (*There's dogs*) – or in some varieties with *were* in all persons (see Text 11.1: ll. 1, 3, 11; cf. Tagliamonte 2009; link: Vernacular universals);
- *never* as a general past tense negator, for example SAfE *I made you a cake, but I never brought it* (Bowerman 2004b: 955);

Table 11.2 Mandative subjunctive (vs. *should*): strongest in AmE, then NZE/AusE, then BrE

| Brown | 88.1% | LOB | 12.9% | WCNZE | 66.7% |
| Frown | 89.5% | FLOB | 39.6% | ACE | 77.7% |

(Hunt et al. 2004: 570)

---

7 This is not the same as increased complexity since the extension of the progressive leads to simplification in the choice of the predicates to which it may be applied.

- the greater use of the past for the present perfect (see Text 11.1: l. 16);
- double comparatives, for example NZE *more ragier, more brighter, most luckiest* (Hundt et al. 2004: 486–487);
- double negatives (see Text 11.1: l. 12).

Not all the non-standard forms are shared in an identical fashion. The adoption of a second person plural personal pronoun is found in all the varieties, but with often differing forms. AusE often has *yiz/youse*, NZE has *yous* and *you guys*, Indian SAfE has *y'all*, and Black SAfE has *you people*. Something of the same nature is involved in the adoption of question tags. All these varieties have non-standard tags, but they differ. SAfE uses the unchanging grammatical tag *is it?* as in *The kittens ran away. Is it?* (Bowerman 2004b: 957). NZE has *eh, ne, (h)okay*; AusE has *eh*; AusCE (Kriol), *ngi* or *intit*; Torres Straits CE, *eh*; and Aboriginal English, *you know, init, inti, ina, na* and *ana* (Malcolm 2004: 675). Since tags such as uniform *innit* are known from ESL varieties as well, this may be a universal of simplification.

All of this is not to say that there are not also features of non-standard morphology and syntax unique to the one or the other variety. SAfE *busy* + V*ing*, as in *busy losing my house* or *busy dying* (Bowerman 2004b: 949) is specifically South African and was presumably borrowed from a parallel construction in Afrikaans with *besig*. Southland NZE has *the baby needs fed*; *Will I close the door?*, both Northern or Scottish in origin (Hundt et al. 2004: 587). Perhaps the use of archaic present progressive active for the passive (see Text 11.1: l. 15) should be seen this way as well.

The following text is an example of non-standard AusE. It has been taken from *True History of the Kelly Gang* (2000), a historical novel by Booker Award-winning author Peter Carey. The novel purports to be Ned Kelly's own account of his doings as a bushranger ("bandit") in the late nineteenth century in the outback ("back country") of Victoria. The words in blue are ***non-standard GenE*** grammar (see comments above); those in blue italics are AusE vocabulary items. The underlined words are rural usages.

Text 11.1 Non-standard General AusE

On the back veranda Harry were *holding out my elastic sided boots. When last I saw* them *boots they* was *muddied and sodden but the old* <u>wombat</u> [AusE "small, bear-like marsupial"; meant offensively] *had been to work on them and that surprised me* <u>mightily</u> *for he had a great aversion to menial labour. If this* were *meant to be apology or payment he did not say but he had scraped and oiled and dubbined them until they* was *soft as a lady's purse.*

   Here said he tossing them to me I <u>reckon</u> *you* forget *these when you* run *away. . . .* 5

   There was nothing for me to do but sit down to pull the boots on. My feet must of * *grown for now they pinched my toes.*

   Comfy?

   Yes Harry. 10

You can try them out with *bringing round my horse.*

> I were pledged not to take his orders no more but fair is fair I did require his assistance in the matter of Bill Frost so I went to the _paddock_ [AusE "field (usually fenced in)"] hunting down his poor old switchtailed mare. . . .
> Where's your own nag he said when I come back. Jesus lad the light is wasting. 15
> I didn't say goodbye yet.

(P. Carey, _True History of the Kelly Gang_. New York: Vintage, 2002, 113)
* _Of_ for '_ve_ (=_have_) is a purely non-standard spelling phenomenon.

11.3 Southern Hemisphere English: pronunciation

Each of the three Southern Hemisphere ENL varieties is conveniently divided into three subtypes, most obviously according to their pronunciation. Cultivated English is typically seen as upper middle class and higher and is used at its upper end particularly by women. The Broad variety is more closely associated with men and the working class – and in South Africa is relatively similar to Afrikaans English. Sandwiched between them but growing at the expense of the other two is General. Yet no one uses exclusively Broad, General, or Cultivated pronunciations; the distinctions are quantitative (cf. esp. for AusE, Horvath 2004: 633). Cultivated pronunciations are relatively closer to RP norms while Broad ones are closer to popular London speech. Indeed, Broad Australian shares very much with Cockney. It seems that each of the national varieties was influenced by the earliest immigrants from the Southeast of England, whether lower or higher in social status, as this threefold distinction shows.[8]

These labels should not lead anyone into thinking that the subdivisions within each national variety are more than generally equivalent. The situations in Australia and New Zealand do share a lot, but South Africa is very different due to the fact that, for one, there were two distinct and geographically separate streams of English-language immigrants (see 11.1.2.2) and, for another, ENL speakers have always been in a minority position in South Africa and have practiced widespread (mostly English–Afrikaans) bilingualism. In the following a few major similarities in pronunciation between the three national varieties will be recounted as will some of the important distinguishing features.

11.3.1 Vowel shifts

These are most noticeable vis-à-vis reference pronunciations such as RP or General American. In observing what has happened it is convenient to look separately at the complex vowels, that is, the long ones and diphthongs, then at the short vowels. The following observations focus on the Broad varieties, for this is where change may be observed most freely[9] according to Wells' _lexical sets_ (link: Lexical sets).

---

8 Horvath (2004: 633) argues for a four-way division in AusE in which she divides General into two.
9 For more detail than follows see Wells (1982) on all three and Horvath (2004) on AusE, Bowerman (2004a) on WSAfE, and Bauer and Warren (2004) on NZE. Horvath reports on changes between the 1960s and the 1990s, not all of which fit in with the results given in the following.

FLEECE	/iː/ → /əɪ/
GOOSE	/uː/ → /ᵊɵ̞ː/
NURSE	/ɜː/ → /ɜ̟ː/
FACE	/eɪ/ → /æe/
GOAT	/əʊ/ → /ɐɵ/
THOUGHT	/ɔː/ → /oː/
MOUTH	/aʊ/ → /æo/
PRICE	/aɪ/ → /ɒe/
START	/ɑː/ → /aː/

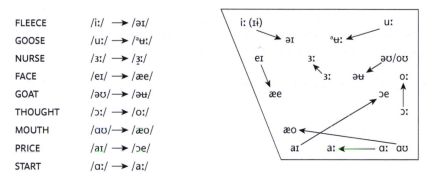

Figure 11.1 The Southern Hemisphere Shift (Australia): long vowels and diphthongs

What Figure 11.1 is intended to suggest is that the starting point for the diphthongs, that is, their first element, has fallen if originally – in the reference accents RP or GenAm – high front (/ɪi/ to /əɪ/; /eɪ/ to /æe/). The move downward to [æe] may influence the move backward of /aɪ/ to /ɒe/. Except for /ɔː/, which rises, the originally back elements move front /uː/ to /ɵ̞ː/ with an on-glide; /əʊ~oʊ/ to /ɐɵ/; /aʊ/ to /æo/; and /ɑː/ to /aː/), whereby even central /ɜː/ moves further front. These moves are congruent with two of the ***principles of vowel change*** (link: Principles of vowel change) advanced by Labov (1991):

II. Lax or short vowels fall = non-peripheral vowels fall
III. Back vowels move to the front.

Figure 11.1 above applies to Broad AusE; however, the shifts in Broad NZE and SAfE conform in part to this even though neither of them show the degree of movement toward a more retracted starting point for /iː/, and the change involved with the START vowel is distinctly different in SAfE.

Not included in Figure 11.1 and Table 11.3 are the centering diphthongs, which are phonological only in non-rhotic accents. All of them have undergone or are undergoing monophthongization in which the off-glide is replaced by lengthening. The NORTH words have become monophthongs in RP and in the three Southern Hemisphere national varieties, even though they have not done so in some of the Southern English vernaculars.

Table 11.3 The long vowels and diphthongs of SAfE and NZE

key	*RP/GenAm*	*Broad SAfE*	*difference to RP/GenAm*	*Broad NZE*	*difference*
FLEECE	iː	iː	none	iː (ɪi)	none
GOOSE	uː	ɵ̞ː ~ yː	fronted	ɵ̞ː, ʏː, ɪɵ, ɐɵ	fronted
NURSE	ɜː	œː	fronted	œː	fronted
FACE	eɪ	ʌɪ	lowered	æe, ɐe, ɐi	lowered
GOAT	əʊ	ʌʊ	fronted	ɐɵ, ɐi	fronted
MOUTH	aʊ	æʊ, aː	fronted	æɵ, ɛɵ	fronted
PRICE	aɪ	ɐə	retracted	ɑe, ɒe, ɐi	retracted
START	ɑː	ɒ, ɔ	shortened, raised	ɐː	fronted
THOUGHT	ɔː	oː	raised	oː, oə, o, ɐ	raised

The other three, NEAR, SQUARE, and CURE are still undergoing this process, which is more advanced in NZE, AusE, and SAfE than in RP. In NZE NEAR and SQUARE are beginning to merge into a single class, probably in the direction of [iə] (Bauer and Warren 2004: 592). CURE, in contrast, is remaining a diphthong where preceded by /j/ as in *cure* or *pure* in NZE but moving to the NORTH class elsewhere (*moor, poor, tour*), much as is the case in RP.

The short vowels may be compared in a similar fashion (Figure 11.2). In their case the opposite direction of shift is in effect. The short vowels seem to have replaced the complex ones as peripheral and then to have begun to move upward in accord with a further principle of Labov's, namely: Peripheral vowels rise. These shifts may explain the astonishment of the American at Wellington Airport who heard Flight 846 announced as "Flight ite four sucks" (Gordon and Deverson 1985: 82). And it may help explain why another visiting American, who when calling a New Zealand colleague, got one of his children on the line. When he asked to speak to his colleague, he understood "He's dead" – when, in fact, the child was saying "Here's Dad" (ibid.).

SAfE shows raising in much the same way as in Broad AusE except for the fronting of the FOOT vowel. The KIT vowel may, in fact be part of a chain shift as shown in Figure 11.3.

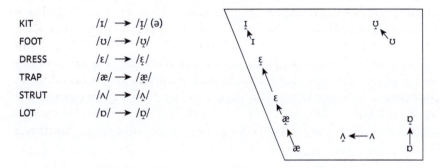

Figure 11.2 The Southern Hemisphere Shift (Australia): the simple or short vowels

Table 11.4 Short vowels of SAfE and NZE (*) Innovative [ɨ], especially in *good day* [gɪd:ɐi]

key	RP/GenAm	Broad SAfE	difference	Broad NZE	difference
KIT	ɪ	ɪ ~ ï, ə	raised, centered	ə, ə̈, ɪ	raised, centered
FOOT	ʊ	ʉ, ʏ	fronted, lowered	ʊ, ɨ (*)	fronted, unrounded
DRESS	e	e (sometimes æ)	raised	e	raised
TRAP	æ	ɛ	raised	ɛ	raised
STRUT	ʌ	ɐ	fronted	ɐ, ɐ̈	fronted
LOT	ɒ	ɔ	raised	ɒ̈	slightly centralized

(Bauer and Warren 2004: 589)

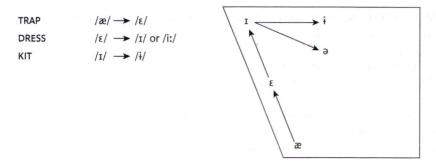

TRAP   /æ/ → /ɛ/

DRESS   /ɛ/ → /ɪ/ or /iː/

KIT   /ɪ/ → /ɨ/

Figure 11.3 The Southern Hemisphere Shift (South Africa) (from Mesthrie et al. 2000: 143; see Lass and Wright 1986: 207ff; Lass 2002: 113) NZE is similar, but AusE /ɪ/ remains high front.

11.3.2 Consonants

All three of the national varieties are basically non-rhotic, even though Otago-Southland NZE may be termed semi-rhotic: it has r-coloring especially in NURSE words. Likewise, Broad Cape SAfE may show some rhoticity, especially in final {-er}. This may be due to influence from Afrikaans, which also gives it flapped or trilled /r/ prevocalically (Bowerman 2004a: 940). In addition, there is little or no H-dropping in any of the three, with the exception of /hw/ which is /w/ virtually everywhere. AusE and NZE group together in having varying degrees of L-vocalization, which, for example, is greater in Adelaide, less in Sydney, and rare in Brisbane (Horvath 2004: 635–636). T-flapping, as in *get up* or *bitter*, where the <t> is flapped [ɾ], is widespread in Broad AusE and NZE (cf. Text 11.4); furthermore, AusE also has instances of glottaling, that is, replacing /t/ with [ʔ], especially before /l/ and /m/ as in *cutlass* or *hitman* (ibid.). Broad SAfE contrasts with the other two by showing instances of final de-voicing of the fricatives /v, ð, z, ʒ/ so that, for example, *love* is /lʌf/ rather than /lʌv/,[10] and by borrowing /x/ especially in loan words, for example Afrikaans *gogga* /xoxə/ "bug" or Xhosa *Gamtoos River* with initial /x-/ (Bowerman 2004a: 939).

11.3.3 High Rising Tone

High Rising Tone (aka Australian Questioning Intonation) is the use of a final rising tone in declarative sentences. It was first reported in Australia among WC girls but has spread well beyond this group. It is also found in New Zealand and seems to be spreading to North America and Great Britain. In AusE it is most frequent in narrative and descriptive texts and seems to be used to secure verification and to ensure heightened participation of the listeners (Horvath 2004: 639). In NZE it is a positive *politeness* marker since it includes the hearer in the discourse (Bauer and Warren 2004: 601).

---

10 NZE shows some de-voicing as with the <s> in *president* (Bauer and Warren 2004: 593).

11.4 Southern Hemisphere English: vocabulary and pragmatics

Like all the other settler societies in which English is spoken as a native language, the major forces affecting the lexicon have been contact-induced ones. The newcomers have always drawn on the indigenous languages for names of plants and animals, places, and social institutions of the indigenous peoples. A further source has been borrowing from the languages of other immigrants. Most widespread, however, have been the processes whereby new expressions have been coined out of native English material, especially compounds. In other cases, the same words are used but the meanings and/or referents have changed vis-à-vis AmE or BrE. A final case is the "re-surfacing" of seemingly archaic words or regional dialect words and expressions which have remained submerged in Britain. Each of these cases will be expanded on in the following sections.

11.4.1 Old words and new

Before moving on it should also be noted that numerous words which apply to aspects of both the natural world and the social and institutional setting of BrE became remote in meaning for Australians, South Africans, and New Zealanders. What Mencken said about AmE applies to the Southern Hemisphere Englishes as well: "Such common English topographical terms as *down, fen, bog, chase, dell* and *common* disappeared, save as fossilized in a few localisms and proper names" (Mencken 1963: 127). Australians, South Africans, and New Zealanders may well recognize these words, however, but not from personal, physical experience, but from (British) literature and/or movies, TV, and the Internet. Much the same applies to the vocabulary which refers to institutional and social phenomena. All three countries focused on in this chapter have a law-giving branch of government. However, the legislative body is not *Parliament* with a *House of Lords* and a *House of Commons* but the *Parliament of Australia* with a *Senate* and a *House of Representatives* and a *Prime Minister* as head of government and a *Governor General* (together with the British monarch) as head of state. South Africa also has a bicameral parliament, the *Democratic Parliament of South Africa* with a *National Assembly* and a *National Council of Provinces* (formerly the *Senate*), and New Zealand, finally, has a unicameral *House of Representatives*, a *Prime Minister*, and a *Governor General* (plus monarch). While Britain has a *BBC* (British Broadcasting Corporation), Australian has an *ABC* (Australian Broadcasting Corporation). The English *GCSE* (General Certificate of Secondary Education) is more or less the *NCEA* (National Certificate of Educational Achievement) in New Zealand. The UK has *pounds* and *pence*; South Africa has *rand* and *cents*. AusE has *alcheringa/alchera* (< Arrernte) "the time in Aboriginal mythology when the Earth received its present form and the patterns and cycles of life and nature began"; SAfE has *indaba* (< Zulu and Xhoso) "a serious meeting between community leaders"; NZE has *marae* (< Māori) "courtyard of a Māori meeting-house; the focus of social life in a Māori community." All of these examples are interesting because they demonstrate how historical, political, and geographic change is reflected in the national varieties of the language.

11.4.2 *Place-names* (link: Place-names; cf. 2.1.2)

The movement of English speakers to these "new" countries brought with it the need for new names. An exemplary look at naming practices (see Table 11.5) illustrates the most common ways of bestowing names. The names used by the indigenous peoples are one major source (Plate 11.4). Others are European place-names, often prefaced by the qualification *New*, the names of important or prominent persons, names which reflect the topography, and, finally, wishful or whimsical names.

11.4.3 Borrowing

One of the chief ways of expanding the vocabulary is borrowing, which can be in the form of *loan words, loan translations* (aka *calques*) (link: Loan translation), and *folk etymologies* (link: Folk etymologies).

11.4.3.1 Loan words from other languages

In addition to the examples just mentioned words for flora, fauna, and topography may also differ considerably from BrE. As with place-names, the terms used in the indigenous languages, which include Afrikaans in the case of South Africa, were one important source, as the following alphabetical list illustrates:

- *cockabully* (< Māori *kokopu*) "a small freshwater fish"
- *gemsbok* (< Afrikaans) "(large) antelope"
- *kangaroo* (< Guugu Yimidhirr *gangurru*)
- *kiwi* (< Māori) "a kind of flightless bird native to New Zealand"
- *koala* (< Dharug *gulawang*) "a furry tree-dwelling marsupial of Australia"
- *kookaburra* (< Wiradjuri *gugubarra*) "an Australian kingfisher"
- *meerkat* (< Afrikaans for "sea cat") "a type of mongoose native to southern Africa"
- *numbat* (< Nyungar) "small, reddish-brown diurnal marsupial"
- *pipi* (< Māori) "an edible New Zealand and Australian mollusc"

Table 11.5 Southern Hemisphere place-names

	Australia	*New Zealand*	*South Africa*
Indigenous names	Wagga Wagga Katoomba	Kaitangata Wanganui	Thabazimbi Umzinto
European place-names	New South Wales Perth	Richmond New Plymouth	East London Aberdeen
Prominent persons	Tasmania Victoria	Wellington Queenstown	Port Elizabeth Prince Albert
Descriptive	Salt Lake Great Sandy Desert	Bluff Cloudy Bay	Silver Streams Oatlands
Wishful, Whimsical	Mt. Curious Disaster Beach	Chaslands Mistake Hen and Chickens Islands	Good Hope Hole in the Wall

- *quagga* (< Khoikhoi/Nama, cf. Xhosa *iqwara*) "a zebra-like animal of southern Africa, now extinct"
- *taniwha* (< Māori) "a mythical water monster"
- *waterbuck* (< Afrikaans *waterbok*) "a type of antelope"
- *wildebeest* (< Afrikaans for "wild beast") "gnu."

Other languages, especially immigrant languages, have also contributed to the word stock of English, for example in SAfE *kugel* "wealthy Jewish woman; usually derogatory" from Yiddish; *kraal* "corral" ultimately from Portuguese for "native village" by way of Afrikaans; *brinjal* ultimately from Sanskrit "eggplant or aubergine"; and *dhobi* "washerman" from Hindi.

AusE has borrowed from various Aboriginal languages, as the list above makes clear. Most borrowings have come from the languages encountered earliest on the east coast of the continent. SAfE has taken over numerous words from Zulu and Xhosa, but even more vocabulary has been borrowed from linguistically closely related Afrikaans. NZE, finally, contains especially many words pertaining to Māori culture (for further examples, see link: Borrowings). Text 11.2 is taken from a recent novel by André Brink, *Praying Mantis* (2005). It is the story of the Hottentot (Khoikhoi) Cupido, set in the second half of the eighteenth and the beginning of the nineteenth centuries. It is linguistically unremarkable except for the large number of loan words for native fauna and one case of topography (*veld*).

Text 11.2 Loan words in SAfE

But it is when it comes to hunting that Heitsi-Eibib [the hunter-god of the Khoikhoi] *really takes him* [Cupido] *in charge. It begins with small buck –* oribi [Afrikaans < Khoikhoi "a small antelope"], grysbok [< Afrikaans "a gray antelope"], suni [< Swahili "a very small antelope"], steenbok [< Afrikaans "a small antelope"] (never a hare, as this repulsive creature with its split lip is the messenger of death). These he catches in ingenious traps. Then follow larger antelopes: springbok [< Afrikaans "gazelle"], blesbok [< Afrikaans "an antelope with 'blazed' marking"], hartebeest [< Afrikaans "a large antelope"]. Heitsi-Eibib helps him carry those home, so that there will be food for him and his people. . . .*

One day, . . . he comes upon a lion in the veld [< Afrikaans "open land with grass, bushes, thin wooding"] *beyond the tract of red earth mottled with anthills where there is a patch of dry bush. . . . That afternoon, as he follows a stray goat, a* meerkat [see above] *suddenly appears before him. Nothing strange about that. Except that the* meerkat *begins to speak.*

(A. Brink, *Praying Mantis*. Ondon: Secker & Warburg, 2005, 25–26)

In this passage, as generally in SAfE, most of the loan words are from Afrikaans; shortly after this text, reference is made to a *tsamma melon* "pie or citron melon" < Nama (Khoikhoi) *tsamas* (p. 27). The boy, who magically kills a lion, takes its skin back to his *baas* ("boss"), and says, "He can't *mos* catch our goats like that [dead], Baas," where *mos* is a discourse marker from Afrikaans "indeed, of course" (p. 28).

11.4.3.2 Vocabulary from other varieties of English

English words which have not entered the stream of GenE often continue to be used in a more traditional and regionally restricted variety. Such lexical items may be carried overseas and come into more general, mainstream use there. The following AusE examples, which may be regarded as "language-internal loan words,"have been borrowed from British dialects or have a specifically Australian colloquial tone, for example:

- *billy* (< Scots dialect *bally* "milk pail") "can or pail"
- *chook* (< British dialect) "chicken"
- *choom* (< British dialect pronunciation of *chum*) "an Englishman"
- *dag* (< British dialect for something odd) "unkempt, untidy person"
- *dinkum* (< British dialect for "work") "genuine"
- *larrikin* (< Warwickshire, Worcestershire dialect "mischievous youth") "rowdy"
- *nong* (< British dialect *(ning-)nang* "foolish person") "idiot"
- *swag* (< British dialect) "tramp's bundle."

11.4.3.3 Loan translation or calquing

This is the second widely recognized means of borrowing. In such cases each distinct morpheme of a word may be translated into English. New Zealand, for example, is also known as *Aotearoa* (< Māori *ao tea roa* or "Land of the Long White Cloud"). In AusE the Aboriginal word *alcheringa/alchera* also appears translated into English as *Dreamtime*. Yet there are relatively few loan translations from Māori and the various Aboriginal languages. SAfE, in contrast, has numerous calques from Afrikaans, again facilitated by the structural similarity of lexical items in the two languages. *A Dictionary of South African English* (Branford 1991) lists many such loan translations, for example:

- *after-ox* < Afr. *agteros* "One of the hindmost pair in a *span* (q.v.) of draught oxen . . ."
- *antheap* < Afr. *miershoop* "anthill"
- *bad friends* < Afr. *kwaaivriende* "at enmity, not on speaking terms: . . . usu. temporarily"
- *to lead water* < Afr. *water lei* "To irrigate, usu. by means of *sloots* (q.v.) or *furrows* (q.v.) from a public supply in towns which have *water erven* (see *erf*) from farm dams or other irrigation schemes"
- *lungsickness* < Afr. *longsiekte* "pleuro-pneumonia, a highly infectious disease of cattle, and horses."

Note how dense the system of terms borrowed may be: the definition of *after-ox* uses *span*; *to lead water* uses *sloots*, *furrows*, and *water erven*.

11.4.3.4 Modified borrowings and folk etymologies

When words are borrowed they usually accommodate to the pronunciation and spelling of the host language. This accounts for the borrowing of the German word for a species of fish found in the waters around Australia, the *Schnapper* (*Chrysophys auratus*), which is now spelled with <s> and not <Sch>. This is a case of assimilation to English spelling patterns

(German common nouns are capitalized) and English phonology (the sound combination /ʃn-/ of <schn-> is not native.[11]

A second process of accommodation is one in which words not only assimilate to English spelling and/or pronunciation, but also take on a new history. This is called *folk etymology*. The spelling of Australian *palberry* looks as if it is a berry like *strawberry, raspberry, blueberry*, and so on; yet, the supposed ***morpheme*** (link: Morpheme){berry} in *palberry* does not come from English, but from an Aboriginal language (Morris 1898), where the word *palbri* by chance coincides with one of the common pronunciations of {-berry}. Turner recounts that the Aboriginal proper name for a creek, *Yel-lo-mun-dee* was reanalyzed as *Yellow Monday Creek*. Eventually it was applied to a kind of cicada that was found living close by. Further species then came to be designated *Yellow Tuesday* or *Green Monday* under the mistaken assumption that the color or the day of the week was somehow relevant (Turner 1989: 216).

11.4.4 Word formation using native English elements

All the varieties of English make use of the same processes of word formation, which consists of compounding and derivation. Despite overall similarity some of these processes seems to be favored in one or the other variety.

11.4.4.1 Compounds

A *compound* (link: Compounding) comes about by combining two (or more) words to form a complex word, and it is perhaps the most common way of expanding vocabulary in English. The word *bush*, which is the usual word for woods or a forest in Australia, South Africa, and New Zealand enters into especially many compounds in AusE. *Bush tucker*, for example, is a word for "plain food, as can be gotten from the woods." Since the meaning of this compound is easy to deduce from the two elements it consists of, its meaning is *transparent*, that is, the resulting meaning is an obvious combination of the meanings of the individual elements of the compound according to the principle of *compositionality*.

In the *Macquarie Dictionary* (Delbridge 1997) {bush} is a frequent element in compounds, with over ninety main entries containing it. Although a few are derived from the meaning of *bush* in the sense of a shrub, most are based on (1) the meaning of "land covered with bushy vegetation or trees" (*Macquarie*, bush, q.v.). A further sense (2), "the countryside in general, as opposed to the towns" (ibid.) is associated with an extended meaning. Finally (3), as is typical of the disdain of city people all over the world for rustic and unrefined country life (though often nostalgically regarded as quaint), *bush* takes on the meaning of "uncivilised; rough; makeshift" (ibid.). Consequently, Australian compounds incorporating *bush* vary between these senses. *Bush bashing*, "clearing virgin bush" makes use of the first meaning. *Bush ballad*, a ballad "dealing with aspects of life in the Australian bush," has the second meaning, while *bush breakfast* represents the third, namely "a rough, improvised breakfast partaken of while camping in the bush" (*Macquarie*, qq.v.).

---

11 The relatively many Yiddish words beginning in <s(c)hl->, <s(c)hm->, or <s(c)hn-> found in AmE and increasingly in other varieties are an exception: *s(c)hlep, s(c)hlock, s(c)hmo(e), s(c)hmuck, s(c)hmal(t)z, s(c)hnook, schnoz.*

11.4.4.2 Derivation *(affixation,* **conversion,** *shortening,* **blending)** (link: Derivation)

In recent additions to ModE, compounds and affixation – the latter a process in which a morpheme is added to the *lexeme* (or base) – account for 54.9%. Conversion, a shift of word class or subclass in which there is no formal change, not even a shift in stress, makes up 19.6%. Shortening is involved in 18%. The remainder comprises new meanings (14.4%; see 11.4.5) and borrowing (7.5%) (cf. Cannon 1987: 279; summarized in Gramley and Pätzold 2004: §2.7). A combination of two factors gives us four different cases of derivation, as shown in Table 11.6.

Conversion, **shift,** and **zero derivation** are fully integrated in the English of Australia, New Zealand, and South Africa. Examples from AusE include the following: *ocker* (n.) "the archetypal uncultivated Australian working man" used attributively as in *ocker humor*; *boomerang* (n.) "throwing stick that returns" and *to boomerang* (v.) "to backfire"; or *kangaroo* (n.), the animal and *to kangaroo* (v.) "(of a car) to move forward in a jerky manner" (*Macquarie*, qq.v.).

Affixation, in which a free morpheme is combined with a prefix or a suffix, is highly productive in ModE, including the Englishes of Australia, New Zealand, and South Africa; {-y} and {-o} are, however, especially typical of AusE.

Shortening (including *abbreviation,* **acronym,** **back-formation,** and **clipping**). The last of these is a strong tendency in ModE (*pants* (< *pantaloons*), *specs* (< *spectacles* or *specifications*), *bra* (< *brassiere*), *gas* (< *gasoline*), *petrol* (< *petroleum*), *bus* (< *omnibus*) and many, many more). In AusE we find clippings such as *Abo* < *Aborigine*, *com* < *communist*, *kanga* (or *roo*) < *kangaroo*. In SAfE we find *trooper* clipped to *troop* with *-ie* added to make *troopie* "lowest military rank"; Afrikaans *tante* > *tann* + *ie* "auntie"; *terrorist* > *terr* + *y*. The resulting form often functions as a diminutive, which serves to make the resulting word more familiar, sometimes endearing (*tannie*); however, it can also be disparaging as with *commie* (< *communist*).

AusE seems, more than other varieties, to add a {-y} or {-o} to clipped forms (Dabke 1976: 40). A central example is the clipping of *Australian* to **Aus* and the subsequent expansion to *Aussy*, or, more familiarly, *Ozzie*. The suffixes are not always used in a positive sense, as we see in AusE *swiftie* ("deceitful trick"). A third way of using these endings is to indicate an animate being that is involved in an activity connected with the base lexeme in some often unpredictable manner. A *bushie* is "a person, usu. unsophisticated and uncultivated, who lives in the bush" (*Macquarie*, q.v.). However, the meaning can be variable and unpredictable: "Among bus and truck drivers *bushy . . .* means 'a stop in the middle of the bush'" (Dabke 1976: 40). Words involving this third use of {-y} are not necessarily endearing or derogatory; they are merely informal and may "evoke the especially

Table 11.6 Processes of word formation

process	combination	deletion	examples (all from AusE)
conversion	–	–	*kangaroo* → *to kangaroo* (v)
affixation	+	–	*milk + o* → *milko*
shortening	–	+	*kangaroo* → *roo*
blending	+	+	*squatter* + ~~aristo~~*cracy* = *squattocracy*

tough world of the Australian male" (ibid.: 41). A fourth and final use of {-y} is as a suffix to adjectives which become nouns and refer to something with the quality of the adjective, see *swiftie* above.

The suffix {-o} can be seen in *this arvo* (or *sarvo*, also *aftie*), which is a clipping of *afternoon* to *af* and then the addition of {-o}. The letter <r> in non-rhotic AusE is not pronounced but only indicates that the <a> is pronounced as long /aː/. The /f/ of *afternoon* has been softened to a voiced /v/, possibly to add an emotive note (cf. the voicing of *Ozzie < Aussie*).

The range of meanings of {-o} is similar to {-y} and the potential list of items is similarly long. The items and the meanings seem to be quite variable. For example, *falsy* is given by Dabke as "faked registration form" (1976: 42), but *falsies* (plural only) show up in the *Australian Concise Oxford Dictionary of Current English* (*ACOD*) and the *Macquarie* only in the meaning of breast contour enhancers, a meaning found in other varieties. Similar conclusions must be drawn when comparing the 1966 list in Baker (1966: 369–373) with

dictionary entries in the *ACOD* or the *Macquarie* (see [link: Shortening](link:Shortening); for more recent material, Angelo et al. 1998: 34ff; Simpson 2004).

Abbreviations and *acronyms* are shortenings which are treated as independent means of word formation. An abbreviation is an expression consisting of the initial letters of a phrase it stands for, each of which is pronounced as a letter. AusE AAP /eɪeɪˈpiː/ is the *Australian Associated Press*; AAT /eɪeɪˈtiː/, *Australian Antarctic Territory*; and ABC /eɪbiːˈsiː/, the *Australian Broadcasting Corporation*. Such abbreviations are not always well known outside their country of origin and use and so belong to the distinct vocabulary of the given national variety. Acronyms differ only inasmuch as the initials which make them up are construed as a pronounceable word. *UPE* /ˈjuːpiːˈiː/, an abbreviation for the South African *University of Port Elizabeth*, is attended by *Uppies*, an acronym for UPE students. And the University

of South Africa is *Unisa* /juːˈniːsə/ or /juːˈnaɪsə/.

Blends or *portmanteau words* ([link: Blending](link:Blending)) are formed by the clipping of one or more words followed by their combination to a new single item. Perhaps the best known South African example is *Soweto* (< *South West Township*). Among the AusE contributions to this area we find *jack + kangaroo = jackaroo* (also: *jackeroo*) "young man working on a sheep or cattle station to gain practical experience needed to become an owner, overseer, manager, etc." and *jill + kangaroo = jillaroo* (also: *jilleroo*) "young woman, as in the preceding."

11.4.5 Lexical-semantic change

This has to do with such processes as the broadening of lexical meaning, as with *bush* (above) or narrowing, as with *corn*, which in AusE refers not to grain in general, but to maize. Transfer in the referent is the case with the European robin (*Erithacus rubecula*), which is not the same as the North American (*Turdus migratorius*) or the Australian one (the *Petroica goodenovii* or the *Eopsaltria australis*). Sometimes lexical-semantic change comes as a result of social changes, for example SAfE *rainbow-X*, where *X* can be any English noun – *rainbow nation*, *rainbow swimming pool*, and so on – and *rainbow* serves to indicate the ethnic mixing aimed at. For further types of **semantic change** and examples, see [link: Meaning change](link:Meaning change).

Long-distance transportation in the days of earliest settlement was chiefly by coach or ship. Consequently, it is no surprise that English vocabulary in this area is relatively unified as the English overseas expansion came after this vocabulary was established. However, the

English-speaking world was geographically divided by the time canal-building developed and, soon afterward, the train came into use. Here the vocabularies of AmE and BrE vary. Car and air travel came in at the high point of separation of AmE and BrE from each other. Not surprisingly, the vocabulary differences in these fields are especially noticeable. How has AusE moved as far as this vocabulary is concerned? There is considerable variation even with such low-tech vehicles as *baby carriages* (older: *baby buggy*) (AmE) or *prams* (older: *perambulator*) (BrE, AusE) for infants and *strollers* (AmE) or *push chairs* (BrE) for young children, where AusE has *strollers*, *pushchairs*, and *pushers*. Older Australian kids *dink* (in South Australia they *donkey*) when they *double* (GenE) on a bike. These examples probably reflect the situation well. AusE usually follows the lead of BrE, sometimes adopts lexemes from AmE, and also sometimes has its own word.

Coupled with semantic change is the question of the lexical influence of AmE and BrE on Southern Hemisphere English. Anglophone European settlement was predominantly from the British Isles. It is therefore understandable that it was from there that vocabulary choices generally came, just as the grammatical ones did. Yet it cannot be overlooked that a certain amount of possible AmE influence is also present. As we saw, the names of the national legislative bodies have variously drawn on American *Senate* and *House of Representatives*. The use of *corn* for maize and *creek* for a small stream is also shared by AmE and AusE. Furthermore, Australia under British administration also divided up the land American-style into *sections* for settlement. And both Australia and New Zealand named their currency the *dollar*; and they and South Africa divided the basic unit up into 100 *cents*, all of which had already been introduced in the United States. There seems to be little doubt that the influence of AmE is, currently, very strong, but it is also accompanied by a certain amount of resentment and rejection. In this context note the following remarks about NZE:

> Given a pair such as *torch* and *flashlight*, the British version is the one most likely to be used in everyday speech, and the American one is likely to be used commercially, to make the product sound more appealing. Thus one would normally pull the *curtains*, but the shop might sell you *drapes*. Other pairs with a similar relationship are *lift/elevator*, *nappy/diaper*, and possibly (although there may be a semantic distinction here) *biscuit/cookie*.
>
> (Bauer 1994: 419)

11.4.6 Pragmatic aspects of Southern Hemisphere ENL varieties

These differ from other ENL varieties most obviously in the formulaic routines used in everyday speech acts like greeting or leave-taking. Leaving-taking formulas give us AusE-NZE *hooroo* "goodbye" (also: *hooray, ooray, ooroo*). For those we want to get rid of (impolitely) there is SAfE *Hamba* (< Zulu "Get you gone!) or *Voetsak*, usually addressed to dogs, but sometimes to people (< Afrikaans *Voort seg ik!* "Get out, I say"). SAfE is also marked by the presence in informal speech of *no* as sentence initiator, for example A: *Can you deliver it?* B: *No, sure, we'll send it this afternoon* (cf. Text 11.3; mentioned in 7.4.2) (Bowerman 2004b: 957). An informal SAfE greeting once typical of white males, but now in more general use is *Howzit!* In New Zealand one might hear Māori *Kia ora*. In AusE (also NZE) *G'day* is widely used (see Text 11.4) and is one of many bits of shared language that make up an intimate part of the local heritage and "documents, and passes on, the attitudes and values which bind the population of Australia together" since anyone, of any heritage may use it (Wierzbicka 1997: 200). Other words like the mildly tabooed "b-words" (*bloody, bastard, bugger, bullshit*) are felt to be "an important means of self-expression, self-identification, and effective communication with others" (cf. Text 11.4). These words serve as genial or even affectionate address between men; and even now by women (ibid.: 217).

11.5 Regional and ethnic variation

Regional variation is generally considered to be minor in AusE (see Gordon and Sudbury 2002 for a different conclusion). In NZE there is some divergence from the rest of the country in Southland-Otago, usually credited to the high proportion of Scottish immigration to that area. South African English consists, as noted, of distinctively different varieties in Natal and at the Cape.

11.5.1 Cape Flats SAfE

Natal English is much closer to StE than Cape English, which is associated strongly with and does indeed share numerous features with Afrikaans English. Indeed, Cape Flats SAfE may be regarded as both a regional and an ethnic (Coloured) variety. Text 11.3 is a sample of Cape Flats English; the speaker is a teacher.

Text 11.3 Cape Flats SAfE

Now me and E. speaks English. And when we went one day to a workshop – and uh, most of the teachers there were Afrikaans – and we were there; they were looking at us like that you know [demonstrates look]. *And I asked E., "Why's this people staring at us?" She said, "No, I don't know." And I asked them, "Look here, excuse me, is there a problem? You want to know something?" They said, "No, it's nothing wrong." Then*   5
this one woman told me, she said "Yes, because if you speak English then we think you so high and mighty." But it wasn't that way, because we don't keep us like that, you know. But it just shows you. So I took it always that way, that's in people's mind, you know.

(Malan 1996: 125)

Among the features which are non-standard are the following:

- conjoined subject *me and E.* for StE *E. and I* (l. 1)
- non-standard concord: plural subject accompanied by a singular verb *speaks* (1); *why's* (3)
- non-standard word order: adverb of time before place: *went one day to a workshop* (1)
- singular demonstrative followed by a plural noun: *this people* (3)

- SAfE pragmatic feature: introductory *no* "well" (4, 5)
- deletion of initial unstressed *do* (a general feature of colloquial English): *You want to know something?* (5)
- expletive *it* rather than standard *there*: *it's nothing wrong* (5)
- non-specific determiner: *this one woman* "one of the women" (6)
- **zero copula**: *you so high and mighty* (6–7)
- *that way* "like that" (7)
- *keep* for *behave* + *us* for *ourselves* (7)
- singular *mind* for the more standard distributional plural *minds* (8).

11.5.2 Māori English

Ethnic varieties are prominent in all three of these national frameworks. In the case of SAfE this has been pointed out throughout this chapter (see esp. 11.1.2.2). In Australia there are varieties often identified with Aboriginal Australians, namely Aboriginal English, Kriol, and Torres Straits Creole. In New Zealand there is Māori English (see Warren and Bauer 2004 on the phonology of this variety). Hulme's 1985 prize-winning novel *The Bone People* is set on South Island and revolves intensely about interaction involving Pakehas (Europeans, whites) and Māoris. Joe is one of the three main protagonists, a Māori. He telephones Kerewin, a Pakeha. They refer to Joe's "adopted" son Haimona/Himi. Later they meet at a pub. Piri is Joe's *coz* (cousin).

Text 11.4 New Zealand English (cum Māori)

On Wednesday, Joe rang at midday.
    "Hello, guess who's got the afternoon off?"
    "You, by the sound of it." . . .
    "E ka pai . . . well, I thought you might like a drink at the pub. Not like last time," he says hastily,
"hell, was I ever sorry about that . . . I was almost glad Himi was hurt, because it meant I didn't have to   5
stay round too long."
    "I'm an ogre?" she asks incredulously.
    "O no," he sounds shocked. "What I meant was that I had behaved badly, and you knew it, and I knew it, and I knew you knew it."
    "Well, to say something very original, that morning I knew you know I know you know, you know.   10
So to speak."
    He giggles.
    "You do have a knack of saying things so unequivocally."
    "Shuddup. I'll see you down at the Duke in about an hour?"
    "Beaudy." . . .   15
    And this afternoon is flowing along nicely on small talk and beer. Two in a row, great! she thinks.
Then Piri comes over.
    "Gidday," she says, grinning happily.

> *"Gidday," he replies, with a grin for her . . .*
> *"Get up. I want to talk to you."*
> *   Joe puts his schooner down slowly. "Why? I'm drinking with Kerewin. What's so important that you think you can interrupt us?"*
> *   "You know bloody well what. Excuse us, Kere."*
> *   "Okay," she says with surprise.*
>
> (K. Hulme (1986) *The Bone People*, London: Picador, 131ff.)

20

There is, in fact, little in this text which reflects Māori English aside from the short phrase in Māori (*E ka pai* (l. 4) "good, great, thanks, mate"). Indeed this is realistic since most Māoris use English which is only occasionally different from Pakeha English. In general, the text has an NZE tone to it, as indicated by the spellings *Shuddup*, *beaudy*, and *gidday* (14, 15, 18, 19), which indicate the T-Flapping of NZE (11.3.2). The pragmatic aspects are among the most obvious: the Māori phrase, the Australasian greeting (*gidday*), the mild, but typical expletive *bloody well* (23) and not just the use of first names among these recent acquaintances, but the hypocoristic shortening *Kere* (< Kerewin; cf. Simpson 2004). On the culture of the pub with its employment of a *schooner* "a large beer glass" and *shouting* "standing someone a drink," Wierzbicka writes: "In the relatively noncompetitive and egalitarian Australian society, 'shouting' was one domain where one could be freely competitive – competing with other people, as it were, in generosity and in the spirit of companionship." That is, there is an expectation of reciprocity, hence a "celebration of relaxed male companionship, and male solidarity over and above any strict reciprocity," including not just drinks – and here not just men (see Wierzbicka 1997: chap. 5 on key words in Australian culture including *bloody* and *shout* – here equally applicable to New Zealand; quotations: 209ff.).

11.5.3 Aboriginal English

In parts of Queensland and Western Australia as well as in the Northern Territory Aboriginals who once spoke mutually unintelligible mother tongues have frequently adopted a common language which varies between a creole such as (Roper) Kriol or Torres Strait Broken (Cape York Creole) and a non-standard form of English often called Aboriginal English. The latter, spoken especially in remote areas, is "used generally to denote speech varieties between so-called St[andard] AusE and creoles" (Sandefur 1983: 55). Both the creoles and Aboriginal English are recognized as mother tongues in bilingual educational programs.

> These Creoles are distinct languages. . . . They show an ingenious blend of English and Australian structural features, producing a language that seems quite appropriate to the bicultural milieu in which many Aboriginal Australians find themselves.
>
> (Dixon 1980: 73–74)

How this blend can work is demonstrated in the system of personal pronouns of Roper Kriol, which has an inclusive and exclusive first person dual and plural. Inclusive means

Table 11.7 The personal pronouns of Roper Krio

	singular	dual			plural	
		inclusive	exclusive		inclusive	exclusive
1st person	mi	yunmi	minim, mindubali		melabat, wi	mibala
2nd person	yu	yundubala			yubala, yumob	
3rd person	im	dubala			olabot	

(Dixon 1980: 73)

"the speaker plus the addressee" (duals) or "address(ees) and others" (plural). Exclusive means the speaker does not include the addressee.

11.6 Summary

The initial historical sketch of the settlement of English-language populations in Australia, South Africa, and New Zealand was followed up by observations on standard and non-standard English in these countries. The discussion of grammar, pronunciation, and vocabulary was carried out in a comparative manner in which both shared features of Southern Hemisphere ENL and some of the individual developments in each of these countries were presented. Particular attention was paid to non-standard grammar, the Southern Hemisphere continuations of the GVS, and vocabulary and meaning change. In the latter area the chapter looked at borrowing, both loan words and loan translations, and at folk etymologies. It was pointed out that borrowing shows up in words used for both the natural and the social world as revealed by examples of expressions from Māori and Afrikaans as well as ones from Australian Aboriginal languages. The major types of word formation as well as semantic change were also introduced and examples of how they were realized in these Englishes were supplied. The chapter closed with a brief look at non-standard varieties in the form of non-standard Cape Flats English, Māori-influenced English, and a short remark on Aboriginal English.

STUDY QUESTIONS

Social and cultural background

1. What were the main motives for emigration to Australia, South Africa, and New Zealand?

2. What were the major regional sources of early population of Australia, South Africa, and New Zealand?
3. What was the social background of the settlers?

Linguistic backgrounds

1. How did the regional origins of the early Anglophone settlers in Australia, South Africa, and New Zealand influence the kind of English that was established there?
2. Discuss how the presence of other peoples and languages affected English in these countries.
3. How might the wider use of the progressive or of the simple past tense (vis-à-vis BrE) be explained?
4. How justified is the comparison of Broad Australian pronunciation and Cockney? What are the major similarities? Differences?
5. These three countries are grouped together despite the numerous differences between them. What justifies treating them separately from North America?

Further reading

De Klerk 1996 contains a number of very readable contributions on English in South Africa including Lanham and Branford with overviews of the language situation there. Gordon and Sudbury provide a short summary of settlement history and of the linguistic features of ENL in Australia, South Africa, and New Zealand. The two reference volumes edited by Schneider et al. offer brief overviews of all the major varieties of English around the world. In the case of Australia, South Africa, and New Zealand there are several articles available on the varieties in each country, several of which have been quoted in chapter 11.

Branford, B. (1996) "English in South African Society: A Preliminary Overview," In: V. De Klerk (ed.) *Focus on South Africa*. Amsterdam: John Benjamins, 35–51.

Gordon, E. and A. Sudbury (2002) "The History of Southern Hemisphere Englishes," In: R.. Watts and P. Trudgill (eds.) *Alternative Histories of English*. London: Routledge, 67–86.

Lanham, L. (1996) "A History of English in South Africa," In: V. De Klerk (ed.) *Focus on South Africa*. Amsterdam: John Benjamins, 19–34.

Schneider, E.W., K. Burridge, B. Kortmann, R. Mesthrie, and C. Upton (eds.) (2004) *A Handbook of Varieties of English*. vol. 1. *Phonology* and vol. 2 *Morphology and Syntax*. Berlin: Mouton de Gruyter.

CHAPTER TWELVE

English in the ESL countries of Africa and Asia (since 1795)

. . . standards are kept in place in "first world" contexts by a technology of reproduction which dissimulates this hegemony through the self-represented neutrality of prestige and precedent whose selectivity is a function of the politics of publication. . . . The non-standard is one of the most accessible means of "natural" resistance, and, therefore, one of the most sensitive indices of de-hegemonization.

(Parakrama 1995: xii–xiii)

The theory of indigenisation has taught us how resistant source culture is to a second language.

(Mbangwana and Sala 2009: 248)

Chapter Overview:

This chapter:

- looks at multilingual societies with English language continuums, code-switching, and the emergence of new national and regional English standards under the influence of non-native as well as non-English cultural and linguistic patterns;
- raises the question of language planning and policy at two levels. First, status planning (official, regional, second, foreign languages) and the question, "Why English?"; second, corpus planning concerning the development of languages in the context of the legacy of colonialism;
- shows examples of nativization, standardization, substratum influences, and the identitarian role of language, including pidgin and creole varieties in some of these societies.

12.1 English as a Second Language

English has a special status in those countries in which the number of speakers of English as a first or *native language* is extremely small or virtually non-existent, but in which English is an official language and plays a central role in helping to ensure a minimum of internal communication and unity as well as promoting higher education and access to the global community. In these countries English plays an important role in the more formal areas of law, commerce, education, and administration, where a command of StE continues to be a prerequisite. For the purposes of this history of English, we will refer to the following geographical groupings of ESL countries:[1]

- *West Africa: Cameroon, Gambia, Ghana, Liberia, Nigeria, and Sierra Leone*
- *Southern Africa: Botswana, Lesotho, Malawi, Namibia, South Africa, Swaziland, Zambia, and Zimbabwe*
- *East Africa: Kenya, Tanzania, and Uganda* (marginally *Madagascar, Rwanda, Somaliland, Sudan*)
- *South Asia: India, Pakistan* (marginally *Bangladesh, Bhutan, the Maldives, Nepal, Sri Lanka*)
- *Southeast Asia* and the Pacific: *Singapore, Hong Kong, and the Philippines.*

The following sections will review the major ESL countries; *language planning and policy* (12.2); linguistic features of selected varieties (12.3); the influence of the substratum languages (12.4), and the identitarian role of language (12.5).

12.1.1 The status of ESL in the former colonial countries of Africa and Asia

English was imposed on the countries reviewed in this chapter as part of the imperialistic project chiefly of Great Britain and to a lesser extent of the United States. StE gained status and prestige in and through the agency of the educational system. Alongside of StE, pidgin and creole forms, present chiefly in West Africa and perhaps in Singapore, are the sources of the spread of particularly vital varieties of English. In most of these countries a kind of indigenization or nativization is currently taking place, a process in which the domains of the language are expanding and in which increasingly endonormative standards are becoming established for usages which were once stigmatized as mistakes. This is opening the way to wider use of English in creative writing and to the institutionalization of local forms in schools, the media, and government (cf. Mazzon 2000b). English may well still be far from being a language of the emotions among the vast majority of its users; indeed, the institutionalization of English may be making it ever more difficult for those without English to close the social gap between "the classes and the masses." All the same, English is more and more firmly a part of everyday linguistic experience.

---

1 The lists could be extended to include countries like Malaysia or Sudan, but this would not have a significant effect on the character of this account of historical developments and linguistic features.

12.1.2 Southern Africa

Already dealt with in 11.1.2.2, Southern Africa is unique among the five groupings listed above because it includes a significant number of speakers from both the Inner Circle and the Outer Circle (see 13.4). The native speakers are, for the most part, descendants of British immigrants and the younger generation of SAf Indians who are increasingly ENL users. ESL speakers, who are the focus of attention in this chapter, come from the largely Bantu-speaking black population, the older generation of SAf Indians, and both white and colored *Afrikaans* speakers. Each of these groups of speakers has its own standards and sub-varieties. The second-language varieties are heavily influenced by the primary languages of their speakers at every level of linguistic structure, but most obviously marked by accent.

The intrusion of Europe into Southern Africa began with almost 150 years of Dutch dominance at the Cape of Good Hope (1652–1795). For a further 150 years, from 1795 to 1948, South Africa was in British hands. This resulted in the widespread use of English in South Africa – even though only about 8% of the South African population speak it as their home language. Estimates about the percentage of Black South Africans who can speak English vary enormously, but probably lie somewhere around one-third of the black population. Of these only a relatively negligible number are ENL speakers (cf. Gough 1996: 53–54). However, English is frequently the unmarked language of inter-ethnic communication. The original center of British presence was Cape Town, whose ethnic and linguistic history is nicely recounted in Finn 2004: 964–967.

Black SAfE has become very prominent in public life since 1994, but is a somewhat diffuse variety moving toward nativization but not yet far enough along the way to be easily described. Its phonology is characterized by the neutralization of tense/lax vowel distinctions and the avoidance of central vowels. In mesolect forms, that is, the English of fluent, educated speakers, consequently, /iː/ and /ɪ/ are not distinguished but are represented by /i/ both in KIT and FLEECE type words. The vowels of TRAP, NURSE, and DRESS all

Table 12.1 Anglophone Southern African countries[2]

country	significant UK contact	beginning of colonial status	independence	total population	English speakers	
					percentage	total number
Botswana	19th century	1885	1966	1,640,000	~ 38%	630,000
Lesotho		protectorate	1966	1,800,000	~ 28%	500,000
Malawi	1878	1891	1964	13,000,000	~ 4%	540,000
Namibia	1878	1920 (S. Afr.)	1990	1,800,000	~ 17%	> 300,000
South Africa	1795	1795	1910	47,850,000	> 28%	13,700,000
Swaziland	1894	1902 (UK)	1968	1,140,000	~ 4.4%	50,000
Zambia	1888	1924	1953, 1964	13,000,000	~ 15%	~ 2,000,000
Zimbabwe	1890	1923	1953, 1980	13,300,000	~ 42%	5,550,000

2 The figures in Tables 12.1–12.5 are only approximate. Probably the best source is the website of Ethnolog, cf. Gordon 2005; Lewis 2009.

converge as /ɛ/ (van Rooy 2004: 943ff). "[T]here are essentially five contrastive vowel phonemes in mesolectal [Black SAfE]: /i/, /ɛ/, /a/, /ɔ/ and /u/" pretty much regardless of the *L1* of the speaker (ibid.: 946). ENL diphthongs are often realized as monophthongs. Consonants are much as in ENL varieties; however, /θ/ and /ð/ may commonly be realized as **plosives**, and /ʃ/ and /ʒ/ may be articulated like /s/ and /z/. The **affricates** /tʃ/ and /dʒ/ are variable and often realized like /ʃ/ and /ʒ/ (ibid.: 948ff). There is also a certain amount of consonant cluster simplification. Black SAfE is syllable- rather than stress-timed (ibid.: 944).

Among speakers of Black SAfE code-switching is quite frequent and serves, among other things, to mark the speakers' self-representation. One can mark oneself as educated and powerful by using English. The following text is taken from a discussion between three students at the University of Witwatersrand in which English–Zulu code-switching takes place.

Text 12.1 SAfE – Zulu code-switching

A   I-*Admin* iyazi ukuthi i-*power* yama-*students* ikwi-*mass-action*. (The Administration knows that student power lies in mass action) *And if they discredit mass action they will have conquered.*

B   Yinye into abangayazi ukuthi *we cannot let them get away with this.* (There is one thing they don't know that . . .)

C   Into ecasulayo ukuthi kube iqenjana elincane eli-*protestayo*. (The annoying thing is that it turns out to be a small group that is involved in the protest action).

(Herbert 1994: 69)

In the other South African countries listed English is for all intents and purposes a second language oriented toward White SAfE, but with features which resemble those of Black SAfE. Zambia, Malawi, and Zimbabwe lie between East Africa and South Africa, but seem more likely to continue to reflect South African influence both economically and linguistically, as Namibia, Swaziland, Botswana, and Lesotho do even more obviously (see Kamwangamalu and Chisanga 1996; Schmied 1996).

12.1.3 West Africa

English is an official language in a number of West African countries: Nigeria, Ghana, Cameroon (together with French in effectively different geographical regions of the country), Sierra Leone, Gambia, and Liberia. Each of these countries has a colonial history in which Great Britain or – in the case of Liberia – the United States had a significant influence on political, economic, and cultural development, including language. Speakers of English reached the West African coast in the first phase of European imperialism as early as the sixteenth century (see 7.1.1, 9.1) when forts and trading posts were established, but their direct sphere of influence was largely limited to the coastal ports, where trade relations, most especially the slave trade, were maintained. It was in this context as well as in the slave economies in the Americas that Pidgin English developed. Because of the historically deep roots of Pidgin English in West Africa it is sometimes seen as an indigenous African language. And, indeed, African languages seem to have had a significant influence on the structure, but also the pronunciation and to a lesser extent the vocabulary of Pidgin English and the creoles that have grown out of it (see 9.5.2). In Cameroon, for example, "Pidgin English is not a problem to acquire or to use because it is tailored to look like the basic structure of the indigenous languages" (Mbangwana and Sala 2009: 270).

12.1.3.1 Colonial expansion into West Africa

This entered its second phase in the nineteenth century. Although the roots of modern European colonialism go back to the fifteenth century and although Britain was a participant from the middle of the sixteenth century on, it was not until the nineteenth that territorial colonies that reached into the inland regions were established. Table 12.2 summarizes some of the key dates and numbers.

The table indicates that the two countries which were initiated as projects for the "repatriation" of freed slaves, Sierra Leone and Liberia, are also the countries which have the highest percentage of English speakers, many of whom are first language speakers of either GenE (Liberia approx. 16%) or an English creole (Sierra Leone approx. 10% Krio) (link: Colonial expansion into West Africa).

In all of these countries political and economic control was reinforced in the 1840s by the establishment of Christian missions, whose efforts, together with the colonial project, helped to establish StE in these countries. Indeed, by the 1860s Nigerian English was presumably well established. Since all of these countries, like most of West Africa, were polyglot, the post-colonial national administrations maintained the language of their former colonial masters as one of their official languages. This helped to strengthen internal (national) unity. At the same time English was seen as a key to higher education and the wider world. In West Africa, English has been associated with the forces of modernization in numerous areas such as private, international enterprise and public administration. All of the Anglophone countries of this region differ from the rest of Africa because of the presence of Pidgin English. West African Pidgin English (WAPE) maintains its function as

Table 12.2 Anglophone West African countries

country	significant UK contact	colonial status	independence	total population	English speakers	
					percentage	total number
Cameroon	1914	1916	1960	18,500,000	~ 42%	7,700,000
Gambia	1661, 1816	1894	1965	1,700,000	~ 2.3%	40,000
Ghana (formerly Gold Coast)	1824, 1850	1874, 1902	1957	23,480,000	~ 6%	1,400,000
Liberia	USA 1822	none	1847	3,750,000	~ 83%	3,100,000
Nigeria	1851	1884, 1900	1960	148,000,000	~ 53%	79,000,000
Sierra Leone	1787	1808	1961	5,800,000	~ 83%	4,900,000

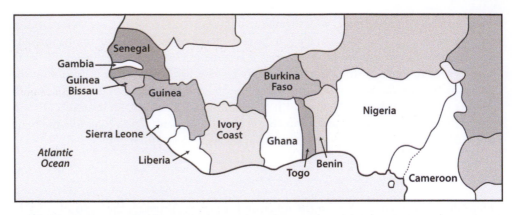

Map 12.1 Anglophone West Africa

a lingua franca between the different ethnic groups throughout the West African region, but especially in the urban populations of Anglophone West Africa.

Today English is an important medium of instruction in most schools once literacy has been attained in the students' native language or in one of the African regional languages. This enables Nigerians, for example, to participate in a diglossic English-language situation with Pidgin as the Low language of everyday (lower-class) urban life and Standard Nigerian English as the High language (link: Diglossia). Since there are further types of English in use such as mixed intermediate forms, it is also tempting to conceive of the overall language situation as a *continuum* with a *basilect*, a series of *mesolects*, and an *acrolect* (link: Continuum). It is, however, hardly likely that the mesolects show the same degree of incremental difference as those of Jamaican Creole and other Caribbean creoles (see 9.4.3). The High language is well established in the domains of secondary and higher education. Pidgin English, specifically NigPE, is used in the mass media and may be undergoing a move toward greater *accommodation* in the direction of the standard. There is also some evidence that NigPE is creolizing as it is used as a first language (Shnukal and Marchese 1983; Agheyisi 1988), often simultaneously with another African mother tongue.

12.1.4 East Africa

East Africa came under European colonial domination at the end of the nineteenth century with the establishment of British and German colonial regimes when the British took over Zanzibar (1890) and the Germans Tanganyika (1891). After World War I the latter came under British mandate. Linguistically, Kiswahili is a widely used lingua franca in the coastal cities which had spread under Arab influence in the slave and ivory trade along the east coast of Africa. Today Tanzania has a trilingual language policy based on the local tribal mother tongues, Kiswahili, and English. Kenya has a similar Arab background followed by British Christian missionary work and the engagement of the British East Africa Company in the second half of the nineteenth century. Arab influence in Uganda did not come until the first half of the nineteenth century, and here the presence of Kiswahili was negligible. The British came soon after the Arabs in explorations to find the source of the Nile. In the neighboring countries of Sudan, Somaliland, Rwanda, and Madagascar, not included in Table 12.3, English has official status, but does not have the British colonial background of the others.

Table 12.3 Anglophone East African countries

country	significant UK contact	colonial status	independence	total population	English speakers	
					percentage	total number
Kenya	1886	1895, 1920	1963	39,000,000	~ 9%	2,700,000
Tanzania	1880s	1890, 1920	1961	42,000,000	~ 11%	4,000,000
Uganda	1860s	1888, 1890	1962	31,000,000	~ 10%	2,500,000

The question of who speaks English can, as everywhere where English is a second language, be answered by: those with a higher level of education and correspondingly a higher social position. The numbers are estimated at 10% in Uganda, 9% in Kenya, and 11% in Tanzania. In the last of these Swahili is widely spoken as a mother tongue and as a lingua franca, thus lessening dependence on an outside language. However, the answer is not always as simple as suggested above. In Nairobi, a linguistic third space has emerged as

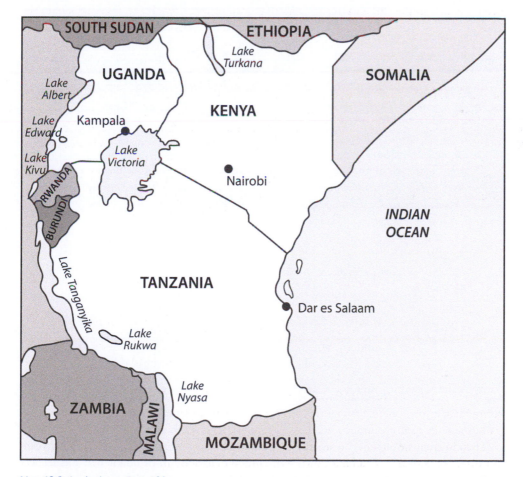

Map 12.2 Anglophone East Africa

the hybrid language *Sheng* (link: Sheng), drawing chiefly on English and Swahili, has developed and spread.

Perhaps the most widely read East African writer, the Kenyan Ngũgĩ wa Thiong'o, has been a vocal advocate of the African vernaculars, in his case Gikuyu and Swahili. Text 12.2 comes from his novel *Weep Not, Child* (1964), the first to be published in English by an East African. In it some of the atmosphere of colonial schooling becomes more tangible, a situation in which learning was largely by rote and insult and punishment, prominent when the results were not those the school wished as we see when one of the teachers, dissatisfied with the children's failure to learn as wished, says, "Look here you stupid and lazy fools. How long do you take to catch things? Didn't we go over all this yesterday? If I come tomorrow and find that you make a single mistake I'll punish you all severely" (*Weep Not, Child*: 45).

Text 12.2 East African English, *Weep Not, Child*

When a teacher came into the class, he greeted them in English.

    Teacher *Good morning children.*

    Class *(standing up, singing the answer) Good morning Sir.*

One day a European woman came to the school. As she was expected the school had been cleaned up and put in good order. The children had been told and shown how to behave. . . . When she entered, the whole class stood up at attention. Some had already opened their mouths to answer the expected greeting.

    "Good afternoon, children."

    "Good morning, Sir."

Lucia [their African teacher] felt like crying. Had she not taught them the correct thing over and over again? She had been let down. The visitor was explaining that since it was after lunch, after twelve o'clock, they should talk of "afternoon", and since she was a woman they should call her "Madam".

    "All right?"

    "Yes Sir!"

    "Madam!" shouted Lucia almost hysterically. She could have killed someone.

    "Yes Madam."

    "Good afternoon."

    "Good afternoon, Madam." But some still clung to "sir". It had come to be part of their way of greeting. Even when one pupil greeted another "Sir" accompanied the answer.

(Ngũgĩ wa Thiong'o, *Weep not, child*. Oxford: Heinemann Educational, chap. 4, 46–47)

The children would soon learn the difference between *sir* and *madam*, as demanded; but even more they would be following the hidden curriculum of obedience and respect toward the omnipotent Europeans.

12.1.5 South Asian English

The presence of English in South Asia goes back very far (Table 12.4), but it was not until the mid-nineteenth century that the language took on a larger role in Nepal and the South Asian British colonial territories (today's Bangladesh, India, Pakistan, and Sri Lanka), especially after the recommendations by Macaulay in his minute of 1835, which proposed that the local elite be "Indian in blood and colour; but English in taste, in opinion, in morals and in intellect" (Macaulay 1967). The colonial civil service and today's Indian Administrative Service use it as an all-India language, and it is recognized in the Constitution. In India, for example, English coexists with fifteen other national languages, one of which, Hindi, is spoken natively by approximately 40% of the population. Indeed, English is important because it offers an alternative in all-India communication in a situation where sensitivities among non-Hindi native speakers play an important role (Plate 12.1).

12.1.6 Southeast and East Asia and the Pacific

Each of the countries in Table 12.5 has a distinctive history and profile of use of English. In Malaysia, English has a colonial past not significantly different from the majority of cases so far reviewed. It is an important foreign language in education, science, technology, and commerce. Within the country Bahasa Malaysia is predominant. Singapore, at the tip of the Malay Peninsula, is a multi-ethnic state whose major groups are Chinese (77%), Malays (14%), and Indians, mostly Tamils (8%). Educational policy (12.2.2) has promoted English as the unifying national language (SingE) and increasingly many people know and use it, including its somewhat creole-like variant *Singlish* (12.3.2 and 12.4.3.3). Hong Kong has long had a Cantonese-speaking population with the consequence that English is clearly a foreign language and is spoken fluently chiefly by the well-educated and socially higher standing (see Text 12.4). The Philippines are one of the two countries in this review which stand in the tradition of AmE. The country itself is multilingual but is making efforts to establish Pilipino, based on Tagalog, as the national language. English was introduced after the Spanish–American War (1898), which ended over 300 years of Spanish colonial rule and introduced half a century of American colonialism. English was at times rigorously imposed and gradually eclipsed Spanish in administrative use. Today English remains an important language and is prominent in the media (news, serious newspapers and magazines, science, and the upper levels of administration).

Table 12.4 Anglophone South Asian countries

country	significant UK contact	colonial status	independence	total population	English speakers	
					percentage	total number
Bangladesh	1690	1858	1947	162,000,000	~ 2%	3,500,000
India	1600	1858	1947	~ 1.2 billion	> 20%	> 230,000,000
Nepal		none		25,000,000	> 25%	7,000,000
Pakistan	1857	1858	1947	164,000,000	~ 11%	18,000,000
Sri Lanka	1796	1802	1948	20,000,000	~ 10%	2,000,000

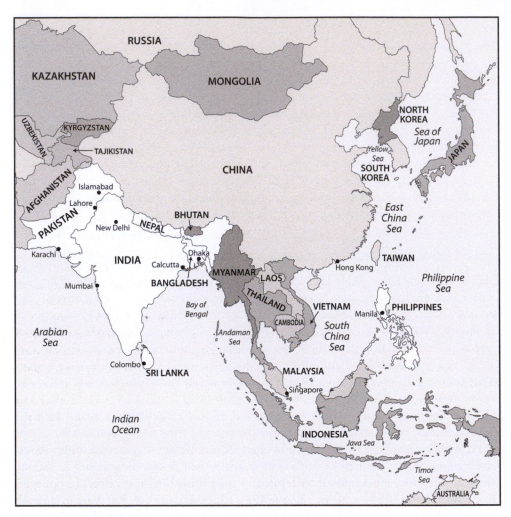

Map 12.3 Anglophone Asia

Table 12.5 Anglophone Southeast Asian countries

country	significant UK contact	colonial status	independence	total population	English speakers	
					percentage	total number
Singapore	1819	1867	1965	5,000,000	~ 80%	~ 4,000,000
Hong Kong	1841	1842	1997	6,900,000	~ 36%	2,500,000
Philippines	USA: 1898	1898	1946	97,000,000	> 50%	50,000,000
Malaysia	1786	1795	1957, 1963	27,000,000	~ 27%	7,400,000

12.2 Language planning and policy

Language planning and policy have taken on a great deal of prominence in ESL countries because of the need to raise the level of general education, which is often viewed as overcoming the local loyalties of polyglot countries (for example: tribalism, regionalism, ethnic rivalries). For these purposes the use of an external language, which does not arouse dangerous jealousies among competing autochthonous languages, is often given official support. In addition to this, in the long term an enlightened language policy provides support and legitimation for the cause of national unity. It is often a colonial language which is chosen – English where Britain or America were the colonial masters. Furthermore, the choice of English also often comes more easily because it is a global language. This gives the ESL-educated access to the world and to modern science and technology. At the same time it helps the outside world to get a foothold in markets in these countries and better access to their work forces.

The major difficulty in instituting English in this sense lies in finding the right balance between it and the regional or local languages. ESL obviously cannot fulfill all the functions language has in a society. Enlightened policy must offer support and developmental opportunities for the L1s of the population. The ideal case is for children to become literate in their first language and only then to begin making the move to a regional language or to a language like English. But developing a multiplicity of local languages requires more resources than most ESL countries have. For this needs a standardized orthography, grammar, and vocabulary; it requires adequate teaching materials; it demands qualified teaching staff; and it presupposes acceptance by parents and children. None of this comes without effort and expense, thus tilting the playing field in favor of English or one of the major regional languages.

The question of acceptance is one of the trickiest, for parents often see the greatest advantages for their children in learning the language which is most likely to ease the way to a good job and a secure future. Resentment toward the one-time colonial language is easily overcome in this context, and the fears of neo-colonialism can be conveniently suppressed. But in the Anglophone countries of West Africa a further problem with regard to acceptance arises, namely the question of which variety of English should be taught. Public policy in all the countries dealt with favors StE, the internationally more widely used form, while the more vital local forms of English are viewed critically. Yet it is the latter – Pidgin English, English creoles, or distinctly local forms of English such Krio in Sierra Leone or Singlish in Singapore (see 12.3.2) – which may well be emotionally closer to the learner. The ideal solution would be the cultivation of *bidialectalism* in the local and the global, but this also faces the problems of limited resources.

12.2.1 The three-language formula in India

This policy was adopted to strengthen the linguistic ties within the country by supporting the learning of English and Hindi. Everyone was supposed to be educated in their mother tongue or the regional standard. Above and beyond this the second and third languages in non-Hindi-speaking states were to be Hindi and English and in Hindi-speaking states, a further modern Indian language and English. In this way English and Hindi were to become all-India languages and indeed, quite a few English-language newspapers (about 100) are

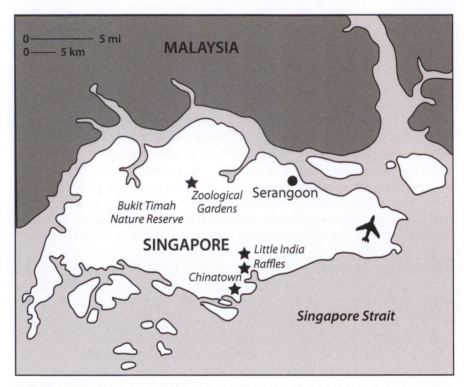

Map 12.4 Singapore

published, and English and Hindi dominate in radio and TV broadcasting and film (Plate 12.1).

12.2.2 Singapore's bilingual education policy

Bilingual education has been practiced since the 1960s. The medium of education in schools is any one of the three major ethnic languages: Chinese (Mandarin), Malay, or Tamil, plus English (Plate 12.2). The result of the application of this policy for half a century is a population with a new supra-ethnic national identity formed not by StE alone, but also by SingE, the vernacular of increasingly many Singaporeans. The higher the educational level of a speaker, the more likely he or she is to speak StE. English had become the home language of over 28% of the ethnic Chinese population, almost 40% of the Indian, and about 12% of the Malay population (*Education and Language* 2010: 17). More and more young people have begun to identify with the local indigenized variety, SingE, which emerged between 1930 and 1960 under the influence of input from school English as taught by teachers from Britain, Ireland, India, and Sri Lanka but also ESL speakers with Tamil, Malay, and Chinese backgrounds. It was highly influenced by the major substrate languages Hokkien Chinese, Bazaar Malay, and Baba Malay (a hybrid lingua franca derived from Hokkien and Malay). According to Platt, Weber, and Ho (1984) young learners were using English – still incompletely learned – in natural communication, hence adopting Chinese features as well as some, but fewer Malay ones. In the following section we will turn to the question of substrate influence.

12.3 Linguistic features of ESL

12.3.1 African English

12.3.1.1 WAfE phonology

It would be mistaken to suppose there is any real unity between varieties spoken over such a large non-contiguous distance. However, WAfE does share the heritage of its exogenous norms, BrE and, in the case of Liberia, AmE or AAVE. This and the use of StE in the schools guarantee a certain degree of similarity. For example, WAfE (with the exception of Liberia) follows RP and other British pronunciations in being non-rhotic, though prevocalic /r/ may well be trilled in contrast to the constricted or retroflex /r/ of most varieties of BrE and AmE.

12.3.1.2 WAfE grammar

WAfE grammar is in general like standard BrE, but different structures are possible, as will be pointed out extensively in 12.3.2. The main distinction lies in the continuum within the various West African ESL countries between the acrolect and pidgin or creole basilect.

12.3.1.3 WAfE vocabulary

WAfE vocabulary includes **borrowing**, both **loan words** (link: Loan words) and **loan translations** (link: Loan translations), which reflect the morphological and semantic structures of the **autochthonous languages** (link: Autochthonous languages). "What actually distinguishes WAVE [West African Vernacular English] from other non-native varieties of English is its lexicon, including the occurrence of certain types of code-mixing and regionally-bound idiomatic expressions" (Bokamba 1991: 503). In addition to the other examples given in this chapter we might add neologisms (link: Neologism) such as *watchnight* for staying up the whole night in order to celebrate something; loans including compounds of English and local vernacular words: *akara ball* "bean cake" or *juju music* for a kind of music; loan translations of local usages such as *father/mother* for a relative, as in *He is staying with his fathers* "He is staying with the relatives of his father"; loan words like *buka* "a food stand" or *wayo* "tricks" both from Hausa or *danfo* "minibus" or *wahala* "trouble" from Yoruba. Local extensions in meaning give NigE *corner* for a curve in the

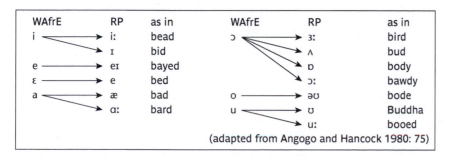

WAfrE		RP	as in	WAfrE		RP	as in
i	→	iː	bead	ɔ	→	ɜː	bird
	→	ɪ	bid		→	ʌ	bud
e	→	eɪ	bayed		→	ɒ	body
ɛ	→	e	bed		→	ɔː	bawdy
a	→	æ	bad	o	→	əʊ	bode
	→	ɑː	bard	u	→	ʊ	Buddha
					→	uː	booed

(adapted from Angogo and Hancock 1980: 75)

Figure 12.1 WAfE vowels

road; *go slow* for a traffic jam, and *to wet plants* for "to water plants." Translation equivalents to the local language(s) provide *to paste / to wash mouth* for "to brush one's teeth with toothpaste" or *buy the market* for "buy goods."

12.3.1.4 Attitudes in West Africa toward English

Attitudes are generally positive since knowledge of English is seen as opening the chances for social advancement and guaranteeing that the language remains internationally intelligible. In addition, the use of English may mask association with any particular ethnic group, thus avoiding tensions. On the other hand English is somewhat the language of the elite whose use creates a feeling of distance. The pidgins are positively regarded as neutral because the pidgin is not connected with any particular ethnic group. They carry a feeling of solidarity and create an atmosphere of intimacy. Among young people the pidgin is a signifier of identity. Yet pidgins are openly regarded as inferior to English and associated with low (overt) prestige.

This can be observed in the controversial status of NigE, whose very existence is denied by some educated Nigerian speakers while others acknowledge that there is such a thing, but see it as an incorrect version of StE. Clearly, it does exist and clearly it does not conform to all the expectations of StE.

12.3.1.5 A textual example: NigE

Text 12.3, taken from a Nigerian blog, illustrates one type of NigE. This blog was started by the remark by georgee at 11:27 a.m. and was followed by a lively discussion (thirty-one exchanges by 7:51 p.m. and continuing). Only a few have been included here.

Text 12.3 Igbo Girls Like Money a Lot

georgee (m) « on: **June 14, 2006, 11:27 AM** »
wt due respect 2 d ibo guys/babes in d house, wuld really love 2 knw y ibo girls r over -money conscious, though all naija babes like money, but ibo girls own just 2 much, no wonder yoruba guys dey run away frm them, they r just 2 demanding, frm their parents ryt 2 thier daughter, i pity them sha, this is naw age,no guys will allow himself 2 b troubled by one yeye ibo girl all 4 one kind unrealistic love,wen there r so many babes out there, wt less demand, ibo chicks its better y'all change, b4 u start running 2 christ embassy @ age 40 ,cos of husband

Damsal (f) « #1 on: **June 14, 2006, 11:57 AM** »
Well i've heard that the money makers in Nigeria are ibo's, and so i do not find it surprising that the women should also be interested in finance the only thing i find wrong. Is taking money from guys for goodness sake women you call yourself independent how about trying to be just that everyone in a while 😊

> dominobaby (f) « #2 on: June 14, 2006, 12:04 PM »
> *Georgee, i bet u are aware of the word 'some'? Dnt start some tribal war here.*
>
> Big Shishi (m) « #3 on: June 14, 2006, 12:33 PM »
> *i think ibo gurls is sexy, kedu ka odi? all my fine ibo thoroughbreds*
> . . .
>
> diddy4 (m) « #19 on: June 14, 2006, 05:46 PM »
> *you better watch ya mouth girl and put a comma when u talking cuzz eerone aint d same. not all igbo girls like money afterall most of them are proud independent women that don't need no ones cash.*
> *@edygirl*
>
> *go easy on him abeg, i am crying with laughter her abeg. u will kill him if u continue. d fool must be broke and he came here to see if he will get a cheap girl.*
>
> *if you don't have anything to offer to a girl, don't bother going to her cuzz all girls have needs and it must be met whether u like it or not. if u don't like it, leave them alone. kapish*
> . . .
>
> 2fine4u (f) « #21 on: June 14, 2006, 05:58 PM »
> *Igbo girls are hardworking, smart, successful and independent so ain't nuffin wrong in them lookin for a hardoworkin, successful man. if u ain't gats the money, they aint gon want u cos u below their level of achievement. so bruh, if u heartbroken by one Igbo girl wey chop ya money it's cos ya lame backside is dumb and puhleeze don't take it out on other Igbo girls. we too cute and sophisticated to be messing with broke backside n199as like u. and we ain't gold diggers cos we gats our own gold.*
>
> (from: Igbo Girls Like Money a Lot, www.nairaland.com/nigeria/topic-15219.0.html)

This blog is characterized by many of the same abbreviations (*2, 4, r, u, y*, etc.) and emoticons found elsewhere in the English-language blogosphere. The use of *d* for *the* is surely less widespread elsewhere, here reflecting Nigerian pronunciation. The use of capitalization varies from participant to participant as does the degree of colloquialism. The frequently used, colloquial word *abeg* is derived from English *I beg* "please." Some of the bloggers, e.g. #1 Damsal are virtually at the acrolect while others like #21 2fine4u switch into NigPE (*one Igbo girl wey chop ya money*). Further code-switching between English and Igbo occurs throughout the blog and varies from person to person, for example in # 3 Big Shishi (*kedu ka odi*). The grammar of these contributions is close to StE, but includes such things as:

- *pleonastic subjects* (link: Pleonastic subjects): *yoruba guys dey run away* (initial blog by georgee);
- non-standard concord: *ibo gurls is sexy* (#3 Big Shishi); *if u ain't gats; cos we gats* (#21 2fine4u);
- zero *be*: *when u talking* (#19 diddy4);
- *ain't*: *so ain't nuffin wrong* (#21 2fine4u and elsewhere).

319

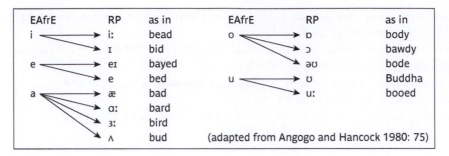

Figure 12.2 EAfE vowels

12.3.1.6 EAfE phonology

EAfE phonology is given here for vowels because of its contrast to WAfE phonology. No distinction between /s/ and /ʃ/ is made, as when *show = so*; likewise /tʃ/ and /ʃ/, /ʒ/ and /z/, /s/ and /dʒ/ may be variably distinguished. The consonants /r/ and /l/ are not distinctive so that *lorry* may be rendered /loli/ or /rori/. While WAfE has seven vowels, EAfE has only five. No further comments on EAfE will, however, be made.

12.3.2 Asian English

12.3.2.1 SingE pronunciation

The most salient differences to the *reference accents* of English (link: Reference accents as standards) are:

- no difference is made between long and short vowels;
- *marry = merry = Mary* (pronounced with an /ɛ/);
- *come = calm* (pronounced with /ʌ/);
- replacement of dental fricatives: /θ/ and /ð/ by /t/ and /d/, sometimes /f/ and /v/, rarely /s/ and /z/;
- word-final cluster simplification: /lift/ →/lif/;
- word-final fricatives are voiceless; no vowel shortening before voiceless fricatives: *rice = rise*; *leaf = leave = live*;
- non-rhotic; but younger speakers tend to use post-vocalic /r/.

12.3.2.2 SingE grammar

- word order in indirect questions: *May I ask where is the stamp counter?*;
- deletion of the indefinite article: *May I apply for car license?*;
- lack of third person singular present tense {-s}: *He always go there every Saturday.*

Singlish usage is more extreme and includes further features not regarded as standard, for example:

- inversion ("*is it*" as a standard *tag question*): *You're teaching us today, is it?*;
- *copula deletion* (link: Zero copula): *X a teacher* instead of *X is a teacher*;

- interrogatives: only *why* and *how* have to be in sentence-initial position, for example *How you on the computer?* vs. *She eat wha?*;
- zero subject (perhaps influenced by Chinese): *so in the end . . . Ø didn't try out the rides, so initially Ø want to take the ferris wheel*;
- deletion of object pronouns: *Sorry, we don't have* instead of *Sorry, we don't have it*;
- lack of *if*: *Got money, I would see the movie*;
- *topic* (link: Topicalization) prominence: *Play soccer he very good also.*

12.3.2.3 SingE vocabulary

SingE vocabulary is marked by the incorporation of loan words from the other languages of Singapore such as *kiasu* = "fear of losing out" from Hokkien (Chinese dialect); *makan* = "to eat" from Malay; hybrid compounds: *botak head* = "bald head." Phraseology may differ as with *catch no ball* "fail to understand"; and there may be a shift in meaning, for example *send* "to accompany someone."

12.3.2.4 A textual example: Hong Kong English

The following text is taken from an interview between the Hong Kong Voice of Democracy and Szeto Wah, the chairperson of the Hong Kong Alliance in Support of Patriotic Democratic Movement of China, which appeared on June 1, 1998. It provides a reasonable sample of acrolect Hong Kong English.

Text 12.4 Hong Kong English

Q *The Alliance has raised a lot of money from the citizens through its activities all these years. What is the financial picture now? What if all the money are spent (1)? Will the Alliance accept foreign sponsorship?*

A *As of April, we still have three million Hong Kong dollars in the bank. . . . However, as Hong Kong is going through (2) an economic down turn recently, we shall have to see. . . . Last year we have raised (3) more than two million Hong Kong dollars. . . . All our past resources are (4) based on the money donated to us directly from the citizens. . . .*

Q *Last May, a debate has been (3) successfully motioned (5) in the Legco to call for (6) Beijing for rectification of the June 4th massacre. . . .*

(Joseph 2004: 141)

The passages in blue show (1) differing subject–verb concord; (2) present progressive for present perfect progressive; (3) present perfect for simple past; (4) present for past; (5) *motioned* for *initiated*; (6) *for* instead of StE *on*. None of these divergences from StE hinder the intelligibility of the text.

12.3.3 Code-switching in the Philippines

In a society in which two languages, English and Pilipino/Filipino, play such a prominent role it is not astonishing that a great deal of code-switching occurs. The use of English may be functional and prestigious, but the intermixture of Tagalog/Filipino establishes sender–receiver solidarity and may mark the speaker as a (Westernized) nationalist. Nevertheless, this mixing is pejoratively referred to as *Mix-Mix* (or *Halo-Halo*). If there is more Tagalog it is sometimes called *Taglish*; if more English, *Engalog* (Gonzalez 1982: 214). The following illustration of it comes from the beginning of a short story:

Text 12.5 Philippine Mix-Mix English

Maniwala ka kaya, pare, kung sabihin ko sa iyo that a mere whisper can cause death. It may even create chaos.

Tipong heavy and intro ko, pero it happened one night dito sa destitute place namin. Ganito iyon, listen carefully. . . .

Can you believe it, friend, if I were to tell you that a mere whisper can cause death. It may even create chaos.

It looks like my introduction is heavy [too serious], but it happened one night here at our destitute place. It was like this, listen carefully.

(qtd. in Gonzalez 1982: 213)

12.3.4 Variation and nativization

A brief look at some numbers from the ESL countries shows how different the status of English is within these as opposed to the ENL countries. Nigeria, the most populous African country with approximately 150 million inhabitants, has around 80 million English speakers, of whom perhaps as many as 4 million have English as (one of) their first language(s). South Africa (see also chapter 11) has a similar number of first language users, but a higher percentage of native speakers, perhaps close to 4 million out of a population approaching 50 million and perhaps as many as a third of the population, who speak English. In Cameroon over 40% can speak English, but virtually no one has it as their first language. India is said to have 200–333 million users of English – depending on the estimates (cf. Crystal 1997; Jenkins 2009a; *Ethnologue* 2009) – in a country of well over a billion people. The point of these examples, which could easily be extended (link: Numbers of speakers), is that ESL must necessarily function differently in such divergent social and political contexts as these countries represent and that the history and development of the language will be fundamentally different there from the course it has taken in ENL countries. In India a percentage of 25–30% means there are more English users in India than in the US. Consequently, many of the researchers working in the area of ***English as a Lingua Franca*** (ELF; cf. 13.4.4) see this as reason enough to regard not only IndE, but a whole range of ESL and EFL (***English as a Foreign Language***) countries as largely independent of ENL and its standards. The range and intensity of ESL and EFL use is, however, clearly different. This does not lessen the importance of English, but it does relativize it. Clearly Indian English (IndE) is not and cannot be an exact copy of ENL, yet IndE and the other ESL types treated in this chapter have grown considerably in global awareness. Just as clearly their development and their features belong to the history of the language.

The varying functions of English in the ESL societies have led to varying constellations. In those countries where English is widely used in domains which presuppose a high degree of education in English, but where a number of regional languages or a national one serve the more everyday needs of the population, there may be fairly clear cases of diglossia or even triglossia. In Cameroon the H (= High) language is English (and French as well, of course) while numerous languages of more restricted currency[3] and a number of lingua francas[4] are the L (= Low) languages. However, when we compare the local languages and the lingua francas, it is perhaps justified to see the latter as Mid-languages, and the local ones, the L in a triglossic H–M–L constellation. In countries such as Sierra Leone, English is also used as an H language, but Krio, which for some people is a pidgin with English as its lexifier and for others a creole, is widely spoken. This makes the variation more like a continuum, but unlike in the Caribbean (cf. 9.4.3).

12.3.5 Standardization

Standardization often accompanies nativization, but is often controversial. The local forms of English may be a "badge of identity" (Gupta 1994) and used "to express emotionality and proximity or to play with, a language of one's heart, an identity carrier" (Schneider 2009). On the other hand, English which does not conform to the exonormative forms may tend toward international unintelligibility and is regarded as a handicap by some, such as the government of Singapore, which launched the "Speak Good English Movement" in an attempt to eradicate Singlish. As Prime Minister Goh remarked:

> If we speak a corrupted form of English that is not understood by others, we will lose a key competitive advantage. My concern is that if we continue to speak Singlish, it will over time become Singapore's common language. Poor English reflects badly on us and makes us seem less intelligent or competent.

> (Goh 2000)

Goh is justified about one point: the popularity of Singlish. According to one study 41% of the respondents stated that they do not need to speak "good" English. Not always, however, do the users of local language forms take such a stance. More often non-standard usage triggers feelings of insecurity and dependence, for education is too often coupled with a kind of "utilitarian elitism with specific political aims." This leads to the development of what has been called *schizoglossia*, in which English represents both modernity and dependence (Mazzon 2000b: 82ff).

---

3 Beti with 2 million speakers is the largest of the autochthonous African languages. Other languages with a large number of speakers are Bulu (858,000), Fulfulde, Adamawa (669,000) and Ewondo (578,000) (*Ethnologue* 2009).

4 Cameroon PE is a widespread lingua franca in the Northwest and Southwest provinces. Fulfulde is used as a lingua franca in the north, and Ewondo in the the center, south, and east.

In ESL countries there are persistent calls for alternative models of English to replace exonormative, that is, non-native, mostly BrE models, especially in teaching. Although everyday communicative practice has de facto established local norms, any serious consideration of codification along the lines of the kind of codification which can be found in ENL countries would require fuller knowledge of the local varieties than usually exists. There are some commonalities among ESL varieties, such as a leveling of StE tense forms, prepositions, word order, and the like (Mesthrie 2004a: 807), but there is dispute over the reasons for them. To what extent are they due to historical language contact, similar substrate influences, and universal tendencies?

"Nativisation is an assessment of how 'unsuccessful' the learning process has been, that is, how the learning [of] English has been resisted. . . . an indigenised English, from a structural perspective, is the restructuring of English structure to fit within the frame of indigenous norms" (Mbangwana and Sala 2009: 261). It is a form of English "used effortlessly, unconsciously, spontaneously and naturally" (ibid.: 274).

> The term indigenisation presupposes that we do not need to consider deviations as errors. It means that deviations are considered to be what the English language has become the evolution and changes it has undergone in a particular region. This is certainly different from the notion of errors, which are learner-problems. Speakers of CamE are no more considered to be learners of English but speakers of a particular brand of English.
>
> (ibid.: 273)

12.4 Substrate influence

It is sometimes questioned whether – or how much – the original language of a speech community can influence English when this speech community comes into contact with English or is subject to the imposition of English (cf. Mesthrie 2004c: 1141). There is no doubt about such influence in the cases of immigrants to English-speaking societies, nor is there in the cases of learners of English as a foreign language. Here new users regularly carry over into English features of their own (original) L1, most especially a "foreign accent." Grammatical constructions show up which are more typical of the L1 than of English, as do borrowings (loan words or loan translations) and *false friends* (<u>link: False friends</u>) in the lexis of these varieties. This kind of transfer is often referred to negatively as *interference* and more positively as *interlanguage* or *learner's language* (<u>link: Interlanguage</u>). It is usually not found in the language of the following generation, for whom English is the L1. If, however, the features of the original heritage language are passed on, this is a case of substrate influence.

Substrate influence is one of the results of language contact in which the language of one community is imposed on another. Quoting again from Mesthrie: "The robustness of the substrate languages in Africa and Asia makes the likelihood of their influence on ESL very great." This is especially the case in phonology "and only slightly less so in syntax, pragmatics and lexis" (Mesthrie 2004a: 808). When imposition is followed by nativization, processes are set in motion in which substratum influences together with universals of language creation shape the form and features of the contact varieties of English. These universals are understood as the principles of language acquisition, including second language acquisition (SLA) (cf. Winford 2009: 209). As Mbangwana and Sala express it, "Cameroonianisms in CamE cannot be helped by Cameroonians and are more or less resources than problems" because they grow out of categories in the L1 which are missing in English (2009: 246).

12.4.1 The phonetics and phonology of Second Language Englishes

These most often reflect the patterns of the autochthonous languages. If we look, as an example, at Cameroon English (CamE), we see that there are various indications of the influence of the speakers' African native languages such as a tendency toward using the intonational features of the tonal systems of West African languages or syllable timing, which shows up in the retention of full vowels in what in Britain or America would be weakly stressed syllables with /ə/ or /ɪ/. Simo Bobda (1994, 2010) explains the latter with the concept of the Trilateral Process, which says the underlying phonological structure of a word will vary according to fixed rules of derivation from an underlying phonological representation (UR), which itself may differ in, for example, RP and CamE. CamE, like most WAfE, lacks central vowels. Consequently, /ʌ/ will be realized as /ɔ/, and /ɔ/ retains its full quality (Figure 12.3).

The same sort of process applies with suitable adjustments in the underlying representation and the derivational rules to other African Englishes (cf. Simo Bobda 2008). In terms of phonetic realization dental fricatives are often articulated as /t/ and /d/ instead of /θ/ and /ð/ "three of these" = "tree of dese." While the diphthongs /aɪ/, /aʊ/, and /ɔɪ/ are present, the diphthongs /eɪ/ and /oʊ ~ əʊ/ are not and the realization is a monophthongal [eː] and [oː]. Phonotactic rules favor single rather than clustered consonants with the consequence that *list* is always *lis'* (link: Substrate phonetic-phonological shift).

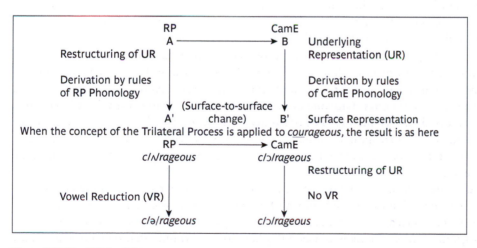

Figure 12.3 The Trilateral Process

12.4.2 Grammar: inflectional morphology and syntax

A synopsis of morphological and syntactic variation in the ESLs of Africa and South and Southeast Asia (see Mesthrie 2004c) reveals a diversity of features which differ fairly much among themselves, yet these ESLs differ even more as a group from ENL varieties, on the one hand, and English pidgins and creoles, on the other. Among the few wider generalizations one "striking and almost universal characteristic among L2 varieties in Africa-Asia is the extension of *BE + -ING* to stative contexts" (ibid.: 1134), as in *What are you wanting?*

Most attention has been paid to the *TMA* (tense, modality, aspect; <u>link: TMA (tense, modality, aspect)</u>) features of the ESL varieties, but inflectional morphology, auxiliary choice, concord, and verb serialization as well as negation, relativization, and complementation have also been treated. Differences in the pronoun system are frequently mentioned (<u>link: Personal pronoun systems of English</u>). In order to escape vague generalities but not to get caught in a morass of detail a selection of data from two ESL varieties, CamE and SingE, is recounted in the following.

12.4.2.1 The case of CamE

The influence of the substratum on educated CamE may be illustrated by a series of constructions in which structures occur which are analogous to ones in the indigenous languages *Cameroon Pidgin English (CPE)* and the Niger-Congo language Lamnso'. Since at least some CamE structures are found in various indigenous languages but not in StE or GenE, a substrate influence may be inferred, possibly together with universal tendencies of language change (for a wider selection of distinct CamE constructions see Mbangwana and Sala 2009: chap. 6).

Thematic Roles

Thematic roles (<u>link: Thematic roles</u>) may be assignment to *smell* differently in CamE than in StE. In the latter *smell* takes the roles Experiencer and Target as in *I* (Experiencer) *smelled the fire* (Target). In CamE, in contrast, the roles Cause and Experiencer may be assigned as in *The fire* (Cause) *smelled me* (Experiencer). This patterns like *The fire frightened me*, that is, "caused me to be afraid/to smell something."

Simplification of transformations

This is a process which may lead to results divergent from StE. This is the case if questions are formed without any change in word order. It may occur in GenE – a so-called echo-question – in which there is no word order change or transformation, but only marking by rising intonation, for example *You're going to town*↑. In CamE there is no final rising intonation; and, furthermore, this is the default form of questions on the model of the substrate language Lamnso'.

A second example is the general avoidance of movement transformations, such as the movement of a preposition with its object, aka *pied piping* (. . . *the book in which I looked*) (<u>link: Pied piping and stranding</u>). If the preposition is left behind this is known as *stranding* (. . . *the book which I looked in*). In CamE there is no pied piping movement and yet the preposition is deleted (. . . *the book which I looked*), a practice also found in Cameroon PE and Lamnso' (Mbangwana and Sala 2009: 237). Movement is also avoided by embedding *wh*-words in indirect questions, for example *I do not know whether he was reading the book*

how (ibid.: 241), where GenE would move *how* to the front of the indirect question in place of *whether* or would keep *whether* but delete *how*.

Covert variance

Covert variance occurs when what looks like StE may have a different interpretation in CamE, one puzzling to a non-CamE speaker. This is the case with *until* in (1) *He was tired until he could not walk*, where a StE temporal understanding of *until* is not the same as the CamE result interpretation "so tired that." In (2) *Until you are in need, then you know your real friends*, a temporal meaning is not available and a non-CamE speaker is unlikely to guess the intended meaning "only when" (ibid.: 241).

Changes independent of substrate influence

Not all innovations in CamE are so clearly due to substrate influence. Avoidance of empty categories aka "trace guilt" may be an independent development. It is the tendency to fill a trace, the "blank" left after an element moves, with a resumptive pronoun (ibid.: 238), as in the example: **The other teacher** *I taught English with* **her** *went* (ibid.: 258). In StE the blank left by moving *the other teacher* would remain empty (a trace) rather than be filled by repetitive or resumption *her*.

12.4.2.2 The case of SingE

The tense and aspect systems of Singapore Colloquial English (SingE) may once again be used to illustrate substrate influence. Both tense and aspect show the strong effect of Chinese, which as a highly analytical language has virtually no inflections. One consequence of this can be seen in the smaller number of inflections in SingE. The third person present tense verb ending {-s} is subject to variable use, but overall it is not used often, for example *He play soccer also very good one leh*.[5] Tense itself is marked chiefly by employing temporal adverbials: the present uses *today, now*; the past usually takes *yesterday*, for example *Yesterday, dey go there oreddy*; and the future is marked by *tomorrow*, for example *Boss, tomorrow can get my pay check or not?* Winford accounts for this partly as SLA simplification and partly as substrate influence. There is a difference in the frequency of the use of past tense {-ed}. Punctual verbs are marked more (56.2%) than stative verbs are (36.9%). Non-punctual verbs are marked with {-ed} least often (14.7%) (see Ho and Platt 1993 for the percentages). The less frequent use of {-ed} accords with the lack of substrate endings, but the variability in inflectional frequency shows the possible influence of a universal tendency to take into account punctuality, which is interpreted as having past time reference if there is no marking to indicate the contrary. State and non-punctual verbs such as *know* are regarded as having present reference, so helping to account for their "resistance" to marking with {-ed}, see *He also know about it mah!*[6]

SingE aspect

SingE aspect is influenced by both Chinese and English, but more by the former. While GenE has two kinds of verbal aspect, progressive and perfect, SingE has at least four distinctly marked types of grammaticalized aspect:

---

5 *Leh* is a downtoner used to make requests and commands less imposing; borrowed directly from Hokkien.
6 *Mah* marks the truth of a statement as something obvious; borrowed from Cantonese.

(1) *progressive* is like GenE except that the auxiliary is optional: (*be*) V-*in*.
(2) *completive perfect* is similar in meaning to the resultative perfect in traditional StE (*He has lost his orientation*), but is formed using *already* (*Yesterday, dey go there oreddy*), which reflects the use of the Chinese perfect marker *le*.
(3) *experiential perfect* is formed using *ever* on the model of Chinese *guo*: *I ever try this type of fruit before*.
(4) *habitual* is marked by *useto* + verb. Unlike GenE, *useto* is present rather than the past habitual:

Text 12.6 SingE with present habitual aspect

SingE speaker: *The tans* [military unit] *use to stay in Serangoon.*
Non-SingE speaker: *Where are they staying now?*
SingE speaker: *I've just told you. In Serangoon.*

(Tongue 1974: 44)

This is motivated by the lack of a past habitual in Chinese, where it is associated with the present.[7]

The passive

The passive is particularly innovative in SingE. To form the passive, *kena*, a verb particle specific to SingE and derived from the Malay word for "come into physical contact" is used. It is used in negative or adversative contexts, and it is followed by a lexical verb in the infinitive or the past participle form, for example *John kena scold (by his boss)* "John was scolded . . ." or *The thief kena caught (by the police)* ". . . was caught by. . . ." A second way of forming the passive in colloquial SingE is to use *give* as in *John give his boss scold* ("John was scolded by his boss"). The two differ both formally and in their meaning. Unlike *kena*, *give* may be followed only by the infinitive. Passives with *give* have an implication that the person affected carries part of the blame for what happened to them (Wee 2004: 1064–1065).

12.4.3 Vocabulary

Vocabulary differs from variety to variety in much the same way regardless of whether we are looking at ENL or ESL. It is customary to borrow items from the indigenous (substrate) as well as other languages just as it is usual to form new words using the same principles of compounding and derivation. Furthermore, words already in the language may undergo various types of semantic change. There is especially much borrowing in the areas of flora, fauna, topography, and social institutions and practices. As in the preceding sections a few samples of borrowing, word formation, and semantic change in a few ESLs will be supplied.

---

7   The auxiliary *will* also expresses present and *would* past habitual in SingE and may be due to Chinese *hui* or Malay *akan* (Deterding, Ling and Brown qtd. in Winford 2009: 221). GenE habitual *will/would* is also a possible source.

12.4.3.1 New words in WAfE

Borrowings ([link: Borrowings](#)) from autochthonous languages include both loan words like *awujor* "ceremony giving the ancestors food" and *calques* or loan translations such as *next tomorrow* "day after tomorrow" (< Yoruba *otunla* "new tomorrow"). From pidgins or creoles, come expressions such as *tai fes* (literally "tie face" for "frown"). Other (*adstrate*) languages have supplied such words as *palaver* "argument, trouble" (< Portuguese). *Word formation processes* ([link: Word formation](#)) include derivation by affixation as with *co-wives* "wives of the same husband," but also reduplication, for example *slow slow* "slowly," and compounding, for example, *bush-meat* "game."

Semantic shift ([link: Meaning change](#)) includes extension of meaning as when *chap* is used to refer to any person, man or woman. Semantic narrowing can be seen where *cane* refers only to bamboo, and pejoration covers the use of *smallboy* for a low servant. (Examples qtd. from Gramley 2001: chap. 6.)

12.4.3.2 New words in South Asian English

Borrowings from South Asian languages are frequently "more informal, more personal, more relaxed, and sometimes more culture-sensitive" (Mehrotra 1982: 160–162); nevertheless, there may be opportunity or need to use Indian terms in formal texts as well, for example:

> **Text 12.7 IndE newspaper business section**
>
> *Urad and moong fell sharply in the grain market here today on stockists offerings. Rice, jowar and arhar also followed suit, but barley forged ahead.*
>
> (Kachru 1984: 362)

The vocabulary of IndE contains numerous borrowed items, which may often "come more naturally and appear more forceful in a given context than their English equivalents. *Sister-in-law* is no match for *sali*, and *idle talk* is a poor substitute for *buk-buk*" (Mehrotra 1982: 160–162). Word formation would include items such as *black money* "illegal gains," hybrid formations like *lathi charge* "police attack with sticks," or even use of otherwise unproductive suffixes such as {-dom} as in *coolidom* "state of being a coolie" (examples from ibid.). Also well known are the blends *Bollywood* < *Bombay* and *Hollywood* and *Lollywood* < *Lahore* + *Hollywood*). In semantic shift English words are used differently, for example *four-twenty* "a cheat, swindler."

12.4.3.3 Borrowing in SingE

The official position of the Singapore government is not to encourage the use of the more colloquial varieties of SingE, which extend on a continuum to Singlish, often regarded as a creolized variety. Indeed, Singlish is avoided in formal settings in favor of Standard Singapore English. Nevertheless, select Singlish phrases are sometimes injected into discussions to build rapport or for their humorous effect, especially when the audience consists mainly of locals. In informal settings Singlish is used without restriction.

Since Singapore English is spoken by a population whose home languages are Malay, Chinese, and Indian languages, it is not surprising to find borrowings from these languages:

- Malay is the source of *jaga* "guard, sentinel," *padang* "field, open area," *kachang* "peanut," *kampong* "village," and *makan* "food."
- Indian languages have supplied *chop* (Hindi) "stamp, seal," *tamby* (Tamil) "office boy, errand boy," *dhobi* (Hindi) "washerman," and *syce* (from Arabic via Hindi) "driver."
- Chinese has provided *towkay* (Hokkien) "employer, business person," *jiak* (Hokkien) "to eat," and *la/lah* (Hokkien) a speech discourse element; see 12.4.4.1 (cf. Tongue 1974: 69; Platt and Weber 1980: 83–87).

12.4.4 Pragmatics

English speech communities with a local, non-European-based culture will adapt not only their pronunciation, grammar, and vocabulary, but also their conversational rules. Local social norms may dictate different stylistic levels and speech act rules. The expression of thanks in IndE, for example, may turn out to be especially profuse as compared to ENL usage, while culturally appropriate and contextually proper in India:

Text 12.8 Expression of gratitude in IndE

I consider it to be my primordial obligation to humbly offer my deepest sense of gratitude to my most revered Guruji and untiring and illustrious guide Professor [-] for the magnitude of his benevolence and eternal guidance.

(Mehrotra 1982: 165)

Rather more difficult for the outsider to comprehend is the subtle way power differences may be expressed. The active voice, which counts as direct, may be used to a subordinate, as in "I request you to look into the case." This would be impertinent if used for someone of higher standing. For one's boss the passive voice, which is indirect, would be normal: "You are requested to look into the case" (ibid.: 166). The familiar rules of **politeness** and *face* (link: Politeness, face) are in force here as in ENL, but they are differently realized.

12.4.4.1 *Discourse particles* (link: Discourse particles) *in SingE*

There is wide use, outside the acrolect, of discourse particles or modal particles borrowed in form and meaning from Chinese. Of these the perhaps most widely known is *lah* < Hokkien, Malay, which indicates mood and attitude as in *Come with us lah* (persuasion), *Wrong lah* (annoyance), or *No lah* (strong objection). The precise mood or attitude depends very much on the situation. In the mesolects *lah* adds a note of politeness as compared to the same examples quoted when they appear without *lah*. In Wee's words, "This has led

Table 12.6 Discourse particles in SingE

oi (attention getter)	*ar/ah* (negative tone; depending on the tone
wat (information is obvious and contradictory)	used, rhetorical (rising) or genuine (mid-level)
mah (see footnote 6; < Cantonese)	question)
lor (obvious; sense of resignation; < Cantonese)	*hah* (question marker; < English)
leh (see footnote 5; < Hokkien)	*meh* (skepticism; < Cantonese)
hor (solicits support; < Hokkien, Cantonese)	*siah* (emphasis, envy; < Malay)

(see Wee 2004: 1068ff, esp. for *lah*, *wat*, and *lor*)

to claims that the particle is a marker of solidarity, functioning to mitigate face-threatening speech acts" (Wee 2004: 1069). Other discourse particles are given in Table 12.6.

12.4.4.2 Yes, no, and negation

The words *yes* and *no* are used throughout the English-speaking world as pro-forms for affirmative and for negative statements. If one person asks whether someone else would like to go for some coffee (*Would you like to go for some coffee?*), *yes* is equivalent to saying *I would like to go for some coffee* and *no*, to saying *I wouldn't like to go for some coffee*. When the question is phrased negatively (*Wouldn't you like to go for some coffee?*), ENL speakers in answering with *yes* mean *I would (like to go . . .)* and in saying *no* mean *I wouldn't (like to go . . .)*. In SingE, in contrast, a *yes* means *I wouldn't* and *no* means *I would*. This lies in the fact that for the ENL the response is congruent with the polarity *yes* = *would like to* and *no* = *wouldn't like to*. In SingE, in contrast, *yes* engages at the pragmatic level and affirms the speech act, namely *Yes, it is the case that I wouldn't (like to . . .)* and *no* negates it, namely *No, it is not the case that I wouldn't (like to . . .)*. This SingE use of *yes* and *no* is also found in WAVE (Angogo and Hancock 1980: 77–78) and in IndE:

A: Didn't I see you yesterday in college?
B: Yes, you didn't see me yesterday in college.

(Kachru 1984: 374)

This suggests that the difference to traditional ENL varieties lies in the substrate languages.

A further pragmatic difference shared by a number of second language Englishes involves the form of the "grammatical" ***tag question*** ([link: Tag questions](#)). In most ENL varieties the tag varies according to the subject and the verb in the clause it is attached to: *We can, can't we? They did, didn't they? You are, aren't you?* As Algeo points out:

Varieties of English that have been heavily influenced by other languages use invariant question tags that superficially resemble the echo tag of mainstream English. An invariant *isn't it?* or *is it?* has been reported for Welsh, Chinese, West African, Indic, and Papua New Guinean English in constructions like "You're going home now, isn't it?"

(Algeo 1988: 174–175)

Compare this to:

- You went there yesterday, isn't it? (IndE; Verma 1982)
- The Director is busy now, is it? (SingE; Tay 1982: 64)

- Das waz a swiit stuori, duonit? "That was a nice story, wasn't it?" (Miskito Coast CE; Holm 1994: 380)

12.4.4.3 Systems of measurement in PakE

The coexistence of two systems of weights and measures is a good example of how *field* or *domain* (link: Field, domain) determines the use of language. "For many Pakistanis, especially those belonging to the older generation, the more familiar systems of measurement are in fact the indigenous and the British" (Baumgardner and Kennedy 1994: 183). For spices, condiments, and foods the traditional measures[8] are:

- *chattank* = 5 *tola*
- *pao* = 4 *chattank*
- *seer* = 4 *pao* (933.12 grams)
- *dhari* = 5 *seer*
- *maund* = 37.3242 kg = 40 *seer* for drugs, flour, wheat, red chilies, cotton.

Compare the following:

Text 12.9 Pakistani English newspaper report

He said that Gujrat police recovered five maunds of charas, one kg heroin, 131 bottles of liquor, two maunds of lehan [raw materials for making liquor] *and raided four distilleries from where five drunkards were arrested*

(*The News*, Lahore August 16, 1991, L 20/1 qtd. in ibid.: 184)

This mixture will remain, for "words are more than just names for things. Words also carry a host of culturally specific associations, attitudes, and values" (Gumperz and Hernández-Chavez qtd. in ibid.: 185).

12.5 Identitarian function of language

One of the consequences of the observation of the numerous smaller and larger differences between the ENL varieties, on the one hand, and ESL varieties, on the other, is the realization that the emergence of such distinctions is a part of how we use language to signal who we are (or want to be in any given encounter). Language is fundamental to communication, but it inevitably serves the need "for establishing and maintaining 'imagined

---

8 Other sets of terms from the areas of length, surface measure, weight, liquid measure, and numerals are in use. English may underdifferentiate vis-à-vis the semantic field in the source language (Baumgardner and Kennedy 1994: 186).

communities', group self-representations" (Joseph 2004: 191). Consequently, "group identities tend strongly to correlate with shared linguistic features" (ibid.: 38). This function of language guarantees that linguistic diversity will continue in our world. The spread of English may indeed hasten the death of some languages, but the diversity of English itself will ensure that variety will remain: "Ultimately, national, ethnic and religious identities themselves will be asserted through linguistic diversity" – diversity which helps people to know and to show who they are (ibid.: 191) in the multiplicity of their encounters.

12.5.1 Language and identity: can English adequately represent African and Asian cultures?

One of the consequences of the imposition of European power on other parts of the world has been a change in traditional modes of thought and belonging. As with Europe itself, most of the rest of the world has developed a perspective which goes considerably beyond the local or regional. Loyalties are increasingly located on a national scale – whereby nation itself is a concept generated by happenings in Europe and its settler communities in other parts of the world. Lord (1987: 11), remarked:

> In Hong Kong, over the past two decades, English has changed from being a purely colonial language whose use was largely restricted to government circles, the law, high-level business, and a few other sectors, to becoming an indispensable language of wider communication, for a growingly large range of people, all the way down from top brass to clerks, from taipans to secretaries.

As Mazrui (1973) says, English helped to detribalize the African mind and to give it a national dimension. Despite the appropriateness of this statement, this has not made the local, the tribal, the traditional simply go away. Rather, it has led, for many people, to a split in loyalties and in the languages associated with their loyalties. Language, in the words of the Kenyan writer, Ngũgĩ wa Thiong'o, is "the collective memory bank of a people's experience in history. Culture is almost indistinguishable from the language that makes possible its genesis, growth, banking, articulation and indeed its transmission from one generation to the next" (1986: 15). Local languages are, consequently, the depository of local culture. English cannot replace this. In fact, English, as the colonial language, is associated for Ngũgĩ wa Thiong'o with humiliation, denunciation, and lessons in being traitors. The English-speaking African elite accepted the English language, which helped to give them power and prestige and was seen by them as a sign of intelligence and ability even though it meant losing their selves in the process (ibid.: 18).

Other writers do not take such a negative stand on the role of English. Nigerian writer Chinua Achebe, for example, accepts English as a historical fact and makes the point that, if sub-Saharan Africa has a "national" language, then that language is English, as English is spoken in more countries than any other language. He promotes the use of an African variety of English, and he deliberately deviates from Standard English and adopts African idioms in his writing. In his words:

> The African writer should aim to use English in a way that brings out his message best without altering the language to the extent that its value as a medium of international

exchange will be lost. He should aim at fashioning out an English which is at once universal and able to carry his peculiar experience.

(1975: 61)

African English must be "a new English, still in full communion with its ancestral home but altered to suit its new African surroundings" (ibid.: 62). While English was indeed imposed by British colonialism and while it did divide some ethnic groups, it, a world language, also united various groups because it allowed communication between them – both within the individual states and on a Pan-African level (ibid.: 57).

12.5.2 Can an ESL or EFL speaker use English effectively?

Despite many who doubt this, the answer seems quite clearly to be *yes*. The consequence of a *yes* is, however, the acceptance of an English which is not understood as a duplicate of ENL. It is, rather, a kind of English which remains internationally comprehensible but flexible enough to express African, Asian, or other experience. That is, it must seek to reflect the history of its users and their relationship to the world, to adopt their images, their rhythms, and their voices. Merely imposing ENL norms means controlling (parts of) speakers' mental reality and extending one more aspect of colonialism into the neo-colonial world.

What has been said here about Anglophone Africa can be applied equally well to other countries which were once colonial possessions. In the opposition between local traditions and languages, on the one hand, and modernization in which English is particularly instrumental, on the other, new generations who are no longer personally affected by British (or American) colonialism have accepted the once-colonial language as an opportunity to be seized without giving up local rootedness. English goes with modernity and education, and is more likely to flourish in the larger towns and the cities while the autochthonous languages remain important carriers of local culture – religion, family, traditional occupations, and village life. For countless people multilingualism with English as one of the languages used is everyday reality. While in this context English may for some be a modern, outsider language associated with higher education and research or with international trade and finance; for others it may be a multi-faceted language which includes local habits of pronunciation, native vocabulary, and semantic and grammatical structures formed according to underlying patterns of thought and expression. "A Cameroonian learns English with a different cultural background, including a different linguistic culture. He may master the English linguistic culture, but when he has to communicate appropriately with his kin of the same culture, he has to mix his linguistic culture with that of English" (Mbangwana and Sala 2009: 252).

12.6 Summary

The colonial background of the ESL countries reviewed here has been critically reviewed and compared in regard to linguistically relevant aspects. This has brought out differences in the number and nature of English users and in the varieties of English spoken in these countries, and in the functions associated with the use of English. Two cases of educational policy, in India and in Singapore, provided an indication of the role of English in education and national politics. A selection of linguistic features from each of the larger areas, South Africa, West Africa, East Africa, South Asia, and Southeast Asia, gave us a hint of how these areas differ from each other. Furthermore, material was chosen which focused on the influence of substrate languages on pronunciation, vocabulary, grammar, and ways of using the language (pragmatics). Emphasis was also laid on how a second language variety of English can serve not only political, educational, and economic purposes, but can also be used to achieve identitarian goals.

STUDY QUESTIONS

Historical and social background

1. English is an instrument of cultural hegemony. Give an example of this.
2. English is suitable for expressing the local. Give an example.
3. How well do standardization and nativization fit together? That is, how do the two reinforce each other and how do they contradict each other?

Linguistic background

1. Give an example of substratum influence.
2. Give an example of universal principles of second language acquisition.
3. Explain whether the continuum model or the diglossia model best fits the situation of English in East Africa, and in West Africa.

Further reading

Jenkins and Mazzon offer a very accessible exploration of the question of standards in Outer Circle and Expanding Circle Englishes. Joseph is a solid introduction of the identitarian function of language. Schneider et al. is, as the title indicates, a reference work, one of whose greatest virtues is making available in one work (two fat volumes) a comprehensive overview of present-day varieties of English throughout the world in a vast collection of short contributions. Winford looks at substrate influences in three different types of English: IrE (ENL), Bajan (post-creole), and SingE (nativizing ESL) in regard to tense and aspect.

Jenkins, J. (2009a) *World Englishes. A Resource Book for Students.* 2nd ed. London: Routledge.
Joseph, J.E. (2004) *Language and Identity. National, Ethnic, Religious.* Houndmills: Palgrave.

Mazzon, G. (2000) "The Ideology of the Standard and the Development of Extraterritorial Englishes," In: L. Wright (ed.) *The Development of Standard English 1300–1800.* Cambridge: CUP, 73–92.

Schneider, E.W., K. Burridge, B. Kortmann, R. Mesthrie, and C. Upton (eds.) *A Handbook of Varieties of English.* vol. 1. *Phonology* and vol. 2 *Morphology and Syntax.* Berlin: Mouton de Gruyter.

Winford, D. (2009) "The Interplay of 'Universals' and Contact-Induced Change in the Emergence of New Englishes," In: M. Filppula, J. Klemoa, and H. Paulasto (eds.) *Vernacular Universals and Language Contacts. Evidence from Varieties of English and Beyond.* Routledge: London, 206–230.

CHAPTER THIRTEEN

Global English (since 1945)

No-one pays attention to what you say unless you speak English, because English is the language of power.
(Gret Haller, Ombudsperson for Human Rights in Bosnia and Herzegovina, 1997)

Chapter Overview:

This chapter:

- reviews the long-term and more immediate roots of the globalization of English, looking at English in comparison with other languages and at StE in comparison to regional forms;

- follows with aspects of English in the Information Society, especially spelling, texting, advertising, scholarly prose, and English for Specific Purposes (ESP);

- focuses on English as a native, second, and a foreign language, and emphasizes the pluricentrism of the language but also some of the most prominent attempts to redefine English in an international context;

- contrasts this with the identitarian functions of English, which are viewed in regard to both inclusiveness and local rootedness;

- finally, sums up the diversity of perspectives in a discussion of the convergent and divergent aspects of present-day English as both global and local.

13.1 The beginnings of Global English

When did Global English arrive on the scene and did this mean the demise of ModE? Chapter 7 on the spread of English might be taken as the beginning of Global English, but it was not until the middle of the twentieth century that the spread was so overpowering that it became possible to speak of a change in quality. The question of why this came about can be productively approached by considering the move from Insular to Global English, a development which came about parallel to the emergence and spread of the Information Society. The expansion in the accessibility of knowledge was closely connected with the advent of printing (see 5.4.4). If this might be seen as an arithmetic increase, then the explosion in availability of information that came with computers and especially with the Internet and the World Wide Web was an increase of geometric dimensions.[1]

Why has English become the medium of global communication? Latin held sway in the Western World as the language of learning and international scholarship throughout the Middle Ages. With the growth of the national vernaculars in Western Europe Latin was gradually displaced, and in post-Renaissance Europe largely replaced by the language associated with the major hegemonic state of that time: the French of France. The second major change was that the world, especially the Western world, was beginning to grow economically closer together. Under these circumstances religion became less important as the glue which held the West together and a replacement was needed that was more closely associated with the great new revolutions, the Commercial and the Industrial Revolutions. The candidate would be the language of one of the great new global imperial masters – Spanish, Portuguese, French, Dutch, or English. In the case of English there was an almost unbelievable constellation of factors which favored its ever more rapid advancement to the status of global language. English had the unique advantage of being the language of the first country in which the Industrial Revolution took place, which meant the early establishment of an industrial basis which led to a positive balance of trade. Furthermore, just as the British Empire with all its consequences for the spread of English had passed its apogee sometime between the beginning of World War I and the end of World War II, the United States effectively took its place as the economic leader of the world and the military, political, and cultural leader of the West; and the language of both was English.

Virtually every text on the subject of English in the world stresses its role as a library language, as a language of wider communication, or as the major language of the Internet and the Information Society. In a book on the history of English it is not enough to repeat this; rather, it is important to point out how this came about and how this development has affected the language.

13.1.1 Vernacularization

Vernacularization affected English as it did virtually every other European language in the late Middle Ages. In many cases this was a move from Latin to French, German, Italian, Spanish, or English, among others. In other cases this process privileged some vernaculars over others. This was the case in Britain, where English had precedence over the Celtic languages, some of which were completely displaced, for example the "original" Celtic language(s) of England, including Cornish, and, for all intents and purposes, Manx. Scottish Gaelic has long been in decline, but Welsh seems to have stabilized. In Britain and

---

1 This is meant metaphorically building on arithmetic increase by addition: $2 + 2 + 2 + 2 = 8$ vs. geometric increase by multiplication: $2 \times 2 \times 2 \times 2 = 16$.

in other countries where English is the major or dominant language immigrant languages have generally yielded to English over the course of three to four generations (link: Generation model). Added to this is the imposition of English in British and American colonial territories (see chapters 7 to 12). All of this may be subsumed under the title of *linguistic imperialism* (see Phillipson 1992: chap. 3; and 7.3.1).

Although political colonialism ended with the granting of independence to the vast majority of once-colonial territories in Africa and Asia in the two and a half decades following World War II, the expansion of English has continued. However, since the world economic order did not change in any fundamental ways with regard to the overall distribution of power, colonial-like relationships (*neo-(neo-)colonialism*; cf. ibid.) have continued not only in commerce, but in language policy. This has privileged not only English, but also French, Portuguese, and marginally other European languages as well. At this point English was more or less on a par with a small group of other European languages.

Two historical accidents of time and place helped put English in the position it presently occupies. The first, as already mentioned, was the Industrial Revolution, which lent English power and prestige beyond what it had gained in its world-wide confrontation with its chief colonial rivals. This was complemented by growing American ascendency. The second was the advent of the Information Society, whose roots lay scattered through Europe[2] and America, but which found its strongest expression in the development of the personal computer, which took place most emphatically in North America, thus linking it with English through the domination of the market by American giants such as Microsoft and Apple. The cultural power of the US is, as the next section makes clear, strongly rooted in the media.

13.2 Media dominance

The advantages of being there first are revealed in the media, both traditional and digital. This has allowed StE to take a position of dominance in relation both to the "dialects" of English and to non-English languages in general.

13.2.1 Publishing

Publishing was more than anything else the domain of StE. Publishing was long dominated by Britain even though copyright law was so much a national matter that British authors had no protection from blatant piracy in the US until 1891, when America extended its copyright laws to non-American authors. In the meantime the United States had developed a healthy literature of its own drawing on both StE and American regional dialects, especially in the last third of the nineteenth century. However, most publishing appeared in StE, and the American version of StE cannot seriously be regarded as different from StE in England. In both countries it was the default written medium for fiction and non-fiction.

---

2 The first programmable computer was developed by Konrad Zuse, a German, in 1941.

In contrast, the vernacular used in the local color movement (<u>link: Local color and regionalism</u>) of late nineteenth century America was a minority phenomenon. Text 13.1 illustrates what is meant by this vernacular. It comes from the perhaps most widely recognized example of American dialect literature, Mark Twain's *Adventures of Huckleberry Finn*. The text describes Huck Finn's response to two rascals who have chanced upon him and his companion, the runaway slave Jim, who were drifting down the Mississippi. This novel, told by Huck, a young uneducated boy, uses regional dialect, including the since thoroughly discredited word *nigger*, throughout the narrative and not just in dialogue, as is the case with most "dialect" writers including British ones such as Dickens or Thackery.

Text 13.1 Local color writing: Twain's *Adventures of Huckleberry Finn* (1885)

THEY asked us considerable many questions; wanted to know what we covered up the raft that way for, and laid by in the daytime instead of running – was Jim a runaway nigger? Says I:

"Goodness sakes! would a runaway nigger run south?"

No, they allowed he wouldn't. I had to account for things some way, so I says:

"My folks was living in Pike County, in Missouri, where I was born, and they all died off but me and pa and my brother Ike. Pa, he 'lowed he'd break up and go down and live with Uncle Ben, who's got a little one-horse place on the river, forty-four mile below Orleans. Pa was pretty poor, and had some debts; so when he'd squared up there warn't nothing left but sixteen dollars and our nigger, Jim. That warn't enough to take us fourteen hundred mile, deck passage nor no other way. Well, when the river rose pa had a streak of luck one day; he ketched this piece of a raft; so we reckoned we'd go down to Orleans on it. Pa's luck didn't hold out; a steamboat run over the forrard corner of the raft one night, and we all went overboard and dove under the wheel; Jim and me come up all right, but pa was drunk, and Ike was only four years old, so they never come up no more. Well, for the next day or two we had considerable trouble, because people was always coming out in skiffs and trying to take Jim away from me, saying they believed he was a runaway nigger. We don't run day-times no more now; nights they don't bother us."

(M. Twain (1885) *The Adventures of Huckleberry Finn*; chap. 20)

The important point about such literature is what it reveals about the relationship between publishing and StE. It shows that the standard holds no monopoly over use in print, and StE is not the only form of the written language even though it clearly dominates.

Dialect literature is, by definition, divergent from the standard language and may make for hard reading not only abroad, but also in the country of its origin. Even literature written fundamentally in StE can also cause difficulties in comprehension when used in connection with code-switching and borrowing from languages other than English. The following text comes from a New Zealand novel and revolves around the complex relationships between Joe, Kerewin, and Joe's son Simon.

Text 13.2 English – Māori code-switching (1983)

Joe was very still; so softly, that it was almost on a level with his breathing,
    "That's the way I feel most of the time." More loudly, "My father's father was English so I'm not yer 100% pure. But I'm Maori. And that's the way I feel too, the way you said, that the *Maoritanga* [Māori culture, Māoriness] *has got lost in the way we live."*
    He shook his head and sighed.
    "God, that's funny. I never said that to anyone before, not to Piri or Marama or Wherahiko, or Ben. Not even to my wife."
    "She was Maori too?"
    "Tuhoe." [a North Island Māori tribe]
    "Yeah."
    He drank the rest of his cocoa at one swallow.
    "Ho well." *He slides his hands under Simon and gently lifts him and stands in a graceful exact movement straight to his feet. The child doesn't stir.*
    "Kerewin . . ."
    "Yes?"
    "I don't know how to say thank you except this way." *He says very formally,* "Ka whakapai au kia koe mo tau atawhai." [Thanks very much for your kindness]
    Kerewin smiles. "Ka pai, e hoa." [That's okay, mate.]

(K. Hulme (1986) *The Bone People*, London: Picador, 62)

This excerpt from a novel written a hundred years later than Twain's shows the continuing use of local color elements in writing. Indeed, in the period treated in this chapter a booming cross-cultural literary market has emerged. Hulme's novel is fitted out with a glossary of Māori words and expressions, though it is not always sufficient for the Māori-ignorati. *The Brief Wondrous Life of Oscar Wao* by the American novelist J. Diaz is laced with Spanish, but often so colloquial that a normal bilingual dictionary does not help much. The Igbo in Adichie's *Purple Hibiscus* (Texts 7.3 and 7.4) is contextualized and/or paraphrased, but not always enough for non-Igbo speakers to understand. The list of authors and works could be expanded without any difficulty.

Globalization and publication have actually contributed importantly to the diversification of English as more and more voices reach a world-wide audience. While there are some difficulties for the reader who is not on more intimate terms with the culture and language which a particular example of such literature is grounded in, globalization of this sort does not call StE into question as the major medium of communication; rather, it embellishes it.

13.2.2 The electronic media

First analog then digital, the electronic media were introduced earliest in the West, but rapidly spread throughout the world. However, the Western origins meant that much of the media retained specifically North Atlantic elements including English-language ones. The telegraph was used practically exclusively for alphabetic symbols. The telephone did not have this restriction, nor did radio or the movies. Yet the complex infrastructures needed (wiring, broadcasting towers, production studios, cinemas) were most fully developed in the industrial countries, and this meant that the media were dominated by the European languages.

13.2.2.1 Telegraphic style

Since communication by telegram and telephone were private, that is, limited basically to an exchange between two people, the influence of the medium on the language used has not been restrictive as such, but it has influenced style. The economics of both the telegraph – pay by word – and the telephone – pay by minute – induced brevity, most clearly in the development of telegraphese. This refers to a style in which sentences are truncated through omission of contextually unnecessary subjects, auxiliaries, articles, conjunctions, and prepositions. It can be seen in telegrams themselves, but also in newspaper headlines, where space is limited:

Telegram style: ARRIVING GRAND CENTRAL TONITE EIGHT STOP PICK-UP APPRECIATED

Newspaper headline style: Out of Latin Roots, An Independent Streak

Both share dependence on the context for full understanding. In the case of the telegram message the recipient needs to know who is arriving, what evening "*tonite*" refers to, and that *appreciated* is an **indirect imperative speech act** (link: Indirect speech acts). In the newspaper headline only reading the following article will inform the reader that Latin refers to Latin American music and that the unnamed subject is the band Calle 13. There is nothing really strange about these shortenings. They conform to patterns practiced in other genres, especially in the spoken language. The patterns used in **baby-talk** (link: Motherese), foreigner-talk, or pidgins seem to follow the same rules of reduction and simplification. More recently telegrams have become obsolete and newspaper headlines are less and less often abbreviated in the way this one is.

13.2.2.2 Movies

The introduction of sound movies had an enormous influence on English inasmuch as wide audiences now had the opportunity to hear varieties of English previously inaccessible to them. Initially this was above all a case of mutual exposure of British and American varieties to each other. The leading influence was Hollywood, which brought American voices to the rest of the world along with the Hollywood concept movie. In the meantime, however, vigorous English-language film industries have grown up elsewhere, especially in India, where Bollywood (< *Bombay Hollywood*) has popularized its own movie formula and made incursions into the Western world.

Movies seem to have had more influence on people's narrative fantasies than on their language. There is little if any evidence of non-Americans picking up American accents, though idioms are more easily borrowed, for example *Okey-dokey, you bet, ...* What began with movies continued with growing momentum in television. Yet, it has become evident that the ultimate TV genre, the sit-com (< *situation comedy*) ([link: Sit com](#)) and soap opera ([link: Soap opera](#)) cannot always be adopted elsewhere without problems. British *Upstairs Downstairs* was a great success in the US and Australian *Neighbours* was popular abroad as well. Other productions proved to be hard to transplant. This was probably not so much a linguistic as a cultural problem. Presumably differences in cultural background, including types of comedy and satire, were the more significant obstacles.

13.2.3 The expansion of functions in the Information Society

The Information Society at the end of the twentieth century was strongly influenced by the advent of the computer, the Internet and the World Wide Web. This changed the structure of information as linearity and libraries were expanded by links and hypertext structures. The popular image of English had become one in which speed and convenience led to the widespread, though certainly not complete, acceptance of abbreviations, smilies (emoticons), rebus-influenced spellings, and much more as well as changes in the realization of genres. The essential points of English in the Information Society are oriented around the genre divide between information vs. entertainment and the difference in addressees who are experts vs. the general public, and the corresponding language is either more scholarly or more popular. This perspective puts great emphasis on the form of the language of e-mails, blogs, chatrooms, tweets, and texting (13.3.1). But this has not changed English; rather it has led to wider usage and greater general awareness of forms already present, though previously less visible. The more fundamental change in the language lies in its sociolinguistic evolution and new, often revolutionary functionality. It is with the latter point we will continue.

13.3 Features of medialized language

13.3.1 Non-standard tendencies in the written language

The concentration of the publication of newspapers, magazines, and books in the hands of publishing houses enabled StE to consolidate what may be regarded as its hegemonic claim to be "the language," a claim supported by the power of the State, the school house, and the pulpit.[3] With the coming of the Internet, control over the medium, which in this context meant control over the language, was decentralized. This is because the Internet is not a hierarchically organized and controlled means of communication. Rather, it is so fragmented, autonomous, and self-controlling as to be able to by-pass the global media concerns and to encourage grass-roots networking. This is not to ignore the fact that there have been many cases in which the State has exercised its control, and it should not be considered to affect only English; it is a global phenomenon ([link: The communication](#)

---

3 Religion was a less reliable ally in this campaign as popular religion has always been a vital vernacular force.

revolution). All the same, the power of the standard language has remained largely intact – as is clear from the basic orientation toward standard grammar and spelling – but the non-standard has also won a number of symbolic victories, as "u kn c" virtually everywhere, where more informal, personal encounters are the rule.

Communication may be either highly individual or addressed to larger groups within the society. E-mailing, texting, chatting, and tweeting differ from spoken communication in being graphic rather than phonetic in nature. They resemble spoken language, and like it they have their rules and regularities, which guarantee successful communication. What is different from pre-Web days is the fact that the sheer mass of written communication has expanded to a previously unimaginable extent. This is, on the one hand, a reinforcement of literacy. On the other, detractors may claim, it jettisons "standards." The quotation marks are important, for while critics are more impressed by the divergence of all those abbreviations and the like, it should be noted that the vast mass of communication in these new media conforms to established standards (see Crystal 2007).

13.3.1.1 Spellings

Attitudes toward innovative spellings vary, as mentioned, from the clearly negative, for example "digital virus, alien, outlandish, slanguage, dyslexia, mental laziness, illiterate," to more neutral evaluations such as "textese, hi-tech lingo, hybrid shorthand," to a positive view that emphasizes non-standard spellings as inexpensive, unobtrusive, personal, quick, and convenient (ibid.). Since things such as text messages and tweets are very limited in space, there is a motivation to be as brief as is feasible.[4] Text messages are generally used to keep in contact or to regulate everyday logistics such as time and place of meeting; consequently, lengthy discussions are seldom necessary. This leads to a change in etiquette such as a greater likelihood of leaving out salutations or closings, but perhaps also a greater, almost mandatory need to ask where the other person is at the moment or to mention where you are.

On the other hand, the very banality of such communication may well stimulate texters to indulge the ludic instinct, that is, the urge to play with language. Such playfulness has been around for centuries and is even more or less standardized in some cases. The use of *IOU* "I owe you," for example, goes back to the end of the eighteenth century. Among the innovations of digital communication is the use of emoticons ("smilies"), so much so that many computers automatically change the combination : +) to < ☺ >. These devices are generally so well known that much of the interest in them lies in the area of "one-upmanship," playfully going one unexpected step further than your partner. Other elements of shortening include logograms such as *2* "to," "too," or, of course "two" and *b* "be." Conventional symbols include @ "at," from the world of business; *x* or *xxx* "kiss(es)," from letter writing; or *zzz* onomatopoeic of snoring "sleeping" from comic books.

The grammar of abbreviated messages is very similar to telegraphese (13.2.2.1): if not absolutely necessary, articles are left out as are contextually clear subjects and auxiliaries, for example *glad trip ok* or *on way to mall*. Furthermore, many people dispense with capitalization, as in the preceding examples, when this requires pushing one more button

4 Crystal estimates that two-thirds of text messages consist of just one sentence (Crystal 2007).

on a cell phone. Add to this the use of abbreviations such as *cu* "see you," *asap* "as soon as possible," *aka* "also known as," or *btw* "by the way," or the omission of letters (usually vowels), for example *msg* "message," *xlnt* "excellent," or *mbrsd* "embarrassed," and you get stereotypical features of e-mails, chats, blogs, tweets, and text messages. Yet one survey, whose representativity is uncertain, suggests that only 6% of texters use abbreviations of any kind (Crystal 2007: 105). While the examples given are relatively well known or easy to interpret, many are not. See **link: Txtng, aka texting**, which offers further comment and examples.

13.3.1.2 Texting literature

Texting literature may serve to give a small insight into the more creative ways of using text messages, which are automatically restricted to 160 characters. Crystal quotes one example from a text-messaging poetry competition:

Text 13.3 Text-message poem

txtin iz messin   *gran not plsed w/letters shes getn,*
mi headnine englis,   *swears I wrote better*
try2rite essays,   *b4 comin2uni.*
they all come out txtis.   *&she's african*

(Crystal 2007: 14)

Clearly there are no restrictions on the spelling, which may be standard or not: note the complete lack of capitalization, the reduced use of apostrophes, the occasional missing spaces between words, the phonetic spelling of *is*, and the colloquial use of <-(i)n> instead of standard <-ing>. As in dialect literature the spelling reflects colloquial (British) pronunciation (*mi* for *my*). Abbreviations are not obligatory and tend to appear in the usual places (*txt, rite, plsed, b4, 2*). Little grammatical deviation shows up: here only the missing verb *is* in line 5.

13.3.1.3 Advertising and comical spelling

These are further areas in which alternatives to the standard orthographic system show up. In advertising the motivation for non-standard spelling lies in the attention which this may potentially generate for the product advertised. It has, for example, reinforced the use of the letter <k> as in the *Kwik-E-Mart* fictional chain of convenience stores in *The Simpsons*, where it is possible to buy *Krusty-Os cereal* – all a take-off of some of the commercial uses of misspelling. Like much else discussed here, the tradition of "misspelling" is not of recent origin. Its beginnings lie close to a tradition that was popular in nineteenth century America. See the spellings in Josh Billings (Text 13.4), one of those who were called the literary comedians, for some of the roots of this tradition.

> ### Text 13.4 J. Billings, "Amerikans" (1868)
>
> *Amerikans love caustic things; they would prefer turpentine tew colone-water, if they had tew drink either.*
>
> *So with their relish of humor; they must hav it on the half-shell with cayenne.*
>
> *An Englishman wants hiz fun smothered deep in mint sauce, and he iz willin tew wait till next day before he tastes it.*
>
> *If you tickle or convince an Amerikan yu hav got tew do it quick.*
>
> *An Amerikan luvs tew laff, but he don't luv tew make a bizzness ov it; he works, eats, and haw-haws on a canter.*
>
> *I guess the English hav more wit, and the Amerikans more humor.*
>
> *We havn't had time, yet, tew bile down our humor and git the wit out ov it.*
>
> *The English are better punsters, but I konsisder punning a sort of literary prostitushun in which future happynesz is swopped oph for the plezzure ov the moment.*
>
> (qtd. in W. Blair (1937, 1960) *Native American Humor*. New York: Chandler, 427)

A comparison of this with some of the spelling regarded as typical of texting shows an astonishing degree of overlap: *hav, luv, hiz/iz*, and the ending *-in*. There is, nonetheless, enough left over in Text 13.4 which would not be appealing to texters, for example *tew* and *colone*; and *you* is not shortened to the digital *u*, but only to *yu*.

13.3.2 Features of Global Standard English

The Internet is the most obvious, but, of course, not the only element in the structure of the Information Society. Newspapers, magazines, and journals as well as radio and television remain strong components. The catchy, zany spellings and expressions which have enlivened digital communication have not necessarily caused major changes in the more staid genres, which also make use of the Internet. Scholarly writing is one of the most central areas in the Information Society (link: Shamefaced scholarship). And here more than in the non-standard tendencies just treated the influence of English is global.

13.3.2.1 Scholarly prose

In the present-day world a huge proportion of serious academic publishing uses the medium of English. While the demands placed on the quality of the writing and publishing according to the norms of AmE or BrE are very high, a great deal of tolerance of variation is normal in spoken presentations at conferences. All the same, the choice of the conference language allows control over the interchange (Coulmas 1987: 100–101); and the question can be asked whether the language "influences the formation of novel scientific concepts – especially in the humanities – and that hence the increasing tendency of scientists to write in English will have a profound impact on the future development of science" (Traxel qtd. in Coulmas 1987: 106).

This objection lies in the fact that English has become the language which the largest number of academics throughout the world are likely to understand. Consequently, a preference for publishing in English, which was once a tendency, has become more and more a necessity. Ammon, a German-language linguist, recognizes this and sees a certain amount of discrimination in the objections by native speakers regarding the English of non-native users. This is something which he regards as *linguicism* ([link: Linguicism](link:Linguicism)) (Ammon 2000: 222). Linguicism, like sexism, ageism, and the like is the unjustified discrimination against someone because of the language they use. Ammon offers support for his argument by noting that in the case of medical dissertations written in Dutch or in English, the latter were evaluated more highly. In addition, in evaluating the "same" text in English and in a Nordic language it was the English version which was considered to be better (ibid.). The consequence which Ammon demands is that native speakers use more tolerance in regard to the standard of written scholarly English.

Another scholar, Clyne, also aware of the German-language tradition of writing, has gone so far as to maintain that the academic styles of these two important scholarly languages are different. Most striking are the textual asymmetry, the lack of linearity, the frequency of digression in German-language papers as compared with the English-language emphasis placed on linearity, the unity and relevance of the material presented, and the responsibility of authors to make their work readable for their intended addressees (Clyne 1987: 214).

> In English-speaking countries, most of the onus falls on writers to make their texts readable, whereas it is the readers who have to make the extra effort in German-speaking countries so that they can understand the texts, especially if the author is an academic.
> (ibid.: 238)

A more recent study (Kalensky 2009) finds German scientific communication to be as participant-oriented as English is said to be, but does not exclude the possibility that there has been change over the last several years and a movement toward an English stylistic approach in writing. However that may be, there seem to be tendencies toward English ways of expression due to internationalization and globalization. This has led, among other things, to an increasingly strict adherence to international English of Science and Technology (EST) text models, which are strongly formalized and achieve textual cohesion by means of highly conventionalized structural divisions. For example, journal articles normally have the following five divisions:

- an introduction, in which the purpose pursued / hypothesis investigated is presented;
- a review section, in which previous work is summarized or evaluated;
- a methods part, in which procedural sequences, criteria, and so on are evaluated;
- a results section, in which the findings are presented;
- a discussion part, in which the findings are evaluated in the framework of the initial hypothesis.

Such models are a part of the use of scholarly English for Specific Purposes.

13.3.2.2 English for Specific Purposes (ESP)

ESP is a functional differentiation of the language which contributes to its international character; as such it caters to the needs of its non-native users. In general, ESP is a subset of the language structured to transfer information in an unambiguous way. As a consequence, the ESP of any given field will draw on a subset of the vocabulary of GenE, a restricted grammatical inventory, and a restricted set of social and thematic areas. ESP focuses on the purposes of a task by drawing on a selection of reading, listening, writing, and talking skills, a selection of text types, and a selection of vocabulary and grammar. ESP may, for example, be restricted to such areas as English for Science and Technology (EST), English for Academic Purposes (EAP), English for Occupational Purposes (EOP), English for Business and Economics (EBE), English for Legal Purposes, or Doctor–Patient communication to name some of the more prominent areas. The following legal text exemplifies the divergence of ESP texts from GenE.

Text 13.5 Excerpt from an American insurance policy

If the Policy does not contain the provisions relating to Owner and Beneficiary as specified on the reverse hereof, the Company is hereby directed to modify the Policy by including such provisions therein, superseding any existing Policy provisions relating to be effective as of the date this is signed upon its recordation at the Home Office of the Company.

(author's own insurance policy)

The capitalization of the words *Owner, Beneficiary, Company, Policy,* and *Home Office* is used to change what would otherwise be common nouns into proper ones, that is, nouns with specific reference. The *Owner* is the person who owns this particular policy – hence, *Policy.* The use of *hereof* "of it"; *hereby* "by means of this statement"; and *therein* "in it" are survivals from an earlier age and have been preserved especially by their still current use in legal English. The construction *relating to be effective* "with a claim to be in effect" is hardly understandable in terms of everyday ModE. The word *recordation* "act of recording," finally, is unlikely to be found in a desk dictionary.

A further look at selected syntactic features will help to clarify some of the differences in ESP vis-à-vis GenE. Non-defining relative clauses, which are rare in spoken English, are much more frequently found in ESP texts. Personal pronouns also have a different frequency, with almost exclusive use of third person forms, relatively few first person pronouns, and only rare examples of the second person. Traditionally uncountable, mass nouns may be used in the plural to indicate "types of," for example *fats, oils, greases,* and so on (cf. Gerbert 1970: 40). Otherwise, infrequent Latin and Greek plurals (*mitochondrion/-ia*; *bacterium/-ia*) are more likely to be found in such texts than in GenE ones. The default sentence type is the declarative; some imperatives are to be found, for example, in instructions; but relatively few interrogatives and virtually no exclamatory sentences occur in EST texts (cf. Huddleston 1971).

The passive, which is relatively uncommon in colloquial English at a rate of about one occurrence in a thousand words, is ten times more frequent in EAP, namely one occurrence per hundred words. The following text, although it has a preponderance of passives (set in blue), does not sound unusual.

Text 13.6 The passive in ESP

In an experimental facility without breeding animals the health status can be restored if healthy animals are issued into a clean fumigated or disinfected room, and the infected room is gradually emptied as experiments are terminated. It is essential during the period that the clean and infected rooms are both in use that a strict barrier is maintained between them. Once the room has been emptied it can be thoroughly cleaned and disinfected or fumigated.

(Biber et al. 1999: 938)

Modal auxiliaries

Modal auxiliaries have a different distribution. *Could* and *will* have a frequency of 40% in EAP as compared with conversational English. The frequency of *can* lies at two-thirds and of *would* at one-third of the rate in conversation. *Be going to* is virtually absent. In contrast, *may*, used in statements of probability, occurs fourteen times more frequently in EAP than in everyday English (Biber et al. 1999: 489).

Nominal style

Nominal style refers to a higher proportion of nouns (also prepositions and adjectives) in a text and makes ESP hard for an "outsider" to read and understand. Sager et al. (1980) found that 44% of all words in EST vs. 28% in GenE texts fall into this category. This includes a higher degree of nominalization, as when clauses are replaced by nominal phrases, for example *because the surface of the retina is spherical* becomes *because of the sphericity of the retinal surface* (example from Gerbert 1970: 36). Furthermore, the tendency to combine a function verb and a noun instead of a simple verb, for example *to make an investigation* rather than *to investigate*, *to give a report* rather than *to report* are a part of nominalization. Note also the frequencies of compound nouns:

Table 13.1 Frequencies of compound nouns in three types of English (Salager 1984: 138–139)

General English	0.87%
Medical English	9.76%
Technical English	15.37%

Word formation processes ([link: Word formation](#))

These processes are similar to those in GenE, for example:

- prefixing (anti-, in-, mis-, non-, semi-, un-)
- suffixing (-ar, -al, -ed, -er, -less, -ment, -ness)
- conversion / zero derivation (*to dimension < dimension*)
- back-formations (*to lase < laser*)
- clippings (*lab < laboratory*)
- abbreviations (FBR < fast breeder reactor)
- acronyms (*laser* "light amplification by stimulated emission of radiation")
- blends (*pulsar* "pulsating radio star")
- composite forms (*aeroplane*).

It is normal to use symbols, for example Σ, ≤, ∀, ±, =, μ, °, π, ® , graphs, tables, and illustrations; and nomenclatures and terminologies such as the Linnean system have higher frequencies, as do borrowing from Greek or Latin (e.g. *apparatus*, *matrix*, or *phenomenon*), and the use of Greek and Latin combining forms as prefixes (*aero-*, *astro-*, *baro-*, *cryo-*, *ferro-*, *gyro-*, *hydro-*, etc.) or suffixes (*-gram*, *-graph*, *-ology*, *-scope*, *-tomy*, etc.). Some disciplines rely on systematic terminologies, for example in chemistry, where the order and status of roots and affixes are strictly defined: "*eth + an + ol* signifies, in that order, a structure with two carbons, simply linked together and with one of these linked to a hydroxyl (-O-H) group, and no other combination of these morphemes describes that structure" (Dermer et al. qtd. in Beier 1980: 32). How extremely different from GenE this may become is illustrated by the following example of military ESP. This text, battle orders quoted in Philip Caputo's autobiographical account of his experience of the Vietnam War, is, in his own words, "written in language that made the Rosetta Stone look like a Dick-and-Jane reader" (Caputo 1977: 14).

Text 13.7 Military jargon

Enemy sit. *Aggressor forces in div strength holding MLR Hill 820 complex gc AT 940713-951716 w/fwd elements est. bn strength junction at gc AT 948715 (See Annex A, COMPHIBPAC intell. summary period ending 25 June) . . .* Mission: *BLT 1/7 seize, hold and defend obj. A gc 948715 . . .* Execution: *BLT 1/7 land LZ X-RAY AT 946710 at H-Hour 310600 . . . A co. GSF estab. LZ security LZ X-Ray H minus 10 . . . B co. advance axis BLUE H plus 5 estab. blocking pos. vic gs AT 948710 . . . A, C, D cos. maneuver element commence advance axis BROWN H plus 10 . . . Bn tacnet freq 52.9 . . . shackle code HAZTRCEGBD . . . div. tacair dir. air spt callsign PLAYBOY . . . Mark friendly pos w/air panels or green smoke. Mark tgt. w/WP.*

(P. Caputo, *A Rumor of War*. New York: Henry Holt, 1996 [1977] 15)

Although English is widely used by many who are not native speakers, the language itself does not have any "special endowments" which somehow entitles it to popularity (Coulmas 1987: 95); rather, he argues, this is the consequence of the colonial past, which threatens to continue as present-day British, American, and Australian cultural colonialism. As Coulmas goes on to remark, the developing international variety he calls Airplane English "is just like airplane food (economy class), dull and tasteless" (ibid.: 105). But is Global English really so bland? The next section offers a different view.

13.4 ENL, ESL, and ELF/EFL

What the previous section has demonstrated is that English is as hard to describe as the people who use it. English is no longer restricted to a community of (native) speakers who are in face-to-face contact with other (native) speakers. Global travel and electronic technology have changed the traditional picture of the language. Today English is, of course, used by communities of *L1* speakers of *English as a Native Language (ENL)*, but also by speakers whose English is a second language or L2 (ESL), and very likely a nativized variety of English (see chapter 12). Furthermore, the language continues to be learned as a foreign language (EFL). Among EFL users there are many who employ English solely to communicate with other users of English as a non-native language. Indeed, this is probably the largest group of English users (cf. Seidlhofer 2009: 237; Jenkins 2009b: 201) – albeit by number rather than according to the total amount of interaction.

A kind of self-perpetuating momentum has gathered around the English language. There are many circumstances in which it turns out to be convenient to use the language. Out of these opportunities a kind of necessity has developed, one fueled not by the power and prestige of the major ENL countries alone, but by the communicative function of English among the leaders of countries in which English has not necessarily played a special historical role. The Bandung Conference of non-aligned countries in 1955, held in English, was a harbinger of further developments of a similar kind that were to come.

For most of the history of English the language was used only by inhabitants of Britain. The later spread to Ireland, to North America, and to the Southern Hemisphere was by way of settlers whose only language was often English. But the imperialistic project of England/the United Kingdom caused the language to be imposed on more and more people – be it as a community language or as a language of trade, administration, education, and work. This led to the developments described in chapters 7 to 12. While the situation is certainly not simple anywhere, it can be portrayed more or less as if it were without distorting the facts beyond recognition.

In the settlements in Ireland, in North America, and in Australia, in parts of South Africa, and in New Zealand, communities of speakers of English as a Native Language (ENL) grew up ([link: English as a Native Language (ENL)](#)). The indigenous populations of these territories were exposed to English, sometimes, in fact, had the language imposed on them (see for example 10.5.1). Furthermore, immigrant communities with few exceptions underwent language shift to English along the lines of the "Generation Model." Throughout the Caribbean and in Papua New Guinea as well as in scattered communities in West Africa English pidgins and creoles grew up which in the majority of the cases were used alongside of StE. In some of these countries English was nativized as the major language and acrolect in a continuum between a creole basilect and itself. This is most prominent in such Caribbean countries as Jamaica and Guyana (chapter 9).

In those countries in which English – often in a continuum with Pidgin English – is used more as a second or an auxiliary language alongside numerous indigenous languages it is common to speak of *English as a Second Language (ESL)*. Although English is part of the colonial legacy of these countries and was imposed or self-imposed on them (cf. Phillipson 1992; link: Linguistic imperialism), the language has frequently undergone varying degrees of nativization, which includes an expansion of the functions of its use in a broader range of stylistic variation and the (sometimes only incipient) recognition of a local standard (chapter 12; link: World Englishes). The following text not only points out that non-native English is likely to change in this context, it also illustrates one such change: *rhymes* is used here – and consistently so throughout a long book – where ENL would probably have *suits* or *is congruent with*.

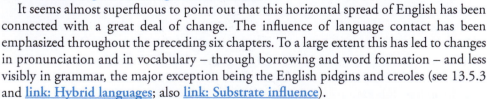

Text 13.8 Foreigner English from an ESL scholar in 2009 showing innovative use of vocabulary

It has been concluded that the structure is transferred from the indigenous languages . . . , and rhymes with other syntactic processes in the variety, ...

(Mbangwana and Sala 2009: 183)

In even more countries, ones in which there may well be no history of colonial domination, English has become an increasingly important language of communication, often between non-native speakers of English, for want of any other shared language. Knowledge of English is usually acquired in classroom type situations; and the status and nature of the language is regulated by practicalities of business, scholarship, travel and tourism, diplomatic relations, and much more. At the beginning of the twenty-first century this function of English as a lingua franca has come more and more into the focus of linguistic attention and is frequently referred to as *English as a Lingua Franca (ELF)*, a term which for some is replacing the idea of *English as a Foreign Language (EFL)* (see next

section; link: English as a Lingua Franca (ELF)).

It seems almost superfluous to point out that this horizontal spread of English has been connected with a great deal of change. The influence of language contact has been emphasized throughout the preceding six chapters. To a large extent this has led to changes in pronunciation and in vocabulary – through borrowing and word formation – and less visibly in grammar, the major exception being the English pidgins and creoles (see 13.5.3

and link: Hybrid languages; also link: Substrate influence).

A large number of models have been proposed to represent the kinds of variation outlined in the preceding paragraphs. Of these Kachru's circle model has, despite some criticism, been most widely adopted (see 7.6; <u>link: Models of World English</u>) and has been reproduced in Figure 13.1 in one of its more recent forms. This particular model has the advantage of combining the present-day global spread of English with the historical depth which is the central interest of this book.

13.4.1 Pluricentricism

The model in Figure 13.1 is not really complete. Not only could the lists in the three upper circles be extended to include further countries, it does not show the power relations between the countries and their varieties of English, which is not only a question of size, but also of the degree of penetration of English into the society in terms of functions and of the country's international presence. The Inner Circle countries – listed in order of size and international standing – are high in power and prestige, and represent three ENL areal linguistic standards: North America, Britain–Ireland, and Australia–New Zealand. In this connection it is worth mentioning that very, very many people who work with the idea of the world-wide spread of English speak about who owns the language. This is an unfortunate metaphor for talking about who sets the standards. But it suggests that it is somehow possible to talk about "possession," which is, in the end, an absurd idea.

Over the last several decades of the twentieth century local norms have developed in a number of further countries or multinational areas: the Caribbean, South and Southeast Asia, West, East, and Southern Africa. This has been reviewed in the preceding chapters. What remains to look at in this chapter is the question of English as a global language, that is, how English as an international medium of communication might look. Theoretically, one might approach this by simplifying the language (Basic English) or one might look for

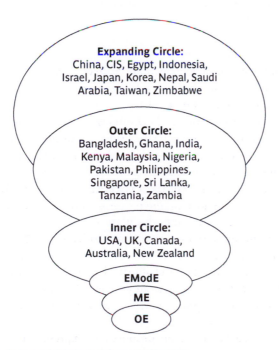

Figure 13.1 Kachru's circle model (adapted from 1992b: 356)

what is shared (Common Core English) or one might simply "loosen" the sometimes too rigid and too Euro-centric standard of the Inner Circle (English as a Lingua Franca).

13.4.2 Basic English

The concept of Basic English was developed by C.K. Ogden in 1930 and updated in cooperation with I. A. Richards after World War II and again by Bill Templer in the 1990s.[5] It was intended to be used as an aid in learning English as a foreign language and as an international auxiliary language, but its impact has been generally very limited. The word *Basic* is itself an acronym for "British American Scientific International Commercial." It consists of 850 words, including only eighteen verbs (*be, do, have, may, will, come, get, give, go, keep, let, make, put, say, see, seem, send, take*) (see Wiktionary's *Appendix: Basic English word list*). Learners were expected to add a further 100 general words and 50 more specialized words from a particular field of science or business which was central to them. Thus the student would have a vocabulary of 1000 words. The restriction to a thousand words is somewhat misleading inasmuch as the headwords listed may represent a word family. For example, *be* includes the forms *been, being, was, were, am, are,* and *is*. Ogden further assumed the knowledge of some 350 "international words" such as – for "g" and "h" – *gas, geography, geology, geometry, gram, glycerin* and *half, hiss, hotel, hundred, hyena, hygiene, hysteria*. There were also to be further general words from business, economics, and science. Altogether this would be 1500 words. Since Ogden calculated that 2000 words were necessary to reach a "standard" level in the language, additional words were then added. The two (or three) thousand word level continues to be important (see below 13.4.3).

The grammatical rules of Basic English were severely reduced (Ogden 1930), and consist principally of the following:

1. Use an "S" to make a noun plural.
2. Adjectives can be extended using "-ER" and "-EST."
3. Verb can end in "-ING" and "-ED."
4. Adjectives become adverbs by adding "-LY."
5. "MORE" and "MOST" are used to talk about amounts.
6. "Opposite" adjectival meaning is expressed using "UN-."
7. To make questions use opposite word order and "DO."
8. Operators and pronouns conjugate as in normal English.
9. Two nouns (e.g. *milkman*) or a noun and a directive (*sundown*) make combined words (compounds).
10. Measures, numbers, money, days, months, years, clock time, and international words are in the British form, for example Date/Time: 20 May 1972 at 21:00.

Text 13.9 is taken from Ogden 1932 and illustrates how one of the verbs, the modal auxiliary *may*, is introduced in a text written in Basic English.

---

5 There are other approaches besides Ogden's, but none so well known.

Text 13.9 A story in Basic English (1932)

One day last May *there was a rat in a hole. It was a good rat which took care of its little ones and kept them out of the way of men, dogs, and poison. About sundown a farmer who was walking that way put his foot into the hole and had a bad fall. "Oh," was his thought, when he got on his legs again, "a rat for my dog, Caesar!" Naturally the rat had the same idea and kept very quiet. After an hour or two, Caesar got tired of waiting, and the farmer put his spade over the top of the hole, so that the rat was shut up till the morning when there might be some sport. But the farmer's daughter, May, had seen him from her window. "What a shame," said May, "Poor rat! there is no sport in letting cruel dogs loose on good mothers! I will take the spade away. There –* the rat may go." *Then she took the spade to her father: "See! your spade was out there in the field, and I went to get it for you. Here it is." "You foolish girl," was his answer, "I put that spade over a rat-hole till the morning and now –* the rat may go."

(C. K. Ogden (1932) *The ABC of Basic English*. London: Kegan Paul, Trench, Trubner, 26–28)

In the story *may* occurs as the name of a month, a girl's name, a deontic modal of permission, and an epistemic modal of possibility (link: Modal auxiliaries). The accompanying text in Ogden 1932 explains these four meanings in the vocabulary of Basic English.

13.4.3 Common Core English

There have been numerous approaches to making the mass of English words more manageable for the non-native speaker. Among these the General Service List (GSL) of English words is one of the best known (West 1953). It consists of 2000 words and is intended to help learners. For example, it is used in so-called easy readers. Here, as with the words of Basic English, there is a differentiation in meanings of any given word form and derivational forms included under single headword entries. This means that there are, in fact, well over 2000 words in the GSL. Some of the entries are clearly dated – words like *shilling* – and others representing changes in our material culture are missing, for example *plastic* or *television*. There is, in other words, a need for reform, but the list represents coverage of about 80% of written English (Billuroğlu and Neufeld 2005).

The General Service List was put together on the basis of frequency, that is, the number of occurrences per 5 million words, but semantic criteria were also used to make the selection and not just frequency. The Academic word list developed by Averil Coxhead at the School of Linguistics and Applied Language Studies, Victoria University, Wellington, New Zealand contains 570 semantic fields which were selected on the basis of frequency from a broad range of academic texts, but adds low-frequency words of general utility such as *area*, *approach*, *create*, *similar*, and *occur*. It goes beyond the General Service List and is specific to academic contexts. This is a useful tool for college and university level students learning English – and for their teachers (cf. also *Simple English Wiktionary*).

The idea of 2000 words is employed by the *Longman Dictionary of Contemporary English* (LDOCE) for its "defining vocabulary," which is used to define all other entries in this learner's dictionary. Oxford uses a list of 3000 keywords, the Oxford 3000. This list, too, is extended with further special words for numerous areas (Oxford 3000).

13.4.4 English as a Lingua Franca (ELF)

This concept, due largely to Jenkins, was undertaken to give learners and users of English as a foreign language a greater say in the norms of their English. Since this group of English users is not geographically definable in the way that ENL and ESL speakers in principle are, they are defined as postmodern, international, global communities. They are often virtual, that is, Internet, "*communities of practice*" (Seidlhofer 2009: 238), ones which do not involve a face-to-face communication within a primary community. As such ELF is less a variety in terms of dialect – region, class, ethnicity, gender – than one in terms of register – how the language is used in particular situations. This English is regarded by ELF adherents as a legitimate linguistic variety within a conceptually new, but legitimate speech community, and as a variety which is not fully in conformity with ENL norms. This relatively recent approach to World English resembles Basic English and the GSL in restricting the extent of English in an international context. While the GSL used limited vocabulary and Basic English included simplified grammar, ELF further adds to this by also taking pronunciation into consideration (see next section). This is justified in two ways. For one it is aimed at describing[6] the English actually used by non-native speakers – especially international professionals, business people, researchers, and chatroom users – communicating among themselves in English, which is said to represent the major use of English in the present world.

It is claimed that ELF is an independent variety both functionally and formally. Functionally it is the result of a very pragmatic need, that of communication in a non-native language. This means its users must engage in accommodation (link: Communication accommodation theory), resolve instances of miscommunication, establish rapport, and employ appropriate communicative strategies such as repetition, silences, and considerate and mutually supportive communicative behavior (ibid.: 241).

On the formal side, ELF is described as following its own non-native standards and even signaling a cultural identity of its own, though it does not become clear just what this is outside of not embracing the "cultural baggage" of native-speaker communities. This would mean, for one, avoiding "local idiomatic language" (ibid.); and, for another, it definitely recommends not regarding non-standard forms such as *She look very sad* or *a book who I like* as errors. This approach accepts *advice* or *information* as countable nouns, hence seeing forms like *advices* or *informations* as perfectly legitimate (cf. Prodromou 2007: 49). Since so many non-native (and even very many native) speakers do not regularly use the phonemes /ð/ and /θ/, they are simply dispensed with in the ELF framework (Jenkins 2000). Words not listed in dictionaries based on ENL usage, such as *transitionary*, *linguistical*, and *increasement*, but employed by ELF-users are regarded as legitimate,

---

6 It is not clear the extent to which the reduced set of grammatical rules and phonological patterns would also constitute teaching goals.

especially since they follow the general principles of English word formation (<u>link: VOICE-project</u>). Needless to say, all of this has led to considerable debate, especially in regard to the point at which a non-native form may or may not be regarded as an "error." Jenkins writes that difference is not deficiency and remarks that what in ENL may be an error "may instead be a legitimate ELF variant." But as she adds, "At present it is still to some extent an empirical question as to which items are ELF variants and which ELF errors, and depends on factors such as systematicity, frequency, and communicative effectiveness" (2009b: 202). For all the optimism of the ELF-adherents, the extent to which ELF can be meaningfully regarded as a variety is clearly controversial. As Jenkins writes, "At present there is insufficient evidence for researchers to be able to predict the extent of the common ELF ground" (ibid.: 201). Many critics point out that ELF is not used by a stable speech community in the same way ENL and ESL are and that a great many – if not all – of the ELF users actually have an ENL variety as their goal.

13.4.5 The phonology of English as an international language

This is conceived of in the framework of ELF as a kind of common denominator pronunciation of English throughout the world. It has been simplified by leaving out a number of clearly shared difficulties, which are declared to be non-essential. The principles employed are (1) intelligibility and (2) teachability and learnability. The justification for this is seen in the fact that English is different from other foreign languages: "Most people quite simply do not learn English to speak to native-speakers," but rather to speak to other non-native speakers. This is different from, say, Spanish, because "people learn Spanish . . . because they are interested in Hispanic culture for some reason (work or pleasure) and will therefore want a spoken and written model which will further this aim. There is a world of difference between English and, in fact, all other living languages at present" (Prodromou 1997: 19).

To determine the pronunciation of English as an International Language (EIL) it is necessary to first describe and analyze pronunciation in lingua franca contexts with regard to mutual intelligibility and acceptability. This then may serve as a basis for determining what the realistic learning and teaching goals (learnability and teachability) are (Jenkins 2000: 2). Jenkins comes to the conclusion that there is no need, as mentioned above, to teach /θ/ and /[ð]/ since most learners find the sounds difficult to master and many native speakers replace them as well (ibid.: 137–138). Furthermore, difficult dark, velar [ɫ] does not belong to the phonology of EIL; it should be replaced either by clear, alveolar [l] or by vocalization as [ʊ] (ibid.: 138–139). A further principle is to favor pronunciations which are consistent with spelling. Consequently, <r> should be pronounced where spelled, thus making this "variety" rhotic and, indeed, using a retroflex GenAm [ɻ] (ibid.: 139). On the other hand <t> should be uniformly pronounced as /t/, thus ruling out the GenAm homophones: *matter* and *madder* (ibid.: 140) – and presumably the glottal stop in those British accents which have it in words like *ma'er* [mæʔə] (see <u>link: The phonology of English as an International Language (EIL)</u> for more detail). Jenkins emphasizes, in addition, that many L2 speakers wish to keep at least some L1 accent so as to mark their identity or nationality.

13.5 The identitarian role of the multiplicity of Englishes

The role of language as a marker of identity may well be important among non-native English users, as just mentioned. It is all the more so among ENL and ESL speakers (13.5.2). Indeed, a variety may be defined as language "used extensively and consistently by a community of speakers with their own sociocultural identity, primarily in regular face-to-face contact" (Seidlhofer 2004: 210; cf. Schneider 2003). Indeed, there is a multiplicity of communities of users for whom one or more marked features of language are highly significant. These groups of users comprise not only national and regional communities and their literatures (as seen in chapters 7 to 12), but also ethnic and gender groups, including what they see as politically correct, inclusive language.

13.5.1 Politically correct and inclusive language

Since the 1960s at the latest an awareness has grown up that language sometimes excludes whole groups of people, for example women, ethnic minorities, vocational groups, and gays and lesbians. It is, of course, not the language which excludes so much as the way the language is used. In many quarters it has, consequently, become more or less programmatic to reverse such practices by using what is termed "politically correct" (PC) language. In the United States, where PC language is perhaps most evident, the indigenous population is more correctly called Native American than Indian, and chairmen may be termed chairpersons in order not to exclude chairwomen. PC language has focused more on vocabulary than other aspects of English, and this is understandable, for it is vocabulary which speakers are most aware of and whose choice lies within their conscious control. Grammatical points such as the use or not of *he* to refer to an indefinite antecedent (*everyone should mind his own business*) is regarded as sexist. The PC remedy might be a totally new third person singular pronoun – suggestions have included *thon, e* or *E, tey, hesh, po, re, xe, jhe,* and *per* – or a conjoined pronoun, for example *he or she* or *s/he*, or the singular use of the third person plural pronoun *they*. New pronouns are doomed since this would require a major planned change in the closed class of personal pronouns. Change has occurred in the past, but based on a different set of motivations (cf. 3.2.3, 4.2.3.3, 5.3, 6.2.5, 6.3.3.2, 6.3.4, 7.4.1) and coming largely from below. The second solution (*he or she* or *s/he*) is frequently seen in writing. The third, singular *they*, is often heard in speech since it is natural to many speakers who interpret indefinite pronouns such as *everybody, whoever, none*, and so on as notionally plural, that is, as referring to more than one person ([link: Personal pronoun](#)). For all the attention, both positive and negative, which this topic has generated, it has had practically no far-reaching effect on the language beyond habits of word choice.

13.5.2 Sharing the world with other languages: growing multilinguality

Today the atmosphere in the English-language world is strongly oriented toward pluralism. This makes it easier for speakers to signal their identities – be they ethnic, sexual, regional, class-driven, national, or other. One of the most common ways of marking linguistic identity is by using features of the language associated with a given group. This may include non-standard, group-specific grammar, though this is less likely to be the case.

More typical among immigrants and L2-users is the often involuntary use of an accent due to the retention of features of L1 pronunciation. Almost all groups can signal identity by using at least some words typical of a particular group or deriving from its cultural practices. In connection with the use of ESL the question has to be raised whether English, as a colonial or neo-(neo-)colonial language, inevitably dominates the mental landscape of the colonized and dictates their self-perception. Does English remain a learned, instrumental language rather than a part of the emotional world of ESL (see 12.5) and EFL users? Does writing in English merely reproduce the bourgeois North Atlantic–Southwest Pacific world?

The Nigerian writer Chinua Achebe, who writes in English rather than in Igbo, has taken a position on the question "Why English?" Achebe concedes that English is an outside and a one-time colonial language, yet he sees it as a means of communication which can unite various groups in Nigeria and in Africa as a whole. Furthermore, it gives the writer access to a global reading public. The further question is whether English belongs to the emotional make-up of such countries as Nigeria. Achebe sees English as part of the project of new nations and sees the local languages as tributaries to English. Furthermore, while ESL and EFL speakers can use the language effectively, it is unlikely that English can reconstruct all the memories, images, rhythms, and associations which are a part of the local language(s). All the same, true African literature need not be written only in an African language. What is important is that African literature in English be able to make associations with the African experience. The African writer need not adopt the standards of ENL to express his or her experience; rather, it is necessary to use English without just imitating it. In any case, "there is no other choice" (Achebe 1975).

13.5.3 Bilingualism, code-switching, and hybrid languages

13.5.3.1 Bilingualism

Bilingualism seems to be a given of English in many parts of the world today. It is one of the consequences of language contact, and, as pointed out throughout this book, it is not something new. Since proficiency in the one or the other language lies at varying degrees of fluency and mastery, the balance between any two linguistic codes will be uneven. One of the results is code-switching.

13.5.3.2 Code-switching

Code-switching is only possible when someone is bilingual. Linguistic material from a language which a speaker does not know can, of course, be used in his or her L1; however, in this case this is not code-switching, but borrowing. Above all, this affects the terms borrowed for new objects and concepts. Code-switching, too, may be motivated by a "skills gap" due to lexical or other blank spots between languages and is one of the reasons for what is sometimes called incompetence code-switching. This may be the case with ESL-speakers and with immigrants who have acquired a limited functional competence in their L2 and have to resort to their L1 to compensate for these L2 gaps (link: Interference; link: Interlanguage). Fluent code-switching, in contrast, is motivated by identity-marking, distance (or solidarity), shifting roles and styles, power and prestige, political solidarity, change in topics, need for communication, focus on some aspect of the message, degree of seriousness, and presumably much more (see Texts 7.4, 8.11, 10.8, 12.1, 12.3 and 12.5). Even for people with a high degree of fluency in their varying languages, there are likely to be noticeable differences in proficiency by domain (family, work, public administration, school, church). Indeed, any number of characteristics may be decisive: features of the speaker such as status, age, gender, education, ethnic awareness and solidarity, on the one hand, and of the speech situation, on the other, for example, locale, medium (spoken only; spoken and written), degree of political, military, or economic imposition of the code, economic advantages (work, mobility), travel, politeness, style (tone, punning, joke-telling, story-telling marked by linguistically different roles and personas including asides and reporting of speech), or repetition (in translation) for emphasis, clarification, to attract attention, and so on.

13.5.3.3 Hybrid Englishes

Hybrid Englishes are forms of the language noticeably influenced by a non-English language. Examples include Franglais (French with English additions), Spanglish (ditto for Spanish), Singlish (Singapore English – with substrate enrichment), TexMex (English with Spanish elements), Mix-Mix (Tagalog/Pilipino English), which may be more English (Engalog) or more Tagalog (Taglish). Such Englishes do not have the extreme structural change typical of pidgins and creoles. Rather, the non-English aspect of these hybrids depends on local systems of pronunciation and vocabulary. Marginally, they will also include structural change. They are likely, in any case, to be difficult for people to understand who are unfamiliar with both languages. In essence hybrid forms are not really different from the nativized Englishes discussed in chapter 12; the justification for a separate term may best be seen in the fact that hybrids are the result of covert norms while nativized Englishes are potentially to be seen on a par with StE (cf. the contrast between GenE and StE in 6.2.2).

13.5.4 Convergence and divergence: a delicate balance

What the years since World War II have shown is that English is involved in developments which are moving in opposite directions. One is the enormous expansion of English as a world-wide language in the form of StE. This has taken place not only in the Inner and Outer Circle countries but also in the Expanding Circle (Figure 13.1). The kind of English which is spreading is highly associated with education and frequently is itself the language of education. Fundamentally, it draws on the StE rules of grammar and StE vocabulary, and the phonology of ESL and EFL is basically comparable to that of ENL varieties.

Yet at the same time English in its differing locations, employed in a broad range of contexts, and used by a wide assortment of speakers also shows variation. In the area of grammar this variation is seldom divergent enough to cause misunderstanding. But basic general vocabulary is enhanced by words reflecting the speakers' often very different cultural and identitarian backgrounds. Pronunciation reveals the most systematic distinctions – be they in the inventory of phonemes, the permissible combinations of sounds (phonotactics), the articulatory realization of sounds (phonetics), or the lexical distribution of phonemes (see 8.2.4). The differences are, overall, relatively small, but they are distinct and are clear evidence of nativization.

Basically, English speakers have at least two language codes at their disposal. *Bilingualism* – and *bidialectalism* (link: Bilingualism) – are more and more often the rule. In the case of the Outer and the Expanding Circles speakers will be bilingual, always with English as a non-native language. For ENL speakers most will have a traditional dialect, an English creole, or non-standard GenE as their mother tongue, but will be more or less well acquainted with StE. Bidialectals, too, have two codes available to themselves. Only a minority of ENL speakers will be restricted to StE alone, but even they can exploit the local and contextual variation of their more limited standard code. In all these cases English speakers have the advantages of a linguistic code which guarantees mutual global intelligibility while allowing speakers to maintain local and individual identities. The two codes permit stylistic differentiation, the standard for communication of a less emotional kind, the local for the expression of in-group solidarity. Of course, the standard can also carry emotions and involve in-group identity, just as the local may also be used in relatively non-emotional communication where solidarity is of subordinate value. The key point is having more than one code at your disposal for use according to situation and function.

13.6 Summary

Global English has been understood in this chapter as a complex phenomenon. Its roots lie in the politically, economically, and culturally dominant position of the United States and Great Britain throughout the Modern period, but also in the momentum that English has generated in the media, here specifically in the Information Society. Two strands have been followed in the chapter: one rather more non-standard, as seen in informal genres and text types, and the other, standard, as in serious, academic writing, including ESP. A number of approaches to World English have been summarized together with comments on their linguistic consequences. In conclusion the perspective has returned to covert and overt norms as we reviewed the identitarian role of language, political correctness in language, and growing multilinguality and their effects on English around the world. The chapter, and with it the book, ends with the prospect of bilingualism and/or bidialectalism as the currently most likely developmental perspective in the long history of English.

STUDY QUESTIONS

Social and cultural background

1. Anglo-American models may influence non-North Atlantic ways of viewing the world. Give an explanation and example of this.
2. It has been suggested that publishing has changed from restricting English to making its diversity more evident. How and when did this happen?

3. Reference has been made to both colonialism and neo-(neo-)colonialism. Even without reading Phillipson (but see further reading) the relationship between the two should be intuitively clear. Give an explanation and exemplify what is meant by these terms and what they have to do with language.

Linguistic background

1. This chapter describes Global English in two contradictory ways, one by limiting it and the other, by opening and expanding it. Explain.
2. How significant is the use of shortening in texting? How innovative is it?
3. Give the pros and cons of teaching to non-ENL standards of use. Use concrete examples to support your own position on this.
4. In 13.5.3 the text speaks of fluent code-switching. Judging by the examples given, what do you think this means?

Further reading

Sager et al. is one of many useful introductions to English for Specific Purposes. Winford introduces contact linguistics. Both are relatively densely written, and less accessible to the novice. Kirkpatrick offers a review of World Englishes. Jenkins and Phillipson were already recommended in the further reading section of chapter 7.

Jenkins, J. (2009a) *World Englishes. A Resource Book for Students.* 2nd ed. London: Routledge.
Kirkpatrick, A. (2007) *World Englishes: Implications for International Communication and ELT.* Cambridge: CUP.
Phillipson, R. (1992) *Linguistic Imperialism.* Oxford: OUP.
Sager, J.C., D. Dungworth, and P.F. McDonald (1980) *English Special Languages.* Wiesbaden: Brandstetter.
Winford, D. (2003). *An Introduction to Contact Linguistics.* Oxford: Blackwell.

THE INTERNATIONAL PHONETIC ALPHABET (2005)

CONSONANTS (PULMONIC)

	LABIAL		CORONAL				DORSAL			RADICAL			LARYNGEAL
	Bilabial	Labio-dental	Dental	Alveolar	Palato-alveolar	Retroflex	Palatal	Velar	Uvular	Pharyngeal	Eip-glottal	Glottal	
Nasal	m	ɱ		n		ɳ	ɲ	ŋ	N				
Plosive	p b			t d		ʈ ɖ	c ɟ	k g	q ɢ			ʔ	ʔ
Fricative	ɸ β	f v	θ ð	s z	ʃ ʒ	ʂ ʐ	ç ʝ	x ɣ	χ ʁ	ħ ʕ	H ʢ	h ɦ	
Approximant		ʋ		ɹ		ɻ	j	ɰ					
Trill	ʙ			r					R				
Tap, Flap		ⱱ		ɾ		ɽ							
Lateral fricative				ɬ ɮ									
Lateral approximant				l		ɭ	ʎ	L					
Lateral flap				ɺ									

Where symbols appear in pairs, the one to the right represents a modally voiced consonant, exept for murmured *ɦ*.
Shaded areas denote articulations judged to be impossible.

CONSONANTS (NON-PULMONIC)

Anterior click releases (require posterior stops)	Voiced implosives	Ejectives
ʘ Bilabial fricated	ɓ Bilabial	ʼ *Examples:*
ǀ Laminal alveolar fricated ("dental")	ɗ Dental or alveolar	pʼ Bilabial
ǃ Apical (post)alveolar abrupt ("retroflex")	ʄ Palatal	tʼ Dental or alveolar
ǂ Laminal postalveolar abrupt ("palatal")	ɠ Velar	kʼ Velar
ǁ Lateral alveolar fricated ("lateral")	ʛ Uvular	sʼ Alveolar fricative

CONSONANTS (CO-ARTICULATED)

ʍ	Voiceless labialized velar approximant
w	Voiced labialized velar approximant
ɥ	Voiced labialized palatal approximant
ɕ	Voiceless palatalized postalveolar (alveolo-palatal) fricative
ʑ	Voiced palatalized postalveolar (alveolo-palatal) fricative
ɧ	Simultaneous x and ʃ (disputed)
k͡p t͡s	Affricates and double articulations may be joined by a tie bar

VOWELS

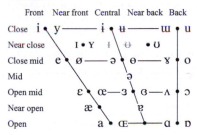

Vowels at right and left of bullets are rounded and unrounded

SUPRASEGMENTALS

ˈ	Primary stress
ˌ	Secondary stress
ː	Long
ˑ	Half-long
ĕ	Extra-short
.	Syllable break
‿	Linking (no break)

[ˌfoʊnəˈtɪʃən]

eː Long
eˑ Half-long
e Short

INTONATION

ǀ	Minor (foot) break
ǁ	Major (intonation) break
↗	Global rise
↘	Global fall

TONE

Level tones		Contour-tone examples:	
e̋ ˥ Top		ě ˩˥ Rising	
é ˦ High		ê ˥˩ Falling	
ē ˧ Mid		e᷄ ˦˥ High rising	
è ˨ Low		e᷅ ˩˨ Low rising	
ȅ ˩ Bottom		e᷇ ˥˧ High falling	
Tone terracing		e᷆ ˩˧ Low falling	
↑ Upstep		e᷈ ˧˦˧ Peaking	
↓ Downstep		e᷉ Dipping	

DIACRITICS   Diacritics may be placed above a symbol with a decender, as ŋ̊.

SYLLABICITY & RELEASES		PHONATION		PRIMARY ARTICULATION		SECONDARY ARTICULATION			
n̩ l̩	Syllabic	n̥ d̥	Voiceless or Slack voice	t̪ b̪	Dental	tʷ dʷ	Labialized	ʔ̹ x̹	More rounded
e̯ ʊ̯	Non-syllabic	s̬ d̬	Modal voice or Stiff voice	t̺ d̺	Apical	tʲ dʲ	Palatalized	ʔ̜ x̹ʷ	Less rounded
tʰ	Aspirated	n̤ a̤	Breathy voice	t̻ d̻	Laminal	tˠ dˠ	Velarized	ẽ z̃	Nasalized
dⁿ	Nasal release	n̰ a̰	Creaky voice	u̟ t̟	Advanced	tˤ dˤ	Pharyngealized	ɚ ɝ	Rhoticity
dˡ	Lateral release			i̠ t̠	Retracted	ɫ z̴	Velarized or pharyngealized	e̝ o̝	Advanced tongue root
t̚	No audible release	n̼ d̼	Linguolabial	ä j̈	Centralized	ü̽	Mid-centralized	e̞ o̞	Retracted tongue root
e̞ β̞	Lowered (β̞ is a bilabial approximant)			e̝ ɹ̝	Raised (ɹ̝ is a voiced alveolar non-sibilant fricative, ɾ̝ a fricative trill)				

Glossary

abduction: a form of logic based largely on association. It is instrumental in the development of new meaning. Example: someone is going (*progressive*) somewhere (movement) to do something (intention); therefore the thing to be done is future. The transfer of future meaning from a consequence of movement and intention to the primary meaning of "be going to do something" is a case of abduction.

ablaut, aka vowel gradation: a change in vowel quality which is connected with the different grammatical forms of the irregular (or strong) verbs. Example: OE present *weorpan* – past sg. *wearp* – past pl. *wurpon* – past part. *worpen* of the verb "throw." See also *derivation; verb classes of OE*.

accent: the pronunciation a speaker or group of speakers has. An accent is independent of grammar and vocabulary. Most important: people may speak *Standard English* (*StE*) with virtually any accent. Example: StE may be delivered in a prestige accent such as *RP* or *GenAm*, but also a local or regional accent or, of course, a foreign (non-native) accent.

accommodation; communication accommodation theory: an approach to understanding and explaining how people assimilate to the way their communication partners use language in order to show closeness. This may involve any aspects of language (pronunciation, grammar, vocabulary, communication strategies, etc.). Features may fully converge with those of other speakers at the one extreme. At the other, people's linguistic behavior may *diverge* and increase the distance to others. Example: an American who says *draughts* rather than *checkers* to show greater closeness to a British interlocutor.

acrolect: the prestige or standard form of a language which stands in a *continuum* with forms (*mesolects*) more divergent from it or as distant from it as possible (*basilect*). Example: Standard Jamaican English is the acrolect while the majority of the Jamaican population speaks a more or less extreme form of mesolectal or basilectal Jamaican Creole.

acronym: a means of *word formation*. The initial letter or letters of a longer expression are used as an independent word. Example: <u>South</u> <u>West</u> <u>Township</u> (of Johannesburg) goes under the acronym. *Soweto*.

adjective: a *part of speech* or *word class*. Adjectives commonly modify (or further describe) nouns. In OE adjectives preceding a noun agreed with them in *case*, *number*, and *gender*. Example: (*man*) *lyswæs hwæt* (*gedō*) "(someone does an) evil deed" (Text 2.1), where *lyswæs* is acc. sg. neuter as is *hwæt*. In ME adjectives were only exceptionally marked in this way, cf. *lowe men* "low men" (Text 4.2), where the final <e> in *lowe* carried no *inflectional* significance. ModE has no inflections of this kind.

adstrate: an "outside" language from which a language might borrow; stands in contrast to *superstrate* and *substrate* language. Example: *Cameroon PE* has English as its superstrate and *lexifier* and numerous indigenous languages as its substrate. Borrowing such as *kaminyon* "truck" are from the adstrate language French.

adverb: a *part of speech* or *word class*. Adverbs commonly modify (or further describe) verbs, adjectives, or other adverbs. In OE adverbs could be derived from adjectives by adding the suffix {-lic}, cf. *wrætlic hongað* "wonderously it hangs" (Text 3.5) or {-ē} as in *sweotule asecgan* "openly speak" (Text 2.4). In ME {-lic} had usually become {-ly}, cf. *And specially from every shires ende* ("Prologue" of *Canterbury Tales*, l. 15) as it remains in ModE.

affricate: a *stop* with *fricative* release at the same place of articulation. Examples: /tʃ, dʒ/

Afrikaans: one of the languages of South Africa. It developed out of Dutch and has been the source of considerable borrowing into English. Examples: *loan words* like *braai* "barbeque"; *loan translations* like *camel thorn* (tree) (< *Kameeldoring*); grammatical constructions like *busy* (< *besig*) *doing something*.

agreement: see *concord*.

Aitken's Law: a phonological rule which explains long vs. short vowel distinctions in Scottish English. A *morpheme* which ends in a vowel (or is followed by /v, ð, z, r/) will be long and remain so after the addition of *inflectional* {-ed}. Elsewhere the vowels are shorter. Examples: *brew + ed* and *toe + ed* have long vowels (/uː/ and /oː/) and differ from *brood* and *toad* (/u/ and /o/). Exceptions: this law does not apply to /ɪ/ and /ʌ/.

allophone: a variant of a phoneme. Although the pronunciation may sound strange, the exchange of allophones does not cause a word to take on a different meaning. Example: the girl's name *Ann* may be pronounced with or with a nasalized vowel as [æn] or [æ̃n] without changing reference. Each is an allophone of /æ/.

alphabet: a system of written symbols which represent sounds. English uses a slightly extended version of the Latin alphabet, distinguishing <i> and <j> as well as <u> and <v> and adding <w> and reintroducing <k>. OE used *runes* in the very early period and a number of letters no longer in use. Examples: thorn <þ> and eth <ð> for /θ/ or /ð/, wynn <ρ> for /w/, and ash <æ> for /æ/. ME used, in addition, yogh <ʒ> for /j/, /g/, and /ɤ/.

American Indian English (AIE): an ethnic variety of AmE. AIE is in no way a unified variety. The features of AIE vary according to the *L1* of the speaker or *speech community*. Example: Lakota (Sioux) AIE might use *word order* such as *What he is doing there is he announcing* (Leap 1993: 77), which differs considerably from *StE* and from AIE with a different language *substrate*.

American Indian Pidgin English: a pidgin which developed in the early period of contact of English speakers with Native Americans. Examples: among its features use of *me* as a subject, pre-verbal *no* for negation, and words like *heap* "very" are well known to the point of being stereotypes.

American language, the: a somewhat misleading designation of American English (AmE), which is not significantly enough different from other varieties of English to be considered a language on its own. The term *American language* was popularized by H.L. Mencken in his book of the same name.

American Vernacular, American Vulgate: a term for that type of AmE which is characterized by non-standard grammar, attempts to represent local-regional pronunciation and uncultivated usage in modified spelling, and its boastful, exaggerated, and somewhat anti-establishment tone, cf. Text 10.4.

Antilles, Greater: Cuba (Spanish), Hispaniola (Spanish and French), Jamaica (English), and Puerto Rico (Spanish with some English). **Lesser**: the crescent of islands stretching southward from the Greater Antilles and including the following Anglophone territories: the American and British Virgin Islands, Anguilla, St. Kitts-Nevis, Antigua-Barbuda, Montserrat, Dominica, St. Lucia, St. Vincent, Barbados, Grenada, and Trinidad-Tobago.

Appalachians: mountain range in eastern North America extending from southeastern Canada to northern Mississippi and Alabama. The once great isolation of the Southern Appalachians – and perhaps the large amount of immigration of Scotch-Irish from Ulster – led to a relatively distinct regional variety of English characterized by numerous now archaic features such as *a-prefixing* (*I'm a-going*) and the retention of irregular verb forms such as *holp* "helped." See also *Old Southwest*.

***a*-prefixing**: a now archaic form of the *progressive*. The source of the prefix is the unstressed form of the preposition *on* + the *-ing* form of the verb. Example: *they were a-singing* "they were engaged in singing."

articles: together with other *specifiers* or *determiners* such as the *demonstratives*, a *part of speech* or *word class*. Articles are distinguished as definite *the* and indefinite *a(n)*. The former developed out of the OE demonstrative; the latter, out of the numeral *one*. In OE both were marked for *case*, *number*, and *gender*.

aspect: a feature of the verb (or predicate) which marks "situation-internal time," which stands in contrast to *tense* (Comrie 1976: 5). Aspect in English may be *habitual, hotnews, perfect(ive), progressive, punctual,* or *stative*. In OE aspect was more likely to be marked lexically, cf. *besettan* "own, keep, occupy" vs. *settan* "set, cause to sit." Grammatical aspect slowly emerged as *StE* simple *they set it down* vs. progressive *they were setting it down* and perfect *they have set it down*.

aspiration: a feature of pronunciation in which a stop (/p, t, k/) is followed by a slight puff of air. Aspiration is marked in phonetic transcription with a following raised <h>, e.g. [pʰ].

assimilation: a process in which a sound becomes more like a neighboring sound. Example: a nasal before a velar stop (/k, g/) may become velar. Example: *in* + *come* /ɪŋkʌm/.

attrition: loss of language, usually due to lack of use. Example: when an immigrant from a non-English language community who does not use his or her original language forgets more and more words.

autochthonous languages: the original languages of a native population of a given territory in contrast to outside languages such as colonial or international languages. Example: Navajo is autochthonous in the Southwest of the United States, but English and Spanish are not.

auxiliary or periphrastic *do*: the grammatical (auxiliary) verb used with lexical verbs to forms negations, questions, and emphatic forms. The auxiliary *do* carries *inflection* for person, i.e. *present tense* {*-s*} or zero or for *tense* {did} in the past. Examples: *Does she like history or doesn't she? Yes, she really does!* See also *auxiliary verbs* and *NICE*. In some varieties periphrastic *do* is used to mark *habitual aspect*, and in EModE it was also used in non-emphatic affirmative statements.

auxiliary verbs: grammaticalized verbs with little or no lexical-semantic content, but a high degree of grammatical meaning. They consist of the primary auxiliaries *be* (used to form the progressive and the passive), *have* (to form the perfect), and *auxiliary* **do** (to mark negation, questions with inverted *word order*, and emphasis) and the *modal auxiliaries*. The wider use of the auxiliary verbs emerged in the ME and EModE periods.

baby-talk, aka motherese or child-directed language: a simplified manner of speaking in which, for example, pronouns may be replaced by nouns, word structures simplified, and some words reduplicated. Example: *Mommy is* [instead of *I am*] *gonna rub oo* [= *your*] *tum-tum* [= *stomach*]. Baby-talk is sometimes suggested as the input of *pidgins* and the reason for their reduced, simplified structures. See also *bioprogram, monogenesis, nautical jargons, polygenesis*.

back-formation: a means of *word formation* in which a "simpler" word which did not previously exist is derived from a more complex one on the basis of a well-established pattern. Example: *edit* is a formation backward from *editor* on the pattern of *bake* forward to *baker*.

backing: a feature of vowel pronunciation. Specifically, there is backing if the highest point of the tongue when producing a *vowel* lies farther to the back of the mouth in comparison to some other pronunciation of the "same" vowel. Example: in SAfE the START vowel is farther back at [ɒː] in comparison to *RP/ GenAm* [ɑː].

basilect: the least prestigious form of a language standing at the opposite extreme from the *acrolect* in a *continuum* with intermediate forms (*mesolects*) in between. Example: Broad Scots (of whatever region) would be the basilect vs. modifications of it right up to the Scottish Standard English acrolect.

bilingualism; bidialectalism: the mastery of more than one language or more than one dialect of a particular language. Neither term presupposes that proficiency in the two or more languages/dialects has to be balanced, that is, equivalent in extent. Both allow *code-switching* and are important motors for language change.

binomials/doublets: multi-word expressions in which two (and sometimes more) words are coordinated. The words are usually from the same *part of speech* and may have overlapping or shared meaning (*þe consuetude and þe custom*, Text 5.6) and be alliterative (*stif & starc & strong*, Text 4.8), or they may rhyme (*harryng and garrying*, Text 5.1). ModE bi- or trinomials are often irreversible, e.g. the *meronyms hook, line, and sinker* or a fixed expression such as *bacon and eggs* from the field of eating.

bioprogram: the theory that there is an innate set of linguistic distinctions which everyone is born with and which determine the way an emerging creole will develop when not subject to the influence of already existing languages. Example: the *TMA* (tense–modality–aspect) system is pre-programmed to be realized by grammatical markers in precisely this order if left "alone." See also *baby-talk, monogenesis, nautical jargons, polygenesis*

bleaching out: a part of the process of *grammaticalization* in which a word loses its lexical meaning as it turns into a grammatical marker. Example: the *going* of *be going to do something* no longer suggests its one-time lexical meaning of movement.

bleeding: a process in which the stock of words to which a rule applies gets smaller. Example: rule (1) says a vowel in a stressed syllable is longer before a voiced than a voiceless consonant, as in *bead* [biːd] vs. *beat* [bit]. Rule (2) says *T-flapping* in *GenAm* occurs between two voiced sounds before an unstressed syllable and leads to the voicing of the [t], as in *latter* [læɖər]. If (1) applies before (2), the vowel length in *latter* [læɖər] is shorter than in *ladder* [læːɖər], i.e. there has been bleeding. If (2) applies before (1) there is *feeding* and the two sound identical.

blending, blend (portmanteau word): a means of *word formation* in which two elements are combined after one or both of them have been clipped (see *clipping*, also *shortening*). Example: *squatter* + ~~aristo~~*cracy* = *squattocracy* (Table 11.6).

borrowing: the process by which words in particular, but also grammatical structures are taken over from a different language. Examples: the use of singular *you* on the model of French singular *vous* in the early ME period or the borrowing of Scandinavian words such a *taka* "take" into OE in the period following the Viking invasions. Borrowing includes *loan words* and *loan translation (calques)*.

calque, see *loan translation.*

Cameroon Pidgin English (CPE): the English pidgin of Cameroon, aka Kamtok. CPE is spoken in both the Anglophone and the Francophone parts of the country. Example: *a bin tanap fɔ kɔna an a bin di kɔnggɔsa* "I was standing at the corner gossiping," where *kɔnggɔsa* "gossip" comes from the Twi language (Todd 1990: 7).

Canadian raising: a phonological rule of CanE which describes the distribution of the allophones (i.e. the variants) of /aɪ/ and /aʊ/: when either is followed by a voiceless consonant, the first element of the diphthong has a half-open starting point: [əi] and [ʌʊ], as is the case with *life* and *about.*

case: a grammatical feature of OE noun phrases (NPs) in which not only the noun head, but also the adjectives and determiners preceding it are marked for the cases nominative (for sentence subjects), genitive (for possession), dative (for indirect objects), and accusative (for direct objects). OE examples: *scip* (nom./acc. sg.), but *scipe* (dat. sg.) and *scipes* (gen. sg.). By ModE times only the genitive (= possessive) continued to be marked as the *inflection* {-s}. ModE has three cases for the *personal pronouns*: nominative/subject, genitive/possessive, and accusative/object, two for the noun (common case and possessive). Adjectives and determiners no longer carry case inflections.

case leveling: the process in which case distinctions gradually ceased to be maintained. Case leveling has led to the replacement of the nominative by the accusative of some of the *personal pronouns*. Examples: *ye* (nom.) has yielded to *you* (orig. only acc.). It has also moved in the opposite directions in *pronoun exchange*. Example: *just between you and I.*

chain shifts: processes in which whole sets of sounds (phonemes) change in accord with each other. Such changes in articulation would cause distinct sounds to merge if the sounds "intruded" upon did not themselves shift, thus maintaining sound distinctions. This may affect both consonants (see *Germanic Sound Shifts*) and vowels (see *Great Vowel Shift, Southern Shift, Northern Cities Shift*).

Chancery English: the written language used in the government chancery in London for public records and documents. It displaced the use of Latin and French and was initiated in the early fifteenth century and gradually became *standardized*, especially under the influence of printing (Caxton).

Chicano English (CE): a Spanish-influenced variety of English spoken in the US. CE is not merely the result of foreign language interference, but has features of its own. Example: the replacement of /tʃ/ by /ʃ/ even though Spanish has /tʃ/ but no /ʃ/ as when *check* is pronounced *sheck.*

class: a social category according to which language use frequently varies. Example: *RP* is largely an accent of the higher standing classes (upper and upper middle).

clipping: a means of *word formation* in which a part of an original word is removed. Example: *mob* is a seventeenth century clipping of Latin *mobile vulgus* "vacillating crowd." See also *shortening.*

CLOTH–NORTH split: although the CLOTH and NORTH sets both had the same vowel in EModE (after R-dropping), they diverged once again in all but older *RP* and

Southern working-class accents (Wells 1982: 234). See also *THOUGHT–NORTH–FORCE Merger*.

code-switching and code-mixing: the former, a communicative strategy in which bilinguals switch languages according to the aims they are pursuing. Code-mixing may refer to more infrequent or individual elements scattered in an otherwise largely monolingual contribution. Examples: switching for stylistic effect, because of the field of discourse or to show identity or solidarity. See Text 8.11.

codification: a part of the process of *standardization* – along with selection, elaboration/expansion, and acceptance. Codification refers to regulation of how the language should look and relies on dictionaries, grammars, and usage guides. Codification was particularly prominent in the eighteenth century. Examples: Johnson's dictionary (1755) and Lowth's (1762) or Murray's (1795) grammars.

Colonial English: a type of English whose further development continued independent of linguistic developments in Britain. After overcoming initial feelings of inferiority, Americans, Australians, New Zealanders, and Anglophone South Africans established new national standards for their once-colonial Englishes.

comparing pronunciation: systematic approaches to pronunciation which take different aspects into consideration. (1) Via contrasts in the *vowel system* or inventory of phonemes of the different accents of English. Example: OE had the velar fricative /x/ while ModE does not. (2) Differences in the articulation or phonetic realization of the sounds. Example: Northern and Scottish varieties of ModE may have monophthongal /eː/ and /oː/ where *RP* and many varieties of *GenAm* have /eɪ/ and /əʊ/ or /oʊ/. (3) Phonotactic rules describe the possible combination of phonemes. Example: the permissible initial *consonant clusters* /hl-/, /hr-/, /hw-/, and /hn-/ of OE and including contextual variants (*allophones*) like initial voiceless *fricatives* (/f, θ, s/) but medial voiced ones (/v, ð, z/), and (4) The lexical sets of words which indicate which words undergo or have undergone particular processes of change. Example: the BATH words, which have [ɑː] in Southern England, but [a] or [æ] in the North or in America.

complementizers: grammatical elements which introduce clausal complements. Examples: the *that* of indirect speech or the *for* which introduces infinitive constructions like *For you to ask* (was nice).

compounding: a means of *word formation* in which two independent words (free *morphemes*) are combined to form a new word. Example: OE *mægð-man* "virgin, maiden" literally *maid +person* (Text 2.1).

concord, aka agreement: a process in which two or more words show their relationship to each other in being marked for the same category. Example: the verb (or predicate) will be plural if its subject is plural, and singular if the subject is singular. Here we can speak of grammatical (plural) concord, (e.g. *soldiers are . . .*); the concord is notional if the meaning, but not the form of the subject is plural (as in *police are . . .*). Finally, it is juxtapositional (by closeness) if the part of a multiple subject nearest the verb determines whether the verb should be singular or plural. Example: *Either the girls or the boy was there*.

consonant clusters: the occurrence of two or more consonants together without intervening vowels. In ME numerous such clusters were simplified. Example: initial /kn-/ to /n-/ or final /-mb/ to /-m/ even though the spelling continues to reflect the earlier pronunciation of the clusters (*know, lamb*)

contact language: a term which emphasizes one of the chief motivations for the creation of a *pidgin*, viz. contact. Such a language is used by speakers who do not share any other language. It is created in the situation of interaction of different languages, all of which may contribute to the new pidgin. Example: West African Pidgin English.

continuum: a series of incrementally different forms of a language within a particular *speech community*. A continuum stretches from the *acrolect* to the *basilect* by way of intermediate *mesolects*. Originally used for creole-speaking communities, but now applied more widely. Example: the continuum from broad (or deep) *Singlish* by way of less extreme forms to standard SingE.

conversion, aka shift and **zero derivation**: a process of *word formation* in which there is change in the *part of speech* (word class) without any formal change. This became more frequent as English lost its distinctive part-of-speech *inflections*. Example: *mob* (n.) > *mob* (v.).

copula deletion: a rule in which any form of the copular (or linking) verb *be* or the progressive auxiliary *be* which can be contracted in *StE* can be deleted. This is also called the zero copula. It is prominent particularly in African American Vernacular English, where it stands in contrast to *invariant* be. Examples: *she hungry; we goin'*.

copular verb: a verb which links the subject with a predicate complement (aka subject complement). Example: *she is hungry*, where the verb *is* links *hungry* with the subject *she*.

core vocabulary: an approach to teaching and learning English as a Foreign Language. Numerous lists of limited size have been compiled in order to ease learning while guaranteeing communicative success. Examples: Ogden's Basic English, West's General Service List, the LDOCE defining vocabulary, or Oxford 3000.

correctness, attitudes toward: see *prescriptivism*.

count vs. mass: a subdivision of nouns according to whether they may take a plural (= count) or not (= mass). Examples: count: *books, words*; mass: *printed matter*.

covert (and overt) norms: *StE* is the public norm for English and is therefore overt. Since many people do not identify with this norm but emulate the often non-standard English of their peers, they are following a covert norm.

creolization: the process in which a *pidgin* becomes a *native language*. Usually this occurs when children are exposed to a pidgin as their primary language. In adopting it they expand its linguistic repertory and its domains of use. Example: in many families in urban Papua New Guinea the parents do not share a native language and must rely on Tok Pisin, which is effectively the only language of the children, for whom it is now a *creole*.

cultural-institutional vocabulary: that part of the word stock of a particular variety which is specific to it because it is used to designate the distinct institutions or cultural practices of the country or society where it is used. Examples: AmE *ABC store* [< Alcoholic Beverage Control] or *brown-bagging* for the practice of concealing alcoholic drinks whose public consumption is prohibited.

declension: the set of *case, number*, and *gender* forms which a noun, a *determiner*, an *adjective*, or a *pronoun* may have. OE had four to five cases, three numbers, three genders. ModE has three cases for the *personal pronouns*, two for the noun, and none for adjectives and determiners. There are now only two number categories.

deictic system (noun: **deixis**): grammaticalized means of locating events and objects in time and space. *Tense* is in this sense basically deictic. Most prominent are the adverbial and *demonstrative* deictics whereby ME and EModE had a three-way system while ModE has a two-way distinction. Examples: earlier *here–there–yonder* or *this–that–yon* vs. modern *here–there* vs. *this–that*.

demonstrative: together with other *specifiers* such as the *articles* a *part of speech* or *word class*. Demonstratives are fundamentally *deictic*. They function as *pronouns* and as *determiners* and are the only determiners which mark singular and plural. Example: *this–these*.

derivation: processes of *word formation*. Derivation is commonly carried out by means of affixation, adding a prefix or a suffix. This was already the case in OE. Examples: prefixing: *ofsloh* "kill" (Text 3.1) < *of* "off" + *sloh*, the past of *slēan* "beat"; suffixing: *softe* "softly" (Text 4.8) < *soft(e)* + *-e*, the adverbial suffix. A further means of derivation is *ablaut* or vowel change. See also *blending, conversion, shortening,* and *compounding*.

determiners: the class name for *articles, demonstratives, possessive adjectives, interrogatives, relatives,* quantifiers (*some, any, both,* etc.), and cardinal (*1, 2, 3*) and ordinal (*1ˢᵗ, 2ⁿᵈ, 3ʳᵈ*) numerals.

dialect: any variety of a language according to speaker group. Without further clarification this is usually understood as referring to region, but includes *ethnicity, gender, class, education,* and more. Examples: Northumberland dialect, AAVE.

dictionaries: resources for retrieving information about vocabulary such as spelling, pronunciation, etymology, style, and meaning. Printed dictionaries are most commonly organized alphabetically.

diglossia, triglossia, polyglossia: the presence of two (or three; or more) languages in a society, each generally reserved for different domains of use. In diglossic settings one language is the High (H) and one, the Low (L) language. Example: in Guyana *StE* is H and Guyanese Creole English is L. Problem: with related languages it may be difficult to distinguish between diglossia and a *continuum*.

diphthong, diphthongization: combinations of two vowels which function as a unit. Example: the vowel of *time* is /aɪ/, a diphthong consisting of /a/ + /ɪ/. In the process of diphthongization new diphthongs emerge. Example: if dark [ɫ] is vocalic [ʊ], as in *milk* [mɪʊk] it contains a new diphthong.

discourse particles: words which structure discourse or help set the tone of what is said. Examples: SAfE initial *no* frequently introduces a reaction to something someone else has said; SingE *leh* downtones requests and commands.

discourse structure: the order in which an encounter is carried out. This may affect the phases of the encounter. Example: in friendly conversational encounters the small talk phase may be different than in a business encounter. See also *thematic structure*.

divergence: (1) an aspect of *accommodation* in which the distance between interlocutors increases; (2) the adoption of a distinctly functional meaning as a lexical word grammaticalizes. Example: grammatical auxiliary *do* vs. lexical *do*.

do-periphrasis: see *auxiliary* do.

double modals: the use of two modal auxiliaries one immediately after the other. This is regarded as non-standard usage. Example: *I might could go*.

double negation, see *multiple negation*.

dual: see *number*.

Dutch: a closely related Germanic language which has been the source of much vocabulary. Examples: ME borrowed a great deal of shipping vocabulary from Dutch, e.g. *boom,* *deck*; AmE borrowed from the Dutch settlers of New Amsterdam (= New York), e.g. *stoop*. See also *Afrikaans*.

East Africa: a region with a number of countries with English as a Second Language and a similar linguistic and colonial background. Specifically: Kenya, Tanzania, and Uganda, marginally Madagascar, Rwanda, Somaliland, and Sudan.

education: a social category according to which language use frequently varies. Example: *StE* is more likely to be used by those familiar with more formal written English.

emblematic markers: the use of symbolic elements from a different language or dialect to show identity with the other speech community even by people otherwise not fluent in the given language or dialect. Example: a Chicano who speaks idiomatic English but refers to his or her *abuelita* "granny."

English as a Foreign Language (EFL): non-native English used in countries in which English does not have any official status. Example: English in China or in Germany.

English as a Lingua Franca (ELF): a term which emphasizes the functional nature of *EFL*. Example: when a Brazilian engineer talks to a German businessperson in English, the important factor is not that English is a foreign language, but that it permits communication.

English as a Native Language (ENL): English spoken by people who grow up using it usually as their home language. Example: the child of Mexican immigrants growing up in Los Angeles whose parents speak English with him or her (rather than, for example, Spanish).

English as a Second Language (ESL): English as used by people whose native language is not English in a country in which English has official status. Example: an ethnic Chinese Singaporean government official whose home language is Hokkien, but whose usual working language is English.

English creole languages: include Jamaican Creole, *London Jamaican*, Krio, Kriol, *Tok Pisin, Gullah, Singlish*, Torres Straits CE, Guyanese CE, Belize CE, HCE, *Plantation Creole, Sranan*, Patois/Patwa, Roper Creole, and many more.

English pidgins: include *American Indian PE, Tok Pisin*, NigPE, WAfPE, Kamtok, Bislama PE, Solomon Island PE and many more. Some of these are well-established extended pidgins, i.e. pidgins used over many generations and often relatively highly conventionalized in grammar and vocabulary.

Estuary English: a *koinéized* form of English that seems to be developing in London and its vicinity (the Thames Estuary and the lower Thames valley, i.e. Essex and northern Kent). It contains some of the less stigmatized features of London English. Example: *L-vocalization, Paul = paw* /pɔː/.

ethnicity, ethnic varieties: a social category according to which language use frequently varies. Example: *London Jamaican* is largely restricted to people of Caribbean heritage. Example: the use of *se* after verbs in the same function as English *that* (*A all white jury found out se 'e was guilty*).

eye dialect: spelling which suggests non-standard language because it violates spelling conventions thus intimating that the speaker to whom the eye dialect is attributed is illiterate, socially low-standing, or humorous. It is dialect for the eye not the ear, for when pronounced a word is no different than the "same" word in standard spelling. Example: *W'at* for *what* (Text 10.6).

false friends: similar looking, perhaps even etymologically related words in two different languages with distinctly different meanings. Non-native speakers use them as in their

L1. Example: a German might say, "I became a new car" using English *became* as if it meant "got" as German *bekam* does.

family model: a way of explaining linguistic similarities between languages which can be traced back to the same source. Example: Dutch and English are sister languages with the same Proto-West Germanic mother.

feeding: a process in which the stock of words to which a rule applies gets larger. Example: rule (1): nouns ending in sibilants (/s, z, ʃ, ʒ, tʃ, dʒ/) form the {s} plural by adding /əz/, as in *bus + es*. Rule (2): in *AAVE* a final *consonant cluster* consisting of /s/ + a *stop* loses the stop, e.g. *desk* is /des/ and *test* is /tes/. These words now fulfill the requirements for rule (1) giving us the plurals /desəz/ and /tesəz/. See also *bleeding*.

field; domain: an aspect of register which helps to define how a language is used. Example: the English of the field/domain of religion will have distinctly different vocabulary from the field of computer science and a statistically different use of grammatical structures.

folk etymology: a means of *word formation* which attributes to a word a fictitious history due to coincidental resemblances. Example: *crayfish*, a kind of freshwater shrimp, mistakenly contains the morpheme {fish} due to the sound similarity with the final syllable of the French source word *crevice*.

FOOT–STRUT Split: in the South of England ME short /u/ became opener + unrounded /ʌ/ in STRUT-words. Examples: *come, luck, putt*. Short /u/ was retained as /ʊ/ in others, chiefly after labials. Examples: *foot, full, put, pulpit, butcher, bush*. In the North /ʊ/ remained in both sets; consequently, *look* and *luck* are homophones.

foreigner-talk: a simplified manner of speaking used toward foreigners and assumed as one of the reasons for the reduced complexity of *pidgins*. Example: the lack of verb *inflection* in *I go [went] there yesterday*.

French: a language which has had great influence on English, particularly in the ME period. French language contact appeared in two distinct varieties: the French of the Norman conquerors and landholders in England after 1066; the Central French of Paris and the French monarchy. The most significant influence was on vocabulary, but French also reinforced or initiated structural innovations. Examples: vocabulary: *catch* (Norman) and *chase* (Central); pronunciation: the distinction between initial /v-/ and /f-/; morphology: the suffix {-ous}; spelling: <ou> for /uː/; grammar: *you* (sg.) as with French *vous*.

fricative: *obstruent* with a continuous flow of air. Examples: /f, θ, s/.

fronting: a feature of vowel pronunciation. Specifically, there is fronting if the highest point of the tongue when producing a *vowel* lies at the front of the mouth in comparison to some other pronunciation of the "same" vowel. Example: in the *Southern Shift* the FOOT-vowel is further front at [ʉ] in comparison to conservative *RP/GenAm* [ʊ].

futhorc: see *runes*.

gender: (1) **a social category** according to which language use frequently varies. Example: lower middle-class women seem to be more strongly oriented toward the overt norm than men of the same class; (2) **a grammatical category** with the terms masculine, feminine, and neuter, which are assigned to all nouns in some languages such as OE, Latin, German, and French (only masc. and fem.). ModE has grammatical gender only in the *personal pronoun system*.

General American (GenAm): a relatively diffuse cluster of accents of North American English which are generally viewed as constituting the standard accent. It is rhotic and is characterized by the lack of specifically *Southern, New England, Appalachian,* or *ethnic* features. Some form of GenAm is spoken by perhaps 70% of the population of the US.

General English (GenE): a blanket designation for a wide assortment of varieties of English which are generally mutually intelligible. GenE is conceived as including both *StE* (the *overt norm*) and non-standard English (a *covert norm*), but excluding the *traditional dialects* and the *English pidgins* and *creoles*. Examples of **non-standard GenE:** *ain't,* which serves as the negative form of *am, are, is, have,* and *has* as in *Mrs. Messenger ain't* [isn't] *callin' me up* (Text 10.3); *The Pearsons ain't* [haven't] *ast,* (same source text slightly further on). Third-person singular *don't* as in *she don't know any-/nothing.*

generation model: describes language shift among (many) immigrant groups. The first generation retains the heritage language as the home language at a rate of about 90%; in the second generation the rate falls to around 60%; in the third, to under 10%.

Germanic languages: one of the branches of the *Indo-European language family.* Examples of Germanic languages: Swedish, Norwegian, and Danish; Dutch, German, and English.

Germanic Sound Shifts: the **First Germanic Sound Shift** describes, for example, the change of voiceless stops /p, t, k/ to voiceless fricatives /f, θ, h/. Examples using Latin and English: Latin *pro* but English *for*; *tu* and *thou*; *cor* and *heart.* The **Second (High Germanic) Sound Shift** describes further changes in the consonants in German including the shift from Germanic /p, t, k/ to High German fricatives /f, s, x/ and affricates /pf, ts, kx/ (/kx/ only in Swiss German). Examples: *pipe* and German *Pfeiffe*; *water* and *Wasser*; OE *ac* and German *auch.* See also *Grimm's Law*; *Verner's Law.*

grammars: resources used to codify *StE.* As part of the *codification* process grammars have been instruments of *prescriptivism.* More recently they have moved closer to a descriptive perspective. Examples: early, more prescriptive grammars of English include Lowth's and Murray's. Recent ones such as the *Longman Grammar of Spoken and Written English* (Biber et al. 1999) are more descriptive.

grammatical categories: the **primary** division of all words into *parts of speech* and the **secondary** association of categories like *tense, modality,* and *aspect* with the verb and *case, number,* and *gender* with the noun.

grammaticalization: the process by which originally lexical items diverge into two, one continuing to be lexical, the other taking on grammatical function while losing its lexical meaning. Example: the word *have* is lexical and means, among other things, "to possess"; it has also been grammaticalized as the auxiliary *have,* where its function is to help form the perfect construction. See also *lexicalization.*

Great Vowel Shift (GVS): a *chain shift* which began in the ME period and was completed in the EModE period. The GVS affected the long vowels of ME leading to raising and/or diphthongization. Example: ME *hus* /huːs/ became ModE *house* /haʊs/.

Grimm's Law: the principal part of the *First Germanic Sound Shift.* Modified by *Verner's Law.*

Gullah: a North American creole spoken along the South Carolina and Georgia coast. Gullah continues to be spoken, but is de-creolizing. Example: *we bes tek we pot wid we so when we kill one deer we ain haf for tote um home n wait for eat.* Note that *we* is used for *we, our,* and *us,* that the indefinite article is *one,* and that the infinitive is marked by *for.*

habitual (aspect), aka iterative: marks a verbal act as one which is repeated. Examples: *StE* marks the habitual past using *used to* or *would* (*he used to/would do such things as that*). SingE uses *use to* to mark present habitual (*I use to work on Saturdays* "do so regularly"); Southwest English marks habitual with the auxiliary *do* (/ðat də kiːp ˈiː daʊn/ "that keeps (h)e [a cart] down").

hard words: learned words of classical origin. Hard words are not transparent in meaning in the way the Germanic words usually are, cf. grandiloquence, *inkhorn terms*. Example: *concurrence* "coming together" (Text 8.1).

H-dropping: the loss of /h/. Although /h/ has generally been lost in consonant clusters like /hr-/ and before consonants as in *right*, it has been retained before vowels. Dropping pre-vocalic /h/ is stereotypically stigmatized as violating the norms of "good English." Example: Cockney '*ous* for *house*.

Hiri Motu: a *lingua franca* of Papua New Guinea.

historical reconstruction and the comparative method: a way of using existing language evidence to show the phonological, lexical, and grammatical relations between languages which evolved out of a common source language. Example: German and English both evolved out of Proto-(West) Germanic. Example: comparing older forms of English *stone*, Dutch *steen*, German *Stein*, Swedish *sten* allow reconstruction of Proto-German **stainaz*.

hot-news perfect (aspect): a type of verbal aspect typical of IrE. It is formed with *after* + verb + *ing* to indicate a recently completed act. Example: *You're after ruinin' me*.

hybrid language: (1) a mixed language such as a *pidgin*; (2) forms of language which show a great deal of *borrowing* are also often referred to as hybrid languages. Examples: Singlish, Taglish or Engalog.

hypercorrection: the erroneous correction of a supposed mistake based on conclusions from other norm violations. Example: Machyn (mid-sixteenth century) writes *harme* for *arm* (Text 6.9) presumably in the belief that he would otherwise be *H-dropping*.

idiom: multi-word expressions which are less than a full sentence and are not semantically transparent. Example: *to pull someone's leg* "to kid someone." The words do not contribute individually to the meaning, that is, replacement of *pull* by the synonym *tug* is not possible. Rather, the meaning of the idiom is derived from the whole.

implicational relationship: a way of gauging how close to the basilect or acrolect a mesolect sample of a creole is. Examinations have revealed that some forms are regularly abandoned early in speakers' accommodation to the acrolect and others much later. Example: in Guyanese CE the indefinite article *wan* is lost long before speakers discontinue pronouncing *car* with an initial /kj-/. Thus retention of *wan* implies retention of /kj-/. This is an implicational relationship.

inclusive, exclusive pronouns: (1) a distinction among first and second person pronouns in which *we* and *you* may include or exclude the addressees. Example: Tok Pisin inclusive *we* is *yumi* and exclusive *we* is *mipela*. (2) a gender issue in which the use of what is called "generic *he*" is criticized because it is more exclusive of females than truly generic. Example: the final pronoun in *Everyone looks out for **himself*** may lead people to think of men only. Remedies vary, but the most widespread change in recent usage has been to replace himself with *him- or herself* or singular *themselves* (or *themself*). A further alternative is to use *oneself*, but this cannot be extended to sentences such as the following: *I asked everyone to leave **his** name with the secretary*.

indefinite pronouns and determiners: a subgrouping of the pronouns and determiners. Examples: *each*, *every*, *any*, *some* (pronouns) or the same with a following noun (determiners).

indicator: a sociolinguistically significant, but unconscious variant. Example: the conjunction *like* (*Do it like I do*) is typical of Southern American usage without speakers' being conscious of it, to say nothing of shifting to more consensual *StE as* in careful speech. See also *marker, shibboleth*, and *stereotype*.

indirect (imperative) speech acts: the mention of accompanying circumstances ("felicity conditions") that might lead to a request, can, in fact, replace a direct request. Example: *It would be nice if x* is virtually the same as saying *Please do x*.

Indo-European language family: perhaps the largest (by number of speakers) of the many language families of today's world, others being Altaic (e.g. Turkish) and Dravidian (e.g. Tamil). Examples of Indo-European language families: Celtic, Italic, Slavic, Indo-Iranian.

inflection in English: the grammatical endings added to verbs, nouns, adjectives, and adverbs. In comparison to other languages, English has very few inflections. It has undergone a long-term shift from a high degree of inflection (typical of a synthetic language) to periphrastic structures (typical of analytic languages). Examples: the comparative of the adjective in {-er} as in *clearer* is inflectional; the comparative with {more} is synthetic as in *more clear*. The different *word forms* of the *personal pronouns* (e.g. *I, me*) are also considered to be inflections.

inkhorn terms/pretentious language: derogatory way of referring to the influx of new Latinate words added to the language in the sixteenth and seventeenth centuries. Some have become quite common; others were not accepted. Examples: *adjuvate* "help" (rejected); *confidence* (retained).

interference: the tendency for language learners to carry over aspects of their *L1* to the new language. In the case of *ESL* this shows up as *substrate* influence. Example: a native speaker of Chinese may fail to distinguish /l/ from /r/ and pronounce *very* like *velly*.

interlanguage; learner's language: a non-native learner's emerging second language system. Such a language is systematic but different from the target language. It may be characterized by *interference*.

interrogative pronouns/determiners: a subgrouping of the pronouns and determiners. Examples: *which, what, who, where, why, how* (pronouns); *which/what book* (determiners).

intersectionality: the presence of more than one determining factor in language use. Example: if a black American woman has a particular feature of pronunciation, is it due to *ethnicity, national variety*, or *gender*? The three intersect.

invariant *be*: the use of uninflected *be* in *AAVE* to indicate repeated or *habitual* state. Example: *they always be talkin'*.

IPA (International Phonetic Alphabet): the set of symbols used to designate sounds unambiguously. If used broadly each phoneme in a language is assigned one symbol. Example: the <j> in *jet*, the <dg> in *lodge*, and the <g> in *privilege* are all /dʒ/. A narrow transcription is more strictly phonemic and distinguishes allophonic variants such as monophthongal [eː] and diphthongal [eɪ] for /eɪ/. See chart on p. 363.

irrealis: a term for unreal conditions, often expressed by use of modals, sometimes by the subjunctive. Example: *If I had known (subjunctive), I would have told you (modal)*.

isogloss: a line on a dialect map separating areas in which differing linguistic forms are used. Where whole bundles of isoglosses co-occur there may be grounds for distinguishing regional dialect areas. Example: the line separating the *Northern Cities Shift* from its southward absence. The isogloss goes north–south through New York, then westward through northern Ohio and southern Michigan.

jargon: (1) the type of language, especially vocabulary, characteristic of vocational language. Example: the jargon of law. (2) a pre-*pidgin* hybrid language. Example: *nautical jargon*.

kinship terms: a convenient insight into the cultural background of English speakers. Traditional English kinship terms are extended to reflect non-English (non-European) family relations. Example: in a society in which polygyny is practiced (as in West Africa) there is a need for a term like *co-wives*.

koinéization, koiné: a leveling of differing dialects usually as the result of migration. Example: London English in the late ME period was surely undergoing koinéization.

L1: a person's first language. The L1 (native language, mother tongue) may not be a person's *primary language*.

language and nation: the major criteria in approaching the historical spread of English. National identity and national forms of English have a great deal of saliency. Example: the widely recognized distinction between AmE and BrE. Although IrE is a part of BrE and CanE is a part of AmE, there is a reluctance on the part of many to see IrE and CanE as regions of the respective larger types.

language attitudes: see *prescriptivism*.

language contact: a major factor in language change. Contact with other languages and other dialectal varieties of one language is a source of alternative pronunciations, grammatical structures, and vocabulary. Examples: the large amount of borrowing from indigenous languages in overseas varieties.

language imposition, shift, loss, and death: the often darker side of the spread of English. The association of English with power has led to its imposition on colonial peoples often resulting in language shift and the death of indigenous languages. Example: the extinction of numerous American Indian languages. Immigrant languages have been subject to loss among immigrants though not to language death because of language maintenance in the countries of origin.

language planning and policy: administrative action which affects the development, maintenance, and sometimes standardization of a language for the purposes of written, educational use and/or national unity. Language planning and policy has often brutally suppressed indigenous languages, but even taking no action weakens minor languages. See also *language imposition, shift, loss, and death*.

language retention: see *generation model*.

lax: a vowel pronounced without any great muscle tension. Examples: /ɪ, e, ʊ/. See also *tense* (2).

lexeme: an abstract concept of the word. It includes all the possible shapes a spoken or written "word" may have. Example: in the sentence *He went yesterday and is going again tomorrow* the lexeme GO occurs twice (as the *word forms* went and going).

lexical gaps: empty spots in the vocabulary for concepts which are familiar, but for which there is no single fitting word. Example: there is no simple lexeme for "brother-in-law's wife."

lexical sets: see *comparing pronunciation*.

lexicalization: a process in which a grammatical word becomes more lexical. Example: the increasingly common use of *need* as a full verb rather than a modal as in *You don't need to say more* (for somewhat old-fashioned *You needn't say more*). See also *grammaticalization*.

lexifier: the language, usually the *superstrate*, which is the main source of the vocabulary of a *pidgin* or *creole*. Example: Tok Pisin's main lexifier is English.

life-cycle theory: the theory that there is a regular progression from *pidgin* to *creole* to post-creole to *acrolect*. Example: *AAVE* began as a pidgin, became *Plantation Creole*, became post-creole AAVE, and continues to de-creolize in the direction of *GenE*. An alternative view emphasizes the coexistence of the basilect, mesolects, and the acrolect throughout their history without implications of succession.

lingua franca: an existing language used in a possibly simplified form for communication between people who have no other language in common. Example: in the Middle Ages scholars from all over Europe used Latin to communicate. Today English is widely used as a world lingua franca. See *ELF*.

linguicism: a prejudicial perspective in which only people who have mastered a particular standard code are regarded as intellectually qualified. Example: non-native English usage is regarded as inferior.

linguistic drift: the supposed tendency of a language to change in a particular direction without any external forces driving this move. Internal typological change of major dimensions in English is often understood in this way. See *chain shifts* and *Germanic Sound Shifts*.

linguistic imperialism: see *language imposition*.

linking-r and intrusive-r: in the first case the continued pronunciation of /r/ in final position in non-rhotic accents when the following word has an initial vowel and there is no pause between. Example: *aware of* /əweərəv/. In the second case an unhistorical /r/ is added after final /ɑː, ɔː, ə/ under similar conditions (cf. *hypercorrection*). Example: *law of* /lɔːrəv/.

loan translation, aka calque: a means of *word formation* in which a foreign expression is translated *morpheme* by morpheme into English. Example: *camel thorn* (tree) < *Afrikaans Kameeldoring*.

loan word: a word borrowed directly from another language. Usually there is some phonetic-phonological or morphological change so that the borrowed item fits the patterns of English better. Example: *raccoon* < Algonquian *raugroughcun / arocoun*.

London Jamaican: a *koinéized* creole spoken by immigrants from the Caribbean and the following generations. Its speakers are fluent *GenE* speakers who can *code-switch* between English and Creole. Example: "and then I just laughed and then 'e – 'e just pulled me for a dance. I didn't mind dancing wiv 'im 'cause *mi nuo se, mi n' av notin ina* my mind but to dance" (Sebba 1986: 165).

loss of /h/: see *H-dropping*.

Low Back Merger: a major shift in vowel pronunciation in AmE. The Low Back Merger is centered in Boston and Pittsburgh, but found throughout the US and Canada and is spreading rapidly; it involves the leveling of the /ɑː/–/ɔː/ distinction. Example: *cot* /kɑːt/ = *caught* /kɑːt/.

Low Dutch: a blanket terms used for Flemish, *Dutch*, Frisian, and Low German.

L-vocalization: the realization of dark [ ] as [ʊ]; see also *diphthongization*.

mandative subjunctive: one of the few vestiges of the subjunctive in ModE. It occurs in subordinate clauses after predicates like *order, demand, be important, be mandatory*. The verb remains uninflected and need not take *do*-periphrasis if negated. Example: *We demanded he not come late again*.

manuals of usage: resources which set standards for formal written English. They include information about vocabulary, spelling and punctuation, style, and meaning. Example: *The King's English* by H.W. and F.G. Fowler originally published in 1906.

marginal language: a designation often given to a *pidgin* because of its use in a reduced set of circumstances. Example: West African PE is used above all in market situations.

Maritimes: the easternmost provinces of Canada. The English of the Maritimes (New Brunswick, Nova Scotia, and Prince Edward Island) is often quite different from Canada west of Quebec. See also *Newfoundland*.

marker: a sociolinguistically significant variant which speakers are aware of. Example: *rhoticity*, which non-rhotic AmE speakers often restore in conscious speech – /kɑː/ becomes /kɑːr/ – and rhotic BrE speakers avoid (the converse of the preceding example).

mass nouns: see *count vs. mass*.

mergers: a process in which two formerly distinct forms unite as one undifferentiated form. Example: *T-flapping* in AmE which flaps and voices both former /t/ and former /d/ in a vocalic context with a following unstressed syllable: *latter* = *ladder* [lædɚ]. Vowel mergers are particularly well known. See *Low Back Merger*, *THOUGH–NORTH–FORCE Merger*, *nurse Merger*.

meronymy: a lexical semantic relationship between words which are both parts of a whole. Example: *nose* and *mouth* are meronyms of superordinate *face*.

mesolects: varieties of a *creole* which lie between the extremes of the *basilect* and the *acrolect*.

metathesis: the reversal in order of two sounds, frequently involving /r/. Example: *forst* for *frost* (OE).

middle passage: the second part of the triangular trade which reaches (1) from England to West Africa, then (2) to the Caribbean, finally (3) back to England. The middle passage was notorious for the abominable conditions under which African slaves were transported to the West Indies.

Midlands: the dialect area in England between the South and the North, often divided into East and West. In the USA the dialect area between New England (and the North) and the South, often further divided into Northern and Southern.

minimal pair: two words with different meanings which are distinguished in pronunciation by a change of one *phoneme*. This is a test for establishing the existence of distinct phonemes. Example: *sharpe–carpe* (Text 5.7b) distinguishes /ʃ/ from /k/.

modal auxiliary: a subcategory of the auxiliary verbs which represents grammaticalized *modality*. Three types are frequently recognized: (1) deontic for permission and obligation. Example: *you may/must stay overnight*. (2) dynamic for ability and volition. Example: *She couldn't/wouldn't speak French*. (3) epistemic for possibility and probability. Example: *They may/must be at home*. A fourth type may be emerging: (4) evidential for hearsay and factual. Example: *Language history can be interesting* (factual). Hearsay is not associated with a full modal, but can be expressed by a *semi-modal*. See also *double modals*.

modality: a category of the verb which expresses uncertainty. Example: *may* in *they may be at home*. Modality is also expressed in other ways, for example by adverbials: *possibly they are at home*. See also *modal auxiliary*.

modes of address: pronouns, names, titles, and descriptive terms used in addressing a person. Modes of address are good indications of how intimate or distant people are toward each other. Examples: polite singular *you* even to a family member as in late ME *I prayed **yow** sende me som tydyngys* (Text 5.5).

monogenesis: a theory that all creoles had a single source. This view cannot be taken fully seriously, but the numerous similarities among the Atlantic creoles (those of West Africa and the Caribbean) do suggest similar origins. See also *baby-talk, bioprogram, nautical jargons, polygenesis*.

monophthongization, monophthong: the process in which diphthongs become monophthongs. A monophthong is a constant vowel sound. Examples: short vowels of English such as /e, ɪ, ʊ/. English long vowels have a tendency to diphthongize. Example: earlier and regional /eː/ has become /eɪ/.

mood: a secondary category of the verb. Traditionally mood in English has included the indicative, the *subjunctive*, and the imperative.

morpheme: a distinctive unit of form in language. Examples: individual words such as *book* or *with* which can stand alone (free morphemes); *inflectional* elements such as the plural {-s} in *books*.

morphology: a branch of linguistics which deals with the form of words, often divided into lexical morphology (see *word formation*) and grammatical morphology (see *inflection*).

motherese: see *baby-talk*.

multiple negation, aka double negation: the use of two or more markers of negation to indicate negation. This was common in OE but is non-standard in ModE. Examples: OE *Nis nu cwicra nan* "Nor is now alive no one" (Text 2.4); non-standard ModE *they . . . don't know no better* (Text 8.3).

nasal: a consonant with air flow exclusively through the nose. Examples: /m, n, ŋ/.

national variety: see *language and nation*.

native language: see *L1*.

Native Speaker Englishes: see *English as a Native Language*.

nautical jargons: simplified *lingua francas* used among polyglot crews on early sailing ships and suggested as part of the input of English *pidgins*. See also *baby-talk, bioprogram, monogenesis, polygenesis*.

New England: a distinct linguistic region of the US. Eastern New England is traditionally *non-rhotic*.

Newfoundland: one of the provinces of Canada. Newfoundland was strongly settled by colonists from the Southwest of England. Consequently, a number of features of *traditional dialect* can be heard there in contrast with virtually all of the rest of North America. Example: the use of *he* (subject case) and *ən* (object case) for count nouns like *book* or *cat* and *it* for mass nouns like *air* or *beer*.

NICE: the features associated with auxiliary verbs, direct <u>n</u>egation with periphrastic do; <u>i</u>nversion in questions; use as <u>c</u>ode for the short forms; use for <u>e</u>mphatic affirmation. Examples: *They can't come* (N); *Did she leave?* (I); *Yes, she did* (C); *They máy return soon* (E).

nominative *you*: the use of a once exclusively accusative/object form as a subject. A similar tendency applies to other accusative *personal pronouns* as well, especially conjoined subjects. Example: *Me and him are goin' out* (often regarded as non-standard).

non-rhotic: see *rhoticity*.

non-standard GenE: see *GenE*; *shibboleth*.

Norman French: see French.

Northern: in England the area north of the Humber River (Northumbria) whose regional English shares much with Scotland without forming a single region. In North America the area (sometimes starting far) north of the Ohio River, whose regional Northern English includes CanE.

Northern Cities Shift: a chain shift which affects chiefly the short vowels in the US Upper North from western New England westward. In its simpler form short vowels lower and /æ/ lengthens and rises. Consequently, *tick* sounds like *tech* (in **GenAm** or **RP**) and *tech* like *tack*, while *tack* becomes *tay-ik*.

Northern Subject Rule: the observation in the English of Northern England that plural subjects take a verb ending in {-s} if the subject is a singular or plural noun or ***demonstrative pronoun***, or even a plural ***personal pronoun*** if the latter is separated from the verb by intervening words. Example: *The boys loves it*.

North Sea Germanic, aka Ingvæonish: the Germanic language(s) spoken along the North Sea in the times of the Anglo-Saxon invasions of England. Examples: Frisian and Saxon.

number: a grammatical category. Its usual terms are singular and plural, but some languages also have dual for two and trial for three. Examples: OE had the dual ***personal pronouns***, *wit* "we two" and *git* "you two." ModE has remnants of the dual in words like *either*, *neither*, and *both*. Tok Pisin has third person, singular *em*, dual *tupela*, trial *tripela*, and plural *ol*.

number of speakers: an extremely difficult phenomenon in regard to English, especially since the population of a(n) (Anglophone) country is not the same as the number of speakers of English there. Estimates of ENL speakers in the world lie at around 350 million; ESL at perhaps as many as 450 million; numbers for EFL would be speculative.

Nurse Merger: the leveling of the vowel in words like *stirred*, *heard*, and *word* to /ɜː(r)/. The spelling reveals that they once were pronounced differently, and in some ***traditional dialects*** they still are. Examples of non-merger: Scottish *stirred* with /ɪr/, *heard* with /ɛr/ and *word* with /ʌr/ (Wells 1982: 200).

obstruent: a cover term for both stops/plosives and fricatives. Examples: /p, t, k/ (stops) and /f, θ, s, ʃ/ (fricatives).

OED (*Oxford English Dictionary*): historical dictionary of English which records usage from the time of King Alfred to the present. The first twelve-volume edition appeared in 1928. Currently available online.

Old Southwest: a regional dialect area in the US at the time when the Mississippi River was still the western border (hence "Old"). The language of this region is generally Mountain or Upland Southern (see ***Appalachian***). Examples from the sub-literature of this area (western Georgia, Alabama, Mississippi, Tennessee, Louisiana, Arkansas, eastern Texas): *thar* for *there*, **a-*prefixing***, *ourn*, *yourn*, and so on.

Open-Syllable Lengthening: the general lengthening and lowering of vowels in open syllables in the early ME period, especially in the South. The short /i/ of *seeke*, for example, became a long /eː/.

origins of language: have to do with both when and how human language came into being. The most widely accepted assumption is that this happened only once and that all present-day languages have the same source. The prerequisites of human language were a changed anatomy with a larger space above the larynx (or voice box) and the development of conscious control over vocalization rather than "instinctive" cries of pain, fear, or warning. Time of origin: approximately 145,000 years ago (± 70,000) (Bickerton 1990: 175).

orthography: see *spelling*.

overt norm: see *covert norms*; ***GenE***; ***StE***.

palatalization: the OE process in which a /k/ or a /g/ followed by a front vowel took on a more palatal pronunciation including affrication (combination of stop and fricative) to /tʃ/ from /k/ and fricativization to /j/ from /g/. Examples: OE *ciste* "chest" with /tʃ/ but *castene* "cabinet, chest" with /k/ and *giefan* with /j/ but *gifa* (< ON) with /g/. Later palatalization (esp. in the EModE period) affected the consonants /s, z, t, d/ which become /ʃ, ʒ, tʃ, dʒ/ when followed by /j/ usually in an unstressed syllable. Examples: *fissure, azure, feature*, and *educate* though not always in all varieties.

parts of speech, aka word class: the primary categories of the language. They are important because membership in a part of speech reveals how a word can be used. Traditionally eight or nine classes are recognized: verb, noun, *adjective, adverb, pronoun, preposition*, conjunction, *determiner* (article), and interjection.

past: see *tense*.

perfect(ive) aspect: the **perfect** is one of the major two *grammaticalized* types of *aspect* in *StE*. It is formed with the auxiliary *have* + past participle and is aspectually distinct from the simple past. Example: *I haven't seen her* (up to now) vs. *I didn't see her* (in the past). In OE, in some creoles, and in AAVE **perfective** aspect refers to a completed action. Example: OE {ge-} as in *geferdon* "enter," which is used for a more "complete" action than *ferdon* "go" (Text 2.5). In AAVE *I done promise Miss Sally* (Text 10.6) indicates an already completed action.

periphrastic *be going to*: a means of expressing the future. It emphasizes the subject's intention or the inevitability of a future action. Example: *He's going to buy a computer. It's going to rain.* See *bleaching out*.

personal pronouns (systems of): a subgrouping of the pronouns which have a deictic function and indicate the person(s) speaking (first person); the person(s) spoken to (second person); and the person(s) spoken about (third person). In English they are marked for case, number, and gender (third person singular only). The possessive pronouns and the reflexive pronouns are also differentiated by person. See also *case, case leveling, declension, gender, inclusive/exclusive pronouns, inflection, nominative* you, *number, pronoun exchange*, and *second person pronoun usage*.

phonemicization: the process in which an *allophone* becomes a distinct sound (*phoneme*). Two words with a sound which once existed as two variations are now distinct. Example: with the loss of final /g/ after /ŋ/ in words like *sing* the phoneme /ŋ/ became distinct from the /n/ of *sin*.

phonetic symbols: see *IPA* chart on p. 363.

phonotactics: see *comparing pronunciation*.

phrasal verb: a combination of a verb and, most usually, an adverbial particle. They have increased by both the number which exist and the frequency of occurrence over time. Examples: *drink up, look out*.

pidginization: a process in which a new language comes into existence which is no one's native language. The resulting pidgin is a *reduced, marginal, hybrid, contact language* and/or *trade language*.

pied piping: a structure in which a *preposition* moves with its object when the object is replaced by a *relative pronoun* and moves to the front of its relative clause. Example: *the man to whom we were talking*. See also *stranding*.

place-names: see *toponyms*.

Plantation Creole: a creole supposed to have been widely spoken by African slaves in the British North American colonies and later US.

pleonastic subject: a repeated subject; considered stylistically undesirable, but widely used in spoken GenE. Example: *she* in *My sister she just left*.

plosive, aka stop: *obstruent* with stoppage of the air flow and then release. Examples: /p, b, t, d/.

plural: see *number*.

plural {-s} and {-th}: earlier present tense Northern and Southern (respectively) plural verb *inflections*. By the EModE period they were only used sporadically, if at all. Example: OE *Hi willað eow to gafole garas syllan* "They want to give you as tribute spears" (Text 3.3).

politeness; face: the avoidance of intrusion is central to politeness and indirectness is a key strategy in mitigating intrusion (= **negative face** or avoidance of imposition); **positive face** includes paying compliments and otherwise establishing solidarity. Examples: using the conditional in a request and embedding it as an indirect statement as in *I was wondering whether you could lend me your book*.

political-social change: affects language. Examples: the loss of the distinction between singular *thou* and singular *you*; the need for new names for new institutions such as *caucus* or *truth commission*.

polygenesis: a theory that creoles had multiple sources. This view emphasizes the similar conditions in West Africa and the Caribbean of the Atlantic creoles suggesting that this explains their similarities. See also *baby-talk, bioprogram, monogenesis, nautical jargons*.

possessive pronouns/adjectives: a subgrouping of the pronouns closely associated with the *personal pronouns*. The possessive adjectives are really *determiners*, not *adjectives*. Examples (pronoun, determiner): *mine, my*; *yours, your*; *his, his*; *hers, her*.

pragmatic idiom: a situationally embedded speech act. Example: greetings such as *kia-ora* in New Zealand English or SAfE *Howzit!*

pragmatics: the branch of linguistics which deals with the way language is employed. This often involves indirect use. Example: a speech act such as a request is often indirectly framed as a question, as in *Wouldn't it be nice to go out for dinner?* See also *pragmatic idiom*.

prepositions: a *part of speech* or word class. English has a large number of prepositions, due perhaps to the typological shift from synthetic to analytic. Analytic languages depend on particles such as prepositions to carry grammatical meaning. Example: OE *wordum mælde* (Text 3.3) consists of the dative plural of *word*; a ModE translation requires a preposition: *spoke with words*.

prescriptivism: a view of language which is largely motivated by the move to define what is correct and to condemn what is, consequently, "incorrect." Prescriptivism is closely related to the standard, and many speakers maintain a high regard for correctness, so defined. Example: There is a prescriptive rule *to never split* an infinitive (as just done). Descriptivism explains usage without such evaluation.

present tense {-s}: may be used with a subject in any person and number in non-standard varieties and informal usage, perhaps with a restriction to narratives or the verb *say*. Example: . . . *and then I says.* . . .

preterite-present verbs: a small group of verbs whose one-time past form became present tense in Proto-Germanic. As a result, for example, the 3rd p. sg. has no ending. New weak class past tense forms emerged to fill the gap. OE examples: *witan* "know," *āgan* "have," *cunnan* "be able," *magan* "be able," *sculan* "have to"; ModE examples: *can, may, must, shall, will*.

pre-verbal markers: markers of verb categories such as *TMA,* but also negation. In *creolization* such markers are placed immediately before the lexical verb, in the case of TMA usually in this order (see *bioprogram*). Example: Belize CE *we mi* (= T; past) *de* (= A; progressive) *luk fu rowp* (Holm 1989: 279).

primary language: a person's dominant language. Example: a native speaker of Igbo living in the Yoruba region of Nigeria may seldom use his or her *L1* but find English (or NigPE) more useful.

principal parts: the main *inflectional* forms of the verb consisting of infinitive, past (in OE two forms), and past participle. Examples: OE *drincan–dranc–druncon–druncen*; ModE: *drink–drank–drunk*.

principles of vowel change: as formulated by Labov 1991. The one or the other of the first five of them apply in describing the *Great Vowel Shift*, the *Northern Cities Shift*, the *Southern Shift*, and the *Low Back Merger*: (I) tense or long vowels, which are peripheral, rise; (II) lax or short ones fall = non-peripheral vowels fall; (III) back vowels move to the front; (IV) in chain shifting, low non-peripheral vowels become peripheral; (V) in chain shifting, high peripheral vowels become non-peripheral before peripheral glides.

progressive (aspect): one of the major grammaticalized types of *aspect* in *StE*. It is formed with the auxiliary *be* + present participle and is aspectually distinct from the simple form. Example: *I am eating lunch* vs. *I eat lunch at one every day.*

pronoun: a *part of speech* or word class with a number of sub-classes including *reflective, interrogative, relative, demonstrative, personal, indefinite*, and *possessive* pronouns

pronoun exchange: see *case leveling.*

pronunciation change: see *chain shifts, mergers, splits.*

Proto-Germanic: a hypothetic source language spoken before the various Germanic languages we know about from concrete evidence developed in their individual ways. Example: Proto-Germanic underwent the *First Germanic Sound Shift* which clearly distinguished the Germanic languages / dialects from those of the other *Indo-European languages. Historical reconstruction* is the tool used to extrapolate how it looked.

proto-language: a simpler and presumably historically older type of language without the creativity of genuine language. Consequently, a proto-language is more parrot-like. Children before the age of two to two and a half years seem to have proto-language rather than true language.

punctual (aspect): marks a verb as designating a singular, complete act. In English this is the case with dynamic (in contrast to stative) verbs and the simple, unmarked form of the verb is used for this, but also for habitual, iterative (repeated) or characteristic acts. Example: *The phone rang.*

reanalysis: a phase in the process of *grammaticalization* in which linguistic elements are differently understood than was originally the case. Example: the reassessment of *got* in a (non-standard) sentence like *I got a bike* as present tense so that negation with periphrastic *do* is possible: *I don't got a bike.*

reduced language: one aspect of a *pidgin* in which missing *grammatical categories*, a reduced phonemic repertory, and a vocabulary insufficient for many types of encounter beyond everyday situations are prominent features.

reduction of strong verb forms: the leveling of the four distinctions in the *principal parts* of strong verbs in OE (see *verb classes of OE*). The resulting forms may retain three, two, or no different vowels. Examples: *sing–sang–sung*; *sting–stung–stung*; *help–helped–helped*. Non-standard and regional forms may vary from *StE*.

reduplication: a means of ***word formation*** in which a word or a part of a word is repeated. Examples: *talk-talk* (or **pidgin** *tók-tók*) or *StE* *helter-skelter*. The effect of reduplication may be an intensification of meaning as with *talk-talk* including plural, repetition, indivisibility, or intensification as with *helter-skelter*.

reference accents: the standard accents generally used in dictionaries and other reference works. See *GenAm* and *RP*.

reflexive pronouns: a subgrouping of the pronouns closely related to the personal pronouns. The reflectives are formed by adding sg. {-self} or plur. {-selves} to the possessive or the object form. Examples: *myself*; *himself*. Only here are the 2nd person sg. and plur. distinct in *StE*: *yourself* vs. *yourselves*.

regionalization: the development of regional distinctions due to demographic effects. Example: Southern American may have emerged due to the particular mix of speakers of European and African heritage. The latter would have contributed non-***rhoticity*** and the merger of /e/ and /ɪ/ before nasals.

register: a means of approaching language use. It takes into consideration the ***field*** or ***domain***, the medium, the ***style***, and the function of a text. Example: an instruction leaflet on how and when to take medication would be the field of medicine, written medium, formal style, and directive function.

relative pronouns: a subgrouping of the pronouns divided among other things into ones with personal and with non-personal reference. Examples: personal: *who(m)*; non-personal: *which*; both: *whose, that*. *That* goes back to OE (*þat*); *who* is derived from the interrogatory pronoun possibly influenced by French, where *qui* is both interrogatory and relative.

relexification: the hypothesis that the similarity between the various Atlantic creoles is the result of an original Portuguese ***pidgin*** having its vocabulary replaced with words from other ***superstrate*** lexifiers while retaining its structure unchanged. Examples: Portuguese perfective *acabar de* > proto-pidgin *kabe* > (via relexification); English pidgin/creole *done* as in *ain't I done tell you 'bout that* (Harris 1881: 211; Text 10.6).

rhoticity, semi-rhoticity, and non-rhoticity: refers to whether /r/ is pronounced only before a vowel (non-rhoticity), only in morpheme-final position (semi-rhoticity), or also freely before consonants and a pause (rhoticity). Examples: *farm* non-rhotic and semi-rhotic /fɑːm/ vs. rhotic /fɑːrm/; *star* (morpheme-final <r>) non-rhotic /stɑː/ vs. semi-rhotic and rhotic /stɑːr/.

Romance languages: languages which developed out of vernacular Latin. Examples: French, Italian, Provençal, Spanish.

RP (Received Pronunciation): the prestigious standard accent of England, spoken in a near-RP form by as many as 25% of the population. RP in a narrower sense (3%) carries strong associations of class and is rejected by many for this reason. The accent is non-rhotic and realizes the ***FOOT–STRUT Split***.

runes, runic alphabet, aka the futhorc: an alphabet used, among others, by the Germanic peoples mostly for inscriptions. Some of the letters resemble ones in the Latin alphabet; other may have come from Northern Italian alphabets. Example: see Text 2.2.

schwa: the default unstressed vowel, transcribed as /ə/. Example: the <a> in *alone* is /ə/.

Scots: the ***traditional dialects*** of Scotland, often very divergent from GenE. Example: Text 8.8.

second person pronoun usage: has, with the loss of the *thou*-forms merged singular and plural in *StE*. Numerous GenE forms have restored the distinction by adding a distinct plural form, which is, however, not mandatory. Examples: *you all, youse, you guys*.

semantic shift or **change**: especially processes such as semantic narrowing and extension or broadening. **Narrowing** is the restriction of reference to fewer things. Example: AmE and AusE *corn* refers not to any kind of edible grain, but only to maize or Indian corn. **Extension** widens the original field of reference. Example: *NigE corner* refers not only to a *StE* corner, but also to a bend in the road.

semi-modals: emerging auxiliary forms which express modality but do not have the *NICE* features of auxiliaries. Examples: *gotta, gonna, hafta, wanna*. Hearsay can be expressed by the semi-modal *supposta*: *Language history is supposta be interesting*. See also **modal auxiliaries**.

Sheng: the Swahili-based **hybrid language** of Nairobi (Kenya). Sheng is basically Swahili with large elements of English, Kikuyu, Luo, Luhya, and Kamba in it. The language is spreading both socially into more public use and geographically into Tanzania and Uganda.

shibboleth: a word or expression which is a **marker** of language-belonging and is often non-standard. Example: *ain't* is considered to be non-standard and seen as a sign of poor education. Hence it is avoided in careful speech. See also **non-standard GenE**.

shift: see **conversion**.

shortening: a means of **word formation** including abbreviation, **acronym**, **back-formation**, and **clipping**. Example: *ABC* is an abbreviation of *Australian Broadcasting Corporation*.

Singlish: the possibly somewhat creolized **basilect** form of English spoken in Singapore. Example: Singlish **zero copula** as in *John a teacher*.

singular: see **number**.

solidarity and power: two major sociolinguistic dimensions. They are not opposites, but somewhat complementary in determining people's relations to each other. Solidarity reduces distance, and power maintains it. Both may operate reciprocally or non-reciprocally. Furthermore, solidarity is more likely to lead to **accommodation** than power is.

sound shift: see **Great Vowel Shift**, the **Germanic Sound Shifts**, the **Northern Cities Shift**, the **Southern Shift**, and the **Low Back Merger**.

South Asia: a region with a number of countries with English as a Second Language and British colonial background. India and Pakistan dominate. Bangladesh, Bhutan, the Maldives, Nepal, and Sri Lanka are more marginal from the point of view of *ESL*.

Southeast Asia: a region with a number of countries with English as a Second Language and a British (Singapore, Hong Kong) or American (the Philippines) colonial background.

Southern Africa: a region with a number of countries with English as a First, a Second, or a Foreign Language and similar linguistic and colonial backgrounds. In Botswana, Lesotho, Malawi, Namibia, Swaziland, Zambia, and Zimbabwe English is an important non-native language; in South Africa it is both a native and a second language.

Southern English: the English spoken in the region south of a line from mid-Shropshire to the Wash in England; the English of the Republic in Ireland; in New Zealand in the South Island; in the US in an area from just north of the Ohio River south to the Gulf and west through Central Texas.

Southern Shift: a chain shift which is vaguely similar in Southern England, the Southern Hemisphere ENLs, and the American South. Different from the GVS it affects the short vowels as well. Example: the raising of the AusE KIT vowel to [ɪ] and the FOOT vowel to [ʊ].

Southwest (England): a conservative and relatively distinct dialect region. It has retained older *gender* distinctions long lost in *StE*. Example: *count nouns* like *book* for distinctly formed things are referred to pronominally with *(h)e* (object case *a(n)*) while *mass nouns* like *air* have *it*.

Spanish: the source of numerous words in AmE. Many AmE speakers are *bilingual* in Spanish and practice *code-switching*. Example: Q (asked in Spanish): *How can you hear everything in Spanish and reply in English?*; A: *Ay, ya no sé, I don't know. I'm surprised to be able to do that* (Silva-Corvalán 1994: 12).

specifier: a subtype of *determiner*. It marks the following noun as known and unique. Example: *my book* as opposed to semi-specified *one of my books* or unspecified *a book*.

speech community, aka language community: the speakers of a given language, whereby "language" is vague and may also be a smaller peer group or regional or social subset of speakers. Examples: everyone who speaks English; the AusE speech community; or upper middle-class Sydney females.

spelling reform: any one of numerous attempts to bring spelling into a closer relation to pronunciation. Some modest reforms have been successful, but the abstractness of the present system and distance from actual pronunciation allows it to more easily represent many accents. Example: the reforms initiated by Noah Webster in the United States.

spelling, aka orthography: the conventional means for representing language in the written medium. English uses the Latin *alphabet* for this, but once also used *runes*. The principle of English spelling is – despite its bad reputation – phonetic. Many of the exceptions are due to *borrowing* or to *sound changes* which have occurred since spelling was fixed. Examples: <ea> is regularly used for /iː/ as in <beat>, but uneven change means that quite a few exceptions exist where the pronunciation is /e/, e.g. <death>, and a few where it is /eɪ/ <great>.

splits: the division of a previously unified class into two (or more) on account of new phonotactic rules. Example: see *FOOT–STRUT Split*.

Sranan: a *creole* of Suriname with English as its *lexifier*, but without standing in a *continuum* with English as the *acrolect* since the official language of Suriname is not English but Dutch.

stable, extended pidgin: a pidgin spoken over several generations. The very act of passing the language on speaks for its conventionality and the likelihood that such a pidgin will be less reduced than a newly emerging one. Example: *Tok Pisin* with its relatively complex grammar is such a pidgin.

Standard English (StE): a highly prestigious form of English which sets relatively narrow limits on what is regarded as acceptable grammar and vocabulary. In contrast, a wide variety of pronunciations may be used with StE. It stands virtually alone for purposes of writing.

standardization: a process in which a particular variety of a language is selected, expanded, *codified*, and eventually accepted as the standard for a speech community. In the case of English it was *StE*, a restricted code within GenE, which was promoted.

stative (aspect): a use of verbs to designate a state. Examples: cognitive verbs like *know* or *understand*, verbs of perception like *see* and *hear* are typically used for states and cannot occur in the progressive form. See also *aspect*.

stereotype: a socially marked form of speech. See *shibboleth* and *marker*. Example: *H-dropping*. See also *hypercorrection*.

stop, aka plosive: *obstruent* with stoppage of the air flow and then release. Examples: /p, b, t, d/.

stranding: constructions in which a preposition appears without its object after it. The preposition is "stranded" at one place in the sentence while its *relative pronoun* object moves to the front of its clause. Example: In *the man who we were talking to* the object of *to* is relative *who*. See also *pied piping*.

strong verbs: see *verb classes of OE*.

style: an aspect of register which helps to define how a language is used, usually on a continuum between formal and informal. Example: formal *a large quantity of* vs. intermediate *lots of* vs. informal *gobs of*.

subjunctive: a parallel paradigm in OE to the indicative. OE example: *Godes feoh and ciricean XII gylde* "(may) it be recompensed to God's property and the church 12-fold"; the indicative is *gylt*. See also *irrealis, mandative subjunctive, mood*.

substrate languages: languages whose speakers have a *superstrate* language imposed on them, typically in a situation of colonial dominance or conquest. English has been imposed on numerous non-English speaking peoples whose languages have influenced the features of English as it nativizes or indigenizes. Example: Gaelic substrate influence on IrE in its use of the *"hot-news" perfect: You're after ruinin' me*.

superstrate: a language of high prestige, often imposed on the speakers of *substrate* languages.

syntax: a branch of linguistics dealing chiefly with the arrangement of grammatical elements and their *morphological* features in sentences. Example: the syntax of a statement in English usually follows the order SV$_{aux}$V (*she has come*), but in a question may invert to V$_{aux}$SV (*Has she come*).

T (T-flapping, post-nasal T-loss): the flapping and voicing of /t/ in a vocalic context before an unstressed syllable. T-flapping is common in AmE, AusE, and increasingly in London English. Example: *matter = madder*. **Post-nasal /t/** is lost before an unstressed syllable in AmE. Example: *winter = winner*.

tag questions: grammatical tag questions include a repeat of the auxiliary of the preceding main verb or the use of *do* if there is no other auxiliary plus a corresponding pronoun subject. Example: *The food's cold, isn't it? The family left, didn't they?* In a number of ESL as well as Welsh Vernacular English the universal tag *isn't it?* is used. Example: *You went there yesterday, isn't it?*

tense: **(1)** a deictic instrument which locates a situation above all in time. English has distinct morphological forms for present and past (or remote); future is indicated in a variety of ways. OE example (Text 2.5): *Brittene igland **is** ehta hund mila lang* (present); *Erest **weron** bugend þises landes Brittes* (past); *þer ge **magon** eardian gif ge willað* (modal future). See also **periphrastic** *be going to*. **(2)** a vowel pronounced with tensed muscles. Examples: the long vowels such as /iː/ or /uː/. See also *lax*.

tertiary hybridization: the use of a *pidgin* (a *hybrid language*) not for communication between speakers of the *superstrate* and *substrate*, but among substrate speakers.

thematic roles: the semantic role of a sentence element. Typical roles are **agent:** the voluntary initiator of some action, e.g. *We decided to go to the movies*; **patient:** the entity affected by some action, e.g. *The **window** got broken*; **instrument:** the means used to do something, e.g. *A crowbar was employed to jimmy open the window*; location: the place in which something is situated, e.g. the book is **on the table**.

thematic structure, theme–rheme: the arrangement of information in a sentence or text. What is known (= the *topic*) usually comes first and represents the theme. What is said about it follows and is new (= the rheme). Example: *Changes in inflectional system* [theme] *continued to simplify the paradigms* [rheme].

THOUGHT–NORTH–FORCE Merger: a merger of the vowels of these *lexical sets* due to phonetic and phonological changes between the EModE and ModE periods. *RP* has undergone this merger, but *GenAm* has not done so completely because it is rhotic. See also *CLOTH–NORTH Split*.

TMA (tense, modality, aspect): categories of the verb which may be *universals*. The *bioprogram* gives them considerable prominence as default categories which human beings draw on in rapid *creolization*, i.e. creolization from a basis which is not an already *stable extended pidgin*. See also *tense*, *modality*, and *aspect*.

Tok Pisin: the **pidgin** (now creolizing in some urban centers) of Papua New Guinea. Its vocabulary, grammar, morphology, and phonology have been continuously expanding.

topicalization, topic: a process in which an element which might otherwise come later in a sentence is moved to initial and thus topical position. OE example: *Mið strelum ʒiwundad ælezdun hi hinæ limwæriʒnæ* (Text 2.2) "With arrows wounded laid they him weary-limbed down." See also *thematic structure*.

toponyms, aka place-names: provide evidence about who once settled or lived on or had control over the land whether in Britain and Ireland (Celtic, Germanic names) or in the US, Canada, Australia, New Zealand, and South Africa (also indigenous names or names suggesting various immigrant groups).

trade language: a term which emphasizes one of the chief motivations for the creation of a *pidgin*, viz. trade. Today Pidgin English continues to be an important market language.

traditional dialects: geographical and usually rural varieties of English which have been passed down in unbroken tradition since Anglo-Saxon times without undergoing major processes of *koinéization* or *accommodation* to GenE. Examples: the Lowlands Scots dialects.

TRAP–BATH Split: a division of words which previously had a shared [a] or [æ] vowel into two distinct vowels, the one class, TRAP, as before, and the new class, BATH, with long [aː] or [æː]. The new class eventually developed into [ɑː]. The split, typical of *RP* and the South of England, was very uneven. Examples: *past* with /ɑː/, but *bast* with /æ/.

trial, see *number*.

typology of language: classification of languages according to shared features. One of the major structural features examined is the *word order* of subject (S), predicate (V; for verb), and object (O), according to whether a language is, for example, an SOV or an SVO language. Example: English has undergone typological change from relatively variable to relatively fixed (SVO) word order.

uni- and multidimensionality: degree of complexity of relations within a social network. The denser relations are, the more likely speakers are to resemble each other in their linguistic features. See also *accommodation*.

universal grammatical categories: categories assumed to occur in all languages. Examples: nouns and verbs; maybe *TMA*.

verb classes of OE: basically divided into *weak verbs* and *strong verbs*. The former mark the past and past participle with an ending, e.g. {-d(e)}; the latter by means of vowel gradation or *ablaut*. Seven classes are commonly recognized. Examples: I. "bid" *bīdan–bād–bidon–biden*; II. "offer" *bēodan–bēad–budon–boden*; III. "bind" *bindan–band–bundon–bunden*; IV. "bear" *beran–bær–bǣron-boren*; V. "give" *giefan–geaf–gēafon–giefen*; VI. "stand" *standan–stōd–stōdon–standen*; VII. "fall" *feallan–fēoll–fēolloon–feallen*. See also *preterite-present verbs*.

vernacular universals: phonological and grammatical processes which occur in a wide variety of English *vernaculars* throughout the world. Vernaculars in this sense include not only GenE but also *traditional dialects* and *creoles* and may be due to innate features of the *bioprogram*. Example: the tendency to realize unstressed {-ing} as /ɪn/ as in *walkin'*.

vernacular: everyday spoken language, often in contrast to a more formal or classical variety (see *diglossia*). Non-standard GenE is a set of world-wide, mutually intelligible vernacular forms.

Verner's Law: an extension of Grimm's Law which factored in the effect of word stress to explain the presence of voiced fricatives where Grimm's Law predicted voiceless ones. Example: *father* with voiced /ð/ rather the voiceless /θ/.

vocabulary: the word stock (the totality of the *lexemes*) of a language. In the case of English, important structural features can be found such as the source of vocabulary which is about 30% Romance and Classical, 60% Germanic, and 10% other languages. This correlates somewhat with style and register, where in general the Germanic words are most common everyday ones while the Romance-Classical ones are more learned. Example: Germanic *help* vs. Romance-Classical *aid/assistance*.

voicing: *obstruents* in English are paired according to whether the vocal cords vibrate (**voiced**) or not (**voiceless**) when they are articulated. Examples of such pairs: /b – p/, /v – f/, /z – s/,

vowel systems: *GenE* in its many varieties shares systems of vowels which are close enough to allow a high degree of mutual intelligibility. The vowel systems of some *traditional dialects* may diverge too strongly for easy comprehension by outsiders. Examples: *RP, GenAm, Northern Cities Shift, Southern Shift*.

wave theory: a model of language or dialect spread in analogy to the rings of waves that spread over the surface of water when someone throws a stone in a pond. This analogy is misleading since there is a significant tendency for forms of a language to jump from city to city and to fill in the space in between much later. Change also spreads socially within identity groups even faster.

weak nouns, weak adjective endings, and weak verbs: the designation given in OE to a class of "regular" **nouns**, i.e. ones ending in {-n} in most of the grammatical *cases*. Example: *nama* "name"(masc. nom. sg.) but *naman* (gen., dat., acc. sg; nom. and acc. plur.); to the endings of adjectives preceded by a *determiner*. Example: *gōda* "good" (masc. nom. sg.) but *gōdan* (as with *naman*); to "regular" verbs, ones taking a {-d(e)} ending in the past and past participle. Example: *lufian* "love"; *lufode* (past); *lufod* (past participle).

West Africa: includes the Anglophone ESL countries Cameroon, Gambia, Ghana, Liberia, Nigeria, and Sierra Leone. All of these countries are polyglot and all of them have English as one of their official languages and in all of them Pidgin English widely spoken.

word class: see *part of speech*

word form: the shape of a *lexeme* on a particular occasion, including an identical sequence of letters or sounds. Example: *Herkneth to me, gode men – Wives, maydnes, and alle men – Of a tale that ich you wile telle* (Text 4.6) has eighteen different word forms; in other words, both occurrences of *men* count separately as do *me* and *ich*, which are two forms of one single lexeme (the 1st person singular personal pronoun).

word formation (processes): including *derivation* (*ablaut*, prefixation, suffixation), *shortening* (abbreviations, *acronyms, back-formation, clipping*), *blending, conversion/zero derivation.*

word order: the relative sequence of Subject, Verb, and Object in a sentence. In OE it was relatively free with SVO, AdvVSO, and SOV as the main variants, often however, conditioned by clause type. ModE is more rigid using chiefly SVO in most declaratives and (Wh-word)V$_{aux}$SVO in most questions.

word stress: the syllable in lexical words which is more strongly accented in English. It is relatively fixed and tends to fall on the first syllable. However, borrowed words, especially ones from Latin may have variable stress, and there may be some differences between varieties of English. Examples: Latinate: *professór*, but *professórial*; varieties: AmE *advertísement*, but BrE *advértisement*.

World Englishes: a blanket term for English of all sorts throughout the world. World Englishes include *English as a Native*, a *Second*, and a *Foreign Language*. See also *English as a Lingua Franca*.

yod-dropping: the loss of /j/ before /uː/. This process has been very uneven. In East Anglia it is largely lost following any consonant. In *GenAm* it has been restricted to /ʊː/ for /juː/ following dental and alveolar phonemes such as /s, z, n, l/. Examples: *sue, resume, new, lewd*. In London English it may occur after /s/ and /n/ as in the preceding examples but not after /d/ and /t/ as in *dew* and *tune*.

zero derivation: see *conversion.*

zero copula: see *copula deletion.*

Bibliography

Note: Bibliographical details on primary literature are provided in the main text.

Abercrombie, D. (1965) *Studies in Phonetics and Linguistics*. Oxford: OUP.

Achebe, C. (1975) "The African Writer and the English Language," In: *Morning Yet on Creation Day*. New York: Anchor, 55–62.

Agheyisi, R.N. (1971) *West African Pidgin English: Simplification and Simplicity*. Dissertation, Stanford University.

Agheyisi, R.N. (1988) "The Standardization of Nigerian English," In: *English World-Wide* 9, 227–241.

Algeo, J. (1988) "The Tag Question in British English: It's Different, I'n't?" In: *English World-Wide* 9, 171–191.

Alleyne, M.C. (1971) "Acculturation and the Cultural Matrix of Creolization," In: D. Hymes (ed.) *Pidginization and Creolization of Languages*. Cambridge: CUP, 169–186.

Ammon, U. (2000) "Toward More Fairness in International English: Linguistic Rights of Non-native Speakers," In: R. Phillipson (ed.) *Rights to Language: Equity, Power, and Education*. Mahwah: Lawrence Erlbaum, 112–116.

Angelo, D. et al. (1998) *Australian Phrasebook*, 2nd ed. Hawthorn, Vic.: Lonely Planet.

Angogo, R. and I. Hancock (1980) "English in Africa: Emerging Standards or Diverging Regionalisms," In: *English World-Wide* 1, 67–96.

Australian Concise Oxford Dictionary of Current English, The (1987), 7th ed., G.W. Turner (ed.), Melbourne: OUP.

Bailey, C.-J.N. and K. Maroldt (1977) "The French Lineage of English," In: J.M. Meisel (ed.) *Langues en contact – Pidgins – Creoles – Language in Contact*. Tübingen: Gunter Narr, 21–53.

Bailey, G. and E. Thomas (1998) "Some Aspects of African-American Vernacular English Phonology," In: S.S. Mufwene, J.R. Rickford, G. Bailey, and J. Baugh (eds.) *African-American English. Structure, History and Use*. London: Routledge, 85–109.

Bailey, R. (2004) "American English: Its Origins and History," In: E. Finegan and J.R. Rickford (eds.) *Language in the USA. Themes for the Twenty-first Century*. Cambridge: CUP, 3–17.

Bailyn, B. (1988) *The Peopling of British North America. An Introduction*. New York: Vintage.

Baker, S.J. (1966) *The Australian Language*, 2nd ed. Sydney: Currawong.

Bambas, R.C. (1998) "Verb Forms in -s and -th in Early Modern English Prose," In: M. Rydén, I. Tieken-Boon van Ostade, and M. Kytö (eds). *A Reader in Early Modern English*. Frankfurt: Lang, 65–71.

Barber, C. (1997 [1976]) *Early Modern English*, rev. ed. Edinburgh: Edinburgh UP.

Barber, C., J.C. Beal, and P.A. Shaw (2009) *The English Language. A Historical Introduction*, 2nd ed. Cambridge: CUP.

Barry, M.V. (1984) "The English Language in Ireland," In: R.W. Bailey and M. Görlach (eds.) *English as a World Language*. Cambridge: CUP, 84–133.

Bassett, S. (1989) "In Search of the Origins of Anglo-Saxon Kingdoms," In: S. Bassett (ed.) *The Origins of Anglo-Saxon Kingdoms*. London: Leicester UP, 3–27.

Bauer, L. (1994) "English in New Zealand," In: R. Burchfield (ed.) *The Cambridge History of the English Language*. vol. 5. *English in Britain and Overseas: Origins and Development*. Cambridge: CUP, 382–429.

Bauer, L. and P. Warren (2004) "New Zealand English: Phonology," In: E.W. Schneider, K. Burridge, B. Kortmann, R. Mesthrie, and C. Upton (eds.) *A Handbook of Varieties of English*. vol. 1. *Phonology*. Berlin: Mouton de Gruyter, 580–602.

Baugh, A.C. (1957) *A History of the English Language*, 2nd ed. New York: Appleton-Century-Crofts.

Baugh, A.C. (1963) "The American Dialects," In: *Linguistics* 1, 104–111.

Baugh, A.C. and T. Cable (1993, 2002). *A History of the English Language*. 4th and 5th eds. London: Routledge.

Baumgardner, R.J. (1998) "Word-Formation in Pakistani English," In: *English World-Wide* 19, 205–246.

Baumgardner, R.J. and A.E.H. Kennedy (1994) "Measure for Measure: Terms of Measurement in Pakistani English," In: *English World-Wide* 15, 173–193.

Beal, J. (2004) "English Dialects in the North of England: Morphology and Syntax," In: B. Kortmann, K. Burridge, R. Mesthrie, E.W. Schneider, and C. Upton (eds.) *A Handbook of Varieties of English*. vol. 2. *Morphology and Syntax*. Berlin: Mouton de Gruyter, 114–141.

Beier, R. (1980) *Englische Fachsprachen*. Stuttgart: Kohlhammer.

Benton, R.A. (1991) "Maori English: a New Zealand Myth?" In: J. Cheshire (ed) *English Around the World. Sociolinguistic Perspectives*. Cambridge: CUP, 187–199.

Bex, T. and R. Watts (eds.) (1999) *Standard English: The Widening Debate*. London: Routledge.

Biber, D., S. Johansson, G. Leech, S. Conrad, and E. Finegan (1999) *Longman Grammar of Spoken and Written English*. Harlow: Longman.

Bickerton, D. (1981) *Roots of Language*. Ann Arbor: Karoma.

Bickerton, D. (1988) "Creole Languages and the Bioprogram," In: F.J. Newmeyer (ed.) *Linguistics: The Cambridge Survey*. vol. 2. *Linguistic Theory: Extensions and Implications*. Cambridge: CUP, 268–284.

Bickerton, D. (1990) *Language and Species*. Chicago: University of Chicago Press.

Billington, R.A. (1974) *Westward Expansion: A History of the American Frontier*, 4th ed. New York: Macmillan.

Billuroğlu, A. and S. Neufeld (2005). "The Bare Necessities in Lexis: A New Perspective on Vocabulary Profiling," at: http://lextutor.ca/vp/BNL_Rationale.doc

Blake, N. (1996) *A History of the English Language*. Houndsmill: Palgrave.

Bliss, A. (1984) "English in the South of Ireland," In: P. Trudgill (ed.) *Language in the British Isles*. Cambridge: CUP, 135–151.

Bokamba, E.G. (1991) "West Africa," In: J. Cheshire (ed.) *English around the World: Sociolinguistic Perspectives*. Cambridge: CUP, 493–508.

Botkin, B.A. (ed.) (1983 [1944]) *A Treasury of American Folklore. Stories, Ballads, and Traditions of the People*. New York: Bonanza Books.

Bowerman, S. (2004a) "White South African English: Phonology," In: E.W. Schneider, K. Burridge, B. Kortmann, R. Mesthrie, and C. Upton (eds.) *A Handbook of Varieties of English*. vol. 1. *Phonology*. Berlin: Mouton de Gruyter, 931–942.

Bowerman S. (2004b) "White South African English: Morphology and Syntax," In: E.W. Schneider, K. Burridge, B. Kortmann, R. Mesthrie, and C. Upton (eds.) *A Handbook of Varieties of English*. vol. 2. *Morphology and Syntax*. Berlin: Mouton de Gruyter, 948–961.

Branford, J. (ed.) (1991) *A Dictionary of South African English* 4th ed. Oxford: OUP.

Branford, J. (1996) "English in South African Society: A Preliminary Overview," In: V. De Klerk (ed.) *Focus on South Africa*. Amsterdam: Benjamins, 35–51.

Brooks, N. (1989) "The Creation and Early Structure of the Kingdom of Kent," In: S. Bassett (ed.) *The Origins of the Anglo-Saxon Kingdoms*. London: Leicester UP, 55–74.

Bruti, S. (2000) "Address Pronouns in Shakespeare's English: A Re-appraisal in Terms of Markedness," In: D. Kastovsky and A. Mettinger (eds.) *The History of English in a Social Context. A Contribution to Historical Sociolinguistics*. Berlin: Mouton de Gruyter, 25–51.

Burnley, D. (ed.) (1992) *The History of the English Language. A Source Book*. London: Longman.

Cannon, G. (1987) *Historical Change and English Word-Formation*. New York: Lang.

Cassidy, F.G. (1971) *Jamaica Talk: Three Hundred Years of the English Language in Jamaica*. London: Macmillan.

Cassidy, F.G. (1980) "The Place of Gullah," In: *American Speech* 55, 3–15.

Chambers, J.K. (1986) "Three Kinds of Standard in Canadian English," In: W.C. Lougheed (ed.) *In Search of a Standard in Canadian English*. Kingston: Queens's University, 1–15.

Chambers, J.K. and M.F. Hardwick (1986) "Comparative Sociolinguistics of a Sound Change in Canadian English," In: *English World-Wide* 7, 23–44.

Cheshire, J. (1979) "Present Tense Verbs in Reading English," In: P. Trudgill (ed.) *Sociolinguistic Patterns in British English*. London: Arnold, 52–68.

Cheshire, J. (1999) "Standard Spoken English," In: T. Bex and R.J. Watts (eds.) *Standard English. The Widening Debate*. London: Routledge, 129–148.

Clyne, M. (1987) "Cultural Differences in the Organisation of Academic Texts," In: *Journal of Pragmatics* 11, 211–247.

Coates, J. (1983) *The Semantics of the Modal Auxiliaries*. London: Croom Helm.

Coghill, N. (1952) "Introduction," In: G. Chaucer *The Canterbury Tales*. Translated by N. Coghill. Baltimore: Penguin, 9–24.

Collins, P. and P. Peters (2004) "Australian English: Morphosyntax," In: E.W. Schneider, K. Burridge, B. Kortmann, R. Mesthrie, and C. Upton (eds.) *A Handbook of Varieties of English*. vol. 2. *Morphology and Syntax*. Berlin: Mouton de Gruyter, 593–610.

Comrie, B. (1976) *Aspect*. Cambridge: CUP.

Coulmas, F. (1987) "Why Speak English," In: K. Knapp, W. Enninger, A. Knapp-Potthoff (eds.) *Analyzing Intercultural Communication*. Berlin: Mouton de Gruyter, 95–107.

Countryman, E. (1985) *The American Revolution*. Harmondsworth: Penguin.

Craig, D.R. (1982) "Toward a Description of Caribbean English," In: B.B. Kachru (ed.) *The Other Tongue. English across Cultures*. Oxford: Pergamon, 198–209.

Crisma, P. (2009) "The Emergence of the Definite Article in English: A Contact-Induced Change?" at: www.hum.uva.nl/template/downloadAsset.cfm?objectid=F3CC72DB-1321-B0BE-A4C25 DDF219CB951

Croft, W. (1990) *Typology and Universals*. Cambridge: CUP.

Crosby, A.W. (2003) *The Columbian Exchange. Biological and Cultural Consequences of 1492*, rev. ed. Westport: Praeger.

Cruttenden, A. (2001) *Gimson's Pronunciation of English*, 6th ed. London: Arnold.

Crystal, D. (1997, 2000) *English as a Global Language*, 1st and 2nd eds. Cambridge: CUP.

Crystal, D. (2007) *Txtng. The Gr8 Db8*. Oxford: OUP.

Cunliffe, B. (1988) *Greeks, Romans and Barbarians. Spheres of Interaction*. London: Batsford.

Curtin, P. (1969) *The Atlantic Slave Trade: A Census*. Madison: University of Wisconsin Press.

Dabke, R. (1976) *Morphology of Australian English*. Munich: Fink.

Danchev, A. and M. Kytö (1998) "The Construction *be going to + infinitive* in Early Modern English," In: M. Rydén, I. Tieken-Boon van Ostade, and M. Kytö (eds.) *A Reader in Early Modern English*. Frankfurt: Lang, 145–163.

DeCamp, D. (1971) "Toward a Generative Analysis of a Post-Creole Continuum," In: D. Hymes (ed.) *Pidginization and Creolization of Languages*. Cambridge: CUP, 349–370.

Delbridge, A. (1970) "The Recent Study of Spoken Australian English," In: W.S. Ramson (ed.) *English Transported*. Canberra: Australian National UP, 15–31.

Delbridge, A. (ed.) (1997) *Macquarie Dictionary*, 3rd ed. Macquarie University: The Macquarie Library.

Denison, D. (1993) *English Historical Syntax: Verbal Constructions*. London: Longman.

Dillard, J.L. (1973) *Black English*. New York: Vintage.

Dillard, J.L. (1975) *All-American English*. New York: Random House.

Dillard, J.L. (1980) "Introduction [to Part Five: 'Pidgin English']" In: J.L. Dillard (ed.) *Perspectives on American English*. The Hague: Mouton, 403–416.

Dillard, J.L. (1992) *A History of American English*. London: Longman.

Dixon, R.M.W. (1980) "The Role of Language in Aboriginal Australian Society Today" [= chap. 4], In: *The Languages of Australia*. Cambridge: CUP, 69–96.

Dobson, E.J. (1955) "Early Modern Standard English," In: *Transactions of the Philological Society* 54, 25–54.

Driver, H.E. (1969) *Indians of North America*, 2nd ed. Chicago: University of Chicago.

Education and Language (2010) at: www.singstat.gov.sg/pubn/popn/ghsr1/chap2.pdf, 11–19.

Ekwall, E. (1970 [1936]) *Concise Oxford Dictionary of English Place-Names*, 4th ed. Oxford: Clarendon.

Ellegård, A. (1953) *The Auxiliary do. The Establishment and Regulation of Its Use in English*. Stockholm: Almqvist and Wiksell.

Ethnologue (2009) at: www.ethnologue.com/show_country.asp?name=CM

Fasold, R.W. (1972) *Tense Marking in Black English. A Linguistic and Social Analysis*. Washington: Center for Applied Linguistics.

Faulkner, H.U. and T. Kepler (1950) *America. Its History and People*, 5th ed. New York: McGraw-Hill.

Fennell, B.A. (2001) *A History of English. A Sociolinguistic Approach*. Malden: Blackwell.

Filppula, M. (2004) "Irish English: Morphology and Syntax," In: B. Kortmann, K. Burridge, R. Mesthrie, E.W. Schneider, and C. Upton (eds.) *A Handbook of Varieties of English*. vol. 2. *Morphology and Syntax*. Berlin: Mouton de Gruyter, 73–101.

Filppula, M., J. Klemola, and H. Paulasto (2008) *English and Celtic in Contact*. New York: Routledge.

Finegan, E. and J.R. Rickford (eds.) (2004) *Language in the USA. Themes for the Twenty-first Century*. Cambridge: CUP.

Finkenstaedt, T. and D. Wolff (1973) *Ordered Profusion. Studies in Dictionaries and the English Lexicon*. Heidelberg: Winter.

Finn, P. (2004) "Cape Flats English: Phonology," In: B. Kortmann, K. Burridge, R. Mestrie, E.W. Schneider, and C. Upton (eds.) *A Handbook of Varieties of English*. vol. 2. *Morphology and Syntax*. Berlin: Mouton de Gruyter, 964–984.

Fischer, O. (1992) "Syntax," In: N. Blake (ed.) *The Cambridge History of the English Language*. vol. 2. *1066–1476*. Cambridge: CUP, 207–408.

Fisher, J.H. (2001) "British and American, Continuity and Divergence," In: J. Algeo (ed.) *The Cambridge History of the English Language*. vol. 6. *English in North America*. Cambridge: CUP, 59–85.

Fought, C. (2003) *Chicano English in Context*. London: Palgrave/Macmillan.

Franklin, J.H. (1980) *From Slavery to Freedom. A History of Negro Americans*, 5th ed. New York: Knopf.

Fries, C.C. (1940) "On the Development of the Structural Use of Word-Order in Modern English," *Language* 16, 199–208.

Fritz, C. (2006) "Resilient or Yielding? Features of Irish English Syntax and Aspect in Early Australia," In: T. Nevalainen, J. Klemola, and M. Laitinen (eds.) *Types of Variation. Diachronic, Dialectal and Typological Interfaces*. Amsterdam: John Benjamins, 281–301.

Geipel, J. (1971) *The Viking Legacy: The Scandinavian Influence on the English and Gaelic Languages*. Newton Abbot: David and Charles.

Gerbert, M. (1970) *Besonderheiten der Syntax in der technischen Fachsprache des Englischen*. Halle: Niemeyer.

Gilbert, G. (1984) "Review of McDavid, R.I. Jr., R.K. O'Cain. *Linguistic Atlas of the Middle and South Atlantic States* fascicles 1 and 2 University of Chicago Press, 1980," In: *Leuvense bijdragen* 73, 407–415.

Giles, H., R. Bourhis, and D. Taylor (1977) "Towards a Theory of Language in Ethnic Group Relations," In: H. Giles (ed.) *Language, Ethnicity*. London: Academic, 307–348.

Godden, M.R. (1992) "Literary Language," In: R.M. Hogg (ed.) *The Cambridge History of the English Language*. vol. 1. *The Beginnings to 1066*. Cambridge: CUP, 490–535.

Goh, C.T. (2000) "Speak Good English Movement," at: www.goodenglish.org.sg/about/over-the-years/2004/official-speeches-2004/pm-goh-chok-tong-2000

Gonzalez, A. (1982) "English in the Philippines," In: J. Pride (ed.) *New Englishes*. Rowley: Newbury House, 211–226.

Gordon, E. and T. Deverson (1985) *New Zealand English*. Auckland: Heinemann.

Gordon, E. and A. Sudbury (2002) "The History of Southern Hemisphere Englishes," In: R. Watts and P. Trudgill (eds.) *Alternative Histories of English*. London: Routledge, 67–86.

Gordon, R.G., Jr. (ed.) (2005) "English," In: *Ethnologue: Languages of the World*, 15th ed. Dallas: SIL International, also at: www.ethnologue.com/show_language.asp?code=eng.

Görlach, M. (1986) "Middle English – A Creole?" In: D. Kastovsky and A. Szwedek (eds.) *Linguistics across Historical and Geographical Boundaries*. Berlin: Mouton de Gruyter, 329–344.

Görlach, M. (1997) *The Linguistic History of English. An Introduction*. London: Macmillan.

Görlach, M. (1998) "Renaissance English (1525–1640)," In: M. Rydén, I. Tieken-Boon van Ostade, and M. Kytö (eds.) *A Reader in Early Modern English*. Frankfurt: Lang, 9–22.

Gough, D. (1996) "Black English in South Africa," In: V. De Klerk (ed.) *Focus on South Africa*. Amsterdam: Benjamins, 53–77.

Gramley, S.E. (2001) *The Vocabulary of World English*. London: Arnold.

Gramley, S.E. and K.-M. Pätzold (2004) *Survey of Modern English*, 2nd ed. London: Routledge.

Green, L. (1998) "Aspect and Predicate Phrases in African-American Vernacular English," In: S.S. Mufwene, J.F. Rickford, G. Bailey, and J. Baugh (eds.) *African-American English. Structure, History, and Use*. London. Routledge, 37–68.

Green, L. (2004) "African American English," In: E. Finegan and J.R. Rickford (eds.) *Language in the USA. Themes for the Twenty-first Century*. Cambridge: CUP, 76–91.

Gupta, A. (1994) *The Step-Tongue: Children's English in Singapore*. Clevedon: Multilingual Matters.

Hall, R.A., Jr. (1966) *Pidgin and Creole Languages*. Ithaca: Cornell UP.

Hancock, I. (1980) "Gullah and Barbadian. Origins and Relationships," In: *American Speech* 55, 17–35.

Hansen, K. (1996). *Die Differenzierung des Englischen in nationale Varianten*. Berlin: Erich Schmidt Verlag.

Herbert, R.K. (1994) "The Meaning of Language Choice(s): Social and Pragmatic Factors Reconsidered," qtd. in: D. Gough "Black English in South Africa," In: V. de Klerk (ed.) *Focus on South Africa*. Amsterdam: Benjamins, 1996, 53–77.

Hill, C. (1972) *The World Turned Upside Down. Radical Ideas during the English Revolution*. Harmondsworth: Penguin.

History of Canada, The (2009) at: www.linksnorth.com/canada-history/theunitedempire.html

Ho, M.L. and J.T. Platt (1993) *Dynamics of a Contact Continuum: Singaporean English*. Oxford: Clarendon.

Hobsbawm, E.J. (1990) *Nations and Nationalism since 1780: Programmes, Myth, Reality*. Cambridge: CUP.

Hogg, R.M. (1992) "Phonology and Morphology," In: R.M. Hogg (ed.) *The Cambridge History of the English Language*. vol. 1. *The Beginnings to 1066*. Cambridge: CUP, 67–167.

Holm, J. (1986) "The Spread of English in the Caribbean Area," In: M. Görlach and J.A. Holm (eds.) *Focus on the Caribbean*. Amsterdam: Benjamins, 1–22.

Holm, J. (1988–89) *Pidgins and Creoles*. vol. 1. *Theory and Structure*, vol. 2. *Reference Survey*. Cambridge: CUP.

Holm, J. (1994) "The History of the English Language in the West Indies," In: R. Burchfield (ed.) *The Cambridge History of the English Language*. vol. 5. *English in Britain and Overseas: Origins and Development*. Cambridge: CUP, 328–281.

Holm, J. (2000) *An Introduction to Pidgins and Creoles*. Cambridge: CUP.

Hopper, P.J. and E.C. Traugott (1993) *Grammaticalization*. Cambridge: CUP.

Horvath, B.M. (2004) "Australian English: Phonology," In: E.W. Schneider, K. Burridge, B. Kortmann, R. Mesthrie, and C. Upton (eds.) *A Handbook of Varieties of English*. vol. 1. *Phonology*. Berlin: Mouton de Gruyter, 625–644.

Huddleston, R.D. (1971) *The Sentence in Written English: A Syntactic Study Based on an Analysis of Scientific Texts*. Cambridge: CUP.

Hundt, M., J. Hay, and E. Gordon (2004) "New Zealand English: Morphosyntax," In: E.W. Schneider, K. Burridge, B. Kortmann, R. Mesthrie, and C. Upton (eds.) *A Handbook of Varieties of English*. vol. 2. *Morphology and Syntax*. Berlin: Mouton de Gruyter, 560–592.

Jenkins, J. (2000) *The Phonology of English as an International Language*. Oxford: OUP.

Jenkins, J. (2009a) *World Englishes. A Resource Book for Students*, 2nd ed. London: Routledge.

Jenkins, J. (2009b) "English as a Lingua Franca: Interpretations and Attitudes," In: *World Englishes* 28, 200–207.

Jespersen, O. (1955 [1905]) *Growth and Structure of the English Language*, 9th ed. Garden City: Doubleday Anchor.

Johnson, F.R. (1998) "Latin versus English: The Sixteenth-Century Debate over Scientific Terminology," In: M. Rydén, I. Tieken-Boon van Ostade, and M. Kytö (eds.) *A Reader in Early Modern English*. Frankfurt: Lang, 255–278.

Joos, M. (1968) *The English Verb. Form and Meanings*. Madison: University of Wisconsin Press.

Joseph, J.E. (2004) *Language and Identity. National, Ethnic, Religious*. Houndmills: Palgrave.

Kachru, B.B. (1984) "Asian English," In: R. Bailey and M. Görlach (eds.) *English as a World Language*. Cambridge: CUP, 353–383.

Kachru, B.B. (1985) "Standard, Codification and Sociolinguistic Realism: The English Language in the Outer Circle," In: R. Quirk and H.G. Widdowson (eds.) *English in the World: Teaching and Learning the Language and Literatures*. Cambridge: CUP, 11–30.

Kachru, B.B. (ed.) (1992a) *The Other Tongue: English across Cultures*, 2nd ed. Urbana: University of Illinois Press.

Kachru, B.B. (1992b) "Teaching World Englishes," In: B.B. Kachru (ed.) *The Other Tongue: English across Cultures,* 2nd ed. Urbana: University of Illinois Press, 355–366.

Kalensky, C. (2009) *Kompliziert – Komplizierter – Wissenschaftsdeutsch?* Diploma thesis, University of Vienna. Philologisch-Kulturwissenschaftliche Fakultät.

Kamwangamalu, N. and T. Chisanga (1996) "English in Swaziland: Form and Functions," In: V. de Klerk (ed.) *Focus on South Africa*. Amsterdam: Benjamins, 285–300.

Kastovsky, D. (1992) "Semantics and Vocabulary," In: R.M. Hogg (ed.) *The Cambridge History of the English Language*. vol. 1. *The Beginnings to 1066*, Cambridge: CUP, 290–408.

Kingsford, C.L. (1905) *Chronicles of London*. Oxford: Clarendon.

Kirkpatrick, A. (2007) *World Englishes: Implications for International Communication and ELT*. Cambridge: CUP.

Knowles, G.O. (1997) *A Cultural History of the English Language*. London: Edward Arnold.

Kretzschmar, W.A., Jr. (2004) "Regional Dialects," In: E. Finegan and J.R. Rickford (eds.) *Language in the USA. Themes for the Twenty-first Century*. Cambridge: CUP, 39–57.

Labov, W. (1972) "The Social Setting of Linguistic Change," In: W. Labov *Sociolinguistic Patterns*. Philadelphia: University of Pennsylvania, 260–325.

Labov, W. (1991) "The Three Dialects of English," In: P. Eckert (ed.) *New Ways of Analyzing Sound Change*. San Diego: Academic, 1–44.

Lanham, L. (1996) "A History of English in South Africa," In: V. De Klerk (ed.) *Focus on South Africa*. Amsterdam: Benjamins, 19–34.

Lass, R. (1992) "Phonology and Morphology," In: N. Blake (ed.) *The Cambridge History of the English Language*. vol. 2. *1066–1476*. Cambridge, CUP, 23–155.

Lass, R. (1999) "Phonology and Morphology," In: R. Lass (ed.) *The Cambridge History of the English Language*. vol. 3. *1476–1776*, Cambridge: CUP, 56–186.

Lass, R. (2000) "A Branching *Path*: Low Vowel Lengthening and Its Friends in the Emerging Standard," In: L. Wright (ed.) *The Development of Standard English 1300–1800*. Cambridge: CUP, 219–229.

Lass, R. (2002) "South African English," In: R. Mesthrie (ed.) *Language in South Africa*. Cambridge: CUP, 104–126.

Lass. R. and S. Wright (1986) "Endogeny vs. Contact: 'Afrikaans Influence' on South African English," *English World-Wide* 7, 201–223.

Leap, W.L. (1981) "American Indian Languages," In: C.A. Ferguson and S.B. Heath (eds.) *Language in the USA*. Cambridge. CUP, 116–144.

Leap, W.L. (1993) *American Indian English*. Salt Lake City: University of Utah Press.

Leith, D. (1983) *A Social History of English*. London: Routledge.

Leith, D. (2007) "The Origins of English," In: D. Graddol, D. Leith, J. Swann, M. Rhys, and J. Gillen (eds) *Changing English*. London: Routledge, 39–73.

Lewis, M.P. (ed.) (2009) *Ethnologue: Languages of the World*, 16th ed. Dallas: SIL International, also at: www.ethnologue.com

Lippi-Green, R. (2004) "Language Ideology and Language Prejudice," In: E. Finegan and J.R. Rickford (eds.) *Language in the USA. Themes for the Twenty-first Century*. Cambridge: CUP, 289–304.

Longman Dictionary of Contemporary English (LDOCE) (various years and editions) London: Longman.

Longmore, P. (2007) "'Good English without Idiom or Tone': The Colonial Origins of American Speech," In: *Journal of Interdisciplinary History* 37, 513–542.

Lord, R. (1987) "Language policy and planning in Hong Kong: Past, Present, and (Especially) Future," In: R. Lord and H.N.L. Cheung (eds.) *Language Education in Hong Kong*. Hong Kong: The Chinese UP.

Lyons, J. (1977) *Semantics*. Cambridge: CUP.

McArthur, A. (1998) *The English Languages*. Cambridge: CUP.

Macaulay, T.B. (1967 [1835]) "Indian Education. Minute of the 2nd of February, 1835," In: G.M. Young (ed.) *Macaulay. Prose and Poetry*. London: Hart-Davis, 719–730.

MacCarthy, P. (1972) *Talking of Speaking. Selected Papers*. Oxford: OUP.

McClure, J.D. (1980) "Developing Scots as a National Language," In: J.D. McClure, A.J. Aitken, and J.T. Low (eds.) *The Scots Language. Planning for Modern Usage*. Edinburgh: Ramsay Head, 11–41.

McDavid, R.I. and R.K. O'Cain (1980) *Linguistic Atlas of the Middle and South Atlantic States*. Chicago: University of Chicago Press.

McKinnon, M. (ed.) (1997) *New Zealand Historical Atlas*. Auckland: Bateman.

MacMahon, M.K.C. (1998) "Phonology," In: S. Romaine (ed.) *The Cambridge History of the English Language*. vol. 4. *1776–1997*. Cambridge: CUP, 373–535.

Malan, K. (1996) "Cape Flats English," In: V. De Klerk (ed.) *Focus on South Africa*. Amsterdam: Benjamins, 125–148.

Malcolm, I.G. (2004) "Australian Creoles and Aboriginal English: Morphology and Syntax," In: E.W. Schneider, K. Burridge, B. Kortmann, R. Mesthrie, and C. Upton (eds.) *A Handbook of Varieties of English,* vol. 2. *Morphology and Syntax*. Berlin: Mouton de Gruyter, 657–681.

Mann, C. (2005) *1491. New Revelations of the Americas before Columbus.* New York: Vintage.

Marckwardt, A.H. (1980) *American English*, 2nd ed. (revised by J.L. Dillard) New York: OUP.

Mazrui, A.A. (1973) *The Political Sociology of the English Language.* The Hague: Mouton.

Mazzon, G. (1994) "OE and ME Multiple Negation. Some Syntactic and Stylistic Remarks," In: F. Fernández, M. Fuster, and J.J. Calvo (eds.) *English Historical Linguistics 1992.* Amsterdam: Benjamins, 157–169.

Mazzon, G. (2000a) "Special Relations and Forms of Address in the *Canterbury Tales*," In: D. Kastovsky and A. Mettinger (eds.) *The History of English in a Social Context. A Contribution to Historical Sociolinguistics.* Berlin: Mouton de Gruyter, 135–167.

Mazzon, G. (2000b) "The Ideology of the Standard and the Development of Extraterritorial Englishes," In: L. Wright (ed.) *The Development of Standard English 1300–1800.* Cambridge: CUP, 73–92.

Mbangwana, P.N. and B.M. Sala (2009) *Cameroon English Morphology and Syntax: Current Trends in Action.* Munich: Lincom Europa.

Mehrotra R.R. (1982) "Indian English: A Sociolinguistic Profile," In: J. Pride (ed.) *New Englishes.* Rowley: Newbury House, 150–173.

Mencken, H.L. (1948) *The American Language*, Supplement II. New York: Knopf.

Mencken, H.L. (1963) *The American Language.* New York: Knopf.

Mesthrie, R. (2004a) "Introduction: Varieties of English in Africa and South and Southeast Asia," In: B. Kortmann, K. Burridge, R. Mestrie, E.W. Schneider, and C. Upton (eds.) *A Handbook of Varieties of English.* vol. 2. *Morphology and Syntax.* Berlin: Mouton de Gruyter, 805–812.

Mesthrie, R. (2004b) "Synopsis: Morphological and Syntactic Variant in Africa, South and Southeast Asia," In: B. Kortmann, K. Burridge, R. Mestrie, E.W. Schneider, and C. Upton (eds.) *A Handbook of Varieties of English.* vol. 2. *Morphology and Syntax.* Berlin: Mouton de Gruyter, 1099–1109.

Mesthrie, R. (2004c) "Synopsis: The Phonology of English in Africa and South and Southeast Asia," In: E.W. Schneider, K. Burridge, B. Kortmann, R. Mesthrie, and C. Upton (eds.) *A Handbook of Varieties of English.* vol. 1. *Phonology.* Berlin: Mouton de Gruyter, 1132–1141.

Mesthrie, R. and R. Bhatt (2008) *World Englishes: The Study of New Linguistic Varieties.* Cambridge: CUP.

Mesthrie, R., J. Swann, A. Deumert, and W.L. Leap (eds.) (2000) *Introducing Sociolinguistics.* Edinburgh: Edinburgh UP.

Metcalf, A. (1972) "Directions of Change in Southern California English," In: *Journal of English Linguistics* 6, 28–34.

Miller, J. (2004) "Scottish English: Morphology and Syntax," In: B. Kortmann, K. Burridge, R. Mesthrie, E.W. Schneider, and C. Upton (eds.) *A Handbook of Varieties of English.* vol. 2. *Morphology and Syntax.* Berlin: Mouton de Gruyter, 47–72.

Millward, C. M. (1996) *A Biography of the English Language,* 2nd ed. Boston: Thomson-Heinle.

Morris, E.E. (1972 [1898]) *A Dictionary of Austral English.* Sydney: Sydney UP.

Mufwene, S.S., J. Rickford, G. Bailey, and J. Baugh (eds.) (1998) *African-American English. Structure, History, and Use.* London. Routledge.

Mühlhäusler, P. (1986a) *Pidgin and Creole Linguistics.* Oxford: Basil Blackwell.

Mühlhäusler, P. (1986b) "English in Contact with Tok Pisin (Papua New Guinea)," In: W. Viereck and W.D. Bald (eds.) *English in Contact with Other Languages.* Budapest. Akadémiai Kiadó, 549–570.

Mustanoja, T.F. (1960) *A Middle English Syntax.* Helsinki: Société Néophilologique.

Nevalainen, T. (1994) "Ladies and Gentlemen: The Generalization of Titles in Early Modern English," In: F. Fernández, M. Fuster, and J.J. Calvo (eds.) *English Historical Linguistics 1992.* Amsterdam: Benjamins, 317–327.

Nevalainen, T. (1998) "Change from Above. A Morphosyntactic Comparison of Two Early Modern English Editions of *The Book of Common Prayer*," In: M. Rydén, I. Tieken-Boon van Ostade, and M. Kytö (eds.) *A Reader in Early Modern English.* Frankfurt: Lang, 165–186.

Nevalainen, T. and H. Raumolin-Brunberg (1994) "*Its* Strength and the Beauty *of It*': The Standardization of the Third Person Neuter Possessive in Early Modern English," In: D. Stein and I. Tieken-Boon van Ostade (eds.) *Towards a Standard English 1600–1800.* Berlin: Mouton de Gruyter, 171–216.

Nevalainen, T. and H. Raumolin-Brunberg (2000) "The Changing Role of London on the Linguistic Map of Tudor and Stuart England," In: D. Kastovsky and A. Mettinger (eds.) *The History of English in a Social Context. A Contribution to Historical Sociolinguistics.* Berlin: Mouton de Gruyter, 279–337.

Ngũgĩ wa Thiong'o (1986) *Decolonizing the Mind: The Politics of Language in African Literature.* London: James Currey.

Officer, L.H. (2009) "Purchasing Power of British Pound from 1264 to Present," at: *Measuring Worth,* www.measuringworth.com/ppoweruk

Ogden, C.K. (1968 [1930]) *Basic English.* London: Kegan Paul, Trench, and Trubner.

Osselton, N.E. (1998a) "Spelling-Book Rules and the Capitalization of Nouns in the Seventeenth and Eighteenth Centuries," In: M. Rydén, I. Tieken-Boon van Ostade, and M. Kytö (eds.) *A Reader in Early Modern English.* Frankfurt: Lang, 447–460.

Osselton, N.E. (1998b) "Informal Spelling Systems in Early Modern English: 1500–1800," In: M. Rydén, I. Tieken-Boon van Ostade, and M. Kytö (eds.) *A Reader in Early Modern English.* Frankfurt: Lang, 33–45.

Oxford English Dictionary (1928) J. Murray (ed.) Oxford: Clarendon.

Oxford 3000 (2006) at: www.oup.com/elt/catalogue/teachersites/oald7/oxford_3000/oxford3000_list?cc=global

Palmer, F.R. (2001) *Mood and Modality,* 2nd ed. Cambridge: CUP.

Parakrama, A. (1995) *De-hegemonizing Language Standards.* Basingstoke: Macmillan.

Pawley, A. (2004) "Australian Vernacular English. Some Grammatical Characteristics," In: E.W. Schneider, K. Burridge, B. Kortmann, R. Mesthrie, and C. Upton (eds.) *A Handbook of Varieties of English.* vol. 2. *Morphology and Syntax.* Berlin: Mouton de Gruyter, 611–642.

Peñalosa, F. (1980) *Chicano Sociolinguistics.* Rowley: Newbury House.

Penhallurick, R. (2004) "Welsh English: Morphology and Syntax," In: B. Kortmann, K. Burridge, R. Mesthrie, E.W. Schneider, and C. Upton (eds.) *A Handbook of Varieties of English.* vol. 2. *Morphology and Syntax.* Berlin: Mouton de Gruyter, 102–113.

Phillipson, R. (1992) *Linguistic Imperialism.* Oxford: OUP.

Pilch, H. (1955) "The Rise of American English Vowel Patterns," In: *Word* 11, 57–93.

Platt, J.T. and H. Weber (1980) *English in Singapore and Malaysia.* Kuala Lampur: OUP.

Platt, J.T., H. Weber, and M.L. Ho (1984) *The New Englishes.* London: Routledge & Paul.

Pohl, W. (2005) *Die Völkerwanderung. Eroberung und Integration,* 2nd ed. Stuttgart: Kohlhammer.

Poplack, S., G. Van Herk, and D. Harvie (2002) "'Deformed in the Dialects,'" In: R. Watts and P. Trudgill (eds.) *Alternative Histories of English.* London: Routledge, 87–110.

Prestwich, M.C. (2005) *Plantagenet England: 1225–1360.* Oxford: OUP.

Price, A.H. (1994) *Germanic Warrior Clubs. An Inquiry into the Dynamics of the Era of Migrations and into the Antecedent of Medieval Society.* Tübingen: UVT Lück und Mauch.

Prodromou, L. (1997) "From Corpus to Corpus," *IATEFL Newsletter* 137, 3–10.

Prodromou, L. (2007) "Is ELF a Variety of English?" In: *English Today* 23 (April), 47–53.

Quirk, R. and C.L. Wrenn (1957) *An Old English Grammar.* 2nd ed. London: Methuen.

Quirk, R., S. Greenbaum, G. Leech, and J. Svartvik (1985) *A Comprehensive Grammar of the English Language.* London: Longman.

Raumolin-Brunberg, H. (1998) "Social Factors and Pronominal Change in the Seventeenth Century: The Civil-War Effect?" In: J. Fisiak and M. Krygier (eds.) *Advances in English Historical Linguistics (1996)* Berlin: Mouton de Gruyter, 361–388.

Rickford, J.R. (1987) *Dimensions of a Creole Continuum. History, Texts, and Linguistic Analysis of Guyanese Creole*. Stanford: Stanford UP.

Rissanen, M. (1998) "Periphrastic *do* in Affirmative Statements in Early American English," In: M. Rydén, I. Tieken-Boon van Ostade, and M. Kytö (eds.) *A Reader in Early Modern English*. Frankfurt: Lang, 201–219.

Rissanen, M. (1999) "Syntax," In: R. Lass (ed.) *The Cambridge History of the English Language*. vol. 3. *1476–1776*. Cambridge: CUP, 187–331.

Ross, A.S.C. (1954) "Linguistic Class-Indicators in Present Day English," In: *Neuphilologische Mitteilungen* 55, 20–56.

Rydén, M., I. Tieken-Boon van Ostade, and M. Kytö (eds.) (1998) *A Reader in Early Modern English*. Frankfurt: Lang.

Sager, J.C., D. Dungworth, and P.F. McDonald (1980) *English Special Languages*. Wiesbaden: Brandstetter.

Salager, F. (1984) "Compound Nominal Phrases in Scientific-Technical Literature: Proportion and Rationale," In: A.K. Pugh and J.M. Ulijn (eds.) *Reading for Professional Purposes: Studies and Practices in Native and Foreign Languages*. London: Heinemann, 136–145.

Samuels, M.L. (1963) "Some Applications of Middle English Dialectology," In: *English Studies* 44, 81–94.

Samuels, M.L. (1972) *Linguistic Evolution with Special Reference to English*. Cambridge: CUP.

Sandefur, J.R. (1983) "Modern Australian Aboriginal Languages: The Present State of Knowledge," In: *English World-Wide* 4, 43–68.

Schmied, J. (1996) "English in Zimbabwe, Zambia and Malawi," In: V. de Klerk (ed.) *Focus on South Africa*. Amsterdam: Benjamins, 301–321.

Schneider, E. (2009) *Postcolonial Englishes*. Cambridge: CUP.

Schneider, E.W., K. Burridge, B. Kortmann, R. Mesthrie, and C. Upton (eds.) (2004) *A Handbook of Varieties of English*. vol. 1. *Phonology* and vol. 2. *Morphology and Syntax*. Berlin: Mouton de Gruyter.

Schneider, G.D. (1967) "West African Pidgin-English – An Overview: Phonology – Morphology," In: *Journal of English Linguistics* 1, 49–56.

Schneider, W. (2003) "The Dynamics of New Englishes: From Identity Construction to Dialect Birth," In: *Language* 79, 233–281.

Schröder, A. (2008) "Investigating the Morphological Productivity of Verbal Prefixation in the History of English," In: *AAA – Arbeiten aus Anglistik und Amerikanistik* 33, 47–69.

Sebba, M. (1986) "London Jamaican and Black London English," In: D. Sutcliffe and A. Wong (eds.) *The Language of Black Experience*. Oxford: Basil Blackwell, 149–167.

Seidlhofer, B. (2004) "Research Perspectives on Teaching English as a Lingua Franca," *Annual Review of Applied Linguistics* 24, 209–239.

Seidlhofer, B. (2009) "Common Ground and Different Realities: World Englishes and English as a Lingua Franca," In: *World Englishes* 28, 236–245.

Shaklee, M. (1980) "The Rise of Standard English," In: T. Shopen and J. Williams (eds.) *Standards and Dialects in English*. Cambridge, Mass.: Winthrop, 33–62.

Shnukal, A. and L. Marchese (1983) "Creolization of Nigerian Pidgin English: A Progress Report," In: *English World-Wide* 4, 17–26.

Siegel, J. (1993) "Introduction: Controversies in the Study of Koines and Koineization," In: *International Journal of the Sociology of Language* 99, 5–8.

Siemund, P. (2004) "Substrate, Superstrate and Universals: Perfect Constructions in Irish English," In: B. Kortmann (ed.) *Dialectology Meets Typology. Dialect Grammar from a Cross-Linguistic Perspective*. Berlin: Mouton de Gruyter, 401–434.

Silva-Corvalán, C. (1994) *Language Contact and Change. Spanish in Los Angeles*. Oxford: Clarendon.

Sim, A. (2009) *Pleasures and Pastimes in Tudor England*. Stroud: History Press.

Simo Bobda, A. (1994) *Aspects of Cameroon English Phonology*. Bern: Lang.

Simo Bobda, A. (2008) "Predictability in African English Word-Stress: Evidence from Nigerian English and Cameroon English," In: A. Simo Bobda (ed.) *Explorations into Language Use in Africa*. Hamburg: Lang, 161–181.

Simo Bobda, A. (2010) "Word Stress in Cameroon English and Nigerian English," In: *World Englishes* 29, 59–74.

Simple English Wiktionary at: http://simple.wiktionary.org/wiki/Main_Page

Simpson, J. (2004) "Hypocoristics in Australian English," In: E.W. Schneider, K. Burridge, B. Kortmann, R. Mesthrie, and C. Upton (eds.) *A Handbook of Varieties of English*. vol. 2. *Morphology and Syntax*. Berlin: Mouton de Gruyter, 643–656.

Singh, I. (2000) *Pidgins and Creoles. An Introduction*. London: Arnold.

Smith; J.J. (2009) *Old English. A Linguistic Introduction*. Cambridge: CUP.

Smith, R.M. (1991) "Demographic Developments in Rural England, 1300–1348: A Survey," In: B.M.S. Campbell (ed.) *Before the Black Death: Studies in the "Crisis" of the Early Fourteenth Century*. Manchester: Manchester UP, 48–49.

Söderlind, J. (1998) "The Attitude to Language Expressed by or Ascertainable from English Writers of the 16th and 17th Centuries," In: M. Rydén, I. Tieken-Boon van Ostade, and M. Kytö (eds.) *A Reader in Early Modern English*. Frankfurt: Lang, 461–474.

Stapleton, M. (1983) *The Cambridge Guide to English Literature*. Cambridge: CUP.

Strang, B.M.H. (1970) *A History of English*. London: Methuen.

Strevens, P. (1992) "English as an International Language: Directions in the 1990s," In: B.B. Kachru (ed.) *The Other Tongue: English across Cultures*, 2nd ed. Urbana: University of Illinois Press, 27–47.

Sutcliffe, D. (1984) "British Black English and West Indian Creoles," In: P. Trudgill (ed.) *Language in the British Isles*. Cambridge: CUP, 219–237.

Tagliamonte, S.A. (2009) "There *Was* Universals; Then There *Weren't*: A Comparative Sociolinguistic Perspective on 'Default Singulars'," In: M. Filppula, J. Klemola, and H. Paulasto (eds.) *Vernacular Universals and Language Contacts. Evidence from Varieties of English and Beyond*. London: Routledge, 103–129.

Tay, M.W.J. (1982) "The Uses, Users, and Features of English in Singapore," In: J. Pride (ed.) *New Englishes*. Rowley: Newbury House, 51–70.

Taylor, A.R. (1981) "Indian Lingua Francas," In: C.A. Ferguson and S.B. Heath (eds.) *Language in the USA*. Cambridge: CUP, 175–195.

Thim, S. (2008) "The Rise of the Phrasal Verb in English: A Case of Scandinavian Influence?" In: K. Stierstorfer (ed.) *Anglistentag 2007, Münster. Proceedings*. Trier: Wissenschaftlicher Verlag, 291–304.

Thomason, S.G. and T. Kaufman (1988) *Language Contact, Creolization, and Genetic Linguistics*. Berkeley: University of California.

Thompson, R.W. (1961) "A Note of Some Possible Affinities between the Creole Dialects of the Old World and Those of the New," In: R.B. LePage (ed.) *Creole Language Studies II*. London: Macmillan, 107–113.

Tibbles, A. (ed.) (1994) *Transatlantic Slavery. Against Human Dignity*. London: HMSO.

Tieken-Boon van Ostade, I. (1998) "Samuel Richardson's Role as Linguistic Innovator: A Sociolinguistic Analysis," In: M. Rydén, I. Tieken-Boon van Ostade, and M. Kytö (eds.). *A Reader in Early Modern English*. Frankfurt: Lang, 407–418.

Todd, L. (1990) *Pidgins and Creoles*. London: Routledge.

Todd, M. (1992) *The Early Germans*. Oxford: Blackwell.

Tongue, R. (1974) *The English of Singapore and Malaysia*. Singapore: Eastern Universities Press.

Trudgill, P. (2004) "The Dialect of East Anglia: Morphology and Syntax," In: B. Kortmann, K. Burridge, R. Mesthrie, E.W. Schneider, and C. Upton (eds.) *A Handbook of Varieties of English*. vol. 2. *Morphology and Syntax*. Berlin: Mouton de Gruyter, 142–153.

Turner, G.W. (1970) "New Zealand English Today," In: W.S. Ramson (ed.) *English Transported*. Canberra: Australian National UP, 84–101.

Turner, L.D. (1949) *Africanisms in the Gullah Dialect*. Chicago: University of Chicago.

Van Rooy, B. (2004) "Black South African English: Phonology," In: E. Schneider, K. Burridge, B. Kortmann, R. Mesthrie, and C. Upton (eds.) *Handbook of Varieties of English*. vol 1. *Phonology*. Berlin: Mouton de Gruyter, 943–952.

Verma, S.K. (1982) "Swadeshi English: Form and Function," In: J. Pride (ed.) *New Englishes*. Rowley: Newbury House, 174–187.

Voorhoeve, J. (1962) *Sranan Syntax*. Amsterdam: North Holland.

Voorhoeve, J. (1973) "Historical and Linguistic Evidence in Favor of the Relexification Theory in the Formation of Creoles," In: *Language in Society* 2, 133–145.

Waggoner, D. (1988) "Language Minorities in the United States in the 1980s," In: S.L. McKay and S.C. Wong (eds.) *Language Diversity. Problem or Resource?* Cambridge, Mass.: Newberry House, 69–108.

Wagner, S. (2004a) "'Gendered' Pronouns in English Dialects – A Typological Perspective," In: B. Kortmann (ed.) *Dialectology Meets Typology. Dialect Grammar from a Cross-Linguistic Perspective*. Berlin: Mouton de Gruyter, 479–496.

Wagner, S. (2004b) "English Dialects in the Southwest: Morphology and Syntax," In: B. Kortmann, K. Burridge, R. Mesthrie, E.W. Schneider, and C. Upton (eds.) *A Handbook of Varieties of English*. vol. 2. *Morphology and Syntax*. Berlin: Mouton de Gruyter, 154–174.

Wales, K. (1994) "Royalese: The Rise and Fall of 'The Queen's English,'" In: *English Today* 10, 3–10.

Wales, K. (2002) "'North of Watford Gap.' A Cultural History of Northern English (from 1700)," In: R. Watts and P. Trudgill (eds.) *Alternative Histories of English*. London: Routledge, 45–66.

Wareing, J. (1980) "Changes in the Geographical Distribution of the Recruitment of Apprentices to the London Companies 1486–1750," In: *Journal of Historical Geography* 6, 241–249.

Warren, P. and L. Bauer (2004) "Maori English: Phonology," In: E.W. Schneider, K. Burridge, B. Kortmann, R. Mesthrie, and C. Upton (eds.) *A Handbook of Varieties of English*. vol. 1. *Phonology*. Berlin: Mouton de Gruyter, 614–624.

Wee, L. (2004) "Singapore English: Morphology and Syntax," In: B. Kortmann, K. Burridge, R. Mestrie, E.W. Schneider, and C. Upton (eds.) *A Handbook of Varieties of English*. vol. 2. *Morphology and Syntax*. Berlin: Mouton de Gruyter, 1058–1072.

Wei, L. (1998) "Banana Split? Variations in language choice and code-switching patterns of two groups of British-born Chinese in Tyneside," In: R. Jacobson (ed.) *Codeswitching Worldwide*. Berlin: Mouton de Gruyter, 153–175.

Wells, J.C. (1982) *Accents of English*. Cambridge: CUP.

West, M. (1953) *General Service List of English Words*. Harlow: Longman.

Whinnom, K. (1965) "The Origins of the European-based Creoles and Pidgins," In: *Orbis* 14, 509–527.

Wierzbicka, A. (1997) *Understanding Cultures through their Key Words*. New York: OUP.

Wiley, T.G. (2004) "Language Planning, Language Policy, and the English-Only Movement," In: E. Finegan and J.R. Rickford (eds.) *Language in the USA. Themes for the Twenty-first Century*. Cambridge: CUP, 319–338.

Williams, R. (1983) *Keywords: A Vocabulary of Culture and Society*, rev. ed. New York: OUP.

Winford, D. (2003) *An Introduction to Contact Linguistics*. Oxford: Blackwell.

Winford, D. (2009) "The Interplay of 'Universals' and Contact-Induced Change in the Emergence of New Englishes," In: M. Filppula, J. Klemoa, and H. Paulasto (eds.) *Vernacular Universals and Language Contacts. Evidence from Varieties of English and Beyond.* London: Routledge, 206–230.

Wolfram, W. (2004) "Social Varieties of American English," In: E. Finegan and J.R. Rickford (eds.) *Language in the USA. Themes for the Twenty-first Century.* Cambridge: CUP, 58–75.

Index

References to footnotes are indicated by n, e.g. 105n. Color illustrations, which appear in the plate section between pp. 214 and 215, are referenced by plate number, e.g. *P2.1*.